❧ CONTENTS ❧

I. THE CLASSICAL TRADITION

Aeschylus, *Prometheus Bound* 1

Niccolò Machiavelli, *Clizia* 21

William Shakespeare, *Hamlet* 51

Molière, *The Misanthrope* 181

II. INFLUENCES ON MODERN DRAMA

Georg Büchner, *Woyzeck* 213

Henrik Ibsen, *A Doll's House* 231

Bernard Shaw, *Major Barbara* 283

Tennessee Williams, *Cat on a Hot Tin Roof* 359

III. THE CURRENT GENERATION

David Mamet, *Glengarry Glen Ross* 417

Jane Wagner, *The Search for Signs of Intelligent Life in the Universe* 453

August Wilson, *Joe Turner's Come and Gone* 541

David Henry Hwang, *M. Butterfly* 583

1

PROMETHEUS BOUND

Aeschylus (?) • about 457 B.C.

Translated by David Grene

PROMETHEUS BOUND IS A PLAY THAT VIRTUALLY reeks with antiquity—yet one that still scorches with its fiery, over-the-top passion.

Once believed to be the world's oldest surviving drama (that honor now goes to Aeschylus' *The Persians*, written in 472 B.C.), *Prometheus Bound* is currently thought to have been written late in its author's career; a few scholars even believe the play is post-Aeschylean. Yet *Prometheus Bound*, with its soulful choruses, thundering soliloquies, and warring gods and demigods still seems to speak from the most ancient theatrical impulses: if in fact it is a later play, it was written in a deliberately antique style.

The story was known by every Athenian: it was, indeed, the primal story of Greek civilization, and the basis of the earliest Greek philosophies. In Aeschylus' accounting, Zeus and Prometheus, Olympian gods, have quarreled over the future of humanity: Zeus, newly crowned as king of the

gods, wishes humans to remain ignorant and subjugated; Prometheus wants humankind to reach its intellectual and artistic potential. Prometheus thus steals fire from the gods and gives it to humankind—and with it, light, warmth, illumination, knowledge, language, literature, and culture. Enraged, Zeus has Prometheus chained to a cliff, where, for the rest of eternity, he is to be torn to shreds by ravenous eagles. It is here that Aeschylus sets his play: at the edge of the universe, with the fate of humankind teetering in the balance.

Pure divinity is rarely shown on stage ("almighty" gods are simply too invulnerable to make interesting dramatic characters), and Zeus does not appear in *Prometheus Bound*; he is instead represented onstage by his servants (Might, Violence, Hephaestus, and Hermes), his sometimes apologist (Oceanos), and one of his victims (Io). Zeus's presence is defined, however, not so much by his representatives as by the defiance of Prometheus, a demigod (and therefore capable of feeling pain) who struggles against his pain, his chains, and the injustice of his punishment. It is in his defiance—his fierce conflict against a superior force—that Prometheus becomes a tragic hero and *Prometheus Bound* becomes a dramatic play.

The structure of *Prometheus Bound* is simple and straightforward. The basic conflict is established physically and scenically in the first scene (the prologue), where Prometheus is nailed to the rock; subsequent scenes depict a series of arguments among Prometheus and his various tormentors, would-be helpers, and fellow victims. The language, which is highly musical, is deeply imagistic and evocative, with some of the most sublime religious poetry and political rhetoric of any era.

Watching everything along with us, of course, is the chorus—a striking invention of Greek dramaturgy, which is both audience to and participant in the action. Like the original Athenian audience, these "daughters of Oceanos" are both friends of Prometheus and subjects of Zeus, torn between their loyalty to the demigod who aided them, and to the king of gods, who terrifies them. Their odes between each scene, which were danced as well as sung, make this battle of deities deeply personal. For the chorus and audience alike, *Prometheus Bound* is both a thrilling and agonizing experience.

Prometheus Bound was originally part of a trilogy (collectively known as the *Prometheia*), which included a now-lost *Prometheus Unbound* that seems to have described the eventual reconciliation of Zeus and Prometheus; this was a subject that caught the fancy of the Romantic poet Percy Shelley, who wrote a long poem on that theme. But the sole surviving play, with its heroic defiance against authority and its sense of unresolved spir-

itual alienation, has proved immensely powerful and meaningful in numerous late twentieth-century productions, particularly in western Europe.

READING THE PLAY

Reading a Greek tragedy requires a certain amount of creative imagination, because we have little knowledge as to how the play was initially staged. Readers should be aware that the text of the play, as with all Greek tragedies of its time, was not simply spoken. Dialogue between characters was musically chanted, and the choral odes were sung outright—in parts and sometimes in unison—to the accompaniment of a flute. The chorus also danced during their odes, and at their entrance and exit as well. Unfortunately, none of the original music or choreography has survived. Some of the original Greek production techniques are a little better known. Principal actors wore masks. Stage effects were highly stylized, and it is likely that the "crag" on which Prometheus was nailed was, in fact, simply a stake erected in the orchestra (dancing circle that served as the main acting area) or on a slightly raised stage behind the orchestra. But we have no idea how Aeschylus intended the earth to "stagger" at the end of the play: the reader's imagination, as the ancient Athenian spectator's, should be enlivened by the challenge.

A NOTE ON THE TRANSLATION

David Grene's translation was initially published in 1941; nearly fifty years later, the translator returned to the text, and what follows is Grene's 1990 revision. "The majestic poetry is beyond the reach of anyone not so great as the play's author," Professor Grene modestly notes, but his translation is a recognized masterpiece in its own right. Grene is also the co-editor, with Richmond Lattimore, of the virtually definitive *The Complete Greek Tragedies* (Chicago: University of Chicago Press, 1992; originally published 1959).

For the six footnotes in this printing, the current editor has in part relied on information in James C. Hogan's *A Commentary on the Complete Greek Tragedies: Aeschylus* (Chicago: University of Chicago Press, 1984), to which the reader is referred for comprehensive annotations on all seven Aeschylean dramas.

⚜ PROMETHEUS BOUND ⚜

─────── **CAST OF CHARACTERS** ───────

MIGHT, a demon, servant of Zeus.

HEPHAESTUS, a blacksmith, employed by Zeus.

VIOLENCE (does not speak), another servant of Zeus.

PROMETHEUS, a demigod; his name means
     "Forethought."

OCEANOS, the god of the sea.

IO, a girl with horns, victim of Zeus.

HERMES, Zeus's messenger.

A CHORUS of the birdlike daughters of Oceanos.

Scene: A bare and desolate crag in the Caucasus. Enter Might and Violence, demons, servants of Zeus, and Hephaestus, the smith.

MIGHT

This is the world's limit that we have come to; this is the Scythian country, an untrodden desolation. Hephaestus, it is you that must heed the commands the Father laid upon you to nail this malefactor to the high craggy rocks in fetters unbreakable of adamantine chain. For it was your flower, the brightness of fire that devises all, that he stole and gave to mortal men; this is the sin for which he must pay the Gods the penalty—that he may learn to endure and like the sovereignty of Zeus and quit his man-loving disposition.

HEPHAESTUS

Might and Violence, in you the command of Zeus has its perfect fulfilment: in you there is nothing to stand in its way. But, for myself, I have not the heart to bind violently a God who is my kin here on this wintry cliff. Yet there is constraint upon me to have the heart for just that, for it is a dangerous thing to treat the Father's words lightly.

High-contriving Son of Themis of Straight Counsel: this is not of your will nor of mine; yet I shall nail you in bonds of indissoluble bronze on this crag far from men. Here you shall hear no voice of mortal; here you shall see no form of mortal. You shall be grilled by the sun's bright fire and change the fair bloom of your skin. You shall be glad when Night comes with her mantle of stars and hides the sun's light; but the sun shall scatter the hoar-frost again at dawn. Always the grievous burden of your torture will be there to wear you down; for he that shall cause it to cease has yet to be born.[1]

Such is the reward you reap of your man-loving disposition. For you, a God, feared not the anger of the Gods, but gave honors to mortals beyond what was just. Wherefore you shall mount guard on this unlovely rock, upright, sleepless, not bending the knee. Many a groan and many a lamentation you shall utter, but they shall not serve you. For the mind of Zeus is hard to soften with prayer and every ruler is harsh whose rule is new.

MIGHT

Come, why are you holding back? Why are you pitying in vain? Why is it that you do not hate a God whom the Gods hate most of all? Why do you not

─────────────

[1] The reference is to Heracles, who frees Prometheus in the legend and presumably also in the subsequent play of the trilogy.

hate him, since it was your honor that he betrayed to men?

HEPHAESTUS
Our kinship has strange power; that, and our life together.

MIGHT
Yes. But to turn a deaf ear to the Father's words—how can that be? Do you not fear that more?

HEPHAESTUS
You are always pitiless, always full of ruthlessness.

MIGHT
There is no good singing dirges over him. Do not labor uselessly at what helps not at all.

HEPHAESTUS
O handicraft of mine—that I deeply hate!

MIGHT
Why do you hate it? To speak simply, your craft is in no way the author of his present troubles.

HEPHAESTUS
Yet would another had had this craft allotted to him.

MIGHT
There is nothing without discomfort except the overlordship of the Gods. For only Zeus is free.

HEPHAESTUS
I know. I have no answer to this.

MIGHT
Hurry now. Throw the chain around him that the Father may not look upon your tarrying.

HEPHAESTUS
There are the fetters, there: you can see them.

MIGHT
Put them on his hands: strong, now with the hammer: strike. Nail him to the rock.

HEPHAESTUS
It is being done now. I am not idling at my work.

MIGHT
Hammer it more; put in the wedge; leave it loose nowhere. He's a cunning fellow at finding a way even out of hopeless difficulties.

HEPHAESTUS
Look now, his arm is fixed immovably!

MIGHT
Nail the other safe, that he may learn, for all his cleverness, that he is duller witted than Zeus.

HEPHAESTUS
No one, save Prometheus, can justly blame me.

MIGHT
Drive the obstinate jaw of the adamantine wedge right through his breast: drive it hard.

HEPHAESTUS
Alas, Prometheus, I groan for your sufferings.

MIGHT
Are you pitying again? Are you groaning for the enemies of Zeus? Have a care, lest some day you may be pitying yourself.

HEPHAESTUS
You see a sight that hurts the eye.

MIGHT
I see this rascal getting his deserts. Throw the girth around his sides.

HEPHAESTUS
I am forced to do this; do not keep urging me.

MIGHT
Yes, I will urge you, and hound you on as well. Get below now, and hoop his legs in strongly.

HEPHAESTUS
There now, the task is done. It has not taken long.

MIGHT
Hammer the piercing fetters with all your power, for the Overseer of our work is severe.

HEPHAESTUS
Your looks and the refrain of your tongue are alike.

MIGHT
You can be softhearted. But do not blame my stubbornness and harshness of temper.

HEPHAESTUS
Let us go. He has the harness on his limbs.

MIGHT
[to Prometheus] Now, play the insolent; now, plunder the Gods' privileges and give them to creatures of a day. What drop of your sufferings can mortals spare you? The Gods named you wrongly when they called you Forethought; you yourself *need* Forethought to extricate yourself from this contrivance. [Prometheus is left alone on the rock.]

PROMETHEUS

Bright light, swift-winged winds, springs of the
    rivers, numberless[2]
laughter of the sea's waves, earth, mother of all, and
    the all-seeing
circle of the sun: I call upon you to see what I, a
    God, suffer
at the hands of Gods—
see with what kind of torture
worn down I shall wrestle ten thousand
years of time—
such is the despiteful bond that the Prince
has devised against me, the new Prince
of the Blessed Ones. Oh woe is me!
I groan for the present sorrow,
I groan for the sorrow to come, I groan
questioning when there shall come a time
when He shall ordain a limit to my sufferings.
What am I saying? I have known all before,
all that shall be, and clearly known; to me,
nothing that hurts shall come with a new face.
So must I bear, as lightly as I can,
the destiny that fate has given me;
for I know well against necessity,
against its strength, no one can fight and win.

I cannot speak about my fortune, cannot
hold my tongue either. It was mortal man
to whom I gave great privileges and
for that was yoked in this unyielding harness.
I hunted out the secret spring of fire
that filled the narthex stem, which when revealed
became the teacher of each craft to men,
a great resource. This is the sin committed
for which I stand accountant, and I pay
nailed in my chains under the open sky.

Ah! Ah!
What sound, what sightless smell approaches me,
God sent, or mortal, or mingled?
Has it come to earth's end
to look on my sufferings,
or what does it wish?
You see me a wretched God in chains,
the enemy of Zeus, hated of all

the Gods that enter Zeus's palace hall,
because of my excessive love for Man.
What is that? The rustle
of birds' wings near? The air whispers
with the gentle strokes of wings.
Everything that comes toward me is occasion for
    fear.

[The Chorus, composed of the daughters of Oceanos,
    enters, the members wearing some formalized
    representation of wings, so that their general
    appearance is birdlike.]

CHORUS

Fear not: this is a company of friends
that comes to your mountain with swift
rivalry of wings.
Hardly have we persuaded our Father's
mind, and the quick-bearing winds
speeded us hither. The sound
of stroke of bronze rang through our cavern
in its depths and it shook from us
shamefaced modesty; unsandaled
we have hastened on our chariot of wings.

PROMETHEUS

Alas, children of teeming Tethys and of him
who encircles all the world with stream unsleeping,
Father Ocean,
look, see with what chains
I am nailed on the craggy heights
of this gully to keep a watch
that none would envy me.

CHORUS

I see, Prometheus: and a mist of fear and tears
besets my eyes as I see your form
wasting away on these cliffs
in adamantine bonds of bitter shame.
For new are the steersmen that rule Olympus:
and new are the customs by which Zeus rules,
customs that have no law to them,
but what was great before he brings to nothingness.

PROMETHEUS

Would that he had hurled me
underneath the earth and underneath
the House of Hades, host to the dead—
yes, down to limitless Tartarus,
yes, though he bound me cruelly
in chains unbreakable,
so neither God nor any other being

---

might have found joy in gloating over me.
Now as I hang, the plaything of the winds,
my enemies can laugh at what I suffer.

CHORUS
Who of the Gods is so hard of heart
that he finds joy in this?
Who is that that does not feel
sorrow answering your pain—
save only Zeus? For he malignantly,
always cherishing a mind
that bends not, has subdued the breed
of Ouranos, nor shall he cease
until he satisfies his heart,
or someone take the rule from him—that hard-to-
    capture rule—
by some device of subtlety.

PROMETHEUS
Yes, there shall come a day for me
when he shall need me, me that now am tortured
in bonds and fetters—he shall need me then,
this president of the Blessed—
to show the new plot whereby he may be spoiled
of his throne and his power.
Then not with honeyed tongues
of persuasion shall he enchant me;
he shall not cow me with his threats
to tell him what I know,
until he free me from my cruel chains
and pay me recompense for what I suffer.

CHORUS
You are stout of heart, unyielding
to the bitterness of pain.
You are free of tongue, too free.
It is my mind that piercing fear has fluttered;
your misfortunes frighten me.
Where and when is it fated
to see you reach the term, to see you reach
the harbor free of trouble at the last?
A disposition none can win, a heart
that no persuasions soften—these are his,
the Son of Kronos.

PROMETHEUS
I know that he is savage: and his justice
a thing he keeps by his own standard: still
that will of his shall melt to softness yet
when he is broken in the way I know,
and though his temper now is oaken hard
it shall be softened: hastily he'll come

to meet my haste, to join in amity
and union with me—one day he shall come.

CHORUS
Reveal it all to us; tell us the story,
on what charges Zeus has laid hold on you
and tortures you so cruelly, with dishonor.
Instruct us if the telling will not harm you.

PROMETHEUS
To speak of this is bitterness. To keep silent
bitter no less; and every way is misery.

When first the Gods began their angry quarrel,
and God matched God in rising faction, some
eager to drive old Kronos from his throne
that Zeus might rule—the fools!—others again
earnest that Zeus might never be their king—
I then with the best counsel tried to win
the Titans, sons of Ouranos and Earth,
but failed. They would have none of crafty schemes
and in their savage arrogance of spirit
thought they would lord it easily by force.
But she that was my mother, Themis, Earth—
she is but one although her names are many—
had prophesied to me how it should be,
even how the fates decreed it: and she said
that "not by strength nor overmastering force
the fates allowed the conquerors to conquer
but by guile only": This is what I told them,
but they would not vouchsafe a glance at me.
Then with those things before me it seemed best
to take my mother and join Zeus's side:
he was as willing as we were:
thanks to my plans the dark receptacle
of Tartarus conceals the ancient Kronos,
him and his allies. These were the services
I rendered to this tyrant and these pains
the payment he has given me in requital.
This is a sickness rooted and inherent
in the nature of a tyranny:
that he that holds it does not trust his friends.
But you have asked on what particular
charge he now tortures me: this I will tell you.
As soon as he ascended to the throne
that was his father's, straightway he assigned
to the several Gods their several privileges
and portioned out the power, but to the unhappy
breed of mankind he gave no heed, intending
to blot the race out and create a new.
Against these plans none stood save I: I dared.

I rescued men from shattering destruction
that would have carried them to Hades' house;
and therefore I am tortured on this rock,
a bitterness to suffer, and a pain
to pitiful eyes. I gave to mortal man
a precedence over myself in pity: I
can win no pity: pitiless is he
that thus chastises me, a spectacle
bringing dishonor on the name of Zeus.

CHORUS
Of iron mind he must be, must be made of stone
who does not sympathize, Prometheus, with your
    sufferings.
Myself, I would not have chosen to look on them;
now that I do, my heart is full of pain.

PROMETHEUS
Yes, to my friends the sight is pitiable.

CHORUS
Did you perhaps go further than you have told us?

PROMETHEUS
Yes, I stopped mortals from foreseeing doom.

CHORUS
What cure did you discover for that sickness?

PROMETHEUS
I sowed in them blind hopes.

CHORUS
That was a great help that you gave to men.

PROMETHEUS
Besides, I myself gave them fire.

CHORUS
Do now creatures of a day own bright-faced fire?

PROMETHEUS
Yes and from it they shall learn many crafts.

CHORUS
So it was on such charges as this that Zeus—

PROMETHEUS
Tortures me, gives me no respite from my pains.

CHORUS
Is there no term prescribed for your suffering?

PROMETHEUS
None save when it seems good to Zeus himself.

CHORUS
How shall it seem good? What hope is there? Do
    you not see

that you were wrong? How you have been wrong, it
    is not
a pleasure for me to say, and pain for you.
Let us let all this be; seek some deliverance
out of your trial.

PROMETHEUS
It is an easy thing for one whose foot
is on the outside of calamity
to give advice and to rebuke the sufferer.
I have known all that you have said: I knew,
I knew when I transgressed nor will deny it.
In helping man I brought my troubles on me;
but yet I did not think that with such tortures
I should be wasted on these airy cliffs,
this lonely mountain top, with no one near.
But do not sorrow for my present suffering;
alight on earth and hear what is to come
that you may know the whole complete: I beg you
alight and join your sorrow with mine: misfortune
wandering the same track lights now upon one
and now upon another.

CHORUS
                                    Willing our ears,
that hear you cry to them, Prometheus.
Now with light foot I leave the rushing car
and sky, the holy path of birds, and light
upon this jutting rock: I long
to hear your story to the end.

[Enter Oceanos, riding on a hippocamp, or
sea monster.][3]

OCEANOS
                                    I come
on a long journey, speeding past the boundaries,
to visit you, Prometheus: with the mind
alone, no bridle needed, I direct
my swift-winged bird; my heart is sore
for your misfortunes; you know that. I think
that it is kinship makes me feel them so.
Besides, apart from kinship, there is no one
I hold in higher estimation: that
you soon shall know and know beside that in me
there is no mere word-kindness: tell me

_____

[3]It is possible, even likely, that Aeschylus employed a giant
crane to provide a flying entrance for Oceanos.

how I can help you, and you will never say
that you have any friend more loyal to you
than Oceanos.

PROMETHEUS
What do I see? Have you, too, come to gape
in wonder at this great display, my torture?
How did you have the courage to come here
to this land, this Iron Mother, leaving the stream
called after you and the rock-roofed, self-
    established
caverns? Was it to feast your eyes upon
the spectacle of my suffering and join
in pity for my pain? Now look and see
the sight, this friend of Zeus, that helped set up
his tyranny, and see what agonies
twist me, by his instructions!

OCEANOS
                  Yes, I see,
Prometheus, and I want, indeed I do,
to advise you for the best, for all your cleverness.
Know yourself and reform your ways to new ways,
for new is he that rules among the Gods.
But if you throw about such angry words,
words that are whetted swords, soon Zeus will hear
    you,
even though his seat in glory is far removed,
and then your present multitude of pains
will seem like child's play. My poor friend, give up
this angry mood of yours and look for means
of getting yourself free of trouble. Maybe
what I say seems to you both old and
    commonplace;
but this is what you pay, Prometheus, for
that tongue of yours which talked so high and
    haughty:
you are not yet humble, still you do not yield
to your misfortunes, and you wish, indeed,
to add some more to them; now, if you follow
me as a schoolmaster you will not kick
against the pricks, seeing that he, the King,
that rules alone, is harsh and sends accounts
to no one's audit for the deeds he does.
Now I will go and try if I can free you:
do you be quiet, do not talk so much.
Since your mind is so subtle, don't you know
that a vain tongue is subject to correction?

PROMETHEUS
I envy you, that you stand clear of blame,
yet shared and dared in everything with me!
Now let me be, and have no care for me.
Do what you will, Him you will not persuade;
He is not easily won over: look,
take care lest coming here to me should hurt you.

OCEANOS
You are by nature better at advising
others than yourself. I take my cue
from deeds, not words. Do not withhold me now
when I am eager to go to Zeus. I'm sure,
I'm sure that he will grant this favor to me,
to free you from your chains.

PROMETHEUS
I thank you and will never cease; for loyalty
is not what you are wanting in. Don't trouble,
for you will trouble to no purpose, and no help
to me—if it so be you want to trouble.
No, rest yourself, keep away from this thing;
because I am unlucky I would not,
for that, have everyone unlucky too.
No, for my heart is sore already when
I think about my brothers' fortunes—Atlas,
who stands to westward of the world, supporting
the pillar of earth and heaven on his shoulders,
a load that suits no shoulders; and the earthborn
dweller in caves Cilician, whom I saw
and pitied, hundred-headed, dreadful monster,
fierce Typho, conquered and brought low by force.
Once against all the Gods he stood, opposing,
hissing out terror from his grim jaws; his eyes
flashed gorgon glaring lightning as he thought
to sack the sovereign tyranny of Zeus;
but upon him came the unsleeping bolt
of Zeus, the lightning-breathing flame, down
    rushing,
which cast him from his high aspiring boast.
Struck to the heart, his strength was blasted dead
and burnt to ashes; now a sprawling mass
useless he lies, hard by the narrow seaway
pressed down beneath the roots of Aetna: high
above him on the mountain peak the smith
Hephaestus works at the anvil. Yet one day
there shall burst out rivers of fire, devouring
with savage jaws the fertile, level plains
of Sicily of the fair fruits; such boiling wrath

with weapons of fire-breathing surf, a fiery
unapproachable torrent, shall Typho vomit,
though Zeus's lightning left him but a cinder.
But all of this you know: you do not need me
to be your schoolmaster: reassure yourself
as you know how: this cup I shall drain myself
till the high mind of Zeus shall cease from anger.

OCEANOS
Do you not know, Prometheus,
that words are doctors for a diseased temper?

PROMETHEUS
Yes, if in season due one soothes the heart,
not violently reduces the swelling temper.

OCEANOS
In loyalty to you and courage to show it
what penalty do you see for me? Now tell me.

PROMETHEUS
Only futile effort and a silly good nature.

OCEANOS
Suffer me to be sick of this complaint,
for it is best for wise ones to seem foolish.

PROMETHEUS
The fault will seem to be mine if you do this.

OCEANOS
It is clear your words would send me home again.

PROMETHEUS
Yes, for lamenting now will lead to enmity.

OCEANOS
With him that now sits on the throne of power?

PROMETHEUS
His is a heart take heed you never vex.

OCEANOS
Your own misfortune, Prometheus, is my teacher.

PROMETHEUS
Off with you, then! Begone! Keep your present
    mind.

OCEANOS
These words of yours reach one who is ready to go.
For my four-footed bird already paws
the level track of heaven with his wings
and gladly will he bend his knee
in his home stable.

CHORUS

Strophe[+]
I cry aloud, Prometheus, and lament your bitter
    fate.
My tender eyes are trickling tears:
their fountains wet my cheek.
This is a tyrant's deed; this is unlovely,
a thing done by a tyrant's private laws,
and with this thing Zeus shows his haughtiness
of temper toward the Gods that were of old.

Antistrophe
Now all the earth has cried aloud, lamenting:
now all that was magnificent of old
laments your fall, laments your brethren's fall—
as many as in holy Asia hold
their stablished habitation, all lament
in sympathy for your most grievous woes.

Strophe
Dwellers in the land of Colchis,
maidens fearless in the fight,
and the host of Scythia, living
round the lake Maeotis, living
on the edges of the world.

Antistrophe
And Arabia's flower of warriors
and the craggy fortress keepers
near Caucasian mountains, fighters
terrible, crying for battle,
brandishing sharp pointed spears.

Strophe
One God and one God only I have seen
before this day, in torture and in bonds
unbreakable: he was a Titan,
Atlas, whose strength and might
ever exceeded; now he bends his back
and groans beneath the load of earth and heaven.

[+]The Greek choral ode was both sung and danced by the
entire chorus, accompanied by a flute. The ode was broken
up into dialectically contrasting rhythmic sections, known as
the *strophe* and *antistrophe* (literally "turning" and "counter-
turning"), which gave the ode a somewhat dialogue-like
pattern.

The wave cries out as it breaks into surf;
the depth cries out, lamenting you; the dark
Hades, the hollow underneath the world,
sullenly groans below; the springs
of sacred flowing rivers all lament
the pain and pity of your suffering.

PROMETHEUS
Do not think from pride and stubbornness I am
    silent.
In self awareness my heart is eaten away
to see myself insulted as I am.
Yet to these new gods who but I assigned
their privileges of honor in full completion?
Of all that I say nothing, for I would speak
to you who know it. But man's tribulation,
that I would have you hear—how I found them
    mindless
and gave them minds, made them masters of their
    wits.
I will tell you this not as reproaching man,
but to set forth the goodwill of my gifts.
First they had eyes but had no eyes to see,
and ears but heard not. Like shapes within a dream
they dragged through their long lives and muddled
    all,
haphazardly. They knew not how to build
brick houses to face the sun, nor work in wood.
They lived beneath the earth like swarming ants
in sunless caves. They had no certain mark
of winter nor of flowery spring nor summer,
with its crops, but did all this without intelligence
until it was I that showed them—yes, it was I—
stars' risings and their settings hard to judge.
And numbering as well, preeminent
of subtle devices, and letter combinations
that hold all in memory, the Muses' mother skilled
    in craft,
I found for them. I was the first to yoke
beasts to be slave to the traces, and with their
    bodies
to be man's substitute in the hardest work. I
    harnessed
to the carriage horses obedient to the rein,
the crowning glory of the rich man's luxury.
And carriages that wander on the sea,
the ships sail-winged, who else but I invented?
Such, to my sorrow, were the devices which

I found for men, but have no clever means
to rid myself of the afflictions now oppressing me.

CHORUS
You have suffered terribly. Bewildered in your mind
you are astray, and like a bad doctor who
has fallen sick, you have lost heart not finding
by what drugs your own disease is curable.

PROMETHEUS
If you hear the rest, you will marvel even more
at what crafts and what resources I contrived.
Greatest was this: when one of mankind was sick,
there was no defense for him—neither healing food
nor drink nor unguent; for lack of drugs they
    wasted,
until I showed them blendings of mild simples
with which they drive away all kinds of sickness.
The many ways of prophesying I charted;
I was the one who first judged what out of dreams
came truly real; and for mankind I gave meaning
to ominous sounds, hard of interpretation,
and to the significance of road encounters.
The flights of hook-taloned birds I analyzed,
which of them were in nature prosperous
and lucky, and what manner of life each led,
their hates and loves, companionships with each
    other;
what smoothness of the entrails and what color
the gall should have if it were to please the Gods,
and also the dappled beauty of the lobe.
It was I bound the thighbones wrapped in fat,
and the long shank; it was I that set mortals on
the murky road of prophecy. Flaming signs
I made visible which till then were only dim.
So much for these things. Then beneath the earth
those hidden blessings for man, bronze, iron, silver
and gold—who can claim to have discovered before
    me?
No one, I am sure, who wants to speak to the
    purpose.
In one short sentence understand it all:
every art of mankind comes from Prometheus.

CHORUS
Do not help mortals beyond due occasion
while careless of your own misfortune.
For I am strong in hope that once released
from these chains you will be no less strong than
    Zeus.

PROMETHEUS

These things the Fate that brings all to fulfilment
has not yet determined that they be accomplished.
I must first be twisted by ten thousand pangs
and agonies before I escape my bondage.
Craft is far weaker than necessity.

CHORUS

Who then is the steersman of necessity?

PROMETHEUS

The three-formed Fates and the remembering
   Furies.

CHORUS

And is Zeus, then, weaker than these?

PROMETHEUS

                                            Yes,
for he too cannot escape what is fated.

CHORUS

But what is fated for Zeus save rule eternal?

PROMETHEUS

You cannot know that yet; do not entreat me.

CHORUS

This must be a solemn secret that you veil.

PROMETHEUS

Think of some other story; this is not seasonable
to utter; it must be wholly hidden.
For only by so keeping it can I
escape these shameful bonds and agonies.

CHORUS

Strophe

May Zeus never, Zeus that all
the universe controls, oppose
his power against *my* mind:
may I never dallying
be slow to give my worship at
the sacrificial feasts
when the bulls are killed beside
quenchless Father Ocean:
may I never sin in word:
may these precepts still abide
in my mind nor melt away.

Antistrophe

It is a sweet thing to draw out
a long, long life in cheerful hopes,
and feed the spirit in the bright

benignity of happiness:
but I shiver when I see you
wasted with ten thousand pains,
all because you did not tremble
at the name of Zeus: your mind
was yours, not his, and at its bidding
you regarded mortal men
too high, Prometheus.

Strophe

Kindness that cannot be requited, tell me,
where is the help in that, my friend? What succor
in creatures of a day? You did not see
the feebleness that draws its breath in gasps,
a dreamlike feebleness by which the race
of man is held in bondage, a blind prisoner.
So the plans of men shall never
pass the ordered law of Zeus.

Antistrophe

This I have learned while I looked on your pains,
deadly pains, Prometheus.
A dirge for you came to my lips, so different
from the other song I sang to crown your marriage
in honor of your couching and your bath,
upon the day you won her with your gifts
to share your bed—of your own race she was,
Hesione—and so you brought her home.

[Enter Io, a girl wearing horns like an ox.][5]

IO

What land is this? what race of men? Who is it
I see here tortured in this rocky bondage?
What is the sin he's paying for? Oh tell me
to what part of the world my wanderings have
   brought me.
O, O, O,
there it is again, there again—it stings me,
the gadfly, the ghost of earth-born Argos:
keep it away, keep it away, earth!
I'm frightened when I see the shape of Argos,
Argos the herdsman with ten thousand eyes.
He stalks me with his crafty eyes: he died,
but the earth didn't hide him; still he comes

---

[5]Io, the helpless victim of the gods (her name is a homonym
for the Greek word that means "alas!"), speaks for the most part
in highly excited rhythmic patterns. Her dance was quite
possibly spectacular.

even from the depths of the Underworld to hunt
    me:
he drives me starving by the sands of the sea.
The reed-woven pipe drones on in a hum
and drones and drones its sleep-giving strain:
O, O, O,
Where are you bringing me, my far-wandering
    wanderings?
Son of Kronos, what fault, what fault
did you find in me that you should yoke me
to a harness of misery like this,
that you should torture me so to madness
driven in fear of the gadfly?

Burn me with fire: hide me in earth: cast me away
to monsters of the deep for food: but do not
grudge me the granting of this prayer, King.
Enough have my much wandering wanderings
exercised me: I cannot find
a way to escape my troubles.
Do you hear the voice of the cow-horned maid?

PROMETHEUS

Surely I hear the voice of the gadfly-haunted
daughter of Inachus who fired with love
the heart of Zeus and now through Hera's hate
is violently driven in courses overlong.

IO

How is it you speak my father's name?
Tell me, who are you? Who are you? Oh
who are you that so exactly accosts me by name?
You have spoken of the disease that the Gods have
    sent to me
which wastes me away, pricking with goads,
so that I am moving always
tortured and hungry, wild bounding,
quick sped I come,
a victim of jealous plots.
Some have been wretched
before me, but who of these
suffered as I do?
But declare to me clearly
what I have still to suffer: what would avail
against my sickness, what drug would cure it:
Tell me, if you know:
tell me, declare it to the unlucky, wandering maid.

PROMETHEUS

I will tell you clearly all that you would know,
weaving no riddles, but in simple story

as it is just to open lips to friends.
You see Prometheus that gave fire to men.

IO

You that have shown yourself a common blessing
to all men, sad Prometheus, why are you punished?

PROMETHEUS

I have but now ceased complaining of my
    sufferings.

IO

Will you grant me this favor?

PROMETHEUS

Say what it is
you ask for. You will learn all from me.

IO

Tell me who nailed you to this cliff.

PROMETHEUS

                                    The plan
was Zeus's, but it was Hephaestus' hand.

IO

What was the offense for which this is punishment?

PROMETHEUS

Enough that I have told you clearly just so far.

IO

Besides this, tell me the limit of my own
    wanderings.

PROMETHEUS

It were better not to know than to know this.

IO

Do not hide from me what it is fated I should suffer.
What shall its term be for this unhappy girl?

PROMETHEUS

It is not I grudge you this gift that you ask.

IO

Then why not tell me everything at once.

PROMETHEUS

No grudging, but I dread to break your spirit.

IO

Do not care for me more than I would have you.

PROMETHEUS

Since you are bent on it, I must speak; Now hear
    me, you.

CHORUS

Not yet. Give to me, too, a share of pleasure.
Let us first question her about her sickness;

let herself tell us her disastrous chances.
Then let her be told by you what she must still
     suffer.

PROMETHEUS

Io, it is your task to gratify
these spirits who are, moreover, your father's
     sisters.
To sorrow and make wail for your ill fortune,
when you will win a tear from those who listen,
is well worthwhile.

IO

I know not how I should distrust you: clearly
you shall hear all you want to know from me.
Yet even as I speak I groan in bitterness
for that storm sent by God on me, that ruin
of my beauty; I must sorrow when I think
who sent all this upon me. There were always
night visions that kept haunting me and coming
into my maiden chamber and exhorting
with winning words, "O maiden greatly blessed,
why are you still a maiden, you who might
make marriage with the greatest? Zeus is stricken
with lust for you; he is afire to try
the bed of love with you: do not disdain him.
Go, child, to Lerna's meadow, deep in grass,
to where your father's flocks and cattle stand,
that Zeus's eye may cease from longing for you."
With such dreams I was cruelly beset
night after night until I took the courage
to tell my father of my nightly terror.
He sent to Pytho many an embassy
and to Dodona seeking to discover
what deed or word of his might please the God,
but those he sent came back with riddling oracles
dark and beyond the power of understanding.
At last the word came clear to Inachus
charging him plainly that he cast me out
of home and country, drive me out footloose
to wander to the limits of the world;
if he should not obey, the oracle said,
the fire-faced thunderbolt would come from Zeus
and blot out his whole race. These were the oracles
of Loxias, and Inachus obeyed them.
He drove me out and shut his doors against me
with tears on both our parts, but Zeus's bit
compelled him to do this against his will.
Immediately my form and mind were changed
and all distorted; horned, as you see,

pricked on by the sharp biting gadfly, leaping
in frenzied jumps I ran beside the river
Kerchneia, good to drink, and Lerna's spring.
The earth-born herdsman Argos followed me
whose anger knew no limits, and he spied
after my tracks with all his hundred eyes.
Then an unlooked-for doom, descending suddenly,
took him from life: I, driven by the gadfly,
that god-sent scourge, was driven always onward
from one land to another: that is my story.
If you can tell me what remains for me,
tell me, and do not out of pity cozen
with kindly lies: there is no sickness worse
for me than words that to be kind must lie.

CHORUS

Hold! Keep away! Alas!
never did I think that such strange
words would come to my ears:
never did I think such intolerable
sufferings, an offense to the eye,
shameful and frightening, so
would chill my soul with a double-edged point.
Alas, Alas, for your fate!
I shudder when I look on Io's fortune.

PROMETHEUS

You groan too soon, you are full of fear too soon.
Wait till you hear what still remains.

CHORUS

Speak, tell us to the end. For the sick it is sweet to
     know
what pain is still to come and to know it clearly.

PROMETHEUS

The first request you made of me you gained
lightly: from her you wished to hear the story
of what she suffered. Now hear what remains,
what sufferings this maid must yet endure
from Hera. Do you listen, child of Inachus,
hear and lay up my words within your heart
that you may know the limits of your journey.
First turn to the sun's rising and walk on
over the fields no plough has broken: then
you will come to the wandering Scythians,
who live in wicker houses built above
their well-wheeled wagons; they are an armed
     people,
armed with the bow that strikes from far away:
do not draw near them; rather let your feet
touch the surf line of the sea where the waves moan,

and cross their country: on your left there live
the Chalybes who work with iron: these
you must beware of; for they are not gentle,
nor people whom a stranger dare approach.
Then you will come to Insolence, a river
that well deserves its name: but cross it not—
It is no stream that you can easily ford—
until you come to Caucasus itself,
the highest mountains, where the river's strength
gushes from its very temples. Cross these peaks,
the neighbors of the stars, and take the road
southward until you reach the Amazons,
the race of women who hate men, who one day
shall live around Thermodon in Themiscyra
where Salmydessos, rocky jaw of the sea,
stands sailor-hating, stepmother of ships.
The Amazons will set you on your way
and gladly: you will reach Cimmeria,
the isthmus, at the narrow gates of the lake.
Leave this with a good heart and cross the channel,
the channel of Maeotis: and hereafter
for all time men shall talk about your crossing,
and they shall call the place for you Cow's-ford.*
Leave Europe's mainland then, and go to Asia.
[To the Chorus]
Do you now think this tyrant of the Gods
is hard in all things without difference?
He was a God and sought to lie in love
with this girl who was mortal, and on her
he brought this curse of wandering: bitter indeed
you found your marriage with this suitor, maid.
Yet you must think of all that I have told you
as still only in prelude.

IO
O, O!

PROMETHEUS
Again you cry out, again you lament? What then
will you do when you learn your other sufferings?

CHORUS
Is there still suffering that you have to tell her?

PROMETHEUS
A wintry sea of agony and ruin.

_____

*Cow's-ford: Bosporus

IO
What is the good of life to me? Why should I not
quickly dash myself down from this blind precipice
to strike the ground and win a quittance
of all my pains? Better at once to die
than suffer torment all the rest of my days.

PROMETHEUS
You would find it hard to bear these trials of mine,
since for me death is not decreed at all.
Death would indeed be a riddance of my suffering,
but, as it is, there is no limit set
for pain, save when Zeus falls from his seat of
    power.

IO
Is there a time when Zeus shall fall?

PROMETHEUS
You would be glad, I think, to see that end.

IO
How should I not, who suffer so cruelly from him?

PROMETHEUS
Know surely, then, that this will come to pass.

IO
Who will despoil him of his sovereign power?

PROMETHEUS
His own light-witted counsels will undo him.

IO
How? Tell me, if there is no harm in telling.

PROMETHEUS
He will make a marriage which one day he will rue.

IO
With god or mortal? Tell me if it may be told.

PROMETHEUS
Why tell what marriage? That may not be spoken.

IO
Will it be by his wife that he shall lose his throne?

PROMETHEUS
Yes. She shall bear a son greater than his father.

IO
Can he not turn aside this doom of his?

PROMETHEUS
No, save only by my release from bondage.

IO
But who will free you against Zeus's will?

PROMETHEUS

That must be one of your own descendants.

IO

What! Will a child of mine free you one day?

PROMETHEUS

Yes, in the generation tenth and third.

IO

No longer can I grasp your prophecy.

PROMETHEUS

Then do not seek to know your own troubles
    further.

IO

Do not offer me the gift and then withhold it.

PROMETHEUS

I will offer you the choice of the two stories.

IO

Which are they? Tell me, give me the choice.

PROMETHEUS

Yes, I will give it you: either to tell you,
clearly, the rest of your troubles or my deliverer.

CHORUS

Give *her* the one of the two and me the other,
a kindly favor. Do not deny the tale.
Tell her what still remains of her wanderings,
and me the deliverer. That is what I want.

PROMETHEUS

Since you have so much eagerness, I will not
refuse to tell you all that you have asked me.
First to you, Io, I shall tell the tale
of your sad wanderings, rich in groans—inscribe
the story in the tablets of your mind.
When you shall cross the channel that divides
Europe from Asia, turn to the rising sun,
to the burnt plains, sun-scorched; cross by the edge
of the foaming sea till you come to Gorgona,
to the flat stretches of Kisthene's country.
There live the ancient maids, children of Phorcys:
these swan-formed hags, with but one common
    eye,
single-toothed monsters, such as nowhere else
the sun's rays look on nor the moon by night.
Near are their winged sisters, the three Gorgons,
with snakes to bind their hair up, mortal-hating:
no mortal that but looks on them shall live:
these are the sentry guards I tell you of.
Hear, too, of yet another gruesome sight,

the sharp-toothed hounds of Zeus, that have no
    bark,
the vultures—them take heed of—and the host
of one-eyed Arimaspians, horse-riding,
that live around the spring which flows with gold,
the spring of Pluto's river: go not near them.
A land far off, a nation of black men,
these you shall come to, men who live hard by
the fountain of the sun where is the river
Aethiops—travel by his banks along
to a waterfall where from the Bibline hills
Nile pours his holy waters, pure to drink.
This river shall be your guide to the triangular
land of the Nile and there, by Fate's decree,
there, Io, you shall find your distant home,
a colony for you and your descendants.
If anything of this is still obscure
or difficult ask me again and learn
clearly: I have more leisure than I wish.

CHORUS

If there is anything further or left over
you have to tell her of her deadly traveling,
tell her. If that is all, grant us again
the favor that we asked for earlier.
You remember?

PROMETHEUS

The limit of her wanderings complete
she now has heard: but so that she may know
that she has not been listening to no purpose
I shall recount what she endured before
she came to us here: this I give as pledge,
a witness to the good faith of my words.
The great part of the story I omit
and come to the very boundary of your travels.
When you had come to the Molossian plains
around the sheer back of Dodona where
is the oracular seat of Zeus Thesprotian,
the talking oaks, a wonder past belief,
by them full clearly, in no riddling terms,
you were hailed glorious wife of Zeus that shall be:
does anything of this wake pleasant memories?
Then, goaded by the gadfly, on you hastened
to the great gulf of Rhea by the track
at the side of the sea; but in returning course
you were storm-driven back: in time to come
that inlet of the sea shall bear your name
and shall be called Ionian, a memorial
to all men of your journeying: these are proofs

for you, of how far my mind sees something farther
than what is visible: for what is left,
to you and you this I shall say in common,
taking up again the track of my old tale.
There is a city, furthest in the world,
Canobos, near the mouth and issuing point
of the Nile: there Zeus shall make you sound of
    mind
touching you with a hand that brings no fear,
and through that touch alone shall come your
    healing.
You shall bear Epaphos, dark of skin, his name
recalling Zeus's touch and his begetting.
This Epaphos shall reap the fruit of all
the land that is watered by the broad flowing Nile.
From him five generations, and again
to Argos they shall come, against their will,
in number fifty, women, flying from
a marriage with their kinsfolk: but these kinsfolk,
their hearts with lust aflutter like the hawks
barely outdistanced by the doves, will come
hunting a marriage that the law forbids:
the God shall grudge the men these women's
    bodies,
and the Pelasgian earth shall welcome them
in death: for death shall claim them in a fight
where women strike in the dark, a murderous vigil.
Each wife shall rob her husband of his life,
dipping in blood her two-edged sword: even so
may Love come, too, upon my enemies.
But one among these girls shall love beguile
from killing her bedfellow, blunting her purpose:
and she shall make her choice—to bear the name
of coward and not murderer: this girl
she shall in Argos bear a race of kings.
To tell this clearly needs a longer story,
but from her seed shall spring one brave and
    famous
for archery, and he shall set me free.[6]
Such was the prophecy which ancient Themis,
my Titan mother, opened up to me;
but how and by what means it shall come true
would take too long to tell, and if you heard
the knowledge would not profit you.

---

[6]Again, Heracles.

IO
Eleleu, eleleu.
It creeps on me again, the twitching spasm,
the mind-destroying madness, burning me up,
and the gadfly's sting goads me on—
steel point by no fire tempered—
and my heart in its fear knocks on my breast.
There's a dazing whirl in my eyes as I run
out of my course by the madness driven,
the crazy frenzy; my tongue ungoverned
babbles, the words in a muddy flow strike
on the waves of the mischief I hate, strike wild
without aim or sense.

CHORUS

Strophe

A wise man indeed he was
that first in judgment weighed this word
and gave it tongue: the best by far
it is to marry in one's rank and station:
let no one working with her hands aspire
to marriage with those lifted high in pride
because of wealth, or of ancestral glory.

Antistrophe

Never, never may you see me,
Fates majestic, drawing nigh
the bed of Zeus, to share it with the King,
nor ever may I know a heavenly wooer:
I dread such things beholding
Io's sad virginity
ravaged, ruined; bitter wandering
hers because of Hera's wrath.

Epode

When a match has equal partners
then I fear not: may the eye
inescapable of the mighty
Gods not look on me.
That is a fight that none can fight: a fruitful
source of fruitlessness: I would not
know what I could do: I cannot
see the hope when Zeus is angry
of escaping him.

PROMETHEUS
Yet shall this Zeus, for all his pride of heart,
be humble yet: such is the match he plans,
a marriage that shall drive him from his power
and from his throne, out of the sight of all.

So shall at last the final consummation
be brought about of Father Kronos' curse
which he, driven from his ancient throne, invoked
against the son deposing him: no one
of all the Gods save I alone can tell
a way to escape this mischief: I alone
know it and how. So let him confidently
sit on his throne and trust his heavenly thunder
and brandish in his hand his fiery bolt.
Nothing shall all of this avail against
a fall intolerable, a dishonored end.
So strong a wrestler Zeus is now equipping
against himself, a monster hard to fight.
This enemy shall find a plan to best
the thunderbolt, a thunderclap to best
the thunderclap of Zeus: and he shall shiver
Poseidon's trident, curse of sea and land.
So, in his crashing fall shall Zeus discover
how different are rule and slavery.

CHORUS
You voice your wishes for the God's destruction.

PROMETHEUS
They are my wishes, yet shall come to pass.

CHORUS
Must we expect someone to conquer Zeus?

PROMETHEUS
Yes, he shall suffer worse than I do now.

CHORUS
Have you no fear of uttering such words?

PROMETHEUS
Why should I fear, since death is not my fate?

CHORUS
But he might give you pain still worse than this.

PROMETHEUS
Then let him do so; all this I expect.

CHORUS
Wise are the worshipers of Adrasteia.

PROMETHEUS
Worship him, pray; flatter whatever king
is king today; but I care less than nothing
for Zeus. Let him do what he likes,
let him be king for his short time: he shall not
be king for long
                Look, here is Zeus's footman,
this fetch-and-carry messenger of him,

the New King. Certainly he has come here
with news for us.

HERMES
                You, subtle-spirit, you
bitterly overbitter, you that sinned
against the immortals, giving honor to
the creatures of a day, you thief of fire:
the Father has commanded you to say
what marriage of his is this you brag about
that shall drive him from power—and declare it
in clear terms and no riddles. You, Prometheus,
do not cause me a double journey; these
[Pointing to the chains.] will prove to you that Zeus is
    not softhearted.

PROMETHEUS
Your speech is pompous sounding, full of pride,
as fits the lackey of the Gods. You are young
and young your rule and you think that the tower
in which you live is free from sorrow: from it
have I not seen two tyrants thrown? the third,
who now is king, I shall yet live to see him
fall, of all three most suddenly, most dishonored.
Do you think I will crouch before your Gods,
—so new—and tremble? I am far from that.
Hasten away, back on the road you came.
You shall learn nothing that you ask of me.

HERMES
Just such the obstinacy that brought you here,
to this self-willed calamitous anchorage.

PROMETHEUS
Be sure of this: when I set my misfortune
against your slavery, I would not change.

HERMES
It is better, I suppose, to be a slave
to this rock, than Zeus's trusted messenger.

PROMETHEUS
Thus must the insolent show their insolence!

HERMES
I think you find your present lot too soft.

PROMETHEUS
Too soft? I would my enemies had it then,
and you are one of those I count as such.

HERMES
Oh, you would blame me too for your calamity?

PROMETHEUS

In a single word, I am the enemy
of all the Gods that gave me ill for good.

HERMES

Your words declare you mad, and mad indeed.

PROMETHEUS

Yes, if it's madness to detest my foes.

HERMES

No one could bear you in success.

PROMETHEUS

Alas!

HERMES

Alas! *Zeus* does not know that word.

PROMETHEUS

Time in its aging course teaches all things.

HERMES

But you have not yet learned a wise discretion.

PROMETHEUS

True: or I would not speak so to a servant.

HERMES

It seems you will not grant the Father's wish.

PROMETHEUS

I should be glad, indeed, to requite his kindness!

HERMES

You mock me like a child!

PROMETHEUS

And are you not
a child, and sillier than a child, to think
that I should tell you anything? There is not
a torture or an engine wherewithal
Zeus can induce me to declare these things,
till he has loosed me from these cruel shackles.
So let him hurl his smoky lightning flame,
and throw in turmoil all things in the world
with white-winged snowflakes and deep bellowing
thunder beneath the earth: me he shall not
bend by all this to tell him who is fated
to drive him from his tyranny.

HERMES

Think, here and now, if this seems to your interest.

PROMETHEUS

I have already thought—and laid my plans.

HERMES

Bring your proud heart to know a true discretion—
O foolish spirit—in the face of ruin.

PROMETHEUS

You vex me by these senseless adjurations,
senseless as if you were to advise the waves.
Let it not cross your mind that I will turn
womanish-minded from my fixed decision
or that I shall entreat the one I hate
so greatly, with a woman's upturned hands,
to loose me from my chains: I am far from that.

HERMES

I have said too much already—so I think—
and said it to no purpose: you are not softened:
your purpose is not dented by my prayers.
You are a colt new broken, with the bit
clenched in its teeth, fighting against the reins,
and bolting. You are far too strong and confident
in your weak cleverness. For obstinacy
standing alone is the weakest of all things
in one whose mind is not possessed by wisdom.
Think what a storm, a triple wave of ruin
will rise against you, if you will not hear me,
and no escape for you. First this rough crag
with thunder and the lightning bolt the Father
shall cleave asunder, and shall hide your body
wrapped in a rocky clasp within its depth;
a tedious length of time you must fulfil
before you see the light again, returning.
Then Zeus's winged hound, the eagle red,
shall tear great shreds of flesh from you, a feaster
coming unbidden, every day: your liver
bloodied to blackness will be his repast.
And of this pain do not expect an end
until some God shall show himself successor
to take your tortures for himself and willing
go down to lightless Hades and the shadows
of Tartarus' depths. Bear this in mind
and so determine. This is no feigned boast
but spoken with too much truth. The mouth of
   Zeus
does not know how to lie, but every word
brings to fulfilment. Look, you, and reflect
and never think that obstinacy is better
than prudent counsel.

CHORUS

Hermes seems to us
to speak not altogether out of season.
He bids you leave your obstinacy and seek
a wise good counsel. Hearken to him. Shame
it were for one so wise to fall in error.

PROMETHEUS

Before he told it me I knew this message:
but there is no disgrace in suffering
at an enemy's hand, when you hate mutually.
So let the curling tendril of the fire
from the lightning bolt be sent against me: let
the air be stirred with thunderclaps, the winds
in savage blasts convulsing all the world.
Let earth to her foundations shake, yes to her root,
before the quivering storm: let it confuse
the paths of heavenly stars and the sea's waves
in a wild surging torrent: this my body
let Him raise up on high and dash it down
into black Tartarus with rigorous
compulsive eddies: death he cannot give me.

HERMES

These are a madman's words, a madman's plan:
is there a missing note in this mad harmony?
is there a slack chord in his madness? You,
you, who are so sympathetic with his troubles,
away with you from here, quickly away!
lest you should find your wits stunned by the
    thunder
and its hard defending roar.

CHORUS

                              Say something else
different from this: give me some other counsel
that I will listen to: this word of yours
for all its instancy is not for us.

How dare you bid us practice baseness? We
will bear along with him what we must bear.
I have learned to hate all traitors: there is no
disease I spit on more than treachery.

HERMES

Remember then my warning before the act:
when you are trapped by ruin don't blame fortune:
don't say that Zeus has brought you to calamity
that you could not foresee: do not do this:
but blame yourselves: now you know what you're
    doing:
and with this knowledge neither suddenly
nor secretly your own want of good sense
has tangled you in the net of ruin, past
all hope of rescue.

PROMETHEUS

Now it is words no longer: now in very truth
the earth is staggered: in its depths the thunder
bellows resoundingly, the fiery tendrils
of the lightning flash light up, and whirling clouds
carry the dust along: all the winds' blasts
dance in a fury one against the other
in violent confusion: earth and sea
are one, confused together: such is the storm
that comes against me manifestly from Zeus
to work its terrors. O Holy mother mine,
O Sky that circling brings the light to all,
you see me, how I suffer, how unjustly.

2
CLIZIA

by Niccolò Machiavelli • 1524

Translated by Robert Cohen

HISTORY HAS PRETTY MUCH OVERLOOKED NICCOLÒ Machiavelli's *Clizia*, which appears here for the first time in a general dramatic anthology; yet the play is certainly a fascinating and important theatre piece by one of history's most brilliant and controversial authors. Moreover, *Clizia* has one of the most impressive pedigrees in theatrical history.

As to the pedigree: *Clizia*'s known origin is a Greek play named *Kleoroumenoi*, or *The Lot Drawers*, by Diphilus. Diphilus' play (between 332 and 320 B.C.) is classed as a New Comedy, a late form of Greek comic drama featuring plots of domestic intrigue, and "stock" dramatic characters who appear in play after play: young lovers, faithful servants, wily slaves, identical twins, lecherous old men, and long-lost children. It was New Comedy—rather than Aristophanes' more political and spectacular Old Comedy—that served as a dramatic model for the future, and that survives comfortably today in certain Broadway (or French boulevard) plays and television situation comedy.

In the centuries after Diphilus, Roman dramatists—Plautus and Terence in particular—revised many of the New Comedies into a Latin form known as *fabula palliata*, or "comedies in Greek clothing." Plautus turned to *Kleoroumenoi* (the text of which has subsequently been lost) in 185 B.C., translating and revising it under the Latin title *Sorientes* (which also means *The Lot Drawers*). At a later revival, Plautus' play was renamed *Casina*, after its (nonappearing) heroine, and the script for that play survived. In 1524, Machiavelli translated and adapted it into *Clizia*.

Clizia is what the Italians called a *commedia erudita*, or "learned comedy." Such plays were "learned" only in the sense that they took some learning (of Latin) to adapt them from Roman models; far from being "erudite," the plays are generally licentious, bawdy, and topical. Both farcical and deliberately offensive, "learned comedies" are made up of gross puns, hilarious confrontations, absurd characters, sexual escapades, visual gags, "stand-up" speeches, and a rambunctious sense of general disrespect, if not outright tastelessness. Eventually the *commedia erudita* gave way to the more refined and professionalized *commedia dell'arte* (literally: the comedy of artists), and *Clizia* somewhat prefigures that mode; Machiavelli's protagonist Nicomaco can be seen as a precursor of the *commedia dell'arte* Pantalone. Meanwhile the theme of *Clizia* was picked up, nearly a century later, by the English dramatist Ben Jonson, who adapted it as *Epicoene, or The Silent Woman*.

Thus the dramatic historian can easily trace a continuous line of development running from Diphilus to Plautus to Machiavelli to Jonson to the *commedia dell'arte* and the present day, with *Clizia* squarely in the middle, if not at the apex. A minor masterpiece, to be sure, but at a major junction in dramatic history.

If *Clizia* has been generally overlooked, its author has suffered no such fate. But destiny has dealt Niccolò Machiavelli a cruel blow. Portrayed internationally, even in his own lifetime, as a conniving, immoral, even evil villain, Machiavelli was actually one of the great social thinkers, diplomats, and writers of all time. Moreover, he was a man of distinctly republican (that is, democratic) views, who opposed tyranny vigorously—in both words and deeds. Born in Florence in 1469, he became secretary to the Florentine Signoria (something like a secretary of state in the United States) in 1498. There, for more than fourteen years, he artfully preserved Florence's republican independence against the machinations of deposed Medici rulers, Papist general Cesare Borgia, Pope Alexander VI (also a Borgia), the kings of Spain and France, the emperor of Germany, and dozens of petty kings,

dukes, and warlords of city-states on all sides: Venice, Milan, Naples, and Pisa, among them. An ideal Renaissance man, he created the first citizen militia in Europe, and theorized the first model (not achieved until the nineteenth century) of a united Italian state. These were amazing times, in which art, science, and politics conjoined: when Florence needed new military weapons, Machiavelli commissioned Leonardo da Vinci to design them; when new town fortifications were desired, Machiavelli sought out his fellow citizen Michelangelo to draw up the blueprints. And when Machiavelli turned his interests to literature, his writing was informed by the entirety of known civilization.

Unfortunately for him, the Medicis returned to power in 1512, and Secretary Machiavelli was thrown out of office, falsely accused of treason, jailed, tortured, and eventually exiled from his beloved Florence. Although he was subsequently exonerated, Machiavelli's political career was over. In a small village outside of town, Machiavelli turned full time to writing, and an unprecedented series of poems, plays, histories, biographies, discourses, letters, and essays flowed from his pen. One manuscript, unpublished in his lifetime, became notorious: *The Prince*, a ruthlessly accurate description of (but not a prescription for) political manipulation, circulated widely throughout Europe. Unlike any author before him, Machiavelli described (but did not prescribe) grisly details of the new statecraft: including the political practices of terrorism, torture, secrecy, fear, deception, and betrayal. Thus "machiavellianism" entered the world's languages as a synonym for political evil.

What has been lost in his notoriety is Machiavelli's literary genius, his absorbing wit, and his wide-ranging sense of delight. Although rigorously clear-minded and unsentimental (this can be seen immediately in *Clizia*, as well as *The Prince*), Machiavelli's creative work includes a romantic and spiritual dimension, and an inspiring passion for freedom—which infused his political life as well as his literary endeavors.

On the surface, *Clizia* reveals more of Plautus than Machiavelli. The play is divided into five acts, which was the Roman standard, and it takes place within a single and near-continuous twenty-four-hour period, as was proper under classical models. All the action is set on a single outdoor street, with characters arriving on stage while on their way to or from their homes, or the market or church: this sort of staging, requiring little or no scenery (and no scene changes), was ideal for uncomplicated stage presentation both in Plautus' time and in Machiavelli's. Most of the characters in Machiavelli's play correspond with counterparts in Plautus' (although Machiavelli was the only one of the two to bring a Cleandro figure onstage), and that the title character (Clizia/Casina) does not appear in either play is also traditional, as unmarried women were not allowed to appear in public in ancient Greece, and so did not appear in New Comedy. Finally, the play ends with a classic *deus ex machina* (literally, a god on a flying machine): the surprise arrival of a character who neatly resolves the plot in a single stroke.

But Machiavelli did make many changes from the Plautus source. His play is actually less bawdy than his predecessor's, and the overtones of homosexual humor in the bedroom scenes of acts 4 and 5 are far less direct than in Plautus, where Lysidamus (the Nicomaco character) is unambiguously bisexual. By bringing Cleandro onto the stage, Machiavelli adds a lover to the plot, and somewhat humanizes the more coldblooded Plautine situation: we are even given to understand that Clizia loves Cleandro, too, making the romantic theme reciprocal, unlike Plautus' play, which was purely lust driven. Machiavelli also adds a prologue, and songs between each act, which lend his play a more presentational style.

The author's major changes from Plautus, however, are in the characterizations of Sofronia and Nicomaco. In Sofronia, Machiavelli has created a woman of more depth, intelligence, wit, fair-mindedness, and human compassion than can be seen in the Plautine original; indeed, Sofronia may be seen as one of the first dominant heroines in modern drama; she is both winning and winsome. And Nicomaco, whose name is, of course, a shorthand version of the author's, is not drawn merely with tottering buffoonery; we surely sense in this role the author's own ironic and self-deprecating laughter at his folly in the waning years of his own life, and a sense of repentance for his excesses.

Nicomaco's repentance and Sofronia's "victory" notwithstanding, however, no one can consider this play terribly enlightened with regard to the role of women in family life. Machiavelli simply accepts and passes on the tradition of the "silent woman" (Clizia) who has little or no say in her own affairs, and looks with comic derision—but not moral outrage—at the specter of forced sexual incest. Is derision enough? Contemporary readers and audiences must arrive at their own verdict.

A NOTE ON THE TRANSLATION AND THE STYLE OF THE PLAY

Clizia is a performance piece, and is meant to be presented with comic imagination, volatile energy, and a racy, bombastic style. The play is fundamentally presentational, calling attention to its own theatricality through numerous devices: direct asides to the audience, a prologue citing the play's historical roots, polemical songs, and the near-continual heralding of character entrances; for example, "Here comes Pirro now!" The *deus ex machina* ending is deliberately sudden and absurd, making a wry parody of the classical dramatic form, and subtly implying (as Bertolt Brecht was to do much later) that the loose ends in real life are never tied up so neatly.

This English adaptation is reasonably faithful, but it is hardly a scholarly version of the play: translator's liberties abound. My effort has been to find equivalents not merely for Machiavelli's line-by-line meaning, but for his total dramaturgy: the *sounds* of his speeches, together with his puns, jokes, rhythms, and tones. Let one example suffice: in act 4, Damone cites Nicomaco's impotence and foolishness by referring to him as "*questo vecchio impazzato, bavoso, ciposo, e sanza denti.*" It is quite proper and literal to render this as "that crazy, slobbering, bleary-eyed toothless old man," but such a rendition eliminates the terminal "o" vowel repetitions of the original, which provide a rolling comic momentum. In rendering the line as "that useless, juiceless, TOOTHLESS, mad old man," I have traded off some of the literal semantics for the escalating assonances of the original; this sort of thinking permeates the rendition. In similar fashion, anyone noting poor grammar ("grabbed the bed so tight") or contemporary slang ("I'm outta here," "monkey business") must understand that Machiavelli used parallel idiomatic devices; indeed, Machiavelli was quite deliberate in showing that this *wasn't* an old play, but a new play about the current times. Contemporary conversational syntax, urban slang, folk proverbs, and clichés of the day are prevalent in the Italian original, as are the mild vulgarities that have provoked comparable ones in this translation. Conversely, the erudite reader may also spot a few literary borrowings employed in this translation, certainly anachronistic to the 1506 setting, but parallelling Machiavelli's own classical references and *erudita*-isms.

Finally, I have added stage directions, lacking in the original, to clarify the action and give a sense of the likely staging. I have added the title of "Dr." to Damone's name, to identify him as a precursor of the *commedia dell'arte* character of Dottore, and I have had Sofronia refer to Nicomaco as a "Pantalone" for the same reason: both these appellations are anachronistic and not in the original. I have also assigned appropriate singers for the songs, as they are not indicated in the original text, but a new producer might well reassign the songs to whomever in the cast has the most appropriate voice(s).

⚹ CLIZIA ⚹

CAST OF CHARACTERS

NICOMACO, a prosperous Florentine businessman, in love with his ward, Clizia

SOFRONIA, Nicomaco's wife

CLEANDRO, his son, also in love with Clizia

DR. DAMONE, Nicomaco's neighbor

SOSTRATA, Dr. Damone's wife

PIRRO, Nicomaco's servant

EUSTACHIO, also Nicomaco's servant, but loyal to Cleandro

DORIA, Sostrata's servant

RAMONDO, a gentleman from Naples

A trestle-type stage, such as is used in the traditional commedia dell'arte, is set up, with a curtain drawn across the back. The setting is of a Florentine street in 1506. Entrances from one side are from the "town," which from time to time includes the marketplace, the church, and Dr. Damone's house. Entrances from the other side are from the house of Nicomaco and his family.

[As the audience has assembled, a chorus of nymphs and shepherds comes out from behind the curtain and sings:]

NYMPHS AND SHEPHERDS
What a happy day today!
When we remember years gone by,
Our voices raised in celebration;
And you, who've come to see our play,
Please know we'll try to satisfy
Your need for sylvan exaltation!
For we are nymphs and shepherds here,
Who love to sing, and sing to love.
And pretty soon we'll disappear
And do . . . just what you're thinking of!

This is a captivating place!
So beautiful and full of joy,
Which we will consummate with singing!
And all you of the human race
Can settle back and just enjoy
The entertainment we'll be bringing!
For we are nymphs and shepherds here,
Who love to sing, and sing to love.
And pretty soon we'll disappear
And do . . . just what you're thinking of!

[The nymphs and shepherds exit. From behind the curtain, a man or woman as prologue comes forward to address the audience.]

PROLOGUE
Well, nothing changes, nothing's ever new, the centuries roll on and on and yet the same things keep happening: "*Déjà* views," one after another! Listen, you recall the old play about the man in ancient Athens who adopted the little girl? Remember? He raised her very carefully until she was seventeen, and then he fell in love with her—and so did his son! What a mess, right? Well, can you believe the exact same thing happened here in Florence just a few years ago? It did! The story was so amazing that our author, Mr. Niccolò Machiavelli, decided to write his own play about it! About the Florence version, I mean, since Athens is pretty much in ruins these days, and also since our author figures that the Athenian language is pretty much Greek to you folks, right? *[pointing to a*

man in the audience] Oh, sir, don't worry, he's changed all the names! Always protecting the innocent, that's Machiavelli! [calling to the actors] OK! Everybody out! [The cast comes out in front of the curtain; the Prologue turns back to the audience.] Well, folks, these are our characters, just so you'll know them when you see 'em later on. Here's our big star: Nicomaco; he's the old goat, throbbing with desire. [Nicomaco comes forward and bows, as do the others when named.] And Cleandro, his only son, now his rival. Here's Palamede, Cleandro's friend; Pirro and Eustachio, the old man's servants; Sofronia, Nicomaco's wife; Doria, her maid; and here're the neighbors, Dr. Damone, and his wife Sostrata. There's one more in the cast, but he's driving up from Naples and hasn't gotten here yet: he doesn't show up 'til the last act, anyway. A randy bunch, all of them. [to the actors] OK, everybody outta' here! [The actors go back behind the curtain.] Our tale is called Clizia 'cause that's the name of the girl I told you about. You won't see her, though; Sofronia, who's in charge of her moral education, keeps her hidden inside the house. So you guys out there: stop panting! [stares accusingly at the men in the audience, then relaxes and continues] One more thing: our author, Mr. Machiavelli, considers himself a very straightlaced and straightforward sort of fellow, and will be most upset if you draw any unintended inferences or "doo-bull in-tenders" from what goes on up here. Not that there are any such things, of course. But just in case you think you hear any slanderous comments, or political wisecracks, or dirty jokes, or anything like that, you should excuse him, and not call the censors—or the vice squad. Because it's Mr. Machiavelli's view that comedy should be educational—but still funny. Educational in the sense that it shows us exactly who we really are: miserly old men, violent lovers, lying servants, greedy hangers-on, ruthless capitalists, beguiling whores, and, what can I say, BASE, LYING, ROTTEN, SLIME-BAGS! Right? Now, that's educational! But, hey, what's a comedy without laughs? Just a lot of moaning and groaning and high-falutin' TALK; all work, and no play. Well, I'm happy to tell you that Mr. M. thinks a comedy should be comic. Of course, you Florentines don't make it easy for him: you only laugh at things that are silly, foul-mouthed, blasphemous, or about sex. The problem is, Mr. M. won't be caught dead writing about people who are silly, or foul-mouthed, or blasphemous. So, I'm afraid, he's been forced into writing about . . . [whispers loudly] SEX. . . ! But ladies: You don't have to worry about blushing: there's no indecency in this play! None! Or if there is, you won't understand it! Unless, of course, you have dirty minds! So, listen, there's nothing to worry about. Well, pay attention, everybody, and enjoy the play!

[The Prologue goes behind the curtain.]

ACT ONE

[Palamede enters from the town, and Cleandro enters from the house; they meet in crossing.]

PALAMEDE
Cleandro! Where're you going?

CLEANDRO
Palamede! Where're you coming from?

PALAMEDE
[with a wink] Oh, just a little private affair . . .

CLEANDRO
That's what I'm after, too. But . . .

PALAMEDE
But? Tell me about it!

CLEANDRO
Easy to tell, hard to do. . . . [he drifts away, as if in a daze.]

PALAMEDE
Well, I'm off. Let me know when you wake up from your dream, Cleandro.

CLEANDRO
I'm not dreaming! I'm in love!

PALAMEDE
In love! I don't believe it!

CLEANDRO
Oh, Palamede, you don't know the half of it! I know I've been acting crazy for a long time, but now I'm beside myself!

PALAMEDE
I'll say!

CLEANDRO
Let me tell you about it!

PALAMEDE
Hey! No way! Listen, Cleandro, there're three kinds of people I can't deal with: Singers, old folks, and lov-

ers. You get in a good conversation with a singer, he starts practicing his *do re mi*'s on you, and warbling songs in your face. And the old folks: they pretend to listen to you, but really they're just running their paternosters over and over inside their heads: "Our Father who art in Heaven, blahbedee blah blah!" And lovers, oh, they're the worst! They tell you their troubles and ask your advice: and then their ears shut down, their eyes glaze over, and they're lost in their dreams. All they want is your sympathy! Go on, Cleandro, tell me about it: It's a girl from the streets, and she's driving you out of your house, right? Or out of your head; yeah, she's killing you and destroying your reputation! No, I've got it, she's a countess, yes! . . . and she's got dozens of lovers, so you're consumed by thousands of jealousies, agonies, mortal perturbations! Oh, no, Cleandro, I've heard it all, I've seen it all. Don't tell me—unless you're ready to listen in return!

CLEANDRO
OK, that's why I haven't told you. Until now. But I'm desperate, Palamede, and I need your help!

PALAMEDE
Well, if I can . . .

CLEANDRO
You can! You know that girl Dad adopted?

PALAMEDE
Clizia? Of course. She's your adopted . . . what?

CLEANDRO
You remember twelve years ago, when King Charles and his soldiers came through here on their way to the battle of Naples?

PALAMEDE
Yes . . .

CLEANDRO
Well, this Gascon general, Bertram, was lodged with us for a time. He was an honorable man, and my father and he became good friends.

PALAMEDE
Lucky you. The ones they put at our house were scum.

CLEANDRO
We were lucky, yes. Bertram went on to Naples with King Charles, but when the battle ended, he had taken on this little orphan girl: five years old, very pretty and apparently well bred. Well, the war kept going, and, right before the battle of Taro, Bertram had the girl sent to our house for safekeeping. We didn't know anything about her except her name: "Clizia." Mom and Dad, having no other children besides me, treated her as if she were their own daughter; soon they fell in love with her . . .

PALAMEDE
As did . . .

CLEANDRO
Oh, yes. I fell in love with her too. It was puppy love, I guess, I was only ten at the time, but pretty soon it was real love all right: overwhelming love, violent love, extraordinary love! Everybody could see it; by the time she was twelve, my parents were watching us like hawks, always keeping the two of us apart. If I even spoke to her, the whole household would get in an uproar! Well, the forbidden fruit is the one most hotly desired, isn't it? And their efforts to restrain me have only intensified my passion. So now I'm in torment, Palamede. I'm in Hell!

PALAMEDE
Didn't Bertram come back for her?

CLEANDRO
Never. He died in battle.

PALAMEDE
Well, what are you going to do? Marry her—or just keep her as a mistress? I mean, she's pretty much at your disposal . . .

CLEANDRO
Well, there's one more thing. But I can't tell you . . .

PALAMEDE
Tell me!

CLEANDRO
Ah, it only hurts when I laugh, Palamede . . . Dad loves her too!

PALAMEDE
Love? As in [*He shimmies suggestively.*] LUH-UV? Your father? Old Nicomaco?

CLEANDRO
The same.

PALAMEDE
Oh my God!

CLEANDRO
Oh my God, and Oh, you Saints, it's true!

PALAMEDE

Well, at least it's all in the family. Does your mother know?

CLEANDRO

Mom knows, I know, the servants know, and now you know!

PALAMEDE

So what are you going to do?

CLEANDRO

I don't know. Dad won't let me marry her—not just because he's in love with her, but because she has no dowry: He's such a miser! Also, because she doesn't have noble blood, and he's a social snob! But I don't care: wife, mistress, live-in girlfriend, whatever; I'd take her anyway I can. So, my friend, that's where things stand.

PALAMEDE

Well, what now?

CLEANDRO

Dad's trying to marry her off to Pirro, our servant! Can you believe that? Married in name only, of course; the idea is that Pirro will let Dad have his way with her whenever he wants! Oh, yes, Dad's been planning this for a year, ever since he fell in love with her. He almost pulled it off last month, but my mother got wind of his plans and threw a wrench in 'em. It's Mom's idea that Clizia should marry our other servant, Eustachio, instead of Pirro; that would keep Clizia out of Dad's hands all right. But now Dad's pressing Pirro's suit; he's called the priest for this evening, scheduled the ceremony, and has even rented out Dr. Damone's cottage next door for the honeymoon! For HIS honeymoon, that is, with MY Clizia!

PALAMEDE

Pirro or Eustachio: why do you care which one she marries?

CLEANDRO

Because Pirro's a scoundrel; the biggest in Florence! He loves my Dad, hates me, and two-times everybody else! I'd rather see her marry the devil than that rat! But I've sent for Eustachio; he's due here any minute. So, where're you going?

PALAMEDE

Like I said, a private affair . . .

CLEANDRO

Ciao, Palamede.

PALAMEDE

Ciao. Hang in there, Cleandro, and let me know if I can do anything.

[Palamede exits to the town.]

CLEANDRO

[to the audience] Owwwwwwwwwwww! Who was it said that lovers are like soldiers? He sure was speaking the truth. The general wants his men young and sturdy; so do women. Old soldiers are a dirty joke; so are old lovers. Soldiers get chewed out by their sergeants; lovers by their ladies. Soldiers sleep out in the rain on the battlefields: as do would-be Romeos, who get sopping wet under the balconies of their Juliets. Soldiers pursue their enemies with total ferocity: just as lovers attack their rivals. Secrecy, faith, and courage are the emblems of both the soldier and the lover: neither blackest night, nor iciest cold, nor driving-est wind, rain, sleet, nor hail will halt either one on the route to conquest! Thus, at the end of that lonely road, the warrior dies cruelly in a ditch: the lover in despair! And so it is with me: Clizia lives in my house, I see her, I eat with her; the closer she gets, the more I want her; the more I want her, the less I have her; the less I have her, the more I am in an agony of passion! But where the hell is my man Eustachio? He has to help me to stop this marriage between Clizia and Pirro, and before tonight, too! Oh, wait, there he is! Eustachio! Eustachio!

[Eustachio enters from the town.]

EUSTACHIO

Who's that? Oh, Cleandro, it's you!

CLEANDRO

I thought you'd never get here!

EUSTACHIO

I came in last night, but I had to hide: your father Nicomaco wrote and asked me to do a whole bunch of things for him; I didn't want him to see me.

CLEANDRO

Good thinking! Listen, I wrote you because Dad's trying to marry Clizia off to that scoundrel Pirro, again. But my mother wants her to marry you instead, and so do I!

EUSTACHIO

Well, thanks. I'll sure be happy to marry her if you and your mother want me to, but, look, I don't want to make an enemy of your Dad; he's still the boss around here, as I understand it.

CLEANDRO
Don't worry about that! My mother and I are completely behind you; we'll take care of old Nicomaco. But you better freshen up a bit. Hey, look here, your coat's falling off, your cap's dirty, you need a shave: Clizia's going to think you're a pig! Go on, Eustachio, take a bath, press your pants, go to the barber's . . .

EUSTACHIO
You're not so great looking yourself, you know . . .

CLEANDRO
Get going! Do what I tell you, and then wait for me in the church. I'm going home to see what that fool, old Nicomaco, my father's up to.

[Eustachio exits to the town, and Cleandro sings.]

CLEANDRO
[sings] The man who's never been in love
Has no idea what it's made of!
Has no idea what wretched things,
What MISERY this passion brings!
That little bastard Cupid's shaft
Is whittled sharp by sheer witchcraft!
It goes in deep! And makes us foolish
Hopeless! Helpless! Ghastly! Ghoulish!
I pray the love-god: Set me free
From love's great asininity!

[Cleandro exits toward the house.]

─────── ACT TWO ───────

[Nicomaco enters the stage, stumbling and almost falling.]

NICOMACO
Ouch! What the hell's the matter with my eyes this morning? Last night I saw great, today I'm bumping into walls. *[directly to the audience]* Maybe I had too much to drink? What do you think? Oh my God, maybe it's old age! You think? Well, at least I'm not too old to point my lance at Clizia! God! Who would have thought it possible? Me, Nicomaco, a lover! But I'm afraid that Sofronia, my wife, has found out about it. And she knows why I want Clizia married to Pirro! Oh Pirro! Come here!

PIRRO
Here I am!

NICOMACO
Pirro, I want you to marry Clizia tonight.

PIRRO
Sure. How about right now?

NICOMACO
Slow down! One step at a time, as the fat lady says. Things are all messed up here right now: Sofronia knows, and she's out to stop us; your fellow servant Eustachio wants to marry Clizia too; and Cleandro, the Devil, seems to be backing HIM for God's sake. But hold firm, Pirro! Have faith! I'll get her for you, don't worry! And if they don't like it they can lump it!

PIRRO
Well? Tell me what to do!

NICOMACO
Just stick around. When I need you, I'll come for you.

PIRRO
OK! But there's just one thing . . .

NICOMACO
What?

PIRRO
Eustachio's in town.

NICOMACO
Eustachio? In Florence? No! Says who?

PIRRO
Old Ambruogio, from next door. They both came into the city last night . . .

NICOMACO
Last night! Where's Eustachio staying?

PIRRO
How would I know?

NICOMACO
Sofronia must have sent for the scoundrel, and he answered HER letter and not MINE. By God I'll pay him back for this! And her! Uh-oh, here she comes: Pirro, get out of here fast!

[Pirro exits hurriedly, and Nicomaco puts on a big grin as Sofronia enters and walks right past him.]

SOFRONIA
[aside to the audience] I've had to lock Clizia in her room: my son's after her, my husband's after her; the

servants are after her: my house is becoming a den of iniquity for God's sake!

[*Sofronia looks back at her husband, snarls and starts off.*]

NICOMACO
Where're you going?

SOFRONIA
To church.

NICOMACO
To church? What on earth for, it's not Lent! It's not even Sunday!

SOFRONIA
It's a day in the life of the wicked, all of whom need our prayers. Including you!

NICOMACO
Me? What's wrong with me?

SOFRONIA
Here we've raised this lovely young girl, for which everyone in town admires us, and now you're trying to marry her off to this brainless idiot Pirro! Who can't even support the fleas in his beard! We'll be the laughingstocks of Florence.

NICOMACO
Sofronia, darling, you're dead wrong as usual. Pirro's young, he's good-looking, and what he doesn't know yet he can learn. Besides, he loves her. He's got the three things a husband should have, youth, looks, and *amore, amore*; who could ask for anything "more, eh"?

SOFRONIA
That's not funny! I could!

NICOMACO
I know, he's not rich, but you know money, it goes from boom to bust, bust to boom, and Pirro's a boomer if I've ever seen one! Indeed, I'm thinking of buying him Dr. Damone's house next door, and setting him up. Hell, it'll only cost four hundred thousand florins, and . . .

SOFRONIA
Ha ha ha!

NICOMACO
You're laughing?

SOFRONIA
Who wouldn't? And what are you "setting him up" IN?

NICOMACO
What do you mean? In business, of course!

SOFRONIA
In monkey business, I bet! You're going to take something away from your son and give it to your cabin steward, right? Something's fishy here, Nicomaco!

NICOMACO
Fishy? What are you saying, fishy?

SOFRONIA
You already know, so I won't tell you.

NICOMACO
What . . . what . . . what do I know?

SOFRONIA
Forget it! Why are you so eager to marry Clizia to Pirro? She's got no dowry, and he's got no prospects! Right?

NICOMACO
Right . . . I guess . . . But I love them both so much, I raised them both; they're both so . . . both so . . . ME! . . . that I know they'll be very happy together.

SOFRONIA
Well, how about your servant Eustachio? You raised him, too, didn't you? Isn't he YOU enough?

NICOMACO
Eustachio's a country yokel; he's spent his life with cows, sheep, and chickens; what kind of husband would he make? Clizia would die of boredom.

SOFRONIA
So? With Pirro she'll die of starvation! Let me remind you, Nicomaco, a husband must know how to DO something; he must have some ability, some know-how, some intelligence! Eustachio can make all sorts of things; he understands the marketplace, how to get people to do things; he can keep his head above water! Look, he's even got some money of his own! Your Pirro, on the other hand, spends all his time drinking and gambling. Pirro would starve in the Garden of Eden![1]

NICOMACO
I told you, I'll set him up!

---

[1]In the original, "in Altopascio." Altopascio is a prosperous farm town northwest of Florence.

SOFRONIA

And I told you, you'd just be throwing good money after bad! And you'd convert all our good work into a public scandal! Listen, we're both involved in this: you may have paid for Clizia's food but I've brought her up, and I'll have my say about what happens to her! Or else there'll be hell to pay all over town: I'll make sure of that!

NICOMACO

Are you crazy? What are you trying to say? I'm telling you they're getting married tonight, no matter what you do.

SOFRONIA

Maybe yes and maybe no.

NICOMACO

Oho, you're threatening to slander me. Watch out, woman, two can play at that game. You're not all that innocent, you know, helping your dear Cleandro out in his little adventures . . .

SOFRONIA

What adventures? What are you talking about?

NICOMACO

Oh ho ho! Don't make me say it, dear wife: You know, and I know, and I know that you know, and you know that I know that. . . . Arghhh! We're none of us idiots here! Let's make a deal before we make ourselves a public spectacle.

SOFRONIA

A spectacle, yes, pure *commedia dell'arte!* And you: old Pantalone! All Florence will be rolling in the aisles!

NICOMACO

[sings] Sofronia! Sofronia! You're so full of macaronia![2] *[imitates a fart]* Pfffffffffffffffffffffft!

SOFRONIA

God forgive you, husband. I'm going to church; I'll see you later.

NICOMACO

Wait! Just a minute. Come on, be agreeable. People'll say we're crazy.

SOFRONIA

Crazy, no. Stupid, yes. And wicked, too!

---

[2]In the original, Machiavelli puns *Sofronia* with *soffiona*—a wind machine.

NICOMACO

I know, let's get some outside advice; talk this through with someone, you know!

SOFRONIA

What someone?

NICOMACO

You know, friends, family . . . Why don't we go get one of them? Someone who can say who's right and who's wrong?

SOFRONIA

And let everybody see how stupid we are?

NICOMACO

OK, forget friends and family: let's get the priest! We'll put it to him in confession!

SOFRONIA

What priest?

NICOMACO

Our family confessor, of course, Friar Timoteo! The man's a virtual saint. He works miracles.

SOFRONIA

Miracles?

NICOMACO

You remember Mona Lucrezia, wife of Signior Nicia? She became pregnant through his prayers!

SOFRONIA

Some miracle: the baby looks a little friarish to me! If a NUN got her pregnant, THAT would be a miracle!

NICOMACO

Is this possible? You're twisting everything I say!

SOFRONIA

I'm going to church! And I'm not going to turn Clizia over to you, or to your fishy friar, or to anybody else!

NICOMACO

Go on, then! Go! I'm going home; I'll see you there later, and we'll settle this once and for all!

[Nicomaco starts toward the house, but noticing Sofronia remaining onstage, stops.]

NICOMACO

She's up to something; I better not go too far away.

[Nicomaco tiptoes off the other way, toward the town, but out of a corner of her eye Sofronia sees him go.]

SOFRONIA

It's amazing, the change in this man! Why, right up through last year, he was serious, consistent, respectful, honorable! He woke up early, got dressed, went to church, and went about his work! In the morning he made his rounds: the market, city hall, maybe a business call or two, or else he'd go to his office and balance his books. Then it'd be a quiet lunch with a few friends, perhaps a visit with his son, giving the boy a few words of advice—worthwhile lessons from history, you know, sage observations on current affairs—and then, home for afternoon chores, evening prayers, a quick visit to the study to plan the next day's events; then, at nine o'clock, a big family dinner in front of the fireplace. An orderly life! A model husband: a father, a citizen! An exemplar of family values! But now look at him! All of a sudden, he's lost in fantasy: all he thinks about is Clizia! He ignores his business, neglects his properties, forgets his friends! All he does now is yell and scream: about what, nobody knows; most of the time he doesn't even know himself! A thousand times a day he comes home, then goes right out again, for no reason at all! He's never here at mealtime: if you talk to him he doesn't respond—or if he does, he doesn't make any sense. The servants laugh at him, and his son's completely written him off; why, everyone in the house now feels they can do whatever they want! Our home has fallen into total anarchy! Well, I'm going to church and pray things get better. Hey: there's Eustachio and Pirro having a fight about something. Great husbands they'd make for my Clizia!

[Sofronia exits to the town, crossing Pirro and Eustachio as they enter; Eustachio is dressed up in fancy new clothes.]

PIRRO
What are you doing in Florence, you scumbag?

EUSTACHIO
None of your business!

PIRRO
Well, you sure look snazzy! Like a gilded pisspot!

EUSTACHIO
You're so stupid, it's amazing you haven't been run out of town yet!

PIRRO
We'll see who's stupid, stupid!

EUSTACHIO
Pray God Nicomaco keeps paying your bills, or you'll be begging in the streets!

PIRRO
Where is Nicomaco?

EUSTACHIO
What's it to you?

PIRRO
You're the one better find out: if he finds you here in Florence, he'll have you run out of town in a hurry.

EUSTACHIO
It really bugs you I'm here, doesn't it?

PIRRO
It bugs someone else more than it does me.

EUSTACHIO
Then let him worry about it.

PIRRO
You're pathetic.

EUSTACHIO
Wipe that sneer off your face!

PIRRO
I'm just thinking what a great husband you'll make Clizia!

EUSTACHIO
And you know what I say? The finest wine comes in the dirtiest bottles! If she marries you, she's REALLY in the gutter: better Nicomaco should drown her in the well; at least she'd die quickly, and with less misery!

PIRRO
God, there's a stink around here! *[sniffs Eustachio]* Manure, I think. But maybe Clizia won't mind a little shit . . .

EUSTACHIO
No, she'd rather have a city dimwit like you. If she married you, I guarantee she'd be looking around for a real man within the year; but now, you wouldn't mind that, would you? You're a born cuckold, Pirro . . .

PIRRO
Leave me alone! You go prepare for a fight, Eustachio, we'll see who comes out on top. I'm going home; if I stayed here I'd have to break your neck.

EUSTACHIO
And I'm headed back to church: sorry you can't come . . .

PIRRO
Go on, then. You might find some sanctuary there . . .

[Pirro exits to the house, Eustachio to the town.]

──────── ACT THREE ────────

[Cleandro enters from the house.]

CLEANDRO
[sings] Romantic love's designed for youth!
And young love's charming to behold!
But there's a corresponding truth:
Such love's appalling in the old!
Passion needs a sturdy heart;
A healthy body filled with life!
An old man's coming all apart!
How can he satisfy a wife?
So listen, Dad, to what I'm sayin':
And leave the world for ME to play in.

[Nicomaco enters from the town.]

NICOMACO
Cleandro! Hey, Cleandro!

CLEANDRO
Yessir!

NICOMACO
Come here! Come here, dammit! What are you doing home? Not messing around with Clizia, are you? You should be ashamed of yourself: it's Carnival time, on days like this young guys like you should be out watching the maskers, or playing football, not moping around the house. What's the matter with you, you look half dead!

CLEANDRO
I'm not like other guys; I never have been. I'm just as happy here at home. Besides, at home I'm available if you need anything.

NICOMACO
I don't need anything, dammit! And if I do, I've got two servants and a steward, so I don't need to bother you.

CLEANDRO
God forbid I should be of any help then! But it's not like I don't know what to do with myself.

NICOMACO
I'm sure you do! But your mother doesn't, I know that! She's gone crazy—maybe you can straighten her out. She's going to ruin our whole family!

CLEANDRO
She won't, but someone else might.

NICOMACO
Which someone else?

CLEANDRO
Which? I'm sure I don't know.

NICOMACO
I'm sure you don't, either. But in this business about Clizia . . .

CLEANDRO
[aside] Now we're getting somewhere!

NICOMACO
What?

CLEANDRO
I said, What about Clizia?

NICOMACO
Don't you think your mother's crazy not to let Clizia marry Pirro?

CLEANDRO
I don't know anything about it.

NICOMACO
Aha! You're on her side! You two are hatching a plot against me! You can't want her to marry Eustachio?

CLEANDRO
I don't know anything about that, either!

NICOMACO
What the hell DO you know, then?

CLEANDRO
Nothing!

NICOMACO
Nothing? Then who brought Eustachio back to Florence, may I ask? Who's been sneaking him around town? You and he are trying to break up Pirro's marriage, aren't you? I'll have both of you thrown in jail! I'll give your mother her dowry back, and ship her home to her father! You listen: Everybody listen: I am going to be master in my own house, you hear? Pirro and Clizia are going to be married this evening, or I'll do something terrible—I'll . . . I'll burn down the house! Yes! I'll wait just five minutes more for your mother: either she goes along with me or . . . or I'll go it alone: What's good for the gander is to cook her goose—or something like that—you wait and see!

CLEANDRO
Dad . . .

NICOMACO

Cleandro, if you want this family to survive, go find your mother, and tell her what's what! She's still in the church; go talk to her. I'll wait here at home. And if you see that rascal Eustachio, tell him I want to see him, post haste and double pronto! Or he'll be more than sorry! Go on! Goodbye! *Au revoir! Ciao!*

CLEANDRO

[starting off to town] I'm on my way . . .

[Nicomaco exits to the house; Cleandro halts, remains onstage.]

Oh the misery of love! All I do is go from one torment to another! I know that anyone in love with a beautiful girl like Clizia is going to have rivals, but . . . my own father! I've never heard of anything like this! Fathers are supposed to help their sons, not compete against them! Mother's on my side—but more because she wants Dad to lose than for me to win! I can't even tell her my plans: she'll think I'm pushing Eustachio's suit for the same reason Dad's pushing Pirro's: she'll think we're pimping for ourselves, and she'll give up on both of us. I'm going to go kill myself! No, wait, there's Mother now, coming out of church. Let me see: maybe she's come up with some way to foul up the old man's scheme!

[Sofronia enters from the town.]

Momma!

SOFRONIA

Ah, Cleandro! Have you just come from the house?

CLEANDRO

Yes . . .

SOFRONIA

You've been there since I left?

CLEANDRO

Yes . . .

SOFRONIA

Where's your father?

CLEANDRO

He's home.

SOFRONIA

Doing what?—He's with Clizia, God knows! Like a boy let loose in a candy shop, I'll bet. Did he say anything to you?

CLEANDRO

Oh, he's gone sky high this time; the Devil's in him for sure! Let's see: He's going to have Eustachio and me thrown in jail, he's going to give you back your dowry and send you home to your father, and he's going to burn down the house: All this if we don't agree to Clizia's marrying Pirro! He's sent me to convince you to go along with this, "or else!"

SOFRONIA

And you said . . . ?

CLEANDRO

What could I say? I love Clizia like a sister, and I can't stand the thought of Pirro getting his dirty hands on her.

SOFRONIA

Like a sister? I hope so: I'm not interested in getting her out of Nicomaco's bed just to put her in yours. But Eustachio loves her himself; he can marry her, and then we'll find you another wife who'll make you forget all about Clizia.

CLEANDRO

Great! Sure! Yes! Just make sure this marriage with Pirro never takes place! Marry her off to Eustachio if you have to! Or, maybe you could let her stay single for a while longer: she's still young, there's plenty of time! I mean, suppose her parents show up after all this: how do you think they'd feel, knowing we married her off to a servant? From the country?

SOFRONIA

You're right. I've thought of that, but your father's going crazy. We have to do something. Let me think some more: I'll work this out. There, look; there's your father waiting for me by the door. I'll go see him; you go to the church and get Eustachio. Tell him to come home and not be afraid . . .

CLEANDRO

Done!

[Cleandro exits toward town, Sofronia following a step with him. Nicomaco enters from the house.]

NICOMACO

[aside] Well, Sofronia's returned. I think I'll try a little sweet talk; women like that sort of thing. *[aloud]* Darling! Awwww, Whatsa' matta', sweety-bird, puddy-twos, you look so boo-boo-eyes today? Gimme' li'l kissy-wissy . . .

[Nicomaco grabs at her, she pulls away.]

SOFRONIA
Let go of me!

NICOMACO
Awww . . . come back to Nico-micko . . .

SOFRONIA
No! What, have you gone completely out of your mind????

NICOMACO
Then I'm coming after youzy-wouzy . . . !

SOFRONIA
Are you crazy?

NICOMACO
Cwazy for you, Cwazy wiv desire . . .

SOFRONIA
Well, I don't desire your desire!

NICOMACO
I can't help myself!

SOFRONIA
I'd die first! You're disgusting!

NICOMACO
You don't mean that . . .

SOFRONIA
Better believe it!

NICOMACO
My love! Just look at me!

SOFRONIA
I'm looking at you, all right, and smelling you too! What, are you wearing perfume, now?

NICOMACO
[aside] Dammit! She noticed; I knew I shouldn't have put this on!

SOFRONIA
[sniffs] Ah, Eau de Whorehouse! You crazy old fool!

NICOMACO
A traveling salesman . . . he bumped into me . . . one of his perfume bottles broke . . .

SOFRONIA
What a lie! Listen, you've been fooling around this whole year, drinking, whoring, gambling, spending recklessly: what kind of example is this for Cleandro? It's like father, like son, right? What kind of husband is HE going to make?

NICOMACO
Look, don't throw the whole book at me today! You won't have anything left to accuse me of tomorrow! Ha ha ha! But really, Sofronia, my pet, doesn't it make more sense for a wife to obey her husband than the other way around?

SOFRONIA
It might, if the husband were an honorable man.

NICOMACO
Well, isn't it honorable to have our young girl married off?

SOFRONIA
Yes, to a decent husband.

NICOMACO
And isn't Pirro decent?

SOFRONIA
No!

NICOMACO
Why not?

SOFRONIA
I've already told you!

NICOMACO
I think I know a bit more about these things than you do. Anyway, I'm about to talk to Eustachio; when I'm through, he won't even want her anymore.

SOFRONIA
Go ahead! But I'm going to talk to Pirro, and, believe me, when I'm through HE won't want her either!

NICOMACO
All right, you're on! And let the best man win!

SOFRONIA
Any day! There's Eustachio, coming out of church; you talk to him. I'll go back to the house and talk with Pirro.

NICOMACO
Go ahead!

[Sofronia goes into the house, and Eustachio comes in from the church.]

EUSTACHIO
[aside, not yet seeing Nicomaco] Well, Cleandro told me I needn't be afraid, so I'm going back to the house. Courage, Eustachio, courage!

NICOMACO

[aside] There's that dirty little rat! I was going to chew him out, but now I have to beg to him, dammit! [aloud, sing-songy] Yoo-hoo, Eustach-io!

EUSTACHIO

Ah, noble master!

NICOMACO

Ah, Eustachio, when did you get into Florence?

EUSTACHIO

Last night.

NICOMACO

You've taken your time getting over to see us, dear boy! Where've you been?

EUSTACHIO

Been? Well, I wasn't feeling so good when I came into town: had a headache, fever, swollen testicles, you know; I got scared maybe I was getting the plague. So, not wanting to infect you or your family with the buboes, I stayed at the inn. But now I feel fine, thank God!

NICOMACO

Thank God! [aside] I have to pretend to believe him. [aloud] Just the right thing! And you're cured now?

EUSTACHIO

Indeed I am, sir.

NICOMACO

[aside] Not of lying, however. [aloud] Well, I'm very glad you've come. I suppose you've heard about this argument between my wife and me: Sofronia wants Clizia to marry you, but I want her to marry Pirro.

EUSTACHIO

You like Pirro better than me?

NICOMACO

Oh, no! I like you better than him! It's just that . . . Listen: You're already thirty-eight; what would you do with a young girl? Use your head, Eustachio: within a month or two, she'd just be out looking for a younger man. Pretty soon you'd become the town joke, you'd lose your job, your standing in the community, and eventually the both of you would be left begging in the streets!

EUSTACHIO

In Florence, my noble master, no one with a beautiful wife—and a "liberal disposition"—will ever go hungry.

NICOMACO

Ah, so you still plan to marry Clizia, just to displease me?

EUSTACHIO

No, just to please me!

NICOMACO

Get out of here! Go on home! [aside] I must have been crazy to expect any satisfaction from this mulehead. [aloud] Turn over your account books, you're fired! Consider yourself my enemy! By God, I'll make you suffer for this!

EUSTACHIO

I don't care, as long as I have Clizia!

NICOMACO

You'll have the rack instead!

[Eustachio leaves for the house, crossing Pirro, who enters from the house in terror, calling offstage behind him.]

PIRRO

[to Sofronia, offstage] No! Never! I'll be skinned alive first!

NICOMACO

[aside] Good news! Pirro's forging ahead! [aloud] What's the matter, Pirro? Who are you fighting with?

PIRRO

As if you didn't know—the one YOU'RE always fighting with!

NICOMACO

My wife? What does she want?

PIRRO

She begged me to stay away from Clizia!

NICOMACO

And what did you say?

PIRRO

I said I'd die before I'd give her up!

NICOMACO

Well done, Pirro!

PIRRO

Yeah, but I'm afraid I'm the one who'll be well done, when she gets through with me! She and your son: they'll fry me in oil!

NICOMACO

Well? [pointing to himself] Stick with Jesus, not his saints!

PIRRO

Just don't you get crucified: your saints'll tear me to pieces.

NICOMACO

Don't worry, I'll take care of the saints, and the law courts too: you just see to it I get to sleep with Clizia!

PIRRO

That'll be the day! Your wife is already going through the roof!

NICOMACO

Look, I know what to do: you two can draw lots for Clizia! Whoever wins can have her: we'll leave it all to Fortune; Sofronia will have to go along with that!

PIRRO

You trust your luck so much?

NICOMACO

We'll win: God will see to it!

PIRRO

[aside] God!!!! What a crazy old goat! As if God serves lechery! *[aloud]* Were God to get involved in this, Nicomaco, I think Sofronia might have a prayer or two . . .

NICOMACO

Hell, let her pray! But it won't just be luck: I have another plan as well. Go, call her! Tell her and Eustachio to come out here!

PIRRO

Sofronia! Eustachio! Come out here, both of you. Master calls!

[Sofronia and Eustachio enter from the house.]

SOFRONIA

Here I am, what do you want this time?

NICOMACO

Wife, let's put an end to this quarreling. Pirro and Eustachio can't come to any agreement, so I'm going to propose a solution right now.

SOFRONIA

What's the big hurry? We'll talk about it tomorrow.

NICOMACO

I want to do it today.

SOFRONIA

All right, let's do it right now. Here are the two suitors: what do you want them to do?

NICOMACO

We'll draw lots!

SOFRONIA

Lots?

NICOMACO

Lots! We'll put the two suitors' names in one bag, and Clizia's name in another, along with a blank slip of paper. Then we'll draw one paper from each bag! Whichever man is drawn with Clizia can marry her! Well? What do you think? Speak up!

SOFRONIA

OK. I accept.

NICOMACO, PIRRO, and EUSTACHIO

[astounded] You do?

SOFRONIA

I know what I'm doing. Go into the house, make up the four slips of paper, and bring them out with two bags. I want to end this matter once and for all.

EUSTACHIO

All right . . . *[runs off to the house]*

NICOMACO

Excellent! Now pray, Pirro, pray hard so God will help you!

PIRRO

So he will help YOU, you mean . . .

NICOMACO

[unhappy that this is overheard] Right! Uh . . . He will help ME because I will be divinely HAPPY that you will have HER . . .

EUSTACHIO

[returning with the bags and the slips] Here are the two bags and the four slips of paper.

NICOMACO

Give them to me. Now, what does this one say? "Clizia." Good. And this one? It's blank, fine. I'm putting them both in this bag here! And now this one? "Eustachio." Excellent. And this one? "Pirro." Terrific! These two go in the other bag. Okay, now close the bags up tight and shake them up. Nothing up your sleeves, now, is there, Sofronia? Keep your eyes open, Pirro: and no cheating, wife!

SOFRONIA

A man without trust is a man without honor.

NICOMACO

Drivel! Only those who trust can truly be deceived. So, now, who's going to draw?

SOFRONIA
Whomsoever you want!

NICOMACO
[to an attendant] Come here, boy.

[A boy comes forward.]

SOFRONIA
No! Whoever draws lots should be a virgin.

NICOMACO
Virgin or not, I've never touched him! What are you insinuating? Come on, my boy, draw a slip from this bag: no, wait, let me pray first. O Saint Appolonia . . .

SOFRONIA
[under her breath] . . . patron of the toothless . . .

NICOMACO
. . . and all you other saints who safeguard holy matrimony, please grant Clizia the noble, handsome Pirro for a husband! OK, draw! [The boy draws a name.] Give it here! Oh God! I'm dying! No, I'm dead! It's Eustachio!

SOFRONIA
What's wrong with you? He hasn't drawn the other one yet!

NICOMACO
Oh, right. Draw the other one. Give it here! Aha! Aha! It's the blank! Resurrection! Victory! Jubilation! Pirro, to the victor belongs the spoils! Eustachio's dead in the water! Sofronia, it seems that God has willed Clizia to Pirro! So you better go along with it now!

SOFRONIA
I will.

NICOMACO
Make plans for the wedding!

SOFRONIA
Don't be in such a hurry. Let it wait till tomorrow!

NICOMACO
No, no, no, no, no! You hear me: NO! What kind of a trick is this?

SOFRONIA
What are we, atheists? Can't you wait until morning mass?

NICOMACO
Mass, my ass! Let her go to mass next week. Next year! She can confess her sins after the fact!

SOFRONIA
But she's in the middle of her period!

NICOMACO
Well? I'll put a period to that! You don't seem to understand, Sofronia: I want her married tonight!

SOFRONIA
Well, go ahead, then, and the hell with you! I'm going home; you better come too, and tell Clizia what you have in mind. But don't expect a reward.

NICOMACO
No, but I do expect a bonus! Ha! Let's go in!

[Nicomaco and Pirro start toward the house; Nicomaco turns back to Sofronia.]

Come on!

SOFRONIA
I'll be right there!

[Nicomaco and Pirro exit toward the house.]

[to Eustachio] Go, find Cleandro! He'll think up some way to get us out of this!

[Eustachio exits toward the church, and Sofronia, alone onstage, sings.]

SOFRONIA
[sings] Prospective lovers, be forewarned:
In order to keep living,
You'd best beware all women scorned,
We're wholly unforgiving!
We women come into this life
With savage pride and fierce desire.
The man who trifles with his wife
Will roast in diabolic fire!
We'll lie, we'll cheat, we'll steal, we'll kill.
Don't underestimate our will!
For we know what we're fighting for:
We know all's fair in love and war.

[Sofronia exits to the house.]

——————— ACT FOUR ———————

[Cleandro and Eustachio enter from the church.]

CLEANDRO
How could my mother be so stupid! Give up Clizia in a lottery? When the honor of our whole house is at stake?

EUSTACHIO
Exactly!

CLEANDRO
How could this happen to me? I'm totally destroyed! If I hadn't run into my friend in the church, I'd've been right over here: but no, I get held up; meanwhile the marriage is arranged, the ceremony is scheduled, and everything's gone just as my father planned! O damn Dame Fortune, I thought you favored young lovers, not old lechers! Aren't you ashamed of yourself, Fortune, offering Clizia's sweet, lovely cheek to an old man's stinking breath, toothless gums, and slobbering lips? Putting Clizia's delicious, dainty, delicate body into a pair of wrinkled, feverish, quivering hands? Because it won't be Pirro, it will be Nicomaco who will have her in the end, I know it! With a single blow, cruel Fortune, you have taken everything from me: oh yes, the woman I love AND the inheritance I deserve—for now my father will leave everything to Pirro! Where's Mother? How could she do this to me?

EUSTACHIO
Take it easy, Cleandro. Sofronia had kind of—well—a strange expression on her face when she left me: so I don't think Nicomaco's "pear" has yet been "plucked," if you know what I mean.

CLEANDRO
Plucked? PLUCKED?

EUSTACHIO
But here comes your father, with Pirro, chipper as they can be . . .

CLEANDRO
Go on in, Eustachio: I'll hide and listen; maybe I can overhear their plans . . .

EUSTACHIO
I'm outta here . . .

[Nicomaco and Pirro enter from the house, passing Eustachio and Cleandro, who have headed off the same way. Eustachio goes on to exit, but Cleandro stops and hides onstage.]

NICOMACO
Oh, how great it is! Did you see how miserable they looked? And how furious Sofronia is? Boy, does that make me happy! But I will be even happier when I get my hands on Clizia tonight: when I can touch her, kiss her, give her a big, big squeeze! Yummmmmmm! Oh, sweet night: I can hardly wait! And you, Pirro, I owe you one for this, don't worry. Hell, I owe you two! Four . . . six . . . eight . . .

CLEANDRO
[aside] The crazy old fool!

PIRRO
I believe you, master, but, TONIGHT. . . ? Aren't you rushing things?

NICOMACO
What do you mean, rushing? I've arranged everything!

PIRRO
Tell me!

CLEANDRO
[aside] And tell ME, so I can spoil your little plan . . . and get Clizia back for myself!

NICOMACO
You know our neighbor, Dr. Damone, whose house I've rented for you and Clizia?

PIRRO
Sure . . .

NICOMACO
Well, you take her over to his house.

PIRRO
But he and his wife haven't moved out yet!

NICOMACO
I've taken care of that!

CLEANDRO
[aside] Ears, do your work . . .

NICOMACO
Listen, I've told Sofronia to ask Dr. Damone's wife, Sostrata, to help with the wedding preparations; that takes care of HER. I'll be having dinner at Dr. Damone's, but after that, I'll invite him to spend the night with me at the inn, so as to leave you two love-birds alone in your nest. So then, after the wedding dinner, Sostrata will escort you and Clizia back to her house, but then, finding her husband gone, she'll come back to our house to spend the night with Sofronia. And you'll be all alone with Clizia!

PIRRO
I will?

NICOMACO
For the moment, yes. You lead her to bed and put out the candle; then, make some undressing noises.

PIRRO
OK!

NICOMACO
Meanwhile, I'll sneak out of the inn, come over to the house, slither into the room, doff my garments, and hop in bed with Clizia!

PIRRO
And what do I do?

NICOMACO
You can go sleep on the couch downstairs. Then, tomorrow morning, just before it gets light, I'll pretend I have to take a pee: I'll get up, get dressed, go down and wake you up: then it'll be your turn to get in bed with her!

CLEANDRO
What a disgusting old man! Thank the Lord I heard what he intends to do! Well, Fortune seems to be changing—for both of us!

PIRRO
Well, that's a great plan. But there's one thing: are you sure, at your age, that you're going to be up for all this?

NICOMACO
Up?

PIRRO
Up. [miming erection] "Up."

CLEANDRO
That's enough for me: I'm going to tell Mother . . . [exits]

NICOMACO
Up, yes, I've made plans for that. For my dinner at Dr. Damone's, I've ordered some special seasonings from the apothecary, beginning with some satyrisis.

PIRRO
Satyrisis? That sounds strange . . .

NICOMACO
Truth is stranger than fiction: just a pinch of satyrisis will turn a ninety-year-old into a crowing cock, and I'm only seventy for God's sake! Then I'll indulge in my little sustenance diet: boiled onion salad, spiced beans . . .

PIRRO
What do they do?

NICOMACO
They'll heat up my engine; they'll get the wind up in my sails . . . Ffffft! Ffffffft! And then I'll eat a fat little roast pigeon; medium rare; bloody, in fact . . .

PIRRO
Who's going to chew it for you?

NICOMACO
Don't worry about me. I may not have too many teeth in my mouth, but I have gums of steel!

PIRRO
That's what worries me. After you've finished with Clizia, what will be left for me? She'll be mashed potatoes!

NICOMACO
[grandly] Consider it my gift, Pirro: that between your sheets I will have done your office.

PIRRO
I thank you, God, for giving me a wife that I won't have to bother making pregnant—or even providing a home for.

NICOMACO
Here comes Dr. Damone now; go in the house, Pirro, get the wedding under way, and let me talk to him alone for a minute.

PIRRO
I'm off.

[Pirro exits toward house, as Dr. Damone enters from his house.]

NICOMACO
Ah, Damone, well, now it's time to demonstrate your friendship. I need you to leave your house—you, your wife, everybody—so that I can . . . proceed . . . you know . . . as we discussed earlier . . .

DR. DAMONE
As you wish.

NICOMACO
I've told Sofronia to ask your wife over to our house to help with the wedding preparations. It's your job to make sure Sostrata goes when she's asked, and that she takes her maid with her, too.

DR. DAMONE
I'll be happy to do whatever I can. Just say the word, Nicomaco.

NICOMACO
"Word." Ah, here comes Sofronia. Just make sure there're no hitches, dammit. Look, I've got to get to

the apothecary; I'll be back soon. Here she is. Be prepared! Good luck! Goodbye!

[Nicomaco hurriedly exits to the town; Sofronia comes in from the house.]

SOFRONIA

[aside] Well, it's no wonder my husband begged me to ask Dr. Damone's wife to come over; he wants Damone's house freed up so he can carry on with Clizia! And there's old Dr. Damone: what a man—offering up his own home for this wickedness! He's nothing but a pimp; shame on him! And shame on my husband! I'll fix their faucets, starting with Dr. Damone . . .

DR. DAMONE

[aside] What's that Sofronia's saying? And why hasn't she come over to ask me for my wife? Well, here she comes. *[aloud]* God be with you, Sofronia!

SOFRONIA

And He with you, Dr. Damone! Where's Sostrata, your good wife?

DR. DAMONE

Ah! She's at home, just waiting for your call . . .

SOFRONIA

My call?

DR. DAMONE

Yes, Nicomaco said you'd be calling on her. Shall I get her now?

SOFRONIA

Oh, no, she must be quite busy . . .

DR. DAMONE

No, no, she's not doing anything particular . . .

SOFRONIA

That's OK, let her be, Damone, I don't want to bother her. I'll come over if I need her . . .

DR. DAMONE

But aren't you getting ready for the wedding?

SOFRONIA

Yes . . .

DR. DAMONE

Well, you must need a little help . . .

SOFRONIA

Oh no, we've got a whole houseful of helpers . . . Cooks, maids, wenches, serving girls . . .

DR. DAMONE

[aside] What on earth do I do now? Damn Nicomaco! Sofronia doesn't need my wife's help at all! How could I have been so stupid as to trust that useless, juiceless, TOOTHLESS mad old man? Good heavens, Sofronia must think I'm just trying to worm my way into the wedding dinner! *[weakly smiling to her]* Well, *ciao*, Sofronia! *[exits confused and talking to himself]*

SOFRONIA

So much for Dr. Damone. Yes, he's ashamed of himself all right: look how he's sneaking off there, his face is hidden under his cloak! And now to make some hay with my husband. Well, speak of the devil, look, there he is, leaving the apothecary's! With something to raise his "spirits" for tonight, I'll bet.

[Nicomaco enters.]

NICOMACO

[aside] So, I have the satyrisis! *[sniffs it]* Oh, true apothecary! And this rubbing lotion he gave me: enough to stiffen a whole battalion! When you go to war, you've gotta have your weapons in working order! *[sees his wife]* Oh, my God, it's Sofronia! I hope she didn't hear me . . .

SOFRONIA

[aside] Oh yes, I heard you, and unless I have a heart attack tonight, you are going to be very miserable tomorrow.

NICOMACO

Wife, is everything ready? Have you called Sostrata in to help you?

SOFRONIA

Well, yes, I did, but your friend, Dr. Damone, told her not to come.

NICOMACO

No, he didn't! She must have misunderstood him.

SOFRONIA

She didn't misunderstand him.

NICOMACO

You must not have asked her the right way . . .

SOFRONIA

I asked her the right way; her husband, Dr. Damone, told her not to come!

NICOMACO

He did? Well, it's your fault! You are too rude to people!

SOFRONIA

I am not rude to people: what do you want me to do, kiss up to Dr. Damone? Drag Sostrata across the street? Go get her yourself, since you enjoy running after other men's wives. I'm going home to finish the wedding preparations!

NICOMACO

Oh, damn! Damn!

[Sofronia exits, and Nicomaco starts to follow as Dr. Damone returns. Nicomaco halts.]

DR. DAMONE

[aside] I've come back to see if loverboy is back from the apothecary's . . . Ah, there he is, about to go in his house. *[aloud]* Nicomaco! I've been looking for you!

NICOMACO

And I've been looking for you, you imbecile! Damone, what did I ask you? What did I tell you? Oh, this is great! Just great!

DR. DAMONE

What's the matter with you?

NICOMACO

You were to send your wife over to our house! You were to get everyone out of your house! *[imitating Damone's voice]* "I'll be happy to do whatever I can!" "Just say the word, Nicomaco!" Oh, God, I'm a dead man.

DR. DAMONE

Well, don't blame me. Didn't you say your wife would call on mine?

NICOMACO

Yes, and that's exactly what she did, but you told your wife not to come.

DR. DAMONE

Not at all! Sostrata offered to come, I offered to go get her, but your wife said she didn't need anybody! So I'M left with egg on my face, and YOU'RE complaining about ME! The hell with you and your wedding!

[Damone starts to leave.]

NICOMACO

Well, look, NOW, just get your family to come over to my house! Please! Please!

[Damone thinks things over a moment, then relents.][3]

DR. DAMONE

Well, all right, the hell with them too! OK, the wife, the maid, the cat, and any visitors that might be around: I'll bring them all over through the garden.

NICOMACO

Good!

[Dr. Damone exits toward his house.]

NICOMACO

It looks like he's a friend again; all is well. Oh God, what's that noise in the house? Doria . . . !

[Doria runs in.]

DORIA

Help! I'm wounded! I'm dead! Run, run! Get that knife from her! *[calling back to the house]* Run, Sofronia, RUN!

[Doria starts to run out again; Nicomaco grabs her.]

NICOMACO

Doria, what's the matter with you? What's going on?

DORIA

I'm dead! I've been killed!

NICOMACO

Killed? What for?

DORIA

I'm murdered! And you're next!

NICOMACO

What the hell are you talking about?

DORIA

I can't. I'm too out of breath . . . Look, I'm perspiring . . . Oh, God, SWEAT! Nicomaco, fan me with your cloak, would you?

[Nicomaco starts fanning her, then realizes how absurd he looks.]

NICOMACO

You tell me what this is all about or I'll fan you with a brick!

---

[3]Machiavelli does not give Damone any motivation for his change of heart here; it is possible that the intention was for Nicomaco to offer—and Damone to accept—a monetary bribe at this point, but there is no evidence to support this.

DORIA

[screaming, and throwing up her hands]
YYIIEEEEEEEEE! Oh, please, master, NO PUBLIC
BRUTALITY! POLICE!

NICOMACO

[shaking her] DAMMIT, DORIA, WHAT THE
HELL'S GOING ON IN MY HOUSE?

DORIA

OK. Well, Pirro had just put the wedding ring on Clizia's finger, and was showing the notary out at the
back door, when Clizia—can you believe this?—Clizia suddenly broke into a frenzy, grabbed a butcher
knife, and started shouting at the top of her lungs:
"Where's Nicomaco? Where's Pirro? I'll kill 'em both!
I'll murder 'em in their own blood!" Cleandro, Sofronia, all of us tried to get the knife from her, but we
couldn't: now she's running around the house
screaming that she's going to kill the two of you, one
way or another. Everybody's scared out of their
wits . . .

NICOMACO

Where's Pirro?

DORIA

He's hiding in the chicken coop. He sent me to warn
you to stay away . . .

NICOMACO

How can this be happening to me? Can't you get the
knife from her?

DORIA

We've tried our best . . .

NICOMACO

And she says she'll kill . . . who?

DORIA

You and Pirro.

NICOMACO

Oh, God; what a mess, what a catastrophe! Listen,
sweetie, lambchuck, honeypuss, I beg you, go back
in the house, try to calm her down a little, see if you
can maybe sweet-talk the itty-bitty knife from her,
won't you please, babykins? And Master Nicomaco
promises to buy you a new pair of shoesies and a
pwetty blouse. OK, Sweetie-love? Angel-pie? Let's go
bye-bye . . . ? Bye-bye . . . ?

DORIA

OK, I'll go, but don't come into the house until I call
you.

*[Doria goes off to the house. Nicomaco turns to
the audience.]*

NICOMACO

Ah misery! What terrible luck . . . Two hours from
the happiest night of my life, and now it's all screwed
up! *[calls to Doria]* Has she given up the knife yet?
Can I come in, now?

DORIA

[offstage, in the house] No, not yet! Stay there!

NICOMACO

O God! What's going to happen? *[to Doria]* Now?

[Doria enters, grim-faced.]

DORIA

OK, now!

[Nicomaco starts off to the house.]

DORIA

[calling after him] But don't go in the house! If you go
inside now, she'll kill you. Go in the chicken coop
with Pirro.

NICOMACO

The chicken coop? [4] Well, all right.

*[Nicomaco goes off. Doria stares after him until he is
gone, and then bursts out laughing.]*

DORIA

How may I fool you? Let me count the ways . . . silly
old man! *[laughs]* Oh, this house is an absolute feast
of follies! The old goat and Pirro are (Ha!) "laying"
low in the chicken coop, cluck, cluck; while Cleandro, Clizia, and Sofronia are "hatching" their little
plan in the bedroom! Clizia's gotten undressed, and
given her clothes to Siro, our serving boy, and Siro
has given HIS clothes to Clizia: that way, Siro can take
Clizia's place in Nicomaco's wedding bed! Meanwhile Nicomaco and Pirro, thinking Clizia is in a
rage, are up to their elbows in chicken shit, completely unawares! A great trick, yes? Brilliant! But
here come Nicomaco and Pirro!

---

[4]Machiavelli sends Nicomaco off to the "kitchen, behind the
chicken crates"; however, to be confined to a fifteenth-century
kitchen in such fashion would be an unbearably "earthy"
experience for a gentleman of the house, hence the rendition
"chicken coop."

[Nicomaco and Pirro enter from the house, brushing off chicken feathers.]

NICOMACO

Doria! What are you doing here, still? Has Clizia quieted down?

DORIA

Master, yes, she has, and she's promised Sofronia that she will do whatever you want her to.

NICOMACO

Whatever?

DORIA

Whatever! But Sofronia says you and Pirro should keep your distance for the time being, just so she doesn't flare up all over again. Then, when she's been put to bed for the night, Pirro can show her who's boss . . . if anyone can!

NICOMACO

Excellent! Sofronia counsels well! You go on in now, Doria; since dinner's prepared, tell everybody to go ahead and eat! Pirro and I are eating at Dr. Damone's.[5] When you've all finished dinner, bring the bride over to her wedding chamber! And hurry everyone along, Doria; it's already nine o'clock; we don't want to wait all night!

DORIA

[suppressing a giggle] No, we sure don't! I'm on my way . . .

[Doria goes back into the house. Nicomaco starts toward Dr. Damone's, and Pirro starts after him.]

NICOMACO

Pirro, you stay here. I'm going to Damone's for a drink or two.

[Pirro starts to go the other way, but is stopped by Nicomaco.]

NICOMACO

And don't go back to the house, either! You'll just get Clizia started up again! Just stay here. If anything happens, you come get me.

PIRRO

Go ahead, then. Whatever you say.

---

[5] The author has evidently forgotten Nicomaco's plan to eat at the inn.

[Nicomaco leaves for Damone's.]

PIRRO

So I have a marriage ceremony but no wife; a wedding banquet but no dinner. Well, so what? At least I've had more excitement today than in the whole year put together: and I don't think it's over yet—not from all the giggling I've overheard at home in the past half hour. Uh-oh, there's a torch: it looks like the wedding procession's coming this way already! I better get the old man . . . *[shouts]* Nicomaco! Dr. Damone! Here comes the bride!!!

[Nicomaco and Dr. Damone run in from Damone's house.]

NICOMACO

Here we are! Pirro, go inside Dr. Damone's: it's best you keep out of sight. Go! Get! *[Pirro exits, Nicomaco hides behind Damone.]* You, Damone, stand in front of me and do the talking. Here they come.

[Sofronia, Sostrata, Doria, and Siro (dressed as Clizia; weeping, holding a handkerchief over her eyes) enter from Nicomaco's house.]

SOFRONIA

Oh, poor girl. The walking weeping! Look what you've done: she can't stop crying!

SOSTRATA

But she'll be laughing tomorrow, if I know young girls!

DR. DAMONE

Wife!

SOSTRATA

Husband! *Buona sera!* And *buona sera* to you too, back there, Messer Nicomaco!

NICOMACO

[bowing as gracefully as he can, hidden behind Damone] Sostrata! *Buona sera* . . .

DR. DAMONE

Well, *ben venute* to you all, and welcome, too, dear Clizia! *[A fresh burst of tears emanates from Siro.]* Go on upstairs, ladies, and escort the bride to the wedding bed, as is the custom of our city. Pirro is "making ready" in the parlor.

SOSTRATA

Praise God for it. Let's go, girls.

[Sostrata, Sofronia, Doria, and Siro exit toward Damone's house.]

NICOMACO

[looking after them] Clizia looks very unhappy! And doesn't she look taller, all of a sudden? Maybe she's wearing high heels?

DR. DAMONE

She does look taller, you're right! All the more woman for you, eh, Nicomaco! You must be delighted: everything's coming up roses . . . As long as you are too.

NICOMACO

Don't worry about that! Since I've eaten my dinner—and taken my medicine!—I'm strong as an ox, and sharp as an axe! Ah, here come the women back again . . .

[Sostrata, Doria, and Sofronia return.]

NICOMACO

You've put Clizia to bed?

SOSTRATA

All tucked in.

DR. DAMONE

Good. Well, let's leave the lovers alone. Sostrata, you go spend the night with Sofronia; Nicomaco and I will sleep at my house.

SOFRONIA

[in mock surprise] What, you want to get rid of us?

DR. DAMONE

Why not? You've been trying to screw us at every chance; so go screw each other for a change!

SOSTRATA

I think you're the ones who have the tools for that sort of thing! Let's go, ladies.

DR. DAMONE

Let's go, Nicomaco.

[Dr. Damone and Nicomaco leave; Sofronia halts, calling after her husband.]

SOFRONIA

Go ahead, Nicomaco! But watch out for bottlenecks![6]

---

[6]In the original: "This woman of yours will be like those pitchers from Santa Maria Impruneta." The pitchers were narrow-necked.

[The women laugh conspiratorially. Doria and Sofronia leave, leaving Sostrata to sing the act closer.]

SOSTRATA

[sings] There's nothing quite so sweet
As elegant deceit,
When taken to conclusion!
There's nothing like a hoax
To bring down haughty folks
And throw 'em in confusion!
O, keen deception rare
O, trickery so fair
It's moral medication!
I'll see my old blowhard
Hoist by his own petard:
A lovely education!
For there is not a soul so flawed
That can't be cured by honest fraud!

[Sostrata leaves.]

ACT FIVE

[Doria enters, breathless.]

DORIA

I have never laughed so hard in my life, and I don't think I ever will again: I'm laughed out, and so's everybody in the house: Sofronia, Sostrata, Cleandro, Eustachio, everybody! We have just about consummated this "marriage" ourselves, counting off the minutes: now Nicomaco must be sneaking into the bedroom, now he's probably taking off his clothes, now he's slipping in bed next to the "bride," now he's mounting his charge, and now . . . now they're going at it, *mano e mano*! And then, as we were rolling on the floor in laughter, Pirro and Siro came over and gave us the details, and we all shrieked ourselves hoarse! It's the prize comedy of the year! Now that it's daylight, the women have sent me to hunt up the old goat, and see how he's surviving. But here he comes with Dr. Damone running after him; I'll hide over here to see what they're saying: even more comic material, I'll bet.

[Nicomaco comes in, followed by Dr. Damone. Doria hides elsewhere onstage.]

DR. DAMONE

Well, what happened last night? How did it go, man? You're awfully quiet! What was all that commotion:

getting dressed, getting undressed, getting in and out of bed, doors opening and closing? I was trying to sleep in the guest room, but it was impossible, so I got up and went out; now I find you here too! What's the matter? You look terrible! What the devil's gotten into you?

NICOMACO

Oh, brother, I don't know where to run, where to hide, what to do: I'M SO ASHAMED! Disgraced for all eternity! It's hopeless! I can't show my face in town, even in my own house! It's my fault: I asked for it! And my wife gave it to me! And the worst part is that I got you involved in it: you'll be destroyed too!

DR. DAMONE

Me?! Nicomaco, what happened? Did you break something?

NICOMACO

I wish. I'd rather I'd broken my neck!

DR. DAMONE

What the devil happened? Why won't you tell me?

NICOMACO

[sobbing] I'm too embarrassed! Boo hoo hoo!

DR. DAMONE

Nicomaco! Stop acting like a baby! How bad can it be? [Nicomaco wails.] SPEAK UP, MAN!

NICOMACO

You know what I'd planned: well, after the women left, I tiptoed into Clizia's bedroom; sent Pirro downstairs to sleep on the couch, very quietly got undressed, and slipped into the bed next to the bride.

DR. DAMONE

And . . . ? [Nicomaco sobs.] Go on . . . !

NICOMACO

Boo hoo hoo! Well, I wriggled up next to her, like this [he demonstrates], and, in the manner of a smug new bridegroom, reached my hands around to her . . . chest, like this . . . when she grabbed my two hands with just one of hers, like this, and wouldn't let go! Well, I thought I'd just soften her up a little with a kiss, but with her other hand she pushed my face back into the pillow! OK, I thought, I'll climb on top of her—and the little devil kneed me in the ribs! [He hits himself, showing where.] Ow! Good Lord, I think one of 'em's broken! Well, when I saw force wasn't going to do me any good, I tried praying: "Oh, darling, oh my sweet love . . ."—disguising my voice, of

course, so she wouldn't recognize me—"Why are you tormenting me? Please, my dearest, why don't you just give me what other women give their husbands? Please? Pretty please????" [a new burst of sobs] Boo hoo hoo!

DR. DAMONE

Stop crying!

NICOMACO

I can't! I feel so horrible! [sniffs back a final sob] Well, as my prayers got me nowhere, I decided to get tough with her, so I threatened to punish her if she didn't give in! So . . .

DR. DAMONE

Yes . . . ?

NICOMACO

So, she stood right up on the bed and kicked me! Twice! Right in the . . . bedsheets!

DR. DAMONE

Unbelievable!

NICOMACO

Well, believe it! And then, BAM, she flopped back down hard on the bed, face to the pillow, and grabbed the frame so tight you couldn't turn her over with a block and tackle! Well, I quickly saw that neither force nor prayers nor threats would make her give way, so, pretty much in desperation, I rolled over on my tummy and left her alone, thinking maybe she'd change her mind in the morning . . .

DR. DAMONE

Well, you should have done that early on. I mean, if she doesn't want you, you shouldn't want her . . .

NICOMACO

But wait, that's not all, you haven't heard the worst part! There I was, flat-out exhausted, confused, upset; well, I finally fell asleep. And then . . . all of a sudden . . .

DR. DAMONE

What? What?

NICOMACO

I felt something stiff, poking at my ass!

DR. DAMONE

No!

NICOMACO

Yes, something was jabbing me, over and over, right in the tail! Still groggy, half asleep, I reached back there and grabbed it! Yieeeeeeeeeeeee! It was hard, pointy; boy, did I wake up! Of course, right away I thought of Clizia's butcher knife: so I jumped out of bed, and shouted down to Pirro to get a lamp or something, or we'd be murdered in the dark! Well, Pirro must have been up already; he came in a moment later with a lamp, and you won't believe what we saw: instead of Clizia, it was my servant Siro there on the bed, yes, stark naked and fully erect, grinning like a wild man and [sobs] giving me the middle finger![7]

DR. DAMONE
[laughing] Ha ha ha!

NICOMACO
What are YOU laughing about?

DR. DAMONE
[restraining himself] I'm sorry. It's very sad, what happened. Very sad . . . [breaking out in laughter again] But I can't stop laughing!

DORIA
[aside] I can't wait to tell Sofronia what happened! She'll split her sides all over again!

NICOMACO
[as Damone continues to laugh] Laugh! Laugh! That's what's so terrible; everybody's laughing at me, and I can't stop crying! Pirro and Siro, my servants, they thought nothing of insulting me! They laughed right there in my face, then they threw on some clothes and went out to tell the women—so they could all laugh some more together! Laugh, clowns, laugh! While Nicomaco weeps!

DR. DAMONE
I know you know I'm sorry—and for myself as well as you, since you got us into this mess, my friend.

NICOMACO
Damone, what should I do? Tell me, please! [Damone turns in reflection.] Don't leave me, for God's sake!

DR. DAMONE
Well, it seems to me that, unless you've got some better plan, you better throw yourself on Sofronia's mercy. Tell her from now on you'll do whatever she says—with regard to Clizia and everything else. Af-

ter all, Sofronia's not going to want your name dragged in the mud, since it's her name too, right? Look, here she comes; talk to her. I'll head over to the market; if I hear anything about last night, I'll try to shut it up as best as I can.

NICOMACO
Oh, thank you, thank you, thank you, Damone! Thank you!

[Dr. Damone exits to the town as Sofronia enters from the house; she carries a basket with breakfast for two.]

SOFRONIA
[aside] My maid Doria told me Nicomaco was out here, moping pitifully about; I sure would like to hear his version of what happened last night! Ah, there he is! [singing his name aloud] Yoo-hoo, Nico-maco!

NICOMACO
What do you want?

SOFRONIA
Well, you're up awfully early! What, have you left Dr. Damone's without saying a word to the bride? Did she and Pirro have a jolly wedding night? Hmmm?

NICOMACO
I have no idea.

SOFRONIA
Well, who does, if you don't—you, who turned all Florence upside down to arrange this match? Well, they're married now, Nicomaco, aren't you happy?

NICOMACO
Leave me alone. Stop torturing me.

SOFRONIA
Torturing you? You're the one torturing me! You got what you wanted, you should comfort me, not shower me with your complaints! And look, here, I've brought the happy couple their wedding breakfast! Scrambled eggs and a big hard pepperoni!

NICOMACO
Will you stop it!

SOFRONIA
What?

NICOMACO
Stop making a fool of me! You've been at it all year, Sofronia, and yesterday, last night, you did it, YOU FINALLY DID IT! Enough, for God's sake! ENOUGH!

---

[7]In the original, the *manichetto*; an aggressive phallic gesture made with the clenched fist.

SOFRONIA

I never wanted to make a fool of you. You tried to make fools of us, and your plans backfired, that's all. And aren't you ashamed of yourself, to raise a decent, sweet, and well-behaved girl in your house, and then try to marry her off to some rascally servant just so you could sleep with her on the side?

NICOMACO

You knew . . . ?

SOFRONIA

Of course we knew! What, did you think we were blind? That we couldn't see through your lies, or confound your dirty tricks? I confess, this little game we played on you was my idea, but there was no other way to wake you up, dear husband, from your dream, but to have you embarrass yourself in front of *[pointing to the audience]* all these people! Public humiliation is a great teacher, isn't it? Well, now, this is how it stands: if you want to wipe the slate clean, and to be the honest, good Nicomaco we all knew last year and before, we're all willing to start fresh again and consider this matter forgotten. And if anyone can't forget—well, they'll forgive.

NICOMACO

Sofronia, my Sofronia, I'll do anything you say. Just make sure nobody else knows what happened!

SOFRONIA

You do your part, I'll do mine.

NICOMACO

Where is Clizia?

SOFRONIA

She's up at the monastery, in Siro's clothes. I sent her there last night after dinner.

NICOMACO

And Cleandro, where is he in all this?

SOFRONIA

He's happy the wedding is spoiled, but miserable that he doesn't yet have Clizia for himself.

NICOMACO

I leave his unhappiness to you: do what you want for him. Still, he can't marry Clizia; she's an orphan, and we don't know anything about her parentage.

SOFRONIA

That's true; we shouldn't marry her to anybody until we can find out more about her. Meanwhile, I'll have yesterday's marriage annulled.

NICOMACO

Whatever you wish. Well, 'twas a rough night; I'm going home to rest before I fall over in the street! Besides, I see Cleandro and Eustachio over there. You talk to them, tell 'em what we've agreed on, and tell 'em to be satisfied with their damn victory and not ask me any more about it!

[Nicomaco exits to the house; Cleandro and Eustachio enter from the town.]

CLEANDRO

[to Eustachio] Did you hear? The old goat went and shut himself up in the house! Sofronia must have really given it to him; he's all humble pie this morning. There she is, let's ask her. *[to Sofronia]* Mother! God save you!

SOFRONIA

And you . . .

CLEANDRO

What did Dad say?

SOFRONIA

The poor man's broken up, he's been completely humiliated, he's given me *carte blanche* to take care of everything.

EUSTACHIO

Fantastic! Then I get Clizia!

CLEANDRO

Hey, not so fast! What do you think she is, a piece of meat?

EUSTACHIO

[sarcastic] Oh, great! First I win her, then I lose her, just like Pirro.

SOFRONIA

Neither you nor Pirro's going to have her. *[Cleandro exults silently.]* Nor you, neither, Cleandro! *[Cleandro is astounded.]* For now, thing's'll stay the way they are.

CLEANDRO

What? Mom???! No!!! *[Sofronia is unmoved.]* Well, let her come back to the house, at least, so I can see her.

SOFRONIA

Maybe I will, maybe I won't. Eustachio, come home with me and straighten up the house. You, Cleandro, go find Dr. Damone. And see if he can keep this business hushed up in town.

CLEANDRO

I HATE THIS!!

SOFRONIA
Just be patient.

[Sofronia goes into the house, dragging Eustachio with her. Cleandro is left onstage.]

CLEANDRO
[to the audience] Just when my ship was sailing into harbor, good ol' Dame Fortune kicks up a hurricane and blows me back into the middle of the sea! I'm drowning in waves of misery! First I have to fight off my father's lust; now it's Mom's social climbing! I had her help against Dad, but who's going to help me against her? I'm all alone: it's hopeless, I'm just a born loser, I'll kill myself! Ever since that girl came into our house, I haven't thought of anything but her: I know no joy but Clizia! God!!! *[sees Damone approaching]* But who's this coming toward me? It's Dr. Damone! And smiling from ear to ear! *[to Damone, who enters from the town]* Damone! What's up? You look happy, what news?

DR. DAMONE
The best! The happiest news! And I, the happiest bearer of it!

CLEANDRO
What??? What???

DR. DAMONE
Clizia's father's in town!

CLEANDRO
Her father???

DR. DAMONE
He's just arrived; his name's Ramondo; he's a noble and rich man from Naples, and he's come to Florence to find his daughter!

CLEANDRO
My God! How did you find out?

DR. DAMONE
I've just been talking with him! There's absolutely no doubt about it: he's Clizia's father!

CLEANDRO
Unbelievable! I'm overcome, I'm crazy with happiness!

DR. DAMONE
You all have to hear it yourselves. Call Nicomaco and Sofronia out here; quick!

CLEANDRO
Mom! Dad! News! Great news!

[Sofronia and Nicomaco come running in from the house.]

NICOMACO
Here we are! What's great news?

DR. DAMONE
Clizia's father is here in Florence looking for her! His name is Ramondo, he's a rich Neapolitan gentleman. I've already talked with him, told him where she is; in fact, I've actually persuaded him to let her marry Cleandro—if you approve, of course.

NICOMACO
OF COURSE, of course! That's wonderful. But where is he?

DR. DAMONE
He's staying at the Corona Hotel, downtown, with a huge entourage of servants. I've told him to come here—and here he comes!

[Ramondo enters from the town, and Nicomaco greets him effusively.]

NICOMACO
God bless you, Sir.

DR. DAMONE
Ramondo, this is Nicomaco, and this is his wife, Sofronia; these are the people that have raised your daughter with such great care. And this is their son, Cleandro, who will become your son-in-law, if it pleases you!

RAMONDO
I'm delighted to meet you all. And I thank God for having led me here—to see my daughter before I die, and to reward this kind couple for having raised her with such loving care. Nothing could please me more than this proposed marriage, for it will only seal our family ties of friendship with noble bonds of matrimony!

[Everyone cheers.]

DR. DAMONE
Let's go inside, so Signior Ramondo can tell us how he came to be here today; then you *[turning to Sofronia and Nicomaco]* can plan a most joyous wedding!

SOFRONIA
Yes, let's go! *[turns to the audience, as the other characters go into the house]* And you, dear audience, you go home too, since we're not coming out again. Not at least until we've planned a new wedding: with a real bride this time!

[Sofronia and the others exit into the house, and the
Prologue comes out and sings.]

PROLOGUE
[sings] So now you've seen our humble story:
Applause—is now obligatory!
All's well up here; no one got hurt,
And you? You're just the more alert!
You know the steps that lead to Heaven:
There's one two three four five six seven—
Go on, climb up, you're almost there!
Our author's play has shown you where!
For man has Hellfire in his belly
So says our great Machi-avelli,
But Hellfire needs a remedy:
Divine, then, is his comedy!

[End of Play]

3

HAMLET

William Shakespeare • About 1600

Edited and with notes by Marilyn F. Moriarty

SHAKESPEARE'S *HAMLET* IS SURELY THE MOST FAMOUS play ever written. First produced around 1600—it may have been the play that opened the Globe Theatre at about that time—it has since been produced, read, analyzed, interpreted, and admired in every language of civilization and in every country that creates a theatre.

And yet *Hamlet* is also a very mysterious play, and the unresolved debates about its meanings, references, and implications have spawned a virtual ocean of literature: the University of California libraries currently list 1,213 individual books specifically about this one play. Few actors—male or female—have failed to at least imagine themselves in the title role of *Hamlet*; many thousands have tackled the introspective Danish prince; none has satisfactorily defined him or his fascinating discontents.

What we *feel* about *Hamlet*, however, is that it is an intensely *personal* play, its royal environment

richly textured with domestic intrigue, philosophical rumination, and psychological insight. No one knows enough about Shakespeare's life to know exactly how personal his *Hamlet* actually is, but it is worth noting that the author had a son named Hamnet (a variant spelling of Hamlet), and that a theatrical legend—unfortunately unprovable—indicates that Shakespeare himself performed the role of Hamlet's father (the Ghost).

As with almost all his plays, Shakespeare did not create the basic story of *Hamlet*, which first appeared in the *Historia Danica* of Saxo Grammaticus, a Danish chronicler of the twelfth century. In 1570 or thereabouts, Saxo's story was translated and adapted into French by François de Belleforest, who included it in his *Histoires Tragiques*; by 1589 an anonymous English play, probably called *Hamlet* and perhaps written by Thomas Kyd, had been based on the Belleforest novella. Unfortunately, only a line or two of the earlier play has come down to us, but it was widely known on the stage in the 1580s and 90s; Shakespeare was undoubtedly familiar with it.

None of these sources, however, could have prepared Shakespeare's audience for the splendors of this play, which, on the one hand, is a gripping and fast-paced melodrama of political assassination and revenge, and on the other is a psychological investigation so profound as to serve as a paradigm for professional psychiatric analysis. Parts of the play are considered sufficiently wise to cite in church sermons; others border on the farcical and obscene. Certainly, no play stares into the face of death with such bravery, wit, and charm. No play until Pirandello wrestles so cogently with the nature of theatre itself, and the nature of "acting" (on stage) as both representation and criticism of "action" (in life).

Nor has any play probed so deeply into human introspection, despair, and renewal. Surely, this is the secret of *Hamlet*'s enormous appeal to actors, readers, and audiences: most of us feel we know the Prince like we might know a brother or sister; we may feel we love Hamlet; sometimes we may even feel we *are* Hamlet. Few plays achieve this universality of appeal beyond their own era or geographic borders: Hamlet, however, has been a "member of the family" for nearly four centuries worldwide.

But then, what IS *Hamlet* about? The multiplicity of responses to that question has circled around a few key questions, none satisfactorily resolved despite literally centuries of discussion. How old is Hamlet? The early scenes strongly suggest a teenage prince; information in the last act, however, indicates that he's thirty years old: How should these differing impressions be reconciled? Does Hamlet's feigned madness include a touch (or more) of the real thing? Does he feel truly betrayed by Ophelia, or is he just trying to protect her? Why does Hamlet, after hearing of his father's murder in act 1, "delay" his revenge until act 5? Or does he delay? Is the Ghost really a ghost? Or is he a goblin damned? And where exactly does Gertrude stand: what does she know (and when did she know it) of her husband's true acts and intents? Hamlet himself asks these questions, and in his soliloquies he invites us to consider them too. Entering into the play's multiple complexities, amid the thrills of its onrushing action and emotion, is one of the profound joys of seeing or reading *Hamlet*. Simply put, the play is the paragon of theatre.

A NOTE ON THE TEXT

As far as we know, neither Shakespeare nor his company ever authorized the publication of any of his plays. This is not surprising, as there was no copyright law at the time to protect a theatre's proprietary interest in the dramatic works it had commissioned and produced. But more than half of Shakespeare's plays did appear in print within his lifetime, in single-play "quarto" versions put out by various London publishers. Some of these are considered "good" quartos, as they seem to have been printed from Shakespeare's actual manuscripts, or authentic playhouse copies, with or without authorial approval. These "good quartos" coexist with "bad" ones, however; pirated versions that were often reconstructed from memory by disgruntled former actors working for a fee.

It was in part to replace these "stol'n and surruptitious copies" that two of his fellow actors, John Heminges and Henry Condell, published a leatherbound "folio" edition of Shakespeare's complete works in 1623, seven years after the dramatist's death.

Shakespeare's *Hamlet* has come down to us in three versions: a (very) "bad" First Quarto of 1603, which is often incomprehensible; a (very) "good" Second Quarto of 1604, described on its title page as "newly imprinted and enlarged . . . according to the true and perfect Coppie"; and the text in the First Folio. Of the three, the Second Quarto, though marred by typographical errors and poor spelling in many places, represents the superior text.

The edited version in this book was prepared by Marilyn F. Moriarty. It is largely based on the Second Quarto, with additional passages and stage directions collated from the Folio and (occasionally) from the First Quarto. Spellings and punctuation have generally been modernized. Moriarty has also provided a running glossary in the right-hand margin to explain words that are now obsolete, or whose meaning has changed over the years, plus footnotes at the bottom of several pages addressing certain thornier interpretational points in greater depth.

As anthology editor, I have added two brief notes of my own (signed *R.C.*) to the commentary on act 5, scene 1. These notes address the question of Hamlet's age, on which I have a rather unorthodox view. The interested reader may find elaboration of these notes in my "Shakespeare's Sixteen-Year-Old Hamlet" (*Educational Theatre Journal*, May 1973, pp. 179–188) and "Coming of Age in Elsinore" (*On-Stage Studies*, 1987, pp. 43–66).

Marilyn F. Moriarty is Assistant Professor of English at Hollins College (Roanoke, Virginia). She has lectured widely on Shakespeare and has served as a dramaturg at the Colorado Shakespeare Festival. She received the Katherine Anne Porter Prize for fiction in 1990.

THE TRAGEDY OF HAMLET, PRINCE OF DENMARK

DRAMATIS PERSONAE

CLAUDIUS, King of Denmark

HAMLET, son to the late King Hamlet and nephew to the present King

POLONIUS, Lord Chamberlain

HORATIO, friend to Hamlet

LAERTES, son of Polonius

VOLTEMAND ⎫
CORNELIUS ⎭ Ambassadors to Norway

ROSENCRANTZ ⎫
GUILDENSTERN ⎭ Hamlet's old schoolfellows

A GENTLEMAN

OSRIC, a courtier

MARCELLUS ⎫
BARNARDO ⎬ soldiers
FRANCISCO ⎭

REYNALDO, servant to Polonius

FORTINBRAS, Prince of Norway

NORWEGIAN CAPTAIN

DOCTOR OF DIVINITY

PLAYERS

TWO CLOWNS, grave-diggers

ENGLISH AMBASSADORS

GERTRUDE, Queen of Denmark, mother to Hamlet

OPHELIA, daughter to Polonius

GHOST of Hamlet's father

LORDS, LADIES, OFFICERS, SOLDIERS, SAILORS, MESSENGERS,
     AND ATTENDANTS

Scene: Denmark

Act One, Scene One

Elsinore: a platform before the castle.

[Enter Barnardo to Francisco.]

BARNARDO
Who's there?

FRANCISCO
Nay, answer me°. Stand, and unfold° yourself.[1]   °*You* answer *me.* °identify

BARNARDO
Long live the King!°   °password

FRANCISCO
Barnardo?

BARNARDO
He.

FRANCISCO
You come most carefully upon your hour°.   °punctually

BARNARDO
'Tis now struck twelve. Get thee to bed, Francisco.

FRANCISCO
For this relief much thanks. 'Tis bitter cold,
And I am sick at heart°.   °wretched

BARNARDO
Have you had quiet guard?

FRANCISCO
                    Not a mouse stirring.

BARNARDO
Well, good night.
If you do meet Horatio and Marcellus,
The rivals° of my watch, bid them make haste.   °partners

FRANCISCO
I think I hear them.

[Enter Horatio and Marcellus.]
                    Stand, ho! Who is there?

HORATIO
Friends to this ground.

---

[1]The challenge "Who's there?" comes from the wrong man, as Francisco's counter-challenge, "Nay, answer me," confirms. Francisco, entering first, has been waiting for relief from guard duty. Barnardo, Francisco's relief, should have expected to find Francisco posted on the wall. Barnardo's nervousness cues the audience that things are not as they should be.

MARCELLUS
                    And liegemen° to the Dane.   °loyal subjects

FRANCISCO
Give you good night.

MARCELLUS
                    O, farewell, honest soldier.
Who hath relieved you?

FRANCISCO
                    Barnardo has my place.
Give° you good night.   °God give you

                              [Exit Francisco.]

MARCELLUS
                    Holla, Barnardo!

BARNARDO
                                   Say—
What, is Horatio there?

HORATIO
                    A piece of him.°   °What's left of him after this night's
                                                                                    cold weather.
BARNARDO
Welcome, Horatio. Welcome, good Marcellus.

MARCELLUS
What, has this thing appeared again tonight?

BARNARDO
I have seen nothing.

MARCELLUS
Horatio says 'tis but our fantasy°,   °imagination
And will not let belief take hold of him
Touching this dreaded sight, twice seen of us:
Therefore I have entreated him along
With us to watch the minutes of this night;
That, if again this apparition come,
He may approve° our eyes, and speak to it.   °corroborate

HORATIO
Tush, tush, 'twill not appear.

BARNARDO
                              Sit down awhile;
And let us once again assail your ears,
That are so fortified against our story,
What we have two nights seen.

HORATIO
                         Well, sit we down,
And let us hear Barnardo speak of this.

BARNARDO
Last night of all,
When yond same star that's westward from the pole°²   ° pole star
Had made his course t'illume that part of heaven
Where now it burns, Marcellus and myself,
The bell then beating one—

                                        [Enter Ghost.]

MARCELLUS
Peace, break thee off. Look, where it comes again.

BARNARDO
In the same figure like the King that's dead.³

MARCELLUS
Thou art a scholar, speak to it, Horatio.⁴

BARNARDO
Looks 'a° not like the King? Mark it, Horatio.   ° he

HORATIO
Most like. It harrows° me with fear and wonder.   ° lacerates, distresses

BARNARDO
It would be spoke to.

MARCELLUS
                    Question it, Horatio.

HORATIO
What art thou that usurp'st this time of night,
Together with that fair and warlike° form   ° dressed for war
In which the majesty of buried Denmark°   ° the late Danish King
Did sometimes° march?⁵ By heaven I charge thee speak!   ° formerly

MARCELLUS
It is offended.

---

²If Barnardo points to the sky at one end of the stage, he can direct the audience's
eyes away from the Ghost's entry point.

³Notice that Barnardo preserves caution: he does not assume the figure to *be* the
King of Denmark. The popular belief that the devil had the power to assume specific
human form underlies Barnardo's caution. The specific nature of the Ghost cannot
be assumed until the Ghost identifies itself; thus, Marcellus prompts Horatio to in-
terrogate it.

⁴A common belief about ghosts held that they could not speak unless they were first
spoken to. Although a scholar would know Latin, and thus be able to exorcise a
ghost if it proved to be evil, Marcellus may simply mean that Horatio knows best
the proper forms of address. Horatio's inquiry has two ends: to determine the
Ghost's identity and to ascertain its business on earth.

⁵Because supernatural beings properly belong in the supernatural realm, Horatio
considers the Ghost's appearance as an invasion of the natural world. Horatio challenges it on two counts: both its presence among mortals and its taking on the appearance of the former King need to be accounted for. "Usurp," meaning "to wrongfully appropriate to oneself," is obliquely apt here, for it foreshadows the coming
story of Claudius's usurpation of the throne.

BARNARDO

        See, it stalks away.

HORATIO

Stay! Speak, speak, I charge thee speak!

                                   [Exit Ghost.]

MARCELLUS

'Tis gone and will not answer.[6]

BARNARDO

How now, Horatio? You tremble, and look pale.
Is not this something more than fantasy°?   ° imagination
What think you on't?

HORATIO

Before my God, I might not this believe
Without the sensible° and true avouch°   ° capable of being confirmed
Of mine own eyes.   through the senses ° empirical
                                           confirmation

MARCELLUS

Is it not like the King?

HORATIO

As thou art to thyself.
Such was the very armor he had on.
When he th'ambitious Norway combated.[7]
So frowned he once, when, in an angry parle°,   ° parley, encounter
He smote the sledded Polacks° on the ice.   ° Poles using sleds
'Tis strange.

MARCELLUS

Thus twice before, and jump° at this dead hour,   ° precisely
With martial stalk hath he gone by our watch.

HORATIO

In what particular thought to work I know not,
But in the gross and scope° of my opinion,   ° totality and range
This bodes some strange eruption to our state.

MARCELLUS

Good now, sit down, and tell me, he that knows,
Why this same strict and most observant watch°   ° vigilance
So nightly toils the subject° of the land,   ° subjects
And why such daily cast° of brazen cannon   ° casting
And foreign mart° for implements of war,   ° trading
Why such impress° of shipwrights, whose sore task ° forced service
Does not divide the Sunday from the week.

---

[6]Although ghosts may speak when addressed, ghosts choose to speak to those for whom they have a message. The Ghost wants to speak to Hamlet, not to Horatio.

[7]Although this account makes us wonder about Horatio's age, Shakespeare, more importantly, gives Horatio the voice of history. This combat between King Hamlet and King Fortinbras occurred on the day that Hamlet was born.

What might be toward°, that this sweaty haste   °imminent
Doth make the night joint-laborer with the day:[8]
Who is't that can inform me?

HORATIO
                        That can I.
At least, the whisper goes so: our last King,
Whose image even but now appeared to us,
Was, as you know, by Fortinbras of Norway,
Thereto pricked on by a most emulate° pride,   °envious, jealous
Dared to the combat; in which our valiant Hamlet—
For so this side of our known world esteemed him—
Did slay this Fortinbras[9]; who, by a sealed compact°,   °mutual agreement
Well ratified by law and heraldry°,   °heraldic law
Did forfeit, with his life, all those his lands
Which he stood seized of°, to the conqueror;   °legally owned
Against the which, a moiety competent°   °an equivalent portion
Was gaged° by our king; which had returned   °wagered
To the inheritance of Fortinbras,
Had he been vanquisher; as, by the same cov'nant,°   °compact
And carriage of the article designed,°   °meaning conveyed by the words
His fell to Hamlet. Now, sir, young Fortinbras,
Of unimproved mettle hot and full,
Hath in the skirts of Norway here and there
Sharked up a list of lawless resolutes°   °Assembled a band of thugs
For food and diet to some enterprise
That hath a stomach in't: which is no other—
As it doth well appear unto our state—
But to recover of us, by strong hand°   °(1) force (2) pun on "Fortinbras"
And terms compulsatory°, those foresaid lands   °compulsory
So by his father lost. And this, I take it,
Is the main motive of our preparations,
The source of this our watch, and the chief head
Of this post-haste° and romage° in the land.   °feverish activity °commotion

---

[8]Marcellus sketches out a picture of Danish military readiness: the state exists in constant vigilance; foundries turn out cannon daily; foreign trade secures armament; shipwrights, in forced labor, work so hard they don't get Sundays off; and, in general, men work day and night.

[9]Horatio explains why preparations for war are so extensive. In the past, King Fortinbras of Norway, envious of King Hamlet, challenged the Danish King to a combat to the death. The terms of the combat were defined and agreed on by both combatants and those terms conformed to the rules of heraldic law. Both men staked an equivalent amount of land in their wager (they wagered their individual private property and not national land holdings). Victorious, King Hamlet seized deceased King Fortinbras's lands. (Reciprocally, had King Hamlet lost, his property would have gone to King Fortinbras.) At this point in the play, young Prince Fortinbras has gathered together a group of men to help him recover the property his father lost. While Prince Fortinbras conducts a type of guerrilla warfare against Denmark, Norway is governed by Prince Fortinbras's uncle.

BARNARDO
I think it be no other but e'en so.
Well may it sort, that this portentous° figure   ° ominous
Comes armed through our watch so like the King
That was and is the question of these wars.

HORATIO
A mote° it is to trouble the mind's eye.   ° speck
In the most high and palmy° state of Rome,   ° flourishing
A little ere the mightiest Julius fell,
The graves stood tenantless and the sheeted dead°   ° ghosts
Did squeak and gibber in the Roman streets.
As, stars with trains of fire, and dews of blood,
Disasters in the sun; and the moist star°,   ° the moon
Upon whose influence Neptune's empire° stands,   ° the seas
Was sick almost to doomsday with eclipse.
And even the like precurse° of fierce events,   ° foreshadowing
As harbingers° preceding still the fates   ° advance messengers
And prologue to the omen coming on,
Have heaven and earth together demonstrated
Unto our climatures° and countrymen.[10]   ° regions

                              [Enter Ghost.]

But, soft, behold! Lo, where it comes again!
I'll cross° it, though it blast me.   ° cross its path, confront

                    [Ghost spreads its arms.]

                         Stay, illusion!
If thou hast any sound or use of voice,
Speak to me.
If there be any good thing to be done
That may to thee do ease, and grace to me,
Speak to me.
If thou art privy to thy country's fate,
Which happily° foreknowing may avoid,   ° perhaps
O, speak!
Or if thou hast uphoarded in thy life
Extorted treasure in the womb of earth,
For which, they say, your spirits oft walk in death,
Speak of it, stay and speak. *[Cock crows.]*
                         Stop it, Marcellus.

MARCELLUS
Shall I strike at it with my partisan°?   ° a long-handled spear

---

[10]Horatio compares the present events in Denmark with the past events of Rome:
the appearance of the Ghost portends disaster just as, in the past, other unnatural
events heralded Caesar's assassination. Ominously, the play casts the epilogue to
Rome as the prologue to Denmark. Horatio does not whimsically impose this par-
allelism, for the Ghost immediately appears, as if Horatio had introduced him
through the account of Rome.

HORATIO
Do, if it will not stand.

BARNARDO
　　　　　'Tis here!

HORATIO
　　　　　　'Tis here!

MARCELLUS
'Tis gone!

　　　　　　　　　　　　　　　　　　[Exit Ghost.]

We do it wrong, being so majestical,
To offer it the show of violence;
For it is as the air, invulnerable,
And our vain blows malicious mockery.

BARNARDO
It was about to speak when the cock crew.

HORATIO
And then it started like a guilty thing
Upon° a fearful summons. I have heard　　　　　　　　　　　　　°At
The cock, that is the trumpet to the morn,
Doth with his lofty and shrill-sounding throat
Awake the god of day, and at his warning,
Whether in sea or fire, in earth or air,
Th'extravagant° and erring spirit hies°　　　　　　　　°wandering °hastens
To his confine°; and of the truth herein　　　　　　　°place of confinement
This present object° made probation°.　　　　　　　　　°sight °proof

MARCELLUS
It faded on the crowing of the cock.
Some say, that ever 'gainst° that season comes　　　　　　　°just before
Wherein our Savior's birth is celebrated,
The bird of dawning° singeth all night long;　　　　　　　°the cock
And then, they say, no spirit stir abroad;
The nights are wholesome°; then no planets strike°,　　　°healthy °destroy
No fairy takes°, nor witch hath power to charm;　　　　　　°bewitches
So hallowed and so gracious° is the time.　　　　　°full of divine grace, blessed

HORATIO
So have I heard, and do in part believe it.
But, look, the morn in russet° mantle clad　　　　°coarse, grayish-brown cloth
Walks o'er the dew of yon high eastward hill.
Break we our watch up, and, by my advice,
Let us impart what we have seen tonight
Unto young Hamlet; for, upon my life,
This spirit, dumb to us, will speak to him.
Do you consent we shall acquaint him with it,
As needful in our loves, fitting our duty?

MARCELLUS
Let's do't, I pray, and I this morning know
Where we shall find him most convenient.

[Exeunt all.]

Act One, Scene Two

A room of state in the castle.

*[Flourish. Enter Claudius King of Denmark, Gertrude the Queen, Prince
Hamlet, council, Polonius, Laertes his son, Voltemand, Cornelius,
Lords, and Attendants.]*

KING
Though yet of Hamlet our dear brother's death
The memory be green°, and that° it us befitted   ° fresh in our minds ° though
To bear our hearts in grief, and our whole kingdom
To be contracted in one brow of woe,
Yet so far hath discretion fought with nature,
That we with wisest sorrow think on him,
Together with remembrance of ourselves.
Therefore our sometime° sister, now our queen,   ° former
Th'imperial jointress° of this warlike state,   ° joint ruler
Have we, as 'twere with a defeated° joy,   ° impaired
With one auspicious° and one dropping° eye,   ° cheerful ° weeping
With mirth in funeral and with dirge in marriage,
In equal scale weighing delight and dole°,   ° grief
Taken to wife. Nor have we herein barred
Your better wisdoms, which have freely gone°   ° unconstrained
With this affair along. For all, our thanks.
Now follows that you know young Fortinbras,
Holding a weak supposal° of our worth,   ° a poor estimation
Or thinking by our late dear brother's death
Our state to be disjoint° and out of frame°,   ° disordered ° in a mess
Colleagued° with the dream of his advantage,   ° Allied
He hath not failed to pester us with message,
Importing° the surrender of those lands   ° Dealing with
Lost by his father, with all bands° of law,   ° bonds
To our most valiant brother. So much for him.
Now for ourself, and for this time of meeting,
Thus much the business is: we have here writ
To Norway, uncle of young Fortinbras—
Who, impotent° and bed-rid, scarcely hears   ° weak
Of this his nephew's purpose—to suppress
His further gait° herein, in that the levies,   ° proceeding
The lists°, and full proportions° are all made   ° troops ° numbers, forces
Out of his subject°; and we here dispatch   ° troops are drawn from the subjects
You, good Cornelius, and you, Voltemand,
For bearers of this greeting to old Norway,

Giving to you no further personal power
To° business with the King, more than the scope
Of these dilated° articles allow.
Farewell, and let your haste commend your duty.

°For
°detailed

CORNELIUS AND VOLTEMAND
In that and all things will we show our duty.

KING
We doubt it nothing°. Heartily farewell.

°not at all

[Exeunt Voltemand and Cornelius.]

And now, Laertes, what's the news with you?
You told us of some suit, what is't, Laertes?
You cannot speak of reason to the Dane,
And lose° your voice. What would'st thou beg, Laertes,
That shall not be my offer, not thy asking?
The head is not more native° to the heart,
The hand more instrumental° to the mouth,
Than is the throne of Denmark to thy father.
What wouldst thou have, Laertes?

°waste

°closely connected
°useful

LAERTES
          My dread lord,
Your leave and favor to return to France,
From whence though willingly I came to Denmark,
To show my duty in your coronation,
Yet now, I must confess, that duty done,
My thoughts and wishes bend° again toward France
And bow them to your gracious leave and pardon°.

°incline
°kind permission

KING
Have you your father's leave? What says Polonius?

POLONIUS
He hath, my lord, wrung from me my slow leave
By laborsome° petition, and, at last,
Upon his will I sealed my hard° consent.
I do beseech you give him leave to go.

°persistent
°reluctant

KING
Take thy fair hour,° Laertes; time be thine,
And thy best graces spend it at thy will.
But now, my cousin° Hamlet, and my son—

°Enjoy your youth

°kinsman

HAMLET
A little more than kin, and less than kind.[11]

-----

[11] Some editors emend this line with "aside," but its obscure barb may be meant to puzzle Claudius. These lines paraphrase a proverb, "The nearer in kin, the less in kindness." Since Hamlet's familial relationship to Claudius has doubled with the King's marriage to Gertrude (Claudius is now uncle-"father"), Claudius is more than kin. Since Hamlet neither likes Claudius nor approves his marriage, Claudius is also unkind (with a play on double meaning of *kind*): not natural and not compassionate.

KING
How is it that the clouds still hang on you?

HAMLET
Not so, my lord, I am too much i'th'sun°.

                       ° (1) the sunshine of kingly favor,
                           (2) the son

QUEEN
Good Hamlet, cast thy nighted color° off,   ° dark clothes and disposition
And let thine eye look like a friend on Denmark.
Do not for ever with thy vailed° lids   ° downcast
Seek for thy noble father in the dust.
Thou know'st 'tis common°, all that lives must die,   ° general
Passing through nature to eternity.

HAMLET
Ay, madam, it is common°.   ° commonplace, vulgar

QUEEN
                If it be,
Why seems it so particular° with thee?   ° personal

HAMLET
Seems, madam? Nay, it is. I know not "seems."
'Tis not along my inky° cloak, good mother,   ° black
Nor customary° suits of solemn black,   ° conventional, formal
Nor windy suspiration of forced breath,°   ° insincere sighs
No, nor the fruitful° river in the eye,   ° copious
Nor the dejected havior° of the visage,   ° expression
Together with all forms, moods°, shows of grief, ° external appearances
That can denote me truly. These, indeed, seem,
For they are actions that a man might play,
But I have that within which passeth° show,   ° surpasses
These but the trappings and the suits of woe.

KING
'Tis sweet and commendable in your nature, Hamlet,
To give these mourning duties to your father.
But, you must know, your father lost a father;
That father lost, lost his; and the survivor bound,
In filial obligation, for some term
To do obsequious sorrow°. But to persevere   ° proper mourning
In obstinate condolement° is a course   ° grief
Of impious stubbornness, 'tis unmanly grief,
It shows a will most incorrect° to heaven,   ° unsubmissive
A heart unfortified°, a mind impatient,   ° lacking the stoic virtue, fortitude
An understanding simple° and unschooled: ° ignorant
For what we know must be, and is as common
As any the most vulgar° thing to sense,   ° ordinary
Why should we, in our peevish opposition,
Take it to heart? Fie, 'tis a fault° to heaven,   ° offense
A fault against the dead, a fault to nature,
To reason most absurd, whose common theme
Is death of fathers, and who still hath cried,

From the first corpse° till he° that died to-day,   °Abel °up to any man
"This must be so." We pray you, throw to earth°   °drop
This unprevailing° woe, and think of us   °unavailing
As of a father, for let the world take note
You are the most immediate° to our throne,   °next in succession
And with no less nobility of love
Than that which dearest father bears his son,
Do I impart° toward you. For° your intent   °offer to share °As for
In going back to school in Wittenberg,[12]
It is most retrograde° to our desire,   °contrary
And we beseech you, bend you° to remain   °incline
Here in the cheer and comfort of our eye,
Our chiefest courtier, cousin, and our son.

QUEEN
Let not thy mother lose her prayers, Hamlet.
I pray thee, stay with us, go not to Wittenberg.

HAMLET
I shall in all my best obey you, madam.

KING
Why, 'tis a loving and a fair reply.
Be as ourself in Denmark. Madam, come.
This gentle and unforced accord of Hamlet
Sits smiling to my heart; in grace whereof,
No jocund health that Denmark drinks today
But the great cannon to the clouds shall tell,
And the King's rouse° the heaven shall bruit° again,   °full draught of liquor °loudly declare
Re-speaking earthly thunder. Come away.

[Exeunt all but Hamlet.]

HAMLET
O, that this too too solid flesh would melt,
Thaw, and resolve° itself into a dew,   °dissolve
Or that the Everlasting had not fixed
His canon° 'gainst self-slaughter. O God, God,   °religious law
How weary°, stale, flat, and unprofitable   °tedious
Seem to me all the uses° of this world!   °activities
Fie on't, ah fie, 'tis an unweeded garden
That grows to seed; things rank and gross in nature
Possess it merely°. That it should come to this!   °entirely
But two months dead—nay, not so much, not two—
So excellent a king, that was to° this   °compared to
Hyperion° to a satyr, so loving to my mother   °god of the sun
That he might not beteem° the winds of heaven   °would not allow

---

[12]Shakespeare's audience would have recognized Wittenberg, a German university, as Martin Luther's alma mater (and the birthplace of Protestantism) and as the university of Dr. Faustus (from Marlowe's *Dr. Faustus*).

Visit her face too roughly. Heaven and earth,
Must I remember? Why, she would hang on him
As if increase of appetite had grown
By what it fed on, and yet, within a month—
Let me not think on't—Frailty, thy name is woman—
A little month, or e'er° those shoes were old   °before
With which she followed my poor father's body,
Like Niobe°, all tears—why she, even she—   °epitome of grief
O God, a beast that wants° discourse of reason   °lacks
Would have mourned longer—married with my uncle,
My father's brother, but no more like my father
Than I to Hercules. Within a month,
Ere yet the salt of most unrighteous° tears   °insincere
Had left the flushing° in her galled° eyes,   °redness °sore
She married. O, most wicked speed, to post°   °hurry
With such dexterity° to incestuous sheets!¹³   °nimbleness
It is not nor it cannot come to good.
But break, my heart, for I must hold my tongue.

[Enter Horatio, Marcellus, and Barnardo.]

HORATIO
Hail to your lordship.

HAMLET
                    I am glad to see you well.
Horatio—or I do forget myself.

HORATIO
The same, my lord, and your poor servant ever.

HAMLET
Sir, my good friend, I'll change° that name with you.   °exchange
And what make you from Wittenberg, Horatio?
Marcellus.

MARCELLUS
My good lord.

HAMLET
I am very glad to see you. *[To Barnardo.]* Good even, sir.—
But what in faith make° you from Wittenberg?   °has brought you

HORATIO
A truant disposition, good my lord.

HAMLET
I would not hear your enemy say so.
Nor shall you do mine ear that violence
To make it truster of your own report
Against yourself. I know you are no truant.

---

¹³Both Catholic and Protestant church law prohibited the widow's marriage to her
deceased husband's brother.

But what is your affair in Elsinore?
We'll teach you to drink deep ere you depart.

HORATIO
My lord, I came to see your father's funeral.

HAMLET
I pray thee do not mock me, fellow-student;
I think it was to see my mother's wedding.

HORATIO
Indeed, my lord, it followed hard upon.

HAMLET
Thrift, thrift, Horatio. The funeral baked meats
Did coldly furnish forth the marriage tables.°   ° Cold leftovers from the funeral fed
Would I had met my dearest foe in heaven   the wedding party.
Or ever I had seen that day, Horatio.
My father—methinks I see my father.

HORATIO
Where, my lord?

HAMLET
                In my mind's eye, Horatio.

HORATIO
I saw him once. He was a goodly king.

HAMLET
He was a man. Take him for all in all°.   ° sum and pattern of excellence
I shall not look upon his like again.

HORATIO
My lord, I think I saw him yesternight.

HAMLET
Saw? Who?

HORATIO
My lord, the King your father.

HAMLET
                  The King my father!

HORATIO
Season your admiration° for a while   ° Restrain your amazement
With an attent° ear till I may deliver,   ° attentive
Upon the witness of these gentlemen,
This marvel to you.

HAMLET
                For God's love, let me hear.

HORATIO
Two nights together had these gentlemen,
Marcellus and Barnardo, on their watch,
In the dead vast and middle of the night,
Been thus encountered. A figure like your father,

Armed at point, exactly, cap-a-pie°,   °head to foot
Appears before them, and with solemn march
Goes slowly and stately° by them. Thrice he walked   °majestically
By their oppressed and fear-surprised eyes
Within his truncheon's° length, whilst they, distilled °military staff
Almost to jelly with the act° of fear,   °effect
Stand dumb and speak not to him. This to me
In dreadful° secrecy impart they did,   °awe-struck
And I with them the third night kept the watch,
Where, as they had delivered, both in time,
Form of the thing, each word made true and good,
The apparition comes. I knew your father;
These hands are not more like.

HAMLET
                              But where was this?

MARCELLUS
My lord, upon the platform° where we watched.   °cannon emplacement

HAMLET
Did you not speak to it?

HORATIO
                 My lord, I did;
But answer made it none. Yet once methought
It lifted up its head and did address°   °prepare
Itself to motion, like as it would speak.
But even then° the morning cock crew loud,   °Precisely at that moment
And at the sound it shrunk in haste away
And vanished from our sight.

HAMLET
                              'Tis very strange.

HORATIO
As I do live, my honored lord, 'tis true;
And we did think it writ down in our duty
To let you know of it.

HAMLET
Indeed, indeed, sirs, but this troubles me.
Hold you the watch tonight?

MARCELLUS AND BARNARDO
                 We do, my lord.

HAMLET
Armed, say you?

MARCELLUS AND BARNARDO
Armed, my lord.

HAMLET
From top to toe?

MARCELLUS AND BARNARDO
                 My lord, from head to foot.

HAMLET
Then saw you not his face?

HORATIO
O, yes, my lord, he wore his beaver° up.   ° visor, face-guard of a helmet

HAMLET
What looked he? Frowningly?

HORATIO
A countenance more in sorrow than in anger.

HAMLET
Pale or red?

HORATIO
Nay, very pale.

HAMLET
                    And fixed his eyes upon you?

HORATIO
Most constantly.

HAMLET
                              I would I had been there.

HORATIO
It would have much amazed° you.   ° astounded

HAMLET
Very like, very like. Stayed it long?

HORATIO
While one with moderate haste might tell° a hundred.   ° count

MARCELLUS AND BARNARDO
Longer, longer.

HORATIO
Not when I saw't.

HAMLET
                    His beard was grizzly°, no?   ° gray

HORATIO
It was as I have seen it in his life,
A sable silvered.

HAMLET
                              I will watch tonight.
Perchance 'twill walk again.

HORATIO
                                        I warrant you it will.

HAMLET
If it assume my noble father's person,
I'll speak to it, though hell itself should gape
And bid me hold my peace. I pray you all,
If you have hitherto concealed this sight°,   ° up to now kept this a secret

Let it be tenable in your silence° still,　　　　　　　　° remain a secret
And whatsoever else shall hap tonight,
Give it an understanding but no tongue.
I will requite your loves.° So fare you well.　　　　° (Love rather than duty sustains
Upon the platform, 'twixt eleven and twelve,　　　　　their friendship.)
I'll visit you.

ALL
　　　　　　　Our duty to your honor.

HAMLET
Your loves, as mine to you. Farewell.

[Exeunt all but Hamlet.]

My father's spirit, in arms! All is not well;
I doubt° some foul play. Would the night were come.　　° fear
Till then sit still, my soul; foul deeds will rise,
Though all the earth o'erwhelm them, to men's eyes.

[Exit Hamlet.]

Act One, Scene Three

A room in Polonius' house.

[Enter Laertes and Ophelia.]

LAERTES
My necessaries° are embarked. Farewell.　　　　　　° luggage
And, sister, as° the winds give benefit　　　　　　　° whenever
And convoy is assistant°, do not sleep　　　　　　　° transportation is available
But let me hear from you.

OPHELIA
　　　　　　　Do you doubt that?

LAERTES
For Hamlet, and the trifling of his favor°,　　　　° his frivolous attention
Hold it a fashion°, and a toy in blood°,　　　　　° courtly game ° passing fancy
A violet in the youth of primy° nature,　　　　　° (1) springtime (2) sexually excited
Forward° not permanent, sweet not lasting,　　　　° Precocious
The perfume and suppliance of a minute,
No more.

OPHELIA
　　　　No more but so?°　　　　　　　　　° No more than that?

LAERTES
　　　　　　　Think it no more.
For nature crescent° does not grow alone　　　　° the natural course of development
In thews and bulk°, but, as his temple waxes,　　° physical strength and size
The inward service° of the mind and soul　　　　° spiritual duty
Grows wide withal°. Perhaps he loves you now,　　° grows extensive with it
And now no soil° nor cautel° doth besmirch　　　° stain ° deceitful purpose

The virtue of his will; but you must fear,
His greatness weighed,° his will is not his own,   ° Considering his rank
For he himself is subject to his birth.
He may not, as unvalued° persons do,   ° unimportant
Carve for himself,° for on his choice depends   ° Do as he likes
The safety and health of this whole state;
And therefore must his choice be circumscribed°   ° restricted
Unto the voice and yielding of that body
Whereof he is the head. Then if he says he loves you,
It fits your wisdom so far to believe it,
As he in his particular act and place
May give his saying deed,° which is no further   ° make good his promise
Than the main voice° of Denmark goes withal.   ° general consent
Then weigh what loss your honor may sustain
If with too credent° ear you list° his songs,   ° trustful ° listen
Or lose your heart, or your chaste treasure° open   ° virginity
To his unmastered importunity.
Fear it, Ophelia, fear it, my dear sister,
And keep you in the rear° of your affection,   ° stay out of range
Out of the shot and danger of desire.
The chariest° maid is prodigal enough   ° shyest
If she unmask her beauty to the moon°.   ° (emblem of virginity)
Virtue itself scapes° not calumnious strokes.   ° escapes, avoids
The canker galls the infants of the spring°   ° blight attacks young plants
Too oft before their buttons be disclosed°,   ° buds open
And in the morn and liquid dew of youth
Contagious blastments° are most imminent.   ° withering blights
Be wary, then; best safety lies in fear;
Youth to° itself rebels, though none else near.   ° against

OPHELIA
I shall th'effect° of this good lesson keep   ° drift, point
As watchman to my heart. But, good my brother,
Do not, as some ungracious° pastors do,   ° wicked
Show me the steep and thorny way to heaven,
Whilst, like a puffed° and reckless libertine,   ° prideful
Himself the primrose path of dalliance treads
And recks not his own rede°.   ° ignores his own advice

LAERTES
                    O, fear me not.

                   [Enter Polonius.]

I stay too long—but here my father comes.
A double blessing is a double grace;
Occasion smiles upon a second leave.

POLONIUS
Yet here, Laertes? Aboard, aboard, for shame!
The wind sits in the shoulders° of your sail,   ° in the back
And you are stayed for°. There—   ° waited for

[Laying his hand on Laertes' head.]

       my blessing with thee;
And these few precepts in thy memory
See thou character°. Give thy thoughts no tongue,   °engrave
Nor any unproportioned° thought his act.   °unruly
Be thou familiar, but by no means vulgar.°   °Associate freely but not
The friends thou hast, and their adoption tried,   promiscuously.
Grapple them to thy soul with hoops of steel,
But do not dull° thy palm with entertainment   °make callous
Of each new-hatched, unfledged comrade. Beware
Of entrance to a quarrel, but being in,
Bear't,° that th'opposed may beware of thee.   °Manage it so that
Give every man thine ear, but few thy voice.
Take each man's censure, but reserve thy judgement.
Costly thy habit° as thy purse can buy,   °clothes
But not expressed in fancy, rich not gaudy,
For the apparel oft proclaims the man,
And they in France of the best rank and station
Are most select and generous, chief in that.
Neither a borrower nor a lender be,
For loan oft loses both itself and friend
And borrowing dulls the edge of husbandry.
This above all—to thine own self be true;
And it must follow, as the night the day,
Thou canst not then be false° to any man.   °faithless
Farewell—my blessing season° this in thee.   °ripen

LAERTES
Most humbly do I take my leave, my lord.

POLONIUS
The time invites you. Go, your servants tend.

LAERTES
Farewell, Ophelia, and remember well
What I have said to you.

OPHELIA
                'Tis in my memory locked,
And you yourself shall keep the key of it.

LAERTES
Farewell.

[Exit Laertes.]

POLONIUS
What is't, Ophelia, he hath said to you?

OPHELIA
So please you, something touching the Lord Hamlet.

POLONIUS
Marry,° well bethought.   °To be sure
'Tis told me he hath very oft of late

Given private time° to you; and you yourself   °time away from public duties
Have of your audience been most free° and bounteous.   °liberal
If it be so—as so 'tis put on me,
And that in way of caution—I must tell you
You do not understand yourself so clearly
As it behooves my daughter and your honor.
What is between you? Give me up the truth.

OPHELIA
He hath, my lord, of late made many tenders°   °offers
Of his affection to me.

POLONIUS
Affection, pooh! You speak like a green° girl   °inexperienced
Unsifted° in such perilous circumstance.   °Untried
Do you believe his tenders°, as you call them?   °(1) offers (2) financial payment

OPHELIA
I do not know, my lord, what I should think.

POLONIUS
Marry, I'll teach you. Think yourself a baby
That you have ta'en these tenders for true pay
Which are not sterling. Tender° yourself more dearly,   °Value
Or—not to crack the wind of the poor phrase,
Running it thus—you'll tender me a fool.°   °make me a fool, make yourself a fool, make a fool (bastard)

OPHELIA
My lord, he hath importuned me with love
In honorable fashion.

POLONIUS
Ay, "fashion" you may call't. Go to, go to.

OPHELIA
And hath given countenance° to his speech, my lord,   °authority
With almost all the holy vows of heaven.

POLONIUS
Ay, springes° to catch woodcocks°. I do know,   °snares °gullible birds
When the blood burns, how prodigal° the soul   °lavishly
Lends the tongue vows. These blazes°, daughter,   °short-lived bursts of flame
Giving more light than heat, extinct in both
Even in their promise as it is a-making,
You must not take for fire. From this time
Be somewhat scanter of your maiden presence,
Set your entreatments° at a higher rate   °interviews
Than a command to parley. For Lord Hamlet,
Believe so° much in him, that he is young,   °thus
And with a larger tether may he walk
Than may be given you. In few, Ophelia,
Do not believe his vows, for they are brokers,°   °procurers
Not of that dye which their investments show,°   °Not what they seem
But mere implorators° of unholy suits,   °out and out procurers

Breathing like sanctified and pious bawds
The better to beguile. This is for all—
I would not, in plain terms, from this time forth,
Have you so slander° any moment leisure   °disgrace
As to give words or talk with the Lord Hamlet.
Look to't, I charge you. Come your ways.°   °Come along.

OPHELIA
I shall obey, my lord.

                                               [Exeunt all.]

Act One, Scene Four

The platform before the castle.

                    [Enter Hamlet, Horatio, and Marcellus.]

HAMLET
The air bites shrewdly°, it is very cold.   °keenly, sharply

HORATIO
It is a nipping and an eager air.

HAMLET
What hour now?

HORATIO
                    I think it lacks of twelve.

MARCELLUS
No, it is struck.

HORATIO
                    Indeed? I heard it not.
Then it draws near the season
Wherein the spirit held his wont to walk.

          [A flourish of trumpets, and ordnance shot off, within.]

What does this mean, my lord?

HAMLET
The king doth wake tonight and takes his rouse°,   °carouses
Keeps wassail° and the swaggering up-spring reels°,   °drinking bouts °dances
And, as he drains his draughts of Rhenish° down,   °Rhine wine
The kettle-drum and trumpet thus bray out
The triumph of his pledge.¹⁴

HORATIO
                    Is it a custom?

---

¹⁴The kettle drum and trumpet, instruments of the Danish military march, sound
when Claudius drains his cup in a single draught. Because the accompaniment to
ceremony, martial music, is used to celebrate Claudius's drinking, Hamlet believes
this degenerate custom were better ignored, especially since foreigners call the
Danes drunks.

HAMLET
Ay, marry, is't.
But to my mind, though I am native here
And to the manner born°, it is a custom   °familiar from birth
More honored in the breach than the observance.°   °Better to break than observe.
This heavy-headed revel east and west
Makes us traduced and taxed° of other nations.   °censured
They clepe° us drunkards, and with swinish phrase   °call
Soil our addition°, and, indeed, it takes°   °titles of honor °detracts
From our achievements, though performed at height°,   °excellently
The pith and marrow of our attribute°.   °reputation
So, oft it chances in particular men,
That, for some vicious mole of nature° in them,   °small natural blemish
As, in their birth, wherein they are not guilty,
Since nature cannot choose his origin,
By the o'ergrowth of some complexion,°   °By the excess of a humor
Oft breaking down the pales° and forts of reason,   °fences
Or by some habit, that too much o'er-leavens
The form of plausive° manners—that these men,   °pleasing
Carrying, I say, the stamp of one defect,
Being nature's livery or fortune's star,°   °Acquired by birth or by misfortune
Their virtues else, be they as pure as grace,
As infinite as man may undergo°,   °sustain
Shall in the general censure° take corruption   °popular opinion
From that particular fault: the dram° of evil   °minute amount
Doth all the noble substance of a doubt°   °extinguishing
To his own scandal.

HORATIO
                    Look, my lord, it comes!

                                        [Enter Ghost.]

HAMLET
Angels and ministers of grace defend us!
Be thou a spirit of health or goblin damned,
Bring with thee airs from heaven or blasts from hell,
Be thy intents wicked or charitable,
Thou comest in such a questionable° shape,   °inviting question
That I will speak to thee. I'll call thee Hamlet,
King, father, royal Dane. O, answer me!
Let me not burst in ignorance, but tell
Why thy canonized° bones, hearsed° in death,   °consecrated °coffined
Have burst their cerements°, why the sepulchre,   °grave clothes
Wherein we saw thee quietly inurned°   °entombed
Hath oped his ponderous and marble jaws
To cast thee up again. What may this mean
That thou, dead corpse, again, in complete steel°,   °full armor
Revisits thus the glimpses of the moon,
Making night hideous°, and we fools of nature°   °terrifying °baffled by the
So horridly to shake our disposition   supernatural

With thoughts beyond the reaches of our souls?
Say, why is this? Wherefore? What should we do?

[Ghost beckons Hamlet.]

HORATIO
It beckons you to go away with it,
As if it some impartment° did desire   °communication
To you alone.

MARCELLUS
          Look with what courteous action
It waves you to a more removed ground°.   °secluded place
But do not go with it.

HORATIO
             No, by no means.

HAMLET
It will not speak. Then I will follow it.

HORATIO
Do not, my lord.

HAMLET
            Why, what should be the fear?°   °what is there to fear?
I do not set my life at a pin's fee°,   °worth
And for my soul, what can it do to that,
Being a thing immortal as itself?
It waves me forth again. I'll follow it.

HORATIO
What if it tempt you toward the flood, my lord,
Or to the dreadful summit of the cliff
That beetles° o'er his base into the sea,   °overhangs threateningly
And there assume some other horrible form,
Which might deprive your sovereignty of reason
And draw you into madness?[15] Think of it.
The very place puts toys of desperation°,   °fancies
Without more motive, into every brain
That looks so many fathoms to the sea,
And hears it roar beneath.

HAMLET
            It waves° me still—   °beckons
Go on, I'll follow thee.

MARCELLUS
You shall not go, my lord.

---

[15] Horatio voices the common belief that malign spirits might tempt people to suicide by providing them with the means and the opportunity to take their own lives. The devil could make people mad by overturning reason, the faculty that rules the mind.

HAMLET

　　　　　　Hold off your hands.

HORATIO

Be ruled, you shall not go.

HAMLET

　　　　　　　My fate cries out,
And makes each petty artery in this body
As hardy as the Nemean lion's nerve.[16]
Still am I called. Unhand me, gentlemen.
By heaven, I'll make a ghost of him that lets° me.　　　　　　　　　　　° hinders
I say, away! —Go on, I'll follow thee.

[Exeunt Ghost and Hamlet.]

HORATIO

He waxes desperate with imagination°.　　　　　　　　　　　　　　° delusion

MARCELLUS

Let's follow. 'Tis not fit thus to obey him.

HORATIO

Have after.° To what issue° will this come?　　　　　° Let's follow him. ° conclusion

MARCELLUS

Something is rotten in the state of Denmark.

HORATIO

Heaven will direct it.

MARCELLUS

　　　　　Nay°, let's follow him.　　　　　　　　° No, we'll act and not wait for
　　　　　　　　　　　　　　　　　　　　　　　　heaven

　　　　　　　　　　　　　　　[Exeunt all.]

Act One, Scene Five

Another part of the platform.

[Enter Ghost and Hamlet.]

HAMLET

Where wilt thou lead me? Speak. I'll go no further.

GHOST

Mark me.

HAMLET

　　　　　I will.

---

[16] In Shakespeare's time, arteries were thought to convey an ethereal fluid called "vital spirits" or "animal spirits," which were the source of courage and nerve. The Nemean lion was a reputedly invulnerable creature (until Hercules strangled it in his first labor). Hamlet feels that his destiny makes every small vessel in his body as strong as the lion's sinew.

GHOST

              My hour is almost come°   °Dawn is coming
When I to sulphurous and tormenting flames°   °purgatory
Must render up myself.

HAMLET

                  Alas, poor ghost!

GHOST

Pity me not, but lend thy serious hearing
To what I shall unfold.

HAMLET

               Speak, I am bound to hear.

GHOST

So art thou to revenge, when thou shalt hear.

HAMLET
What?

GHOST

I am thy father's spirit,
Doomed for a certain term to walk the night,
And for the day confined to fast° in fires,   °do penance
Till the foul crimes° done in my days of nature   °sins
Are burnt and purged away. But that I am forbid°   °Were I not forbidden
To tell the secrets of my prison-house,
I could a tale unfold, whose lightest word
Would harrow up thy soul, freeze thy young blood,
Make thy two eyes, like stars, start from their spheres°,   °sockets
Thy knotted and combined locks to part,[17]
And each particular hair to stand on end,
Like quills upon the fretful° porcupine.   °frightened
But this eternal blazon[18] must not be
To ears of flesh and blood. List,° Hamlet, O, list!   °Listen
If thou didst ever thy dear father love—

HAMLET
O God!

---

[17] The Ghost gives us a glimpse of Hamlet as the "glass of fashion." Remarking on Hamlet's appearance, the Ghost describes his "knotty and combined locks." "Combined" refers to hair wound together rather than combed out into separate hairs, so Hamlet may be wearing curls.

[18] "Blazon" literally means the description of a coat of arms on a heraldic shield. The coat of arms identifies the bearer and his family by a visual, iconographic design in which colors, shapes, figures, and location on the shield all carry meaning. A blazon connotes publication (making public) or proclamation. By "eternal blazon," the Ghost refers to a disclosure of eternal, or supernatural, matters.

GHOST
Revenge his foul and most unnatural[19] murder.

HAMLET
Murder!

GHOST
Murder most foul, as in the best it is,°   ° At its best, murder is foul
But this most foul, strange, and unnatural.

HAMLET
Haste me to know it,° that I, with wings as swift   ° Hurry to tell me
As meditation° or the thoughts of love,   ° thought
May sweep to my revenge.

GHOST
                    I find thee apt°;   ° quick to get the point
And duller shouldst thou be than the fat weed
That roots itself in ease on Lethe wharf°,   ° banks of the river of forgetfulness
Wouldst thou not stir in this. Now, Hamlet, hear.
'Tis given out that, sleeping in my orchard°,   ° garden
A serpent stung me. So the whole ear of Denmark
Is by a forged process° of my death   ° a lying account
Rankly abused°. But know, thou noble youth,   ° deceived
The serpent that did sting thy father's life
Now wears his crown.

HAMLET
                    O my prophetic soul![20]
My uncle!

GHOST
Ay, that incestuous, that adulterate° beast,   ° adulterous
With witchcraft of his wit, with traitorous gifts—
O wicked wit and gifts, that have the power
So to seduce! —won to his shameful lust
The will of my most seeming-virtuous queen.
O Hamlet, what a falling-off° was there,   ° change for the worse
From me, whose love was of that° dignity°   ° such ° worthiness

---

[19] This murder is unnatural on several counts. First, murder is unnatural because it
violates natural law, which maintains that humans ought not kill their own kind.
The horrific nature of that act gains force because this murder is also fratricide,
echoing back to the primal murder of Abel by Cain. Furthermore, this murder was
executed so relentlessly that King Hamlet had no opportunity to prepare his soul
for the spiritual afterlife by receiving the relevant sacraments: confession, communion, or extreme unction (last rites). The play's repetition of "strange" reinforces
"unnatural."

[20] Hamlet's soul is prophetic because he intuited his uncle's wicked nature, not because he intuited the fratricide.

That it went hand-in-hand even with the vow
I made to her in marriage, and to decline°   ° sink down
Upon a wretch, whose natural gifts[21] were poor
To those of mine.
But virtue, as it never will be moved,
Though lewdness court it in a shape of heaven°,   ° angelic form
So lust, though to a radiant angel linked,
Will sate itself in a celestial bed
And prey on garbage.
But, soft, methinks I scent the morning air.
Brief let me be. Sleeping within my orchard,
My custom always in the afternoon,
Upon my secure° hour thy uncle stole   ° carefree
With juice of cursed hebenon° in a vial,   ° substance with poisonous juice
And in the porches of mine ears did pour
The leperous distilment°, whose effect   ° liquid producing effects of leprosy
Holds such an enmity with blood of man,
That, swift as quicksilver, it courses through
The natural gates and alleys of the body,
And with a sudden vigor it doth posset°   ° curdle
And curd, like eager° droppings into milk,   ° sour
The thin and wholesome blood. So did it mine;
And a most instant tetter° barked about°,   ° skin rash ° encrusted (as with
Most lazar-like°, with vile and loathsome crust   bark)
All my smooth body.   ° leper-like
Thus was I, sleeping, by a brother's hand
Of life, of crown, of queen, at once dispatched°,   °deprived
Cut off even in the blossoms of my sin,
Unhouseled, disappointed, unaneled,°   ° Without the Eucharist (housel),
No reckoning made, but sent to my account   confession, or last rites
With all my imperfections on my head.
O horrible, O horrible, most horrible!
If thou hast nature° in thee, bear it not;   ° natural feeling
Let not the royal bed of Denmark be
A couch for luxury° and damned incest.   °lust
But howsoever thou pursuest this act,
Taint not thy mind, nor let thy soul contrive
Against thy mother aught—leave her to heaven,
And to those thorns that in her bosom lodge
To prick and sting her. Fare thee well at once.
The glow-worm shows the matin° to be near,   ° morning
And 'gins to pale° his uneffectual fire.   ° dim
Adieu, adieu, adieu! Remember me.

                          [Exit Ghost.]

---

[21] King Hamlet's natural gifts, his virtue and good character, contrast with Claudius's traitorous gifts, presents given to Gertrude to woo her.

HAMLET
O all you host of heaven! O earth! What else?
And shall I couple hell? O, fie! Hold°, hold, my heart,   °Be firm
And you, my sinews, grow not instant old,
But bear me stiffly up. Remember thee?
Ay, thou poor ghost, while memory holds a seat
In this distracted globe°. Remember thee?   °(1) his head (2) the Globe Theater
Yea, from the table° of my memory   °writing tablet
I'll wipe away all trivial fond° records,   °foolish
All saws of books°, all forms, all pressures° past,   °maxims °impressions
That youth and observation copied there,
And thy commandment all alone shall live
Within the book and volume of my brain,
Unmixed with baser matter. Yes, yes, by heaven!
O most pernicious° woman!   °wicked
O villain, villain, smiling, damned villain!
My tables°—meet it is I set it down   °note tablet
That one may smile, and smile, and be a villain.
At least I'm sure it may be so in Denmark.

                                  [He writes.]

So, uncle, there you are. Now to my word°;   °watchword
It is, "Adieu, adieu, remember me."
I have sworn't.

HORATIO *[within]*
My lord, my lord!

MARCELLUS *[within]*
          Lord Hamlet!

HORATIO *[within]*
                    Heaven secure him!

HAMLET
So be it.

HORATIO *[within]*
Hillo, ho, ho, my lord!

HAMLET
Hillo, ho, ho, boy! Come, bird, come.°   °(falconer's call to his hawk)

              [Enter Horatio and Marcellus.]

MARCELLUS
How is't, my noble lord?

HORATIO
                    What news, my lord?

HAMLET
O, wonderful!

HORATIO
Good my lord, tell it.

HAMLET

No, you'll reveal it.

HORATIO
Not I, my lord, by heaven.

MARCELLUS

Nor I, my lord.

HAMLET
How say you, then, would heart of man once think it?
But you'll be secret?

HORATIO AND MARCELLUS

Ay, by heaven, my lord.

HAMLET
There's ne'er a villain dwelling in all Denmark
But he's an arrant knave.²²

HORATIO
There needs no ghost, my lord, come from the grave
To tell us this.

HAMLET

Why, right; you are i' th'right.
And so, without more circumstance at all
I hold it fit that we shake hands and part:
You, as your business and desire shall point° you,   °direct
For every man hath business and desire,
Such as it is; and for mine own poor part,
Look you, I'll go pray.

HORATIO
These are but wild and whirling° words, my lord.   °agitated

HAMLET
I'm sorry they offend you, heartily—
Yes, faith, heartily.

HORATIO

There's no offence, my lord.

HAMLET
Yes, by Saint Patrick,²³ but there is, Horatio,
And much offence too. Touching this vision here—
It is an honest° ghost, that let me tell you.   °reliable, trustworthy
For your desire to know what is between us°,   °(Hamlet and the Ghost)
O'ermaster't as you may. And now, good friends,

---

²²Hamlet seems about to disclose the particulars of the arrant knave, Claudius, but
then he turns his speech to jest.

²³According to lore, St. Patrick kept Purgatory in an Irish cave. He was visited by
pilgrims who believed that by spending a night and a day there, they would be
purged of their sins and receive visions of the damned and the blessed.

As you are friends, scholars, and soldiers,
Give me one poor request.

HORATIO
What is't, my lord? We will.

HAMLET
Never make known what you have seen tonight.

HORATIO AND MARCELLUS
My lord, we will not.

HAMLET
            Nay, but swear't.

HORATIO
                 In faith,
My lord, not I.°   °I will not reveal the secret.

MARCELLUS
           Nor I, my lord, in faith.

HAMLET
Upon my sword.°   °(The sword's hilt forms a cross.)

MARCELLUS
          We have sworn, my lord, already.

HAMLET
Indeed, upon my sword, indeed.

GHOST [cries under the stage]
Swear.

HAMLET
Ah, ha, boy, say'st thou so? Art thou there, truepenny°?   °trusty fellow
Come on. You hear this fellow in the cellarage.
Consent to swear.

HORATIO
           Propose the oath, my lord.

HAMLET
Never to speak of this that you have seen,
Swear by my sword.

GHOST [beneath]
Swear.

HAMLET
Hic et ubique°? Then we'll shift our ground.   °Here and everywhere
Come hither, gentlemen,
And lay your hands again upon my sword:
Never to speak of this that you have heard.
Swear by my sword.

GHOST [beneath]
Swear.

HAMLET
Well said, old mole. Canst work i' th'earth so fast?
A worthy pioneer°! Once more remove°, good friends.   °military miner °move to another
                                                    place again

HORATIO
O day and night, but this is wondrous strange.

HAMLET
And therefore as a stranger give it welcome.
There are more things in heaven and earth, Horatio,
Than are dreamt of in your philosophy°. But come,   ° science
Here, as before, never, so help you mercy,
How strange or odd soe'er I bear myself—
As I, perchance, hereafter shall think meet
To put an antic disposition on°—   ° act mad
That you, at such times seeing me, never shall,
With arms encumbered° thus, or this head-shake,   ° folded
Or by pronouncing of some doubtful° phrase,   ° ambiguous
As "Well, we know," or "We could an if° we would,"   ° if only
Or "If we list to speak," or "There be an if they might,"
Or such ambiguous giving out°, to note°   ° insinuation ° indicate
That you know aught of me—this not to do,
So grace and mercy at your most need help you,
Swear.

GHOST
Swear.

HAMLET
Rest, rest, perturbed spirit. So, gentlemen,
With all my love I do commend me to you;
And what so poor a man as Hamlet is
May do t'express his love and friending° to you,   ° friendliness
God willing, shall not lack. Let us go in together;
And still° your fingers on your lips, I pray.   ° always; that is, keep silent
The time is out of joint. O cursed spite,
That ever I was born to set it right!
Nay, come, let's go together.

                    [Exeunt all.]

————————————— **ACT TWO** —————————————

Act Two, Scene One

Elsinore: a room in Polonius' house.

                    [Enter Polonius and Reynaldo.]

POLONIUS
Give him this money and these notes, Reynaldo.

REYNALDO
I will, my lord.

POLONIUS
You shall do marvellous wisely, good Reynaldo,
Before you visit him, to make inquiry
Of his behavior.

REYNALDO
                    My lord, I did intend it.

POLONIUS
Marry, well said, very well said. Look you, sir,
Inquire me first what Danskers° are in Paris,   °Danes
And how, and who, what means, and where they keep°,   °lodge
What company, at what expense; and finding,
By this encompassment° and drift of question   °roundabout approach
That they do know my son, come you more nearer
Than your particular demands° will touch it.   °direct questions
Take° you, as 'twere, some distant knowledge of him, °Assume
As thus, "I know his father and his friends,
And in part him." Do you mark this, Reynaldo?

REYNALDO
Ay, very well, my lord.

POLONIUS
"And in part him, but," you may say, "not well,
But, if't be he I mean, he's very wild,
Addicted so and so"; and there put on° him   °ascribe to
What forgeries° you please. Marry, none so rank   °false accusations
As may dishonor him—take heed of that—
But, sir, such wanton, wild, and usual slips
As are companions noted and most known
To youth and liberty.

REYNALDO
                    As gaming, my lord.

POLONIUS
Ay, or drinking, fencing, swearing,
Quarrelling, drabbing°—you may go so far.   °whoring

REYNALDO
My lord, that would dishonor him.

POLONIUS
Faith, no, as you may season° it in the charge.   °temper, qualify
You must not put another scandal on him,
That he is open to incontinency°—   °sexual profligacy
That's not my meaning—but breathe his faults so quaintly° °artfully
That they may seem the taints of liberty,
The flash and outbreak of a fiery mind,
A savageness in unreclaimed° blood,   °untamed
Of general assault.°   °Common to men in general

REYNALDO
                    But, my good lord—

POLONIUS
Wherefore should you do this?

REYNALDO
                    Ay, my lord,
I would know that.

POLONIUS
                    Marry, sir, here's my drift°,   °underlying purpose
And, I believe, it is a fetch of warrant°.   °legitimate trick
You laying these slight sullies on my son,
As 'twere a thing a little soil'd i' th'working,
Mark you, your party in converse, him you would sound,
Having ever seen in the prenominate° crimes   °aforementioned
The youth you breathe of guilty, be assured
He closes with you in this consequence°:   °to this end
"Good sir," or so, or "friend," or "gentleman,"
According to the phrase and the addition°   °form of address
Of man and country.

REYNALDO
                    Very good, my lord.

POLONIUS
And then, sir, does he this—he does—what was I about to
say? By the mass, I was about to say something. Where did
I leave?

REYNALDO
At "closes in the consequence," at "friend or so," and
"gentleman."

POLONIUS
At "closes in the consequence," ay, marry!
He closes with you thus: "I know the gentleman,
I saw him yesterday, or t'other day,
Or then, or then, with such and such; and, as you say,
There was he gaming, there o'ertook in's rouse°,   °drink
There falling out at tennis," or perchance,
"I saw him enter such a house of sale,"
Videlicet, a brothel, or so forth.
See you now,
Your bait of falsehood takes° this carp of truth: °catches
And thus do we of wisdom and of reach°,   °comprehension
With windlasses° and with assays of bias°,   °roundabout course °indirect
By indirections find directions out.   attempts
So, by my former lecture° and advice,   °lesson
Shall you my son. You have me, have you not?

REYNALDO
My lord, I have.

POLONIUS
                    God buy you°, fare ye well.   °God be with you (goodbye)

REYNALDO
Good my lord!

POLONIUS
Observe his inclination in yourself.°   ° Accommodate him.

REYNALDO
I shall, my lord.

POLONIUS
And let him ply° his music.   ° work on

REYNALDO
                        Well, my lord.

POLONIUS
Farewell!

                                        [Exit Reynaldo.]

                                        [Enter Ophelia.]

How now, Ophelia, what's the matter?

OPHELIA
O, my lord, my lord, I have been so affrighted!

POLONIUS
With what, i' th'name of God?

OPHELIA
My lord, as I was sewing in my chamber,
Lord Hamlet, with his doublet all unbraced°,   ° unbuttoned
No hat upon his head, his stockings fouled°,   ° dirty
Ungartered, and down-gyved to his ankle,°   ° hanging around his ankles like
Pale as his shirt, his knees knocking each other,   fetters
And with a look so piteous in purport
As if he had been loosed out of hell
To speak of horrors, he comes before me.

POLONIUS
Mad for thy love?

OPHELIA
                        My lord, I do not know;
But, truly, I do fear it.

POLONIUS
                        What said he?

OPHELIA
He took me by the wrist, and held me hard.
Then goes he to the length of all his arm,
And, with his other hand thus o'er his brow,
He falls to such perusal° of my face   ° scrutiny
As he would draw it. Long stayed he so.
At last, a little shaking of mine arm,
And thrice his head thus waving up and down,

He raised a sigh so piteous and profound,
That it did seem to shatter all his bulk°,   °body
And end his being. That done, he lets me go,
And, with his head over his shoulder turned,
He seemed to find his way without his eyes;
For out o' doors he went without their help,
And, to the last, bended their light on me.

POLONIUS
Come, go with me. I will go seek the King.
This is the very ecstasy° of love,   °madness
Whose violent property fordoes° itself,   °destroys
And leads the will to desperate undertakings
As oft as any passion under heaven
That does afflict our natures. I am sorry—
What, have you given him any hard words of late?

OPHELIA
No, my good lord, but, as you did command
I did repel his letters, and denied
His access to me.

POLONIUS
                    That hath made him mad.
I am sorry that with better heed and judgement
I had not quoted him. I feared he did but trifle
And meant to wrack° thee. But, beshrew my jealousy°!   °ruin °curse my suspicion
By heaven, it is as proper to our age°   °natural for old men
To cast beyond ourselves° in our opinions   °go too far
As it is common for the younger sort
To lack discretion. Come, go we to the King.
This must be known, which, being kept close°, might move   °secret
More grief to hide than hate to utter love.
Come.

                              [Exeunt all.]

Act Two, Scene Two

A room in the castle.

        [Enter King, Queen, Rosencrantz, Guildenstern, and Attendants.]

KING
Welcome, dear Rosencrantz and Guildenstern.
Moreover° that we much did long to see you,   °Besides
The need we have to use you did provoke
Our hasty sending. Something have you heard
Of Hamlet's transformation—so call it,
Since nor th'exterior nor the inward man
Resembles that it was. What it should be,
More than his father's death, that thus hath put him

So much from th'understanding of himself
I cannot dream of. I entreat you both,
That, being of so young days brought up with him,
And sith° so neighbored° to his youth and havior, °since °familiar with
That you vouchsafe your rest° here in our court °consent to stay
Some little time, so by your companies
To draw him him on to pleasures, and to gather,
So much as from occasion° you may glean, °opportunity
Whether aught, to us unknown, afflicts him thus
That, opened, lies within our remedy.

QUEEN
Good gentlemen, he hath much talked of you,
And sure I am two men there are not living
To whom he more adheres°. If it will please you °is more attached
To show us so much gentry° and good will °courtesy
As to expend your time with us awhile
For the supply and profit° of our hope, °support and advancement
Your visitation shall receive such thanks
As fits a king's remembrance.

ROSENCRANTZ
                    Both your majesties
Might, by the sovereign power you have of us,
Put your dread pleasures more into command
Than to entreaty.

GUILDENSTERN
            But we both obey,
And here give up ourselves, in the full bent°, °fully devote ourselves
To lay our service freely° at your feet, °willingly
To be commanded.

KING
Thanks, Rosencrantz and gentle Guildenstern.

QUEEN
Thanks, Guildenstern and gentle Rosencrantz.
And I beseech you instantly to visit
My too-much-changed son. Go, some of you,
And bring these gentlemen where Hamlet is.

GUILDENSTERN
Heavens make our presence and our practices° °activities
Pleasant and helpful to him!

QUEEN
              Ay, amen!

[Exeunt Rosencrantz, Guildenstern, and some Attendants.]

[Enter Polonius.]

POLONIUS
Th'ambassadors from Norway, my good lord,
Are joyfully returned.

KING
Thou still° hast been the father of good news.   °always

POLONIUS
Have I, my lord? Assure you, my good liege,
I hold my duty, as I hold my soul,
Both to my God and to my gracious King.
And I do think—or else this brain of mine
Hunts not the trail of policy° so sure   °statecraft
As it hath used to do—that I have found
The very cause of Hamlet's lunacy.

KING
O, speak of that, that do I long to hear.

POLONIUS
Give first admittance to th'ambassadors;
My news shall be the fruit° to that great feast.   °dessert

KING
Thyself do grace° to them, and bring them in.   °honor

                        [Exit Polonius.]

He tells me, my dear Gertrude, he hath found
The head and source of all your son's distemper.

QUEEN
I doubt° it is no other but the main°—   °suspect °obvious reason
His father's death and our o'erhasty marriage.

KING
Well, we shall sift him°.   °examine Polonius

              [Enter Polonius, with Voltemand and Cornelius.]

              Welcome, my good friends!
Say, Voltemand, what from our brother Norway?

VOLTEMAND
Most fair return of greetings and desires.
Upon our first, he sent out to suppress
His nephew's levies, which to him appeared
To be a preparation 'gainst the Polack°;   °King of Poland
But, better looked into, he truly found
It was against your highness: whereat grieved°,   °aggrieved, offended
That so his sickness, age, and impotence°   °infirmity
Was falsely borne in hand°, sends out arrests   °taken advantage of
On Fortinbras, which he, in brief, obeys,
Receives rebuke from Norway, and, in fine°,   °finally
Makes vow before his uncle never more
To give th'assay° of arms against your majesty.   °challenge
Whereon old Norway, overcome with joy,
Gives him three thousand crowns in annual fee
And his commission° to employ these soldiers   °authorization

So levied as before, against the Polack,
With an entreaty, herein further shown,
[gives a paper]
That it might please you to give quiet pass° °safe passage
Through your dominions for this enterprise,
On such regards of safety and allowance° °with safeguards and provisos
As therein are set down.

KING
                    It likes° us well; °pleases
And at our more considered° time we'll read, °suitable for consideration
Answer, and think upon this business.
Meantime, we thank you for your well-took labor.
Go to your rest; at night° we'll feast together. °tonight
Most welcome home.

                    [Exeunt Voltemand and Cornelius.]

POLONIUS
                    This business is well ended.
My liege, and madam, to expostulate° °expound
What majesty should be, what duty is,
Why day is day, night night, and time is time.
Were nothing but to waste night, day, and time.
Therefore, since brevity is the soul of wit°, °good sense
And tediousness the limbs and outward flourishes,
I will be brief. Your noble son is mad.
Mad call I it, for, to define true madness,
What is't but to be nothing else but mad?
But let that go.

QUEEN
                    More matter with less art°. °rhetorical artfulness

POLONIUS
Madam, I swear I use no art at all.
That he is mad, 'tis true; 'tis true 'tis pity;
And pity 'tis 'tis true—a foolish figure°. °figure of speech
But farewell it, for I will use no art.
Mad let us grant him then: and now remains
That we find out the cause of this effect,
Or rather say the cause of this defect,
For this effect defective comes by cause.
Thus it remains, and the remainder thus.
Perpend.° °Consider.
I have a daughter—have whilst she is mine—
Who, in her duty and obedience, mark,
Hath given me this. Now gather and surmise°. °draw your own conclusion
[Reads.]
"To the celestial and my soul's idol, the most beautified° °beautiful
Ophelia"—That's an ill phrase, a vile phrase, "beautified"

is a vile phrase. But you shall hear. Thus: *[Reads.]* "In
her excellent white bosom, these, etc."

QUEEN
Came this from Hamlet to her?

POLONIUS
Good madam, stay a while; I will be faithful.
[Reads.]

> *"Doubt° thou the stars are fire,*   ° Suspect
> *Doubt that the sun doth move²⁴*
> *Doubt truth to be a liar,*
> *But never doubt I love.*

O dear Ophelia, I am ill at these numbers°. I have not   ° bad at versifying
art to reckon° my groans. But that I love thee best, O   ° count
most best, believe it. Adieu.

> Thine evermore, most dear lady, whilst this machine° is to him,   ° body
> Hamlet."

This, in obedience, hath my daughter shown me,
And more above°, hath his solicitings,   ° moreover
As they fell out by time, by means, and place,
All given to mine ear.

KING
                     But how hath she
Received his love?

POLONIUS
                What do you think of me?

KING
As of a man faithful and honorable.

POLONIUS
I would fain prove so. But what might you think,
When I had seen this hot love on the wing,
As I perceived it—I must tell you that—
Before my daughter told me, what might you,
Or my dear majesty your queen here, think,
If I had played the desk or table-book°,   ° acted as an intermediary
Or given my heart a winking mute and dumb°,   ° shut my eyes to
Or looked upon this love with idle sight—
What might you think? No, I went round° to work,   ° straightforwardly
And my young mistress thus I did bespeak:
"Lord Hamlet is a prince, out of thy star°.   ° beyond your station
This must not be." And then I precepts° gave her,   ° instructions

---

²⁴The Ptolemaic universe informs Hamlet's cosmology. In this system, the fixed
earth centered the universe. Although Hamlet urges Ophelia to doubt the most
common truths (including the movement of the sun around the earth) before she
doubts his love, the astronomical irony is unintentional on Shakespeare's part.

That she should lock herself from his resort,
Admit no messengers, receive no tokens.
Which done, she took the fruits of my advice;
And he, repulsed—a short tale to make—
Fell into a sadness, then into a fast,
Thence to a watch°, thence into a weakness,   ° sleeplessness
Thence to a lightness°, and, by this declension,   ° lightheadedness
Into the madness wherein now he raves,
And all we mourn for.

KING
                    Do you think 'tis this?

QUEEN
It may be—very likely.

POLONIUS
Hath there been such a time—I'd fain know that—
That I have positively said " 'Tis so,"
When it proved otherwise?

KING
                    Not that I know.

POLONIUS [pointing to his head and shoulder]
Take this from this, if this be otherwise.
If circumstances lead me, I will find
Where truth is hid, though it were hid indeed
Within the centre°.   ° center of the earth

KING
                    How may we try° it further?   ° test

POLONIUS
You know, sometimes he walks four hours together
Here in the lobby.

QUEEN
                    So he does, indeed.

POLONIUS
At such a time I'll loose my daughter to him.
Be you and I behind an arras° then,   ° hanging tapestry
Mark the encounter. If he love her not,
And be not from his reason fallen thereon°,   ° on that account
Let me be no assistant for a state,
But keep a farm and carters.

KING
                    We will try it.

QUEEN
But, look, where sadly° the poor wretch comes reading. ° seriously

POLONIUS
Away, I do beseech you both, away.
I'll board° him presently. O give me leave.   ° address

[Exeunt King, Queen, and Attendants.]

[Enter Hamlet, reading on a book.]

How does my good Lord Hamlet?

HAMLET
Well, God-a-mercy.

POLONIUS
Do you know me, my lord?

HAMLET
Excellent, excellent well. You are a fishmonger°.   ° a seller of fish, a bawd

POLONIUS
Not I, my lord.

HAMLET
Then I would you were so honest a man.

POLONIUS
Honest, my lord?

HAMLET
Ay, sir. To be honest, as this world goes, is to be one man picked out of
ten thousand.

POLONIUS
That's very true, my lord.

HAMLET
For if the sun breed maggots in a dead dog,[25] being a good kissing car-
rion°—Have you a daughter?   ° carrion good for kissing

POLONIUS
I have, my lord.

HAMLET
Let her not walk i' th'sun.[26] Conception[27] is a blessing, but not as your
daughter may conceive—friend, look to't.

POLONIUS *[aside]*
How say you by that? Still harping on my daughter. Yet he knew me not
at first; he said I was a fishmonger. He is far gone, far gone. And truly
in my youth I suffered much extremity for love, very near this. I'll speak
to him again. —What do you read, my lord?

HAMLET
Words, words, words.

---

[25] Hamlet alludes to spontaneous generation, the then-current belief that the sun
shining on dead matter produced maggots. A dead dog provides raw material, carrion, good for kissing by the sun.

[26] Polonius should keep Ophelia out of public places lest she become pregnant.
"Sun" refers to (1) the sun, which breeds maggots, that is, brings forth life; and (2)
the sun as an emblem of royalty.

[27] "Conception" puns on (1) the power to form ideas and (2) pregnancy.

POLONIUS
What is the matter°, my lord?   °subject

HAMLET
Between who?

POLONIUS
I mean, the matter that you read, my lord.

HAMLET
Slanders, sir. For the satirical rogue says here that old men have gray
beards, that their faces are wrinkled, their eyes purging thick amber
and plum-tree gums, and that they have a plentiful lack of wit, together
with most weak hams—all which, sir, though I most powerfully and
potently believe, yet I hold it not honesty° to have it thus set down; for   °proper
yourself, sir, should be as old as I am—if, like a crab, you could go
backward.

POLONIUS [aside]
Though this be madness, yet there is method° in't. —Will you walk out   °order
of the air,²⁸ my lord?

HAMLET
Into my grave?

POLONIUS
Indeed that is out o' th'air.
[aside] How pregnant° sometimes his replies are! A happiness that   °apt, pointed
often madness hits on, which reason and sanity could not so prosper-
ously be delivered of. I will leave him, and suddenly contrive the means
of meeting between him and my daughter. —My honorable lord, I will
most humbly take my leave of you.

HAMLET
You cannot, sir, take from me any thing that I will more willingly part
withal—except my life, except my life, except my life.

POLONIUS
Fare you well, my lord.

HAMLET
These tedious old fools!

                    [Enter Rosencrantz and Guildenstern.]

POLONIUS
You go to seek the Lord Hamlet. There he is.

ROSENCRANTZ [to Polonius]
God save you, sir.

                                        [Exit Polonius.]

GUILDENSTERN
My honored lord!

---

²⁸Because fresh air was thought to be bad for invalids, Polonius implies that Hamlet
is mad by suggesting that Hamlet walk indoors.

ROSENCRANTZ
My most dear lord!

HAMLET
My excellent good friends! How dost thou, Guildenstern? O, Rosencrantz! Good lads, how do you both?

ROSENCRANTZ
As the indifferent° children of the earth.   ° ordinary

GUILDENSTERN
Happy in that we are not overhappy,
On Fortune's cap we are not the very button.

HAMLET
Nor the soles of her shoe?

ROSENCRANTZ
Neither, my lord.

HAMLET
Then you live about her waist, or in the middle of her favors?

GUILDENSTERN
Faith, her privates° we.   ° (pun: private parts and private
                                                                    citizens)

HAMLET
In the secret parts of Fortune? O, most true, she is a strumpet°. What's   ° (because Fortune is fickle)
the news?

ROSENCRANTZ
None, my lord, but that the world's grown honest.

HAMLET
Then is doomsday near. But your news is not true. Let me question
more in particular. What have you, my good friends, deserved at the
hands of Fortune, that she sends you to prison hither?

GUILDENSTERN
Prison, my lord?

HAMLET
Denmark's a prison.

ROSENCRANTZ
Then is the world one.

HAMLET
A goodly one, in which there are many confines, wards°, and dun-   ° cells
geons, Denmark being one o'th'worst.

ROSENCRANTZ
We think not so, my lord.

HAMLET
Why, then, 'tis none to you; for there is nothing either good or bad, but
thinking makes it so. To me it is a prison.

ROSENCRANTZ
Why, then, your ambition makes it one; 'tis too narrow for your mind.

HAMLET
O God, I could be bounded in a nutshell and count myself a king of
infinite space, were it not that I have bad dreams.

GUILDENSTERN
Which dreams, indeed, are ambition; for the very substance of the ambitious is merely the shadow of a dream.

HAMLET
A dream itself is but a shadow.

ROSENCRANTZ
Truly, and I hold ambition of so airy and light a quality, that it is but a
shadow's shadow.

HAMLET
Then are our beggars bodies, and our monarchs and outstretched heroes the beggars' shadows.[29] Shall we to th'court? For, by my fay, I cannot reason.

ROSENCRANTZ AND GUILDENSTERN
We'll wait upon you.

HAMLET
No such matter.° I will not sort° you with the rest of my servants, for,   ° I won't have that. ° associate
to speak to you like an honest man, I am most dreadfully attended°.   ° badly waited on
But, in the beaten way of friendship, what make you at Elsinore?

ROSENCRANTZ
To visit you, my lord, no other occasion.

HAMLET
Beggar that I am, I am even poor in thanks, but I thank you. And sure,
dear friends, my thanks are too dear a halfpenny°. Were you not sent   ° not worth much
for? Is it your own inclining? Is it a free° visitation? Come, deal justly   ° voluntary
with me. Come, come. Nay, speak.

GUILDENSTERN
What should we say, my lord?

HAMLET
Why, anything but to the purpose°. You were sent for, and there is a   ° except your purpose
kind of confession in your looks, which your modesties° have not craft   ° decency
enough to color. I know the good King and Queen have sent for you.

ROSENCRANTZ
To what end, my lord?

HAMLET
That you must teach me. But let me conjure you, by the rights of our
fellowship, by the consonancy° of our youth, by the obligation of our   ° similarity

---

[29] If ambition is a shadow, then monarchs and heroes, who are ambitious, are shadows; and only beggars, who lack ambition, possess substance. But since a shadow
must be cast from a body—and only beggars have bodies—the shadows of ambition must fall from beggars.

ever-preserved love, and by what more dear a better proposer could charge you withal, be even and direct with me whether you were sent for or no.

ROSENCRANTZ [aside to Guildenstern]
What say you?

HAMLET [aside]
Nay, then, I have an eye of° you. If you love me, hold not off°.   ° on ° don't hold back

GUILDENSTERN
My lord, we were sent for.

HAMLET
I will tell you why. So shall my anticipation prevent your discovery°,   ° forestall disclosure
and your secrecy to the King and Queen moult no feather°. I have of   ° remain intact
late—but wherefore I know not—lost all my mirth, forgone all custom
of exercises; and, indeed, it goes so heavily with my disposition° that   ° I am so depressed
this goodly frame°, the earth, seems to me a sterile promontory. This   ° structure
most excellent canopy, the air, look you, this brave° o'erhanging fir-   ° splendid
mament, this majestical roof fretted° with golden fire—why, it appears   ° adorned
no other thing to me than a foul and pestilent congregation of vapors.
What a piece of work° is man, how noble in reason, how infinite in fac-   ° masterpiece
ulty, in form and moving how express and admirable, in action how
like an angel, in apprehension how like a god—the beauty of the
world, the paragon of animals! And yet, to me, what is this quintes-
sence° of dust? Man delights not me—no, nor woman neither, though   ° essence
by your smiling you seem to say so.

ROSENCRANTZ
My lord, there was no such stuff in my thoughts.

HAMLET
Why did you laugh, then, when I said "Man delights not me"?

ROSENCRANTZ
To think, my lord, if you delight not in man, what lenten entertain-
ment° the players shall receive from you. We coted° them on the way,   ° poor reception ° overtook them
and hither are they coming, to offer you service.

HAMLET
He that plays the King shall be welcome—his majesty shall have tribute of me; the Adventurous Knight shall use his foil and target°; the   ° light shield
Lover shall not sigh gratis; the Humorous Man shall end his part in
peace; the Clown shall make those laugh whose lungs are tickle o'
th'sere;[30] and the Lady shall say her mind freely, or the blank verse shall
halt for't. What players are they?

ROSENCRANTZ
Even those you were wont to take such delight in, the tragedians of the
city.

---

[30]"Sere," a gunsmith's word, refers to the catch, which is released by squeezing the trigger. If a gun fires with just a tickle on the sere, it goes off easily. This clown Hamlet describes can get people to laugh at anything.

HAMLET

How chances it they travel°? Their residence, both in reputation and
profit, was better both ways.   °tour

ROSENCRANTZ

I think their inhibition° comes by the means of the late innovation.[31]   °formal prohibition

HAMLET

Do they hold the same estimation they did when I was in the city? Are
they so followed?

ROSENCRANTZ

No, indeed, they are not.

HAMLET

How comes it? Do they grow rusty?

ROSENCRANTZ

Nay, their endeavour keeps in the wonted pace. But there is, sir, an ae-
rie of children,[32] little eyases°, that cry out on the top of question, and   °young hawks
are most tyrannically° clapped for't. These are now the fashion, and so   °outrageously
berattle the common stages—so they call them—that many wearing
rapiers are afraid of goose-quills, and dare scarce come thither.

HAMLET

What, are they children? Who maintains 'em? How are they escoted°?   °supported
Will they pursue the quality° no longer than they can sing? Will they   °acting profession
not say afterwards, if they should grow themselves to common play-
ers—as it is most like, if their means are no better—their writers do
them wrong to make them exclaim against their own succession°?   °future

ROSENCRANTZ

Faith, there has been much to do on both sides; and the nation holds it
no sin to tar° them to controversy. There was, for a while, no money bid   °incite
for argument, unless the poet and the player went to cuffs in the
question.[33]

---

[31] The tragedians of the city are on tour because they have been prohibited from
playing in town, perhaps as a result of the Essex rebellion. In 1601, Essex staged a
rebellion against the Queen. Essex had commissioned Shakespeare's company to
stage a private performance of *Richard II*, a play about the deposition of a monarch,
on the eve of the uprising. Shakespeare's company, though, was not touched by this
"inhibition."
   "Innovation" might refer to the recent popularity of the boy companies, which
threatened the business of the adult companies. "Inhibition" might also refer to the
Act of the Privy Council (1600), which limited theatrical performances to two a
week and which limited the number of London playhouses to two.

[32] These juvenile birds of prey, so highly applauded, are the Children of the Chapel,
the company of boy actors that began performing at the Blackfriars Playhouse in
1600. Blackfriars was a private theatre, in contrast to the Globe and the Fortune,
which were public theatres.

[33] During the War between the Theaters, the money-making plays were those in
which the authors of the adult companies and the writers for the children's companies attacked one another. "Argument" plays on the double sense of (1) controversy and (2) the plot or summary of the play.

HAMLET
Is't possible?

GUILDENSTERN
O, there has been much throwing about of brains.

HAMLET
Do the boys carry it away°?   °triumph

ROSENCRANTZ
Ay, that they do, my lord—Hercules and his load too.³⁴

HAMLET
It is not very strange; for my uncle is King of Denmark, and those that
would make mouths° at him while my father lived, give twenty, forty,   °derisive faces
fifty, a hundred ducats a-piece for his picture in little°. 'Sblood, there is   °miniature
something in this more than natural, if philosophy could find it out.

[*flourish of trumpets°*]   °announces the Players' arrival

[*Enter Players.*]

GUILDENSTERN
There are the players.

HAMLET
Gentlemen, you are welcome to Elsinore. Your hands. Come. The ap-
purtenance° of welcome is fashion and ceremony. Let me comply with   °proper accompaniment
you in this garb, lest my extent° to the players, which, I tell you, must   °extension of welcome (and stage
show fairly outward, should more appear like entertainment than   direction)
yours. You are welcome. But my uncle-father and aunt-mother are
deceived.

GUILDENSTERN
In what, my dear lord?

HAMLET
I am but mad north-north-west; when the wind is southerly, I know a
hawk from a handsaw.³⁵

[*Enter Polonius.*]

POLONIUS
Well be with you, gentlemen.

---

³⁴During the course of his labors, Hercules supported the world for Atlas; if the child
companies "carry it away" like Hercules and his load, they are extremely successful.
At the same time, the emblem for Shakespeare's own theatre, the Globe, is thought
to be Hercules bearing the world. This allusion suggests that Shakespeare's own
theatre was feeling the pinch of competition from the boy companies.

³⁵Hamlet is only slightly off balance, like a compass whose needle points north-
northwest instead of directly north. Because he is not mad, as his uncle-father and
aunt-mother believe, he can tell the difference between a hawk and a handsaw or
between a friend and an enemy. If "handsaw" is a corruption of "heronshaw" (besides its meaning as carpentry tool), Hamlet uses a metaphor of predation: hawks
preyed on herons.

HAMLET
Hark you, Guildenstern, and you too—at each ear a hearer; that great baby you see there is not yet out of his swaddling-clouts°.   ° swaddling clothes

ROSENCRANTZ
Happily° he's the second time come to them; for they say an old man is twice a child°.   ° Perhaps
° in his second childhood

HAMLET
I will prophesy he comes to tell me of the players. Mark it. —You say right, sir; for o' Monday morning, 'twas so, indeed.

POLONIUS
My lord, I have news to tell you.

HAMLET
My lord, I have news to tell you. When Roscius was an actor in Rome—[36]

POLONIUS
The actors are come hither, my lord.

HAMLET
Buzz, buzz.°   ° (contemptuous exclamation responding to old news)

POLONIUS
Upon mine honor—

HAMLET
Then came each actor on his ass—[37]

POLONIUS
The best actors in the world, either for tragedy, comedy, history, pastoral, pastoral-comical, historical-pastoral, tragical-historical, tragical-comical-historical-pastoral, scene individable°, or poem unlimited. Seneca cannot be too heavy nor Plautus too light.[38] For the law of writ and the liberty,[39] these are the only men.   ° observing unity of place

HAMLET
O Jephthah, judge of Israel, what a treasure hadst thou![40]

---

[36] Roscius was a famous Roman actor (d. 62 B.C.), a legend in antiquity, and a type for the Renaissance players. Hamlet undercuts Polonius' announcement of the Players by getting in the word *actor* first. Hamlet also insults Polonius by offering him such ancient "news"—"When Roscius was an actor."

[37] Possibly a line from a lost ballad, Hamlet's remark is a rejoinder to Polonius' "Upon my honor."

[38] The Renaissance models for drama were Roman rather than Greek. Seneca was considered the master of tragedy; Plautus (and Terence) was the master of comedy.

[39] For plays that were written according to rules and for plays that ignore the rules, Seneca and Plautus were the best.

[40] From Judges 11 comes the story: Jephthah promised God that he would sacrifice the first thing he met when he returned home if God would grant him martial victory over the Ammonites. Jephthah was victorious, but he encountered his daughter on the way home. Keeping his promise to God, Jephthah sacrificed her.

POLONIUS
What a treasure had he, my lord?

HAMLET
Why,
"One fair daughter, and no more,
The which he loved passing° well."   °exceedingly

POLONIUS [aside]
Still on my daughter.

HAMLET
Am I not i' th'right, old Jephthah?

POLONIUS
If you call me Jephthah, my lord, I have a daughter that I love passing°   °exceedingly
well.

HAMLET
Nay, that follows not.

POLONIUS
What follows, then, my lord?

HAMLET
Why,
        "As by lot, God wot."
and then, you know,
        "It came to pass, as most like it was"—
the first row° of the pious chanson° will show you more; for look, where   °stanza °song, ballad
my abridgement° comes.   °interruption, pastime

                        [Enter four or five Players.]

You are welcome, masters, welcome, all. —I am glad to see thee
well. —Welcome, good friends. —O, my old friend! Thy face is val-
anced° since I saw thee last. Com'st thou to beard° me in Denmark?   °bearded
—What, my young lady° and mistress? By'r lady, your ladyship is   °defy
nearer to heaven° than when I saw you last by the altitude of a cho-   °boy who plays women
pine°. Pray God, your voice, like a piece of uncurrent gold, be not   °taller °a platform shoe
cracked within the ring.[41] Masters, you are all welcome. We'll e'en
to't like French falconers, fly at any thing we see. We'll have a
speech straight. Come, give us a taste of your quality°. Come, a pas-   °professional skill
sionate speech.

FIRST PLAYER
What speech, my good lord?

------

[41] Before coins were milled (1662), the monarch's head would be stamped inside a
circle. Because people might shave or clip (crack) the metal from the coin, only coins
in which both the head and the circle were intact were considered legal currency.
If the crack extended into the ring, the coin was *uncurrent* (not legal currency).
When a boy actor's voice cracks because he reaches adolescence, his maturity
makes him uncurrent for women's parts.

102   WILLIAM SHAKESPEARE

HAMLET

I heard thee speak me a speech once, but it was never acted, or, if it was, not above once; for the play, I remember, pleased not the million, 'twas caviare to the general°. But it was—as I received it, and others, whose judgements in such matters cried in the top of mine—an excellent play, well digested° in the scenes, set down with as much modesty as cunning. I remember one said there were no sallets° in the lines to make the matter savory, nor no matter in the phrase that might indict the author of affection, but called it an honest method, as wholesome as sweet, and by very much more handsome than fine. One speech in it I chiefly loved: 'twas Aeneas' tale to Dido, and thereabout of it especially where he speaks of Priam's slaughter. If it live in your memory, begin at this line—let me see, let me see:
"The rugged° Pyrrhus, like th'Hyrcanian beast°,"
It is not so. It begins with Pyrrhus—
"The rugged Pyrrhus, he whose sable° arms,
Black as his purpose, did the night resemble
When he lay couched° in the ominous horse,
Hath now this dread and black complexion smeared
With heraldry more dismal. Head to foot
Now is he total gules°, horridly tricked°
With blood of fathers, mothers, daughters, sons,
Baked and impasted° with the parching streets,
That lend a tyrannous° and damned light
To their vile murders. Roasted in wrath and fire,
And thus o'er-sized° with coagulate gore,
With eyes like carbuncles°, the hellish Pyrrhus
Old grandsire Priam seeks."
So, proceed you.

° too good for the general public

° organized
° sallies

° savage ° tiger

° blackened

° in ambush

° red (bloody) all over ° smeared

° encrusted
° cruel

° covered
°jewels that mythically glow in the dark

POLONIUS

Fore God, my lord, well spoken, with good accent and good discretion.

FIRST PLAYER
                    "Anon he finds him,
Striking too short at Greeks. His antique sword,
Rebellious to his arm, lies where it falls,
Repugnant° to command. Unequal matched,
Pyrrhus at Priam drives, in rage strikes wide;
But with the whiff and wind of his fell° sword
Th'unnerved° father falls. Then senseless° Ilium,
Seeming to feel this blow, with flaming top
Stoops to his base, and with a hideous crash
Takes prisoner Pyrrhus' ear. For, lo! his sword,
Which was declining on the milky head
Of reverend Priam, seem'd i' th'air to stick:
So, as a painted tyrant, Pyrrhus stood,
And, like a neutral to his will and matter°,
Did nothing.
But, as we often see, against° some storm,

° resistant

° cruel
° weakened ° insensible

° losing his motivation

° just before

A silence in the heavens, the rack° stand still,   ° clouds
The bold winds speechless, and the orb° below   ° earth
As hush as death, anon the dreadful thunder
Doth rend the region°; so, after Pyrrhus' pause,   ° air
Aroused vengeance sets him new a-work;
And never did the Cyclops'° hammers fall   ° giants in Vulcan's smithy
On Mars his armor, forged for proof eterne°,   ° impenetrable forever
With less remorse° than Pyrrhus' bleeding sword   ° pity
Now falls on Priam.
Out, out, thou strumpet, Fortune! All you gods,
In general synod, take away her power,
Break all the spokes and fellies° from her wheel,   ° pieces that form the rim
And bowl the round nave down the hill of heaven,
As low as to the fiends!"

POLONIUS
This is too long.

HAMLET
It shall to th'barber's, with your beard. —Prithee, say on. He's for a jig
or a tale of bawdry, or he sleeps. Say on, come to Hecuba.

FIRST PLAYER
"But who, O, who had seen the mobled° queen"—   ° muffled

HAMLET
"The mobled queen"?

POLONIUS
That's good; "mobled queen" is good.

FIRST PLAYER
"Run barefoot up and down, threat'ning the flames
With bisson rheum°; a clout° upon that head   ° blinding tears ° cloth
Where late the diadem stood; and for a robe,
About her lank and all o'er-teemed° loins,   ° worn-out
A blanket, in th'alarum° of fear caught up—   ° excitement
Who this had seen, with tongue in venom steep'd,
'Gainst Fortune's state° would treason have pronounced. ° rule
But if° the gods themselves did see her then,   ° If only
When she saw Pyrrhus make malicious sport
In mincing with his sword her husband's limbs,
The instant burst of clamor that she made—
Unless things mortal move them not at all—
Would have made milch° the burning eyes of heaven, ° moist (milky)
And passion in the gods."

POLONIUS
Look, whe'er he has not turned his color, and has tears in's eyes. —Pray
you, no more.

HAMLET
'Tis well. I'll have thee speak out the rest soon. —Good my lord, will
you see the players well bestowed°? Do you hear, let them be well used, ° lodged
for they are the abstract° and brief chronicles of the time. After your ° epitomes

death you were better have a bad epitaph than their ill report while you live.

POLONIUS
My lord, I will use them according to their desert.

HAMLET
God's bodykins,° man, much better. Use every man after his desert, and who should scape whipping? Use them after your own honor and dignity—the less they deserve, the more merit is in your bounty. Take them in.

° By God's body

POLONIUS
Come, sirs.

HAMLET
Follow him, friends: we'll hear a play to-morrow.

[Exit Polonius with all the Players but the First.]

Dost thou hear me, old friend. Can you play *The Murder of Gonzago?*

FIRST PLAYER
Ay, my lord.

HAMLET
We'll ha't to-morrow night. You could, for a need,° study° a speech of some dozen or sixteen lines, which I would set down and insert in't, could you not?

° if required °learn

FIRST PLAYER
Ay, my lord.

HAMLET
Very well. Follow that lord, and look you mock him not.

[Exit First Player.]

My good friends, I'll leave you till night. You are welcome to Elsinore.

ROSENCRANTZ
Good my lord.

HAMLET
Ay, so, God buy you.

[Exeunt Rosencrantz and Guildenstern.]

　　　　Now I am alone.
O, what a rogue and peasant slave am I!
Is it not monstrous, that this player here,
But in a fiction, in a dream of passion,
Could force his soul so to his own conceit°
That from her working all his visage wanned,
Tears in his eyes, distraction in's aspect,
A broken voice, and his whole function° suiting
With forms° to his conceit? And all for nothing.
For Hecuba!°
What's Hecuba to him, or he to Hecuba,

° imagination

° physical expressiveness
° expressions
° the most sorrowful Trojan woman

That he should weep for her? What would he do,
Had he the motive and the cue for passion
That I have? He would drown the stage with tears
And cleave the general ear with horrid speech,
Make mad the guilty, and appal the free°,   °innocent
Confound the ignorant and amaze°, indeed,   °bewilder
The very faculties of eyes and ears. Yet I,
A dull and muddy-mettled° rascal, peak°,   °dull-spirited °mope
Like John-a-dreams°, unpregnant° of my cause,   °a sleepy fellow °unquickened
And can say nothing; no, not for a king,
Upon whose property and most dear life
A damned defeat° was made. Am I a coward?   °destruction
Who calls me villain, breaks my pate across,
Plucks off my beard, and blows it in my face,
Tweaks me by th'nose, gives me the lie i' th'throat
As deep as to the lungs°? Who does me this?   °calls me a liar
Ha? 'Swounds°, I should take it. For it cannot be   °By God's wounds
But I am pigeon-liver'd and lack gall°   °wrathfulness
To make oppression bitter, or, ere this
I should have fatted all the region kites°   °kites (vultures) of the air
With this slave's offal°. Bloody, bawdy villain!   °entrails
Remorseless, treacherous, lecherous, kindless° villain!   °unnatural
O, vengeance!
Why, what an ass am I! This is most brave°,   °a fine performance
That I, the son of a dear father murdered,
Prompted to my revenge by heaven and hell,
Must, like a whore, unpack my heart with words,
And fall a-cursing like a very drab°,   °whore
A scullion!° Fie upon't, foh!   °menial kitchen servant
About°, my brain. I have heard   °Get busy, work
That guilty creatures sitting at a play
Have by the very cunning of the scene
Been struck so to the soul, that presently
They have proclaimed their malefactions;
For murder, though it have no tongue, will speak
With most miraculous organ. I'll have these players
Play something like the murder of my father
Before mine uncle. I'll observe his looks,
I'll tent° him to the quick. If he but blench°,   °probe °flinch
I know my course. The spirit that I have seen
May be the devil, and the devil hath power
T'assume a pleasing shape; yea, and perhaps
Out of my weakness and my melancholy,
As he is very potent with such spirits,
Abuses° me to damn me. I'll have grounds   °Deludes
More relative° than this. The play's the thing   °conclusive
Wherein I'll catch the conscience of the King.

[Exit Hamlet.]

Act Three, Scene One

Elsinore: a room in the castle.

[Enter King, Queen, Polonius, Ophelia, Rosencrantz, and Guildenstern.]

KING
And can you, by no drift of circumstance°,   °leading conversation
Get from him why he puts on this confusion,
Grating so harshly all his days of quiet
With turbulent and dangerous lunacy?

ROSENCRANTZ
He does confess he feels himself distracted,
But from what cause he will by no means speak.

GUILDENSTERN
Nor do we find him forward° to be sounded,   °willing
But with a crafty° madness keeps aloof   °cunning, feigned
When we would bring him on to some confession
Of his true state.

QUEEN
        Did he receive you well?

ROSENCRANTZ
Most like a gentleman.

GUILDENSTERN
But with much forcing of his disposition°.   °inclination

ROSENCRANTZ
Niggard of question°, but, of our demands,   °Reluctant to start a conversation
Most free in his reply.

QUEEN
        Did you assay° him   °interest him in
To any pastime?

ROSENCRANTZ
Madam, it so fell out that certain players
We o'er-raught° on the way. Of these we told him;   °passed
And there did seem in him a kind of joy
To hear of it. They are about the court,
And, as I think, they have already order
This night to play before him.

POLONIUS
        'Tis most true;
And he beseeched me to entreat your majesties
To hear and see the matter.

KING
With all my heart; and it doth much content me
To hear him so inclined.

Good gentlemen, give him a further edge°,   °stimulus
And drive his purpose on to these delights.

POLONIUS

ROSENCRANTZ
We shall, my lord.

[Exeunt Rosencrantz and Guildenstern.]

KING
    Sweet Gertrude, leave us too;
For we have closely° sent for Hamlet hither,   °privately
That he, as 'twere by accident, may here
Affront° Ophelia.   °Meet face to face
Her father and myself, lawful espials°,   °spies
Will so bestow ourselves that, seeing unseen,
We may of their encounter frankly° judge,   °freely
And gather by him, as he is behaved,
If't be th'affliction of his love or no
That thus he suffers for.

QUEEN
    I shall obey you.
And for your part, Ophelia, I do wish
That your good beauties be the happy cause
Of Hamlet's wildness: so shall I hope your virtues
Will bring him to his wonted way again,
To both your honors.

OPHELIA
    Madam, I wish it may.

[Exit Queen.]

POLONIUS
Ophelia, walk you here. —Gracious, so please you,
We will bestow ourselves.— *[to Ophelia]* Read on this book,
That show of such an exercise° may color°   °religious exercise °make natural
Your loneliness. We are oft to blame in this,
'Tis too much proved°, that with devotion's visage   °all too true
And pious action we do sugar o'er
The devil himself.

KING
    O, 'tis too true.
[aside] How smart a lash that speech doth give my conscience.
The harlot's cheek, beautied with plastering art°,   °cosmetics
Is not more ugly to the thing that helps it
Than is my deed to my most painted word.
O heavy burden.

POLONIUS
I hear him coming: let's withdraw, my lord.

[Exeunt King and Polonius.]

[Enter Hamlet.]

HAMLET
To be, or not to be—that is the question:
Whether 'tis nobler in the mind to suffer
The slings and arrows of outrageous fortune,
Or to take arms against a sea of troubles,
And by opposing end them? To die, to sleep—
No more; and by a sleep to say we end
The heartache, and the thousand natural shocks
That flesh is heir to—'tis a consummation°   ° completion, end
Devoutly to be wished. To die, to sleep.
To sleep, perchance to dream. Ay, there's the rub°;   ° obstacle
For in that sleep of death what dreams may come,
When we have shuffled off° this mortal coil°,   ° freed ourselves of ° (1) turmoil
Must give us pause°. There's the respect°   (2) body   ° make us stop and
That makes calamity of so long life°.   think ° consideration
                                                        ° so long-lived
For who would bear the whips and scorns of time,
The oppressor's wrong, the proud man's contumely,
The pangs of despised° love, the law's delay,   ° unprized
The insolence of office, and the spurns
That patient merit of the unworthy takes,
When he himself might his quietus° make   ° "paid in full"
With a bare bodkin°? Who would these fardels° bear   ° mere dagger ° burdens
To grunt and sweat under a weary life,
But that the dread of something after death,
The undiscovered country°, from whose bourn°   ° undisclosed ° frontier
No traveller returns, puzzles° the will,   ° bewilders, paralyzes
And makes us rather bear those ills we have
Than fly to others that we know not of?
Thus conscience does make cowards of us all;
And thus the native hue° of resolution   ° natural color
Is sicklied o'er with the pale cast° of thought,   ° pallor
And enterprises of great pith and moment,
With this regard, their currents turn awry,
And lose the name of action. —Soft you now,
The fair Ophelia. Nymph, in thy orisons°   ° prayers
Be all my sins remembered.

OPHELIA
                    Good my lord,
How does your honor for this many a day°?   ° all this time

HAMLET
I humbly thank you, well, well, well.

OPHELIA
My lord, I have remembrances° of yours   ° love-tokens, souvenirs
That I have longed long to re-deliver.
I pray you now receive them.

HAMLET

No, not I.

I never gave you aught.

OPHELIA

My honored lord, you know right well you did,
And, with them, words of so sweet breath composed
As made the things more rich. Their perfume lost,
Take these again; for to the noble mind
Rich gifts wax poor when givers prove unkind.
There, my lord.

HAMLET

Ha, ha? Are you honest°?

° (1) speaking the truth (2) chaste

OPHELIA

My lord?

HAMLET

Are you fair?

OPHELIA

What means your lordship?

HAMLET

That if you be honest and fair, your honesty should admit no discourse
to your beauty.

OPHELIA

Could beauty, my lord, have better commerce than with honesty?

HAMLET

Ay, truly; for the power of beauty will sooner transform honesty from
what it is to a bawd than the force of honesty can translate° beauty into
his likeness. This was sometime° a paradox°, but now the time gives it
proof. I did love you once.

° transform
° formerly ° tenet contrary to
   popular belief

OPHELIA

Indeed, my lord, you made me believe so.

HAMLET

You should not have believed me. For virtue cannot so inoculate° our
old stock, but we shall relish of it. I loved you not.

° be engrafted on

OPHELIA

I was the more deceived.

HAMLET

Get thee to a nunnery°. Why, wouldst thou be a breeder of sinners? I
am myself indifferent honest°, but yet I could accuse me of such things
that it were better my mother had not borne me. I am very proud, re-
vengeful, ambitious, with more offences at my beck° than I have
thoughts to put them in, imagination to give them shape, or time to act
them in. What should such fellows as I do crawling between earth and
heaven? We° are arrant knaves, all. Believe none of us. Go thy ways to
a nunnery. Where's your father?

° convent
° tolerably virtuous

° waiting to be committed

° Men

OPHELIA
At home, my lord.

HAMLET
Let the doors be shut upon him, that he may play the fool no where but in's own house. Farewell.

OPHELIA
O, help him, you sweet heavens!

HAMLET
If thou dost marry, I'll give thee this plague for thy dowry: be thou as chaste as ice, as pure as snow, thou shalt not escape calumny. Get thee to a nunnery, go, farewell. Or, if thou wilt needs marry, marry a fool; for wise men know well enough what monsters° you make of them. To a nunnery, go, and quickly too. Farewell.

°cuckolds

OPHELIA
O heavenly powers, restore him!

HAMLET
I have heard of your paintings too, well enough. God has given you° one face, and you make yourselves another. You jig, you amble, and you lisp°, and nickname God's creatures°, and make your wantonness your ignorance. Go to, I'll no more on't, it hath made me mad. I say we will have no more marriages. Those that are married already—all but one—shall live. The rest shall keep as they are. To a nunnery, go.

°you women

°you assume affectations °who already have names

[Exit Hamlet.]

OPHELIA
O, what a noble mind is here o'erthrown!
The courtier's, soldier's, scholar's eye, tongue, sword;
Th'expectancy and rose° of the fair state,
The glass° of fashion and the mould of form°,
Th'observed of all observers—quite, quite down!
And I, of ladies most deject and wretched,
That sucked the honey of his music vows,
Now see that noble and most sovereign reason,
Like sweet bells jangled, out of tune and harsh;
That unmatched form and feature of blown° youth
Blasted with ecstasy°. O woe is me
T'have seen what I have seen, see what I see!

°hope and ornament
°mirror °pattern of courtliness

°in full bloom
°Withered with madness

[Enter King and Polonius.]

KING
Love? His affections° do not that way tend;
Nor what he spake, though it lacked form a little,
Was not like madness. There's something in his soul
O'er which his melancholy sits on brood;
And I do doubt° the hatch and the disclose°
Will be some danger: which for to prevent,
I have in quick determination
Thus set it down°: he shall with speed to England

°feelings

°suspect °disclosure

°resolved

For the demand of our neglected tribute.
Haply the seas, and countries different,
With variable objects°, shall expel   ° various sights
This something-settled matter in his heart,
Whereon his brains still beating puts him thus
From fashion of himself. What think you on't?

POLONIUS
It shall do well. But yet do I believe
The origin and commencement of his grief
Sprung from neglected° love. How now, Ophelia?   ° unrequited
You need not tell us what Lord Hamlet said;
We heard it all. —My lord, do as you please;
But, if you hold it fit, after the play
Let his queen mother all alone entreat him
To show his griefs. Let her be round° with him;   ° blunt
And I'll be placed, so please you, in the ear
Of all their conference. If she find him not,
To England send him; or confine him where
Your wisdom best shall think.

KING
                        It shall be so:
Madness in great ones must not unwatched go.

                                        [Exeunt all.]

Act Three, Scene Two

A hall in the castle.

                [Enter Hamlet and two or three of the Players.]

HAMLET
Speak the speech, I pray you, as I pronounced it to you, trippingly on
the tongue. But if you mouth° it, as many of your players do, I had as   ° declaim
lief the town-crier spoke my lines. Nor do not saw the air too much
with your hand, thus, but use all gently: for in the very torrent, tempest,
and, as I may say, the whirlwind of passion, you must acquire and beget
a temperance that may give it smoothness. O, it offends me to the soul
to hear a robustious periwig-pated fellow tear a passion to tatters, to
very rags, to split the ears of the groundlings°, who, for the most part,   ° audience in the pit
are capable of nothing but inexplicable dumb-shows and noise. I
would have such a fellow whipped for o'erdoing Termagant.[42] It out-
herods Herod°. Pray you, avoid it.   ° (typified by anger)

FIRST PLAYER
I warrant your honor.

---

[42] In the mystery plays, Termagant is the noisy violent companion of Mahound, false
deity of the Mohammedans.

HAMLET

Be not too tame neither, but let your own discretion be your tutor. Suit the action to the word, the word to the action, with this special observance, that you o'erstep not the modesty° of nature. For any thing so overdone is from° the purpose of playing, whose end, both at the first and now, was and is, to hold, as 'twere, the mirror up to nature: to show virtue her own feature, scorn her own image, and the very age and body of the time his form and pressure°. Now, this overdone, or come tardy off°, though it make the unskilful° laugh, cannot but make the judicious grieve; the censure° of the which one must, in your allowance, o'erweigh a whole theatre of others. O, there be players that I have seen play—and heard others praise, and that highly—not to speak it profanely, that neither having the accent of Christians°, nor the gait of Christian, pagan, nor man, have so strutted and bellowed, that I have thought some of nature's journeymen° had made them, and not made them well, they imitated humanity so abominably.

°moderation
°contrary to

°impression, as of a seal
°inadequately °indiscriminate
°opinion

°ordinary human beings

°common laborers

FIRST PLAYER

I hope we have reformed that indifferently° with us, sir.

°pretty well

HAMLET

O reform it altogether. And let those that play your clowns speak no more than is set down for them: for there be of them that will themselves laugh, to set on some quantity of barren spectators to laugh too; though, in the mean time, some necessary question of the play be then to be considered. That's villainous°, and shows a most pitiful ambition in the fool° that uses it. Go make you ready.

°objectionable
°(1) silly person and (2) person playing the fool

[Exeunt Players.]

[Enter Polonius, Rosencrantz, and Guildenstern.]

How now, my lord? Will the king hear this piece of work?

POLONIUS

And the queen too, and that presently°.

°at once

HAMLET

Bid the players make haste.

[Exit Polonius.]

Will you two help to hasten them?

ROSENCRANTZ AND GUILDENSTERN

We will, my lord.

[Exeunt Rosencrantz and Guildenstern.]

HAMLET

What, ho, Horatio!

[Enter Horatio.]

HORATIO

Here, sweet lord, at your service.

HAMLET

Horatio, thou art e'en as just° a man
As e'er my conversation coped withal.°

°precise, ideal man
°As my association with people has brought me into contact with.

HORATIO

O, my dear lord—

HAMLET

                  Nay, do not think I flatter;
For what advancement may I hope from thee
That no revenue hast, but thy good spirits
To feed and clothe thee? Why should the poor be flattered?
No, let the candied° tongue lick absurd° pomp,   °flattering °tasteless
And crook° the pregnant° hinges of the knee   °bend °readily inclined (to be bent)
Where thrift° may follow fawning. Dost thou hear?   °profit
Since my dear soul was mistress of her choice,
And could of men distinguish, her election
Hath sealed thee for herself. For thou hast been
As one, in suffering all, that suffers nothing,
A man that fortune's buffets and rewards
Hast ta'en with equal thanks; and blest are those
Whose blood and judgement° are so well commingled,   °passion and reason
That they are not a pipe for fortune's finger
To sound what stop she please. Give me that man
That is not passion's slave, and I will wear him
In my heart's core, ay, in my heart of heart°,   °heart's heart
As I do thee. Something too much of this.
There is a play tonight before the King.
One scene of it comes near the circumstance
Which I have told thee of my father's death.
I prithee, when thou seest that act afoot,
Even with the very comment° of thy soul   °greatest concentrated attention
Observe my uncle. If his occulted° guilt   °hidden
Do not itself unkennel° in one speech,   °reveal itself
It is a damned ghost that we have seen,
And my imaginations are as foul
As Vulcan's stithy°. Give him heedful note;   °forge
For I mine eyes will rivet to his face;
And, after, we will both our judgements join
In censure of his seeming.°   °interpret his response

HORATIO

                  Well, my lord.
If he steal aught° the whilst this play is playing,   °gets away with being unobserved
And scape detecting, I will pay the theft°.   °take the blame

HAMLET

They're coming to the play. I must be idle°.   °(1) act mad (2) be unoccupied
Get you a place.

       *[Danish march. A flourish. Enter King, Queen, Polonius, Ophelia,
             Rosencrantz, Guildenstern, and other Lords attendant,
                     with the Guard carrying torches.]*

KING

How fares our cousin Hamlet?

HAMLET

Excellent, i'faith, of the chameleon's dish. I eat the air, promise-crammed. You cannot feed capons so.[43]

KING

I have nothing with this answer,° Hamlet; these words are not mine°.

°do not understand °an answer to his question

HAMLET

No, nor mine now. *[to Polonius]* My lord, you played once i' th'university, you say?

POLONIUS

That did I, my lord, and was accounted a good actor.

HAMLET

And what did you enact?

POLONIUS

I did enact Julius Caesar. I was kill'd i' th'Capitol. Brutus killed me.

HAMLET

It was a brute part° of him to kill so capital a calf there.—Be the players ready?

°brutal action

ROSENCRANTZ

Ay, my lord, they stay upon your patience°.

°await your permission

QUEEN

Come hither, my dear Hamlet, sit by me.

HAMLET

No, good mother, here's metal more attractive.

POLONIUS *[to the King]*

O, ho! Do you mark that?

HAMLET

Lady, shall I lie in your lap?

[Lying down at Ophelia's feet.]

OPHELIA

No, my lord.

HAMLET

I mean, my head upon your lap?

OPHELIA

Ay, my lord.

HAMLET

Do you think I meant country matters°?

°sexual intercourse

---

[43] It was believed that chameleons lived by eating nothing but air. Hamlet's "air" quibbles on *air/heir*, suggesting that Claudius's naming him "most immediate to our throne" has brought Hamlet nothing but air. Even capons, castrated cocks, reputedly stupid because they were fattened for the table, require more substance than air. A prince, Hamlet suggests, has greater needs than a capon.

OPHELIA

I think nothing, my lord.

HAMLET

That's a fair° thought to lie between maids' legs.   ° modest

OPHELIA

What is, my lord?

HAMLET

No-thing.⁴⁴

OPHELIA

You are merry, my lord.

HAMLET

Who, I?

OPHELIA

Ay, my lord.

HAMLET

O God, your only° jig-maker°. What should a man do but be merry?   ° very best ° master of foolish
For look you how cheerfully my mother looks, and my father died with-   entertainment
in's° two hours.   ° this

OPHELIA

Nay, 'tis twice two months, my lord.

HAMLET

So long? Nay, then, let the devil wear black, for I'll have a suit of sables.
O heavens, die two months ago, and not forgotten yet? Then there's
hope a great man's memory may outlive his life half a year. But, by'r
lady, he must build churches, then, or else shall he suffer not thinking
on, with the hobby-horse, whose epitaph is "For O, for O, the hobby-
horse is forgot."⁴⁵

[Trumpets sound. The dumb-show enters. Enter a King and a Queen very
   lovingly; the Queen embracing him, and he her. She kneels, and makes
   show of protestation unto him. He takes her up, and declines his head
   upon her neck; lays him down upon a bank of flowers: she, seeing him
   asleep, leaves him. Anon comes in a fellow, takes off his crown, kisses
   it, and pours poison in the King's ears, and exits. The Queen returns;
   finds the King dead, and makes passionate action. The Poisoner,
   with some two or three Mutes, comes in again, seeming to lament
   with her. The dead body is carried away. The Poisoner woos
   the Queen with gifts: she seems loth and unwilling awhile, but in the
   end accepts his love. Exeunt.]

OPHELIA

What means this, my lord?

----

⁴⁴Hamlet's "No-thing" may be read to accommodate the word-play on "thing"
(penis).

⁴⁵During the May Day celebrations, taking part in the morris dances, the hobby
horse was a male dancer wearing a pasteboard horse. This line probably originated
as the refrain from a ballad, now lost.

HAMLET
Marry, this is miching mallecho°. That means mischief.   ° sneaking mischief

OPHELIA
Belike this show imports the argument° of the play.   ° plot

[Enter Prologue.]

HAMLET
We shall know by this fellow. The players cannot keep counsel°; they'll   ° secrets
tell all.

OPHELIA
Will he tell us what this show meant?

HAMLET
Ay, or any show that you'll show him. Be not you ashamed to show,
he'll not shame to tell you what it means.

OPHELIA
You are naught, you are naught°. I'll mark the play.   ° offensive

PROLOGUE
For us, and for our tragedy,
Here stooping to your clemency,
We beg your hearing patiently.

[Exit.]

HAMLET
Is this a prologue, or the posy of a ring°?   ° verse motto inscribed in a finger
                                                       ring

OPHELIA
'Tis brief, my lord.

HAMLET
As woman's love.

[Enter two Players, King and Queen.]

PLAYER KING
Full thirty times hath Phoebus' cart° gone round   ° the sun
Neptune's salt wash° and Tellus' orbed ground°,   ° the sea ° the earth
And thirty dozen moons with borrowed sheen°   ° radiance
About the world have times twelve thirties been,
Since love our hearts, and Hymen° did our hands,   ° goddess of marriage
Unite commutual° in most sacred bands°.   ° reciprocal ° bonds

PLAYER QUEEN
So many journeys may the sun and moon
Make us again count o'er ere love be done.
But woe is me, you are so sick of late,
So far from cheer and from your former state,
That I distrust° you. Yet, though I distrust,   ° am worried about you
Discomfort° you, my lord, it nothing must;   ° sadden, distress
For women's fear and love hold quantity°,   ° are proportional to each other
In neither aught, or in extremity°.   ° in absence or in excess

Now what my love is, proof° hath made you know,
And as my love is sized°, my fear is so.
Where love is great, the littlest doubts are fear;
Where little fears grow great, great love grows there.

PLAYER KING
Faith, I must leave thee, love, and shortly too;
My operant° powers their functions leave to do°.
And thou shalt live in this fair world behind,
Honored, beloved; and, haply, one as kind
For husband shalt thou—

PLAYER QUEEN
                                    O, confound the rest!
Such love must needs be treason in my breast.
In second husband° let me be accurst;
None wed the second but who killed the first.

HAMLET [aside]
Wormwood, wormwood.°

PLAYER QUEEN
The instances° that second marriage move°
Are base respects of thrift°, but none of love.
A second time I kill my husband dead
When second husband kisses me in bed.

PLAYER KING
I do believe you think what now you speak;
But what we do determine oft we break.
Purpose is but the slave to memory,
Of violent birth, but poor validity°;
Which now, like fruit unripe, sticks on the tree,
But fall unshaken when they mellow be.
Most necessary 'tis that we forget
To pay ourselves what to ourselves is debt.
What to ourselves in passion we propose,
The passion ending, doth the purpose lose.
The violence of either grief or joy
Their own enactures° with themselves destroy.
Where joy most revels, grief doth most lament;
Grief joys, joy grieves, on slender accident°.
This world is not for aye; nor 'tis not strange
That even our loves should with our fortunes change;
For 'tis a question left us yet to prove°,
Whether love lead fortune, or else fortune love.
The great man down, you mark his favorite flies;
The poor advanced makes friends of enemies.
And hitherto° doth love on fortune tend,
For who not needs shall never lack a friend,
And who in want a hollow friend doth try,
Directly seasons° him his enemy.

° experience
° of a particular size

° vital ° stop functioning

° If I marry a second time

° bitter to the taste; bitter truth

° motives ° give rise to
° economic matters

° weak staying power

° fulfillments

° with the slightest excuse

° ascertain

° up to now (in the argument)

° ripens, converts

But, orderly to end where I begun,
Our wills and fates do so contrary run
That our devices° still° are overthrown;   °intentions °always
Our thoughts are ours, their ends° none of our own.   °consequences
So think thou wilt no second husband wed;
But die thy thoughts when thy first lord is dead.

PLAYER QUEEN
Nor earth to me give food, nor heaven light,
Sport and repose lock from me day and night,
To desperation turn my trust and hope.
An anchor's cheer° in prison be my scope.   °hermit's accommodation
Each opposite that blanks° the face of joy   °blanches
Meet what I would have well, and it destroy,
Both here and hence° pursue me lasting strife,   °in this world and the next
If, once a widow, ever I be wife!

HAMLET
If she should break it now!

PLAYER KING
'Tis deeply sworn. Sweet, leave me here awhile.
My spirits grow dull, and fain I would beguile
The tedious day with sleep.

                                        [Sleeps.]

PLAYER QUEEN
                        Sleep rock thy brain,
And never come mischance between us twain!

                                        [Exit.]

HAMLET
Madam, how like you this play?

QUEEN
The lady doth protest too much, methinks.

HAMLET
O, but she'll keep her word.

KING
Have you heard the argument? Is there no offence° in't?   °offensive matter

HAMLET
No, no, they do but jest°, poison in jest. No offence i' th'world.   °pretend

KING
What do you call the play?

HAMLET
The Mousetrap. Marry, how? Tropically°. This play is the image° of a   °Figuratively °exact representation
murder done in Vienna. Gonzago is the duke's name; his wife, Baptista.
You shall see anon. 'Tis a knavish piece of work. But what o'that? Your

majesty, and we that have free souls°, it touches us not. Let the galled
jade wince, our withers are unwrung.⁴⁶

° clear consciences

[Enter Player, as Lucianus.]

This is one Lucianus, nephew to the king.

OPHELIA
You are as good as a chorus°, my lord.

*° one who explains the coming
action*

HAMLET
I could interpret° between you and your love, if I could see the puppets
dallying.⁴⁷

° (1) write dialogue for (2) pander

OPHELIA
You are keen°, my lord, you are keen.

° sharp-tongued

HAMLET
It would cost you a groaning° to take off my edge.

° sexual act

OPHELIA
Still better, and worse°.

*° more pointed and thus more
offensive*

HAMLET
So you mistake° your husbands. —Begin, murderer, leave thy damnable faces and begin. Come, "the croaking raven doth bellow for
revenge."⁴⁸

° wrongfully take

LUCIANUS
Thoughts black, hands apt, drugs fit, and time agreeing,
Confederate season, else no creature seeing;
Thou mixture rank, of midnight weeds collected,
With Hecate's ban° thrice blasted, thrice infected,
Thy natural magic and dire property
On wholesome life usurp immediately.

*° the curse of Hecate, goddess of
witchcraft*

[Pours the poison in his ears.]

HAMLET
He poisons him i th'garden for's estate. His° name's Gonzago. The story
is extant, and writ in choice Italian. You shall see anon how the murderer gets the love of Gonzago's wife.

° the sleeper's

OPHELIA
The King rises.

HAMLET
What, frighted with false fire°!

° a blank shot

---

⁴⁶A horse with saddle sores (galls) will wince if something rubs against its sores.
Withers are the part at the junction of a horse's neck and back. Hamlet, like a horse,
has no reason to wince because he has no sores (guilty conscience) that can be
irritated.

⁴⁷At this point, the players speak Hamlet's words and Claudius is about to fall into
the trap, so Hamlet figuratively pulls everyone's strings. He proposes to Ophelia, by
way of ambiguous jest, that he fashion her a lover and write dialogue for them.

⁴⁸Misquote from an anonymous play, *True Tragedy of Richard III*.

QUEEN
How fares my lord?

POLONIUS
Give o'er the play.

KING
Give me some light. Away!

ALL
Lights, lights, lights.

[Exeunt all but Hamlet and Horatio.]

HAMLET
> *Why, let the stricken° deer go weep,*   ° wounded
> *The hart ungalled° play;*   ° the unwounded deer
> *For some must watch°, while some must sleep,*   ° stay awake
> *So runs the world away.*

Would not this, sir, and a forest of feathers°—if the rest of my fortunes   ° actors' plumes
turn Turk° with me—with two Provincial roses on my razed° shoes, get   ° go bad ° decorated with slashes
me a fellowship in a cry° of players, sir?   ° company

HORATIO
Half a share.

HAMLET
A whole one, I.

> *For thou dost know, O Damon dear,*
> *This realm dismantled° was*   ° deprived
> *Of Jove himself, and now reigns here*
> *A very, very—pajock°.*   ° peacock, instead of the expected
>   rhyme, "ass"

HORATIO
You might have rhymed.

HAMLET
O good Horatio, I'll take the ghost's word for a thousand pound. Didst
perceive?

HORATIO
Very well, my lord.

HAMLET
Upon the talk of the poisoning?

HORATIO
I did very well note him.

HAMLET
Ah, ha! Come, some music. Come, the recorders.

> *For if the King like not the comedy,*
> *Why, then, belike, he likes it not, pardie°.*   ° assuredly, "By God"

Come, some music.

[Enter Rosencrantz and Guildenstern.]

GUILDENSTERN
Good my lord, vouchsafe me a word with you.

HAMLET
Sir, a whole history.

GUILDENSTERN
The King, sir—

HAMLET
Ay, sir, what of him?

GUILDENSTERN
Is in his retirement marvellous distempered.

HAMLET
With drink, sir?

GUILDENSTERN
No, my lord, with choler°.   °anger

HAMLET
Your wisdom should show itself more richer to signify this to his doc-
tor, for, for me to put him to his purgation° would perhaps plunge him   °prescribe a remedy
into far more choler.

GUILDENSTERN
Good my lord, put your discourse into some frame°, and start not so   °logical structure
wildly from my affair.

HAMLET
I am tame, sir. Pronounce.

GUILDENSTERN
The Queen, your mother, in most great affliction of spirit, hath sent me
to you.

HAMLET
You are welcome.

GUILDENSTERN
Nay, good my lord, this courtesy is not of the right breed. If it shall
please you to make me a wholesome° answer, I will do your mother's   °rational
commandment. If not, your pardon and my return shall be the end of
the business.

HAMLET
Sir, I cannot.

GUILDENSTERN
What, my lord?

HAMLET
Make you a wholesome answer. My wit's diseased. But, sir, such answer
as I can make, you shall command, or, rather, as you say, my mother.
Therefore no more, but to the matter. My mother, you say—

ROSENCRANTZ
Then thus she says: your behavior hath struck her into amazement and
admiration°.   °bewilderment and wonder

HAMLET
O wonderful son, that can so astonish a mother! But is there no sequel
at the heels of this mother's admiration? Impart.

ROSENCRANTZ
She desires to speak with you in her closet° ere you go to bed.   °private room

HAMLET
We shall obey, were she ten times our mother. Have you any further
trade with us?

ROSENCRANTZ
My lord, you once did love me.

HAMLET
And do still, by these pickers and stealers°.   °hands

ROSENCRANTZ
Good my lord, what is your cause of distemper? You do freely bar the
door upon your own liberty if you deny your griefs to your friend.

HAMLET
Sir, I lack advancement.

ROSENCRANTZ
How can that be, when you have the voice of the King himself for your
succession in Denmark?

HAMLET
Ay, sir, but "While the grass grows"—the proverb° is something   °"While the grass grows, the steed
musty°.   starves."
                                                                     °stale

[Enter Players with recorders.]

O, the recorders. Let me see one. To withdraw with you. Why do you
go about to recover the wind° of me, as if you would drive me into a   °get windward
toil°?[49]   °snare

GUILDENSTERN
O, my lord, if my duty be too bold, my love is too unmannerly.

HAMLET
I do not well understand that. Will you play upon this pipe?

GUILDENSTERN
My lord, I cannot.

HAMLET
I pray you.

GUILDENSTERN
Believe me, I cannot.

HAMLET
I do beseech you.

GUILDENSTERN
I know no touch of it, my lord.

---

[49] Hunting analogy: when a hunter allows the quarry to get windward of him, the
quarry scents the hunter, turns away, and runs in the opposite direction, into the
snare (toil).

HAMLET

'Tis as easy as lying. Govern these ventages° with your finger and   ° stops
thumb, give it breath with your mouth, and it will discourse most eloquent music. Look you, these are the stops.

GUILDENSTERN

But these cannot I command to any utterance of harmony. I have not
the skill.

HAMLET

Why, look you now, how unworthy a thing you make of me. You would
play upon me, you would seem to know my stops, you would pluck
out the heart of my mystery, you would sound me from my lowest note
to the top of my compass; and there is much music, excellent voice, in
this little organ°, yet cannot you make it speak. 'Sblood, do you think I   ° instrument
am easier to be played on than a pipe? Call me what instrument you
will, though you can fret° me, you cannot play upon me.   ° (1) finger (2) vex

[Enter Polonius.]

God bless you, sir.

POLONIUS

My lord, the Queen would speak with you, and presently°.   ° at once

HAMLET

Do you see yonder cloud that's almost in shape of a camel?

POLONIUS

By th'mass, and 'tis like a camel, indeed.

HAMLET

Methinks it is like a weasel.

POLONIUS

It is backed like a weasel.

HAMLET

Or like a whale?

POLONIUS

Very like a whale.

HAMLET

Then will I come to my mother by and by. *[aside.]* They fool me° to the   ° make me play the fool
top of my bent°. —I will come by and by.   ° to my utmost capacity

POLONIUS

I will say so.

HAMLET

"By and by" is easily said.

[Exit Polonius.]

Leave me, friends,

[Exeunt Rosencrantz, Guildenstern, Horatio, and Players.]

'Tis now the very witching time° of night,   ° when evil is loose
When churchyards yawn, and hell itself breathes out

Contagion to this world. Now could I drink hot blood,
And do such bitter business as the day
Would quake to look on. Soft, now to my mother.
O heart, lose not thy nature°. Let not ever   ° natural affection
The soul of Nero° enter this firm bosom.   ° (a matricide)
Let me be cruel, not unnatural.
I will speak daggers to her, but use none.
My tongue and soul in this be hypocrites—
How in my words soever she be shent°,   ° rebuked
To give them seals never my soul consent.

[Exit Hamlet.]

Act Three, Scene Three

A room in the castle.

[*Enter King, Rosencrantz, and Guildenstern.*]

KING
I like him° not, nor stands it safe with us   ° his behavior
To let his madness range. Therefore prepare you.
I your commission will forthwith dispatch°,   ° have drawn up
And he to England shall along with you.
The terms of our estate° may not endure   ° my position as King
Hazard so dangerous as doth hourly grow
Out of his lunacies.

GUILDENSTERN
                    We will ourselves provide.
Most holy and religious fear it is
To keep those many many bodies safe
That live and feed upon your majesty.

ROSENCRANTZ
The single and peculiar life is bound
With all the strength and armor of the mind
To keep itself from noyance°; but much more   ° injury
That spirit upon whose weal° depends and rests   ° welfare
The lives of many. The cess° of majesty   ° cessation
Dies not alone, but like a gulf° doth draw   ° whirlpool
What's near it with it. Or, it is a massy wheel,
Fixed on the summit of the highest mount,
To whose huge spokes ten thousand lesser things
Are mortised° and adjoined, which, when it falls,   ° fixed
Each small annexment, petty consequence,
Attends° the boisterous ruin°. Never alone   ° Accompanies ° massive fall
Did the King sigh, but with a general groan.

KING
Arm° you, I pray you, to this speedy voyage,   ° Prepare
For we will fetters put upon this fear
Which now goes too free-footed.

We will haste us.

[Exeunt Rosencrantz and Guildenstern.]

[Enter Polonius.]

POLONIUS
My lord, he's going to his mother's closet.
Behind the arras I'll convey myself
To hear the process°. I"ll warrant she'll tax him home°.   °proceedings °take him to task
And, as you said, and wisely was it said,
'Tis meet that some more audience than a mother,
Since nature makes them partial, should o'erhear
The speech of vantage°. Fare you well, my liege.   °(1) in addition (2) from a vantage
I'll call upon you ere you go to bed,   position
And tell you what I know.

KING
               Thanks, dear my lord.

[Exit Polonius.]

O, my offence is rank, it smells to heaven.
It hath the primal eldest curse upon't°—   °God's curse on Cain
A brother's murder. Pray can I not;
Though inclination be as sharp as will°,   °desire is as strong as resolve
My stronger guilt defeats my strong intent,
And, like a man to double business bound,
I stand in pause where I shall first begin,
And both neglect°. What if this cursed hand   °omit
Were thicker than itself with brother's blood,
Is there not rain enough in the sweet heavens
To wash it white as snow? Whereto serves mercy
But to confront the visage of offence?
And what's in prayer but this twofold force,
To be forestalled ere we come to fall,
Or pardoned being down? Then I'll look up.
My fault is past—but, O, what form of prayer
Can serve my turn? "Forgive me my foul murder"?
That cannot be, since I am still possessed
Of those effects° for which I did the murder: °fruits of the murder
My crown, mine own ambition, and my queen.
May one be pardoned and retain th'offence°?   °the fruits of the act
In the corrupted currents of this world
Offence's gilded° hand may shove by justice,   °with gold for bribery
And oft 'tis seen the wicked prize itself
Buys out the law. But 'tis not so above.
There is no shuffling°, there the action lies   °evasion
In his true nature, and we ourselves compelled,
Even to the teeth and forehead of our faults,
To give in evidence. What then? What rests°?   °remains

Try what repentance can. What can it not?
Yet what can it when one can not repent?
O wretched state! O bosom black as death!
O limed° soul, that struggling to be free   ° caught (as birds are trapped in
Art more engaged°! Help, angels! Make assay.   birdlime)
Bow, stubborn knees, and heart, with strings of steel,   ° entangled
Be soft as sinews of the new-born babe.
All may be well.

[King kneels.]

[Enter Hamlet.]

HAMLET
Now might I do it pat, now he is praying;
And now I'll do't. And so he goes to heaven,
And so am I revenged. That would be scanned°.   ° carefully considered
A villain kills my father, and for that,
I, his sole son, do this same villain send
To heaven.
O, this is hire and salary, not revenge.
He took my father grossly°, full of bread,   ° spiritually unprepared
With all his crimes° broad blown°, as flush as May,   ° sins ° in full bloom
And how his audit° stands who knows save heaven?   ° spiritual account
But, in our circumstance and course of thought°   ° to the best of our knowledge
'Tis heavy with him. And am I then revenged,
To take him in the purging of his soul,
When he is fit and seasoned for his passage?
No. Up°, sword, and know thou a more horrid hent°:   ° into the sheath ° a more dreadful
When he is drunk, asleep, or in his rage,   time
Or in th'incestuous pleasure of his bed,
At gaming, swearing, or about some act
That has no relish of salvation in't—
Then trip him, that his heels may kick at heaven,
And that his soul may be as damned and black
As hell, whereto it goes. My mother stays°.   ° waits
This physic° but prolongs thy sickly days.   ° remedy (prayer)

[Exit Hamlet.]

KING *[rising]*
My words fly up, my thoughts remain below.
Words without thoughts never to heaven go.

[Exit King.]

Act Three, Scene Four

The Queen's closet.

[Enter Queen and Polonius.]

POLONIUS
He will come straight. Look you lay home° to him: ° severely reprove
Tell him his pranks have been too broad° to bear with,   ° unrestrained
And that your Grace hath screened and stood between
Much heat and him. I'll silence me even here.
Pray you, be round° with him.   ° direct

HAMLET *[within]*
Mother, mother, mother.

QUEEN
I'll warrant you. Fear me not.
Withdraw. I hear him coming.

[Polonius hides behind the arras.]

[Enter Hamlet.]

HAMLET
Now, mother, what's the matter?

QUEEN
Hamlet, thou hast thy father much offended.

HAMLET
Mother, you have my father much offended.

QUEEN
Come, come, you answer with an idle° tongue.   ° foolish

HAMLET
Go, go, you question with a wicked tongue.

QUEEN
Why, how now, Hamlet?

HAMLET
                    What's the matter now?

QUEEN
Have you forgot me?

HAMLET
                    No, by the rood°, not so.   ° cross
You are the Queen, your husband's brother's wife;
And would it were not so, you are my mother.

QUEEN
Nay, then, I'll set those to you that can speak.

HAMLET
Come, come, and sit you down. You shall not budge.
You go not till I set you up a glass°   ° mirror
Where you may see the inmost part of you.

QUEEN
What wilt thou do? Thou wilt not murder me?
Help, help, ho!

POLONIUS [behind]
What, ho! Help, help, help!

HAMLET [drawing]
How now? A rat? Dead, for a ducat°, dead!   ° I'll wager a ducat.

[Makes a pass through the arras.]

POLONIUS [behind]
O, I am slain. *[Falls and dies.]*

QUEEN
                O me, what hast thou done?

HAMLET
Nay, I know not. Is it the King?

QUEEN
O, what a rash and bloody deed is this!

HAMLET
A bloody deed—almost as bad, good mother,
As kill a king, and marry with his brother.

QUEEN
As kill a king!

HAMLET
       Ay, lady, it was my word.

[Lifts up the arras, and sees Polonius.]

Thou wretched, rash, intruding fool, farewell.
I took thee for thy better. Take thy fortune.
Thou find'st to be too busy° is some danger.—   ° meddlesome
Leave wringing of your hands. Peace, sit you down,
And let me wring your heart. For so I shall
If it be made of penetrable stuff,
If damned custom° have not brazed° it so   ° wicked customs ° hardened
That it is proof° and bulwark against sense°.   ° armor ° feeling

QUEEN
What have I done, that thou darest wag thy tongue
In noise so rude against me?

HAMLET
            Such an act
That blurs the grace and blush of modesty,
Calls virtue hypocrite, takes off the rose
From the fair forehead of an innocent love,
And sets a blister° there, makes marriage-vows   ° brand of shame
As false as dicers' oaths. O, such a deed
As from the body of contraction° plucks   ° the making of contracts
The very soul, and sweet religion makes

A rhapsody° of words. Heaven's face doth glow°　　　　°jumble °(with anger)
O'er this solidity and compound mass
With tristful° visage, as against the doom°,　　　　°sad °anticipating Judgment Day
Is thought-sick° at the act.　　　　°sick at the thought

QUEEN
　　　　　　　　　　Ay me, what act
That roars so loud and thunders in the index°?　　　　°table of contents (that is, opening
　　　　　　　　　　　　　　　　　　　　　　　　statement)

HAMLET
Look here, upon this picture, and on this,
The counterfeit presentment° of two brothers.　　　　°miniature portraits
See, what a grace was seated on this brow—
Hyperion's° curls, the front° of Jove himself,　　　　°sun god's °forehead
An eye like Mars to threaten and command,
A station° like the herald Mercury　　　　°bearing
New-lighted on a heaven-kissing hill;
A combination and a form indeed
Where every god did seem to set his seal
To give the world assurance of a man.
This was your husband. Look you now what follows.
Here is your husband, like a mildewed ear°　　　　°(of grain)
Blasting° his wholesome° brother. Have you eyes?　　　　°infecting °healthy
Could you on this fair mountain leave° to feed,　　　　°cease
And batten° on this moor°? Ha? Have you eyes?　　　　°glut yourself °fen
You cannot call it love; for at your age
The heyday° in the blood is tame, it's humble,　　　　°sexual intensity
And waits upon° the judgement; and what judgement　　　　°subservient to
Would step from this to this? Sense°, sure, you have,　　　　°sense perception
Else could you not have motion; but, sure, that sense
Is apoplexed°, for madness would not err,　　　　°paralyzed
Nor sense to ecstasy° was n'er so thralled　　　　°state of hallucination
But it reserved some quantity of choice
To serve in such a difference.⁵⁰ What devil was't
That thus hath cozened° you at hoodman-blind°?　　　　°deceived °blind man's bluff
Eyes without feeling, feeling without sight,
Ears without hands or eyes, smelling sans° all,　　　　°without
Or but a sickly part of one true sense
Could not so mope°. O shame, where is thy blush?　　　　°be dazed
Rebellious hell,°⁵¹　　　　°Rampant feminine desire
If thou canst mutine° in a matron's bones,　　　　°mutiny
To flaming youth let virtue be as wax
And melt in her own fire. Proclaim no shame°　　　　°Don't call it sin

---

⁵⁰ In questions that are also accusations, Hamlet wants to know what possessed Gertrude to take up with Claudius; from Hamlet's point of view, Gertrude's bad judgment goes beyond madness.

⁵¹ Shakespeare sometimes uses "rebellion" in the context of sexual matters to describe male erection. Sexual desire is an insurrection because it undermines the sovereignty of reason. In *King Lear*, Shakespeare refers to female genitalia as "hell."

When the compulsive ardor gives the charge°,   °makes the attack
Since frost° itself as actively doth burn,   °age, numbed desire
And reason panders will°.   °reason (which should restrain
                                                         desire) pimps for it.

QUEEN
                      O Hamlet, speak no more.
Thou turn'st mine eyes into my very soul,
And there I see such black and grained° spots   °ingrained, indelible
As will not leave their tinct°.   °lose their color, be erased

HAMLET
                      Nay, but to live
In the rank sweat of an enseamed° bed,   °greasy
Stewed in° corruption, honeying° and making love   °steeped in °calling each other
Over the nasty sty—   "honey"

QUEEN
                      O, speak to me no more.
These words like daggers enter in mine ears.
No more, sweet Hamlet.

HAMLET
                      A murderer and a villain,
A slave that is not twentieth part the tithe
Of your precedent° lord, a vice of kings,   °former
A cutpurse° of the empire and the rule,   °thief
That from a shelf the precious diadem stole,
And put it in his pocket—

QUEEN
                      No more.

HAMLET
A king of shreds and patches°—   °Clownish (in motley) or beggarly
                                                         (patched together)

                                   [Enter Ghost.]

Save me, and hover o'er me with your wings,
You heavenly guards! What would your gracious figure?

QUEEN
Alas, he's mad!

HAMLET
Do you not come your tardy son to chide,
That, lapsed in time and passion°, lets go by   °let time slip away and passion cool
Th'important° acting of your dread command?   °urgent
O, say!

GHOST
Do not forget. This visitation
Is but to whet thy almost blunted purpose
But, look, amazement° on thy mother sits.   °bewilderment
O, step between her and her fighting soul.
Conceit° in weakest bodies strongest works.   °Imagination
Speak to her, Hamlet.

HAMLET
How is it with you, lady?

QUEEN
Alas, how is't with you,
That you do bend your eye on vacancy°,   ° empty air
And with th'incorporal air do hold discourse?
Forth at your eyes your spirits wildly peep,
And, as the sleeping soldiers in th'alarm°,   ° called to arms
Your bedded° hair like life in excrements°,   ° lying flat ° outgrowths
Start up, and stand on end. O gentle son,
Upon the heat and flame of thy distemper
Sprinkle cool patience. Whereon do you look?

HAMLET
On him, on him! Look you, how pale he glares.
His form and cause conjoined, preaching to stones,
Would make them capable°. Do not look upon me,   ° capable of feeling
Lest with this piteous action you convert
My stern effects°. Then what I have to do   ° purposed actions
Will want true color°—tears perchance for blood.   ° lack its proper appearance

QUEEN
To whom do you speak this?

HAMLET
Do you see nothing there?

QUEEN
Nothing at all; yet all that is I see.

HAMLET
Nor did you nothing hear?

QUEEN
No, nothing but ourselves.

HAMLET
Why, look you there. Look, how it steals away.
My father, in his habit as he lived!
Look where he goes even now out at the portal.

[Exit Ghost.]

QUEEN
This is the very coinage° of your brain.   ° creation
This bodiless creation ecstasy°   ° madness
Is very cunning in.

HAMLET
Ecstasy?
My pulse as yours doth temperately keep time,
And makes as healthful music. It is not madness
That I have uttered. Bring me to the test,
And I the matter will re-word°, which madness   ° repeat

Would gambol° from. Mother, for love of grace,   ° shy away
Lay not that flattering unction° to your soul,   ° soothing ointment
That not your trespass but my madness speaks.
It will but skin and film° the ulcerous place   ° cover over
Whilst rank corruption, mining° all within,   ° undermining
Infects unseen. Confess yourself to heaven;
Repent what's past; avoid what is to come;
And do not spread the compost° on the weeds   ° manure
To make them ranker. Forgive me this my virtue;
For in the fatness of these pursy° times   ° corpulent, puffy
Virtue itself of vice must pardon beg,
Yea, curb and woo° for leave to do him good.   ° bow and entreat

QUEEN
O Hamlet, thou hast cleft my heart in twain.

HAMLET
O, throw away the worser part of it,
And live the purer with the other half.
Good night—but go not to my uncle's bed.
Assume° a virtue if you have it not.   ° Pretend
That monster, custom, who all sense doth eat
Of habits devil, is angel yet in this,
That to the use° of actions fair and good   ° habit
He likewise gives a frock or livery
That aptly is put on.⁵² Refrain to-night,
And that shall lend a kind of easiness
To the next abstinence, the next more easy;
For use° almost can change the stamp of nature,   ° habit
And either lodge° the devil or throw him out   ° accommodate
With wondrous potency. Once more, good night,
And when you are desirous to be blessed,
I'll blessing beg of you. For this same lord,
[Pointing to Polonius.]
I do repent. But heaven hath pleased it so,
To punish me with this and this with me,
That I must be their scourge and minister°.   ° instruments of chastisement
I will bestow° him, and will answer well   ° dispose of
The death I gave him. So, again, good night.
I must be cruel only to be kind.
Thus bad begins, and worse remains behind.
One word more, good lady.

QUEEN
                    What shall I do?

---

⁵²Although routine dulls one's sense of evil, one may also become virtuous through
habit.

HAMLET
Not this, by no means, that I bid you do:
Let the bloat° king tempt you again to bed,   ° bloated, flabby
Pinch wanton on your cheek, call you his mouse°,   ° (endearment)
And let him, for a pair of reechy° kisses,   ° filthy
Or paddling° in your neck with his damned fingers,   ° fondling
Make you to ravel° all this matter out,   ° unravel (explain)
That I essentially am not in madness,
But mad in craft. 'Twere good you let him know;
For who, that's but a queen, fair, sober, wise,
Would from a paddock°, from a bat, a gib°,   ° toad ° tom cat
Such dear concernings° hide? Who would do so?   ° matters of great concern
No, in despite of sense and secrecy,
Unpeg the basket on the house's top,
Let the birds fly, and, like the famous ape,[53]
To try conclusions°, in the basket creep,   ° see what will happen
And break your own neck down°.   ° (at the bottom of the fall)

QUEEN
Be thou assured, if words be made of breath,
And breath of life, I have no life to breathe
What thou hast said to me.

HAMLET
I must to England. You know that?

QUEEN
                                        Alack,
I had forgot. 'Tis so concluded on.

HAMLET
There's letters sealed, and my two schoolfellows,
Whom I will trust as I will adders fanged,
They bear the mandate, they must sweep my way°,   ° as escorts
And marshal° me to knavery°. Let it work,   ° conduct ° plot against Hamlet
For 'tis the sport to have the enginer°   ° munitions expert
Hoist with his own petar°; and't shall go hard   ° blown up with his own bomb
But I will delve one yard below their mines,
And blow them at the moon. O, 'tis most sweet
When in one line two crafts° directly meet.   ° cunning plots
This man° shall set me packing°;   ° dead Polonius ° off in a hurry
I'll lug the guts into the neighbor room.
Mother, good night indeed°. This counsellor   ° earnestly
Is now most still, most secret, and most grave,
Who was in life a foolish prating knave.

_____

[53] The actual story has been lost, but it plays upon the ape's propensity for imitation:
an ape, having seen birds fly when released from a cage, attempted to copy them,
fell, and broke its neck. Hamlet offers Gertrude a warning by way of this analogy. If
she tells Claudius everything about Hamlet (unpegs the basket to let Hamlet's secrets out), she runs the risk of self-injury.

Come, sir, to draw toward an end° with you.   ° finish my conversation
Good night, mother.

> *[Exeunt severally; Hamlet lugging out Polonius.]*

--- **ACT FOUR** ---

Act Four, Scene One

A room in the castle.

> *[Enter King, Queen, Rosencrantz, and Guildenstern.]*

KING
There's matter in these sighs, these profound heaves,
You must translate. 'Tis fit we understand them.
Where is your son?

QUEEN
Bestow this place on us a little while.

> *[Exeunt Rosencrantz and Guildenstern.]*

Ah, mine own lord, what have I seen tonight!

KING
What, Gertrude? How does Hamlet?

QUEEN
Mad as the sea and wind when both contend
Which is the mightier. In his lawless fit,
Behind the arras hearing something stir,
Whips out his rapier, cries "A rat, a rat!"
And in this brainish° apprehension kills   ° deluded
The unseen good old man.

KING
              O heavy deed!
It had been so with us had we been there.
His liberty is full of threats to all—
To you yourself, to us, to every one.
Alas, how shall this bloody deed be answered°?   ° publicly accounted for
It will be laid to us,° whose providence°   ° Responsibility will fall to us
Should have kept short°, restrained, and out of haunt°   ° foresight
This mad young man. But so much was our love,   ° tethered ° secluded
We would not understand what was most fit,
But, like the owner of a foul disease,
To keep it from divulging°, let it feed   ° becoming public
Even on the pith° of life. Where is he gone?   ° essential substance

QUEEN
To draw apart the body he hath killed:
O'er whom his very madness—like some ore
Among a mineral° of metals base,   ° mine
Shows itself pure—he weeps for what is done.

KING
O Gertrude, come away!
The sun no sooner shall the mountains touch,
But we will ship him hence; and this vile deed
We must, with all our majesty and skill
Both countenance° and excuse. Ho, Guildenstern!   °face out

[Enter Rosencrantz and Guildenstern.]

Friends both, go join you with some further aid.
Hamlet in madness hath Polonius slain,
And from his mother's closet hath he dragged him.
Go seek him out, speak fair, and bring the body
Into the chapel. I pray you haste in this.

[Exeunt Rosencrantz and Guildenstern.]

Come, Gertrude, we'll call up our wisest friends
And let them know both what we mean to do
And what's untimely done. So, haply, slander—
Whose whisper o'er the world's diameter
As level° as the cannon to his blank°,   °with aim as good °target
Transports his poisoned shot—may miss our name,
And hit the woundless air°. O, come away!   °incapable of injury
My soul is full of discord and dismay.

[Exeunt all.]

Act Four, Scene Two

Another room in the castle.

[Enter Hamlet.]

HAMLET
Safely stowed.

ROSENCRANTZ AND GUILDENSTERN *[within]*
Hamlet! Lord Hamlet!

HAMLET
What noise? Who calls on Hamlet? O, here they come.

[Enter Rosencrantz and Guildenstern.]

ROSENCRANTZ
What have you done, my lord, with the dead body?

HAMLET
Compounded it with dust, whereto 'tis kin.

ROSENCRANTZ
Tell us where 'tis, that we may take it thence,
And bear it to the chapel.

HAMLET
Do not believe it.

ROSENCRANTZ
Believe what?

HAMLET
That I can keep your counsel and not mine own. Besides, to be de-
manded of° a sponge[54]—what replication° should be made by the son   ° questioned by ° reply
of a king?[55]

ROSENCRANTZ
Take you me for a sponge, my lord?

HAMLET
Ay, sir, that soaks up the King's countenance°, his rewards, his author-   ° favors
ities. But such officers do the King best service in the end. He keeps
them, like an ape an apple in the corner of his jaw; first mouthed, to be
last swallowed. When he needs what you have gleaned, it is but squeezing you, and, sponge, you shall be dry again.

ROSENCRANTZ
I understand you not, my lord.

HAMLET
I am glad of it. A knavish speech sleeps in a foolish ear.

ROSENCRANTZ
My lord, you must tell us where the body is, and go with us to the King.

HAMLET
The body is with the King, but the King is not with the body.[56] The King
is a thing—

GUILDENSTERN
A thing, my lord?

HAMLET
Of nothing. Bring me to him. Hide fox, and all after.°   ° (a cry in a game like hide and seek)

[Exeunt all.]

[54]"Sponge" was a commonplace term for a flatterer. A ruler might squeeze the
sponge when it was full and let it soak when it was dry.

[55]Hamlet reminds Rosencrantz of his rank because, in the preceding lines, Rosencrantz neglected to use the proper form of address to Hamlet. For the rest of the
scene, Hamlet is addressed as "my lord."

[56]Hamlet's lines allude to the "king's two bodies," a political fiction with theological
roots dating back to the twelfth century. This doctrine attempted to accommodate
and describe the rights and responsibilities of kingship by separating the *office* of
the king (the immortal and divinely sanctioned symbol of governance) from the *person* of the king (the mortal, perhaps even errant bearer of that symbol).

Act Four, Scene Three

Another room in the castle.

[Enter King, attended.]

KING
I have sent to seek him, and to find the body.
How dangerous is it that this man goes loose.
Yet must not we put the strong law° on him.   °full force of law
He's loved of the distracted multitude°,   °irrational populace
Who like not° in their judgement but their eyes;   °bestow their affections
And where 'tis so, th'offender's scourge is weighed,
But never the offence. To bear all smooth and even°, °handle all with grace
This sudden sending him away must seem
Deliberate pause°. Diseases desperate grown   °result of careful deliberation
By desperate appliance° are relieved,   °remedies
Or not at all.

[Enter Rosencrantz.]

How now! What hath befallen?

ROSENCRANTZ
Where the dead body is bestowed, my lord,
We cannot get from him.

KING
But where is he?

ROSENCRANTZ
Without, my lord, guarded, to know your pleasure.

KING
Bring him before us.

ROSENCRANTZ
Ho, Guildenstern, bring in my lord.

[Enter Hamlet and Guildenstern.]

KING
Now, Hamlet, where's Polonius?

HAMLET
At supper.

KING
At supper? Where?

HAMLET
Not where he eats, but where he is eaten. A certain convocation of pol-
itic° worms are e'en° at him. Your worm is your only emperor for diet°.   °crafty °even now °a pun on the
We fat all creatures else to fat us, and we fat ourselves for maggots. Your   Diet of Worms
fat king and your lean beggar is but variable service—two dishes, but
to one table. That's the end.

KING
Alas, alas!

HAMLET
A man may fish with the worm that hath eat of a king, and eat of the
fish that hath fed of that worm.

KING
What dost thou mean by this?

HAMLET
Nothing but to show you how a king may go a progress° through the   °state journey
guts of a beggar.

KING
Where is Polonius?

HAMLET
In heaven. Send thither to see. If your messenger find him not there,
seek him i' th'other place yourself. But, indeed, if you find him not
within this month, you shall nose him as you go up the stairs into the
lobby.

KING [to some Attendants]
Go seek him there.

HAMLET
He will stay till you come.

[Exeunt Attendants.]

KING
Hamlet, this deed, for thine especial safety—
Which we do tender° as we dearly° grieve   °hold dear °deeply
For that which thou hast done—must send thee hence
With fiery quickness. Therefore prepare thyself.
The bark° is ready, and the wind at help°,   °ship °favorable
Th'associates tend°, and every thing is bent   °wait
For England.

HAMLET
          For England?

KING
                    Ay, Hamlet.

HAMLET
                              Good.

KING
So is it, if thou knew'st our purposes.

HAMLET
I see a cherub that sees them. But, come; for England!
Farewell, dear mother.

KING
Thy loving father, Hamlet.

HAMLET
My mother. Father and mother is man and wife; man and wife is one
flesh; and so, my mother. Come, for England!

[Exit Hamlet.]

KING
Follow him at foot. Tempt him with speed aboard.
Delay it not. I'll have him hence tonight.
Away, for every thing is sealed and done
That else leans° on th'affair. Pray you, make haste.   °relates to

[Exeunt Rosencrantz and Guildenstern.]

And, England°, if my love thou hold'st at aught—   °King of England
As my great power thereof may give thee sense,
Since yet thy cicatrice° looks raw and red   °scar
After the Danish sword, and thy free° awe   °uncompelled
Pays homage to us°—thou mayst not coldly set°   °fear of Denmark commands
Our sovereign process°, which imports at full°,   English foreign policy °coolly
By letters conjuring to that effect,   disregard
The present° death of Hamlet. Do it, England;   °royal command °explicitly
For like the hectic° in my blood he rages,   specifies
And thou must cure me. Till I know 'tis done,   °immediate
Howe'er my haps°, my joys were ne'er begun.   °fever
                                                              °fortune

[Exit King.]

Act Four, Scene Four

A plain in Denmark.

[Enter Fortinbras with his army over the stage.]

FORTINBRAS
Go, captain, from me greet the Danish king.
Tell him that by his license Fortinbras
Claims the conveyance° of a promised march   °escort
Over his kingdom. You know the rendezvous.
If that his majesty would aught with us,
We shall express our duty in his eye°;   °presence
And let him know so.

CAPTAIN
                    I will do't, my lord.

FORTINBRAS
Go softly on.

[Exeunt all but Captain.]

[Enter Hamlet, Rosencrantz, Guildenstern, and others.]

HAMLET
Good sir, whose powers° are these?   °forces

CAPTAIN
They are of Norway, sir.

HAMLET
How purposed, sir, I pray you?

CAPTAIN
Against some part of Poland.

HAMLET
Who commands them, sir?

CAPTAIN
The nephew to old Norway, Fortinbras.

HAMLET
Goes it against the main° of Poland, sir,   ° main territory
Or for some frontier?

CAPTAIN
Truly to speak, sir, and with no addition,
We go to gain a little patch of ground
That hath in it no profit but the name.
To pay five ducats, five, I would not farm it;
Nor will it yield to Norway or the Pole
A ranker° rate, should it be sold in fee°.   ° higher ° outright

HAMLET
Why, then, the Polack never will defend it.

CAPTAIN
Yes, it is already garrisoned.

HAMLET
Two thousand souls and twenty thousand ducats
Will not debate° the question of this straw.   ° decide, settle
This is th'imposthume° of much wealth and peace,   ° abscess
That inward breaks, and shows no cause without
Why the man dies. I humbly thank you, sir.

CAPTAIN
God be wi' you, sir.

[Exit Captain.]

ROSENCRANTZ
                    Will't please you go, my lord?

HAMLET
I'll be with you straight. Go a little before.

[Exeunt all but Hamlet.]

How all occasions do inform° against me,   ° denounce
And spur my dull revenge. What is a man
If his chief good and market° of his time   ° profit
Be but to sleep and feed? A beast, no more.
Sure, He that made us with such large discourse°,   ° reasoning power
Looking before and after, gave us not

That capability and godlike reason
To fust° in us unused. Now, whether it be   ° grow moldy
Bestial oblivion°, or some craven scruple   ° forgetfulness
Of thinking too precisely on th'event°—   ° outcome
A thought which, quartered, hath but one part wisdom
And ever three parts coward—I do not know
Why yet I live to say "This thing's to do,"
Sith I have cause, and will, and strength, and means
To do't. Examples gross° as earth exhort me.   ° obvious
Witness this army, of such mass and charge°,   ° size and expense
Led by a delicate and tender prince,
Whose spirit with divine ambition puffed,
Makes mouths at° the invisible event°,   ° Makes faces at, mocks
Exposing what is mortal and unsure   ° unforseeable outcome
To all that fortune, death, and danger dare,
Even for an eggshell. Rightly to be great
Is not to stir without great argument°,   ° cause
But greatly to find quarrel in a straw
When honor's at the stake.[57] How stand I, then,
That have a father killed, a mother stained,
Excitements of my reason and my blood,
And let all sleep, while, to my shame, I see
The imminent death of twenty thousand men
That, for a fantasy° and trick° of fame,   ° illusion ° trifle
Go to their graves like beds, fight for a plot
Whereon the numbers cannot try the cause,
Which is not tomb enough and continent°   ° container
To hide the slain?[58] O, from this time forth,
My thoughts be bloody or be nothing worth!

[Exit Hamlet.]

Act Four, Scene Five

Elsinore. A room in the castle.

[Enter Queen, Horatio, and Gentleman.]

QUEEN
I will not speak with her.

GENTLEMAN
She is importunate, indeed distract°.   ° out of her mind
Her mood will needs be pitied.

---

[57] The construction is "*not* this, *but* that": greatness exists not in being slow to anger
but in finding great cause for quarrel in a small matter to defend honor.

[58] The soldiers fight for a plot of ground that is so small that it cannot physically contain all who fight for it nor entomb all the bodies of those who died for it.

QUEEN

What would she have?

GENTLEMAN
She speaks much of her father, says she hears
There's tricks i' th'world, and hems, and beats her heart,
Spurns enviously at straws, speaks things in doubt°   °Makes no clear sense
That carry but half sense. Her speech is nothing°,   °She speaks nonsense
Yet the unshaped use° of it doth move   °incoherent manner
The hearers to collection°. They aim° at it,   °try to understand °guess
And botch° the words up fit to their own thoughts,   °patch
Which°, as her winks and nods and gestures yield° them, °which words °affect the meaning
Indeed would make one think there might be thought°,   °inferred
Though nothing sure, yet much unhappily.

QUEEN
'Twere good she were spoken with, for she may strew
Dangerous conjectures in ill-breeding° minds.   °prone to think the worst
Let her come in.

                    [Exit Gentleman.]

          To my sick soul, as sin's true nature is,
Each toy° seems prologue to some great amiss°.   °trifle °calamity
So full of artless jealousy° is guilt,   °uncontrolled suspicion
It spills° itself in fearing to be spilt.   °destroys

          [Enter Ophelia, distracted and playing on a lute.]

OPHELIA
Where is the beauteous majesty of Denmark?

QUEEN
How now, Ophelia?

OPHELIA [sings]
          How should I your true love know
                    From another one?
          By his cockle hat and staff,
                    And his sandal shoon°.   °shoes

QUEEN
Alas, sweet lady, what imports this song?

OPHELIA
Say you? Nay, pray you, mark.

          [sings] He is dead and gone, lady,
                    He is dead and gone,
          At his head a grass-green turf,
                    At his heels a stone.

QUEEN
Nay, but, Ophelia—

OPHELIA
Pray you, mark.

          [sings] White his shroud as the mountain snow—

[Enter King.]

QUEEN
Alas, look here, my lord.

OPHELIA *[sings]*
> Larded° with sweet flowers,   °Adorned
>   Which bewept to the grave did not go
> With true-love showers.

KING
How do you, pretty lady?

OPHELIA
Well, God dild° you! They say the owl was a baker's daughter.[59] Lord,   °reward
we know what we are, but know not what we may be. God be at your
table!

KING
Conceit upon her father.°   °Wild delusions caused by her
                                       father's death.

OPHELIA
Pray you, let's have no words of this. But when they ask you what it
means, say you this:

> *[sings]* To-morrow is Saint Valentine's day,
>   All in the morning betime,
> And I a maid at your window,
>   To be your Valentine.
>
> Then up he rose, and donned his clothes,
>   And dupped° the chamber-door;   °opened
> Let in the maid, that out a maid
>   Never departed more.

KING
Pretty Ophelia—

OPHELIA
Indeed, la, without an oath, I'll make an end on't.

> *[sings]* By Gis° and by Saint Charity[60]   °contraction of *Jesus*
>   Alack, and fie for shame!
> Young men will do't°, if they come to't,   °have sex
>   By Cock°, they are to blame.   °By God (with play on *penis*)
>
> Quoth she, "Before you tumbled me,
>   You promised me to wed."
> "So would I ha' done, by yonder sun,
>   An° thou hadst not come to my bed."   °If

KING
How long hath she been thus?

---

[59] A folktale recounts that Christ went to a baker's shop and asked for food. When
the baker's daughter rebuked her mother for giving him too much, Christ turned
the daughter into an owl.

[60] Not a real saint but a mild oath derived from the French *par sainte charité* (by holy
charity).

OPHELIA
I hope all will be well. We must be patient. But I cannot choose but weep to think they should lay him i' th'cold ground. My brother shall know of it. And so I thank you for your good counsel. Come, my coach! Good night, ladies. Good night, sweet ladies, good night, good night.

[Exit Ophelia.]

KING
Follow her close. Give her good watch, I pray you.

[Exit Horatio.]

O, this is the poison of deep grief; it springs
All from her father's death. O Gertrude, Gertrude,
When sorrows come, they come not single spies°,   °as scouts
But in battalions. First, her father slain;
Next, your son gone, and he most violent author°   °causer
Of his own just remove°: the people muddied°,   °dismissal °confused
Thick and unwholesome in their thoughts and whispers,
For good Polonius' death; and we have done but greenly°   °unwisely
In hugger-mugger° to inter him; poor Ophelia   °secretly
Divided from herself and her fair judgement,
Without the which we are pictures° or mere beasts;   °soulless imitations
Last, and as much containing as all these,
Her brother is in secret come from France,
Feeds on this wonder°, keeps himself in clouds°,   °encourages the people's view
And wants° not buzzers° to infect his ear   °remains inscrutable
With pestilent speeches of his father's death,   °lacks °informers
Wherein necessity, of matter beggared°,   °without facts
Will nothing stick our person to arraign°   °blame Claudius
In ear and ear. O my dear Gertrude, this°,   °these troubles
Like to a murdering-piece°, in many places   °small cannon with scatter shot
Gives me superfluous death. [A noise within.]

QUEEN
                    Alack, what noise is this?

KING
Where are my Switzers°? Let them guard the door.   °Swiss guards

[Enter a Gentleman.]

What is the matter?

GENTLEMAN
                    Save yourself, my lord.
The ocean, overpeering of his list°,   °rising above its shore
Eats not the flats with more impetuous haste
Than young Laertes, in a riotous head°,   °insurrection
O'erbears your officers. The rabble call him lord;
And, as° the world were now but to begin,   °as if
Antiquity forgot, custom not known,
The ratifiers and props of every word,

They cry, "Choose we! Laertes shall be king!"
Caps, hands, and tongues applaud it to the clouds,
"Laertes shall be king, Laertes king!"

QUEEN
How cheerfully on the false trail they cry!
O, this is counter°, you false Danish dogs!   °on the wrong scent

KING
The doors are broke. *[Noise within.]*

[Enter Laertes, armed; Danes following.]

LAERTES
Where is this king? —Sirs, stand you all without.

DANES
No, let's come in.

LAERTES
                    I pray you give me leave.

DANES
We will, we will.

[Danes retire without the door.]

LAERTES
I thank you. Keep° the door. O thou vile king,   °Guard
Give me my father.

QUEEN
                    Calmly, good Laertes.

LAERTES
That drop of blood that's calm proclaims me bastard,
Cries cuckold to my father, brands the harlot
Even here, between the chaste unsmirched brow
Of my true mother.

KING
                    What is the cause, Laertes,
That thy rebellion looks so giant-like?
Let him go, Gertrude. Do not fear° our person.   °(to Gertrude) fear for
There's such divinity doth hedge a king
That treason can but peep to what it would,°   °God protects kings even from
Acts little of his will. —Tell me, Laertes,   treason
Why thou art thus incensed. —Let him go, Gertrude.
—Speak, man.

LAERTES
Where's my father?

KING
                    Dead.

QUEEN
                    But not by him.

146   WILLIAM SHAKESPEARE

KING
Let him demand his fill.

LAERTES
How came he dead? I'll not be juggled with.
To hell, allegiance! Vows, to the blackest devil!
Conscience and grace, to the profoundest pit!
I dare damnation. To this point I stand°,   °I am resolved
That both the worlds I give to negligence°,   °I have no fear of consequences here
Let come what comes; only I'll be revenged   or hereafter
Most throughly° for my father.   °thoroughly

KING
                              Who shall stay° you?   °stop

LAERTES
My will, not all the world°;   °world's will
And for my means, I'll husband them so well
They shall go far with little.

KING
                              Good Laertes,
If you desire to know the certainty
Of your dear father's death, is't writ in your revenge,
That, swoopstake°, you will draw both friend and foe,   °indiscriminately
Winner and loser?

LAERTES
None but his enemies.

KING
                              Will you know them then?

LAERTES
To his good friends thus wide I'll ope my arms,
And, like the kind life-rendering pelican[61]
Repast° them with my blood.   °Feed

KING
                              Why, now you speak
Like a good child° and a true gentleman.   °faithful son
That I am guiltless of your father's death,
And am most sensibly° in grief for it,   °feelingly
It shall as level° to your judgement 'pear   °plain
As day does to your eye.

DANES [within]
                              Let her come in.

LAERTES
How now! What noise is that?

---

[61] The generous pelican reputedly fed her young with blood from her own breast.

[*Enter Ophelia.*]

O heat, dry up my brains! Tears seven-times salt
Burn out the sense and virtue° of mine eye!   ° natural power
By heaven, thy madness shall be paid by weight,
Till our scale turn the beam. O rose of May,
Dear maid, kind sister, sweet Ophelia!
O heavens, is't possible a young maid's wits
Should be as mortal as an old man's life?
Nature is fine° in love, and, where 'tis fine,   ° refined, spiritualized by
It sends some precious instance° of itself   ° proof
After the thing it loves.

OPHELIA [*sings*]
    They bore him barefaced on the bier,
    Hey non nonny, nonny, hey nonny;
    And in his grave rain'd many a tear—
        Fare you well, my dove.

LAERTES
Hadst thou thy wits and didst persuade revenge,
It could not move thus.

OPHELIA
You must sing, "Down a-down," an you call him a-down-a. O, how the
wheel° becomes it! It is the false steward, that stole his master's   ° refrain
daughter.

LAERTES
This nothing's more than matter.°   ° This nonsense has significance.

OPHELIA [*to Laertes*]
There's rosemary, that's for remembrance. Pray you, love, remember.
And there is pansies, that's for thoughts.⁶²

LAERTES
A document in madness°—thoughts and remembrance fitted.   ° lesson containing mad talk

OPHELIA
There's fennel for you, and columbines. There's rue° for you; and here's   ° herb signifying repentance
some for me. We may call it herb-grace° o' Sundays. O, you must wear   ° another name for rue
your rue with a difference°. There's a daisy. I would give you some vi-   ° for a different reason
olets but they withered all when my father died. They say he made a
good end.

    [*sings*] *For bonny sweet Robin is all my joy.*

---

⁶² Flower symbolism was commonplace in Elizabethan England. As Ophelia calls up
the common flower meanings, she also deliberately chooses the appropriate flower
for each person. Rosemary (remembrance) and pansies (thoughts) might go to
Laertes. (In the following lines) fennel (flattery) and columbines (cuckoldry) might
go to Gertrude. Rue, the bitter plant (with associated meanings of sorrow and repentance), suits Claudius. The recipients of violets (faithfulness) and daisies (dis-
sembling) are not clear.

LAERTES
Thought° and affliction, passion°, hell itself,   °Melancholy °suffering
She turns to favor° and to prettiness.   °grace, charm

OPHELIA [sings]
 And will a' not come again?
 And will a' not come again?
  No, no, he's dead,
  Go to thy death-bed,
 He never will come again.

 His beard was as white as snow,
 All flaxen° was his poll°.   °white °head
  He is gone, he is gone,
  And we cast away° moan.   °throw away
 God ha' mercy on his soul.

And of all Christian souls, I pray God. God be wi'you.

[Exit Ophelia.]

LAERTES
Do you see this, O God?

KING
Laertes, I must commune with° your grief,   °share in
Or you deny me right. Go but apart,
Make choice of whom your wisest friends you will,
And they shall hear and judge 'twixt you and me.
If by direct or by collateral° hand   °indirect
They find us touched°, we will our kingdom give,   °involved
Our crown, our life, and all that we call ours,
To you in satisfaction. But if not,
Be you content to lend your patience to us,
And we shall jointly labor with your soul
To give it due content.

LAERTES
   Let this be so.
His means° of death, his obscure burial—   °cause and manner
No trophy°, sword, nor hatchment° o'er his bones,   °memorial °plaque with coat of
No noble rite nor formal ostentation°—   arms
Cry to be heard, as 'twere from heaven to earth,   °ceremony
That° I must call't in question.   °So that

KING
    So you shall;
And where th'offence is let the great axe fall.
I pray you, go with me.

[Exeunt.]

Act Four, Scene Six

Another room in the castle.

[Enter Horatio and a Servant.]

HORATIO
What are they that would speak with me?

SERVANT
Seafaring men, sir. They say they have letters for you.

HORATIO
Let them come in.

[Exit Servant.]

I do not know from what part of the world
I should be greeted, if not from Lord Hamlet.

[Enter Sailors.]

FIRST SAILOR
God bless you, sir.

HORATIO
Let Him bless thee too.

FIRST SAILOR
He shall, sir, an't please Him. There's a letter for you, sir. It comes from
the ambassador that was bound for England—if your name be Horatio,
as I am let to know it is.

HORATIO *[reads]*
> "Horatio, when thou shalt have overlook'd° this, give these fellows some   ° read
> means to the King. They have letters for him. Ere we were two days old
> at sea, a pirate of very warlike appointment gave us chase. Finding our-
> selves too slow of sail, we put on a compelled valor. In the grapple I
> boarded them. On the instant they got clear of our ship; so I alone be-
> came their prisoner. They have dealt with me like thieves of mercy°. But   ° merciful thieves
> they knew what they did: I am to do a good turn for them. Let the King
> have the letters I have sent; and repair thou to me with as much speed
> as thou wouldest fly death. I have words to speak in thine ear will make
> thee dumb; yet are they much too light for the bore° of the matter. These   ° caliber, size
> good fellows will bring thee where I am. Rosencrantz and Guildenstern
> hold their course for England. Of them I have much to tell thee.
> Farewell.
>
> *He that thou knowest thine, Hamlet.*"

Come, I will make you way for these your letters,
And do't the speedier that you may direct me
To him from whom you brought them.

[Exeunt all.]

Act Four, Scene Seven

Another room in the castle.

[Enter King and Laertes.]

KING
Now must your conscience my acquittance seal°,   °acknowledge my innocence
And you must put me in your heart for friend,
Sith you have heard, and with a knowing ear,
That he which hath your noble father slain
Pursued my life.

LAERTES
            It well appears. But tell me
Why you proceeded not against these feats°,   °actions
So crimeful and so capital in nature,
As by your safety°, wisdom, all things else,   °regard for safety
You mainly were stirred up.

KING
            O, for two special reasons,
Which may to you, perhaps, seem much unsinewed°,   °weak
But yet to me they are strong. The Queen his mother
Lives almost by his looks; and for myself—
My virtue or my plague, be it either which°—   °one or the other
She's so conjunctive° to my life and soul   °closely connected
That, as the star moves not but in his sphere°,   °from Ptolemaic cosmology
I could not but by her. The other motive,
Why to a public count° I might not go,   °reckoning
Is the great love the general gender° bear him,   °common people
Who, dipping all his faults in their affection,
Would, like the spring that turneth wood to stone,
Convert his gyves° to graces; so that my arrows,   °fetters
Too slightly timbered for so loud a wind,
Would have reverted to my bow again,
And not where I had aimed them.

LAERTES
And so have I a noble father lost,
A sister driven into desperate terms°,   °condition
Whose worth, if praises may go back again°,   °refer to her before her madness
Stood challenger on mount° of all the age   °preeminent
For her perfections. But my revenge will come.

KING
Break not your sleeps for that.° You must not think   °(for fear of losing your revenge)
That we are made of stuff so flat° and dull   °spiritless
That we can let our beard be shook with danger,
And think it pastime. You shortly shall hear more.
I loved your father, and we love ourself;
And that, I hope, will teach you to imagine—

[Enter a Messenger.]

How now? What news?

MESSENGER

      Letters, my lord, from Hamlet.
This to your majesty, this to the Queen.

KING

From Hamlet? Who brought them?

MESSENGER

Sailors, my lord, they say. I saw them not.
They were given me by Claudio. He received them
Of him that brought them.

KING

      Laertes, you shall hear them.
Leave us.

       [Exit Messenger.]

[reads] "High and mighty, you shall know I am set naked° on your king-   ° destitute
dom. Tomorrow shall I beg leave to see your kingly eyes, when I shall,
first asking your pardon, thereunto recount the occasion of my sudden
and more strange return.

         Hamlet."

What should this mean? Are all the rest come back?
Or is it some abuse°, and no such thing?   ° deceit

LAERTES

Know you the hand?

KING

    'Tis Hamlet's character°. "Naked"—   ° handwriting
And in a postscript here, he says, "alone."
Can you advise me?

LAERTES

I'm lost in it, my lord. But let him come.
It warms the very sickness in my heart,
That I shall live and tell him to his teeth,
"Thus didest thou."

KING

    If it be so, Laertes—
As how should it be so, how otherwise?°—   ° How could he have returned?
Will you be ruled by me?

LAERTES

    Ay, my lord.
So° you will not o'errule me to a peace.   ° Provided that

KING

To thine own peace. If he be now returned,
As checking° at his voyage, and that he means   ° As a result of stopping
No more to undertake it, I will work him
To an exploit, now ripe in my device,

Under the which he shall not choose but fall;
And for his death no wind of blame shall breathe;
But even his mother shall uncharge° the practice°,   °exonerate °deception
And call it accident.

LAERTES
               My lord, I will be ruled,
The rather, if you could devise it so,
That I might be the organ°.   °instrument

KING
             It falls right.
You have been talked of since your travel much,
And that in Hamlet's hearing, for a quality
Wherein, they say, you shine. Your sum of parts°   °All your other accomplishments
Did not together pluck such envy from him
As did that one, and that, in my regard,
Of the unworthiest siege°.   °least important position

LAERTES
            What part is that, my lord?

KING
A very riband° in the cap of youth,   ·   °A mere ornament
Yet needful too, for youth no less becomes
The light and careless livery that it wears
Than settled age his sables and his weeds°,   °garb
Importing health and graveness°. Two months since,   °Signifying prosperity and dignity
Here was a gentleman of Normandy.
I've seen myself, and served against, the French,
And they can well on horseback°; but this gallant   °are excellent riders
Had witchcraft in't. He grew unto his seat,
And to such wondrous doing brought his horse
As he had been incorpsed° and demi-natured°   °made into one body °became half
With the brave beast. So far he topped my thought,   of
That I, in forgery° of shapes° and tricks,   °fabrication °figures
Come short of what he did.

LAERTES
           A Norman was't?

KING
A Norman.

LAERTES
Upon my life, Lamord.

KING
          The very same.

LAERTES
I know him well. He is the brooch°, indeed,   °jewel
And gem of all the nation.

KING

He made confession of you°,
And gave you such a masterly report
For art and exercise in your defence°,
And for your rapier most especially,
That he cried out, 'twould be a sight indeed,
If one could match you. The scrimers° of their nation,
He swore, had neither motion, guard, nor eye,
If you opposed them. Sir, this report of his
Did Hamlet so envenom with his envy
That he could nothing do but wish and beg
Your sudden coming o'er to play with you.
Now, out of this—

LAERTES

What out of this, my lord?

KING

Laertes, was your father dear to you?
Or are you like the painting of a sorrow,
A face without a heart?

LAERTES

Why ask you this?

KING

Not that I think you did not love your father,
But that I know love is begun by time,
And that I see, in passages of proof°,
Time° qualifies° the spark and fire of it.
There lives within the very flame of love
A kind of wick or snuff that will abate it,
And nothing is at a like goodness still°,
For goodness, growing to a plurisy°,
Dies in his own too-much. That we would do,
We should do when we would; for this "would" changes,
And hath abatements and delays as many
As there are tongues, are hands, are accidents;
And then this "should" is like a spendthrift sigh°
That hurts by easing°. But, to th'quick o' th'ulcer—
Hamlet comes back. What would you undertake
To show yourself your father's son in deed
More than in words?

LAERTES

To cut his throat i' th'church.

KING

No place, indeed, should murder sanctuarize°;
Revenge should have no bounds. But, good Laertes,
Will you do this? —Keep close within your chamber.
Hamlet returned shall know you are come home.
We'll put on° those shall praise your excellence,

° acknowledged your excellence

° fencing

° fencers

° actual examples
° Circumstances ° diminishes

° nothing remains always at the same
  level of perfection
° plethora

° (sighs took blood from the heart)
° injures by relieving

° give asylum to

° incite

And set a double varnish° on the fame   °a second coat
The Frenchman gave you; bring you, in fine°, together,   °finally
And wager on your heads. He, being remiss°,   °careless
Most generous°, and free from all contriving,   °noble-minded
Will not peruse° the foils; so that with ease,   °examine
Or with a little shuffling°, you may choose   °sleight of hand
A sword unbated°, and, in a pass of practice°,   °not blunted °treacherous thrust
Requite him for your father.

LAERTES
                    I will do't:
And for that purpose I'll anoint my sword.
I bought an unction° of a mountebank°,   °ointment °quack
So mortal that but dip a knife in it,
Where it draws blood no cataplasm° so rare,   °salve
Collected from all simples that have virtue°   °medicinal herbs
Under the moon, can save the thing from death
That is but scratched withal. I'll touch my point
With this contagion, that, if I gall° him slightly,   °graze
It may be death.

KING
              Let's further think of this;
Weigh what convenience both of time and means
May fit us to our shape°. If this should fail,   °best suit our purpose
And that our drift° look through° our bad performance,   °plot °exposes
'Twere better not essayed. Therefore this project
Should have a back or second°, that might hold   °alternative plan
If this should blast in proof°. Soft, let me see.   °blow up in our faces
We'll make a solemn wager on your cunnings—I ha't.
When in your motion you are hot and dry—
As° make your bouts more violent to that end—   °And you should
And that he calls for drink, I'll have prepared him
A chalice for the nonce°; whereon but sipping,   °occasion
If he by chance escape your venomed stuck°,   °thrust
Our purpose may hold there. But stay. What noise?

[Enter Queen.]

How now, sweet queen?

QUEEN
One woe doth tread upon another's heel,
So fast they follow. Your sister's drowned, Laertes.

LAERTES
Drowned! O, where?

QUEEN
There is a willow° grows aslant° a brook,   °(emblem of mourning and forsaken
That shows his hoar° leaves in the glassy stream.   love) °slanting across
There with fantastic garlands did she come   °gray-white
Of crow-flowers, nettles, daisies, and long purples°   °wild orchids

That liberal° shepherds give a grosser name,   °free-spoken
But our cold° maids do dead men's fingers call them.   °chaste
There, on the pendent boughs her coronet weeds°   °wreath
Clambering to hang, an envious sliver broke;
When down her weedy trophies° and herself   °garlands
Fell in the weeping brook. Her clothes spread wide,
And, mermaid-like, awhile they bore her up;
Which time she chanted snatches of old tunes,
As one incapable° of her own distress,   °insensible to
Or like a creature native and indued
Unto that element°. But long it could not be   °habituated to water
Till that her garments, heavy with their drink,
Pulled the poor wretch from her melodious lay
To muddy death.

LAERTES

        Alas, then, she is drowned?

QUEEN
Drowned, drowned.

LAERTES
Too much of water hast thou, poor Ophelia,
And therefore I forbid my tears. But yet
It° is our trick°; nature her custom holds,   °Crying °natural response
Let shame say what it will. When these° are gone,   °tears
The woman° will be out. Adieu, my lord.   °the "woman" side of Laertes
I have a speech of fire that fain would blaze,
But that this folly drowns it.

                                        [Exit Laertes.]

KING

                Let's follow, Gertrude.
How much I had to do to calm his rage!
Now fear I this will give it start again;
Therefore let's follow.

                                        [Exeunt all.]

———— ACT FIVE ————

Act Five, Scene One

Elsinore: a churchyard.

               [Enter two Clowns°, with spades.]   °rustics

FIRST CLOWN
Is she to be buried in Christian burial when she willfully seeks her own
salvation?

SECOND CLOWN
I tell thee she is, and therefore make her grave straight°. The crowner° | °immediately °coroner
hath sat° on her, and finds it Christian burial.⁶³ | °held an inquest

FIRST CLOWN
How can that be, unless she drowned herself in her own defence°? | °in self-defense

SECOND CLOWN
Why 'tis found so.

FIRST CLOWN
It must be *se offendendo*°; it cannot be else. For here lies the point: if I | °(blunder for *se defendendo*, in self-
drown myself wittingly°, it argues an act; and an act hath three | defense)
branches—it is to act, to do, and to perform. Argal°, she drowned her- | °intentionally
self wittingly. | °Ergo

SECOND CLOWN
Nay, but hear you, Goodman Delver—

FIRST CLOWN
Give me leave. Here lies the water—good. Here stands the man—
good. If the man go to this water and drown himself, it is, will he, nill
he°, he goes. Mark you that. But if the water come to him and drown | °will he not
him, he drowns not himself. Argal, he that is not guilty of his own death
shortens not his own life.⁶⁴

SECOND CLOWN
But is this law?

FIRST CLOWN
Ay, marry, is't—crowner's quest-law°. | °coroner's inquest law

SECOND CLOWN
Will you ha' the truth on't? If this had not been a gentlewoman, she
should have been buried out o' Christian burial.

FIRST CLOWN
Why, there thou sayst; and the more pity that great folk should have
countenance° in this world to drown or hang themselves, more than | °be privileged
their even-Christian°. Come, my spade. There is no ancient gentlemen | °fellow Christian
but gardeners, ditchers, and grave-makers. They hold up° Adam's | °carry on
profession.

SECOND CLOWN
Was he a gentleman?

FIRST CLOWN
A'° was the first that ever bore arms°. | °He °had a coat of arms

SECOND CLOWN
Why, he had none.

---

⁶³Suicides were denied the full ceremonies of the Church and burial in consecrated
ground.

⁶⁴This passage alludes to a 1554 suicide when common law judge Sir James Hales
killed himself by walking into a river. His case, brought to trial, turned on the question of his forfeiting a lease as punishment for his suicide.

FIRST CLOWN

What, art a heathen? How dost thou understand the Scripture? The Scripture says Adam digged. Could he dig without arms? I'll put another question to thee. If thou answerest me not to the purpose, confess thyself—

SECOND CLOWN

Go to.

FIRST CLOWN

What is he that builds stronger than either the mason, the shipwright, or the carpenter?

SECOND CLOWN

The gallows-maker; for that frame° outlives a thousand tenants.   ° gallows

FIRST CLOWN

I like thy wit well, in good faith. The gallows does well°. But how does   ° is a good answer
it well? It does well to those that do ill. Now, thou dost ill to say the
gallows is built stronger than the church. Argal, the gallows may do
well to thee. To't again, come.

SECOND CLOWN

Who builds stronger than a mason, a shipwright, or a carpenter?

FIRST CLOWN

Ay, tell me that, and unyoke°.   ° have done with it

SECOND CLOWN

Marry, now I can tell.

FIRST CLOWN

To't.

SECOND CLOWN

Mass°, I cannot tell.   ° By the Mass

[Enter Hamlet and Horatio, far off.]

FIRST CLOWN

Cudgel thy brains no more about it, for your dull ass will not mend his
pace with beating. And when you are ask'd this question next, say "a
grave-maker." The houses that he makes lasts till doomsday. Go, get
thee to Yaughan; fetch me a stoop of liquor.

[Exit Second Clown.]

[First Clown digs, and sings.]

> In youth, when I did love, did love,
>   Methought it was very sweet,
> To contract°, O, the time, for, ah, my behove°,   ° shorten ° advantage
>   O, methought there was nothing meet.

HAMLET

Has this fellow no feeling of his business that he sings at grave-making?

HORATIO

Custom hath made it in him a property of easiness.°   ° He's used to his work.

HAMLET

'Tis e'en so; the hand of little employment hath the daintier sense°.   ° is more sensitive

FIRST CLOWN [sings]
> But age, with his stealing steps
>   Hath claw'd me in his clutch,
> And hath shipp'd me intil the land,
>   As if I had never been such.

[First Clown throws up a skull.]

HAMLET

That skull had a tongue in it, and could sing once. How the knave
jowls° it to the ground, as if it were Cain's jaw-bone, that did the first   ° dashes
murder. It might be the pate of a politician° which this ass now o'er-   ° schemer
reaches, one that would circumvent God°, might it not?   ° bypass God's law

HORATIO

It might, my lord.

HAMLET

Or of a courtier, which could say, "Good morrow, sweet lord. How dost
thou, good lord?" This might be my Lord Such-a-one, that praised my
Lord Such-a-one's horse when he meant to beg it, might it not?

HORATIO

Ay, my lord.

HAMLET

Why, e'en so, and now my Lady Worm's, chapless°, and knocked about   ° lacking the lower jaw
the mazard° with a sexton's spade. Here's fine revolution°, an we had   ° head ° change
the trick° to see't. Did these bones cost no more° the breeding but to   ° knack ° Were they worth no more
play at loggats° with 'em? Mine ache to think on't.   than
      ° (throwing game)

FIRST CLOWN [sings]
> A pickaxe, and a spade, a spade,
>   For and° a shrouding-sheet;   ° And furthermore
> O, a pit of clay for to be made
>   For such a guest is meet.

[Throws up another skull.]

HAMLET

There's another. Why may not that be the skull of a lawyer? Where be
his quiddities° now, his quillets°, his cases, his tenures°, and his tricks?   ° quibbles ° fine distinctions ° titles
Why does he suffer this rude knave now to knock him about the   to real estate
sconce° with a dirty shovel, and will not tell him of his action of battery?   ° head
Hum! This fellow might be in's time a great buyer of land, with his statutes, his recognizances, his fines, his double vouchers, his recoveries.[65]
Is this the fine° of his fines, and the recovery of his recoveries°, to have   ° net result ° profit from land
his fine pate full of fine dirt? Will his vouchers vouch° him no more of   transaction
      ° assure

---

[65] Statutes are bonds securing debts by attaching land and property. Recognizances
are bonds that testify that one party owes another money. Fines and recoveries are
procedures for converting an entailed estate to freehold.

his purchases, and double ones° too, than the length and breadth of a
pair of indentures°? The very conveyances° of his lands will hardly lie
in this box°; and must the inheritor° himself have no more, ha?

HORATIO
Not a jot more, my lord.

HAMLET
Is not parchment made of sheep-skins?

HORATIO
Ay, my lord, and of calf-skins too.

HAMLET
They are sheep and calves which seek out assurance in that. I will speak
to this fellow. Whose grave's this, sirrah?

FIRST CLOWN
Mine, sir. [sings]

> O, a pit of clay for to be made
> For such a guest is meet.

HAMLET
I think it be thine, indeed, for thou liest in't.

FIRST CLOWN
You lie out on't, sir, and therefore it is not yours. For my part, I do not
lie in't, and yet it is mine.

HAMLET
Thou dost lie in't, to be in't, and say it is thine. 'Tis for the dead, not for
the quick°; therefore thou liest.

FIRST CLOWN
'Tis a quick lie, sir. 'Twill away again, from me to you.

HAMLET
What man dost thou dig it for?

FIRST CLOWN
For no man, sir.

HAMLET
What woman, then?

FIRST CLOWN
For none, neither.

HAMLET
Who is to be buried in't?

FIRST CLOWN
One that was a woman, sir, but, rest her soul, she's dead.

HAMLET
How absolute° the knave is! We must speak by the card° or equivoca-
tion° will undo us. By the Lord, Horatio, this three years I have taken
note of it; the age is grown so picked that the toe of the peasant comes
so near the heel of the courtier, he galls his kibe°. —How long hast thou
been a grave-maker?

° signed by two people
° contracts ° documents relating to
   property transfer
° the skull itself ° owner

° living

° stickler for accuracy ° with
   absolute precision
° ambiguity
° rubs his chilblain

FIRST CLOWN
Of all the days i' th'year, I came to't that day that our last King Hamlet
o'ercame Fortinbras.

HAMLET
How long is that since?

FIRST CLOWN
Cannot you tell that? Every fool can tell that. It was that very day that
young Hamlet was born—he that was mad and sent into England.

HAMLET
Ay, marry, why was he sent into England?

FIRST CLOWN
Why, because a' was mad. A' shall recover his wits there; or, if a' do not,
'tis no great matter there.

HAMLET
Why?

FIRST CLOWN
'Twill not be seen in him there. There the men are as mad as he.

HAMLET
How came he mad?

FIRST CLOWN
Very strangely, they say.

HAMLET
How strangely?

FIRST CLOWN
Faith, e'en with losing his wits.

HAMLET
Upon what ground?

FIRST CLOWN
Why, here in Denmark. I have been sexton here, man and boy, thirty
years.[66]

HAMLET
How long will a man lie i' th'earth ere he rot?

FIRST CLOWN
I'faith, if a' be not rotten before a' die—as we have many pocky° corses   ° pox-ridden
now-a-days that will scarce hold the laying in°—a' will last you some   ° hold together long enough to be
eight year or nine year. A tanner will last you nine year.   buried

---

[66] This line apparently indicates that Hamlet's age is thirty (since the sexton has said
he became a gravemaker on the day Hamlet was born). But there is some textual
confusion here: the line in the First Folio reads (with emphasis added), "I have bin
sixteene heere, man and Boy thirty years," indicating that Hamlet is sixteen, and the
gravedigger is thirty. This Folio reading has never been accepted as correct (the Second Quarto, which is preferred, reads "Sexten" at that point), but a sixteen-year-old
Hamlet may make more sense than a thirty-year-old in light of earlier lines in the
play (see preface). —R.C.

HAMLET

Why he more than another?

FIRST CLOWN

Why, sir, his hide is so tann'd with his trade that a' will keep out water a great while; and your water is a sore decayer of your whoreson dead body. Here's a skull now hath lain you i' th'earth three-and-twenty years.[67]

HAMLET

Whose was it?

FIRST CLOWN

A whoreson mad fellow's it was. Whose do you think it was?

HAMLET

Nay, I know not.

FIRST CLOWN

A pestilence on him for a mad rogue! A' pour'd a flagon of Rhenish on my head once. This same skull, sir, was Yorick's skull, the King's jester.

HAMLET

This?

FIRST CLOWN

E'en that.

HAMLET

Let me see. *[takes the skull]* Alas, poor Yorick. I knew him, Horatio, a fellow of infinite jest, of most excellent fancy. He hath borne me on his back a thousand times. And now, how abhorred in my imagination it is! My gorge rises at it. Here hung those lips that I have kissed I know not how oft. Where be your gibes now, your gambols, your songs, your flashes of merriment, that were wont to set the table on a roar? Not one now to mock your own grinning? Quite chop-fall'n?° Now get you to my lady's chamber and tell her, let her paint an inch thick, to this favor she must come. Make her laugh at that. Prithee, Horatio, tell me one thing.

° (1) lacking the lower jaw (2) dejected

HORATIO

What's that, my lord?

HAMLET

Dost thou think Alexander look'd o' this fashion i' th'earth?

HORATIO

E'en so.

HAMLET

And smelt so? Pah! *[Puts down the skull.]*

---

[67] This line also sets a parameter for Hamlet's age, implying the Prince must be about twenty-seven or so, as he remembers a servant who died twenty-three years ago as having carried him on his back—the sort of thing servants do with four-year-olds. The relevant line in the First Quarto, however, indicates Yorick's skull "hath bin here this dozen years"—again suggesting an age for Hamlet of about sixteen. —*R.C.*

HORATIO
E'en so, my lord.

HAMLET
To what base uses we may return, Horatio. Why may not imagination trace the noble dust of Alexander° till he find it stopping a bung-hole°?

° (emblem of earthly greatness)
° mouth of a cask

HORATIO
'Twere to consider too curiously° to consider so.

° precisely

HAMLET
No, faith, not a jot; but to follow him thither with modesty° enough, and likelihood to lead it. As thus; Alexander died, Alexander was buried, Alexander returneth into dust. The dust is earth: of earth we make loam; and why of that loam whereto he was converted might they not stop a beer-barrel?

° moderation

> Imperious° Caesar, dead and turn'd to clay,
> Might stop a hole to keep the wind away.
> O, that that earth which kept the world in awe
> Should patch a wall t'expel the winter's flaw.

° Imperial

But soft, but soft. Aside. Here comes the King,

[Enter King, Queen, Laertes, and the Corse; Priests and Lords attendant.]

The Queen, the courtiers. Who is that they follow?
And with such maimed rites°? This doth betoken
The corse they follow did with desperate hand
Fordo° its own life. 'Twas of some estate°.
Couch° we awhile, and mark.

° lack of proper ceremony

° Destroy ° rank
° Hide

[Hamlet retires with Horatio.]

LAERTES
What ceremony else?

HAMLET
                    That is Laertes,
A very noble youth. Mark.

LAERTES
What ceremony else?

FIRST PRIEST
Her obsequies have been as far enlarged
As we have warranty. Her death was doubtful°;
And, but that great command o'er sways the order°,
She should in ground unsanctified have lodged
Till the last trumpet. For° charitable prayers,
Shards°, flints, and pebbles should be thrown on her.
Yet here she is allowed her virgin crants°,
Her maiden strewments°, and the bringing home
Of bell and burial°.

° suspicious
° customary procedure

° Instead of
° broken pottery pieces
° garlands
° flowers strewn on a virgin's grave
° burial in consecrated ground, with
  bells tolling

LAERTES
Must there no more be done?

FIRST PRIEST

                    No more be done.
We should profane the service of the dead
To sing a requiem°, and such rest to her   ° dirge
As to peace-parted souls.

LAERTES

                    Lay her i' th'earth,
And from her fair and unpolluted flesh
May violets spring. I tell thee, churlish priest,
A ministering angel shall my sister be,
When thou liest howling.

HAMLET

                  What, the fair Ophelia!

QUEEN

Sweets° to the sweet. Farewell.   ° Flowers

[Scattering flowers.]

I hoped thou shouldst have been my Hamlet's wife.
I thought thy bride-bed to have decked, sweet maid,
And not have strewed thy grave.

LAERTES

                    O, treble woe
Fall ten times treble on that cursed head
Whose wicked deed thy most ingenious° sense   ° intelligent
Depriv'd thee of. —Hold off the earth awhile,
Till I have caught her once more in mine arms.

[Laertes leaps into the grave.]

Now pile your dust upon the quick and dead,
Till of this flat a mountain you have made
T'o'ertop old Pelion or the skyish head
Of blue Olympus.[68]

HAMLET *[advancing]*

                What is he whose grief
Bears such an emphasis, whose phrase of sorrow
Conjures° the wandering stars, and makes them stand   ° Puts a spell on
Like wonder-wounded hearers? This is I,
Hamlet the Dane°.   ° (this title usually signifies the King)

[Hamlet leaps into the grave.]

LAERTES

              The devil take thy soul!

---

[68] According to classical mythology, the giants attempted to reach heaven by piling Mount Pelion and Mount Ossa on top of Mount Olympus.

[Laertes grapples with Hamlet.]

HAMLET
Thou pray'st not well.
I prithee, take thy fingers from my throat;
For, though I am not splenitive° and rash,   °impetuous
Yet have I something in me dangerous,
Which let thy wisdom fear. Hold off thy hand.

KING
Pluck them asunder.

QUEEN
           Hamlet, Hamlet!

ALL
                Gentlemen!

HORATIO
Good my lord, be quiet.

[The Attendants part them, and they come out of the grave.]

HAMLET
Why, I will fight with him upon this theme
Until my eyelids will no longer wag.

QUEEN
O my son, what theme?

HAMLET
I loved Ophelia. Forty thousand brothers
Could not, with all their quantity of love,
Make up my sum. What wilt thou do for her?

KING
O, he is mad, Laertes.

QUEEN
For love of God, forbear him°.   °leave him alone

HAMLET
'Swounds, show me what thou'lt do.
Woo't° weep? Woo't fight? Woo't fast? Woo't tear thyself?   °wilt thou
Woo't drink up eisel°? Eat a crocodile?   °vinegar
I'll do't. Dost thou come here to whine,
To outface me with leaping in her grave?
Be buried quick with her, and so will I.
And if thou prate of mountains, let them throw
Millions of acres on us, till our ground,
Singeing his pate against the burning zone°,   °sun's orbit
Make Ossa like a wart! Nay, an thou'lt mouth°,   °talk bombast
I'll rant as well as thou.

QUEEN
           This is mere° madness;   °utter
And thus awhile the fit will work on him.

Anon, as patient° as the female dove
When that her golden couplets° are disclosed°,
His silence will sit drooping.

HAMLET
                              Hear you, sir,
What is the reason that you use me thus?
I loved you ever. But it is no matter.
Let Hercules himself do what he may,
The cat will mew, and dog will have his day.°

° calm
° pair of baby birds ° hatched

° Creatures act according to their
nature.

[Exit Hamlet.]

KING
I pray you, good Horatio, wait upon him.

[Exit Horatio.]

[to Laertes] Strengthen your patience in our last night's speech.
We'll put the matter to the present push°.—
Good Gertrude, set some watch over your son.
This grave shall have a living° monument.
An hour of quiet shortly shall we see;
Till then, in patience our proceeding be.

° immediate test

° lasting

[Exeunt all.]

Act Five, Scene Two

A hall in the castle.

[Enter Hamlet and Horatio.]

HAMLET
So much for this, sir. Now shall you see the other.
You do remember all the circumstance?

HORATIO
Remember it, my lord!

HAMLET
Sir, in my heart there was a kind of fighting,
That would not let me sleep. Methought I lay
Worse than the mutines in the bilboes°. Rashly,
And praised be rashness for it, let us know,
Our indiscretion sometime serves us well,
When our deep plots do pall°; and that should learn° us
There's a divinity that shapes our ends,
Rough-hew them how we will.

° mutineers in fetters

° fail ° teach

HORATIO
                              That is most certain.

HAMLET
Up from my cabin,
My sea-gown scarfed° about me, in the dark

° loosely wrapped

Groped I to find out them, had my desire,
Fingered° their packet; and, in fine°, withdrew   °Stole °finally
To mine own room again, making so bold,
My fears forgetting manners, to unseal
Their grand commission; where I found, Horatio—
O royal knavery! —an exact command,
Larded° with many several sorts of reasons,   °Enriched
Importing Denmark's health, and England's too,
With, ho, such bugs and goblins in my life,⁶⁹
That, on the supervise°, no leisure bated°,   °perusal °wasting no time
No, not to stay° the grinding of the axe,   °wait for
My head should be struck off.

HORATIO
                        Is't possible?

HAMLET
Here's the commission; read it at more leisure.
But wilt thou hear me how I did proceed?

HORATIO
I beseech you.

HAMLET
Being thus benetted round with villains,
Ere° I could make a prologue to my brains,   °Before
They had begun the play. I sat me down,
Devised a new commission, wrote it fair°.   °clearly
I once did hold it, as our statists° do,   °statesmen
A baseness to write fair, and labored much
How to forget that learning; but, sir, now
It did me yeoman's° service. Wilt thou know   °substantial
The effect° of what I wrote?   °purpose

HORATIO
                        Ay, good my lord.

HAMLET
An earnest conjuration from the King,
As England was his faithful tributary,
As love between them like the palm might flourish,
As peace should still her wheaten garland° wear,   °(emblem of peace)
And stand a comma° 'tween their amities,   °connecting
And many such-like "As"-es of great charge,⁷⁰
That, on the view and knowing of these contents,
Without debatement° further, more or less,   °delay

---

⁶⁹Claudius paints a picture of imaginary terrors (goblins) and bugaboos that would
come to pass should Hamlet live.

⁷⁰"As-es of great charge" parodies Claudius's bureaucratic language. "As-es of great
charge" refers to clauses beginning with "as" at the same time that it puns on "ass."

He should the bearers put to sudden death,
Not shriving-time° allowed.

HORATIO

How was this sealed?

HAMLET

Why, even in that was heaven ordinant°.
I had my father's signet in my purse,
Which was the model° of that Danish seal,
Folded the writ up in the form of th'other,
Subscribed° it, gave't th'impression, placed it safely,
The changeling° never known. Now, the next day
Was our sea-fight; and what to this was sequent
Thou know'st already.

HORATIO

So Guildenstern and Rosencrantz go to't°.

HAMLET

Why, man, they did make love to this employment.
They are not near my conscience. Their defeat
Does by their own insinuation° grow.
'Tis dangerous when the baser° nature comes
Between the pass° and fell° incensed points
Of mighty opposites°.

HORATIO

Why, what a king is this!

HAMLET

Does it not, thinks 't thee, stand me now upon°—
He that hath killed my king, and whored my mother,
Popped in between th'election and my hopes,
Thrown out his angle° for my proper° life,
And with such cozenage° —is't not perfect conscience
To quit° him with this arm? And is't not to be damned
To let this canker of our nature come
In further evil?

HORATIO

It must be shortly known to him from England
What is the issue of the business there.

HAMLET

It will be short. The interim is mine;
And a man's life's no more than to say "one."
But I am very sorry, good Horatio,
That to Laertes I forgot myself;
For, by the image of my cause, I see
The portraiture of his. I'll court his favors.
But, sure, the bravery° of his grief did put me
Into a towering passion.

HORATIO

Peace! who comes here?

°absolution

°looking out for me

°counterpart

°Signed
°substitution

°go to their deaths

°meddling
°inferior (that is, the courtiers')
°thrust °fierce
°(that is, Hamlet and Claudius)

°become incumbent on me

°fishing hook °own
°deception
°pay back

°bravado

[Enter Osric.]

OSRIC
Your lordship is right welcome back to Denmark.

HAMLET
I humbly thank you, sir. *[aside to Horatio]* —Dost know this water-fly°?   °pest

HORATIO *[aside to Hamlet]*
No, my good lord.

HAMLET *[aside to Horatio]*
Thy state is the more gracious, for 'tis a vice to know him. He hath much
land, and fertile. Let a beast be lord of beasts, and his crib° shall stand   °manger
at the king's mess°. 'Tis a chough°; but, as I say, spacious in the posses-   °table °jackdaw, chatterer
sion of dirt.

OSRIC
Sweet lord, if your lordship were at leisure, I should impart a thing to
you from his majesty.

HAMLET
I will receive it, sir, with all diligence of spirit. Put your bonnet to his
right use. 'Tis for the head.

OSRIC
I thank your lordship, it is very hot.

HAMLET
No, believe me, 'tis very cold. The wind is northerly.

OSRIC
It is indifferent cold, my lord, indeed.

HAMLET
But yet methinks it is very sultry and hot for my complexion°.   °constitution

OSRIC
Exceedingly, my lord. It is very sultry, as 'twere—I cannot tell how.
But, my lord, his majesty bade me signify to you, that he has laid a great
wager on your head. Sir, this is the matter—

HAMLET
I beseech you, remember—

[Hamlet moves Osric to put on his hat.]

OSRIC
Nay, good my lord: for mine ease, in good faith. Sir, here is newly come
to court Laertes. Believe me, an absolute gentleman, full of most ex-
cellent differences°, of very soft° society and great showing. Indeed, to   °personal qualities °agreeable
speak feelingly° of him, he is the card or calendar° of gentry, for you   °justly °chart
shall find in him the continent° of what part a gentleman would see.   °summary

HAMLET
Sir, his definement° suffers no perdition° in you; though I know, to di-   °description °loss
vide him inventorially would dizzy the arithmetic of memory, and yet
but yaw° neither, in respect of his quick sail. But, in the verity of ex-   °deviate from a course
tolment°, I take him to be a soul of great article, and his infusion of such   °praise him truly

dearth and rareness, as, to make true diction of him, his semblable° is
his mirror; and who else would trace him, his umbrage°, nothing more.   °likeness
                                                                          °shadow

OSRIC
Your lordship speaks most infallibly of him.

HAMLET
The concernancy°, sir? Why do we wrap the gentleman in our more   °point
rawer breath°?   ° (a medium too base for Laertes's
                                                                             praise)
OSRIC
Sir?

HORATIO
Is't not possible to understand in another tongue? You will to't,° sir,   °get there
really.

HAMLET
What imports the nomination of this gentleman?°   °Why do you bring him up?

OSRIC
Of Laertes?

HORATIO [aside to Hamlet]
His purse is empty already. All's golden words are spent.

HAMLET
Of him, sir.

OSRIC
I know you are not ignorant—

HAMLET
I would you did, sir; yet, in faith, if you did, it would not much ap-
prove° me. Well, sir?   °commend

OSRIC
You are not ignorant of what excellence Laertes is—

HAMLET
I dare not confess that, lest I should compare with him in excellence;
but to know a man well were to know himself.

OSRIC
I mean, sir, for his weapon, but in the imputation° laid on him by them,   °reputation
in his meed° he's unfellowed°.   °merit °unparalleled

HAMLET
What's his weapon?

OSRIC
Rapier and dagger.

HAMLET
That's two of his weapons—but well.

OSRIC
The King, sir, hath wagered with him six Barbary horses; against the
which he has impawned°, as I take it, six French rapiers and poniards,   °staked

with their assigns°, as girdle, hangers, and so.[71] Three of the carriages°, in faith, are very dear to fancy, very responsive° to the hilts, most delicate carriages, and of very liberal conceit°.

°accessories °hangers
°corresponding
°elaborate design

HAMLET
What call you the carriages?

HORATIO [aside to Hamlet]
I knew you must be edified by the margent° ere you had done.

°marginal comment (footnote, as it were)

OSRIC
The carriages, sir, are the hangers.

HAMLET
The phrase would be more german to the matter, if we could carry cannon by our sides. I would it might be hangers till then. But on. Six Barbary horses against six French swords, their assigns, and three liberal-conceited carriages—that's the French bet against the Danish. Why is this "impawned," as you call it?

OSRIC
The king, sir, hath laid, that in a dozen passes° between yourself and him, he shall not exceed you three hits. He hath laid on twelve for nine;[72] and it would come to immediate trial if your lordship would vouchsafe the answer.

°bouts

HAMLET
How if I answer no?

OSRIC
I mean, my lord, the opposition of your person in trial.

HAMLET
Sir, I will walk here in the hall. If it please his majesty, 'tis the breathing time of day° with me. Let the foils be brought, the gentleman willing, and the King hold his purpose, I will win for him if I can. If not, I'll gain nothing but my shame and the odd hits.

°exercise time

OSRIC
Shall I re-deliver you e'en so°?

°take your words back to the King

HAMLET
To this effect, sir, after what flourish° your nature will.

°with whatever embellishment

OSRIC
I commend my duty to your lordship.

---

[71] The rapier was attached to the belt (girdle) by straps (hangers). "Carriage" is an affected word for hanger, but in the course of the following lines, Hamlet will also use "carriage" as it denotes gun carriages. Osric emphasizes not only the beauty and fine craftsmanship in these weapons but also their coordination—the pieces match. And he thus reveals himself to be foolishly affected.

[72] In order to win, Laertes must win eight of twelve bouts; this stipulation cannot be clearly brought into line with "twelve for nine." Although the precise terms of the odds are not clear, the point conveyed through them is that Claudius insults Hamlet's skill.

HAMLET
Yours, yours.

[Exit Osric.]

He does well to commend° it himself; there are no tongues else for's   °submit
turn.

HORATIO
This lapwing runs away with the shell on his head.[73]

HAMLET
He did comply with his dug° before he sucked it. Thus has he—and   °courted his mother's breast
many more of the same bevy, that I know the drossy° age dotes on—   °worthless
only got the tune of the time, and outward habit of encounter,[74] a kind
of yeasty° collection, which carries them through and through the most   °frothy
fanned and winnowed° opinions; and do but blow them to their trial,   °sieved
the bubbles are out.

[Enter a Lord.]

LORD
My lord, his majesty commended him to you by young Osric, who
brings back to him, that you attend him in the hall. He sends to know
if your pleasure hold to play with Laertes, or that you will take longer
time°.   °you are ready now

HAMLET
I am constant to my purposes; they follow the King's pleasure. If his
fitness speaks, mine is ready°, now or whensoever, provided I be so   °I'm ready when he is
able as now.

LORD
The King and Queen and all are coming down.

HAMLET
In happy time.

LORD
The Queen desires you to use some gentle entertainment° to Laertes   °be polite
before you fall to play.

HAMLET
She well instructs me.

---

[73] The young of the lapwing, who begin to run about shortly after they are hatched,
give the bird its reputation for precocity. Osric, the lapwing in this exaggerated
comparison, is so foolishly precocious that he runs before he's completely out of the
shell. Osric has finally put on his hat.

[74] Osric has picked up the stylish language of the time (got the tune) and acquired
slick manners for dealing with other people (outward habit of encounter). Osric is
one of a larger group of people, full of air and without substance (yeasty collection).
Such courtiers may finesse their way through serious conversations with considered thinkers (fanned and winnowed opinions); but if tested, the courtiers will not
stand up to trial, just as bubbles (yeasty, frothy) will pop when one blows on
them—as Hamlet has been doing with Osric.

HORATIO
You will lose this wager, my lord.

HAMLET
I do not think so. Since he went into France, I have been in continual
practice. I shall win at the odds. But thou wouldst not think how ill all's
here about my heart. But it is no matter.

HORATIO
Nay, good my lord—

HAMLET
It is but foolery. But it is such a kind of gain-giving° as would perhaps   ° misgiving
trouble a woman.

HORATIO
If your mind dislike any thing, obey it. I will forestall their repair hither
and say you are not fit°.   ° ready

HAMLET
Not a whit, we defy° augury. There's a special providence in the fall of   ° reject
a sparrow.[75] If it be now, 'tis not to come. If it be not to come, it will be
now. If it be not now, yet it will come. The readiness is all. Since no man
knows aught of what he leaves, what is't to leave betimes°? Let be.   ° early

[Enter King, Queen, Laertes, Lords, Osric, and Attendants with foils and
                 gauntlets: a table and flagons of wine on it.]

KING
Come, Hamlet, come, and take this hand from me.

[The King puts Laertes' hand into Hamlet's.]

HAMLET
Give me your pardon, sir, I've done you wrong;
But pardon't, as you are a gentleman.
This presence° knows,   ° the assembled court
And you must needs have heard, how I am punished°   ° afflicted with
With sore distraction. What I have done,
That might your nature, honor, and exception°   ° disapproval
Roughly awake, I here proclaim was madness.
Was't Hamlet wronged Laertes? Never Hamlet.
If Hamlet from himself be ta'en away,
And when he's not himself does wrong Laertes,
Then Hamlet does it not, Hamlet denies it.
Who does it, then? His madness. If't be so,
Hamlet is of the faction° that is wronged;   ° party
His madness is poor Hamlet's enemy.
Sir, in this audience,

---

[75]Allusion to Matthew 10:29, which reads, "Are not two little sparrows sold for a
farthing? And one of them shall not light on the ground without your Father."

Let my disclaiming from° a purposed evil   °disavowal of
Free me so far in your most generous thoughts,
That I have shot mine arrow o'er the house,
And hurt my brother.

LAERTES
                    I am satisfied in nature,
Whose motive, in this case, should stir me most
To my revenge. But in my terms of honor
I stand aloof and will no reconcilement
Till by some elder masters, of known honor,
I have a voice and precedent° of peace,   °opinion backed by precedent
To keep my name ungored°. But till that time   °undamaged
I do receive your offered love like love,
And will not wrong it.

HAMLET
                    I embrace it freely°,   °without constraint
And will this brother's wager frankly play.—
Give us the foils. —Come on.

LAERTES
                    Come, one for me.

HAMLET
I'll be your foil, Laertes.[76] In mine ignorance
Your skill shall, like a star i' th'darkest night,
Stick fiery off° indeed.   °Stand out brightly

LAERTES
                    You mock me, sir.

HAMLET
No, by this hand.

KING
Give them the foils, young Osric. Cousin Hamlet,
You know the wager?

HAMLET
                    Very well, my lord.
Your Grace hath laid the odds o' th'weaker side.

KING
I do not fear it; I have seen you both.
But since he is bettered°, we have therefore odds.   °has improved (in France)

                    [Hamlet and Laertes choose foils.]

LAERTES
This is too heavy, let me see another.

---

[76]"Foil" carries a number of meanings: (1) a sword or instrument; (2) a thin sheet
of metallic paper set behind a jewel to set it off; and (3) parallel characters.

174   WILLIAM SHAKESPEARE

HAMLET
This likes me well. These foils have all a length°?   °have the same length

[Hamlet and Laertes prepare to play.]

OSRIC
Ay, my good lord.

KING
Set me the stoups of wine upon that table.
If Hamlet give the first or second hit,
Or quit° in answer of the third exchange,   °hit back
Let all the battlements their ordnance° fire.   °cannon
The King shall drink to Hamlet's better breath,
And in the cup an union° shall he throw,   °a large pearl
Richer than that which four successive kings
In Denmark's crown have worn. Give me the cups;
And let the kettle° to the trumpet speak,   °kettledrum
The trumpet to the cannoneer without,
The cannons to the heavens, the heaven to earth,
"Now the King drinks to Hamlet." Come, begin—
And you, the judges, bear a wary eye.

HAMLET
[to Laertes] Come on, sir.

LAERTES
                    Come, my lord. [They play.]

HAMLET
                                One.

LAERTES
                                    No.

HAMLET
                        [to Osric]
    Judgement.

OSRIC
A hit, a very palpable hit.

LAERTES
                    Well, again.

KING
Stay. Give me drink. Hamlet, this pearl is thine.
Here's to thy health.

[Trumpets sound, and shot goes off.]
                Give him the cup.

HAMLET
I'll play this bout first. Set it by awhile.
Come.

[They play.]

Another hit. What say you?

LAERTES
A touch, a touch, I do confess.

KING
Our son shall win.

QUEEN
              He's° fat, and scant of breath.   ° Laertes
Here, Hamlet, take my napkin°, rub thy brows.   ° handkerchief
The Queen carouses to thy fortune, Hamlet.

HAMLET
Good madam.

KING
              Gertrude, do not drink.

QUEEN
I will, my lord, I pray you, pardon me. *[Drinks.]*

KING *[aside]*
It is the poisoned cup. It is too late.

HAMLET
I dare not drink yet, madam—by and by.

QUEEN
Come, let me wipe thy face.

LAERTES
[to Claudius] My lord, I'll hit him now.

KING
                     I do not think't.

LAERTES *[aside]*
And yet 'tis almost 'gainst my conscience.

HAMLET
Come, for the third, Laertes. You but dally.
I pray you pass° with your best violence   ° make a thrust
I am afeared you make a wanton° of me.   ° trifle with me

LAERTES
Say you so? Come on.

                              [They play.]

OSRIC
Nothing, neither way.

LAERTES
Have at you now!°   ° (warning of attack)

[Laertes wounds Hamlet; then, in scuffling they change rapiers, and Ham-
                        let wounds Laertes.]

KING
             Part them. They are incensed.

HAMLET
Nay, come, again.

[The Queen falls.]

OSRIC

Look to the Queen there, ho!

HORATIO

They bleed on both sides. How is it, my lord?

OSRIC

How is't, Laertes?

LAERTES

Why, as a woodcock to mine own springe°, Osric.   °snare
I am justly killed with mine own treachery.

HAMLET

How does the Queen?

KING

She swoons to see them bleed.

QUEEN

No, no, the drink, the drink! O my dear Hamlet!
The drink, the drink! I am poisoned.

[Queen dies.]

HAMLET

O villainy! Ho! Let the door be locked.

[Exit Osric.]

Treachery! Seek it out.

[Laertes falls.]

LAERTES

It is here, Hamlet. Hamlet, thou art slain.
No medicine in the world can do thee good,
In thee there is not half an hour of life.
The treacherous instrument is in thy hand,
Unbated and envenomed. The foul practice
Hath turned itself on me. Lo, here I lie,
Never to rise again. Thy mother's poisoned.
I can no more. The King, the King's to blame.

HAMLET

The point envenomed too!
Then, venom, to thy work.

[Hamlet stabs the King.]

ALL

Treason! Treason!

KING

O, yet defend me, friends, I am but hurt.

HAMLET

Here, thou incestuous, murderous, damned Dane,
Drink off this potion.

[*Hamlet forces Claudius to drink.*]

Is thy union here?
Follow my mother.

[*King dies.*]

LAERTES

He is justly served.
It is a poison tempered° by himself.   °mixed
Exchange forgiveness with me, noble Hamlet.
Mine and my father's death come not upon thee.
Nor thine on me.

[*Laertes dies.*]

HAMLET

Heaven make thee free° of it! I follow thee.   °absolve your guilt
I am dead, Horatio. Wretched° Queen, adieu!   °Unhappy
You that look pale and tremble at this chance,
That are but mutes° or audience to this act,   °actors who have no words
Had I but time—as this fell sergeant°, Death,   °dread sheriff's officer
Is strict in his arrest—O, I could tell you—
But let it be. Horatio, I am dead;
Thou livest; report me and my cause aright
To the unsatisfied°.   °uninformed

HORATIO

Never believe it.
I am more an antique Roman° than a Dane.   °Stoic
Here's yet some liquor left.

HAMLET

As th' art a man,
Give me the cup. Let go. By heaven, I'll have't.
O good Horatio, what a wounded name,
Things standing thus unknown, shall live behind me!
If thou didst ever hold me in thy heart,
Absent thee from felicity° awhile,   °the felicity of death
And in this harsh world draw thy breath in pain,
To tell my story.

[*March afar off, and shot within.*]

What warlike noise is this?

OSRIC

Young Fortinbras, with conquest come from Poland,
To the ambassadors of England gives
This warlike volley.

HAMLET

O, I die, Horatio.
The potent poison quite o'er-crows° my spirit.   °overpowers
I cannot live to hear the news from England,
But I do prophesy th'election° lights   °succession of kingship

On Fortinbras. He has my dying voice.
So tell him, with the occurrents°, more and less,   °occurrences
Which have solicited°—the rest is silence.   °solicited, urged

[Hamlet dies.]

HORATIO
Now cracks a noble heart. Good night, sweet prince,
And flights° of angels sing thee to thy rest.   °companies
Why does the drum come hither?

[March within.]

*[Enter Fortinbras and the English Ambassadors, with drum, colors, and
Attendants, Osric.]*

FORTINBRAS
Where is this sight?

HORATIO
                    What is it you would see?
If aught of woe or wonder, cease your search.

FORTINBRAS
This quarry° cries on havoc. O proud Death,   °heap of bodies
What feast is toward° in thine eternal° cell,   °being prepared °infernal
That thou so many princes at a shot
So bloodily hast struck?

FIRST AMBASSADOR
                    The sight is dismal;
And our affairs from England come too late.
The ears are senseless that should give us hearing,
To tell him his commandment is fulfilled,
That Rosencrantz and Guildenstern are dead.
Where should we have our thanks?

HORATIO
                    Not from his° mouth.   °Claudius's
Had it th'ability of life to thank you:
He never gave commandment for their death.
But since, so jump° upon this bloody question,   °precisely
You from the Polack wars, and you from England,
Are here arrived, give order that these bodies
High on a stage° be placed to the view,   °platform
And let me speak to th'yet unknowing world
How these things came about. So shall you hear
Of carnal, bloody, and unnatural acts,
Of accidental judgements, casual° slaughters,   °by chance
Of deaths put on° by cunning and forced cause°,   °instigated °foul means
And, in this upshot, purposes mistook
Fall'n on the inventors' heads. All this can I
Truly deliver.

FORTINBRAS

        Let us haste to hear it,
And call the noblest to the audience.
For me, with sorrow I embrace my fortune.
I have some rights of memory° in this kingdom,   ° traditional rights
Which now to claim my vantage° doth invite me.   ° favorable opportunity

HORATIO

Of that I shall have also cause to speak,
And from his mouth whose voice will draw on more.
But let this same° be presently performed   ° what I have suggested
Even while men's minds are wild, lest more mischance
On plots and errors happen.

FORTINBRAS

        Let four captains
Bear Hamlet like a soldier to the stage;
For he was likely, had he been put on°,   ° put to the test
To have proved most royally: and, for his passage°,   ° death
The soldiers' music and the rites of war
Speak loudly for him.
Take up the bodies. Such a sight as this
Becomes the field°, but here shows much amiss.   ° battlefield
Go, bid the soldiers shoot.

    [A death march. Exeunt, bearing off the dead bodies: after which a peal of
                        ordnance is shot off.]

                         [End of Play]

4

THE MISANTHROPE

Molière (Jean-Baptiste Poquelin) • 1666

Translated by Robert Cohen

MOLIÈRE IS, BY FAR, THE MOST FREQUENTLY PRO-duced French playwright of all time. After Shakespeare, he is the most-often-produced playwright in the United States, and probably in the world.

He was born Jean-Baptiste Poquelin in 1622, the son of an official upholsterer to King Louis XIII; his family wealth and royal connections had led him to a superb education at the Jesuit College of Clermont and a law degree at Orleans. All this he abandoned at the age of twenty-one, however, when he changed his name to Molière and with a few friends founded a dramatic troupe, the "Illustre-Théâtre," in Paris. The venture quickly proved less than illustrious financially, however, landing Molière in debtor's prison for a short time, but the young theatre artists were undeterred: after Molière's release, the troupe left Paris and toured the French provinces for thirteen years, developing, on the road, a varied repertory of plays. Molière served as the leader of his company—director, principal actor, and playwright—and when the company came to Paris in 1658 to play before King Louis XIV, it was Molière's own play, *The Doctor in Love*, which proved the company's triumph.

Molière and his troupe remained in Paris for the rest of the dramatist's life; the king took on Molière as a personal favorite, serving as godfather for Molière's child, giving Molière's company a public theatre to perform in, and frequently inviting them to perform at royal palaces in and out of town. Molière went on to write dozens of plays during the next fifteen years: *The Precious Ladies*, *The School for Wives*, *The Doctor in Spite of Himself*, *Tartuffe*, *The Miser*, *The Bourgeois Gentleman*, and *The Misanthrope* are only a few of the best known. Molière died in 1673—collapsing onstage during a performance of *The Imaginary Invalid*—but the theatre company he founded at twenty-one survives to this day, where it is known as the Comedie Française, the "House of Molière."

Yet, although the life of Molière seems as a dream of successive triumphs, it was often contorted with problems and despair. Molière's often-stormy marriage with his leading ingenue actress, Armande Béjart, who was twenty years his junior and possibly his daughter as well, caused him the agonizing social embarrassment reflected in his plays. And while the dramatist was favored by the king, that favor was not shared by all of the royal family nor the clergy, and Molière's *Tartuffe*, a satire on religious hypocrisy, was subjected to forced revisions by the cultural authorities. Out of favor with the Church at his death, Molière was not permitted a Christian burial, and his final resting place is unknown.

And therefore it is not surprising that Molière had the material for a comedy as ironic, unsettling, and even bitter as is *The Misanthrope*. This work, first performed in 1666, portrays its protagonist as helplessly in love with a flirtatious, attractive, and presumably younger woman: it is not coincidental that Molière played Alceste and his wife, Armande, played Célimène. *The Misanthrope* is a comedy, but only on the surface. It seems to be a satire, but we are not always certain what is being satirized: of whom do we finally approve, in this play? And whom among the principal characters can we wholly condemn? Our own shifting loyalties and appreciations are part of the intricate dance of feelings Molière choreographs in *The Misanthrope*, as we, a modern audience, toy over issues as ancient—and contemporary—as honesty versus tactfulness, proper gender roles and rights, and what is the appropriate exclusivity of one's personal and sexual commitments. Molière has managed to probe into the deepest personal issues, yet with the lightest possible touch, which makes *The Misanthrope* the play that most modern critics—and audiences—usually consider his masterpiece.

ON THE TRANSLATION

No plays are more strictly composed than those, like *The Misanthrope*, that are ruled by French neoclassicism. The rules for such works demand a five-act structure, with the stage clearing between each act; a single "setting" and virtually continuous action, complete within twenty-four hours; and no physical stage violence. Language (talk) dominates such plays, and the talk is tightly structured into verse; specifically in paired rhyming couplets known as alexandrines. Alexandrine lines universally contain six iambic (dah-DAH) feet, with a caesura (break) after the third foot; the couplets all rhyme, with masculine (one-syllable) rhymes (for example, "blow" and "go") followed by feminine two-syllable ("nested" and "tested") ones. Molière fudged a little on the act structure and the single setting (sometimes we seem to be in front of Célimène's house, sometimes within it), but not on the verse, which, apart from Oronte's so-called sonnet, is perfect.

As translator, I have rendered the play in rhyming couplets (my view being that if it doesn't rhyme, it isn't *The Misanthrope*); however, like most translators of French alexandrines, I have for the most part employed a pentameter five-foot) line of iambs, which is more felicitous in English. Yet I have not been as strict in this as Molière; and have also employed a few rhythmic variations—some anapestic lines, and some two-, three-, and six-footers—to break up the sing-song quality that rigidly consistent rhymed pentameters often create in our language. English is a consonant-pulsed language, whereas French is vowel-pulsed, and the variations in rhythm in this version, which should not be noticed in actual performance, are intended to give the speeches the same sort of propulsion and flow they have in the original French.

❧ THE MISANTHROPE ❧

CAST OF CHARACTERS

CÉLIMÈNE, a young widow

ALCESTE, her suitor

ORONTE, another suitor, a poet

ACASTE, another suitor, a marquis

CLITANDRE, another suitor, also a marquis

PHILINTE, Alceste's friend

ELIANTE, Célimène's friend

ARSINOÉ, a prudish woman

BASQUE, a servant of Célimène

DU BOIS, Alceste's servant

The action is set in Paris, variously in front of and inside the house of Célimène. Time is the present; that is, 1666.

ACT ONE

[Philinte and Alceste enter in the midst of an argument.]

PHILINTE
What is it? What's the matter?

ALCESTE
Leave me be!

PHILINTE
Come on, Alceste! This is insanity!

ALCESTE
Leave me alone, I said! Get out of here!

PHILINTE
I'm staying put until you make this clear!

ALCESTE
Oh no, Philinte, you'd never understand!

PHILINTE
Now this, my friend, is getting out of hand . . .

ALCESTE
"My friend?" You think that I'm a FRIEND of yours?
That sort of "friendship"—decency deplores!
Our amity was utterly disrupted
When you became so morally corrupted!

PHILINTE
What have I done, Alceste, that's so to blame?

ALCESTE
How can you ask that and not die of shame?
Your integrity's been permanently bruised,
And what you did can NEVER be excused!
That man today! You gave him lavish greetings:
And flow'ry praise; extravagant entreatings!
But when I asked you what his claim to fame was,
You couldn't tell me what his bloody NAME
    was!
And when he left! Your smile—evaporated!
"Can't stand that imbecile!" you blithely stated.
My God, Philinte, it's utterly pernicious
To act so nice, yet deep down be so vicious!
If I did that—betrayed my honest feelings—
I'd HANG myself for moral double-dealings!

PHILINTE
[lightly] Well, I don't think this justifies a
    HANGING,
Nor all this uninhibited haranguing.
Let's call a truce, Alceste! And let's both say:
We'll NEITHER of us hang ourselves today!

ALCESTE

Philinte, your humor's sickening at best.

PHILINTE

Well, tell me what to do then, dear Alceste!

ALCESTE

Just be sincere! Just say the words you mean!
And nothing more! Nor less! Nor in-between!

PHILINTE

But when a neighbor greets you in the street
You have to be A LITTLE BIT discreet.
You can't say: "Oh, my God, you're looking old!"
Or: "Your wife's drinking GIN again, I'm told!"

ALCESTE

Well, what's better, showing false affections?
Groveling in social genuflections?
Those oily "thee and thou" words, how I hate 'em!
And flatterers and cowards: Heaven grate 'em
Into shreds!
With all their vile pretensions in their heads!
Those stuck-on-smiling, so-beguiling faces!
Those amorous, gregarious embraces!
Those horribly inflated salutations
That lead to more exalted protestations!
Why should I care if a man speaks me well,
When I am just one of his vast clientele?
Why soak up flattering praises from one
Who equally flatters ALL UNDER THE SUN!
Ah no, Philinte, I'm one who quite abhors
The flatteries of social snobs and bores.
Give me a friend who's mind is still his own—
Who'll give his love to ME, and ME ALONE!
If words of praise are those that will be heard,
Why, then I—dammit!—want to be PREFERRED,
Not mixed among the lot of common men!
Well, then, Philinte: what's YOUR position then?
Do you prefer ME to that simpleton?
The man who loves ALL men cannot love ONE!

PHILINTE

But in the real world, "virtuous" Alceste,
A little tact might—don't you think—be best?

ALCESTE

No tact! We must explicitly rebuke
These flatterers; Good Lord, they make me puke!
Let men be free to say just what they mean;
Reveal their hearts, abjuring all obscene
Hypocrisies: And speak, in sooth,

The truth, th'whole truth, and nothing but the
    truth!

PHILINTE

You're crazy! Honesty like that would cause
An overthrow of all the social laws!
What would you say to someone you despise:
"Of all the jerks in town, you take the prize!"?
Or to that smiling hypocrite you hate,
"It's you, you ass, that I abominate!"?

ALCESTE

I would!

PHILINTE

            Oh sure. Then tell your old aunt Nelly
"Your teeth are rotten, dear, your breath is smelly;
It's appalling just how UGLY you've become!"

ALCESTE

I will!

PHILINTE

            Then tell Dorilas just how dumb
He sounds each time he speaks! "I say there, Dor!
It seems you've turned a most egregious bore!"

ALCESTE

I shall!

PHILINTE

            You joke!

ALCESTE

                        I do not jest, Philinte!
There's no one here in Paris that I can't
Condemn with every fiber of my being!
My eyes fill up with tears at what they're seeing!
My blood heats up, my spleen explodes with bile!
Black clouds descend, there's no way I can smile
Or fawn, or grin, or whimper modestly,
There's no participating honestly
In all these treacherous deceptions!
I hate society receptions!
I hate this place!
I hate your face!
I hate the wholly-stinking holy-human race!

PHILINTE

[pause]Alceste, you're really going overboard!
These little things: they're easily ignored;
I laugh them off a hundred times a day,
Just like that pleasant chap in Molière's play!
[laughs]Remember him?

ALCESTE

                    You dare to quote Molière?

PHILINTE

I do indeed! HE'S never doctrinaire!
Alceste, you can't just change the world around you
By proving that hypocrisies surround you!
And when your rage goes astronomical
It only serves to make you comical!
When you besiege your own society
It's viewed as—laughable anxiety!

ALCESTE

That's fine with me; exactly what I wish!
Yes, let them call my railing gibberish,
For those who say so—aren't worth a fart!
I'd be insulted if they thought me smart!

PHILINTE

[softly]You really hate mankind, don't you, Alceste?

ALCESTE

[mocking]My God, Philinte! How did you
    know . . . ? YOU GUESSED!

PHILINTE

And is that ALL of us? Ladies and men?
All of the seventeenth century then?
All of us—burned in the blaze of your wrath?

ALCESTE

All I have ever seen crossing my path!
The evil ones: of course! But there adjacent—
The thousands who are silently complacent!
Those indulging menial corruptions!
Those whose pleasures brook no interruptions!
Those who down at court are screwing me—
By rooting for that pervert suing me.

[Philinte nods sympathetically at the mention of
Alceste's ongoing lawsuit; Alceste is lost in his imitation
of his enemies.]

They say [affected tone]"Oh, he's so elegantly
    dressed!"
When his mendacity is manifest!
It's clothes, sweet words, EXPRESSIONS he has
    mastered!
Oh, he can smile and smile, and be a bastard!
I'm deeply wounded, sir; I'll be succinct:
I find integrity's become extinct!
There're times that all I think about is flight:
Of heading off alone into the night.

PHILINTE

All right! You've got a bone to pick with man,
But how about ASSISTING where you can?
Some UNDERSTANDING of our mortal flaws,
And when mankind improves, well, some applause!
Some sympathy should temper icy reason:
But no, you treat each pleasantry as treason!
You view our daily pairings and disbandments
As if we're breaking all the ten commandments!
You've got this—medieval idée fixe:
Good Lord, Alceste, it's 1666!
Well, I'm not perfect, nor are you!
And we've got better things to do
Than remoralize the world!
Like—get our hair-wigs curled!
And get ourselves some dinner,
While still faring to look thinner!

[Alceste snorts in ridicule.]

Okay, I'm just joking, there're hundreds of things
That we could improve—if we were but kings!
But since we are NOT, why not take my advice?
Suffer fools gladly, it's quite a small price!
Discharge your high dudgeon, this IDIOCY,
And CALM DOWN, my friend: Be phlegmatic, like
    me!

ALCESTE

Your phlegm, Philinte: What, does it never boil?
On troubled waters, does it turn to oil?
Suppose YOUR friend betrayed you; sued in court
To have your wealth and property cut short,
And mocked your reputation, wouldn't you
Determine then to bid your phlegm adieu?

PHILINTE

Well, yes and no. Alceste; I understand
That human foibles can get out of hand,
And must be countered, but that doesn't mean
That every one deserves the guillotine!
I know: All men are predatory whores—
But so are all the other carnivores!

ALCESTE

They've robbed me, Philinte; they've torn me in
    two,
They've taken my . . . Oh, Hell! Why bother you?
You'll just speak of REASON! and CAUTION! and
    PHLEGM!!!!

PHILINTE
Yes! But your fury—it gratifies them!
[a quick change of subject]
Restrain your indignation; make a journey
To the court—but get a good attorney!

ALCESTE
Oh, nothing doing there, I stand alone!

PHILINTE
Alceste, have you gone mad? That's quite
  unknown!

ALCESTE
Reason's my lawyer: and justice my case.

PHILINTE
Meet with the judge—and explain, face to face.

ALCESTE
Ah! You don't think my case is any good?

PHILINTE
It may be so, but there's a likelihood
That evil men will . . .

ALCESTE
                          . . . Let them do their best!
I'll win or lose . . .

PHILINTE
                    You're so—god damn "Alceste!"

ALCESTE
Yes, to myself I'm true . . .

PHILINTE
                          But truly wrong!
Your enemies conspire . . .

ALCESTE
                          But I'm strong!

PHILINTE
Oh, no . . .

ALCESTE
          Oh, yes!*[pause]* Oh, no! *[pause]* Ho ho!
[pause] I'M MUSING . . .

PHILINTE
On . . . ?

ALCESTE
[rapturously] On how much pleasure I could take—
  in LOSING . . .

PHILINTE
Good Lord, Alceste . . .

ALCESTE
                    . . . It needs to be surveyed:
How deeply can a good man be betrayed!
How evil, how maliciously perverse
Man shows himself against the universe!

PHILINTE
Unbelievable!

ALCESTE
          It's utter beauty!
To LOSE! Why it's my misanthropic duty!

PHILINTE
And what good would that do? On whose behalf?
The more you suffer, why, the more they laugh!

ALCESTE
Too bad for them!

PHILINTE
                Oh, no, my dear Alceste!
Too bad for you! But put this to a rest—
Let's speak of you-know-who, ah, what's-her-name?
That girl you dote on! Does she share the same
Distaste that you do for our human faults?
And does she join in your outraged assaults?
Ah no! My feeling is, Alceste, that she
Is more in tune with base humanity!
I must say I'm amazed that your sharp eye
Would light on HER—that social butterfly!
And what astounds me even more, my friend,
Is just how strangely you misapprehend!
The honest Eliante, I know, still likes you,
And affable Arsinoé still strikes you
Fair,
unless I err . . .
But you refuse her!
Flirtatious Célimène: that's who you choose, Her!
The cocktease of the town, DID I SAY THAT?
Well, coquette, then; sweet Mistress Tit-for-Tat!
How can it be, with all of her wrongdoing
The two of you are always rendezvous-ing?
You don't perceive her many faults? God love us,
But she's as bad as—well—as ANY of us!

ALCESTE
I don't ignore, and can't forgive her flaws
But that sweet widow's got me in her claws,
And passion overwhelms me! No, I'm first
In line to name her faults the worst
That can be seen—and yet, Philinte, I'm weak.
She knows the art of pleasing me. Don't speak

Of my denouncing her,
    Nor new faults I'll discover,
Nor, please, of my renouncing her:
    OH GOD, PHILINTE, I LOVE HER!
Her beauty compensates a bit, that's sure.
What flaws remain, my love's hot flame will cure.

PHILINTE
CURE Célimène? Oh no, Alceste, you can't!
Does she love *you*?

ALCESTE
                    How DARE you ask, Philinte?
How could I love her, unless she loves me?

PHILINTE
If she loves you, it's quite curiously!
You know, Alceste, she's seeing other men.

ALCESTE
My rivals, yes! She's testing me again!
That's why I've come today: to clear them out!
I'll have no more contenders hereabout!

PHILINTE
If it were me . . . I recapitulate:
I think Eliante would make the better mate!
She loves you, and her heart is bona fide;
Use reason, man! She's more than qualified!

ALCESTE
My reason, yes! But reason's here above!
What good is REASON to a man IN LOVE?

PHILINTE
[after a pause] I fear for you, Alceste, and for your
    suit!
I hope . . .

        [But Oronte enters, and speaks flamboyantly
                                        to Alceste.]

ORONTE
            . . . That servant girl downstairs is
    CUTE!
She says Eliante has gone, with Célimène.
So I'm alone with you two brilliant men!
My dear Alceste, I say it from the heart:
You are to me a total work of art!
A man of magnitude! I say again:
YOU ARE THE MOST MAGNIFICENT OF MEN!
Alceste, I feel my happiness depends
On your accepting you and me as friends!
A friend like me: so dear, of such good birth;
Is like none other you could have on earth!

[Alceste, however, is daydreaming, and has paid no
attention to Oronte's appeal. Oronte clears his throat
                                        and says:]
It's to YOU, my good sir, that I make this speech!

ALCESTE
To me?

ORONTE
            Yes, to you. But do I—overreach?

ALCESTE
No, no! But, sir . . . I'm just surprised
To be so eloquently advertised.

ORONTE
It shouldn't startle you! Why, I would say
That all the WORLD appraises you this way!

ALCESTE
Oronte . . .

ORONTE
            Why, France itself considers you
As worthy of its grandest bally-hoo!

ALCESTE
Monsieur . . .

ORONTE
            Ah, yes! And I, dear friend, esteem
Your—oh-so-many—virtues as—SUPREME!

ALCESTE
ORONTE! . . .

ORONTE
            Let heaven strike me if I lie!
And now to prove my love, indeed, will I,
[turning politely to Philinte]
If you'll allow, embrace my counterpart here,
Exchanging purest friendship, heart-to-heart here!
[turning back to Alceste, proffering his bosom]
So take me, sir! I'm PROUD that you would choose
    me!
And . . .

ALCESTE
            Monsieur!

ORONTE
                    Monsieur? Do you refuse me?

ALCESTE
I'm honored, sir, and don't mean to be blistery
But I think friendship needs a little mystery!
We make the name of "friend," well, obsolete

By using it for everyone we meet!
For friendship: TIME's the only true begettor:
Let's wait then till we know each other better!
We might find out we're each so different
As to become unendingly belligerent!
*[laughs wildly as Oronte thinks this over,
deadpan. Then]*

ORONTE
Oh my God, how SMART!—I say, Alceste
Why now I find you better than the best!
I know in time our friendship shall ensue,
So, till that time, I GIVE MYSELF TO YOU!
[confidentially, luxuriating in his anapests]
If, say, at court, you have something to tell
I'm happy to help you; I know the King well!
He listens to me, as, in fact, they all do.
And I'm happy to lend you my influence too.
[more formal, back to pentameters]
In short, I'm yours to taste and savor,
And since that's so, I'd like to ask a favor!
Oh PRETTY PLEASE, with cream and sugar on it,
I'd like to read to you, NOW, my newest sonnet!
I'd think of publication if you said . . .

ALCESTE
Oh no, Oronte, ask someone else instead!
Not me!

ORONTE
              Why not?

ALCESTE
                        I'll criticize immodestly.
I have this fault, Oronte, of speaking honestly.

ORONTE
Exactly what I want! I LOVE THE TRUTH!
Mere flattery, I feel, is just uncouth!
I want your sharpest criticism, Sir!

ALCESTE
Well, go on if you wish, my dear Monsieur.

ORONTE
"SONNET!"—It's a sonnet! "HOPE!"—See, there's
    this girl
Who sets my hopes and fantasies awhirl!
"HOPE!"—Well, I'm afraid it's nothing MAJOR,
    really.
Some simple lines, and versified—well, . . . freely!

ALCESTE
Well, well, we'll see.

ORONTE
              "HOPE!"—I hope the style
Will not appear to you too infantile!
And for the words, they're not so bad, I think . . .

ALCESTE
We'll see, go on . . .

ORONTE
                        Oh what the hell, they stink!
I wrote the whole damn thing in half an hour!

ALCESTE
Remarkable, Oronte, your staying power!

ORONTE
    *HOPE, it's true, it keeps us going
    And keeps sadness out of doors.
    But Phyllis, like a river flowing,
    Holds my joy upon her shores.*

PHILINTE
An absolutely charming start, Oronte!

ALCESTE
[astonished, aside to Philinte] How dare you praise
    this flagrant dilettante?

ORONTE
    *You've seduced me, sweetest darling,
    Filling my poor soul with HOPE,
    But leaving me alone and snarling:
    I'll become a misanthrope!*

PHILINTE
What beautiful and rare lucidity!

ALCESTE
[hissing to Philinte] Philinte! You ass! It's rank
    stupidity!

ORONTE
    *If you want, I'll wait forever!
    I'll follow you—well—wheresoever!
    Until I take my final breath!
    O Phyllis, dearest: In despair
    I TRUST my HOPE unto your care,
    And HOPE you'll TRUST it unto death!*

PHILINTE
Oronte! A most magnificent conclusion!

ALCESTE
[to Philinte] A plague on you, Philinte! It's mere
    effusion!
One commendation more, I'll break your nose!

PHILINTE
[still to Oronte] I NEVER have heard lines as good as
    those!

ALCESTE
Oh, God!

ORONTE
Don't flatter, now; you should aim higher . . .

PHILINTE
Flattery? Oh, no . . . !

ALCESTE
[hissing to Philinte] Outrageous liar!

ORONTE
But you, Alceste, you haven't spoken yet!
YOUR thoughts on my—poetical vignette?

ALCESTE
It's a terribly delicate matter, Oronte,
But I'm pleased it's not flattering phrases you want!
As I said to this "poet" a few days ago
(Can't remember his name—well, it's not apropos):
Why must everyone become a poet?
And if you write a poem, WHY MUST YOU SHOW IT?
And thus inflict on OTHERS your bad verses.
It isn't praise this exercise coerces!
Reciting poems—it's verbal harassment!
And proves at best—a sheer embarrassment!

ORONTE
[after a brief pause] To HIM, you said! But, are you telling ME
That my work's—poor?

ALCESTE
Not necessarily.
I said to HIM, though, that his reputation
Would be destroyed by sweeping condemnation
Of his bad verse; his trite, redundant lines,
His vapid thought, and immature designs.

ORONTE
That's HIM! But ME, MY sonnet, is it—BAD?

ALCESTE
I haven't said! To HIM, though, I did add
"The itch to write is loathsome! It destroys
ALL in its path: All happiness! All joys!"

ORONTE
So I write BADLY! Oh, I cannot bear it!

ALCESTE
I DON'T SAY THAT! . . . But, if the shoe fits—wear it!

Why must all men possess this urge to rhyme?
To see oneself in print! Why it's a crime—
I told him—to publish all this drivel,
Unless to earn your living! It's uncivil!
Take my advice, I said, resist temptation
And find a more—rewarding occupation!
And don't, for God's sake, seek to thwart
The reputation you've achieved at court,
Just 'cause some cunning publisher might hint
That "now's the time to rush you into print!"
You'll just appear ridiculous! . . . I said!

ORONTE
To HIM, to HIM! But talk of ME instead!
My sonnet, "HOPE." What do you think of IT?

ALCESTE
What do I think, Oronte? I think it's . . .
. . . Unnatural, mere verbiage, corrupt!
Your hackneyed phrasings make my blood erupt!
And what is "trust my hope" supposed to mean?
Or "Holds my joy upon her shores?" Obscene!

        "If you want I'll wait forever
          . . . Follow you—well—wheresoever"

You're grabbing for a rhyme!
And that "well!"
Well,
It's just a stall for time!
It's just a nonsense syllable
To make the meter "metri-fillable!"
This modern style that everyone adores,
With bogus, sentimental metaphors,
It's only affectation: plays on words;
It leaves you wholly empty afterwards!
I hate this century and all its fashions!
Our ancestors, though coarse, had deeper passions.
And I still love—above all poems today,
This old refrain my grandfather would say:

        Old King Henry
        Gave me Paris City
        Gave me Paris City
        So he could have my Girl!

        "No, King Henry,
        Keep your Paris City!
        Keep your Paris City!
        But I shall keep my Girl!"

It's not much of a rhyme; the style is crude
And certainly the imagery's rough-hewed,
But hear this junk that's now held up as art?
At least "King Henry's" spoken from the heart!

Old King Henry
Gave me Paris City,
Gave me Paris City,
So he could have my Girl!

"No, King Henry,
Keep your Paris City!
Keep your Paris City!
But I shall keep my Girl!"

Now THAT is what a loving heart would say.

                    [Oronte laughs.]

Laugh on, Oronte; this merry roundelay
Ranks far above your imprudent invention,
Which seems, to me, mere insincere pretension.

ORONTE
Ah . . . hah! Well, I, I think my verse is good!

ALCESTE
Of course you do, Oronte, that's understood!
But you have asked MY views, and now you've got
   'em!
You think you're tops, and me: I think you're
   bottom!

ORONTE
But lots of people find my verse terrific!

ALCESTE
Sheer flattery; and not at all specific!

ORONTE
You've got some nerve; you think you're so damn
   smart!

ALCESTE
To praise YOU'd take the genius of Descartes!

ORONTE
I'll do without your praise, since you are loath.

ALCESTE
I've sworn—an "anti-Hypocritic Oath!"

ORONTE
Well, then, Alceste, I'd like to see YOU write
A poem on this subject that's NOT trite.

ALCESTE
I'm sure, Oronte, I'd write as bad as you,
But then, there's NO ONE I WOULD SHOW IT
   TO!

ORONTE
Your wild denunciations leave me shattered!

ALCESTE
Call other men if you want to be flattered!

ORONTE
You little prune, scale down that lofty tone!

ALCESTE
And you, big fart, suck back what's overblown!

        [They begin to grapple, and Philinte comes
                      between them.]

PHILINTE
My friends! Good sirs, enough! Let go his sleeve!

ORONTE
Oh pardon me! I'm sorry, I will leave!
[flowery, to Alceste, as though nothing had happened]
I am your servant, Sir, in every way.

ALCESTE
*[snarling]*And I, your most obedient valet.

PHILINTE
You happy now, Alceste? You may be "right,"
But here you are—in an inane fistfight!
And with Oronte, who only wanted praising . . .

ALCESTE
Shut up.

PHILINTE
        I'll . . .

ALCESTE
               Please! No moral conscience-raising!

PHILINTE
I say . . .

ALCESTE
       Leave me alone.

PHILINTE
              If I . . .

ALCESTE
                 . . . Away!

PHILINTE
Let me . . .

ALCESTE
       I'm deaf! *[starts to go]*

PHILINTE
       Come here!

ALCESTE
           [going] I'll go . . .

PHILINTE
                 No!
Stay!

ALCESTE

[stops] I'll stay if then YOU leave! Leave me,
    Philinte!

PHILINTE

Leave YOU, Alceste? Oh, no, my friend: I can't!

[They stand, adamant. But Célimène enters and
    Philinte then quickly disappears.]

——————— **ACT TWO** ———————

ALCESTE

Good Lady Célimène! May I be frank?
The way you acted yesterday? It stank!
I must tell you I am totally disgusted:
Your actions demonstrate you can't be trusted;
In fact, I would be lying if I didn't tell you
That our relationship is through! You—jezebel,
    you!
No matter if I promised otherwise:
I won't be, by these rivals, compromised!

CÉLIMÈNE

Is that why you came here, to start a fight?
I thought we talked this all out—just last night!

ALCESTE

I will not quarrel. But you seem to be driven
To bad behavior that can't be forgiven!
You give the whole world access to your house
Where troops of lovers seek to be your spouse!

CÉLIMÈNE

You're angry that they find me—affable?
You think I'm wrong, I think you're laughable!
What should I do, then, hit them with a stick?
Drive them from my home? Why are you so thick?

ALCESTE

It's not a stick, Madame, that you must brandish
You must be hard of heart, and less outlandish!
They're drawn to you because you're beautiful,
But your response—it's amply more than dutiful:
Yes, your sweet words, and cooing affectations,
Lead them to elevated aspirations!
And you attract them! They're your panting harem;
This bunch of lisping fops; God, I can't bear 'em!
Ah, Célimène! I don't know what to do!
You LIKE to have these bastards chasing you?
Tell me, my dear, what idiotic pleasure

Does Clitandre provide? Oh, boy, he's a treasure!
You like the curling fingernail he's grown?
Perhaps the horrid wigs he calls his own?
With cannon rolls that fall down to the floor
Those all the demoiselles at court adore!
Maybe his ribboned codpieces amuse you!
His puffed-out German sleeves: do they enthuse
    you?
Or maybe it's his smile, that flat falsetto?
His smarmy, slavelike spirit of the ghetto?

CÉLIMÈNE

You're so infuriatingly UNJUST!
You know I have him here because I MUST!
It's for my lawsuit: Clitandre's support—
His and his friends'—will help my case at court!

ALCESTE

Forget your case! I'd just as soon you lost!
To have Clitandre's help; you'd pay the cost!

CÉLIMÈNE

Well, you're just jealous, all the world knows that.

ALCESTE

Who's "all the world?" Those you make passes at?

CÉLIMÈNE

I don't see why this makes you so depressed!
You should be HAPPY that I love them ALL,
    Alceste!
By not identifying any one as best,
I love, but don't become BY love possessed!

ALCESTE

Real clever, Célimène, but tell me—say:
What on earth do I get more than THEY?

CÉLIMÈNE

The happiness of knowing that you're loved!

ALCESTE

I won't know that—till OUT THE DOOR
    THEY'RE SHOVED!

CÉLIMÈNE

How selfish! No, Alceste, for you've just heard
My testimony here: I've given you my word!

ALCESTE

To me—and to the others too! You love—
    MANKIND!
For you, dear Célimène, love's REALLY blind!

CÉLIMÈNE

Why, how romantic! Sweetie, I'm delighted!
You sure can make a girl get all excited!

And just so's you won't fret your little head—
I TAKE BACK EVERY LITTLE THING I SAID!
Ugh! What an imbecilic fool you are!
Is this your wish?

ALCESTE

This isn't love: it's war!
My heart is trapped; I want it free again!
O God! God!! Set me free from Célimène!
Yes, free from this immoderate attraction,
This passion, poison, puerile stupefaction!
Free from this despicable obsession
Which brings me to the point of indiscretion!

CÉLIMÈNE

Its' true, Alceste, you love me much too much!

ALCESTE

There's no one in the world enraptured such!
My love for you can barely be conceived!
It's cataclysmic! Not to be believed!

CÉLIMÈNE

All right!—But your TECHNIQUE, Alceste, is
    rotten!
When you find fault with me, your love's forgotten!
You quarrel bitterly, and come out fighting!
Is this what "love" is? It's so uninviting!

ALCESTE

But you, it's your fault, Célimène!
You, and your—seraglio of men!
But let's stop fighting, please, and let's begin . . .

[Basque enters.]

CÉLIMÈNE

Yes, Basque?

BASQUE

Acaste is here!

CÉLIMÈNE

Well, let him in!

[Basque exits.]

ALCESTE

WHAT? Can't I ever speak with you alone?
Is this some sort of occupation zone,
Where you receive men ANY TIME OF DAY?
Please, Célimène: just tell him you're away!

CÉLIMÈNE

Alceste! You want him to get mad at me?

ALCESTE

My God, you treat me so despicably!

CÉLIMÈNE

You're only thinking of yourself, Alceste!
I can't afford to aggravate a guest!

ALCESTE

Why not? What's he to you? I just began . . .

CÉLIMÈNE

You're BLIND, Alceste??? He's an IMPORTANT
    MAN!
A man who, though he's physically short
Is six-foot-seven when he speaks at Court!
And there, my dear Alceste, I must alert you,
He cannot help—but certainly can HURT you.
And even if YOU'RE not out on a limb,
You can't afford offending men like him!

ALCESTE

I see. No matter what, I must presume,
You'll make your home the world's reception room!
You'll see them all, just—matter-of-factly . . .

[Basque re-enters.]

BASQUE

Clitandre's here as well, Madame . . .

ALCESTE

Exactly!

[Célimène motions for Basque to bring in the men;
Basque leaves to do so, as Alceste moves to leave
the room.]

CÉLIMÈNE

Where are you going?

ALCESTE

Out!

CÉLIMÈNE

No, stay!

ALCESTE

Stay? Why?

CÉLIMÈNE

Please stay!

ALCESTE

I can't!

CÉLIMÈNE

I want you here!

ALCESTE

Not I!
Accept my most obsequious regrets!
I hate these damned, obnoxious tête à têtes!

CÉLIMÈNE
I want you here! With me!

ALCESTE
So you can flaunt?

CÉLIMÈNE
Well, go on then! Do what the hell you want!

[Eliante barges in.]

ELIANTE
Dear Célimène. *[They kiss.]* Guess who I found
downstairs!

*[Indicating Acaste and Clitandre, who enter grandly,
followed by Philinte and the servant, Basque.]*

Your two marquises!

CÉLIMÈNE
[welcoming them] Friends! Good Basque, get chairs!

*[Basque goes off for chairs, as Célimène speaks
privately to Alceste.]*

CÉLIMÈNE
Well, you're still here, Alceste!

ALCESTE
Admittedly!
It's ultimatum time: it's them or me!

CÉLIMÈNE
Stop it!

ALCESTE
No I won't! Today you choose!

CÉLIMÈNE
You've lost your mind!

ALCESTE
No, FOUND IT!
Witch, *j'accuse!*

CÉLIMÈNE
Alceste!

ALCESTE
Well, make your choice!

CÉLIMÈNE
I don't know how!

ALCESTE
Oh yes you do! Just send them packing—NOW!

CLITANDRE
MY DEAR! You'll never guess where I've come
from!

The King's TOILETTE! Gossips—ad nauseum!
Your friend CLEONTE was absolutely CRASS!
That fool ROUTINELY makes himself an ass!

CÉLIMÈNE
It's true; while in details he's quite meticulous
In overall behavior, he's ridiculous!

ACASTE
But there's an even more outrageous dunce
Who's never known a single thought: not once!
It's blabbermouth Damon! With no idea—
But with this ghastly VERBAL diarrhea!

CÉLIMÈNE
He talks and talks, it's utterly absurd:
His POINT comes at the forty thousandth word!

ELIANTE
[to Philinte]
Not bad, for a start!
High Gossip as art!

CLITANDRE
Then there's Timante, a peculiar one there!

CÉLIMÈNE
Oh yes, and his weird, enigmatical stare!
A "man of mystery"—a superspy
Implying intrigue when he just says "Hi!"
Those whispered greetings and those covert
warnings!
Those mocking, supercilious "Good mornings!"
All those embellishments: they make my soul ill:
Those MOUNTAINS that he makes from every
molehill!

ACASTE
Ahah! Geralde, then?

CÉLIMÈNE
God, he's such a bore!
Does ANYBODY listen anymore?
"I only travel in the best societies,"
He gurgles, drooling improprieties.
He says he only speaks with dukes and princes,
But really—it's with any fop who minces!
He wears this perfume—whoa boy! What a stench!
And when HE says "hello," he speaks—IN
FRENCH!

CLITANDRE
It's said he has the ear of old Belise . . .

CÉLIMÈNE
Ah! "Madame Total Silence," if you please.
She's nothing on her mind nor on her tongue;
Her conversation's utterly hamstrung!
Each time she's here, or when I visit her
I play the role of Grand Inquisitor!
She just sits there! I have to string together
These idiotic questions on the weather:
"Think it will rain?" Or, "Warm enough for you?"
"I hear they're having fog in Timbuktu!"
"Do you think Scotland's having thundershowers?"
It's on and on like this for, god knows, HOURS!
You yawn, you check the clock; SHE SMILES AT
      YOU,
As if you have no better things to do!

ACASTE
Well, then, Adraste?

CÉLIMÈNE
                    Adraste? Outlandish hubris!
Its' self-infatuation up the gluteus!
He pesters everyone around the throne
Just so's he'll get increasingly "well known."
But let some other fellow be appointed,
And Adraste's nose gets totally disjointed!

CLITANDRE
Well, how about young Cleon, who these days
Gets lots of social calls and flowery praise?

CÉLIMÈNE
The praises? They are only for his cook!
It's for the MEALS those calls are undertook!

ELIANTE
The SERVICE at his suppers is expert . . .

CÉLIMÈNE
'Til Cleon serves HIMSELF as the dessert!
I even half-enjoy myself, almost,
Until out comes our Cleon, fried, on toast.

PHILINTE
His uncle Damis, EVERYONE commends.
What do you think of him?

CÉLIMÈNE
                    Damis? We're friends.

PHILINTE
Ah good! Damis, an honest man, and true!

CÉLIMÈNE
He's honest, but a little witless too.
A pseudointellectual to boot.

One always sees him TRYING to be cute.
And now it's in his head that he's a critic,
He's gone insufferably analytic!
He finds these DEFECTS everywhere he looks!
Despising this man's poems, and this one's books!
He thinks it wrong to find the simple, good!
True works of art—must be misunderstood!
Until, of course, he gives HIS explanation.
It seems he's got aesthetic constipation!
Our conversations, too, they draw his ire.
Our little chitchats—BOY, they fuel his fire!
His arms cross thus, his nostrils flare in rage . . .
It's quite an intellectual rampage!

ACASTE
God damn, Madame! I say, you've caught Damis!

CLITANDRE
Damn Damn!! I say, that's him, impeccably!

ALCESTE
Go on, my friends, go! Carp and criticize!
Rip 'em to pieces; cut 'em down to size!
BUT let just one SHOW UP by happenstance:
You'd make him feel he was God's gift to France!
You'd kiss his hand, you'd turn all oily-clever,
And then you'd fawn: "Your loyal servant ever!"

CLITANDRE
And why say this to us, sir? 'Cause we're men?
Those "ripping words"—were said by Célimène.

ALCESTE
But caused by you! Oh, yes, you egged her on!
Your fawning laughs, your gossips-liaison.
She likes to jest, but your crude flatteries
Turned jesting to assaults and batteries!
She'd never be a character-marauder
Except that all you pervert fops applaud her!
ALL felonies, ALL sins, ALL misdemeanors;
Are causd by self-indulgent interveners!

PHILINTE
[to Alceste] But, surely, you're not rushing to defend
Those fools to whom YOU ALSO condescend!

CÉLIMÈNE
[to the crowd] Well, so he contradicts himself a bit?
Alceste is always playing opposite!
He's only happy as an adversary;
It's Heaven, he says, makes him so contrary.
When any new thought breaches his dominion
He spouts at once the contrary opinion!
He'd be appalled to find HIS point of view

Appropriated by the likes of you!
No, just say something clever; I predict it:
And instantly Alceste will contradict it!
His mind is haunted: there's this little elf
That makes him take up arms against himself!
[Everyone laughs but Alceste.]

ALCESTE

The laughs have it, dear, you've cooked my goose.
Come on, then: LET'S HAVE MORE ALCESTE-
    ABUSE!

PHILINTE

[to Alceste] But Célimène, you know, speaks
    truthfully.
Whatever WE could say, you'd disagree!
Nor will you suffer fools; or remain silent
When others garner praises: You get—violent!

ALCESTE

When praise becomes the mass's opiate,
Then violence becomes—appropriate!
I'd love to shatter modern narcissism:
Inflated praise, and timid criticism!

CÉLIMÈNE

But . . .

ALCESTE

        No, by God, they are abominations!
And these, your character assassinations!
And those who egg you on, look at them, do:
YOU'RE laughing at others . . . THEY'RE laughing
    at YOU!

CLITANDRE

WELL! As for me, Madame, uhhhh . . . let me say,
I find you CONSUMMATE in every way!

ACASTE

With MARVELOUS features and attributes!
I can't see ANY fault that he imputes!

ALCESTE

No? I see them all! And I don't hide 'em!
I love her much too deeply to abide 'em!
The more one loves, the LESS that one should
    flatter,
PURE love should make you find out what's the
    matter!
Were it me, I'd ostracize all lovers
Who'd shove MY faults beneath the covers,
Who'd give MY shortcomings their blind approval
When they should be demanding their removal!

CÉLIMÈNE

Ah hah! Therefore, if someone REALLY loves,
Then he, or she, should just—RIP OFF THEIR
    GLOVES,
and have a go at it! Why it's COMPASSION
To beat each other up in just this fashion!

ELIANTE

Love, I'm afraid, doesn't follow such laws.
Lovers are blind to their counterpart's flaws.
They never call their passions into question
"Amour" is not pedantic—nor Alcest-ian!
A lover thinks his lover's faults are blessings!
And clothes them in sweet names and fancy
    dressings!
The gaunt one—has a pure angelic whiteness
The skinny runt—has effervescent lightness!
Old fatty there is royally substantial
That miser—"has a mind for things financial."
Miss "Past-Her-Prime," whose hair is coming out—
Still looks terrific when the lights are out.
The giantess? A goddess in their eyes!
The dwarf? That's God's most precious size!
The egoist? He glows with confidence!
The jerk? He's clever! And the lout? Intense!
The talkative bore's got a wonderful zest!
And the dummy? SERENE, so unlike Alceste!
Thus ALL of us lovers, who love to extremes
LOVE the faults of the boy—or the girl—of our
    dreams.

ALCESTE

Well, as for me . . .

CÉLIMÈNE

            Shut up, Alceste! Talk! Talk!
Let's all go outside for a little walk!
Yes? What? You're leaving, sirs?

CLITANDRE

                        Oh, no!

ACASTE

                            Not me!

ALCESTE

Their leaving frightens you so terribly?
Leave anytime you wish, Monsieurs, but know
I'LL never leave until I see YOU go.

ACASTE

Unless it aggravates you, Célimène,
I've nothing else to do today! Amen!

CLITANDRE
To leave you, Célimène? It would appall me!
I'm staying; lest, of course, the King should call
   me.

CÉLIMÈNE
[to Alceste] You're joking, right?

ALCESTE
                        I certainly am not!
I'm staying here with Galahad and Lancelot!

                               [Basque enters.]

BASQUE
Sir, there's a man here wants to speak with you.
Real bad: Says it's an urgent interview.

ALCESTE
Send him away! This interruption's true to form!

BASQUE
Send him away? I can't! No, he's in uniform!
A big gold badge! And braid!

CÉLIMÈNE
                 Why, how gallant!

      [Basque leaves and Célimène calls after him.]
Please, Basque, send him in!

            ·   [A Guard comes to the door.]

ALCESTE
                 WELL? What do you
  want?
Come in . . .

GUARD
         If you would please to come
  outside . . .

ALCESTE
Speak up, you fool, I've nothing here to hide!

GUARD
All right: The Royal Marshals summon you!
To Small Claims Court today, at half past two!
Monsieur . . .

ALCESTE
    Who, me, Monsieur?

GUARD
                Yes, you.

ALCESTE
                 Why me?

PHILINTE
Uh-oh! Oronte's charged you with calumny!

CÉLIMÈNE
What?

PHILINTE
       Oronte read him a sonnet, and Alceste
Tore it to shreds! Oronte is so distressed
He calls for full retraction . . .

ALCESTE
                   No, Philinte!
I meant each word! I never will recant!

PHILINTE
But you must follow orders, so let's go!

ALCESTE
I'm not retracting; not a word, No, NO!
What do these "poet marshals" hope to do?
Make me admire—Japanese haiku?
Or modern verse? Or sentimental trash?
I hate them all. . . .

PHILINTE
               Aren't you a little rash?

ALCESTE
No! Them all! I hate! I hate! I hate!

PHILINTE
[playfully understating] You don't find ONE you can
  appreciate?

ALCESTE
[roars in anguish]

PHILINTE
Let's go. Come on.

ALCESTE
            I'm coming. But I'm not
Retracting anything . . .

PHILINTE
              Nor need you ought!

            [and, simultaneously]

CÉLIMÈNE
What a crackpot!

ACASTE
Right, I forgot!

CLITANDRE
No, not a lot.

ELIANTE
What hath God wrought?

ALCESTE

The poem was vile! I won't say anything
Beside that—unless ordered by the King!
He'll read the poem and come unstuck himself!
And if he doesn't, let him go and f . . .

ACASTE AND CLITANDRE

[They laugh hysterically, to cover.]

ALCESTE

You find me funny, sirs? Oronte should hang!
And you should join him there . . .

CÉLIMÈNE

                                    End this harangue,
Alceste, and go!

ALCESTE

                    Yes, Madame, I'll retire
But I'll still hold your feet right to the fire!

*[Alceste exits, taking Célimène, Eliante, and Philinte
with him, giving instructions to Eliante as he goes.
Clitandre and Acaste remain on stage.]*

─────────── **ACT THREE** ───────────

CLITANDRE

Marquis, you seem to be a happy gent!
You're satisfied: seem utterly content.
But tell me, can things really be that great?
Might you conceivably miscalculate?

ACASTE

Oh no! Sometimes I get all scientific
About myself; and find that I'm—TERRIFIC!
I'm young, I'm rich, my pedigree is tops!
I'm MUCH more noble than MOST Paris fops!
And my family is so well connected
Positions come to me all unexpected!
And when the situation's advantageous,
I'm capable of being SO courageous:
That I will FIGHT for what is right and fair,
And STILL be absolutely debonair!
And witty? HAH! My aptitude's top-rated
Though being—happily—uneducated!
And at the theatre??? EVERY opening night
I'm there to hiss what's bad and cheer what's
    right!
I criticize precisely: BY MY NOSE!
Then holler "Boo's," or thunderous "Bravo's"!
I also have great teeth—no overbite,

A fair complexion, and the PERFECT height.
And for my wardrobe, WELL, I cannot hide it:
Magnificent!—'Least since I dandified it!
I think that NO ONE here in town's above me!
(And Lord, the LADIES, THEY sure seem to love
    me!)
And Louis X-I-V ranks me real high!
I fear— I'm just one HELL of a great guy!

CLITANDRE

Well, yes, but with your other prospects, then
Why are you wasting time on Célimène?

ACASTE

I? Waste my time? It's your gross misperception—
To think I'd tolerate a cool reception!
No, unrequited love's a BORE, I think.
I leave it to the *hoi polloi*, to slink
About their lovers' balconies and doors,
Write sonnets filled with smarmy "*je t'adore*"s,
Weep tears, heave sighs, and manifest their passion
In asininely sentimental fashion.
No, men like me, Marquis, are not afraid
To view ourselves as articles of trade!
No matter how fair, beautiful, or nice
Every woman has her asking price!
And I have mine, thank God! And therefore, she
Will have to pay a price for seeing ME!
So what I give HER, and what remains as MINE
Must end up EQUAL on the bottom line!

CLITANDRE

You think you still have prospects here, *ergo*?

ACASTE

There're lots of things she says make me thinks so!

CLITANDRE

Well, . . . how can I say this, sir? I will be kind:
You flatter yourself, Marquis! You've grown blind!

ACASTE

Oh, my God, you're RIGHT! She hates me, doesn't
    she?

CLITANDRE

Well . . . how could you conjecture differently?

ACASTE

You're right, I FLATTERED myself . . .

CLITANDRE

                                    Why was
    that?

ACASTE
GROWN BLIND!

CLITANDRE
[beginning to realize Acaste is being sarcastic]
         . . . I'm not sure what you're
driving at . . .

ACASTE
I'LL KILL MYSELF!

CLITANDRE
        So, Célimène's not shown
You ANY token you could call your own?

ACASTE
SHE HATES ME!

CLITANDRE
      Answer my damn question,
dammit!

ACASTE
HATES ME!!!!

CLITANDRE
      Shut up, Acaste! Acaste, JUST CRAM
IT!
Has she given you ANY cause for hope?

ACASTE
No! YOU'RE the lucky one! And I'm the dope!
Here, I was hoping to fulfil myself,
But no! I'M GOING OUTSIDE NOW TO KILL
    MYSELF!
[But he stays put, grinning broadly.]

CLITANDRE
ALL RIGHT! Marquis, I'll make a proposition.
We shouldn't have to act in opposition.
Look, let's agree: which of us first can PROVE
That Célimène prefers HIM—makes his move;
The other stands aside; and leaves the field,
The vanquishing Conquistador revealed!

ACASTE
Clitandre! That's a very good idea!
And I'll agree to it! Ave Maria!
But shush . . .

                [Célimène enters.]

CÉLIMÈNE
      Still here?

CLITANDRE
         Love never takes its leave!

CÉLIMÈNE
There's someone at the door, I do believe.
D'you know who?

CLITANDRE
      No . . .

                [Basque enters.]

BASQUE
         Arsinoé, Madame,
She's coming up to see you.

CÉLIMÈNE
         Not her! Damn!

BASQUE
Yes! Eliante is with her at the door.

                [Basque leaves.]

CÉLIMÈNE
Arsinoé! That witch! What's SHE here for?

ACASTE
To take a turn at character-detracting!
She's such a prude . . .

CÉLIMÈNE
         Oh no! She's only acting!
Her holier-than-thou's? They aren't real!
It's just that she thinks they have—sex appeal!
She wants a MAN, although she'll never get one.
She's envied ALL her friends each time they've MET
    one!
And now that she's alone (she's out of suitors)
She's joined the breed of moral persecutors!
Where fun appears, Arsinoé intrudes!
She'd run a Great Society—of prudes!
Romance to her's a rat: and she's the eagle!
She'd make all feminine allure—illegal!
But when a MAN comes round, well, there's the
    test:
Just watch her blushes when she gets around
    Alceste!
Indeed, each time he looks at me and drools,
She acts as though I've robbed her family jewels!
Such envy, rage, and fury: she can't hide it!
Medea's jealousy is trivial beside it!
She's just a bitch, she's positively bad!
And crazy, too; I think she's going mad!
And . . .

[Arsinoé enters.]

. . . How DELIGHTFUL seeing you, my
dear!
Arsinoé, I'm SO glad that you're here!

[Acaste and Clitandre leave.]

ARSINOÉ
My dear, there're things I think you need to
know . . .

CÉLIMÈNE
Arsinoé,—my dear, I've missed you so . . .

ARSINOÉ
They've gone, I see. Their timing's legendary . . .

CÉLIMÈNE
Sit down, my dear . . .

ARSINOÉ
That won't be necessary.
Unfortunately friendship makes demands
To give our friends infrequent reprimands.
My dear, I am especially attuned
To ANY friend whose honor is impugned;
Regrettably—and don't misapprehend,
I now must PROVE myself your foremost friend:
Last night I went to this big, high-class "do,"
In which—surprise!—the talk soon turned to you!
Your "conduct," shall I say, was put in question!
It wasn't—praiseworthy—was the suggestion!
Your crowd of suitors and their foolish chatter
Was PART of what my friends thought was the
matter.
But the critique grew fierce; you, dear, were—
dished
Much more completely than I would have wished!
Of course, you know what side I took:
I leapt right in to get you off the hook!
I said you meant well, had a heart of gold,
Were not the sort to blow both hot and cold,
But you must know that there is some behavior
That simply can't be saved by—ANY saviour!
And so I, after all that, had to give in!
I know that it's a NASTY world we live in.
And it looks bad from every spot you see it!·
Why, Dante's Hell is PLEASANT vis-à-vis it!
Gossip, innuendos, moral looseness!
Rampant intellectual obtuseness!
Of course, YOUR honor still—I think's—intact;
Your virtue wasn't FLAGRANTLY attacked,

But, dear, a shadow of contamination
Is more than darkening your reputation!
Enough! I think you surely know the price
Of disregarding this sincere advice!
I hate to rub salt in a wound that's sore,
But it's my duty: It's what friends are FOR!

CÉLIMÈNE
Well, thanks, Arsinoé! Thanks very much!
One doesn't want to get TOO out of touch.
Please know that I feel some responsibility
To speak with YOU—about your (false?) humility.
Yes, let me demonstrate MY love for YOU:
By doing just exactly what YOU do!
I went to this salon the other day
And there was *tout* Paris, chatting away!
The talk was philosophical and deep—
But then it turned to you! Well, I will keep
This short: your rampant, overwhelming zeal
Was not considered totally—ideal.
Your upturned nose they thought an affectation!
Your prudery? Just morbid fascination!
Your counting up of every indiscretion
They thought a hidden sexual obsession!
Your condescending, patronizing pity,
They thought was sublimation city!
As with your daily lecture on morality:
How kissing has become obscene orality!
May I speak frankly? May I plant a seed?
On ALL these charges, NO ONE disagreed!
One said: "Because HER face is rather—plain
Does that mean that we ALL must now abstain?
Another: "Why, she stays in church all day,
So when the bill collectors come, SHE NEEDN'T
PAY!
She prays: 'God, lead me not into disgrace,'
And then puts tons of makeup on her face!
She hates nude statues in the Jeu de Paume
But in the nighttime, SHE TURNS PEEPING
TOM!"
Of course, dear, I defended you completely
Against these lies tossed out so—indiscreetly.
But up against this—UNIVERSAL view
Why, what on earth was I supposed to do?
They ALL believed that you should cast your stone
Not first at THEIR transgressions, but YOUR
OWN.
They think that one should practice introspection
Before proceeding in a vivisection,

And say that those who register complaints
Had better be anointed, first, as SAINTS!
For YOU to sermonize, they say, is fraud!
Morality, they feel's—BEST LEFT TO GOD!
My dear, I'm sure you know that my concern
Is only that you have the chance to learn
From this advice. So, please—don't misconstrue:
All this hurts ME far WORSE than it hurts YOU!

ARSINOÉ
Well! Mighty clever language you've employed!
I never thought you'd be so—paranoid!
You seem to fear, my dear, this frank exposure.
I fear I rattled your refined composure!

CÉLIMÈNE
No! not at all! I totally agree.
Let's both "advise" each other RUTHLESSLY!
Exchange reproofs, and take it to extremes:
Annihilate each other's self-esteems!
But, you, have YOU the bravery and zeal
To tell me EVERYTHING you feel?
And I, have I the courage to be true?
Tell you exactly what I think of YOU?

ARSINOÉ
Ah . . . Madam . . . Well . . . I don't know what to
    say!
I didn't mean to bother you in any way . . .

CÉLIMÈNE
But praise and blame—how big a scold you are—
They're relative to just how OLD you are.
My own's a "live and let live" attitude.
Perhaps, when I am old, I'll be a prude;
When I am wrinkled, gray, and sag like you
I'm sure I'll get derogatory, too!
YOUR time is running out, but I've got plenty!
And I've no wish to be a prude at twenty!

ARSINOÉ
Yes. Adolescence makes you SO high-strung!
My dear, you're just so awfully, AWFULLY young!
You seem, my little child, just filled with rage.
I know: you're at that "very awkward age,"
But still, I fail to understand your ire,
Or why it's I who's in your line of fire.

CÉLIMÈNE
And I, I fail to understand why you
Come here to roast me on this moral barbecue!
Can I help it if men find me attractive?
And don't you think your anger's—retroactive?

Oh yes! Men follow me, and you're—"concerned,"
That's just the envy of a woman spurned!
You'd like to bring their visits to a halt:
It's jealousy, that's all! IT'S NOT MY FAULT!
The field is free to all, Arsinoé:
Go get a man; I won't be in your way.

ARSINOÉ
You really think I'm desperate like you?
My dear, I've got much better things to do!
What, don't you think I have a comprehension
Of what you PAY to get all this attention?
You think you're intellectually endowed?
Enough to captivate THIS snobbish crowd?
You think they find you virtuous? Or witty?
Or pay you court because you're young and pretty?
Ah, no, dear, people aren't quite THAT blind—
You think these beaux are all excited by your
    MIND?
You get my points—I think. That flock of suitors?
They're nothing but a gaggle of freebooters!
Fine ladies should be gentle, pure, complex,
Not driven to seduce the whole male sex.
Accumulating "conquests" may be nice—
Until you total up the final price!
So don't disdain those women who stay chaste;
Conceit bequeathes a bitter aftertaste.
If I were ENVIOUS of your affairs,
I'd find some WHORE, and study what SHE
    wears.
I'd put it on, and then make my advance
On every undulating thing in pants!

CÉLIMÈNE
Go right ahead, my dear, if that's your—bent.
It seems a riveting experiment!!!!
Go on . . . !

ARSINOÉ
[barely restraining herself from coming to blows]
        ENOUGH, my dear, of this discussion!
Before we live to see its repercussion!
I'll take my leave. I would have left before
But I don't hear my coachman at the door!

CÉLIMÈNE
Don't leave on MY account. Why don't you stay?
You're not demanded elsewhere, anyway!
But I won't tire you with further talk,
For here's Alceste: I know him by his walk.

[Alceste storms in, and is immediately distracted by seeing Arsinoé.]

CÉLIMÈNE

This gentleman is known for 's perfect timing
He comes when there's NO CHANCE for social
   climbing!
Alceste, I'm going off to—write a letter,
But YOU can entertain this "lady" better.
Excuse my rudeness, dear Arsinoé,
But let me tell you: YOU HAVE MADE MY DAY!

[Célimène leaves.]

ARSINOÉ

Monsieur, I don't mean to be burdensome
I'm just here waiting for my coach to come . . .
But I'm thrilled, finally, to have the chance
To tell you: YOU'RE THE GREATEST MAN IN
   FRANCE!
I'm sorry; you must hear this all the time,
But—GOD PROTECT ME!—You're sublime!
I've not confessed this to a sole inquirer,
But I'm your secretest admirer.
And I have NO IDEA why the court
Makes fun of you and always cuts you short!
They treat you like some sort of pest!
You've every right to rage at them, Alceste!

ALCESTE

I, Madame? Rage? What do you think I am?
Condemn the court? You think I give a damn?
I haven't done, nor would do, ANYTHING
To seek consideration from the King.

ARSINOÉ

Not EVERYONE obtaining royal praise
Acquires it in underhanded ways.
Surely merit, brains, ability,
And intellectual facility,
Must . . .

ALCESTE

      No! They don't! They won't BUY royal
   love!
Let's DROP this subject that you're speaking of.
You think the King's the wisdom, or the time
To render up a "merit" paradigm?

ARSINOÉ

But merit rises to the top, I say!
And YOUR worth's spoken of 'most every day!
Why just last night I was at two fine houses,
And oh, the PRAISE that just your NAME arouses!

ALCESTE

Come down to earth, Madam! Praise now is cheap.
The voice of criticism's gone to sleep!
EVERYTHING is totally FANTASTIC!
Ovations? Standing! Reviews? Bombastic!
Everyman's a hero: hear what they say
About my ineffectual valet!

ARSINOÉ

But YOU, Alceste, deserve the King's attention.
An office! Not just honorable mention!
Indeed, I volunteer to be the ointment
To lubricate the wheels for your appointment!
I have some friends who'll press your case at court;
One's just been named the King's latrine escort!

ALCESTE

What would I DO at court, Madam, I pray?
My sentiments go all the other way.
I fear the God who made me didn't plant
My seed to bloom as "royal sycophant."
I don't have the necessary graces
The oily words, the multiplying faces;
I only can be—you see—very frank.
In Court, that means that you're known as a crank!
And those whose frank opinions remain STRONG?
They just don't stick around for very long.
Outside the Court, of course, one lives without
Those privileges that much now's made about.
And yet I think it infinitely better
NOT to be a socialite pacesetter!
Not to be, in other words, always obsequious,
Nor in praising others: always devious;
Nor to bow and scrape to every Mademoiselle,
Nor flatter those god damn marquises from Hell!

ARSINOÉ

Let's drop the subject of the court. Agreed!
But your affair HERE must be remedied.
I hate, Alceste, to speak—well—out of school
But Célimène! She plays you for a fool!
Her scorn! Her other men! Alceste, forget her!
You certainly deserve—well—SOMEONE
   BETTER!

ALCESTE
[through gritted teeth]
I'm just afraid I don't qute comprehend . . .
Good **Madame**, isn't Célimène—your friend?

ARSINOÉ

YES! She is! But my conscience makes me say it!
The passion in my heart: I must obey it!

I've suffered long enough: you've suffered too!
You cherish her, but SHE DOES *NOT* LOVE YOU!

ALCESTE

*[pause]*Thank you, Madam, for that information.
I'm very grateful for this conversation.

ARSINOÉ

Despite the fact that Célimène's my friend
I fear that I—no longer can pretend:
Alceste, she has been faking from the start!

ALCESTE

Perhaps. Who REALLY knows what's in her heart?
But why are YOU now telling me all this?
Do you delight in setting things amiss?

ARSINOÉ

Well, wallow in ignorance, then, if you want!
I'm happy NOT to be your confidant . . .

ALCESTE

NO! But this assertion you've brought up:
It's still just rumors, hints, and wild gossip.
I need—before exploding through the roof,
Dammit, Arsinoé, I NEED SOME PROOF!

ARSINOÉ

You've said enough, my friend. Leave it to me!
You soon will see—all you could wish to see:
Ocular proof of her inconstancies!
Her rampant, faithless infidelities!
Her lovers' names! They'd fill a hefty tome . . .
I'll tell you more, but please, first, take me home.
And if this throws you into desolation . . .
I'm sure I can provide SOME consolation.

[Arsinoé and Alceste leave.]

——————— ACT FOUR ———————

[Eliante and Philinte enter.]

PHILINTE

There's NO ONE who's more bullheaded than he!
No, no one, Eliante! Nor could there be!
No compromise, no deals; what did he want?
He wouldn't take back ONE WORD to Oronte!
And never has there been a dumber case!
Bizarre in court; imprudent anyplace!
"Oh, no," he stated, "I meant what I said.
Oronte should give up writing— and go
    lawnbowling instead!
Why must he come to me? That neophyte?

Why must he versify? WHY MUST HE WRITE?
There're lots of things to do to pass the time,
Why must he try to be profound—IN RHYME?
Oronte's a fashionable sort, a noble fop,
But then he grabs a pen: WHY, WHY? STOP!
    STOP!
You want some praise, Oronte? OKAY! You're great
At dancing, riding, fencing, dining late.
But for your verse: Well, I'm your loyal servant
So let me say—my feeling here is fervent—
Your verses stink; a poet you are not!
And you—if you continue—should be shot!"
Well, that's Alceste. But then he settled down.
And with a milder tone, made his concession to the
    crown.
"Oronte, I really do apologize
I'm very difficult, I realize.
I only wish your poem was—somewhat better."
And then they EACH claimed EACH each other's
    debtor!
Alceste's outrageous! nonetheless, endearing.
And that concluded this outlandish hearing.

ELIANTE

I must admit, I cannot help admiring
A man who's honesty is so—inspiring.
I think Alceste's integrity's heroic.
Unknown today: it's ancient; protozoic!
His eccentricities are only—good!
I think he's mostly just misunderstood.

PHILINTE

You just amaze me speaking in this fashion!
Alceste's a man CONSUMED by violent passion.
He's filled with rage, with jealousy and hate;
What kind of "love" can this man contemplate?
Much less to love your cousin, Célimène!
Why he's the most UNREASONABLE of men!

ELIANTE

The heart, you must admit, though, has its reasons,
And those who love must love in all four seasons.
There's not one book of rules to give direction
As to just what comprises true affection.

PHILINTE

You think she actually loves him then?

ELIANTE

You never really know with Célimène.
How do you ever know if it's "true love"?
Do lovers know what they are thinking of?

She may not know herself—why very often
We rail at love—but then our feelings soften . . .

PHILINTE

I think Alceste can only ask for trouble!
Your cousin ALWAYS seems to burst his bubble!
And that's just how she is! I wish Alceste
Would turn his eye to someone—less obsessed
With social standing. Eliante, I feel
A match 'twixt him and YOU would be—ideal!

ELIANTE

Let me be honest. In all verity . . .
In total, absolute sincerity . . .
I don't oppose his love for Célimène!
Why, he loves her, and she loves—lots of men!
Indeed, were *I* the only one involved
I'd strive to have her other loves—dissolved!
But if she WON'T, and if Alceste should stray . . .
Why then, sure . . . let him cast his eye MY way,
I would be open to his proposition,
Since I've a—pro-Alceste predisposition.

PHILINTE

And I, I don't oppose his love—or yours!
But may we move beyond these metaphors?
There's more than just the two of you, or three!
I'm saying, Eliante, please, think of ME.
If things between YOU two do not work out
Then THIS is what I'd like to talk about:
If you don't love Alceste, or if you can't,
Why then I ask you: THINK ABOUT PHILINTE,
Whose happiness would bloom, and never cease!
You've no IDEA what passions you'd release!

ELIANTE

No metaphors? . . .

PHILINTE

                    Madam, I use no art.
I'm speaking from the bottom of my heart.
Here comes Alceste, he's in a state of pique . . .
I'll wait for an occasion; THEN I'll speak.

[Alceste enters.]

ALCESTE

Eliante! Thank God you're here! I'm so upset!
I want them all thrown down the oubliette!

ELIANTE

Who? What? What on earth has happened to you?

ALCESTE

It kills me just to think it might be true!
The world could break apart; it could explode,
Yet be but preface to THIS episode. . . .
I'm through . . . She loves . . . I don't know how to
    say it!

ELIANTE

Relax, Alceste. Try, maybe, to downplay it . . .

ALCESTE

O, Unjust God! How could you mix such grace
With all the vices of the human race?

ELIANTE

Alceste, what happened?

ALCESTE

                    I've been devastated!
Betrayed, Destroyed, Annulled, Assassinated!
You never will believe this, Eliante:
But Célimène's betrayed me—with Oronte!

ELIANTE

Do you have any—evidence for this?

PHILINTE

Perhaps your judgment is a bit remiss:
A jealous lover's fantasy, I'm sure . . .

ALCESTE

Mind your own damn business here, Monsieur!
Her guilt is all but irrefutable!
[pulling out a letter and showing it to Eliante]
Her writing: look: it's indisputable!
This letter to Oronte—your cousin wrote!
I'm utterly disgraced. I'll cut my throat!
Oronte, that ostentatious, fey "artiste"
Oronte, the one I thought she liked the least!

PHILINTE

Appearances, Alceste, can be misleading.
And letters lend themselves to gross misreading.

ALCESTE

I'm telling you once more, Philinte, BUTT OUT!
There's nothing here that YOU can talk about.

ELIANTE

Compose yourself, Alceste. What you must do . . .

ALCESTE

Not me! What's to be done now's up to YOU.
You, Eliante: YOU'll help me free my soul
From Célimène's contemptible control!
Avenge me for your cousin's treachery!

Avenge my love: and her foul lechery!
Avenge me on that lying, cheating tart!

ELIANTE
Avenge you? How?

ALCESTE
                 Here, Madam, take my heart!
Accept it, Eliante, and make me free;
We'll make your cousin BURN with jealousy!
I'll—smother you with amorous attentions,
Kiss you in public, defy all the conventions,
Write poems to you, write elegies as well;
We'll make that rotten bitch—just MAD AS HELL.

ELIANTE
You're suffering, so I'm at your disposal,
But THIS, Alceste, 's a very strange proposal.
And are you CERTAIN that you aren't WRONG?
In which case you'll soon sing a different song:
"YESSSS, what's-your-name???! Oh, what a fool am
    I!
We've—well—MADE UP, you see! So, sorry! 'Bye!"
Love that bounces back from a rejection
Rarely leads to PERMANENT affection!
The love that's turned to hate—comes back again,
HATE's what's inconstant—certainly in men!

ALCESTE
No! Never! With me? No! I'm resolute!
There is no turning back; that's absolute!
NOTHING can alter my mind about this!
And any OTHER thoughts you have: dismiss!

[Célimène enters.]

Ah, there she is. Look, see how riled I am?
I'll throw the book at her; you'll see, Madame!
I'll shame her; taunt her; damn her too,
And THEN I'll give my loving heart to you.

[Philinte and Eliante leave.]

O God, please keep me calm and politic . . .

CÉLIMÈNE
Alceste! What's wrong? You look as if you're—sick!
Breathe deeply, there! Now, please, regain
   control . . .
You look like you just crawled out of a hole . . .

ALCESTE
I did! A hole where all the horrors dwell!
A hole that was my heart! A hole of Hell!

It's Hell on Earth. There're devils here, it's true,
Who've never seen a creature vile as you!

CÉLIMÈNE
Is this some sort of ploy—or social gaffe?

ALCESTE
Stop making fun of me! Goddamn, don't laugh!
You should be red with shame for what you've
   done!
In wickedness, there's no comparison!
O Célimène, I knew it from the start.
From day one I felt—tremors in my heart,
And so I've been tormented with suspicion,
I've tossed and turned with hopeless indecision,
And, quite despite your supersubtle lying,
I quickly found you—slightly horrifying.
So—don't you think I'll let this matter rest.
No, "Vengeance is mine"—here saith Alceste!
You see, we've no control of our emotions!
We're tossed, we little dinghies, on love's oceans,
And each of us is free to drop our anchor
Anywhere we choose: so why this rancor?
Okay, I'll tell you why! YOU LED ME ON!
When you did that, you crossed the Rubicon!
Why couldn't you refuse me from the start?
Why did you need to break my foolish heart?
But no! You gave such tender looks and sighs
As to ensnare my soul through those pure eyes.
It's treason! Rape! Emotional seduction!
Which should call forth a terrible destruction!
Oh yes! Oh, yes! And don't think I won't do it!
You think I can restrain myself? Yes??? SCREW IT!
You've stabbed me through the heart, I cannot
   breathe!
I cannot think: I RAGE! I STORM! I SEETHE!
Prepare yourself: Pray GOD takes care of you,
For I—no longer care what harm I do!

CÉLIMÈNE
What is this nonsense? Has your wit declined,
Or is it, Alceste, that you've lost your mind?

ALCESTE
I've lost it, Yes! The moment that we met!
My mind was poisoned by a cheap coquette!
Whom I believed in all sincerity
But she succeeded in bewitching me.

CÉLIMÈNE
Bewitched? Betrayed? Alceste, what's this about?

ALCESTE

Oh don't pretend, two-timer, truth will out!
I've evidence, you see, to prove my case.
Here, look at this! Your guilt here's prima-face!
This love note here, this *billet-doux*, I found it!
It's in your hand: don't try to sneak around it!

CÉLIMÈNE

Is THIS the matter's put you in this snit?

ALCESTE

You should be mortified! Just look at it!

CÉLIMÈNE

And why on earth should I be mortified?

ALCESTE

So! Lying and audacity collide!
It's—yes—unsigned, but do you disown this note?

CÉLIMÈNE

Disown what I unquestionably wrote?

ALCESTE

You wrote it! Yes! Then don't act so confused!
By your own writing you are self-accused!

CÉLIMÈNE

You're just the strangest man I've ever known.

ALCESTE

ME! Me, strange? YOU'RE brazen to the bone!
This letter to Oronte: why, it's outrageous!
I'm only glad that shame is not contagious!

CÉLIMÈNE

Oronte! Who said this letter was for him?

ALCESTE

So I was told. Perhaps—a pseudonym.
Well, say it's NOT for him then: Fine! Okay!
For someone else: there's still all hell to pay
'Cause it's to someone, see, with whom you're
smitten!

CÉLIMÈNE

Suppose that to a WOMAN it was written?
Would you be hurt? Or would that be perversion?

ALCESTE

Bravo! A clever twist! A sly diversion!
A detour from the muddy road ahead
Which proves, precisely, EVERYTHING I SAID!
You think I'd fall for that debating trick?
You think I'm—What? Some gauche, provincial
hick?
Come on then, try again, dare number two:

A second ruse to make your lies look true!
Prove that these words of love—this is terrific—
Could ever NOT be thought gender-specific!
This is to a WOMAN? 'Scuse me while I throw up!
Explain these words . . .

CÉLIMÈNE

Alceste, why don't you
grow up?!
Just who are you? The Grand Inquisitor?
Your NOSE offends me, Sir. And there's the door.

ALCESTE

There's no point getting angry! Just explain
To WHOM, exactly, these words here pertain . . .

CÉLIMÈNE

No! Give it up, Alceste, it's only ink!
And no one gives a damn here WHAT you think.

ALCESTE

Just tell me, please; PLEASE, and this'll be the end;
Tell me this letter's to a FEMALE friend!

CÉLIMÈNE

Oh, no; it's to Oronte. And you should know it!
He's one terrific guy—and super poet!
I LOVE Oronte; he's beautiful and kind;
I LOVE to probe his graceful, brilliant mind!
WHATEVER you accuse me of: it's true!
And I'll admit—each crime you want me to!

ALCESTE
[aside]
Ahhhhhhh!
Has anybody ever been so cruel?
Has any man endured such ridicule?
I show her proof of her perfidity,
And she responds—by castigating ME!
MY pain, MY fears—she knows just where to
poke . . .
And yet she thinks that everything's a JOKE!
Good God; why can't I—put her, now, behind me?
It's just my heart—can't break the ties that bind
me;
Nor work up to the hatred it should hold
Towards this—*femme fatale* that I behold.
[to Célimène]
Well! You have learned a very subtle art:
You know how to orchestrate my heart!
And how to take the best advantage of
My catastrophically excessive love!
All right! Just tell me you don't love Oronte!

And no more feigning guilt: I only want
To hear this letter's NOT FOR HIM; Okay?
I will accept—whatever you might say.
In fact; if you could just PRETEND it's true,
I'll do my utmost to believe in you.

CÉLIMÈNE

Are you some kind of NUT? This hoop-de-do
Is what I get, I see, for loving you!
What monumental nerve! You recommend
That I should sink so low as to PRETEND?
If I loved someone ELSE; and don't you doubt it,
I'd tell you so; Why would I LIE about it?
I SAID I loved you—you remain nonplussed!
I thought I'd earned, by now, a little trust!
Don't my assurances have any weight?
Must words of love be turned to words of hate?
Besides, you know it's difficult these days
For girls to talk to men in tender ways.
The laws state ANY ardent sentiments
May be construed as giving our "consents"
To all that follows: This you'd have me do?
Right? Let myself get raped because of you?
But even so, I gave to you my promise,
And YOU continued playing Doubting Thomas!
Get out! I've had it with your dark suspicions!
You don't deserve my love with these conditions!
Oh, GOD, I'm stupid! I just can't BELIEVE
That I'm still fond of you. I'M SO NAIVE!
You wait: there're LOTS of young guys hereabout;
I'll give you something to get mad about!

ALCESTE

You wanton witch! Who has me on my knees.
You still can charm and torture as you please.
It doesn't matter. Destiny is all.
At your seductive feet, I hereby fall.
Do with me as you will, I am your own.
Trample me, kick me, beat me till I moan.

CÉLIMÈNE

No. You don't love me the right way at all.

ALCESTE

I LOVE YOU! Past all law or protocol!
Indeed, dear Célimène, I have this dream:
With sort of a Pygmalion-like theme.
I fantasize that you were born dirt poor;
Unloved, and plain, and treated like a whore,
No rank, no name, a horrible existence,
You smell so bad that DOGS would keep their
    distance.

Then in this dream, I'd reach far down to save you.
And then, you'd say, a whole new life I gave you!
So there's my fantasy! True love, true glory!
The planet's most magnificent love story!

CÉLIMÈNE

A putrifying form of love, indeed!
Please, let me pray to God you don't succeed!

*[Du Bois enters furtively, dressed for travel and
carrying a suitcase.]*

But look, your man Du Bois, why's he tip-toeing?

ALCESTE

Du Bois? What is this get-up? Where're you going?
What's up?

DU BOIS

                        Monsieur . . .

ALCESTE

                                    What's going on?

DU BOIS

                                                Strange
    things!

ALCESTE

Like what?

DU BOIS

                        There's lots of trouble in the wings!

ALCESTE

Like what?

DU BOIS

                        . . . In front of her?

ALCESTE

                                    Of course! Speak out!

DU BOIS

We must . . . The lady . . .

ALCESTE

                                    Damn! What's this
    about??
"We must . . ." WHAT, man?

DU BOIS

                                        We've got to hit the
    street!

ALCESTE

We WHAT?

DU BOIS

                        . . . Must sound the trumpet of retreat!

ALCESTE
But why?

DU BOIS
                And get the Hell—'scuse—out of here!

ALCESTE
Because . . . ?

DU BOIS
                    Andiamo! Schnell! Il faut partir!

ALCESTE
But what's the REASON for your saying so?

DU BOIS
The reason, sir, is that you have to go!

ALCESTE
Please don't count, Du Bois, on my apologies
If I should STRANGLE YOU for these tautologies!

DU BOIS
Oh, Sir! There was a man, sir! In a cape,
He had an evil smile and grotesque shape!
He left a paper in your dining room!
It was the Devil's writing, I assume,
All legal language, and about your suit!
I think the Devil, sir, will prosecute!

ALCESTE
You fool! What does this paper have to do
With skipping town? What's this world coming to?

DU BOIS
Ah, well, there was another man, you see,
Who came an hour later. That man, he—
You know him well, he visits all the time,
And when he can't find you about, then I'm
The one he sees: he thinks it's all the same
If you or I . . . Wait! I forgot his name!

ALCESTE
I don't care WHAT his name is! Idiot!

DU BOIS
One of your friends, anyway. A pity; it
Will come to me, I think. [Alceste roars at him.]
                Ah, yes! Alceste,
He told me you were threatened with arrest!

ALCESTE
For what? I haven't broken any laws!

DU BOIS
He didn't say: he said it's just "because."
He did ask me for paper, then he wrote
Sort of an all-explanatory note.

ALCESTE
Well, give it to me.

                [Du Bois fumbles for the letter.]

CÉLIMÈNE
                What's all this about?

ALCESTE
Who knows? Let's only hope the truth comes out.
Well, where's the note then, imbecile?

                [Du Bois panics, unable to find it.]

DU BOIS
I think I left it on the windowsill!

ALCESTE
I'll kill him!!!

CÉLIMÈNE
                . . . Please! Control yourself, Alceste.
You'll straighten things out first, if you know best.

ALCESTE
So, fate, again, whatever I might do
Prevents my winding up this talk with you!
But I'm not giving up without a fight!
And so, my dear, expect me back tonight.

[Alceste leaves with Du Bois; then Célimène also leaves
                the stage. Alceste enters with Philinte.]

————————— ACT FIVE —————————

ALCESTE
My mind's entirely made up, I tell you!

PHILINTE
But nothing's happened yet that should compel
    you . . .

ALCESTE
No! I'm out of here! Talk all you wish!
This place is HIDEOUS! No, nightmarish!
This century's gone totally perverse!
Society has plunged from bad to worse!
I'm getting out! You were at court today:
I stood for honor, truth, and dignity: Okay?
They all agreed that I was in the right:
I should have won my case with scarce a fight!
The Scales of Justice, though, must have criss-
    crossed:
A nod here, wink there; suddenly, I'd LOST!
A slimy rat that you and I despise

Had had his way: through influence and lies!
What good are all the rules when THIS begins?
He cuts my throat; and, in return, HE WINS!
You saw his diamond ring, his ermine gown
'Round HERE they'd beat the ten commandments
    down!
And then he claimed that I should be arrested
'Cause he had been, can you believe, "Alcested!"
Oh yes! And then he shows this obscene book
He says I wrote: well you, Philinte, can look
At it and know that I could NEVER write it.
But how in Hell am I supposed to fight it?
When, then, Oronte, who's on his side, attests:
"Oh yes, I recognize the writing: it's Alceste's!"
Oronte! who dines bi-weekly with the King,
To whom I've been sincere in everything,
Who comes to me, unasked, so's I'd advise
Him on his "literary merchandise!"
And just because I tell him what I think,
Not coloring my each word primrose-pink,
He joins my enemies in this sedition
Saying I have spoiled his First Edition!
He won't forgive me! It's unbearable!
And just because I thought his poem was terrible!
It's ALL HUMANITY that's been corrupted!
Yes: ever since man's arrogance erupted:
This zeal for fame, for riches, for positions;
For cartloads of expensive acquisitions!
And so it's: "Goodbye, sick society!"
This world is too unscrupulous for me!
We're turning cannibal; it's man eat man
I'm getting out, Philinte, while I still can.

PHILINTE
Just wait, Alceste; slow down a little bit.
't's not QUITE so awful—when you think of it!
Those patent lies you heard in court today—
They've not yet caused you harm—in any way!
In fact, if you would just hold off till later
Those lies will come to haunt their procreator.

ALCESTE
Who, him? Why should he care? The gall he has!
Another scandal gives him more—pizzazz!
He has a license to prevaricate
As long as he can—"socially communicate!"

PHILINTE
No, look, Alceste; this case has just begun.
You're not in jail; what's done can be UNdone.
The whole world knows you got a rotten deal;

You're bound to win your case—on an appeal!
So take a deep breath, reapproach the bar,
And plead your . . .

ALCESTE
                           No! I'll leave things as they are!
Let's let the world see JUST how underhand
The court behaved. I'll let the verdict stand!
Let history record that I was cheated—
And show how cavalierly I was treated!
And let posterity evaluate me then:
A martyr to the wickedness of men!
Yes, it will cost me twenty thousand francs!
The price is cheap, if I can say "No thanks!"
I hereby abdicate the human race!
I hate its smarmy, stinking, slimy face!

PHILINTE
But . . . in the end . . .

ALCESTE
                           . . . WE END! I'm AT my
    end.
You've any other plan to recommend?
Are you still thinking I can find excuses
For these more-than-despicable abuses?

PHILINTE
No: I agree with everything you said
It's influence that puts a man ahead.
Plus bribes, and courtroom tricks, and social ties—
You're right! and men SHOULD function
    otherwise.
But if morality is undermined
You still can't just withdraw from all mankind!
Though human weakness isn't great to see
At least it promulgates philosophy!
And with YOUR intellectual persistence
You could examine all human existence
With objectivity! With charm and wit!
With elegant dispasssion: think of it!
Consider all life adult education!
Abstractions, great ideas, argumentation!
A man with your opinions should be heard . . .

ALCESTE
Your reasoning's so good—that you're absurd!
You're oratorically correct, Philinte,
But wasting time with sentimental cant!
Good "reasoning" would have me step aside;
I don't know what to say, or what to hide,
I'm either flailing for some long-lost cause

Or inanely making horrible *faux pas*.
But leave me now to wait for Célimène.
I've asked her here to speak with me again
About a new proposal I have made.
Tonight, I plan to end this—masquerade.

PHILINTE
Let's first get Eliante; I know she's waited . . .

ALCESTE
No, no! You go! I'm far too agitated.
Go on, find Eliante! *[Philinte starts to speak.]* Put it to
  rest!
I'll find some corner and just be depressed.

PHILINTE
You aren't, for yourself, much company!
I'll get Eliante to come down presently.

*[Philinte leaves; Oronte enters with Célimène; they
don't, at first, see Alceste in his corner.]*

ORONTE
Madam, it's up to YOU to formally declare
If you and I . . . if WE . . . comprise—a pair!
I cannot tolerate much more suspense—
You shouldn't STILL be sitting on the fence!
And if my blazing heart has won your passion
Then tell me so, in some—straightforward fashion!
And give me PROOF, which, in your situation
Means keeping that ALCESTE from visitation!
Please, Madam, end these silly capers
By sending the buffoon his walking papers!

CÉLIMÈNE
But how can you speak of Alceste that way?
You said you LOVED him earlier today!

ORONTE
I don't think I can make things any clearer.
The question is: just whom do you hold dearer?
Choose, Célimène, which one of us you want:
I yield to you: it's Alceste or Oronte!

[Alceste comes forward.]

ALCESTE
Oronte is right, Madame, it's time to choose.
One of us must win, and one must lose.
Our passions are the same: we need to know
SPECIFICALLY, which way YOUR passions flow.
We must know NOW; we're not endlessly long-
  lived
So, Célimène: the moment has arrived!

ORONTE
I'd no IDEA, Monsieur, that you were here!
I'd NEVER think, you know, to interfere!

ALCESTE
Well, jealous or not, I have no plans to
Cut Célimène in half to share with you.

ORONTE
Of course not! So, if she prefers you, then . . .

ALCESTE
Or you, Oronte . . . Which is it, Célimène? . . .

ORONTE
If it's not me—I'll leave here right away!

ALCESTE
If it's not me—It's over yesterday!

ORONTE
Madame: Proceed: You may speak freely here!

ALCESTE
Madame: Agreed! You may speak without fear!

ORONTE
You only have to say who you'll anoint!

ALCESTE
It only takes one word! Or, you can POINT!

ORONTE
Well . . . ? Your silence seems almost . . . derisive.

ALCESTE
Well . . . ? You're altogether INDECISIVE!

CÉLIMÈNE
Good God! Have you completely lost your minds?
Are your heads embedded deep up your behinds?
I have no problem making such a choice,
Nor does it bother me to give my views a voice;
I am not SPLIT between you two at all;
In truth, this is a very SIMPLE call,
But yet, to tell the truth, it would be rude,
And would produce but little gratitude
To give you two some phobia-abatement
By making such a naked public statement!
I think my heart is in a better place
Here, in my breast; not thrown in someone's face!
Those that I love don't need my words in print.
Those who love ME, know how to take a hint.

ORONTE
No hints! Your solemn word: I'll understand it!
I'll take what comes . . .

ALCESTE

               YES, me, too; I demand it!
Your PUBLIC vow is what I want the most!
Ah, Célimène, I've got you diagnosed:
You'd like to have us ALL! All—at your feet!
You LOVE it when your paramours compete!
But "playing time" is past: now you must show:
Say "yes" to one, and to the other, "No!"
Or don't say anything! Look, I'll construe
Your SILENCE as your answer: THAT WE'RE
    THROUGH!

ORONTE

Yes, right, Alceste! Right, yes, I agree!
And, Célimène; I say: THE SAME WITH ME!

CÉLIMÈNE

I find "confessions" irritating, sirs.
Is this to what St. Augustine refers?
I think I TOLD YOU why you'll have to wait;

[Eliante arrives.]

Here's Eliante: Ask HER to arbitrate!
Oh, Cousin, Look! You see—I am attacked!
They're both in league: How'm I s'posed to react?
They're forcing me to straightaway decide
Which one of THEM I want HERE at my side!
And just like that! I'm s'posed to indicate
Which one I'll love, and which one—terminate.
Have you ever heard of ANYTHING so dumb?

ELIANTE

Please, don't ask me. I might turn quarrelsome.
Or overidealistic. Or uncouth.
For MY heart stands with those—who speak the
    truth.

ORONTE

[to Célimène] You see, there're no excuses now for
    stalling.

ALCESTE

Your "little detours" now are REALLY galling.

ORONTE

Just speak! Two words. Ad lib! Speak off the cuff!

ALCESTE

Or just say NOTHING: THAT will be enough!

ORONTE

ONE word. Just one! One word and I will go!

ALCESTE

Or with your SILENCE, Madam: JUST SAY NO!

[Acaste, Clitandre, Arsinoé, and Philinte arrive.]

ACASTE

Good madam, by your leave, we both have come
To settle something . . . Well, it's troublesome!

CLITANDRE

It's fortunate, Monsieurs, that YOU'RE here too:
This matter's also of concern to you!

ARSINOÉ

You must be shocked at seeing ME again,
But I've been brought by these two gentlemen,
Who found me at my house, and said that you . . .
But, Célimène, I KNEW it wasn't true!
Your honor's unimpeachable; sublime!
You NEVER could commit so vile a crime!
So I rejected ALL their savage claims,
And as your FRIEND (forGET you called me
    names!!),
I'm here with them, to watch you speak with
    candor
Repudiating all their vicious slander!

ACASTE

Madame, will it rattle your composure
If I give this document exposure?
Your letter to Clitandre, Friday last?

CLITANDRE

And your *billet-doux*, last Thursday, to Acaste?

ACASTE

Gentlemen. I think we know the writing.
We ALL, in days gone by, found it exciting
To see this dainty little hand! Agreed?
But things have changed, I think, sirs: let me read:

> *"Dear Clitandre. It's very silly of you to get angry
> at me just for having a good time, and for having
> fun when you're not there! That's absurd; you
> should apologize. That idiotic Viscount . . ."*

I wish he were here!

> *"That idiotic Viscount, who told you about this, is a
> total fool; he spent our entire visit the other day
> spitting into the punchbowl, so he could watch those
> stupid little concentric rings spread out! Disgusting!
> And as for that little Marquis . . ."*

That's me, I'm afraid . . .

> *"As for that little Marquis, who limply held my hand
> most of yesterday afternoon, his mind is even tinier
> than his you-know-what (his body, of course!), and
> his notion of chivalry is some sort of idiotic cloak-*

and-dagger routine. And the horrible man with the green ribbons . . ."

[to Alceste] That's you, sir:

"And the ribbon man: well, he's at least amusing with his hilarious tirades about this and that; sometimes he's almost cute, but most of the time, I must say, he's the most BORING man on the face of the earth. Then, of course, there's the 'man of the golden vest . . .'"

[to Oronte] That's you . . .

"Old vest-i-coat thinks himself a writer, no matter what anybody says, and despite the fact that he hasn't got a single TRACE of talent! I HATE having to listen to him recite, or even speak; his prose is even more repulsive than his verse!

Understand, therefore, my dear Clitandre: My life these days is nowhere NEAR as exciting as you imagine; it's actually quite dreary, and I long for YOUR company, so as to season these tedious days wiuth the attentions of someone who truly loves me. Your dearest, Célimène."

CLITANDRE
Now hear what she REALLY thinks of ME:

"Dear Acaste. That marquis Clitandre you keep worrying about: he's the last man in the WORLD I would ever be interested in! He must be crazy to think I love him: YOU must be even crazier to have the remotest concern about it! Please come and see me more often, Acaste, so that the old fool finally catches on! Your loving Célimène."

Quite elegantly put. Aren't we enthralled?
I think we ALL know JUST what this is called!
Enough! Come on, Acaste, we'll find a crowd
Who'd LOVE to hear these letters read out aloud.

ACASTE
My sentiments exactly, dear Marquis.
Madame, now, THIS [snaps his fingers] is what you
    mean to me!
You aren't worth my anger. So—goodbye!
You'll find that we—have better fish to fry!

[Acaste and Clitandre leave.]

ORONTE
So, after all those tender words to me—
You've TORN ME ALL TO SHREDS! What
    treachery!
You've got your moral values upside-down:
You save your heart—for EVERY MAN IN TOWN!
Goodbye. I've been your dupe too long, it's true

But THANKS—for showing me the (puke) real
    you.
My heart's my own again: I won't be back,
You—literary nymphomaniac!
[to Alceste] Of course, you know that I won't
    meddle, sir,
In any plans that YOU could have for her.

[Oronte leaves.]

ARSINOÉ
How simply horrible! Disgusting! Cheap!
I can't keep quiet! No! It makes me—weep!
Has anyone behaved so badly—ever?
I'd never stick MY nose in . . . No, I'd NEVER . . .
BUT, poor Alceste, just see how he's been hurt!
He worshipped you; you tawdry little flirt!
But he—a man of honor, grace, and skill,
Deserves . . .

ALCESTE
                Good Lord, Arsinoé! Be still!
I'll handle my OWN business, if you please
Without unnecessary flatteries!
There's no need YOU should join in this attack,
Since there's no way that I could pay you back.
For if I were to seek another's love,
It never would be YOURS that I'd think of!

ARSINOÉ
And what makes you presume, sir, as you do,
That I've the slightest interest in YOU?
What vanity! Conceit! You egotist!
No wonder you were utterly dismissed!
You think I'd go for somone SHE rejected?
You really thought that YOU'RE what I expected?
Don't fool yourself: And get off that high horse!
No, you and I: we'll have NO intercourse!
Go on, pant after Célimène! Yes, Sir,
I think you've made a PROPER MATCH with her!
    [exits]

ALCESTE
Please notice that I haven't yet been heard,
Though everybody ELSE has had his word!
Acaste, Clitandre, Arsinoé, Oronte,
They've spoken. Now . . .

CÉLIMÈNE
                            Go on, say what you
    want!
You're in the right this time, so have your say!
Reproach me, scold me, have a holiday!

I'm in the wrong, you're right! I've no defense,
I've wronged you and accept the consequence!
The others made me mad, they're just like me;
But YOU sir, have this great integrity.
I KNOW just how my guilt looks in your eyes,
Your anger's justified; go on, chastise:
I've sinned; yes! And I know what must await me
Since you have every reason now to hate me.
Go on, rip me apart . . .

ALCESTE

                I wish I could!
I wish, vile traitor, that my heart was wood,
Or that my tenderness could turn to hate,
So that my anger would predominate!
[to Eliante and Philinte] You see, I'm so infatuated
My sense of justice has deactivated!
Nor is that all; you know I can't forgo her!
So: stay, and watch me sink down even lower;
We men! We're not so wise; no, we're the dregs:
Our minds remain somewhere between our legs.
[to Célimène] Well, traitor, I'll forgive you one more
    time,
And, in my heart, absolve you from all crime,
The which, in what I'll call a "lover's truth"
I'll count—an indiscretion of your youth;
As long, that is, as you become, with me
Expatriated from humanity.
Yes, I shall flee the madding multitude
And go to find some—desert solitude,
And you can follow me! And in that way
You can repair the harm you've done today.
This scandal is atrocious, yes, it's true,
But I'll still take a crack at loving you.

CÉLIMÈNE

Renounce the world? The Court? And at my age?
I'd just as soon be buried in a cage!

ALCESTE

But if you love me, what else do you need?
Upon what meat must Célimène still feed?
What? Can't you be contented just with me?

CÉLIMÈNE

At twenty, solitude is agony!
I've not the bravery, nor inclination
To suffer premature expatriation!

If, however, you still wish my hand
In marriage, HERE, your wish is my command,
I'll marry . . .

ALCESTE

         No! I hate you! Understood?
Your cold refusal's turned me off for good!
If I can't be enough for you, we're through!
Since you can't live alone with me: Adieu!
Go, leave me. I am thoroughly enraged:
I now pronounce us wholly disengaged!

    [Célimène leaves; Alceste speaks to Eliante.]

Eliante! Madame, yes, YOU'RE the beauty here,
Among your many virtues: you're sincere!
For many years I've known you were—the best;
And now I see that you surpass the rest
Of humankind; but let me not be bold;
You cannot wish to hear your gifts extolled
By such as me: I am unworthy, poor
At tête-à-têtes, disastrous in amour.
And this proposal from a man like me
Must be beneath you: an indignity,
Which, finally . . .

ELIANTE

          Yes, true enough, Alceste.
In any case, you'd come out second-best.
For your friend here's more equal to that task
And I would marry HIM, if he would ask.

PHILINTE

Madam! What an honor if you would be my wife!
I here give you my soul, my blood, my life.

ALCESTE

Have joy in them, Eliante. And you, Philinte,
Be trusting in her constancy. I can't!
Abandoned on each side; betrayed since birth
I leave forever this abyss that's earth.
I'll find some secret hideout, where I can
Live, reflect, and die an honest man. [exits]

PHILINTE

Well, madam, let us go then. You and I
Must hurry up and tell Alceste goodbye.

        [They exit.]

        [End of Play]

5

WOYZECK

Georg Büchner • left unfinished, 1837

Translated by Henry J. Schmidt

WOYZECK IS NOT ONLY THE WORLD'S FIRST MODern play, it contains abundant seeds of postmodernism as well. Yet what is astonishing is that the play exists at all: *Woyzeck* was not published until forty-two years after its author's death, and did not receive its stage premiere until another thirty-four years after that. "Ahead of its time" applies to no play in dramatic history as to this amazing drama.

Georg Büchner lived intensely and died young. Born near Darmstadt, Germany, in 1813, he studied medicine at the University of Strassburg (then in Germany) and became a social radical; by the age of twenty-one, he had founded a Society for Human Rights and co-authored a political manifesto based on the political theories of the French Revolution. For the rest of his life Büchner was preoccupied with evading arrest, a fate that fell to many of his friends and co-workers. During the mid 1830s, Büchner managed to complete his doctorate and earn a faculty post at the University of Zurich: he also wrote several scientific papers, a

prose fragment, and three plays—of which only two were finished (*Danton's Death* and *Leonce and Lena*), and none published or produced when he died of typhoid in 1837; he had only just reached the age of twenty-three.

Büchner's masterpiece, *Woyzeck*, was the play left unfinished and untitled; it was so fragmentary and illegible in its initial (and substantially differing) manuscript versions that it was not included in the first publication of the author's "complete works" in 1850. But Büchner's growing posthumous reputation finally led to a restoration and reconstruction of the *Woyzeck* fragments for publication in 1875, and finally to the play's stage premiere in 1913. With its stark portrayal of social estrangement, lowlife brutality, and hallucinatory insanity, combined with its *Sturm und Drang* (literally: "storm and stress") Romanticism and its kaleidoscopic medley of seemingly disconnected scenes, *Woyzeck* quickly proved influential to social activists, neo-Romanticists, and early German expressionists alike. Today, the play may be seen as a precursor to many of the avant-garde and post-modern theatre movements of the middle and late twentieth century, certainly including the epic theatre of Bertolt Brecht.

The play is based on a true event. In 1822, Johann Christian Woyzeck, a mercenary foot soldier with various Dutch, Swedish, and Prussian regiments, seems to have become enraged at his mistress's infidelities. Mounting a broken sword blade onto a wooden handle, Johann killed her in a flurry of seven blows. At trial, Woyzeck's lawyer pleaded his client's medical and mental deficiencies, citing a history of hallucinations, homelessness, alcoholism, and dementia. Although Woyzeck was ultimately beheaded, the case became popularly known throughout Germany, combining as it did themes of sex, violence, madness, and betrayal.

Büchner's fascination with the case clearly stemmed from both its medical and political aspects. What is the relation between mental health and social morality? Individual freedom and social responsibility? To what extent are poor people exploited by political (military, academic, scientific, theatrical) institutions? Büchner's concerns center on the crossroads of ethics and economics: "Virtue must be nice, Cap'n. But I'm just a poor guy," says Woyzeck, anticipating Marx as well as Brecht. *Woyzeck* is, among many other things, a prescient paradigm of social and moral alienation.

Style as well as theme marks *Woyzeck* as pre-Expressionistic. Forgoing the tight, organic plot construction of his predecessors, Büchner structures his action in a vivid mosaic of very short, pithy, and violent scenes, taking place in a melange of disparate locales, and incorporating a huge range of speaking styles: epigrammatic, folksong, nursery rhyme, buddy talk, ethnic dialect, carnival barkery, and professorial pomposity. Cause and effect are only hinted at, if suggested at all, from ep-

isode to episode, and the significance of many of the play's scenes and speeches is subject to multiple interpretations. This apparent randomness is, of course, the brilliance of *Woyzeck*; it's a play that pushes questions rather than answers, and forcefully implies that the social problems of postindustrial society are not going to be solved by any simple moral law or *deus ex machina*. The time is clearly out of joint, in *Woyzeck*, but there is nobody born to set it right: this fact more than anything signals the beginning of the modern (and postmodern) age.

A NOTE ON THE TEXT AND TRANSLATION

As noted, *Woyzeck* comes to us in four posthumous, untitled, and partly illegible manuscripts, none of which presents anything resembling a complete text for reading or performing. All modern versions of the play, therefore, are creative as well as scholarly reconstructions of the author's best intentions at the time of his death.

Büchner's fourth (and final) draft presents his fullest version of the play (in his last letter, Büchner claimed to be within a week of having "two dramas"—one presumably this last draft of *Woyzeck*—ready for publication), but even this draft leaves one and a half scenes blank, and stops abruptly after scene 17. All published versions of *Woyzeck*, including this one, reconstruct an entire play by adding to this fourth draft certain scenes from the first, second, and third (see additional note below).

The translation, reviewed in the *New York Times* as the best English version of the play, is by Henry J. Schmidt, late professor of German at Ohio State University. Written in 1969 and revised in 1986 after additional study of the original manuscripts now in Weimar, Schmidt's translation has been performed on the stage with great success, most recently at the Hartford Stage Company (1990) and the New York Public Theatre under the direction of JoAnne Akalaitis (1992). Schmidt, a stage director as well as a critic, translator, and editor, is also the author of the fine dramaturgical study, *How Dramas End*, published shortly after his untimely death in 1992. His translation is included here by kind permission of Cynthia Schmidt-Shilling.

I have taken the liberty of including (as scenes 1 and 22) two scenes from the third draft that Schmidt considers optional for a "final" version, and I've also included (as scene 8) one scene (known as 2,7) from Büchner's second draft.

❧ WOYZECK ❧

———— **CAST OF CHARACTERS** ————

FRANZ WOYZECK, a soldier

MARIE, his mistress

ANDRES, his friend

CAPTAIN

DOCTOR (also called PROFESSOR)

DRUM MAJOR

SERGEANT

MARGRET

CARNIVAL BARKER

ANNOUNCER

OLD MAN

CHILD

JEW

INNKEEPER

FIRST APPRENTICE

SECOND APPRENTICE

KARL, an idiot

KATEY

GRANDMOTHER

FIRST CHILD

SECOND CHILD

FIRST PERSON

SECOND PERSON

COURT CLERK

JUDGE

SOLDIERS, STUDENTS, YOUNG MEN, GIRLS, CHILDREN

———————— **1** ————————

The Professor's courtyard.

[Students below, the Professor at the attic window.]

PROFESSOR

Gentlemen, I am on the roof like David when he saw Bathsheba, but all I see is underwear on a clothesline in the garden of the girls' boarding house. Gentlemen, we are dealing with the important question of the relationship of subject to object. If we take only one of the things in which the organic self-affirmation of the Divine manifests itself to a high degree, and examine its relationship to space, to the earth, to the planetary system—gentlemen, if I throw this cat out of the window, how will this organism relate to the *centrum gravitationis* and to its own instinct? Hey, Woyzeck. *[Shouts.]* Woyzeck!

WOYZECK

Professor, it bites!

PROFESSOR

The fellow holds the beast so tenderly, like it was his grandmother!

WOYZECK

Doctor, I've got the shivers.

DOCTOR[1]

[Elated.] Say, that's wonderful, Woyzeck! *[Rubs his hands. He takes the cat.]* What's this I see, gentlemen—a new species of rabbit louse, a beautiful species, quite different, deep in the fur. [He pulls out a

———————

[1] The Professor and the Doctor are the same character.

magnifying glass.] Ricinus, gentlemen! *[The cat runs off.]* Gentlemen, that animal has no scientific instinct. Ricinus—the best examples—bring your fur collars. Gentlemen, instead of that you can see something else: take note of this man—for a quarter of a year he hasn't eaten anything but peas. Notice the result—feel how uneven his pulse is. There—and the eyes.

WOYZECK
Doctor, everything's getting black. *[He sits down.]*

DOCTOR
Courage, Woyzeck—just a few more days, and then it'll be all over. Feel him, gentlemen, feel him. *[Students feel his temples, pulse, and chest.]* Apropos, Woyzeck, wiggle your ears for the gentlemen; I meant to show it to you before. He uses two muscles. Come on, hop to it!

WOYZECK
Oh, Doctor!

DOCTOR
You dog, shall I wiggle them for you, are you going to act like the cat? So, gentlemen, this represents a transition to the donkey, frequently resulting from being brought up by women and from the use of the mother tongue. How much hair has your mother pulled out for a tender memory? It's gotten very thin in the last few days. Yes, the peas, gentlemen.

2

Open field. The town in the distance.

> *[Woyzeck and Andres are cutting branches in the bushes.]*

WOYZECK
Yes, Andres—that stripe there across the grass, that's where heads roll at night; once somebody picked one up, he thought it was a hedgehog. Three days and three nights, and he was lying in a coffin. *[Softly.]* Andres, it was the Freemasons, that's it, the Freemasons—shh!

ANDRES
[Sings.]

> I saw two big rabbits
> Chewing up the green, green grass . . .

WOYZECK
Shh! Something's moving!

ANDRES

> Chewing up the green, green grass
> Till it was all gone.

WOYZECK
Something's moving behind me, under me. *[Stamps on the ground]* Hollow—you hear that? It's all hollow down there. The Freemasons!

ANDRES
I'm scared.

WOYZECK
It's so strangely quiet. You feel like holding your breath. Andres!

ANDRES
What?

WOYZECK
Say something! *[Stares off into the distance.]* Andres! Look how bright it is! There's fire raging around the sky, and a noise is coming down like trumpets. It's coming closer! Let's go! Don't look back! *[Drags him into the bushes.]*

ANDRES
[After a pause.] Woyzeck! Do you still hear it?

WOYZECK
Quiet, it's all quiet, like the world was dead.

ANDRES
Listen! They're drumming. We've got to get back.

3

The town.

> *[Marie with her Child at the window. Margret. A military patrol goes by, the Drum Major leading.]*

MARIE
[Rocking the Child in her arms.] Hey, boy! Ta-ra-ra-ra! You hear it? They're coming.

MARGRET
What a man, like a tree!

MARIE
He stands on his feet like a lion.

> *[The Drum Major greets them.]*

MARGRET
Say, what a friendly look you gave him, neighbor—we're not used to that from you.

MARIE
[Sings.]

>A soldier is a handsome fellow . . .

MARGRET
Your eyes are still shining.

MARIE
So what? Why don't you take *your* eyes to the Jew and have them polished—maybe they'll shine enough to sell as two buttons.

MARGRET
What? Why, Mrs. Virgin, I'm a decent woman, but you—you can stare through seven pairs of leather pants!

MARIE
Bitch! [Slams the window shut.] Come, my boy. What do they want from us, anyway? You're only the poor child of a whore, and you make your mother happy with your bastard face. Ta-ta! [Sings.]

>Maiden, now what's to be done?
>You've got no ring, you've a son.
>Oh, why worry my head,
>I'll sing here at your bed:
>Rockabye baby, my baby are you,
>Nobody cares what I do.
>
>Johnny, hitch up your six horses fleet,
>Go bring them something to eat.
>From oats they will turn,
>From water they'll turn,
>
>Only cool wine will be fine, hooray!
>Only cool wine will be fine.

[A knock at the window.]

MARIE
Who's that? Is that you, Franz? Come on in!

WOYZECK
I can't. Have to go to roll call.

MARIE
What's the matter with you, Franz?

WOYZECK
[Mysteriously.] Marie, there was something out there again—a lot. Isn't it written: "And lo, the smoke of the country went up as the smoke of a furnace"?

MARIE
Man alive!

WOYZECK
It followed me until I reached town. What's going to happen?

MARIE
Franz!

WOYZECK
I've got to go.

[He leaves.]

MARIE
That man! He's so upset. He didn't look at his own child. He'll go crazy with those thoughts of his. Why are you so quiet, son? Are you scared? It's getting so dark, you'd think you were blind. Usually there's a light shining in. I can't stand it. I'm frightened.

[Goes off.]

———————— 4 ————————

Carnival booths. Lights. People.

OLD MAN, DANCING CHILD

>How long we live, just time will tell,
>We all have got to die,
>We know that very well!

WOYZECK
Hey! Whee! Poor man, old man! Poor child! Young child! Hey, Marie, shall I carry you? . . . Beautiful world!

CARNIVAL BARKER
[In front of a booth.] Gentlemen! Gentlemen! [Points to a monkey.] Look at this creature, as God made it: he's nothing, nothing at all. Now see the effect of art: he walks upright, wears coat and pants, carries a sword! Ho! Take a bow! Good boy. Give me a kiss! [Monkey, trumpets.] The little dummy is musical!

Ladies and gentlemen, here is to be seen the astronomical horse and the little cannery-birds[2]—they're favorites of all potentates of Europe and members of all learned societies. They'll tell you everything: how old you are, how many children you have, what kind of illnesses. [Points to the monkey.] He shoots a pistol, stands on one leg. It's all a matter of upbringing; he has merely a beastly reason, or rather a very reasonable beastliness—he's no brutish individual like a lot of people, present company ex-

_____
[2] The Barker says *Canaillevögel* instead of *Kanarienvögel*, which means "canaries." *Canaille* means "scoundrel."

cepted. Enter! The presentation will begin. The commencement of the beginning will start immediately.

Observe the progress of civilization. Everything progresses—a horse, a monkey, a cannery-bird. The monkey is already a soldier—that's not much, it's the lowest level of the human race!

WOYZECK
Want to?

MARIE
All right. It ought to be good. Look at his tassels, and the woman's got pants on!

[Sergeant. Drum Major. Marie. Woyzeck.]

SERGEANT
Hold it! Over there. Look at her! What a piece!

DRUM MAJOR
Damn! Good enough for the propagation of cavalry regiments and the breeding of drum majors.

SERGEANT
Look how she holds her head—you'd think that black hair would pull her down like a weight. And those eyes, black . . .

DRUM MAJOR
It's like looking down a well or a chimney. Come on, after her!

MARIE
Those lights!

WOYZECK
Yeah, like a big black cat with fiery eyes. Hey, what a night!

[Inside the booth.]

CARNIVAL ANNOUNCER
[Presenting a horse.] Show your talent! Show your beastly wisdom! Put human society to shame! Gentlemen, this animal that you see here, with a tail on his body, with his four hooves, is a member of all learned societies, is a professor at our university, with whom the students learn to ride and fight duels. That was simple comprehension! Now think with double *raison*. What do you do when you think with double *raison*? Is there in the learned *société* an ass? (*The horse shakes its head.*) Now you understand double *raison*! That is beastiognomy.[3] Yes, that's no brutish individ-

ual, that's a person! A human being, a beastly human being, but still an animal, a *bête*. (*The horse behaves improperly.*) That's right, put *société* to shame! You see, the beast is still nature, unspoiled nature! Take a lesson from him. Go ask the doctor, it's very unhealthy![4] It is written: man, be natural; you were created from dust, sand, dirt. Do you want to be more than dust, sand, dirt? Observe his power of reason! He can add, but he can't count on his fingers—why is that? He simply can't express himself, explain himself—he's a transformed person! Tell the gentlemen what time it is. Who among the ladies and gentlemen has a watch—a watch?

DRUM MAJOR
A watch! [*Slowly and grandly he pulls a watch out of his pocket.*] There you are, sir.

MARIE
This I've got to see. [*She climbs into the first row. The Drum Major helps her.*]

———————— 5 ————————

Room.

[*Marie sits with her Child on her lap, a piece of mirror in her hand.*]

MARIE
[*Looks at herself in the mirror.*] These stones really sparkle! What kind are they? What did he say?—Go to sleep, son! Shut your eyes tight. [*The Child covers his eyes with his hands.*] Tighter—stay quiet or he'll come get you. [*Sings.*]

> Close up your shop, fair maid,
> A gypsy boy's in the glade.
> He'll lead you by the hand
> Off into gypsyland.

[*Looks in the mirror again.*] It must be gold. The likes of us only have a little corner in the world and a little piece of mirror, but I have just as red a mouth as the great ladies with their mirrors from top to toe and their handsome lords who kiss their hands. I'm just a poor woman. [*The Child sits up.*] Shh, son, eyes shut—look, the sandman! He's running along the

---

[3] *Viehsionomik*: a pun on "beast" and "physiognomy."

[4] Meaning "to hold it in."

wall. [She flashes with the mirror.] Eyes shut, or he'll look into them, and you'll go blind.

[Woyzeck enters behind her. She jumps up with her hands over her ears.]

WOYZECK
What's that you got there?

MARIE
Nothing.

WOYZECK
Something's shining under your fingers.

MARIE
An earring—I found it.

WOYZECK
I've never found anything like that. Two at once.

MARIE
What am I—a whore?

WOYZECK
It's all right, Marie.—Look, the boy's asleep. Lift him up under his arms, the chair's hurting him. There are shiny drops on his forehead; everything under the sun is work—sweat, even in our sleep. Us poor people! Here's some more money, Marie, my pay and some from my captain.

MARIE
Bless you, Franz.

WOYZECK
I have to go. See you tonight, Marie. Bye.

MARIE
[Alone, after a pause.] What a bitch I am. I could stab myself.—Oh, what a world! Everything goes to hell anyhow, man and woman alike.

――――――― 6 ―――――――

The Captain. Woyzeck.

[The Captain in a chair, Woyzeck shaves him.]

CAPTAIN
Take it easy, Woyzeck, take it easy. One thing at a time; you're making me quite dizzy. You're going to finish early today—what am I supposed to do with the extra ten minutes? Woyzeck, just think, you've still got a good thirty years to live, thirty years! That's

360 months, and days, hours, minutes! What are you going to do with that ungodly amount of time? Get organized, Woyzeck.

WOYZECK
Yes, Cap'n.

CAPTAIN
I fear for the world when I think about eternity. Activity, Woyzeck, activity! Eternal, that's eternal, that's eternal—you realize that, of course. But then again it's not eternal, it's only a moment, yes, a moment.— Woyzeck, it frightens me to think that the earth rotates in one day—what a waste of time, what will come of that? Woyzeck, I can't look at a mill wheel anymore or I get melancholy.

WOYZECK
Yes, Cap'n.

CAPTAIN
Woyzeck, you always look so upset. A good man doesn't act like that, a good man with a good conscience. Say something, Woyzeck. What's the weather like today?

WOYZECK
It's bad, Cap'n, bad—wind.

CAPTAIN
I can feel it, there's something rapid out there. A wind like that reminds me of a mouse. [Cunningly.] I believe it's coming from the south-north.

WOYZECK
Yes, Cap'n.

CAPTAIN
Ha! Ha! Ha! South-north! Ha! Ha! Ha! Oh, are you stupid, terribly stupid. [Sentimentally.] Woyzeck, you're a good man, a good man—[With dignity.] but Woyzeck, you've got no morality. Morality—that's when you are moral, you understand. It's a good word. You have a child without the blessing of the church, as our Reverend Chaplain says, without the blessing of the church—I didn't say it.

WOYZECK
Cap'n, the good Lord isn't going to look at a poor little kid only because amen was said over it before it was created. The Lord said: "Suffer little children to come unto me."

CAPTAIN
What's that you're saying? What kind of a crazy answer is that? You're getting me all confused with your answer. When I say you, I mean you—you!

WOYZECK

Us poor people. You see, Cap'n—money, money. If you don't have money. Just try to raise your own kind on morality in this world. After all, we're flesh and blood. The likes of us are wretched in this world and in the next; I guess if we ever got to Heaven, we'd have to help with the thunder.

CAPTAIN

Woyzeck, you have no virtue, you're not a virtuous person. Flesh and blood? When I'm lying at the window after it has rained, and I watch the white stockings as they go tripping down the street—damn it, Woyzeck, then love comes all over me. I've got flesh and blood, too. But Woyzeck, virtue, virtue! How else could I make time go by? I always say to myself: you're a virtuous man, *[Sentimentally.]* a good man, a good man.

WOYZECK

Yes, Cap'n, virtue! I haven't figured it out yet. You see, us common people, we don't have virtue, we act like nature tells us—but if I was a gentleman, and had a hat and a watch and an overcoat and could talk refined, then I'd be virtuous, too. Virtue must be nice, Cap'n. But I'm just a poor guy.

CAPTAIN

That's fine, Woyzeck. You're a good man, a good man. But you think too much, that's unhealthy—you always look so upset. This discussion has really worn me out. You can go now—and don't run like that! Slow, nice and slow down the street.

——————— 7 ———————

Marie. Drum Major.

DRUM MAJOR

Marie!

MARIE

[Looking at him expressively.] Go march up and down for me.—A chest like a bull and a beard like a lion. Nobody else is like that.—No woman is prouder than me.

DRUM MAJOR

Sundays when I have my plumed helmet and my white gloves—goddamn, Marie! The prince always says: man, you're quite a guy!

MARIE

[Mockingly.] Aw, go on! *[Goes up to him.]* What a man!

DRUM MAJOR

What a woman! Hell, let's breed a race of drum majors, hey? *[He embraces her.]*

MARIE

[Moody.] Leave me alone!

DRUM MAJOR

You wildcat!

MARIE

[Violently.] Just try to touch me!

DRUM MAJOR

Is the devil in your eyes?

MARIE

For all I care. What does it matter?

——————— 8 ———————

Captain, Doctor.

> *[The Captain comes panting down the street, stops, pants, looks around.]*

CAPTAIN

Where to so fast, most honorable Mr. Coffin Nail?

DOCTOR

Where to so slowly, most honorable Mr. Drillprick?

CAPTAIN

Take your time, honorable tombstone.

DOCTOR

I don't waste my time like you, honorable . . .

CAPTAIN

Don't run like that, Doctor—a good man doesn't go so fast, sir, a good man. *[Pants.]* A good man. You'll run yourself to death that way. You're really frightening me.

DOCTOR

I'm in a hurry, Captain, I'm in a hurry.

CAPTAIN

Mr. Coffin Nail, you're wearing out your little legs on the pavement. Don't ride off in the air on your cane.

DOCTOR

She'll be dead in four weeks. She's in her seventh month—I've had twenty patients like that already. In four weeks—you can count on that.

CAPTAIN
Doctor, don't frighten me—people have been known to die of fright, of pure, sheer fright!

DOCTOR
In four weeks, the stupid beast. She'll be an interesting specimen. I'm telling you . . .

CAPTAIN
May you get struck by lightning! I'll hold you by the wing, I won't let you go. Dammit, four weeks? Doctor, coffin nail, shroud, I'll live as long as I exist—four weeks—and the people with their hats in their hands, but they'll say, he was a good man, a good man.

DOCTOR
Say, good morning, Captain. [Swinging his hat and cane.] Cock-a-doodle-doo! My pleasure! My pleasure! [Holds out his hat.] What's this, Captain? That's brain-less. Ha?

CAPTAIN
[Makes a crease.] What's this, Doctor? That's an increase! Ha-ha-ha! No harm meant. I'm a good man—but I can when I want to, Doctor, ha-ha-ha, when I want to. [Woyzeck comes running down the street.] Hey, Woyzeck, why are you running past me like that? Stay here, Woyzeck. You're running around like an open razor blade—you might cut someone! You're running like you had to shave a regiment of Cossacks and would be hanged by the last hair. But about those long beards—what was I going to say? Woyzeck—those long beards . . .

DOCTOR
A long beard on the chin—Pliny already speaks of it. Soldiers should be made to give them up.

CAPTAIN
[Continues.] Hey? What about those long beards? Say, Woyzeck, haven't you found a hair from a beard in your soup bowl yet? Hey? You understand of course, a human hair, from the beard of an engineer, a sergeant, a—a drum major? Hey, Woyzeck? But you've got a decent wife. Not like others.

WOYZECK
Yes, sir! What are you trying to say, Cap'n?

CAPTAIN
Look at the face he's making! Now, it doesn't necessarily have to be in the soup, but if you hurry around the corner, you might find one on a pair of lips—a pair of lips, Woyzeck. I know what love is, too, Woyzeck. Say! You're as white as chalk!

WOYZECK
Cap'n, I'm just a poor devil—and that's all I have in the world. Cap'n, if you're joking . . .

CAPTAIN
Joking? Me? Who do you think you are?

DOCTOR
Your pulse, Woyzeck, your pulse—short, hard, skipping, irregular.

WOYZECK
Cap'n, the earth is hot as hell—for me it's ice cold, ice cold—hell is cold, I'll bet. It can't be! God! God! It can't be!

CAPTAIN
Listen, fellow, how'd you like to be shot, how'd you like to have a couple of bullets in your head? You're looking daggers at me, but I only mean well, because you're a good man, Woyzeck, a good man.

DOCTOR
Facial muscles rigid, tense, occasionally twitching. Posture tense.

WOYZECK
I'm going. A lot is possible. A human being! A lot is possible. The weather's nice, Cap'n. Look: such a beautiful, hard, gray sky—you'd almost feel like pounding a block of wood into it and hanging yourself on it, only because of the hyphen between yes and no—yes and no. Cap'n, yes and no? Is no to blame for yes, or yes for no? I'll have to think about that. [Goes off with long strides, first slowly, then ever faster.]

DOCTOR
[Races after him.] A phenomenon, Woyzeck! A raise!

CAPTAIN
These people make me dizzy. Look at them go—that tall rascal takes off like the shadow before a spider, and the short one—he's trotting along. The tall one is lightning and the short one is thunder. Ha-ha! After them. I don't like that! A good man loves life, a good man has no courage! A scoundrel has courage! I just went to war to strengthen my love for life . . . Grotesque! Grotesque!

Marie. Woyzeck.

WOYZECK
[Stares at her, shakes his head.] Hm! I don't see anything, I don't see anything. Oh, I should be able to see it; I should be able to grab it with my fists.

MARIE
[Intimidated.] What's the matter, Franz? You're out of your mind, Franz.

WOYZECK
A sin so fat and so wide—it stinks enough to smoke the angels out of Heaven. You've got a red mouth, Marie. No blister on it? Good-bye, Marie, you're as beautiful as sin. —Can mortal sin be so beautiful?

MARIE
Franz, you're delirious.

WOYZECK
Damn it!—Was he standing here like this, like this?

MARIE
As the day is long and the world is old, lots of people can stand on one spot, one after another.

WOYZECK
I saw him.

MARIE
You can see all sorts of things if you've got two eyes and aren't blind, and the sun is shining.

WOYZECK
With my own eyes!

MARIE
[Fresh.] So what!

——————— **10** ———————

Woyzeck. The Doctor.

DOCTOR
What's this I saw, Woyzeck? A man of his word!

WOYZECK
What is it, Doctor?

DOCTOR
I saw it, Woyzeck—you pissed on the street, you pissed on the wall like a dog. And even though you get two cents a day. Woyzeck, that's bad. The world's getting bad, very bad.

WOYZECK
But Doctor, the call of nature . . .

DOCTOR
The call of nature, the call of nature! Nature! Haven't I proved that the *musculus constrictor vesicae* is subject to the will? Nature! Woyzeck, man is free; in man alone is individuality exalted to freedom. Couldn't hold it in! *[Shakes his head, puts his hands behind his back, and paces back and forth.]* Did you eat your peas already, Woyzeck?—I'm revolutionizing science, I'll blow it sky-high. Urea ten per cent, ammonium chloride, hyperoxidic. Woyzeck, don't you have to piss again? Go in there and try.

WOYZECK
I can't, Doctor.

DOCTOR
[With emotion.] But pissing on the wall! I have it in writing, here's the contract. I saw it all, saw it with my own eyes—I was just holding my nose out the window, letting the sun's rays hit it, so as to examine the process of sneezing. *[Starts kicking him.]* No, Woyzeck, I'm not getting angry; anger is unhealthy, unscientific. I am calm, perfectly calm—my pulse is beating at its usual sixty, and I'm telling you this in all cold-bloodedness! Who on earth would get excited about a human being, a human being! Now if it were a Proteus lizard that were dying! But you shouldn't have pissed on the wall . . .

WOYZECK
You see, Doctor, sometimes you've got a certain character, a certain structure.—But with nature, that's something else, you see, with nature—*[He cracks his knuckles.]* that's like—how should I put it—for example . . .

DOCTOR
Woyzeck, you're philosophizing again.

WOYZECK
[Confidingly.] Doctor, have you ever seen anything of double nature? When the sun's standing high at noon and the world seems to be going up in flames, I've heard a terrible voice talking to me!

DOCTOR
Woyzeck, you've got an *aberratio!*

WOYZECK

[Puts his finger to his nose.] The toadstools, Doctor. There—that's where it is. Have you seen how they grow in patterns? If only someone could read that.

DOCTOR

Woyzeck, you've got a marvelous *aberratio mentalis partialis*, second species, beautifully developed. Woyzeck, you're getting a raise. Second species: obsession with a generally rational condition. You're doing everything as usual—shaving your captain?

WOYZECK

Yes, sir.

DOCTOR

Eating your peas?

WOYZECK

Same as ever, Doctor. My wife gets the money for the household.

DOCTOR

Going on duty?

WOYZECK

Yes, sir.

DOCTOR

You're an interesting case. Subject Woyzeck, you're getting a raise. Now behave yourself. Show me your pulse! Yes.

——————— **11** ———————

The guardroom.

[*Woyzeck. Andres.*]

ANDRES

[*Sings.*]

> *Our hostess has a pretty maid,*
> *She's in her garden night and day,*
> *She sits inside her garden . . .*

WOYZECK

Andres!

ANDRES

Huh?

WOYZECK

Nice weather.

ANDRES

Sunday weather. There's music outside town. All the broads are out there already, everybody's sweating—it's really moving along.

WOYZECK

[*Restlessly.*] A dance, Andres, they're dancing.

ANDRES

Yeah, at the Horse and at the Star.

WOYZECK

Dancing, dancing.

ANDRES

Big deal. [*Sings.*]

> *She sits inside her garden,*
> *Until the bells have all struck twelve,*
> *And stares at all the soo-ooldiers.*

WOYZECK

Andres, I can't keep still.

ANDRES

Fool!

WOYZECK

I've got to get out of here. Everything's spinning before my eyes. How hot their hands are. Damn it, Andres!

ANDRES

What do you want?

WOYZECK

I've got to go.

ANDRES

With that whore.

WOYZECK

I've got to get out. It's so hot in here.

——————— **12** ———————

Inn.

[*The windows are open, a dance. Benches in front of the house. Apprentices.*]

FIRST APPRENTICE

> *This shirt I've got, I don't know whose,*
> *My soul it stinks like booze . . .*

SECOND APPRENTICE

Brother, shall I in friendship bore a hole in your nature? Dammit, I want to bore a hole in your nature. I'm quite a guy, too, you know—I'm going to kill all the fleas on his body.

FIRST APPRENTICE

My soul, my soul it stinks like booze.—Even money eventually decays. Forget-me-not! Oh, how beautiful this world is. Brother, I could cry a rain barrel full of tears. I wish our noses were two bottles and we could pour them down each other's throats.

OTHERS
[In chorus.]

> *A hunter from the west*
> *Once went riding through the woods.*
> *Hip-hip, hooray! A hunter has a merry life,*
> *O'er meadow and o'er stream,*
> *Oh, hunting is my dream!*

[Woyzeck stands at the window. Marie and the Drum Major dance past without seeing him.]

MARIE
[Dancing by.] On! and on, on and on!

WOYZECK
[Chokes.] On and on—on and on! *[Jumps up violently and sinks back on the bench.]* On and on, on and on. *[Beats his hands together.]* Spin around, roll around. Why doesn't God blow out the sun so that everything can roll around in lust, man and woman, man and beast. Do it in broad daylight, do it on our hands, like flies.—Woman!—That woman is hot, hot! On and on, on and on. *[Jumps up.]* The bastard! Look how he's grabbing her, grabbing her body! He—he's got her now, like I used to have her.

FIRST APPRENTICE
[Preaches on the table.] Yet when a wanderer stands leaning against the stream of time or gives answer for the wisdom of God, asking himself: Why does man exist? Why does man exist?—But verily I say unto you: how could the farmer, the cooper, the shoemaker, the doctor exist if God hadn't created man? How could the tailor exist if God hadn't given man a feeling of shame? How could the soldier exist, if men didn't feel the necessity of killing one another? Therefore, do not ye despair, yes, yes, it is good and pleasant, yet all that is earthly is passing, even money eventually decays.—In conclusion, my dear friends, let us piss crosswise so that a Jew will die.

——————— 13 ———————

Open field.

WOYZECK
On and on! On and on! Shh—music. *[Stretches out on the ground.]* Ha—what, what are you saying? Louder, louder—stab, stab the bitch to death? Stab, stab the bitch to death. Should I? Must I? Do I hear it over there too, is the wind saying it too? Do I hear it on and on—stab her to death, to death.

——————— 14 ———————

Night.

[Andres and Woyzeck in a bed.]

WOYZECK
[Shakes Andres.] Andres! Andres! I can't sleep—when I close my eyes, everything starts spinning, and I hear the fiddles, on and on, on and on. And then there's a voice from the wall—don't you hear anything?

ANDRES
Oh, yeah—let them dance! God bless us, amen. *[Falls asleep again.]*

WOYZECK
And it floats between my eyes like a knife.

ANDRES
Drink some brandy with a painkiller in it. That'll bring your fever down.

——————— 15 ———————

Inn.

[Drum Major. Woyzeck. People.]

DRUM MAJOR
I'm a man! *[Pounds his chest.]* A man, I say. Who wants to start something? If you're not drunk as a lord, stay away from me. I'll shove your nose up your ass. I'll . . . *[To Woyzeck.]* Man, have a drink. A man gotta drink. I wish the world was booze, booze.

WOYZECK
[Whistles.]

DRUM MAJOR
You bastard, you want me to pull your tongue out of your throat and wrap it around you? *[They wrestle, Woyzeck loses.]* Shall I leave you as much breath as an old woman's fart? Shall I?

[Woyzeck sits on the bench, exhausted and trembling.]

DRUM MAJOR
He can whistle till he's blue in the face. Ha!

Oh, brandy, that's my life,
Oh, brandy gives me courage!

A PERSON
He sure got what was coming to him.

ANOTHER
He's bleeding.

WOYZECK
One thing after another.

———————— 16 ————————

[*Woyzeck. The Jew.*]

WOYZECK
The pistol costs too much.

JEW
Well, do you want it or don't you?

WOYZECK
How much is the knife?

JEW
It's good and straight. You want to cut your throat with it? Well, how about it? I'll give it to you as cheap as anybody else; your death'll be cheap, but not for nothing. How about it? You'll have an economical death.

WOYZECK
That can cut more than just bread.

JEW
Two cents.

WOYZECK
There! [*Goes off.*]

JEW
There! Like it was nothing. But it's money! The dog.

———————— 17 ————————

[*Marie. Karl, the idiot. Child.*]

MARIE
[*Leafs through the Bible.*] "And no guile is found in his mouth" . . . My God, my God! Don't look at me. [*Pages further.*] "And the scribes and Pharisees brought unto him a woman taken in adultery, and set her in the midst. . . . And Jesus said unto her, 'Neither do I condemn thee: go, and sin no more.'"

[*Clasps her hands together.*] My God! My God! I can't. God, just give me enough strength to pray. [*The Child snuggles up to her.*] The boy is like a knife in my heart. Karl! He's sunning himself!

KARL
[*Lies on the ground and tells himself fairy tales on his fingers.*] This one has a golden crown—he's a king. To-morrow I'll go get the queen's child. Blood sausage says, come, liver sausage! [*He takes the Child and is quiet.*]

MARIE
Franz hasn't come, not yesterday, not today. It's getting hot in here. [*She opens the window.*] "And stood at his feet weeping, and began to wash his feet with tears, and did wipe them with the hairs of her head, and kissed his feet, and anointed them with ointment." [*Beats her breast.*] It's all dead! Savior, Savior, I wish I could anoint your feet.

———————— 18 ————————

The barracks.

[*Andres. Woyzeck rummages through his things.*]

WOYZECK
This jacket isn't part of the uniform, Andres; you can use it, Andres. The crucifix is my sister's, and the little ring. I've got an icon, too—two hearts and nice gold. It was in my mother's Bible, and it says:

May pain be my reward,
Through pain I love my Lord.
Lord, like Thy body, red and sore,
So be my heart forevermore.

My mother can only feel the sun shining on her hands now. That doesn't matter.

ANDRES
[*Blankly, answers to everything.*] Yeah.

WOYZECK
[*Pulls out a piece of paper.*] Friedrich Johann Franz Woyzeck, enlisted infantryman in the second regiment, second battalion, fourth company, born. . . . Today I'm thirty years, seven months, and twelve days old.

ANDRES
Franz, you better go to the infirmary. You poor guy—drink brandy with a painkiller in it. That'll kill the fever.

WOYZECK
You know, Andres, when the carpenter nails those boards together, nobody knows who'll be laying his head on them.

——————— **19** ———————

Street.

> [*Marie with girls in front of the house door.*
> *Grandmother. Then Woyzeck.*]

GIRLS

> *How bright the sun on Candlemas Day,*
> *On fields of golden grain.*
> *As two by two they marched along*
> *Down the country lane.*
> *The pipers up in front,*
> *The fiddlers in a chain.*
> *Their red socks . . .*

FIRST CHILD
That's not nice.

SECOND CHILD
What do you want, anyway?

OTHERS
Why'd you start it?

Yeah, why?

I can't.

Because!

Who's going to sing?

Why because?

Marie, you sing to us.

MARIE
Come, you little shrimps.

> [*Children's games: "Ring-around-a-rosy" and*
> *"King Herod."*]

Grandmother, tell a story.

GRANDMOTHER
Once upon a time there was a poor child with no father and no mother, everything was dead, and no one was left in the whole world. Everything was dead, and it went and searched day and night. And since nobody was left on the earth, it wanted to go up to the heavens, and the moon was looking at it so friendly, and when it finally got to the moon, the moon was a piece of rotten wood and then it went to the sun and when it got there, the sun was a wilted sunflower and when it got to the stars, they were little golden flies stuck up there like the shrike sticks 'em on the black-thorn and when it wanted to go back down to the earth, the earth was an overturned pot and was all alone and it sat down and cried and there it sits to this day, all alone.

WOYZECK
Marie!

MARIE
[*Startled.*] What is it?

WOYZECK
Marie, we have to go. It's time.

MARIE
Where to?

WOYZECK
How do I know?

——————— **20** ———————

[*Marie and Woyzeck.*]

MARIE
So the town is over there—it's dark.

WOYZECK
Stay here. Come on, sit down.

MARIE
But I have to get back.

WOYZECK
You won't get sore feet.

MARIE
What's gotten into you!

WOYZECK
Do you know how long it's been, Marie?

MARIE
Two years since Pentecost.

WOYZECK
And do you know how long it's going to be?

MARIE
I've got to go, the evening dew is falling.

WOYZECK
Are you freezing, Marie? But you're warm. How hot your lips are!—Hot, the hot breath of a whore—and yet I'd give heaven and earth to kiss them once more.

And when you're cold, you don't freeze anymore. The morning dew won't make you freeze.

MARIE
What are you talking about?

WOYZECK
Nothing. *[Silence.]*

MARIE
Look how red the moon is.

WOYZECK
Like a bloody blade.

MARIE
What are you up to? Franz, you're so pale. *[He pulls out the knife.]* Franz—wait! For God's sake—help!

WOYZECK
Take that and that! Can't you die? There! There! Ah—she's still twitching—not yet? Not yet? Still alive? *[Stabs once again.]* Are you dead? Dead! Dead! *[People approach, he runs off.]*

───────────── 21 ─────────────

[Two people.]

FIRST PERSON
Wait!

SECOND PERSON
You hear it? Shh! Over there.

FIRST PERSON
Ooh! There! What a sound.

SECOND PERSON
That's the water, it's calling. Nobody has drowned for a long time. Let's go—it's bad to hear things like that.

FIRST PERSON
Ooh! There it is again. Like someone dying.

SECOND PERSON
It's weird. It's so fragrant—some gray fog, and the beetles humming like broken bells. Let's get out of here!

FIRST PERSON
No—it's too clear, too loud. Up this way. Come on.

───────────── 22 ─────────────

[Karl, the idiot. The Child. Woyzeck.]

KARL
[Holds the Child on his lap.] He fell in the water, he fell in the water, he fell in the water.

WOYZECK
Son—Christian!

KARL
[Stares at him.] He fell in the water.

WOYZECK
[Wants to caress the Child, who turns away and screams.] My God!

KARL
He fell in the water.

WOYZECK
Christian, you'll get a hobbyhorse. Da-da! *[The Child resists. To Karl.]* Here, go buy the boy a hobbyhorse.

KARL
[Stares at him.]

WOYZECK
Hop! Hop! Horsey!

KARL
[Cheers.] Hop! Hop! Horsey! Horsey! *[Runs off with the Child.]*

───────────── 23 ─────────────

The inn.

[Woyzeck. Katey. Karl. Innkeeper. People.]

WOYZECK
Dance, all of you, on and on, sweat and stink—he'll get you all in the end. *[Sings.]*

> *Our hostess has a pretty maid,*
> *She's in her garden night and day,*
> *She sits inside her garden,*
> *Until the bells have all struck twelve,*
> *And stares at all the soldiers.*

[He dances.] Come on, Katey! Sit down! I'm hot! Hot. *[He takes off his jacket.]* That's the way it is: The devil takes one and lets the other go. Katey, you're hot! Why? Katey, you'll be cold someday, too. Be reasonable. Can't you sing something?

KATEY

> *For Swabian hills I do not yearn,*
> *And flowing gowns I always spurn,*
> *For flowing gowns and pointed shoes*
> *A servant girl should never choose.*

WOYZECK

No, no shoes—you can go to hell without shoes, too.

KATEY

> *For shame, my love, I'm not your own,*
> *Just keep your money and sleep alone.*

WOYZECK

Yes, that's right, I don't want to make myself bloody.

KATEY

But what's that on your hand?

WOYZECK

Who? Me?

KATEY

Red! Blood! [*People gather around.*]

WOYZECK

Blood? Blood?

INNKEEPER

Ooh, blood.

WOYZECK

I guess I must have cut myself, there on my right hand.

INNKEEPER

But how'd it get on your elbow?

WOYZECK

I wiped it off.

INNKEEPER

What, with your right hand on your right elbow? You're talented.

KARL

And then the giant said: I smell, I smell, I smell human flesh. Phew! That stinks already.

WOYZECK

Damn it, what do you want? What's it got to do with you? Get away, or the first one who—damn it! You think I killed someone? Am I a murderer? What are you staring at? Look at yourselves! Out of my way! [*He runs out.*]

—————— 24 ——————

[*Children.*]

FIRST CHILD

Come on! Marie!

SECOND CHILD

What is it?

FIRST CHILD

Don't you know? Everybody's gone out there already. Someone's lying there!

SECOND CHILD

Where?

FIRST CHILD

To the left through the trench, near the red cross.

SECOND CHILD

Let's go, so we can still see something. Otherwise they'll carry her away.

—————— 25 ——————

[*Woyzeck alone.*]

WOYZECK

The knife? Where's the knife? Here's where I left it. It'll give me away! Closer, still closer! What kind of a place is this? What's that I hear? Something's moving. Shh! Over there. Marie? Ah—Marie! Quiet. Everything's quiet! Why are you so pale, Marie? Why is that red thread around your neck? Who helped you earn that necklace, with your sins? They made you black, black! Now I've made you white. Why does your black hair hang so wild? Didn't you do your braids today? Something's lying over there! Cold, wet, still. Got to get away from here. The knife, the knife—is that it? There! People—over there. [*He runs off.*]

—————— 26 ——————

[*Woyzeck at a pond.*]

WOYZECK

Down it goes! [*He throws the knife in.*] It sinks into the dark water like a stone! The moon is like a bloody blade! Is the whole world going to give me away? No, it's too far in front—when people go swimming—

[He goes into the pond and throws it far out.] All right, now—but in the summer, when they go diving for shells—bah, it'll rust. Who'll recognize it? I wish I'd smashed it! Am I still bloody? I've got to wash myself. There's a spot—and there's another.

[Court Clerk. Barber. Doctor. Judge.]

CLERK

A good murder, a real murder, a beautiful murder— as good a murder as you'd ever want to see. We haven't had one like this for a long time.

6

A DOLL'S HOUSE

Henrik Ibsen • 1879

Translated by Eva Le Gallienne

EVERY WRITTEN INTRODUCTION TO A PLAY RISKS spoiling the play's ending somewhat, but especially in regard to Henrik Ibsen's *A Doll's House*, which has a particularly surprising conclusion. Readers unacquainted with this play, therefore, are urged to skip ahead and read the play *now*, returning to this introductory material afterward.

A Doll's House is, at one time, old-fashioned and revolutionary. Up through the final scene, it's a "well-made" (that is, conventionally plotted) domestic drama, beginning as somewhat of a Christmas comedy, and turning into a melodrama about a gullible housewife and a greedy loan shark. Then, halfway through its final act, *A Doll's House* bursts suddenly into a radical and intense discussion of a woman's role (and women's rights) in marriage and society. The discussion—frank, unsparing, and icily unsentimental—profoundly shocked nineteenth-century audiences, both from Ibsen's frontal attack on ingrained male chauvinism, and his bold violation of conventional dramatic technique. The impact on Western drama was broad and immediate: George Bernard Shaw announced to the world that modern drama began at the moment when Nora, Ibsen's heroine, "stops her emotional acting and says, 'Sit down, Torvald; we have a lot to talk about.'" By Ibsen's transformation of the well-made play into a battleground for contemporary social values, "*A Doll's House* conquered Europe and founded a new school of dramatic art," Shaw declared.[1]

Ibsen hardly invented feminism: John Stuart Mill had published his *Subjection of Women* in 1869, at which time heroic struggles for women's suffrage and legal rights were well under way throughout Europe and America. Nor did Ibsen even consider himself a card-carrying feminist. Nonetheless, his exploration of Victorian-era gender discrimination was profound and passionate.

---

[1] In *The Quintessence of Ibsenism* (1913), in *Major Critical Essays* (New York: Penguin, 1986), pp. 163–164.

In his preliminary notes for the play, Ibsen wrote, "A woman is judged by man's law, as though she were not a woman but a man. . . . A woman cannot be herself in the society of the present day, which is an exclusively masculine society, with laws framed by men and with a judicial system that judges feminine conduct from a masculine point of view."[2] Ibsen's consequent depiction of the agony of a young wife (Nora), virtually imprisoned in her "doll's house" of a home by Norway's (and Europe's) suppressive gender codes, is brilliantly realized.

There's more in A Doll's House than just Nora's case, of course. There's also Torvald's case; it is a mark of Ibsen's humanistic realism (as opposed to propagandistic fervor) that Torvald is not a shallow villain from the world of melodrama, but rather a simple-minded and—by the standards of his time—a generally well-intentioned young businessman and husband. Ibsen certainly takes aim at the laws of his day, which certainly disenfranchised women, and particularly wives, but he also aims much deeper, attacking the unthinking and unconscious prejudices of male chauvinism: a series of so-called moral standards, that were (and in some cases still are) sustained by deeply buried linguistic and social codes; these are the true villains of this play. Torvald, like Nora, is a victim of his culture's limitations.

Ibsen (1828–1906) is generally thought of as a realistic playwright, but that term only takes in a small portion of his vast career: specifically four social plays he wrote between 1879 and 1890: A Doll's House, Ghosts, An Enemy of the People, and Hedda Gabler. Ibsen was in fact a prolific playwright who worked in a variety of styles: his verse dramas, Brand and Peer Gynt, are poetic master-

pieces, and Peer is often considered the greatest literary work in the Norwegian language. His later dramas, including Little Eyeolf and When We Dead Awaken, are dense with mystery, nuance, and non-realistic imagery. Thus it is not surprising that the apparent lifelikeness of A Doll's House is tempered and elevated by poetic elements that raise the play to a theatrically elevated level: Nora is defined as much by the passion with which she dances the tarantella as the logic with which she argues her case to Torvald, and there is a whiff of Greek tragedy in the ecstasy of her revolt. There is also, beyond a plotted necessity of the minor characters, an air of mystery and intrigue: the curious Doctor Rank and the not-always-forthcoming Mrs. Linde are, like Peer Gynt, ancestrally descended from the Kingdom of the Trolls.

Ibsen's inquiry, finally, is philosophical: What is the difference between being "happy" and being "only merry," after all? At the heart of this husband–wife debate, at play's end, is no less than an attempt to define a meaning for life. A Doll's House is not just a play about a wife who leaves home; it is a dramatic work that equally transcends its apparent subject (feminism) and most visible style (realism), and faces the world from a wide variety of philosophical, aesthetic, and socially activist perspectives.

A NOTE ON THE TRANSLATOR

Eva Le Gallienne (1899–1991) was one of America's finest stage actresses, earning her greatest reputation in the plays of Ibsen, Chekhov, and Shakespeare. In New York, she founded America's first true classical repertory company—the Civic Repertory Theatre—where over seven seasons she produced and directed more than thirty classic and modern plays. Scandinavian by background, Le Gallienne was able to read Ibsen in the original, and eventually translated eight of his plays for pro-

---

[2]Collected Works of Henrik Ibsen, Vol. 12, trans. A. G. Chater (New York: Scribner's, 1913), pp. 91–95.

duction and publication. In 1981, nearing the end of her illustrious career, she wrote, "To a great actress the Isben repertoire is as stimulating and rewarding as the Shakespearean repertoire is to a great [male] actor. The range and variety of Ibsen's portraits of women are incomparable. His grasp of the intricacies of female psychology is miraculous. . . . It was indeed as if he had the power to transmute himself and in his imagination actually to become these women of whom he wrote, so intimate and so accurate in every small detail is his knowledge of them."[3]

Ibsen wrote the play in a form of Dano-Norwegian known as Riksmål, a literary language now largely absorbed into colloquial Norwegian. Thus, as Errol Durbach points out, "It is Ibsen's fate to exist almost exclusively in translation, even in his own country."[4] The original-language title, *Et Dukkehjem*, is usually translated into English as "a doll's house" (or "a doll house") owing to the familiarity of that English phrase, but "a doll's *home*" would be a closer approximation of the original meaning.

[3] *Eight Plays of Henrik Ibsen* (New York: Modern Library, 1982), pp. xii–xiii.

[4] *A Doll's House: Ibsen's Myth of Transformation* (Boston: Twayne, 1991), p. ix.

❧ A DOLL'S HOUSE ❧

─── **CHARACTERS** ───

TORVALD HELMER, a lawyer

NORA, his wife

DOCTOR RANK

MRS. KRISTINE LINDE

NILS KROGSTAD, an attorney

HELMER'S THREE SMALL CHILDREN

ANNE-MARIE,* nurse at the Helmers

HELENE, maid at the Helmers

A PORTER

The action takes place in the Helmer residence.

─── **ACT ONE** ───

Scene

A comfortable room furnished with taste, but not expensively. In the back wall a door on the right leads to the hall, another door on the left leads to Helmer's study. Between the two doors a piano. In the left wall, center, a door; farther downstage a window. Near the window a round table with an armchair and a small sofa. In the right wall upstage a door, and further downstage a porcelain stove round which are grouped a couple of armchairs and a rocking chair. Between the stove and the door stands a small table. Engravings on the walls. A whatnot with china objects and various bric-a-brac. A

───

* For stage purposes, often ANNA-MARIA.

234

small bookcase with books in fancy bindings. The floor is carpeted; a fire burns in the stove. A winter day.

NORA

Be sure and hide the Christmas tree carefully, Helene, the children mustn't see it till this evening, when it's all decorated. *[To the Porter, taking out her purse]* How much?

PORTER

Fifty, Ma'am.

NORA

Here you are. No—keep the change. *[The Porter thanks her and goes. Nora closes the door. She laughs gaily to herself as she takes off her outdoor things. Takes a bag of macaroons out of her pocket and eats a couple, then she goes cautiously to the door of her husband's study and listens]* Yes—he's home. *[She goes over to the table right, humming to herself again.]*

HELMER

[From his study] Is that my little lark twittering out there?

NORA

[Busily undoing the packages] Yes, it is.

HELMER

Is that my little squirrel bustling about?

NORA

Yes.

HELMER

When did my squirrel get home?

NORA

Just this minute. *[She puts the bag of macaroons back in her pocket and wipes her mouth.]* Oh, Torvald, do come in here! You must see what I have bought.

HELMER

Now, don't disturb me! *[A moment afterwards he opens the door and looks in—pen in hand.]* Did you say "bought"? That—all *that*? Has my little spendthrift been flinging money about again?

NORA

But, Torvald, surely this year we ought to let ourselves go a bit! After all, it's the first Christmas we haven't had to be careful.

HELMER

Yes, but that doesn't mean we can afford to *squander* money.

NORA

Oh, Torvald, we can squander a bit, can't we? Just a little tiny bit? You're going to get a big salary and you'll be making lots and lots of money.

HELMER

After the first of the year, yes. But remember there'll be three whole months before my salary falls due.

NORA

We can always borrow in the meantime.

HELMER

Nora! *[Goes to her and pulls her ear playfully]* There goes my little featherbrain! Let's suppose I borrowed a thousand crowns today, you'd probably squander it all during Christmas week; and then let's suppose that on New Year's Eve a tile blew off the roof and knocked my brains out—

NORA

[Puts her hand over his mouth] Don't say such frightful things!

HELMER

But let's suppose it happened—then what?

NORA

If anything as terrible as *that* happened, I shouldn't care whether I owed money or not.

HELMER

But what about the people I'd borrowed from?

NORA

Who cares about them? After all they're just strangers.

HELMER

Oh, Nora, Nora! What a little woman you are! But seriously, Nora, you know my feelings about such things. I'll have no borrowing—I'll have no debts!

There can be no freedom—no, nor beauty either—in a home based upon loans and credit. We've held out bravely up to now, and we shall continue to do so for the short time that remains.

NORA

[Goes toward the stove] Just as you like, Torvald.

HELMER

[Following her] Come, come; the little lark mustn't droop her wings. Don't tell me my little squirrel is sulking! *[He opens his purse.]* Nora! Guess what I have here!

NORA

[Turns quickly] Money!

HELMER

There you are! *[He hands her some notes.]* Don't you suppose I know that money is needed at Christmas time.

NORA

[Counts the notes] Ten, twenty, thirty, forty. Oh thank you, thank you, Torvald—this'll last me a long time!

HELMER

Better see that it does!

NORA

Oh, it will—I know. But do come here. I want to show you everything I've bought, and all so cheap too! Here are some new clothes for Ivar, and a little sword—and this horse and trumpet are for Bob, and here's a doll for Emmy—and a doll's bed. They're not worth much, but she's sure to tear them to pieces in a minute anyway. This is some dress material and handkerchiefs for the maids. Old Anne-Marie really should have had something better.

HELMER

And what's in that other parcel?

NORA

[With a shriek] No, Torvald! You can't see that until this evening!

HELMER

I can't, eh? But what about you—you little squanderer? Have you thought of anything for yourself?

NORA

Oh, there's nothing I want, Torvald.

HELMER

Of course there is!—now tell me something sensible you'd really like to have.

NORA

But there's nothing—really! Except of course—

HELMER

Well?

NORA

[She fingers the buttons on his coat, without looking at him.] Well—if you really want to give me something—you might—you might—

HELMER

Well, well, out with it!

NORA

[Rapidly] You might give me some money, Torvald—just anything you feel you could spare; and then one of these days I'll buy myself something with it.

HELMER

But Nora—

NORA

Oh, please do, dear Torvald—I beg you to! I'll wrap it up in beautiful gold paper and hang it on the Christmas tree. Wouldn't that be fun?

HELMER

What's the name of the bird that eats up money?

NORA

The Spendthrift bird—I know! But do let's do as I say, Torvald!—it will give me a chance to choose something I really need. Don't you think that's a sensible idea? Don't you?

HELMER

[Smiling] Sensible enough—providing you really do buy something for yourself with it. But I expect you'll fritter it away on a lot of unnecessary household expenses, and before I know it you'll be coming to me for more.

NORA

But, Torvald—

HELMER

You can't deny it, Nora dear. [Puts his arm round her waist] The Spendthrift is a sweet little bird—but it costs a man an awful lot of money to support one!

NORA

How can you say such nasty things—I save all I can!

HELMER

Yes, I dare say—but that doesn't amount to much!

NORA

[Hums softly and smiles happily] You don't know, Torvald, what expenses we larks and squirrels have!

HELMER

You're a strange little creature; exactly like your father. You'll go to any lengths to get a sum of money—but as soon as you have it, it just slips through your fingers. You don't know yourself what's become of it. Well, I suppose one must just take you as you are. It's in your blood. Oh, yes! such things are hereditary, Nora.

NORA

I only wish I had inherited a lot of Father's qualities.

HELMER

And I wouldn't wish you any different than you are, my own sweet little lark. But Nora, it's just occurred to me—isn't there something a little—what shall I call it—a little guilty about you this morning?

NORA

About me?

HELMER

Yes. Look me straight in the eye.

NORA

[Looking at him] Well?

HELMER

[Wags a threatening finger at her] Has my little sweet-tooth been breaking rules today?

NORA

No! What makes you think that?

HELMER

Are you sure the sweet-tooth didn't drop in at the confectioner's?

NORA

No, I assure you, Torvald—

HELMER

She didn't nibble a little candy?

NORA

No, really not.

HELMER

Not even a macaroon or two?

NORA

No, Torvald, I assure you—really—

HELMER

There, there! Of course I'm only joking.

NORA

[Going to the table right] It would never occur to me to go against your wishes.

HELMER

Of course I know that—and anyhow—you've given me your word—[*Goes to her*] Well, my darling, I won't pry into your little Christmas secrets. They'll be unveiled tonight under the Christmas tree.

NORA

Did you remember to ask Dr. Rank?

HELMER

No, it really isn't necessary. He'll take it for granted he's to dine with us. However, I'll ask him, when he stops by this morning. I've ordered some specially good wine. I am so looking forward to this evening, Nora, dear!

NORA

So am I—And the children will have such fun!

HELMER

Ah! How nice it is to feel secure; to look forward to a good position with an ample income. It's a wonderful prospect—isn't it, Nora?

NORA

It's simply marvelous!

HELMER

Do you remember last Christmas? For three whole weeks—you locked yourself up every evening until past midnight—making paper flowers for the Christmas tree—and a lot of other wonderful things you wanted to surprise us with. I was never so bored in my life!

NORA

I wasn't a bit bored.

HELMER

[*Smiling*] But it all came to rather a sad end, didn't it, Nora?

NORA

Oh, do you have to tease me about that again? How could I help the cat coming in and tearing it all to pieces.

HELMER

Of course you couldn't help it, you poor darling! You meant to give us a good time—that's the main thing. But it's nice to know those lean times are over.

NORA

It's wonderful!

HELMER

Now I don't have to sit here alone, boring myself to death; and you don't have to strain your dear little eyes, and prick your sweet little fingers—

NORA

[*Claps her hands*] No, I don't—do I, Torvald! Oh! How lovely it all is. [*Takes his arm*] I want to tell you how I thought we'd arrange things after Christmas. [*The doorbell rings.*] Oh there's the bell. [*Tidies up the room a bit*] It must be a visitor—how tiresome!

HELMER

I don't care to see any visitors, Nora—remember that.

HELENE

[*In the doorway*] There's a lady to see you, Ma'am.

NORA

Well, show her in.

HELENE

[*To Helmer*] And the Doctor's here too, Sir.

HELMER

Did he go straight to my study?

HELENE

Yes, he did, Sir.

[*Helmer goes into his study. Helene ushers in Mrs. Linde, who is dressed in traveling clothes, and closes the door behind her.*]

MRS. LINDE

[*In subdued and hesitant tone*] How do you do, Nora?

NORA

[*Doubtfully*] How do you do?

MRS. LINDE

You don't recognize me, do you?

NORA

No, I don't think—and yet—I seem to—[*With a sudden outburst*] Kristine! Is it really you?

MRS. LINDE

Yes; it's really I!

NORA

Kristine! And to think of my not knowing you! But how could I when—[*More softly*] You've changed so, Kristine!

MRS. LINDE

Yes I suppose I have. After all—it's nine or ten years—

NORA

Is it *that* long since we met? Yes, so it is. Oh, these last eight years have been such happy ones! Fancy your being in town! And imagine taking that long trip in midwinter! How brave you are!

MRS. LINDE

I arrived by the morning boat.

NORA

You've come for the Christmas holidays, I suppose— what fun! Oh, what a good time we'll have! Do take off your things. You're not cold, are you? *[Helping her]* There; now we'll sit here by the stove. No, you take the arm-chair; I'll sit here in the rocker. *[Seizes her hands]* Now you look more like yourself again. It was just at first—you're a bit paler, Kristine—and perhaps a little thinner.

MRS. LINDE

And much, much older, Nora.

NORA

Well, perhaps a *little* older—a tiny, tiny bit—not much, though. *[She suddenly checks herself; seriously.]* Oh, but, Kristine! What a thoughtless wretch I am, chattering away like that—Dear, darling Kristine, do forgive me!

MRS. LINDE

What for, Nora, dear?

NORA

[Softly] You lost your husband, didn't you, Kristine! You're a widow.

MRS. LINDE

Yes; my husband died three years ago.

NORA

Yes, I remember; I saw it in the paper. Oh, *I did* mean to write to you, Kristine! But I kept on putting it off, and all sorts of things kept coming in the way.

MRS. LINDE

I understand, dear Nora.

NORA

No, it was beastly of me, Kristine! Oh, you poor darling! What you must have gone through!— And he died without leaving you anything, didn't he?

MRS. LINDE

Yes.

NORA

And you have no children?

MRS. LINDE

No.

NORA

Nothing then?

MRS. LINDE

Nothing— Not even grief, not even regret.

NORA

[Looking at her incredulously] But how is that possible, Kristine?

MRS. LINDE

[Smiling sadly and stroking her hair] It sometimes happens, Nora.

NORA

Imagine being so utterly alone! It must be dreadful for you, Kristine! I have three of the loveliest children! I can't show them to you just now, they're out with their nurse. But I want you to tell me all about yourself—

MRS. LINDE

No, no; I'd rather hear about you, Nora—

NORA

No, I want you to begin. I'm not going to be selfish today. I'm going to think only of you. Oh! but one thing I *must* tell you. You haven't heard about the wonderful thing that's just happened to us, have you?

MRS. LINDE

No. What is it?

NORA

My husband's been elected president of the Joint Stock Bank!

MRS. LINDE

Oh, Nora— How splendid!

NORA

Yes; isn't it? You see, a lawyer's position is so uncertain, especially if he refuses to handle any cases that are in the least bit—shady; Torvald is very particular about such things—and I agree with him, of course! You can imagine how glad we are. He's to start at the Bank right after the New Year; he'll make a big salary and all sorts of percentages. We'll be able to live quite differently from then on—we'll have everything we want. Oh, Kristine! I'm so happy and excited! Won't it be wonderful to have lots and lots of money, and nothing to worry about!

MRS. LINDE
It certainly would be wonderful to have enough for one's needs.

NORA
Oh, not just for one's *needs*, Kristine! But heaps and heaps of money!

MRS. LINDE
[With a smile] Nora, Nora, I see you haven't grown up yet! I remember at school you were a frightful spendthrift.

NORA
[Quietly; smiling] Yes; that's what Torvald always says. [Holding up her forefinger] But I haven't had much chance to be a spendthrift. We have had to work hard—both of us.

MRS. LINDE
You too?

NORA
Oh yes! I did all sorts of little jobs: needlework, embroidery, crochet—that sort of thing. [Casually] And other things as well. I suppose you know that Torvald left the Government service right after we were married. There wasn't much chance of promotion in his department, and of course he had to earn more money when he had me to support. But that first year he overworked himself terribly. He had to undertake all sorts of odd jobs, worked from morning till night. He couldn't stand it; his health gave way and he became deathly ill. The doctors said he absolutely *must* spend some time in the South.

MRS. LINDE
Yes, I heard you spent a whole year in Italy.

NORA
Yes, we did. It wasn't easy to arrange, I can tell you. It was just after Ivar's birth. But of course we had to go. It was a wonderful trip, and it saved Torvald's life. But it cost a fearful lot of money, Kristine.

MRS. LINDE
Yes, it must have.

NORA
Twelve hundred dollars! Four thousand eight hundred crowns! That's an awful lot of money, you know.

MRS. LINDE
You were lucky to have it.

NORA
Well, you see, we got it from Father.

MRS. LINDE
Oh, I see. Wasn't it just about that time that your father died?

NORA
Yes, it was, Kristine. Just think! I wasn't able to go to him—I couldn't be there to nurse him! I was expecting Ivar at the time and then I had my poor sick Torvald to look after. Dear, darling Papa! I never saw him again, Kristine. It's the hardest thing I have had to go through since my marriage.

MRS. LINDE
I know you were awfully fond of him. And after that you went to Italy?

NORA
Yes; then we had the money, you see; and the doctors said we must lose no time; so we started a month later.

MRS. LINDE
And your husband came back completely cured?

NORA
Strong as an ox!

MRS. LINDE
But—what about the doctor then?

NORA
How do you mean?

MRS. LINDE
Didn't the maid say something about a doctor, just as I arrived?

NORA
Oh, yes; Dr. Rank. He's our best friend—it's not a professional call; he stops in to see us every day. No, Torvald hasn't had a moment's illness since; and the children are strong and well, and so am I. [Jumps up and claps her hands] Oh Kristine, Kristine! How lovely it is to be alive and happy! But how disgraceful of me! Here I am talking about nothing but myself! [Seats herself upon a footstool close to Kristine and lays her arms on her lap] Please don't be cross with me— Is it really true, Kristine, that you didn't love your husband? Why did you marry him, then?

MRS. LINDE
Well, you see—Mother was still alive; she was bedridden; completely helpless; and I had my two younger brothers to take care of. I didn't think it would be right to refuse him.

NORA

No, I suppose not. I suppose he had money then?

MRS. LINDE

Yes, I believe he was quite well off. But his business was precarious, Nora. When he died it all went to pieces, and there was nothing left.

NORA

And then—?

MRS. LINDE

Then I had to struggle along as best I could. I had a small shop for a while, and then I started a little school. These last three years have been one long battle—but it is over now, Nora. My dear mother is at rest— She doesn't need me any more. And my brothers are old enough to work, and can look after themselves.

NORA

You must have such a free feeling!

MRS. LINDE

No—only one of complete emptiness. I haven't a soul to live for! [Stands up restlessly] I suppose that's why I felt I had to get away. I should think here it would be easier to find something to do—something to occupy one's thoughts. I might be lucky enough to get a steady job here—some office work, perhaps—

NORA

But that's so terribly tiring, Kristine; and you look so tired already. What you need is a rest. Couldn't you go to some nice watering-place?

MRS. LINDE

[Going to the window] I have no father to give me the money, Nora.

NORA

[Rising] Oh, please don't be cross with me!

MRS. LINDE

[Goes to her] My dear Nora, you mustn't be cross with me! In my sort of position it's hard not to become bitter. One has no one to work for, and yet one can't give up the struggle. One must go on living, and it makes one selfish. I'm ashamed to admit it—but, just now, when you told me the good news about your husband's new position—I was glad—not so much for your sake as for mine.

NORA

How do you mean? Oh of course—I see! You think Torvald might perhaps help you.

MRS. LINDE

That's what I thought, yes.

NORA

And so he shall, Kristine. Just you leave it to me. I'll get him in a really good mood—and then bring it up quite casually. Oh, it would be such fun to help you!

MRS. LINDE

How good of you, Nora dear, to bother on my account! It's especially good of you—after all, you've never had to go through any hardship.

NORA

I? Not go through any—?

MRS. LINDE

[Smiling] Well— Good Heavens—a little needlework, and so forth— You're just a child, Nora.

NORA

[Tosses her head and paces the room] You needn't be so patronizing!

MRS. LINDE

No?

NORA

You're just like all the rest. You all think I'm incapable of being serious—

MRS. LINDE

Oh, come now—

NORA

You seem to think I've had no troubles—that I've been through nothing in my life!

MRS. LINDE

But you've just told me all your troubles, Nora dear.

NORA

I've only told you trifles! [Softly] I haven't mentioned the important thing.

MRS. LINDE

Important thing? What do you mean?

NORA

I know you look down on me, Kristine; but you really shouldn't. You take pride in having worked so hard and so long for your mother.

MRS. LINDE

I don't look down on anyone, Nora; I can't help feeling proud and happy too, to have been able to make Mother's last days a little easier—

NORA

And you're proud of what you did for your brothers, too.

MRS. LINDE

I think I have a right to be.

NORA

Yes, so do I. But I want you to know, Kristine—that I, too, have something to be proud of.

MRS. LINDE

I don't doubt that. But what are you referring to?

NORA

Hush! We must talk quietly. It would be dreadful if Torvald overheard us! He must never know about it! No one must know about it, except you.

MRS. LINDE

And what is it, Nora?

NORA

Come over here. [Draws her down beside her on the sofa] Yes, I have something to be proud and happy about too. I saved Torvald's life, you see.

MRS. LINDE

Saved his life? But how?

NORA

I told you about our trip to Italy. Torvald would never have recovered if it hadn't been for that.

MRS. LINDE

Yes, I know—and your father gave you the necessary money.

NORA

[Smiling] That's what everyone thinks—Torvald too; but—

MRS. LINDE

Well—?

NORA

Papa never gave us a penny. I raised the money myself.

MRS. LINDE

All that money! You?

NORA

Twelve hundred dollars. Four thousand eight hundred crowns. What do you think of that?

MRS. LINDE

But, Nora, how on earth did you do it? Did you win it in the lottery?

NORA

[Contemptuously] The lottery! Of course not! Any fool could have done that!

MRS. LINDE

Where did you get it then?

NORA

[Hums and smiles mysteriously] H'm; tra-la-la-la.

MRS. LINDE

You certainly couldn't have borrowed it.

NORA

Why not?

MRS. LINDE

A wife can't borrow without her husband's consent.

NORA

[Tossing her head] Oh I don't know! If a wife has a good head on her shoulders—and has a little sense of business—

MRS. LINDE

I don't in the least understand, Nora—

NORA

Well, you needn't. I never said I borrowed the money. I may have got it in some other way. [Throws herself back on the sofa] Perhaps I got it from some admirer. After all when one is as attractive as I am—!

MRS. LINDE

What a mad little creature you are!

NORA

I'm sure you're dying of curiosity, Kristine—

MRS. LINDE

Nora, are you sure you haven't been a little rash?

NORA

[Sitting upright again] Is it rash to save one's husband's life?

MRS. LINDE

But mightn't it be rash to do such a thing behind his back?

NORA

But I couldn't tell him—don't you understand that? He wasn't even supposed to know how ill he was. The doctors didn't tell him—they came to me privately, told me his life was in danger and that he could only be saved by living in the South for a while. At first I tried persuasion; I cried, I begged, I cajoled—I said how much I longed to take a trip abroad like other young wives; I reminded him of my condition and told him he ought to humor me—and finally, I came right out and suggested that we borrow the money. But then, Kristine, he was almost angry; he said I was being frivolous and that it was his duty as my husband not to indulge my whims and fancies—I think that's what he called them. Then I made up my mind he must be saved in spite of himself—and I thought of a way.

MRS. LINDE

But didn't he ever find out from your father that the money was not from him?

NORA

No; never. You see, Papa died just about that time. I was going to tell him all about it and beg him not to give me away. But he was so very ill—and then, it was no longer necessary—unfortunately.

MRS. LINDE

And you have never confided all this to your husband?

NORA

Good heavens, no! That's out of the question! He's much too strict in matters of that sort. And besides—Torvald could never bear to think of owing anything to me! It would hurt his self-respect—wound his pride. It would ruin everything between us. Our whole marriage would be wrecked by it!

MRS. LINDE

Don't you think you'll ever tell him?

NORA

[Thoughtfully; half-smiling] Perhaps some day—a long time from now when I'm no longer so pretty and attractive. No! Don't laugh! Some day when Torvald is no longer as much in love with me as he is now; when it no longer amuses him to see me dance and dress-up and act for him—then it might be useful to have something in reserve. [Breaking off] Oh, what nonsense! That time will never come! Well—what do you think of my great secret, Kristine? Haven't I something to be proud of too? It's caused me endless worry, though. It hasn't been easy to fulfill my obligations. You know, in business there are things called installments, and quarterly interest—and they're dreadfully hard to meet on time. I've had to save a little here and there, wherever I could. I couldn't save much out of the housekeeping, for of course Torvald had to live well. And I couldn't let the children go

about badly dressed; any money I got for them, I spent on them, the darlings!

MRS. LINDE

Poor Nora! I suppose it had to come out of your own allowance.

NORA

Yes, of course. But after all, the whole thing was my doing. Whenever Torvald gave me money to buy some new clothes, or other things I needed, I never spent more than half of it; I always picked out the simplest cheapest dresses. It's a blessing that almost anything looks well on me—so Torvald never knew the difference. But it's been hard sometimes, Kristine. It's so nice to have pretty clothes—isn't it?

MRS. LINDE

I suppose it is.

NORA

And I made money in other ways too. Last winter I was lucky enough to get a lot of copying to do. I shut myself up in my room every evening and wrote far into the night. Sometimes I was absolutely exhausted—but it was fun all the same—working like that and earning money. It made me feel almost like a man!

MRS. LINDE

How much have you managed to pay off?

NORA

Well, I really don't know exactly. It's hard to keep track of things like that. All I know is—I've paid every penny I could scrape together. There were times when I didn't know which way to turn! [Smiles] Then I used to sit here and pretend that some rich old gentleman had fallen madly in love with me—

MRS. LINDE

What are you talking about? *What* old gentleman?

NORA

I'm just joking! And then he was to die and when they opened his will, there in large letters were to be the words: "I leave all my fortune to that charming Nora Helmer to be handed over to her immediately."

MRS. LINDE

But who *is* this old gentleman?

NORA

Good heavens, can't you understand? There never *was* any such old gentleman; I just used to make him up, when I was at the end of my rope and didn't know where to turn for money. But it doesn't matter now—the tiresome old fellow can stay where he is as far as I am concerned. I no longer need him nor his money; for now my troubles are over. *[Springing up]* Oh, isn't it wonderful to think of, Kristine. No more troubles! No more worry! I'll be able to play and romp about with the children; I'll be able to make a charming lovely home for Torvald—have everything just as he likes it. And soon spring will be here, with its great blue sky. Perhaps we might take a little trip—I might see the ocean again. Oh, it's so marvelous to be alive and to be happy!

[The hall doorbell rings.]

MRS. LINDE

[Rising] There's the bell. Perhaps I had better go.

NORA

No, no; do stay! It's probably just someone for Torvald.

HELENE

[In the doorway] Excuse me, Ma'am; there's a gentleman asking for Mr. Helmer—but the doctor's in there—and I didn't know if I should disturb him—

NORA

Who is it?

KROGSTAD

[In the doorway] It is I, Mrs. Helmer.

[Mrs. Linde starts and turns away to the window.]

NORA

[Goes a step toward him, anxiously; in a low voice] You? What is it? Why do you want to see my husband?

KROGSTAD

It's to do with Bank business—more or less. I have a small position in the Joint Stock Bank, and I hear your husband is to be the new president.

NORA

Then it's just—?

KROGSTAD

Just routine business, Mrs. Helmer; nothing else.

NORA

Then, please be good enough to go into his study.

[Krogstad goes. She bows indifferently while she closes the door into the hall. Then she goes to the stove and tends the fire.]

MRS. LINDE

Who was that man, Nora?

NORA

A Mr. Krogstad—he's a lawyer.

MRS. LINDE

I was right then.

NORA

Do you know him?

MRS. LINDE

I used to know him—many years ago. He worked in a law office in our town.

NORA

Yes, so he did.

MRS. LINDE

How he has changed!

NORA

He was unhappily married, they say.

MRS. LINDE

Is he a widower now?

NORA

Yes—with lots of children. There! That's better! *[She closes the door of the stove and moves the rocking chair a little to one side.]*

MRS. LINDE

I'm told he's mixed up in a lot of rather questionable business.

NORA

He may be; I really don't know. But don't let's talk about business—it's so tiresome.

[Dr. Rank comes out of Helmer's room.]

RANK

[Still in the doorway] No, no, I won't disturb you. I'll go in and see your wife for a moment. *[Sees Mrs. Linde]* Oh, I beg your pardon. I seem to be in the way here, too.

NORA

Of course not! *[Introduces them]* Dr. Rank—Mrs. Linde.

RANK

Well, well, I've often heard that name mentioned in this house; didn't I pass you on the stairs when I came in?

MRS. LINDE

Yes; I'm afraid I climb them very slowly. They wear me out!

RANK

A little on the delicate side—eh?

MRS. LINDE

No; just a bit overtired.

RANK

I see. So I suppose you've come to town for a good rest—on a round of dissipation!

MRS. LINDE

I have come to look for work.

RANK

Is that the best remedy for tiredness?

MRS. LINDE

One has to live, Doctor.

RANK

Yes, I'm told that's necessary.

NORA

Oh, come now, Dr. Rank! You're not above wanting to live yourself!

RANK

That's true enough. No matter how wretched I may be, I still want to hang on as long as possible. All my patients have that feeling too. Even the *morally* sick seem to share it. There's a wreck of a man in there with Helmer now—

MRS. LINDE

[Softly] Ah!

NORA

Whom do you mean?

RANK

A fellow named Krogstad, he's a lawyer—you wouldn't know anything about him. He's thoroughly depraved—rotten to the core— Yet even he declared, as though it were a matter of paramount importance, that he must live.

NORA

Really? What did he want with Torvald?

RANK

I've no idea; I gathered it was some Bank business.

NORA

I didn't know that Krog—that this man Krogstad had anything to do with the Bank?

RANK

He seems to have some sort of position there. *[To Mrs. Linde]* I don't know if this is true in your part of the country—but there are men who make it a practice of prying about in other people's business, searching for individuals of doubtful character—and having discovered their secret, place them in positions of trust, where they can keep an eye on them, and make use of them at will. Honest men—men of strong moral fiber—they leave out in the cold.

MRS. LINDE

Perhaps the weaklings need more help.

RANK

[Shrugs his shoulders] That point-of-view is fast turning society into a clinic.

[Nora, deep in her own thoughts, breaks into half-stifled laughter and claps her hands.]

RANK

Why should that make you laugh? I wonder if you've any idea what "society" is?

NORA

Why should I care about your tiresome old "society"? I was laughing at something quite different—something frightfully amusing. Tell me, Dr. Rank—will all the employees at the Bank be dependent on Torvald now?

RANK

Is *that* what strikes you as so amusing?

NORA

[Smiles and hums] Never you mind! Never you mind! *[Walks about the room]* What fun to think that we—that Torvald—has such power over so many people. *[Takes the bag from her pocket]* Dr. Rank, how about a macaroon?

RANK

Well, well— Macaroons, eh? I thought they were forbidden here.

NORA

These are some Kristine brought—

MRS. LINDE

What! I—

NORA

Now, you needn't be so frightened. How could you possibly know that Torvald had forbidden them? He's afraid they'll spoil my teeth. Oh, well—just for once! Don't you agree, Dr. Rank? There you are! *[Puts a macaroon into his mouth]* You must have one too, Kristine. And I'll have just one—just a tiny one, or at most two. [*Walks about again*] Oh dear, I am so happy! There's just one thing in all the world that would give me the greatest pleasure.

RANK
What's that?

NORA
It's something I long to say in front of Torvald.

RANK
What's to prevent you?

NORA
Oh, I don't dare; it isn't nice.

MRS. LINDE
Not nice?

RANK
It might be unwise, then; but you can certainly say it to us. What is it you so long to say in front of Torvald?

NORA
I'd so love to say "Damn!—damn!—damn it all!"

RANK
Have you gone crazy?

MRS. LINDE
Good gracious, Nora—

RANK
Go ahead and say it—here he comes!

NORA
[*Hides the macaroons*]Hush—sh—sh.

> [*Helmer comes out of his room; he carries his hat and overcoat.*]

NORA
[*Going to him*] Well, Torvald, dear, did you get rid of him?

HELMER
He has just gone.

NORA
Let me introduce you—this is Kristine, who has just arrived in town—

HELMER
Kristine? I'm sorry—but I really don't—

NORA
Mrs. Linde, Torvald, dear—Kristine Linde.

HELMER
Oh yes! I suppose you're one of my wife's school friends?

MRS. LINDE
Yes; we knew each other as children.

NORA
Imagine, Torvald! She came all that long way just to talk to you.

HELMER
How do you mean?

MRS. LINDE
Well, it wasn't exactly—

NORA
Kristine is tremendously good at office-work, and her great dream is to get a position with a really clever man—so she can improve still more, you see—

HELMER
Very sensible, Mrs. Linde.

NORA
And when she heard that you had become president of the Bank—it was in the paper, you know—she started off at once; you *will* try and do something for Kristine, won't you, Torvald? For my sake?

HELMER
It's by no means impossible. You're a widow, I presume?

MRS. LINDE
Yes.

HELMER
And you've already had business experience?

MRS. LINDE
A good deal.

HELMER
Then, I think it's quite likely I may be able to find a place for you.

NORA
[*Clapping her hands*] There, you see! You see!

HELMER
You have come at a good moment, Mrs. Linde.

MRS. LINDE
How can I ever thank you—?

HELMER
[*Smiling*] Don't mention it. [*Puts on his overcoat*] But just now, I'm afraid you must excuse me—

RANK
I'll go with you. [*Fetches his fur coat from the hall and warms it at the stove*]

NORA

Don't be long, Torvald, dear.

HELMER

I shan't be more than an hour.

NORA

Are you going too, Kristine?

MRS. LINDE

[Putting on her outdoor things] Yes; I must go and find a place to live.

HELMER

We can all go out together.

NORA

[Helping her] How tiresome that we're so cramped for room, Kristine; otherwise—

MRS. LINDE

Oh, you mustn't think of that! Good-bye, dear Nora, and thanks for everything.

NORA

Good-bye for the present. Of course you'll come back this evening. And you too, Dr. Rank—eh? If you're well enough? But of course you'll be well enough! Wrap up warmly now! [They go out talking, into the hall; children's voices are heard on the stairs] Here they come! Here they come! [She runs to the outer door and opens it. The nurse, Anne-Marie, enters the hall with the children] Come in, come in—you darlings! Just look at them, Kristine. Aren't they sweet?

RANK

No chattering in this awful draught!

HELMER

Come along, Mrs. Linde; you have to be a mother to put up with this!

[Dr. Rank, Helmer, and Mrs. Linde go down the stairs; Anne-Marie enters the room with the children; Nora comes in too, shutting the door behind her.]

NORA

How fresh and bright you look! And what red cheeks! Like apples and roses. [The children chatter to her during what follows.] Did you have a good time? Splendid! You gave Emmy and Bob a ride on your sled? Both at once? You are a clever boy, Ivar! Let me hold her for a bit, Anne-Marie. My darling little doll-baby. [Takes the smallest from the nurse and dances with her] All right, Bobbie! Mama will dance with you too. You threw snowballs, did you? I should have been in on

that! Never mind, Anne; I'll undress them myself— oh, do let me—it's such fun. Go on into the nursery, you look half-frozen. There's some hot coffee in there on the stove. [The nurse goes into the room on the left. Nora takes off the children's things and throws them down anywhere, while the children all talk together.] Not really! You were chased by a big dog? But he didn't bite you? No; dogs don't bite tiny little doll-babies! Don't touch the packages, Ivar. What's in them? Wouldn't you like to know! No. No! Careful! It might bite! Come on, let's play. What will we play? Hide-and-seek? Let's play hide-and-seek. Bob, you hide first! Do you want me to? All right! I'll hide first then.

[She and the children play, laughing and shouting, all over the room and in the adjacent room to the left. Finally Nora hides under the table; the children come rushing in, look for her, but cannot find her, hear her half-suppressed laughter, rush to the table, lift up the cover and see her. Loud shouts of delight. She creeps out, as though to frighten them. More shouts. Meanwhile there has been a knock at the door leading into the hall. No one has heard it. Now the door is half-opened and Krogstad appears. He waits a little—the game continues.]

KROGSTAD

I beg your pardon, Mrs. Helmer—

NORA

[With a stifled scream, turns round and half jumps up] Oh! What do you want?

KROGSTAD

Excuse me; the outer door was ajar—someone must have forgotten to close it—

NORA

[Standing up] My husband is not at home, Mr. Krogstad.

KROGSTAD

I know that.

NORA

Then, what do you want here?

KROGSTAD

I want a few words with you.

NORA

With—? [To the children, softly] Go in to Anne-Marie. What? No—the strange man won't do Mama any harm; when he's gone we'll go on playing. [She leads the children into the right-hand room, and shuts the door *behind them; uneasy, in suspense.]* You want to speak to me?

KROGSTAD
Yes, I do.

NORA
Today? But it's not the first of the month yet—

KROGSTAD
No, it is Christmas Eve. It's up to you whether your Christmas is a merry one.

NORA
What is it you want? Today I can't possibly—

KROGSTAD
That doesn't concern me for the moment. This is about something else. You have a few minutes, haven't you?

NORA
I suppose so; although—

KROGSTAD
Good. I was sitting in the restaurant opposite, and I saw your husband go down the street—

NORA
Well?

KROGSTAD
—with a lady.

NORA
What of it?

KROGSTAD
May I ask if that lady was a Mrs. Linde?

NORA
Yes.

KROGSTAD
She's just come to town, hasn't she?

NORA
Yes. Today.

KROGSTAD
Is she a good friend of yours?

NORA
Yes, she is. But I can't imagine—

KROGSTAD
I used to know her too.

NORA
Yes, I know you did.

KROGSTAD
Then you know all about it. I thought as much. Now, tell me: is Mrs. Linde to have a place in the Bank?

NORA
How dare you question me like this, Mr. Krogstad—you, one of my husband's employees! But since you ask—you might as well know. Yes, Mrs. Linde is to have a position at the Bank, and it is I who recommended her. Does that satisfy you, Mr. Krogstad?

KROGSTAD
I was right, then.

NORA
[Walks up and down] After all, one has a little influence, now and then. Even if one is only a woman it doesn't always follow that—people in subordinate positions, Mr. Krogstad, ought really to be careful how they offend anyone who—h'm—

KROGSTAD
—has influence?

NORA
Precisely.

KROGSTAD
[Taking another tone] Then perhaps you'll be so kind, Mrs. Helmer, as to use your influence on *my* behalf?

NORA
What? How do you mean?

KROGSTAD
Perhaps you'll be good enough to see that I *retain* my subordinate position?

NORA
But, I don't understand. Who wants to take it from you?

KROGSTAD
Oh, don't try and play the innocent! I can well understand that it would be unpleasant for your friend to associate with me; and I understand too, whom I have to thank for my dismissal.

NORA
But I assure you—

KROGSTAD
Never mind all that—there is still time. But I advise you to use your influence to prevent this.

NORA
But, Mr. Krogstad, I *have* no influence—absolutely none!

KROGSTAD

Indeed! I thought you just told me yourself—

NORA

You misunderstood me—*really* you did! You must know my husband would never be influenced by me!

KROGSTAD

Your husband and I were at the University together—I know him well. I don't suppose he's any more inflexible than other married men.

NORA

Don't you dare talk disrespectfully about my husband, or I'll show you the door!

KROGSTAD

The little lady's plucky.

NORA

I'm no longer afraid of you. I'll soon be free of all this—after the first of the year.

KROGSTAD

[*In a more controlled manner*] Listen to me, Mrs. Helmer. This is a matter of life and death to me. I warn you I shall fight with all my might to keep my position in the Bank.

NORA

So it seems.

KROGSTAD

It's not just the salary; that is the least important part of it— It's something else— Well, I might as well be frank with you. I suppose you know, like everyone else, that once—a long time ago—I got into quite a bit of trouble.

NORA

I have heard something about it, I believe.

KROGSTAD

The matter never came to court; but from that time on, all doors were closed to me. I then went into the business with which you are familiar. I had to do something; and I don't think I've been among the worst. But now I must get away from all that. My sons are growing up, you see; for their sake I'm determined to recapture my good name. This position in the Bank was to be the first step; and now your husband wants to kick me back into the mud again.

NORA

But I tell you, Mr. Krogstad, it's not in my power to help you.

KROGSTAD

Only because you don't really want to; but I can compel you to do it, if I choose.

NORA

You wouldn't tell my husband that I owe you money?

KROGSTAD

And suppose I were to?

NORA

But that would be an outrageous thing to do! [*With tears in her voice*] My secret—that I've guarded with such pride—such joy! I couldn't bear to have him find it out in such an ugly, hateful way—to have him find it out from you! I couldn't bear it! It would be too horribly unpleasant!

KROGSTAD

Only unpleasant, Mrs. Helmer?

NORA

[*Vehemently*] But just you do it! You'll be the one to suffer; for then my husband will *really* know the kind of man you are—there'll be no chance of keeping your job then!

KROGSTAD

Didn't you hear my question? I asked if it were only unpleasantness you feared?

NORA

If my husband got to know about it, he'd naturally pay you off at once, and then we'd have nothing more to do with you.

KROGSTAD

[*Takes a step towards her*] Listen, Mrs. Helmer: Either you have a very bad memory, or you know nothing about business. I think I'd better make the position clear to you.

NORA

What do you mean?

KROGSTAD

When your husband fell ill, you came to me to borrow twelve hundred dollars.

NORA

I didn't know what else to do.

KROGSTAD

I promised to find you the money—

NORA

And you did find it.

KROGSTAD

I promised to find you the money, on certain conditions. At that time you were so taken up with your husband's illness and so anxious to procure the money for your journey, that you probably did not give much thought to details. Perhaps I'd better remind you of them. I promised to find you the amount in exchange for a note, which I drew up.

NORA

Yes, and I signed it.

KROGSTAD

Very good. But then I added a clause, stating that your father would stand sponsor for the debt. This clause your father was to have signed.

NORA

Was to—? He did sign it.

KROGSTAD

I left the date blank, so that your father himself should date his signature. You recall that?

NORA

Yes, I believe—

KROGSTAD

Then I gave you the paper, and you were to mail it to your father. Isn't that so?

NORA

Yes.

KROGSTAD

And you must have mailed it at once; for five or six days later you brought me back the document with your father's signature; and then I handed you the money.

NORA

Well? Haven't I made my payments punctually?

KROGSTAD

Fairly—yes. But to return to the point: That was a sad time for you, wasn't it, Mrs. Helmer?

NORA

It was indeed!

KROGSTAD

Your father was very ill, I believe?

NORA

Yes—he was dying.

KROGSTAD

And he did die soon after, didn't he?

NORA

Yes.

KROGSTAD

Now tell me, Mrs. Helmer: Do you happen to recollect the date of your father's death: the day of the month, I mean?

NORA

Father died on the 29th of September.

KROGSTAD

Quite correct. I have made inquiries. Now here is a strange thing, Mrs. Helmer—[Produces a paper] something rather hard to explain.

NORA

What do you mean? What strange thing?

KROGSTAD

The strange thing about it is, that your father seems to have signed this paper three days after his death!

NORA

I don't understand—

KROGSTAD

Your father died on the 29th of September. But look at this: his signature is dated October 2nd! Isn't that rather strange, Mrs. Helmer? [Nora is silent] Can you explain that to me? [Nora continues silent] It is curious, too, that the words 'October 2nd' and the year are not in your father's handwriting, but in a handwriting I seem to know. This could easily be explained, however; your father might have forgotten to date his signature, and someone might have added the date at random, before the fact of your father's death was known. There is nothing wrong in that. It all depends on the signature itself. It is of course genuine, Mrs. Helmer? It was your father himself who wrote his name here?

NORA

[After a short silence, throws her head back and looks defiantly at him] No, it wasn't. I wrote father's name.

KROGSTAD

I suppose you realize, Mrs. Helmer, what a dangerous confession that is?

NORA

Why should it be dangerous? You will get your money soon enough!

KROGSTAD

I'd like to ask you a question: Why didn't you send the paper to your father?

NORA

It was impossible. Father was too ill. If I had asked him for his signature, he'd have wanted to know what the money was for. In his condition I simply could not tell him that my husband's life was in danger. That's why it was impossible.

KROGSTAD

Then wouldn't it have been wiser to give up the journey?

NORA

How could I? That journey was to save my husband's life. I simply couldn't give it up.

KROGSTAD

And it never occurred to you that you weren't being honest with me?

NORA

I really couldn't concern myself with that. You meant nothing to me— In fact I couldn't help disliking you for making it all so difficult—with your cold, business-like clauses and conditions—when you knew my husband's life was at stake.

KROGSTAD

You evidently haven't the faintest idea, Mrs. Helmer, what you have been guilty of. Yet let me tell you that it was nothing more and nothing worse that made me an outcast from society.

NORA

You don't expect me to believe that you ever did a brave thing to save your wife's life?

KROGSTAD

The law takes no account of motives.

NORA

It must be a very bad law, then!

KROGSTAD

Bad or not, if I produce this document in court, you will be condemned according to the law.

NORA

I don't believe that for a minute. Do you mean to tell me that a daughter has no right to spare her dying father worry and anxiety? Or that a wife has no right to save her husband's life? I may not know much about it—but I'm sure there must be something or other in the law that permits such things. You as a lawyer should be aware of that. You don't seem to know very much about the law, Mr. Krogstad.

KROGSTAD

Possibly not. But business—the kind of business we are concerned with—I *do* know something about. Don't you agree? Very well, then; do as you please. But I warn you: if I am made to suffer a second time, you shall keep me company. [*Bows and goes out through the hall*]

NORA

[*Stands a while thinking, then tosses her head*] What nonsense! He's just trying to frighten me. I'm not such a fool as all that! [*Begins folding the children's clothes. Pauses*] And yet—? No, it's impossible! After all—I only did it for love's sake.

CHILDREN

[*At the door, left*] Mamma, the strange man has gone now.

NORA

Yes, yes, I know. But don't tell anyone about the strange man. Do you hear? Not even Papa!

CHILDREN

No, Mamma; now will you play with us again?

NORA

No, not just now.

CHILDREN

But Mamma! You promised!

NORA

But I can't just now. Run back to the nursery; I have so much to do. Run along now! Run along, my darlings! [*She pushes them gently into the inner room, and closes the door behind them. Sits on the sofa, embroiders a few stitches, but soon pauses*] No! [*Throws down the work, rises, goes to the hall door and calls out*] Helene, bring the tree in to me, will you? [*Goes to table, right, and opens the drawer; again pauses*] No, it's utterly impossible!

HELENE

[*Carries in the Christmas tree*] Where shall I put it, Ma'am?

NORA

Right there; in the middle of the room.

HELENE

Is there anything else you need?

NORA

No, thanks; I have everything. [*Helene, having put down the tree, goes out.*]

NORA

[Busy dressing the tree] We'll put a candle here—and some flowers here—that dreadful man! But it's just nonsense! There's nothing to worry about. The tree will be lovely. I'll do everything to please you, Torvald; I'll sing for you, I'll dance for you—

[Enter Helmer by the hall door, with a bundle of documents.]

NORA

Oh! You're back already?

HELMER

Yes. Has somebody been here?

NORA

No. Nobody.

HELMER

That's odd. I just saw Krogstad leave the house.

NORA

Really? Well—as a matter of fact—Krogstad was here for a moment.

HELMER

Nora—I can tell by your manner—he came here to ask you to put in a good word for him, didn't he?

NORA

Yes, Torvald.

HELMER

And you weren't supposed to tell me he'd been here— You were to do it as if of your own accord— isn't that it?

NORA

Yes, Torvald; but—

HELMER

Nora, Nora! How could you consent to such a thing! To have dealings with a man like that—make him promises! And then to lie about it too!

NORA

Lie!

HELMER

Didn't you tell me that nobody had been here? [Threatens with his finger] My little bird must never do that again! A song-bird must sing clear and true! No false notes! [Puts arm around her] Isn't that the way it should be? Of course it is! [Lets her go] And now we'll say no more about it. [Sits down before the fire] It's so cozy and peaceful here! [Glances through the documents]

NORA

[Busy with the tree, after a short silence] Torvald!

HELMER

Yes.

NORA

I'm so looking forward to the Stenborgs' fancy dress party, day after tomorrow.

HELMER

And I can't wait to see what surprise you have in store for me.

NORA

Oh, it's so awful, Torvald!

HELMER

What is?

NORA

I can't think of anything amusing. Everything seems so silly, so pointless.

HELMER

Has my little Nora come to that conclusion?

NORA

[Behind his chair, with her arms on the back] Are you very busy, Torvald?

HELMER

Well—

NORA

What are all those papers?

HELMER

Just Bank business.

NORA

Already!

HELMER

The board of directors has given me full authority to do some reorganizing—to make a few necessary changes in the staff. I'll have to work on it during Christmas week. I want it all settled by the New Year.

NORA

I see. So that was why that poor Krogstad—

HELMER

H'm.

NORA

[Still leaning over the chair-back and slowly stroking his hair] If you weren't so very busy, I'd ask you to do me a great, great favor, Torvald.

HELMER

Well, let's hear it! Out with it!

NORA

You have such perfect taste, Torvald; and I do so want to look well at the fancy dress ball. Couldn't you take me in hand, and decide what I'm to be, and arrange my costume for me?

HELMER

Well, well! So we're not so self-sufficient after all! We need a helping hand, do we?

NORA

Oh, please, Torvald! I know I shall *never* manage without your help!

HELMER

I'll think about it; we'll hit on something.

NORA

Oh, how sweet of you! [Goes to the tree again; pause] Those red flowers show up beautifully! Tell me, Torvald; did that Krogstad do something very wrong?

HELMER

He committed forgery. Have you any idea of what that means?

NORA

Perhaps he did it out of necessity?

HELMER

Or perhaps he was just fool-hardy, like so many others. I am not so harsh as to condemn a man irrevocably for one mistake.

NORA

No, of course not!

HELMER

A man has a chance to rehabilitate himself, if he honestly admits his guilt and takes his punishment.

NORA

Punishment—

HELMER

But that wasn't Krogstad's way. He resorted to tricks and evasions; became thoroughly demoralized.

NORA

You really think it would—?

HELMER

When a man has that sort of thing on his conscience his life becomes a tissue of lies and deception. He's forced to wear a mask—even with those nearest to him—his own wife and children even. And the children—that's the worst part of it, Nora.

NORA

Why?

HELMER

Because the whole atmosphere of the home would be contaminated. The very air the children breathed would be filled with evil.

NORA

[Closer behind him] Are you sure of that?

HELMER

As a lawyer, I know it from experience. Almost all cases of early delinquency can be traced to dishonest mothers.

NORA

Why—only mothers?

HELMER

It usually stems from the mother's side; but of course it can come from the father too. We lawyers know a lot about such things. And this Krogstad has been deliberately poisoning his own children for years, by surrounding them with lies and hypocrisy—that is why I call him demoralized. [Holds out both hands to her] So my sweet little Nora must promise not to plead his cause. Shake hands on it. Well? What's the matter? Give me your hand. There! That's all settled. I assure you it would have been impossible for me to work with him. It literally gives me a feeling of physical discomfort to come in contact with such people. [Nora draws her hand away, and moves to the other side of the Christmas tree.]

NORA

It's so warm here. And I have such a lot to do.

HELMER

[Rises and gathers up his papers] I must try and look through some of these papers before dinner. I'll give some thought to your costume too. Perhaps I may even find something to hang in gilt paper on the Christmas tree! [Lays his hand on her head] My own precious little song-bird! [He goes into his study and closes the door after him.]

NORA

[Softly, after a pause] It can't be—! It's impossible. Of course it's impossible!

ANNE-MARIE

[At the door, left] The babies keep begging to come in and see Mamma.

NORA

No, no! Don't let them come to me! Keep them with you, Anne-Marie.

ANNE-MARIE

Very well, Ma'am. [Shuts the door]

NORA

[Pale with terror] Harm my children!—Corrupt my home! [Short pause. She throws back her head.] It's not true! I know it's not! It could never, never be true!

[Curtain]

ACT TWO

Scene

The same room. In the corner, beside the piano, stands the Christmas tree, stripped and with the candles burnt out. Nora's outdoor things lie on the sofa. Nora, alone, is walking about restlessly. At last she stops by the sofa, and picks up her cloak.

NORA

[Puts the cloak down again] Did someone come in? [Goes to the hall and listens] No; no one; of course no one will come today, Christmas Day; nor tomorrow either. But perhaps—[Opens the door and looks out] No, there's nothing in the mailbox; it's quite empty. [Comes forward] Oh nonsense! He only meant to frighten me. There won't be any trouble. It's all impossible! Why, I—I have three little children!

[Anne-Marie enters from the left, with a large cardboard box.]

ANNE-MARIE

Well—I found the box with the fancy dress clothes at last, Miss Nora.

NORA

Thanks; put it on the table.

ANNE-MARIE

[Does so] I'm afraid they're rather shabby.

NORA

If I had my way I'd tear them into a thousand pieces!

ANNE-MARIE

Good gracious! They can be repaired—just have a little patience.

NORA

I'll go and get Mrs. Linde to help me.

ANNE-MARIE

I wouldn't go out again in this awful weather! You might catch cold, Miss Nora, and get sick.

NORA

Worse things might happen—How are the children?

ANNE-MARIE

The poor little things are playing with their Christmas presents; but—

NORA

Have they asked for me?

ANNE-MARIE

They're so used to having Mamma with them.

NORA

I know, but, you see, Anne-Marie, I won't be able to be with them as much as I used to.

ANNE-MARIE

Well, little children soon get used to anything.

NORA

You really think so? Would they forget me if I went away for good?

ANNE-MARIE

Good gracious!—for good!

NORA

Tell me something, Anne-Marie—I've so often wondered about it—how could you bear to part with your child—give it up to strangers?

ANNE-MARIE

Well, you see, I had to—when I came to nurse my little Nora.

NORA

Yes—but how could you *bear* to do it?

ANNE-MARIE

I couldn't afford to say "no" to such a good position. A poor girl who's been in trouble must take what comes. Of course *he* never offered to help me—the wicked sinner!

NORA

Then I suppose your daughter has forgotten all about you.

ANNE-MARIE

No—indeed she hasn't! She even wrote to me—once when she was confirmed and again when she was married.

NORA

[Embracing her] Dear old Anne-Marie—you were a good mother to me when I was little.

ANNE-MARIE

But then my poor little Nora *had* no mother of her own!

NORA

And if ever my little ones were left without—you'd look after them, wouldn't you?—Oh, that's just nonsense! [Opens the box] Go back to them. Now I must— Just you wait and see how lovely I'll look tomorrow!

ANNE-MARIE

My Miss Nora will be the prettiest person there! [She goes into the room on the left.]

NORA

[Takes the costume out of the box, but soon throws it down again] I wish I dared go out—I'm afraid someone might come. I'm afraid something might happen while I'm gone. That's just silly! No one will come. I must try not to think— This muff needs cleaning. What pretty gloves—they're lovely! I must put it out of my head! One, two, three, four, five, six— [With a scream] Ah! They're here!

[Goes toward the door, then stands irresolute. Mrs. Linde enters from the hall, where she has taken off her things.]

NORA

Oh, it's you, Kristine! There's no one else out there, is there? I'm so glad you have come!

MRS. LINDE

I got a message you'd been asking for me.

NORA

Yes, I just happened to be passing by. There's something I want you to help me with. Sit down here on the sofa. Now, listen: There's to be a fancy dress ball at the Stenborgs' tomorrow evening—they live just overhead—and Torvald wants me to go as a Neapolitan peasant girl, and dance the tarantella; I learned it while we were in Capri.

MRS. LINDE

So you're going to give a real performance, are you?

NORA

Torvald wants me to. Look, here's the costume; Torvald had it made for me down there. But it's all torn, Kristine, and I don't know whether—

MRS. LINDE

Oh, we'll soon fix that. It's only the trimming that has come loose here and there. Have you a needle and thread? Oh, yes. Here's everything I need.

NORA

It's awfully good of you!

MRS. LINDE

[Sewing] So you're going to be all dressed up, Nora—what fun! You know—I think I'll run in for a moment—just to see you in your costume— I haven't really thanked you for last night. I had such a happy time!

NORA

[Rises and walks across the room] Somehow it didn't seem as nice to me as usual. I wish you'd come to town a little earlier, Kristine. Yes—Torvald has a way of making things so gay and cozy.

MRS. LINDE

Well—so have you. That's your father coming out in you! But tell me—is Doctor Rank always so depressed?

NORA

No; last night it was worse than usual. He's terribly ill, you see—tuberculosis of the spine, or something. His father was a frightful man, who kept mistresses and all that sort of thing—that's why his son has been an invalid from birth—

MRS. LINDE

[Lets her sewing fall into her lap] Why, Nora! what do you know about such things?

NORA

[Moving about the room] After all—I've had three children; and those women who look after one at childbirth know almost as much as doctors; and they love to gossip.

MRS. LINDE

[Goes on sewing; a short pause] Does Doctor Rank come here every day?

NORA

Every single day. He's Torvald's best friend, you know—always has been; and he's *my* friend too. He's almost like one of the family.

MRS. LINDE
Do you think he's quite sincere, Nora? I mean—isn't he inclined to flatter people?

NORA
Quite the contrary. What gave you that impression?

MRS. LINDE
When you introduced us yesterday he said he had often heard my name mentioned here; but I noticed afterwards that your husband hadn't the faintest notion who I was. How could Doctor Rank—?

NORA
He was quite right, Kristine. You see Torvald loves me so tremendously that he won't share me with anyone; he wants me all to himself, as he says. At first he used to get terribly jealous if I even mentioned any of my old friends back home; so naturally I gave up doing it. But I often talk to Doctor Rank about such things—he likes to hear about them.

MRS. LINDE
Listen to me, Nora! In many ways you are still a child. I'm somewhat older than you, and besides, I've had much more experience. I think you ought to put a stop to all this with Doctor Rank.

NORA
Put a stop to what?

MRS. LINDE
To the whole business. You said something yesterday about a rich admirer who was to give you money—

NORA
One who never existed, unfortunately. Go on.

MRS. LINDE
Has Doctor Rank money?

NORA
Why yes, he has.

MRS. LINDE
And he has no one dependent on him?

NORA
No, no one. But—

MRS. LINDE
And he comes here every single day?

NORA
Yes—I've just told you so.

MRS. LINDE
It's surprising that a sensitive man like that should be so importunate.

NORA
I don't understand you—

MRS. LINDE
Don't try to deceive me, Nora. Don't you suppose I can guess who lent you the twelve hundred dollars?

NORA
You must be out of your mind! How could you ever think such a thing? Why, he's a friend of ours; he comes to see us every day! The situation would have been impossible!

MRS. LINDE
So it wasn't he, then?

NORA
No, I assure you. Such a thing never even occurred to me. Anyway, he didn't have any money at that time; he came into it later.

MRS. LINDE
Perhaps that was just as well, Nora, dear.

NORA
No—it would never have entered my head to ask Doctor Rank— Still—I'm sure that if I did ask him—

MRS. LINDE
But you won't, of course.

NORA
No, of course not. Anyway—I don't see why it should be necessary. But I'm sure that if I talked to Doctor Rank—

MRS. LINDE
Behind your husband's back?

NORA
I want to get that thing cleared up; after all, that's behind his back too. I must get clear of it.

MRS. LINDE
That's just what I said yesterday; but—

NORA
[Walking up and down] It's so much easier for a man to manage things like that—

MRS. LINDE
One's own husband, yes.

NORA
Nonsense. [Stands still] Surely if you pay back everything you owe—the paper is returned to you?

MRS. LINDE
Naturally.

NORA

Then you can tear it into a thousand pieces, and burn it up—the nasty, filthy thing!

MRS. LINDE

[Looks at her fixedly, lays down her work, and rises slowly] Nora, you are hiding something from me.

NORA

You can see it in my face, can't you?

MRS. LINDE

Something's happened to you since yesterday morning, Nora, what is it?

NORA

[Going towards her] Kristine—! *[Listens]* Hush! Here comes Torvald! Go into the nursery for a little while. Torvald hates anything to do with sewing. Get Anne-Marie to help you.

MRS. LINDE

[Gathers the things together] Very well; but I shan't leave until you have told me all about it. *[She goes out to the left, as Helmer enters from the hall.]*

NORA

[Runs to meet him] Oh, I've missed you so, Torvald, dear!

HELMER

Was that the dressmaker—?

NORA

No, it was Kristine. She's helping me fix my costume. It's going to look so nice.

HELMER

Wasn't that a good idea of mine?

NORA

Splendid! But don't you think it was good of me to let you have your way?

HELMER

Good of you! To let your own husband have his way! There, there, you crazy little thing; I'm only teasing. Now I won't disturb you. You'll have to try the dress on, I suppose.

NORA

Yes—and I expect you've work to do.

HELMER

I have. *[Shows her a bundle of papers]* Look. I've just come from the Bank— *[Goes towards his room]*

NORA

Torvald.

HELMER

[Stopping] Yes?

NORA

If your little squirrel were to beg you—with all her heart—

HELMER

Well?

NORA

Would you do something for her?

HELMER

That depends on what it is.

NORA

Be a darling and say "Yes", Torvald! Your squirrel would skip about and play all sorts of pretty tricks—

HELMER

Well—out with it!

NORA

Your little lark would twitter all day long—

HELMER

She does that anyway!

NORA

I'll pretend to be an elf and dance for you in the moonlight, Torvald.

HELMER

Nora—you're surely not getting back to what we talked about this morning?

NORA

[Coming nearer] Oh, Torvald, dear, I do most humbly beg you!

HELMER

You have the temerity to bring that up again?

NORA

You must give in to me about this, Torvald! You *must* let Krogstad keep his place!

HELMER

I'm giving his place to Mrs. Linde.

NORA

That's awfully sweet of you. But instead of Krogstad—couldn't you dismiss some other clerk?

HELMER

This is the most incredible obstinacy! Because you were thoughtless enough to promise to put in a good word for him, am I supposed to—

NORA

That's not the reason, Torvald. It's for your own sake. Didn't you tell me yourself he writes for the most horrible newspapers? He can do you no end of harm. Oh! I'm so afraid of him—

HELMER

I think I understand; you have some unpleasant memories—that's why you're frightened.

NORA

What do you mean?

HELMER

Aren't you thinking of your father?

NORA

Oh, yes—of course! You remember how those awful people slandered poor Father in the newspapers? If you hadn't been sent to investigate the matter, and been so kind and helpful—he might have been dismissed.

HELMER

My dear Nora, there is a distinct difference between your father and me. Your father's conduct was not entirely unimpeachable. But mine is; and I trust it will remain so.

NORA

You never know what evil-minded people can think up. We could be so happy now, Torvald, in our lovely, peaceful home—you and I and the children! Oh! I implore you, Torvald—!

HELMER

The more you plead his cause the less likely I am to keep him on. It's already known at the Bank that I intend to dismiss Krogstad. If I were to change my mind, people might say I'd done it at the insistence of my wife—

NORA

Well—what of that?

HELMER

Oh, nothing, of course! As long as the obstinate little woman gets her way! I'd simply be the laughing-stock of the whole staff; they'd think I was weak and easily influenced—I should soon be made to feel the consequences. Besides—there is one factor that makes it quite impossible for Krogstad to work at the Bank as long as I'm head there.

NORA

What could that be?

HELMER

His past record I might be able to overlook—

NORA

Yes, you might, mightn't you, Torvald—?

HELMER

And I'm told he's an excellent worker. But unfortunately we were friendly during our college days. It was one of those impetuous friendships that subsequently often prove embarrassing. He's tactless enough to call me by my first name—regardless of the circumstances—and feels quite justified in taking a familiar tone with me. At any moment he comes out with "Torvald" this, and "Torvald" that! It's acutely irritating. It would make my position at the Bank intolerable.

NORA

You're surely not serious about this, Torvald?

HELMER

Why not?

NORA

But—it's all so petty.

HELMER

Petty! So you think I'm petty!

NORA

Of course not, Torvald—just the opposite; that's why—

HELMER

Never mind; you call my motives petty; so I must be petty too! Petty! Very well!—We'll put an end to this now—once and for all. [Helmer goes to the door into the hall and calls Helene.]

NORA

What do you want?

HELMER

[Searching among his papers] I want this thing settled. [Helene enters.] Take this letter, will you? Get a messenger and have him deliver it at once! It's urgent. Here's some money.

HELENE

Very good, Sir. [Goes with the letter]

HELMER

[Putting his papers together] There, little Miss Obstinacy.

NORA

[Breathless] Torvald—what was in that letter?

HELMER

Krogstad's dismissal.

NORA

Call her back, Torvald! There's still time. Call her back! For my sake, for your own sake, for the sake of the children, don't send that letter! Torvald, do you hear? You don't realize what may come of this!

HELMER

It's too late.

NORA

Too late, yes.

HELMER

Nora, dear; I forgive your fears—though it's not exactly flattering to me to think I could ever be afraid of any spiteful nonsense Krogstad might choose to write about me! But I forgive you all the same—it shows how much you love me. *[Takes her in his arms]* And that's the way it should be, Nora darling. No matter what happens, you'll see—I have strength and courage for us both. My shoulders are broad—I'll bear the burden.

NORA

[Terror-struck] How do you mean?

HELMER

The whole burden, my darling. Don't you worry any more.

NORA

[With decision] No! You mustn't—I won't let you!

HELMER

Then we'll share it, Nora, as man and wife. That is as it should be. *[Petting her]* Are you happy now? There! Don't look at me like a frightened little dove! You're just imagining things, you know— Now don't you think you ought to play the tarantella through—and practice your tambourine? I'll go into my study and close both doors, then you won't disturb me. You can make all the noise you like! *[Turns round in doorway]* And when Rank comes, just tell him where I am. *[He nods to her, and goes with his papers to his room, closing the door.]*

NORA

[Bewildered with terror, stands as though rooted to the ground, and whispers] He'd do it too! He'd do it—in spite of anything! But he mustn't—never, never! Anything but that! There must be some way out! What shall I do? *[The hall bell rings]* Dr. Rank—! Anything but that—anything, *anything* but that!

[Nora draws her hands over her face, pulls herself together, goes to the door and opens it. Rank stands outside hanging up his fur coat. During the following scene, darkness begins to fall.]

NORA

How are you, Doctor Rank? I recognized your ring. You'd better not go in to Torvald just now; I think he's busy.

RANK

How about you? *[Enters and closes the door]*

NORA

You know I always have an hour to spare for you.

RANK

Many thanks. I'll make use of that privilege as long as possible.

NORA

What do you mean—as long as possible?

RANK

Does that frighten you?

NORA

No—but it's such a queer expression. Has anything happened?

RANK

I've been expecting it for a long time; but I never thought it would come quite so soon.

NORA

What is it you have found out? Doctor Rank, please tell me!

RANK

[Sitting down by the stove] I haven't much time left. There's nothing to do about it.

NORA

[With a sigh of relief] Oh! Then—it's about you—?

RANK

Of course. What did you think? It's no use lying to one's self. I am the most miserable of all my patients, Mrs. Helmer. These past few days I've been taking stock of my position—and I find myself completely bankrupt. Within a month, I shall be rotting in the church-yard.

NORA

What a ghastly way to talk!

RANK

The whole business is pretty ghastly, you see. And the worst of it is, there are so many ghastly things to be gone through before it's over. I've just one last examination to make, then I shall know approximately when the final dissolution will begin. There's something I want to say to you: Helmer's sensitive nature is repelled by anything ugly. I couldn't bear to have him near me when—

NORA
But Doctor Rank—

RANK
No, I couldn't bear it! I won't have him there—I shall bar my door against him— As soon as I am absolutely certain of the worst, I'll send you my visiting-card marked with a black cross; that will mean the final horror has begun.

NORA
Doctor Rank—you're absolutely impossible today! And I did so want you to be in a good humor.

RANK
With death staring me in the face? And why should I have to expiate another's sins! What justice is there in that? Well—I suppose in almost every family there are some such debts that have to be paid.

NORA
[Stopping her ears] Don't talk such nonsense! Come along! Cheer up!

RANK
One might as well laugh. It's really very funny when you come to think of it—that my poor innocent spine should be made to suffer for my father's exploits!

NORA
[At table, left] He was much addicted to asparagus-tips and paté de foie gras, wasn't he?

RANK
Yes; and truffles.

NORA
Oh, of course—truffles, yes. And I suppose oysters too?

RANK
Oh, yes! Masses of oysters, certainly!

NORA
And all the wine and champagne that went with them! It does seem a shame that all these pleasant things should be so damaging to the spine, doesn't it?

RANK
Especially when it's a poor miserable spine that never had any of the fun!

NORA
Yes, that's the biggest shame of all!

RANK
[Gives her a searching look] H'm—

NORA
[A moment later] Why did you smile?

RANK
No; you were the one that laughed.

NORA
No; you were the one that smiled, Doctor Rank!

RANK
[Gets up] You're more of a rogue than I thought you were.

NORA
I'm full of mischief today.

RANK
So it seems.

NORA
[With her hands on his shoulders] Dear, dear Doctor Rank, don't go and die and leave Torvald and me.

RANK
Oh, you won't miss me long! Those who go away—are soon forgotten.

NORA
[Looks at him anxiously] You really believe that?

RANK
People develop new interests, and soon—

NORA
What do you mean—new interests?

RANK
That'll happen to you and Helmer when I am gone. You seem to have made a good start already. What was that Mrs. Linde doing here last evening?

NORA
You're surely not jealous of poor old Kristine!

RANK
Yes, I am. She will be my successor in this house. When I'm gone she'll probably—

NORA
Sh—hh! She's in there.

RANK

She's here again today? You see!

NORA

She's just helping me with my costume. Good heavens, you *are* in a unreasonable mood! [*Sits on sofa*] Now do try to be good, Doctor Rank. Tomorrow you'll see how beautifully I'll dance; and then you can pretend I'm doing it all to please you—and Torvald too, of course—that's understood.

RANK

[*After a short silence*] You know—sitting here talking to you so informally—I simply can't imagine what would have become of me, if I had never had this house to come to.

NORA

[*Smiling*] You really *do* feel at home with us, don't you?

RANK

[*In a low voice—looking straight before him*] And to be obliged to leave it all—

NORA

Nonsense! You're not going to leave anything.

RANK

[*In the same tone*] And not to be able to leave behind one even the smallest proof of gratitude; at most a fleeting regret—an empty place to be filled by the first person who comes along.

NORA

And supposing I were to ask you for—? No—

RANK

For what?

NORA

For a great proof of your friendship.

RANK

Yes?—Yes?

NORA

No, I mean—if I were to ask you to do me a really tremendous favor—

RANK

You'd really, for once, give me that great happiness?

NORA

Oh, but you don't know what it is.

RANK

Then tell me.

NORA

I don't think I can, Doctor Rank. It's much too much to ask—it's not just a favor—I need your help and advice as well—

RANK

So much the better. I've no conception of what you mean. But tell me about it. You trust me, don't you?

NORA

More than anyone. I know you are my best and truest friend—that's why I can tell you. Well then, Doctor Rank, there is something you must help me prevent. You know how deeply, how intensely Torvald loves me; he wouldn't hesitate for a moment to give up his life for my sake.

RANK

[*Bending towards her*] Nora—do you think he is the only one who—?

NORA

[*With a slight start*] Who—what?

RANK

Who would gladly give his life for you?

NORA

[*Sadly*] I see.

RANK

I was determined that you should know this before I—went away. There'll never be a better chance to tell you. Well, Nora, now you know, and you must know too that you can trust me as you can no one else.

NORA

[*Standing up; simply and calmly*] Let me get by—

RANK

[*Makes way for her, but remains sitting*] Nora—

NORA

[*In the doorway*] Bring in the lamp, Helene. [*Crosses to the stove*] Oh, dear Doctor Rank, that was really horrid of you.

RANK

[*Rising*] To love you just as deeply as—as someone else does; is that horrid?

NORA

No—but the fact of your telling me. There was no need to do that.

RANK

What do you mean? Did you know—?

[Helene enters with the lamp; sets it on the table and goes out again.]

RANK

Nora—Mrs. Helmer—tell me, did you know?

NORA

Oh, how do I know what I knew or didn't know. I really can't say— How could you be so clumsy, Doctor Rank? It was all so nice.

RANK

Well, at any rate, you know now that I stand ready to serve you body and soul. So—tell me.

NORA

[Looking at him] After this?

RANK

I beg you to tell me what it is.

NORA

I can't tell you anything now.

RANK

But you must! Don't punish me like that! Let me be of use to you; I'll do anything for you—anything within human power.

NORA

You can do nothing for me now. Anyway—I don't really need help. I was just imagining things, you see. Really! That's all it was! *[Sits in the rocking chair, looks at him and smiles]* Well—you're a nice one, Doctor Rank! Aren't you a bit ashamed, now that the lamp's been lit?

RANK

No; really not. But I suppose I'd better go now—for good?

NORA

You'll do no such thing! You must come here just as you always have. Torvald could never get on without you!

RANK

But how about *you?*

NORA

You know I always love to have you here.

RANK

Yes—I suppose that's what misled me. I can't quite make you out. I've often felt you liked being with me almost as much as being with Helmer.

NORA

Well—you see— There are the people one loves best—and yet there are others one would almost rather *be* with.

RANK

Yes—there's something in that.

NORA

When I was still at home, it was of course Papa whom I loved best. And yet whenever I could, I used to slip down to the servants' quarters. I loved being with them. To begin with, they never lectured me a bit, and it was such fun to hear them talk.

RANK

I see; and now you have me instead!

NORA

[Jumps up and hurries towards him] Oh, dear, darling Doctor Rank. I didn't mean it like that! It's just that now, Torvald comes first—the way Papa did. *You* understand—!

[Helene enters from the hall.]

HELENE

I beg your pardon, Ma'am— *[Whispers to Nora, and gives her a card]*

NORA

[Glancing at card] Ah! *[Puts it in her pocket]*

RANK

Anything wrong?

NORA

No, nothing! It's just—it's my new costume—

RANK

Isn't that your costume—there?

NORA

Oh, that one, yes. But this is a different one. It's one I've ordered—Torvald mustn't know—

RANK

So *that's* the great secret!

NORA

Yes, of course it is! Go in and see him, will you? He's in his study. Be sure and keep him there as long as—

RANK

Don't worry; he shan't escape me. *[Goes into Helmer's room]*

NORA

[To Helene] He's waiting in the kitchen?

HELENE

Yes, he came up the back stairs—

NORA

Why didn't you tell him I was busy?

HELENE

I did, but he insisted.

NORA

He won't go away?

HELENE

Not until he has spoken to you, Ma'am.

NORA

Very well, then; show him in; but quietly, Helene—
and don't say a word to anyone; it's about a surprise
for my husband.

HELENE

I understand, Ma'am. [She goes out.]

NORA

It's coming! It's going to happen after all! No, no! It
can't happen. It *can't*!

[She goes to Helmer's door and locks it. Helene opens
the hall door for Krogstad, and shuts it after him. He
wears a traveling-coat, boots, and a fur cap.]

NORA

[Goes towards him] Talk quietly; my husband is at
home.

KROGSTAD

What's that to me?

NORA

What is it you want?

KROGSTAD

I want to make sure of something.

NORA

Well—what is it? Quickly!

KROGSTAD

I suppose you know I've been dismissed.

NORA

I couldn't prevent it, Mr. Krogstad. I did everything
in my power, but it was useless.

KROGSTAD

So that's all your husband cares about you! He must
realize what I can put you through, and yet, in spite
of that, he dares to—

NORA

You don't imagine my husband knows about it?

KROGSTAD

No—I didn't really suppose he did. I can't imagine
my friend Torvald Helmer showing that much
courage.

NORA

I insist that you show respect when speaking of my
husband, Mr. Krogstad!

KROGSTAD

With all due respect, I assure you! But am I right in
thinking—since you are so anxious to keep the matter secret—that you have a clearer idea today than
you had yesterday, of what you really did?

NORA

Clearer than *you* could ever give me!

KROGSTAD

Of course! I who know so little about the law—!

NORA

What do you want of me?

KROGSTAD

I just wanted to see how you were getting on, Mrs.
Helmer. I've been thinking about you all day. You
see—even a mere money-lender, a cheap journalist—in short, someone like me—is not entirely
without feeling.

NORA

Then prove it; think of my little children.

KROGSTAD

Did you or your husband think of mine? But that's
not the point. I only wanted to tell you not to take this
matter too seriously. I shan't take any action—for the
present, at least.

NORA

You won't, will you? I was sure you wouldn't!

KROGSTAD

It can all be settled quite amicably. It needn't be made
public. It needn't go beyond us three.

NORA

But, my husband must never know.

KROGSTAD

How can you prevent it? Can you pay off the balance?

NORA

No, not immediately.

KROGSTAD

Have you any way of raising the money within the
next few days?

NORA

None—that I will make use of.

KROGSTAD

And if you had, it would have made no difference. Even if you were to offer me the entire sum in cash—I still wouldn't give you back your note.

NORA

What are you going to do with it?

KROGSTAD

I shall simply keep it—I shall guard it carefully. No one, outside the three of us, shall know a thing about it. So, if you have any thought of doing something desperate—

NORA

I shall.

KROGSTAD

—of running away from home, for instance—

NORA

I shall!

KROGSTAD

—or perhaps even something worse—

NORA

How could you guess that?

KROGSTAD

—then put all such thoughts out of your head.

NORA

How did you know that I had thought of *that*?

KROGSTAD

Most of us think of *that*, at first. I thought of it, too; but I didn't have the courage—

NORA

[Tonelessly] I haven't either.

KROGSTAD

[Relieved] No; you haven't the courage for it either, have you?

NORA

No! I haven't, I haven't!

KROGSTAD

Besides, it would be a very foolish thing to do. You'll just have to get through one domestic storm—and then it'll all be over. I have a letter for your husband, here in my pocket—

NORA

Telling him all about it?

KROGSTAD

Sparing you as much as possible.

NORA

[Quickly] He must never read that letter. Tear it up, Mr. Krogstad! I will manage to get the money somehow—

KROGSTAD

Excuse me, Mrs. Helmer, but I thought I just told you—

NORA

Oh, I'm not talking about the money I owe you. Just tell me how much money you want from my husband—I will get it somehow!

KROGSTAD

I want no money from your husband.

NORA

What *do* you want then?

KROGSTAD

Just this: I want a new start; I want to make something of myself; and your husband shall help me do it. For the past eighteen months my conduct has been irreproachable. It's been a hard struggle—I've lived in abject poverty; still, I was content to work my way up gradually, step by step. But now I've been kicked out, and now I shall not be satisfied to be merely reinstated—taken back on sufferance. I'm determined to make something of myself, I tell you. I intend to continue working in the Bank—but I expect to be promoted. Your husband shall create a new position for me—

NORA

He'll never do it!

KROGSTAD

Oh, yes he will; I know him—he'll do it without a murmur; he wouldn't dare do otherwise. And then—you'll see! Within a year I'll be his right-hand man. It'll be Nils Krogstad, not Torvald Helmer, who'll run the Joint Stock Bank.

NORA

That will never happen.

KROGSTAD

No? Would you, perhaps—?

NORA

Yes! I have the courage for it now.

KROGSTAD

You don't frighten me! A dainty, pampered little lady such as you—

NORA

You'll see, you'll see!

KROGSTAD

Yes, I dare say! How would you like to lie there under the ice—in that freezing, pitch-black water? And in the spring your body would be found floating on the surface—hideous, hairless, unrecognizable—

NORA

You can't frighten me!

KROGSTAD

You can't frighten me either. People don't do that sort of thing, Mrs. Helmer. And, anyway, what would be the use? I'd still have your husband in my power.

NORA

You mean—afterwards? Even if I were no longer—?

KROGSTAD

Remember—I'd still have your reputation in my hands. [Nora stands speechless and looks at him.] Well, I've given you fair warning. I wouldn't do anything foolish, if I were you. As soon as Helmer receives my letter, I shall expect to hear from him. And just remember this: I've been forced back into my former way of life—and your husband is responsible. I shall never forgive him for it. Good-bye, Mrs. Helmer.

[Goes out through the hall. Nora hurries to the door, opens it a little, and listens.]

NORA

He's gone. He didn't leave the letter. Of course he didn't—that would be impossible! [Opens the door further and further] What's he doing? He's stopped outside the door. He's not going down the stairs. Has he changed his mind? Is he—? [A letter falls into the box. Krogstad's footsteps are heard gradually receding down the stairs. Nora utters a suppressed shriek, and rushes forward towards the sofa table; pause.] It's in the letter-box! [Slips shrinkingly up to the hall door] It's there!—Torvald, Torvald—now we are lost!

[Mrs. Linde enters from the left with the costume.]

MRS. LINDE

There, I think it's all right now. If you'll just try it on—?

NORA

[Hoarsely and softly] Come here, Kristine.

MRS. LINDE

[Throws down the dress on the sofa] What's the matter with you? You look upset.

NORA

Come here. Do you see that letter? Do you see it—in the letter-box?

MRS. LINDE

Yes, yes, I see it.

NORA

It's from Krogstad—

MRS. LINDE

Nora—you don't mean Krogstad lent you the money!

NORA

Yes; and now Torvald will know everything.

MRS. LINDE

It'll be much the best thing for you both, Nora.

NORA

But you don't know everything. I committed forgery—

MRS. LINDE

Good heavens!

NORA

Now, listen to me, Kristine; I want you to be my witness—

MRS. LINDE

How do you mean "witness"? What am I to—?

NORA

If I should go out of my mind—that might easily happen—

MRS. LINDE

Nora!

NORA

Or if something should happen to me—something that would prevent my being here—!

MRS. LINDE

Nora, Nora, you're quite beside yourself!

NORA

In case anyone else should insist on taking all the blame upon himself—the whole blame—you understand—

MRS. LINDE

Yes, but what makes you think—?

NORA

Then you must bear witness to the fact that that isn't true. I'm in my right mind now; I know exactly what I'm saying; and I tell you nobody else knew anything about it; I did the whole thing on my own. Just remember that.

MRS. LINDE

Very well—I will. But I don't understand at all.

NORA

No—of course—you couldn't. It's the wonderful thing— It's about to happen, don't you see?

MRS. LINDE

What "wonderful thing"?

NORA

The wonderful—wonderful thing! But it must never be allowed to happen—never. It would be too terrible.

MRS. LINDE

I'll go and talk to Krogstad at once.

NORA

No, don't go to him! He might do you some harm.

MRS. LINDE

There was a time—he would have done anything in the world for me.

NORA

He?

MRS. LINDE

Where does he live?

NORA

How do I know—? Yes— [Feels in her pocket] Here's his card. But the letter, the letter—!

HELMER

[From his study; knocking on the door] Nora!

NORA

[Shrieks in terror] Oh! What is it? What do you want?

HELMER

Don't be frightened! We're not coming in; anyway, you've locked the door. Are you trying on?

NORA

Yes, yes, I'm trying on. I'm going to look so pretty, Torvald.

MRS. LINDE

[Who has read the card] He lives just round the corner.

NORA

But it won't do any good. It's too late now. The letter is in the box.

MRS. LINDE

I suppose your husband has the key?

NORA

Of course.

MRS. LINDE

Krogstad must ask for his letter back, unread. He must make up some excuse—

NORA

But this is the time that Torvald usually—

MRS. LINDE

Prevent him. Keep him occupied. I'll come back as quickly as I can. [She goes out hastily by the hall door.]

NORA

[Opens Helmer's door and peeps in] Torvald!

HELMER

[In the study] Well? May one venture to come back into one's own living-room? Come along, Rank—now we shall see—[In the doorway] Why—what's this?

NORA

What, Torvald dear?

HELMER

Rank led me to expect some wonderful disguise.

RANK

[In the doorway] That's what I understood. I must have been mistaken.

NORA

Not till tomorrow evening! Then I shall appear in all my splendor!

HELMER

But you look quite tired, Nora, dear. I'm afraid you've been practicing too hard.

NORA

Oh, I haven't practiced at all yet.

HELMER

You ought to, though—

NORA

Yes—I really should, Torvald! But I can't seem to manage without your help. I'm afraid I've forgotten all about it.

HELMER

Well—we'll see what we can do. It'll soon come back to you.

NORA

You will help me, won't you, Torvald? Promise! I feel so nervous—all those people! You must concentrate on me this evening—forget all about business. *Please*, Torvald, dear—promise me you will!

HELMER

I promise. This evening I'll be your slave—you sweet, helpless little thing—! Just one moment, though—I want to see— *[Going to hall door]*

NORA

What do you want out there?

HELMER

I just want to see if there are any letters.

NORA

Oh, don't, Torvald! Don't bother about that now!

HELMER

Why not?

NORA

Please don't, Torvald! There aren't any.

HELMER

Just let me take a look— *[Starts to go]*

[Nora, at the piano, plays the first bars of the tarantella.]

HELMER

[Stops in the doorway] Aha!

NORA

I shan't be able to dance tomorrow if I don't rehearse with you!

HELMER

[Going to her] Are you really so nervous, Nora, dear?

NORA

Yes, I'm terrified! Let's rehearse right away. We've plenty of time before dinner. Sit down and play for me, Torvald, dear; direct me—guide me; you know how you do!

HELMER

With pleasure, my darling, if you wish me to. *[Sits at piano]*

[Nora snatches the tambourine out of the box, and hurriedly drapes herself in a long parti-colored shawl; then, with a bound, stands in the middle of the floor and cries out.]

NORA

Now play for me! Now I'll dance!

[Helmer plays and Nora dances. Rank stands at the piano behind Helmer and looks on.]

HELMER

[Playing] Too fast! Too fast!

NORA

I can't help it!

HELMER

Don't be so violent, Nora!

NORA

That's the way it *should* be!

HELMER

[Stops] No, no; this won't do at all!

NORA

[Laughs and swings her tambourine] You see? What did I tell you?

RANK

I'll play for her.

HELMER

[Rising] Yes, do—then I'll be able to direct her.

[Rank sits down at the piano and plays; Nora dances more and more wildly. Helmer stands by the stove and addresses frequent corrections to her; she seems not to hear. Her hair breaks loose, and falls over her shoulders. She does not notice it, but goes on dancing. Mrs. Linde enters and stands spellbound in the doorway.]

MRS. LINDE

Ah—!

NORA

[Dancing] We're having such fun, Kristine!

HELMER

Why, Nora, dear, you're dancing as if your life were at stake!

NORA

It is! It is!

HELMER

Rank, stop! This is absolute madness. Stop, I say!

[Rank stops playing, and Nora comes to a sudden standstill.]

HELMER

[Going towards her] I never would have believed it. You've forgotten everything I ever taught you.

NORA

[Throws the tambourine away] I told you I had!

HELMER

This needs an immense amount of work.

NORA

That's what I said; you see how important it is! You must work with me up to the very last minute. Will you promise me, Torvald?

HELMER

I most certainly will!

NORA

This evening and all day tomorrow you must think of nothing but me. You mustn't open a single letter—mustn't even *look* at the mail-box.

HELMER

Nora! I believe you're still worried about that wretched man—

NORA

Yes—yes, I am!

HELMER

Nora— Look at me—there's a letter from him in the box, isn't there?

NORA

Maybe—I don't know; I believe there is. But you're not to read anything of that sort now; nothing must come between us until the party's over.

RANK

[Softly, to Helmer] Don't go against her.

HELMER

[Putting his arm around her] Very well! The child shall have her way. But tomorrow night, when your dance is over—

NORA

Then you'll be free.

[Helene appears in the doorway, right.]

HELENE

Dinner is served, Ma'am.

NORA

We'll have champagne, Helene.

HELENE

Very good, Ma'am. *[Goes out]*

HELMER

Quite a feast, I see!

NORA

Yes—a real feast! We'll stay up till dawn drinking champagne! *[Calling out]* Oh, and we'll have macaroons, Helene—lots of them! Why not—for once!

HELMER

[Seizing her hand] Come, come! Not so violent! Be my own little lark again.

NORA

I will, Torvald. But now—both of you go in—while Kristine helps me with my hair.

RANK

[Softly, as they go] Is anything special the matter? I mean—anything—?

HELMER

No, no; nothing at all. It's just this childish fear I was telling you about. *[They go out to the right.]*

NORA

Well?

MRS. LINDE

He's gone out of town.

NORA

I saw it in your face.

MRS. LINDE

He'll be back tomorrow evening. I left a note for him.

NORA

You shouldn't have bothered. You couldn't prevent it anyway. After all, there's a kind of joy in waiting for the wonderful thing to happen.

MRS. LINDE

I don't understand. What *is* this thing you're waiting for?

NORA

I can't explain. Go in and join them. I'll be there in a moment.

[Mrs. Linde goes into the dining room. Nora stands for a moment as though pulling herself together; then looks at her watch.]

NORA

Five o'clock. Seven hours till midnight. Twenty-four hours till the next midnight and then the tarantella will be over. Twenty-four and seven? I've thirty-one hours left to live.

[Helmer appears at the door, right.]

HELMER
Well! What has become of the little lark?

NORA
[Runs to him with open arms] Here she is!

[Curtain]

─────────── **ACT THREE** ───────────

Scene

The same room. The table, with the chairs around it, has been moved to stage-center. A lighted lamp on the table. The hall door is open. Dance music is heard from the floor above. Mrs. Linde sits by the table absent-mindedly turning the pages of a book. She tries to read, but seems unable to keep her mind on it. Now and then she listens intently and glances towards the hall door.

MRS. LINDE
[Looks at her watch] Where can he be? The time is nearly up. I hope he hasn't— [Listens again] Here he is now. [She goes into the hall and cautiously opens the outer door; cautious footsteps are heard on the stairs; she whispers.] Come in; there is no one here.

KROGSTAD
[In the doorway] I found a note from you at home. What does it mean?

MRS. LINDE
I simply *must* speak to you.

KROGSTAD
Indeed? But why here? Why in this house?

MRS. LINDE
I couldn't see you at my place. My room has no separate entrance. Come in; we're quite alone. The servants are asleep, and the Helmers are upstairs at a party.

KROGSTAD
[Coming into the room] Well, well! So the Helmers are dancing tonight, are they?

MRS. LINDE
Why shouldn't they?

KROGSTAD
Well—why not!

MRS. LINDE
Let's have a talk, Krogstad.

KROGSTAD
Have we two anything to talk about?

MRS. LINDE
Yes. A great deal.

KROGSTAD
I shouldn't have thought so.

MRS. LINDE
But then, you see—you have never really understood me.

KROGSTAD
There wasn't much to understand, was there? A woman is heartless enough to break off with a man, when a better match is offered; it's quite an ordinary occurrence.

MRS. LINDE
You really think me heartless? Did you think it was so easy for me?

KROGSTAD
Wasn't it?

MRS. LINDE
You really believed that, Krogstad?

KROGSTAD
If not, why should you have written to me as you did?

MRS. LINDE
What else could I do? Since I was forced to break with you, I felt it was only right to try and kill your love for me.

KROGSTAD
[Clenching his hands together] So that was it! And you did this for money!

MRS. LINDE
Don't forget I had my mother and two little brothers to think of. We couldn't wait for you, Krogstad; things were so unsettled for you then.

KROGSTAD
That may be; but, even so, you had no right to throw me over—not even for their sake.

MRS. LINDE
Who knows? I've often wondered whether I did right or not.

KROGSTAD

[More softly] When I had lost you, I felt the ground crumble beneath my feet. Look at me. I'm like a ship-wrecked man clinging to a raft.

MRS. LINDE

Help may be nearer than you think.

KROGSTAD

Help was here! Then you came and stood in the way.

MRS. LINDE

I knew nothing about it, Krogstad. I didn't know until today that I was to replace *you* at the Bank.

KROGSTAD

Very well—I believe you. But now that you do know, will you withdraw?

MRS. LINDE

No; I'd do you no good by doing that.

KROGSTAD

"Good" or not—I'd withdraw all the same.

MRS. LINDE

I have learnt to be prudent, Krogstad—I've had to. The bitter necessities of life have taught me that.

KROGSTAD

And life has taught me not to believe in phrases.

MRS. LINDE

Then life has taught you a very wise lesson. But what about deeds? Surely you must still believe in them?

KROGSTAD

How do you mean?

MRS. LINDE

You just said you were like a shipwrecked man, cling-ing to a raft.

KROGSTAD

I have good reason to say so.

MRS. LINDE

Well—I'm like a shipwrecked *woman* clinging to a raft. I have no one to mourn for, no one to care for.

KROGSTAD

You made your choice.

MRS. LINDE

I *had* no choice, I tell you!

KROGSTAD

What then?

MRS. LINDE

Since we're both of us shipwrecked, couldn't we join forces, Krogstad?

KROGSTAD

You don't mean—?

MRS. LINDE

Two people on a raft have a better chance than one.

KROGSTAD

Kristine!

MRS. LINDE

Why do you suppose I came here to the city?

KROGSTAD

You mean—you thought of me?

MRS. LINDE

I can't live without work; all my life I've worked, as far back as I can remember; it's always been my one great joy. Now I'm quite alone in the world; my life is empty—aimless. There's not much joy in working for one's self. You could help me, Nils; you could give me something and someone to work for.

KROGSTAD

I can't believe all this. It's an hysterical impulse—a woman's exaggerated craving for self-sacrifice.

MRS. LINDE

When have you ever found me hysterical?

KROGSTAD

You'd really be willing to do this? Tell me honestly—do you quite realize what my past has been?

MRS. LINDE

Yes.

KROGSTAD

And you know what people think of me?

MRS. LINDE

Didn't you just say you'd have been a different person if you'd been with me?

KROGSTAD

I'm sure of it.

MRS. LINDE

Mightn't that still be true?

KROGSTAD

You really mean this, Kristine, don't you? I can see it in your face. Are you sure you have the courage—?

MRS. LINDE

I need someone to care for, and your children need a mother. We two need each other, Nils. I have faith in your fundamental goodness. I'm not afraid.

KROGSTAD

[Seizing her hands] Thank you—thank you, Kristine. I'll make others believe in me too—I won't fail you! But—I'd almost forgotten—

MRS. LINDE

[Listening] Hush! The tarantella! You must go!

KROGSTAD

Why? What is it?

MRS. LINDE

Listen! She's begun her dance; as soon as she's finished dancing, they'll be down.

KROGSTAD

Yes—I'd better go. There'd have been no need for all that—but, of course, you don't know what I've done about the Helmers.

MRS. LINDE

Yes, I do, Nils.

KROGSTAD

And yet you have the courage to—?

MRS. LINDE

I know you were desperate—I understand.

KROGSTAD

I'd give anything to undo it!

MRS. LINDE

You can. Your letter's still in the mail-box.

KROGSTAD

Are you sure?

MRS. LINDE

Quite, but—

KROGSTAD

[Giving her a searching look] Could that be it? You're doing all this to save your friend? You might as well be honest with me! Is that it?

MRS. LINDE

I sold myself once for the sake of others, Nils; I'm not likely to do it again.

KROGSTAD

I'll ask for my letter back unopened.

MRS. LINDE

No, no.

KROGSTAD

Yes, of course. I'll wait till Helmer comes; I'll tell him to give me back the letter—I'll say it refers to my dismissal—and ask him not to read it—

MRS. LINDE

No, Nils; don't ask for it back.

KROGSTAD

But wasn't that actually your reason for getting me to come here?

MRS. LINDE

Yes, in my first moment of fear. But that was twenty-four hours ago, and since then I've seen incredible things happening here. Helmer must know the truth; this wretched business must no longer be kept secret; it's time those two came to a thorough understanding; there's been enough deceit and subterfuge.

KROGSTAD

Very well, if you like to risk it. But there's one thing I can do, and at once—

MRS. LINDE

[Listening] You must go now. Make haste! The dance is over; we're not safe here another moment.

KROGSTAD

I'll wait for you downstairs.

MRS. LINDE

Yes, do; then you can see me home.

KROGSTAD

Kristine! I've never been so happy! *[Krogstad goes out by the outer door. The door between the room and the hall remains open.]*

MRS. LINDE

[Arranging the room and getting her outdoor things together] How different things will be! Someone to work for, to live for; a home to make happy! How wonderful it will be to try!—I wish they'd come— *[Listens]* Here they are! I'll get my coat— *[Takes bonnet and cloak. Helmer's and Nora's voices are heard outside, a key is turned in the lock, and Helmer drags Nora almost by force into the hall. She wears the Italian costume with a large black shawl over it. He is in evening dress and wears a black domino, open.]*

NORA

[Struggling with him in the doorway] No, no! I don't want to come home; I want to go upstairs again; I don't want to leave so early!

HELMER

Come—Nora dearest!

NORA

I beg you, Torvald! Please, *please*—just one hour more!

HELMER

Not one single minute more, Nora darling; don't you remember our agreement? Come along in, now; you'll catch cold.

[He leads her gently into the room in spite of her resistance.]

MRS. LINDE

Good evening.

NORA

Kristine!

HELMER

Why, Mrs. Linde! What are you doing here so late?

MRS. LINDE

Do forgive me. I did so want to see Nora in her costume.

NORA

Have you been waiting for me all this time?

MRS. LINDE

Yes; I came too late to catch you before you went upstairs, and I didn't want to go away without seeing you.

HELMER

[Taking Nora's shawl off] And you *shall* see her, Mrs. Linde! She's worth looking at I can tell you! Isn't she lovely?

MRS. LINDE

Oh, Nora! How perfectly—!

HELMER

Absolutely exquisite, isn't she? That's what everybody said. But she's obstinate as a mule, is my sweet little thing! I don't know what to do with her. Will you believe it, Mrs. Linde, I had to drag her away by force?

NORA

You'll see—you'll be sorry, Torvald, you didn't let me stay, if only for another half-hour.

HELMER

Do you hear that, Mrs. Linde? Now, listen to this: She danced her tarantella to wild applause, and she deserved it, too, I must say—though, perhaps, from an artistic point of view, her interpretation was a bit too realistic. But never mind—the point is, she made a great success, a phenomenal success. Now—should I have allowed her to stay on and spoil the whole effect? Certainly not! I took my sweet little Capri girl—

my capricious little Capri girl, I might say—in my arms; a rapid whirl round the room, a low curtsey to all sides, and—as they say in novels—the lovely apparition vanished! An exit should always be effective, Mrs. Linde; but I can't get Nora to see that. Phew! It's warm here. [Throws his domino on a chair and opens the door to his room] Why—there's no light on in here! Oh no, of course— Excuse me— [Goes in and lights candles]

NORA

[Whispers breathlessly] Well?

MRS. LINDE

[Softly] I've spoken to him.

NORA

And—?

MRS. LINDE

Nora—you must tell your husband everything—

NORA

[Tonelessly] I knew it!

MRS. LINDE

You have nothing to fear from Krogstad; but you must speak out.

NORA

I shan't.

MRS. LINDE

Then the letter will.

NORA

Thank you, Kristine. Now I know what I must do. Hush—!

HELMER

[Coming back] Well, have you finished admiring her, Mrs. Linde?

MRS. LINDE

Yes, and now I must say good-night.

HELMER

Oh—must you be going already? Does this knitting belong to you?

MRS. LINDE

[Takes it] Oh, thank you; I almost forgot it.

HELMER

So you knit, do you?

MRS. LINDE

Yes.

HELMER

Why don't you do embroidery instead?

MRS. LINDE
Why?

HELMER
Because it's so much prettier. Now watch! You hold the embroidery in the left hand—so—and then, in the right hand, you hold the needle, and guide it—so—in a long graceful curve—isn't that right?

MRS. LINDE
Yes, I suppose so—

HELMER
Whereas, knitting can never be anything but ugly. Now, watch! Arms close to your sides, needles going up and down—there's something Chinese about it!— That really was splendid champagne they gave us.

MRS. LINDE
Well, good-night, Nora; don't be obstinate any more.

HELMER
Well said, Mrs. Linde!

MRS. LINDE
Good-night, Mr. Helmer.

HELMER
[Accompanying her to the door] Good-night, good-night; I hope you get home safely. I'd be only too glad to—but you've such a short way to go. Good-night, good-night. [She goes; Helmer shuts the door after her and comes forward again.] Well—thank God we've got rid of her; she's a dreadful bore, that woman.

NORA
You must be tired, Torvald.

HELMER
I? Not in the least.

NORA
But, aren't you sleepy?

HELMER
Not a bit. On the contrary, I feel exceedingly lively. But what about you? You seem to be very tired and sleepy.

NORA
Yes, I am very tired. But I'll soon sleep now.

HELMER
You see! I was right not to let you stay there any longer.

NORA
Everything you do is always right, Torvald.

HELMER
[Kissing her forehead] There's my sweet, sensible little lark! By the way, did you notice how gay Rank was this evening?

NORA
Was he? I didn't get a chance to speak to him.

HELMER
I didn't either, really; but it's a long time since I've seen him in such a jolly mood. [Gazes at Nora for a while, then comes nearer her] It's so lovely to be home again—to be here alone with you. You glorious, fascinating creature!

NORA
Don't look at me like that, Torvald.

HELMER
Why shouldn't I look at my own dearest treasure? — at all this loveliness that is mine, wholly and utterly mine—mine alone!

NORA
[Goes to the other side of the table] You mustn't talk to me like that tonight.

HELMER
[Following] You're still under the spell of the tarantella—and it makes you even more desirable. Listen! The other guests are leaving now. [More softly] Soon the whole house will be still, Nora.

NORA
I hope so.

HELMER
Yes, you do, don't you, my beloved. Do you know something—when I'm out with you among a lot of people—do you know why it is I hardly speak to you, why I keep away from you, and only occasionally steal a quick glance at you; do you know why that is? It's because I pretend that we love each other in secret, that we're secretly engaged, and that no one suspects there is anything between us.

NORA
Yes, yes; I know your thoughts are always round me.

HELMER
Then, when it's time to leave, and I put your shawl round your smooth, soft, young shoulders—round that beautiful neck of yours—I pretend that you are my young bride, that we've just come from the wedding, and that I'm taking you home for the first time—that for the first time I shall be alone with

you—quite alone with you, in all your tremulous beauty. All evening I have been filled with longing for you. As I watched you swaying and whirling in the tarantella—my pulses began to throb until I thought I should go mad; that's why I carried you off—made you leave so early—

NORA

Please go, Torvald! Please leave me. I don't want you like this.

HELMER

What do you mean? You're teasing me, aren't you, little Nora? Not want me—! Aren't I your husband—?

[A knock at the outer door]

NORA

[Starts] Listen—!

HELMER

[Going toward the hall] Who is it?

RANK

[Outside] It is I; may I come in a moment?

HELMER

[In a low tone, annoyed] Why does he have to bother us now! *[Aloud]* Just a second! *[Opens door]* Well! How nice of you to look in.

RANK

I heard your voice, and I thought I'd like to stop in a minute. *[Looks round]* These dear old rooms! You must be so cozy and happy here, you two!

HELMER

I was just saying how gay and happy you seemed to be, upstairs.

RANK

Why not? Why shouldn't I be? One should get all one can out of life; all one can, for as long as one can. That wine was excellent—

HELMER

Especially the champagne.

RANK

You noticed that, did you? It's incredible how much I managed to get down.

NORA

Torvald drank plenty of it too.

RANK

Oh?

NORA

It always puts him in such a jolly mood.

RANK

Well, why shouldn't one have a jolly evening after a well-spent day?

HELMER

Well-spent! I'm afraid mine wasn't much to boast of!

RANK

[Slapping him on the shoulder] But mine was, you see?

NORA

Did you by any chance make a scientific investigation, Doctor Rank?

RANK

Precisely.

HELMER

Listen to little Nora, talking about scientific investigations!

NORA

Am I to congratulate you on the result?

RANK

By all means.

NORA

It was good then?

RANK

The best possible, both for the doctor and the patient—certainty.

NORA

[Quickly and searchingly] Certainty?

RANK

Absolute certainty. Wasn't I right to spend a jolly evening after that?

NORA

You were quite right, Doctor Rank.

HELMER

I quite agree! Provided you don't have to pay for it, tomorrow.

RANK

You don't get anything for nothing in this life.

NORA

You like masquerade parties, don't you, Doctor Rank?

RANK

Very much—when there are plenty of amusing disguises—

NORA

What shall we two be at our next masquerade?

HELMER
Listen to her! Thinking of the next party already!

RANK
We two? I'll tell you. You must go as a precious talisman.

HELMER
How on earth would you dress that!

RANK
That's easy. She'd only have to be herself.

HELMER
Charmingly put. But what about you? Have you decided what you'd be?

RANK
Oh, definitely.

HELMER
Well?

RANK
At the next masquerade party I shall be invisible.

HELMER
That's a funny notion!

RANK
There's a large black cloak—you've heard of the invisible cloak, haven't you? You've only to put it around you and no one can see you any more.

HELMER
[With a suppressed smile] Quite true!

RANK
But I almost forgot what I came for. Give me a cigar, will you, Helmer? One of the dark Havanas.

HELMER
Of course—with pleasure. *[Hands cigar case]*

RANK
[Takes one and cuts the end off] Thanks.

NORA
[Striking a wax match] Let me give you a light.

RANK
I thank you. *[She holds the match. He lights his cigar at it.]* And now, I'll say good-bye!

HELMER
Good-bye, good-bye, my dear fellow.

NORA
Sleep well, Doctor Rank.

RANK
Thanks for the wish.

NORA
Wish me the same.

RANK
You? Very well, since you ask me— Sleep well. And thanks for the light. *[He nods to them both and goes out.]*

HELMER
[In an undertone] He's had a lot to drink.

NORA
[Absently] I dare say. *[Helmer takes his bunch of keys from his pocket and goes into the hall.]* Torvald! What do you want out there?

HELMER
I'd better empty the mail-box; it's so full there won't be room for the papers in the morning.

NORA
Are you going to work tonight?

HELMER
No—you know I'm not. —Why, what's this? Someone has been at the lock.

NORA
The lock—?

HELMER
Yes—that's funny! I shouldn't have thought that the maids would— Here's a broken hair-pin. Why—it's one of yours, Nora.

NORA
[Quickly] It must have been the children—

HELMER
You'll have to stop them doing that— There! I got it open at last. *[Takes contents out and calls out towards the kitchen]* Helene? —Oh, Helene; put out the lamp in the hall, will you? *[He returns with letters in his hand, and shuts the door to the hall.]* Just look how they've stacked up. *[Looks through them]* Why, what's this?

NORA
[At the window] The letter! Oh, Torvald! No!

HELMER
Two visiting cards—from Rank.

NORA
From Doctor Rank?

HELMER
[Looking at them] Doctor Rank, physician. They were right on top. He must have stuck them in just now, as he left.

NORA

Is there anything on them?

HELMER

There's a black cross over his name. Look! What a gruesome thought. Just as if he were announcing his own death.

NORA

And so he is.

HELMER

What do you mean? What do you know about it? Did he tell you anything?

NORA

Yes. These cards mean that he has said good-bye to us for good. Now he'll lock himself up to die.

HELMER

Oh, my poor friend! I always knew he hadn't long to live, but I never dreamed it would be quite so soon—! And to hide away like a wounded animal—

NORA

When the time comes, it's best to go in silence. Don't you think so, Torvald?

HELMER

[Walking up and down] He'd become such a part of us. I can't imagine his having gone for good. With his suffering and loneliness he was like a dark, cloudy background to our lives—it made the sunshine of our happiness seem even brighter— Well, I suppose it's for the best—for him at any rate. [Stands still] And perhaps for us too, Nora. Now we are more than ever dependent on each other. [Takes her in his arms] Oh, my beloved wife! I can't seem to hold you close enough. Do you know something, Nora. I often wish you were in some great danger—so I could risk body and soul—my whole life—everything, everything, for your sake.

NORA

[Tears herself from him and says firmly] Now you must read your letters, Torvald.

HELMER

No, no; not tonight. I want to be with you, my beloved wife.

NORA

With the thought of your dying friend—?

HELMER

Of course— You are right. It's been a shock to both of us. A hideous shadow has come between us—

thoughts of death and decay. We must try and throw them off. Until then—we'll stay apart.

NORA

[Her arms round his neck] Torvald! Good-night! Good-night!

HELMER

[Kissing her forehead] Good-night, my little songbird; sleep well! Now I'll go and read my letters. [He goes with the letters in his hand into his room and shuts the door.]

NORA

[With wild eyes, gropes about her, seizes Helmer's domino, throws it round her, and whispers quickly, hoarsely, and brokenly] I'll never see him again. Never, never, never. [Throws her shawl over her head] I'll never see the children again. I'll never see them either—Oh the thought of that black, icy water! That fathomless—! If it were only over! He has it now; he's reading it. Oh, not yet—please! Not yet! Torvald, good-bye—! Good-bye to you and the children!

[She is rushing out by the hall; at the same moment Helmer flings his door open, and stands there with an open letter in his hand.]

HELMER

Nora!

NORA

[Shrieks] Ah—!

HELMER

What does this mean? Do you know what is in this letter?

NORA

Yes, yes, I know. Let me go! Let me out!

HELMER

[Holds her back] Where are you going?

NORA

[Tries to break away from him] Don't try to save me, Torvald!

HELMER

[Falling back] So it's true! It's true what he writes? It's too horrible! It's impossible—it can't be true.

NORA

It *is* true. I've loved you more than all the world.

HELMER

Oh, come now! Let's have no silly nonsense!

NORA

[A step nearer him] Torvald—!

HELMER

Do you realize what you've done?

NORA

Let me go—I won't have you suffer for it! I won't have you take the blame!

HELMER

Will you stop this play-acting! *[Locks the outer door]* You'll stay here and give an account of yourself. Do you understand what you have done? Answer me! Do you understand it?

NORA

[Looks at him fixedly, and says with a stiffening expression] I think I'm beginning to understand for the first time.

HELMER

[Walking up and down] God! What an awakening! After eight years to discover that you who have been my pride and joy—are no better than a hypocrite, a liar—worse than that—a criminal! It's too horrible to think of! *[Nora says nothing, and continues to look fixedly at him.]* I might have known what to expect. I should have foreseen it. You've inherited all your father's lack of principle—be silent!—all of your father's lack of principle, I say!—no religion, no moral code, no sense of duty. This is my punishment for shielding him! I did it for your sake; and this is my reward!

NORA

I see.

HELMER

You've destroyed my happiness. You've ruined my whole future. It's ghastly to think of! I'm completely in the power of this scoundrel; he can force me to do whatever he likes, demand whatever he chooses; order me about at will; and I shan't dare open my mouth! My entire career is to be wrecked and all because of a lawless, unprincipled woman!

NORA

If I were no longer alive, then you'd be free.

HELMER

Oh yes! You're full of histrionics! Your father was just the same. Even if you "weren't alive," as you put it,

what good would that do me? None whatever! He could publish the story all the same; I might even be suspected of collusion. People might say I was behind it all—that I had prompted you to do it. And to think I have you to thank for all this—you whom I've done nothing but pamper and spoil since the day of our marriage. Now do you realize what you've done to me?

NORA

[With cold calmness] Yes.

HELMER

It's all so incredible, I can't grasp it. But we might try and come to some agreement. Take off that shawl. Take it off, I say! Of course, we must find some way to appease him—the matter must be hushed up at any cost. As far as we two are concerned, there must be no change in our way of life—in the eyes of the world, I mean. You'll naturally continue to live here. But you won't be allowed to bring up the children— I'd never dare trust them to you—God! to have to say this to the woman I've loved so tenderly— There can be no further thought of happiness between us. We must save what we can from the ruins—we can save appearances, at least—*[A ring; Helmer starts]* What can that be? At this hour! You don't suppose he—! Could he—? Hide yourself, Nora; say you are ill.

[Nora stands motionless. Helmer goes to the door and opens it.]

HELENE

[Half dressed, in the hall] It's a letter for Mrs. Helmer.

HELMER

Give it to me. *[(Seizes the letter and shuts the door]* It's from him. I shan't give it to you. I'll read it myself.

NORA

Very well.

HELMER

[By the lamp] I don't dare open it; this may be the end—for both of us. Still—I must know. *[Hastily tears the letter open; reads a few lines, looks at an enclosure; with a cry of joy]* Nora! *[Nora looks inquiringly at him.]* Nora! —I can't believe it—I must read it again. But it's true—it's really true! Nora, I am saved! I'm saved!

NORA

What about me?

HELMER

You too, of course; we are both of us saved, both of us. Look! —he's sent you back your note—he says he's sorry for what he did and apologizes for it—that due to a happy turn of events he—Oh, what does it matter what he says! We are saved, Nora! No one can harm you now. Oh, Nora, Nora—; but let's get rid of this hateful thing. I'll just see— *[Glances at the I.O.U.]* No, no—I won't even look at it; I'll pretend it was all a horrible dream. *[Tears the I.O.U. and both letters in pieces. Throws them into the fire and watches them burn]* There! Now it's all over— He said in his letter you've known about this since Christmas Eve—you must have had three dreadful days, Nora!

NORA

Yes. It's been very hard.

HELMER

How you must have suffered! And you saw no way out but—No! We'll forget the whole ghastly business. We'll just thank God and repeat again and again: It's over; all over! Don't you understand, Nora? You don't seem to grasp it: It's over. What's the matter with you? Why do you look so grim? My poor darling little Nora, I understand; but you mustn't worry—because I've forgiven you, Nora; I swear I have; I've forgiven everything. You did what you did because you loved me—I see that now.

NORA

Yes—that's true.

HELMER

You loved me as a wife should love her husband. You didn't realize what you were doing—you weren't able to judge how wrong it was. Don't think this makes you any less dear to me. Just you lean on me; let me guide you and advise you; I'm not a man for nothing! There's something very endearing about a woman's helplessness. And try and forget those harsh things I said just now. I was frantic; my whole world seemed to be tumbling about my ears. Believe me, I've forgiven you, Nora—I swear it—I've forgiven everything.

NORA

Thank you for your forgiveness, Torvald. *[Goes out, to the right]*

HELMER

No! Don't go. *[Looking through the doorway]* Why do you have to go in there?

NORA

[Inside] I want to get out of these fancy-dress clothes.

HELMER

[In the doorway] Yes, do, my darling. Try to calm down now, and get back to normal, my poor frightened little song-bird. Don't you worry—you'll be safe under my wings—they'll protect you. *[Walking up and down near the door]* How lovely our home is, Nora! You'll be sheltered here; I'll cherish you as if you were a little dove I'd rescued from the claws of some dreadful hawk. You'll see—your poor fluttering little heart will soon grow calm again. Tomorrow all this will appear in quite a different light—things will be just as they were. I won't have to keep on saying I've forgiven you—you'll be able to sense it. You don't really think I could ever drive you away, do you? That I could even so much as reproach you for anything? You'd understand if you could see into my heart. When a man forgives his wife wholeheartedly—as I have you—it fills him with such tenderness, such peace. She seems to belong to him in a double sense; it's as though he'd brought her to life again; she's become more than his wife—she's become his child as well. That's how it will be with us, Nora—my own bewildered, helpless little darling. From now on you mustn't worry about anything; just open your heart to me; just let me be both will and conscience to you. *[Nora enters in everyday dress.]* What's all this? I thought you were going to bed. You've changed your dress?

NORA

Yes, Torvald; I've changed my dress.

HELMER

But what for? At this hour?

NORA

I shan't sleep tonight.

HELMER

But, Nora dear—

NORA

[Looking at her watch] It's not so very late— Sit down, Torvald; we have a lot to talk about. *[She sits at one side of the table.]*

HELMER

Nora—what does this mean? Why that stern expression?

NORA

Sit down. It'll take some time. I have a lot to say to you.

[Helmer sits at the other side of the table.]

HELMER

You frighten me, Nora. I don't understand you.

NORA

No, that's just it. You don't understand me; and I have never understood you either—until tonight. No, don't interrupt me. Just listen to what I have to say. This is to be a final settlement, Torvald.

HELMER

How do you mean?

NORA

[After a short silence] Doesn't anything special strike you as we sit here like this?

HELMER

I don't think so—why?

NORA

It doesn't occur to you, does it, that though we've been married for eight years, this is the first time that we two—man and wife—have sat down for a serious talk?

HELMER

What do you mean by serious?

NORA

During eight whole years, no—more than that—ever since the first day we met—we have never exchanged so much as one serious word about serious things.

HELMER

Why should I perpetually burden you with all my cares and problems? How could you possibly help me to solve them?

NORA

I'm not talking about cares and problems. I'm simply saying we've never once sat down seriously and tried to get to the bottom of anything.

HELMER

But, Nora, darling—why should you be concerned with serious thoughts?

NORA

That's the whole point! You've never understood me— A great injustice has been done me, Torvald; first by Father, and then by you.

HELMER

What a thing to say! No two people on earth could ever have loved you more than we have!

NORA

[Shaking her head] You never loved me. You just thought it was fun to be in love with me.

HELMER

This is fantastic!

NORA

Perhaps. But it's true all the same. While I was still at home I used to hear Father airing his opinions and they became my opinions; or if I didn't happen to agree, I kept it to myself—he would have been displeased otherwise. He used to call me his doll-baby, and played with me as I played with my dolls. Then I came to live in your house—

HELMER

What an expression to use about our marriage!

NORA

[Undisturbed] I mean—from Father's hands I passed into yours. You arranged everything according to your tastes, and I acquired the same tastes, or I pretended to—I'm not sure which—a little of both, perhaps. Looking back on it all, it seems to me I've lived here like a beggar, from hand to mouth. I've lived by performing tricks for you, Torvald. But that's the way you wanted it. You and Father have done me a great wrong. You've prevented me from becoming a real person.

HELMER

Nora, how can you be so ungrateful and unreasonable! Haven't you been happy here?

NORA

No, never. I thought I was; but I wasn't really.

HELMER

Not—not happy!

NORA

No; only merry. You've always been so kind to me. But our home has never been anything but a playroom. I've been your doll-wife, just as at home I was Papa's doll-child. And the children in turn, have been my dolls. I thought it fun when you played games with me, just as they thought it fun when I played games with them. And that's been our marriage, Torvald.

HELMER

There may be a grain of truth in what you say, even though it is distorted and exaggerated. From now on things will be different. Play-time is over now; tomorrow lessons begin!

NORA

Whose lessons? Mine, or the children's?

HELMER

Both, if you wish it, Nora, dear.

NORA

Torvald, I'm afraid you're not the man to teach me to be a real wife to you.

HELMER

How can you say that?

NORA

And I'm certainly not fit to teach the children.

HELMER

Nora!

NORA

Didn't you just say, a moment ago, you didn't dare trust them to me?

HELMER

That was in the excitement of the moment! You mustn't take it so seriously!

NORA

But you were quite right, Torvald. That job is beyond me; there's another job I must do first: I must try and educate myself. You could never help me to do that; I must do it quite alone. So, you see, that's why I'm going to leave you.

HELMER

[Jumping up] What did you say—?

NORA

I shall never get to know myself—I shall never learn to face reality—unless I stand alone. So I can't stay with you any longer.

HELMER

Nora! Nora!

NORA

I am going at once. I'm sure Kristine will let me stay with her tonight—

HELMER

But, Nora—this is madness! I shan't allow you to do this. I shall forbid it!

NORA

You no longer have the power to forbid me anything. I'll only take a few things with me—those that belong to me. I shall never again accept anything from you.

HELMER

Have you lost your senses?

NORA

Tomorrow I'll go home—to what *was* my home, I mean. It might be easier for me there, to find something to do.

HELMER

You talk like an ignorant child, Nora—!

NORA

Yes. That's just why I must educate myself.

HELMER

To leave your home—to leave your husband, and your children! What do you suppose people would say to that?

NORA

It makes no difference. This is something I *must* do.

HELMER

It's inconceivable! Don't you realize you'd be betraying your most sacred duty?

NORA

What do you consider that to be?

HELMER

Your duty towards your husband and your children—I surely don't have to tell you that!

NORA

I've another duty just as sacred.

HELMER

Nonsense! What duty do you mean?

NORA

My duty towards myself.

HELMER

Remember—before all else you are a wife and mother.

NORA

I don't believe that anymore. I believe that before all else I am a human being, just as you are—or at least that I should try and become one. I know that most people would agree with you, Torvald—and that's what they say in books. But I can no longer be satisfied with what most people say—or what they write in books. I must think things out for myself—get clear about them.

HELMER

Surely your position in your home is clear enough? Have you no sense of religion? Isn't that an infallible guide to you?

NORA

But don't you see, Torvald—I don't really know what religion is.

HELMER

Nora! How *can* you!

NORA

All I know about it is what Pastor Hansen told me when I was confirmed. He taught me what he thought religion was—said it was *this* and *that*. As soon as I get away by myself, I shall have to look into that matter too, try and decide whether what he taught me was right—or whether it's right for *me*, at least.

HELMER

A nice way for a young woman to talk! It's unheard of! If religion means nothing to you, I'll appeal to your conscience; you must have some sense of ethics, I suppose? Answer me! Or have you none?

NORA

It's hard for me to answer you, Torvald. I don't think I know—all these things bewilder me. But I *do* know that I think quite differently from you about them. I've discovered that the law, for instance, is quite different from what I had imagined; but I find it hard to believe it can be right. It seems it's criminal for a woman to try and spare her old, sick father, or save her husband's life! I can't agree with that.

HELMER

You talk like a child. You have no understanding of the society we live in.

NORA

No, I haven't. But I'm going to try and learn. I want to find out which of us is right—society or I.

HELMER

You are ill, Nora; you have a touch of fever; you're quite beside yourself.

NORA

I've never felt so sure—so clear-headed—as I do tonight.

HELMER

"Sure and clear-headed" enough to leave your husband and your children?

NORA

Yes.

HELMER

Then there is only one explanation possible.

NORA

What?

HELMER

You don't love me any more.

NORA

No; that is just it.

HELMER

Nora!— What are you saying!

NORA

It makes me so unhappy, Torvald; for you've always been so kind to me. But I can't help it. I don't love you any more.

HELMER

[Mastering himself with difficulty] You feel "sure and clear-headed" about this too?

NORA

Yes, utterly sure. That's why I can't stay here any longer.

HELMER

And can you tell me how I lost your love?

NORA

Yes, I can tell you. It was tonight—when the wonderful thing didn't happen; I knew then you weren't the man I always thought you were.

HELMER

I don't understand.

NORA

For eight years I've been waiting patiently; I knew, of course, that such things don't happen every day. Then, when this trouble came to me—I thought to myself: Now! Now the wonderful thing will happen! All the time Krogstad's letter was out there in the box, it never occurred to me for a single moment that you'd think of submitting to his conditions. I was absolutely convinced that you'd defy him—that you'd tell him to publish the thing to all the world; and that then—

HELMER

You mean you thought I'd let my wife be publicly dishonored and disgraced?

NORA

No. What I thought you'd do, was to take the blame upon yourself.

HELMER

Nora—!

NORA

I know! You think I never would have accepted such a sacrifice. Of course I wouldn't! But my word would have meant nothing against yours. That was the wonderful thing I hoped for, Torvald, hoped for with such terror. And it was to prevent that, that I chose to kill myself.

HELMER

I'd gladly work for you day and night, Nora—go through suffering and want, if need be—but one doesn't sacrifice one's honor for love's sake.

NORA

Millions of women have done so.

HELMER

You think and talk like a silly child.

NORA

Perhaps. But you neither think nor talk like the man I want to share my life with. When you'd recovered from your fright—and you never thought of me, only of yourself—when you had nothing more to fear—you behaved as though none of this had happened. I was your little lark again, your little doll—whom you would have to guard more carefully than ever, because she was so weak and frail. [Stands up] At that moment it suddenly dawned on me that I had been living here for eight years with a stranger and that I'd borne him three children. I can't bear to think about it! I could tear myself to pieces!

HELMER

[Sadly] I see, Nora—I understand; there's suddenly a great void between us— Is there no way to bridge it?

NORA

Feeling as I do now, Torvald—I could never be a wife to you.

HELMER

But, if I were to change? Don't you think I'm capable of that?

NORA

Perhaps—when you no longer have your doll to play with.

HELMER

It's inconceivable! I *can't* part with you, Nora. I can't endure the thought.

NORA

[Going into room on the right] All the more reason it should happen. [She comes back with outdoor things and a small traveling-bag, which she places on a chair.]

HELMER

But not at once, Nora—not now! At least wait till tomorrow.

NORA

[Putting on cloak] I can't spend the night in a strange man's house.

HELMER

Couldn't we go on living here together? As brother and sister, if you like—as friends.

NORA

[Fastening her hat] You know very well that wouldn't last, Torvald. [Puts on the shawl] Good-bye. I won't go in and see the children. I know they're in better hands than mine. Being what I am—how can I be of any use to them?

HELMER

But surely, some day, Nora—?

NORA

How can I tell? How do I know what sort of person I'll become?

HELMER

You are my wife, Nora, now and always!

NORA

Listen to me, Torvald—I've always heard that when a wife deliberately leaves her husband as I am leaving you, he is legally freed from all responsibility towards her. At any rate, I release you now from all responsibility. You mustn't feel yourself bound, any more than I shall. There must be complete freedom on both sides. Here is your ring. Now give me mine.

HELMER

That too?

NORA

That too.

HELMER
Here it is.

NORA
So—it's all over now. Here are the keys. The servants know how to run the house—better than I do. I'll ask Kristine to come by tomorrow, after I've left town; there are a few things I brought with me from home; she'll pack them up and send them on to me.

HELMER
You really mean it's over, Nora? *Really* over? You'll never think of me again?

NORA
I expect I shall often think of you; of you—and the children, and this house.

HELMER
May I write to you?

NORA
No—never. You mustn't! Please!

HELMER
At least, let me send you—

NORA
Nothing!

HELMER
But, you'll let me help you, Nora—

NORA
No, I say! I can't accept anything from strangers.

HELMER
Must I always be a stranger to you, Nora?

NORA
[Taking her traveling-bag] Yes. Unless it were to happen—the most wonderful thing of all—

HELMER
What?

NORA
Unless we both could change so that— Oh, Torvald! I no longer *believe* in miracles, you see!

HELMER
Tell me! Let *me* believe! Unless we both could change so that—?

NORA
So that our life together might truly be a marriage. Good-bye. [She goes out by the hall door.]

HELMER
[Sinks into a chair by the door with his face in his hands] Nora! Nora! [He looks around the room and rises.] She is gone! How empty it all seems! [A hope springs up in him.] The most wonderful thing of all—?

[From below is heard the reverberation of a heavy door closing.]

[Curtain]

7

MAJOR BARBARA

Bernard Shaw • 1905

"I CAN EXPLAIN ANYTHING TO ANYBODY, AND WHAT is more I enjoy doing it." This is more than a quotation from George Bernard Shaw; it is virtually the celebrated author's creed. No playwright, surely, has been more effusively Promethean: "I want to be thoroughly used up when I die, for the harder I work, the more I live. I rejoice in life for its own sake. Life is no 'brief candle' for me. It is a sort of splendid torch, which I have got hold of for the moment; and I want to make it burn as brightly as possible before handing it on to future generations."

It is axiomatic to note that Shaw's is a "theatre of ideas," for it was the "technical novelty . . . of discussion" that Shaw had championed in Ibsen (see introduction to *A Doll's House*), and it was Shaw's emphasis on the social and political relevance of his plays that demanded he categorize many of them as "discussions" rather than "comedies" or "dramas." Shaw himself was an avid polemicist long before he turned to writing for the stage, and there is no such thing as a wholly apo-

litical Shavian play. But Shaw's drama is anything but dry debate. His more than fifty plays—all highly idiosyncratic—radiate with humor, wit, fantasy, satire, rare eloquence, and all-but-bursting intensities of feeling. Ideas become passions in Shaw, and assume a stage life of great emotional richness and complexity.

Shaw was born in Dublin, Ireland, in 1856, and after an admittedly miserable childhood moved with his mother to London at the age of twenty. There, living in relative poverty, the young Shaw embarked on an intensive self-education at the British Museum. Within a few years, he had begun a career in journalistic criticism, written a series of unpublished novels, and joined the Fabian Society, a group of English Marxists with extensive plans for social reform. By the late 1880s, Shaw's reputation as a writer and public speaker had begun to grow, and his critical essays began to appear with great frequency: by the mid 1890s, Shaw was increasingly considered the best music and drama critic in England. It was just at this time that he began to write plays: *Widower's Houses* in 1892, and *Arms and the Man* in 1894, both plays demonstrating the social iconoclasm and witty intellectual disputation that became his trademarks. From then until his death in 1950, Shaw was rarely far from the stage: as playwright, frequent director, and always dramaturg of his many works, subsequently supervising their print publication as well, and adding voluminous prefaces and/or afterwords to drive home the social, political, and aesthetic points the plays (to him) were meant to exemplify.

Major Barbara, which Shaw typically categorized as "A Discussion in Three Acts," (and for which he—also typically—wrote a preface nearly half as long as the play itself) presents three presumed ideologies of its time: Victorian morality (exemplified by Lady Britomart), "Crosstianity" (Undershaft's term for the Salvation Army ethic, as exemplified by Barbara), and neo-Nietzscheanism (exemplified by Undershaft.) No one should mistake the play for a real debate, however. Not only does Shaw load the dice, but he also gaily skips over countless contradictions and logical gaps: Undershaft's ideology somehow mixes Marxism with supercapitalism, and fascism with democracy; Undershaft's eloquence cannot, in fact, stand up to very much reality. All the characters, in the end, are treated with both satire and indulgence; they divide the truth, none fully possesses it. Shaw's goal, finally, is to fascinate, not to proselytize; to entertain contemporary audiences with a dance of ideas, personalities who embody them, and our own projections of the future. The play "works" today because its major themes remain fully debatable, and because Shaw's brilliant, irreverent, and witty observations remain shocking and apt.

A NOTE ON THE PRINTING

Shaw's idiosyncratic spellings, stage directions, and punctuation have been retained exactly as written in the definitive text, which was prepared under the editorial supervision of Dan H. Laurence. The author's preface is likewise included in full.

In adding a few footnotes to the play, I have relied in part on the excellent glosses contained in Warren Sylvester Smith's edition of the play (New York: Norton, 1970).

❧ MAJOR BARBARA ❧

CAST OF CHARACTERS

LADY BRITOMART UNDERSHAFT, a Victorian matriarch

STEPHEN, her son

BARBARA, her daughter

SARAH, her other daughter

CHARLES LOMAX, a young man about town, attracted to Sarah

ADOLPHUS CUSINS, a student of Greek, bent on marrying Barbara

ANDREW UNDERSHAFT, a rich industrialist; long separated from Lady Britomart, his wife

SNOBBY PRICE, an unemployed workman

RUMMY MITCHENS, a poor woman

JENNY HILL, an overwrought, young Salvation lass

PETER SHIRLEY, an elderly man, half worn out

BILL WALKER, an ill-tempered young man

MRS. BAINES, the Salvation Army Commissioner

MORRISON, Lady Britomart's butler

BILTON, a factory foreman

PREFACE

First Aid to Critics

Before dealing with the deeper aspects of Major Barbara, let me, for the credit of English literature, make a protest against an unpatriotic habit into which many of my critics have fallen. Whenever my view strikes them as being at all outside the range of, say, an ordinary suburban church-warden, they conclude that I am echoing Schopenhauer, Nietzsche, Ibsen, Strindberg, Tolstoy, or some other heresiarch in northern or eastern Europe.

I confess there is something flattering in this simple faith in my accomplishment as a linguist and my erudition as a philosopher. But I cannot countenance the assumption that life and literature are so poor in these islands that we must go abroad for all dramatic material that is not common and all ideas that are not superficial. I therefore venture to put my critics in possession of certain facts concerning my contact with modern ideas.

About half a century ago, an Irish novelist, Charles Lever, wrote a story entitled A Day's Ride: A Life's Romance. It was published by Charles Dickens in Household Words, and proved so strange to the public taste that Dickens pressed Lever to make short work of it. I read scraps of this novel when I was a child; and it made an enduring impression on me. The hero was a very romantic hero, trying to live bravely, chivalrously, and powerfully by dint of mere romance-fed imagination, without courage, without means, without knowledge, without skill, without anything real except his bodily appetites. Even in my childhood I found in this poor devil's unsuccessful encounters with the facts of life, a poignant quality that romantic fiction lacked. The book, in spite of its first failure, is not dead: I saw its title the other day in the catalogue of Tauchnitz.

Now why is it that when I also deal in the tragicomic irony of the conflict between real life and the romantic imagination, critics never affiliate me to my countryman and immediate forerunner, Charles Lever, whilst they confidently derive me from a Norwegian author of whose language I do not know three words, and of whom I knew nothing until years after the Shavian *Anschauung* was already unequivocally declared in books full of what came, ten years later, to be perfunctorily labelled Ibsenism? I was not Ibsenist even at second hand; for Lever, though he may have read Henri Beyle, *alias* Stendhal, certainly never read Ibsen. Of the books that made Lever popular, such as Charles O'Malley and Harry Lorrequer, I know nothing but the names and some of the illustrations. But the story of the day's ride and life's romance of Potts (claiming alliance with Pozzo di Borgo) caught me and fascinated me as something strange and significant, though I already knew all about Alnaschar and Don Quixote and Simon Tappertit and many another romantic hero mocked by reality. From the plays of Aristophanes to the tales of Stevenson that mockery has been made familiar to all who are properly saturated with letters.

Where, then, was the novelty in Lever's tale? Partly, I think, in a new seriousness in dealing with Potts's disease. Formerly, the contrast between madness and sanity was deemed comic: Hogarth shews us how fashionable people went in parties to Bedlam to laugh at the lunatics. I myself have had a village idiot exhibited to me as something irresistibly funny. On the stage the madman was once a regular comic figure: that was how Hamlet got his opportunity before Shakespear touched him. The originality of Shakespear's version lay in his taking the lunatic sympathetically and seriously, and thereby making an advance towards the eastern consciousness of the fact that lunacy may be inspiration in disguise, since a man who has more brains than his fellows necessarily appears as mad to them as one who has less. But Shakespear did not do for Pistol and Parolles what he did for Hamlet. The particular sort of madman they represented, the romantic make-believer, lay outside the pale of sympathy in literature: he was pitilessly despised and ridiculed here as he was in the east under the name of Alnaschar, and was doomed to be, centuries later, under the name of Simon Tappertit. When Cervantes relented over Don Quixote, and Dickens relented over Pickwick, they did not become impartial: they simply changed sides, and became friends and apologists where they had formerly been mockers.

In Lever's story there is a real change of attitude. There is no relenting towards Potts: he never gains our affections like Don Quixote and Pickwick: he has not even the infatuate courage of Tappertit. But we dare not laugh at him, because, somehow, we recognize ourselves in Potts. We may, some of us, have enough nerve, enough muscle, enough luck, enough tact or skill or address or knowledge to carry things off better than he did; to impose on the people who saw through him; to fascinate Katinka (who cut Potts so ruthlessly at the end of the story); but for all that, we know that Potts plays an enormous part in ourselves and in the world, and that the social problem is not a problem of story-book heroes of the older pattern, but a problem of Pottses, and of how to make men of them. To fall back on my old phrase, we have the feeling—one that Alnaschar, Pistol, Parolles, and Tappertit never gave us—that Potts is a piece of really scientific natural history as distinguished from funny story telling. His author is not throwing a stone at a creature of another and inferior order, but making a confession, with the effect that the stone hits each of us full in the conscience and causes our self-esteem to smart very sorely. Hence the failure of Lever's book to please the readers of Household Words. That pain in the self-esteem nowadays causes critics to raise a cry of Ibsenism. I therefore assure them that the sensation first came to me from Lever and may have come to him from Beyle, or at least out of the Stendhalian atmosphere. I exclude the hypothesis of complete originality on Lever's part, because a man can no more be completely original in that sense than a tree can grow out of air.

Another mistake as to my literary ancestry is made whenever I violate the romantic convention that all women are angels when they are not devils; that they are better looking than men; that their part in courtship is entirely passive; and that the human female form is the most beautiful object in nature. Schopenhauer wrote a splenetic essay which, as it is neither polite nor profound, was probably intended to knock this nonsense violently on the head. A sentence denouncing the idolized form as ugly has been largely quoted. The English critics have read that sentence; and I must here affirm, with as much gentleness as the implication will bear, that it has yet to be proved that they have dipped any deeper. At all events, whenever an English playwright represents a young and marriageable woman as being anything but a romantic heroine, he is disposed of without further thought as an echo of Schopenhauer. My own case is a specially hard one, because, when I implore the critics who are obsessed with the Schopenhauerian formula to remember that playwrights, like sculptors, study their figures from life, and not from philosophic essays, they reply passionately that I am not a playwright and that my stage figures do not live. But even so, I may and do ask them why, if they must give the credit of my plays to a philosopher, they do not give it to an English philosopher? Long before I ever read a word by Schopenhauer, or even knew whether he was a philosopher or a chemist, the Socialist revival of the eighteen-eighties brought me into contact, both literary and personal, with Ernest Belfort Bax, an English Socialist and philosophic essayist, whose handling of modern feminism would provoke romantic protests from Schopenhauer himself, or even Strindberg. As a matter of fact I hardly noticed Schopenhauer's disparagements of women when they came under my notice later on, so thoroughly had Bax familiarized me with the homoist attitude, and forced me to recognize the extent to which public opinion, and consequently legislation and jurisprudence, is corrupted by feminist sentiment.

Belfort Bax's essays were not confined to the Feminist question. He was a ruthless critic of current morality. Other writers have gained sympathy for dramatic criminals by eliciting the alleged 'soul of goodness in things evil'; but Bax would propound some quite undramatic and apparently shabby violation of our commercial law and morality, and not merely defend it with the most disconcerting ingenuity, but actually prove it to be a positive duty that nothing but the certainty of police persecution should prevent every right-minded man from at once doing on principle. The Socialists were naturally shocked, being for the most part morbidly moral people; but at all events they were saved later on from the delusion that nobody but Nietzsche had ever challenged our mercanto-Christian morality. I first heard the name of Nietzsche from a German mathematician, Miss Borchardt, who had read my Quintessence of Ibsenism, and told me that she saw what I had been reading: namely, Nietzsche's Jenseits von Gut und Böse. Which I protest I had never seen, and could not have read with any comfort, for want of the necessary German, if I had seen it.

Nietzsche, like Schopenhauer, is the victim in England of a single much quoted sentence containing the phrase 'big blonde beast.' On the strength of this alliteration it is assumed that Nietzsche gained his European reputation by a senseless glorification of selfish bullying as the rule of life, just as it is assumed, on the strength of the single word Superman (Übermensch) borrowed by me from Nietzsche, that I look for the salvation of society to the despotism of a single Napoleonic Superman, in spite of my careful demonstration of the folly of that outworn infatuation. But even the less recklessly superficial critics seem to believe that the modern objection to Christianity as a pernicious slave-morality was first put forward by Nietzsche. It was familiar to me before I ever heard of Nietzsche. The late Captain Wilson, author of several queer pamphlets, propagandist of a metaphysical system called Comprehensionism, and inventor of the term 'Crosstianity' to distinguish the retrograde element in Christendom, was wont thirty years ago, in the discussions of the Dialectical Society, to protest earnestly against the beatitudes of the Sermon on the Mount as excuses for cowardice and servility, as destructive of our will, and consequently of our honor and manhood. Now it is true that Captain Wilson's moral criticism of Christianity was not a historical theory of it, like Nietzsche's; but this objection cannot be made to Stuart-Glennie, the successor of Buckle as a philosophic historian, who devoted his life to the elaboration and propagation of his theory that Christianity is part of an epoch (or rather an aberration, since it began as recently as 6000 B.C. and is already collapsing) produced by the necessity in which the numerically inferior white races found themselves to impose their domination on the colored races by priestcraft, making a virtue and a popular religion of drudgery and submissiveness in this world not only as a means of achieving saintliness of character but of securing a reward in heaven. Here was the slave-morality view formulated by a Scotch philosopher of my acquaintance long before we all began chattering about Nietzsche.

As Stuart-Glennie traced the evolution of society to the conflict of races, his theory made some sensation among Socialists—that is, among the only people who were seriously thinking about historical evolution at all—by its collision with the class-conflict theory of Karl Marx. Nietzsche, as I gather, regarded the slave-morality as having been invented and imposed on the world by slaves making a virtue of necessity and a religion of their servitude. Stuart-

Glennie regarded the slave-morality as an invention of the superior white race to subjugate the minds of the inferior races whom they wished to exploit, and who would have destroyed them by force of numbers if their minds had not been subjugated. As this process is in operation still, and can be studied at first hand not only in our Church schools and in the struggle between our modern proprietary classes and the proletariat, but in the part played by Christian missionaries in reconciling the black races of Africa to their subjugation by European Capitalism, we can judge for ourselves whether the initiative came from above or below. My object here is not to argue the historical point, but simply to make our theatre critics ashamed of their habit of treating Britain as an intellectual void, and assuming that every philosophical idea, every historic theory, every criticism of our moral, religious and juridical institutions, must necessarily be either a foreign import, or else a fantastic sally (in rather questionable taste) totally unrelated to the existing body of thought. I urge them to remember that this body of thought is the slowest of growths and the rarest of blossomings, and that if there be such a thing on the philosophic plane as a matter of course, it is that no individual can make more than a minute contribution to it. In fact, their conception of clever persons parthenogenetically bringing forth complete original cosmogonies by dint of sheer 'brilliancy' is part of that ignorant credulity which is the despair of the honest philosopher, and the opportunity of the religious imposter.

The Gospel of St Andrew Undershaft

It is this credulity that drives me to help my critics out with Major Barbara by telling them what to say about it. In the millionaire Undershaft I have represented a man who has become intellectually and spiritually as well as practically conscious of the irresistible natural truth which we all abhor and repudiate: to wit, that the greatest of our evils, and the worst of our crimes is poverty, and that our first duty, to which every other consideration should be sacrificed, is not to be poor. 'Poor but honest,' 'the respectable poor,' and such phrases are as intolerable and as immoral as 'drunken but amiable,' 'fraudulent but a good after-dinner speaker,' 'splendidly criminal,' or the like. Security, the chief pretence of civilization, cannot exist where the worst of dangers, the danger of poverty,

hangs over everyone's head, and where the alleged protection of our persons from violence is only an accidental result of the existence of a police force whose real business is to force the poor man to see his children starve whilst idle people overfeed pet dogs with the money that might feed and clothe them.

It is exceedingly difficult to make people realize that an evil is an evil. For instance, we seize a man and deliberately do him a malicious injury: say, imprison him for years. One would not suppose that it needed any exceptional clearness of wit to recognize in this an act of diabolical cruelty. But in England such a recognition provokes a stare of surprise, followed by an explanation that the outrage is punishment or justice or something else that is all right, or perhaps by a heated attempt to argue that we should all be robbed and murdered in our beds if such stupid villainies as sentences of imprisonment were not committed daily. It is useless to argue that even if this were true, which it is not, the alternative to adding crimes of our own to the crimes from which we suffer is not helpless submission. Chickenpox is an evil; but if I were to declare that we must either submit to it or else repress it sternly by seizing everyone who suffers from it and punishing them by inoculation with smallpox, I should be laughed at; for though nobody could deny that the result would be to prevent chickenpox to some extent by making people avoid it much more carefully, and to effect a further apparent prevention by making them conceal it very anxiously, yet people would have sense enough to see that the deliberate propagation of smallpox was a creation of evil, and must therefore be ruled out in favor of purely humane and hygienic measures. Yet in the precisely parallel case of a man breaking into my house and stealing my wife's diamonds I am expected as a matter of course to steal ten years of his life, torturing him all the time. If he tries to defeat that monstrous retaliation by shooting me, my survivors hang him. The net result suggested by the police statistics is that we inflict atrocious injuries on the burglars we catch in order to make the rest take effectual precautions against detection; so that instead of saving our wives' diamonds from burglary we only greatly decrease our chances of ever getting them back, and increase our chances of being shot by the robber if we are unlucky enough to disturb him at his work.

But the thoughtless wickedness with which we scatter sentences of imprisonment, torture in the solitary cell and on the plank bed, and flogging, on moral invalids and energetic rebels, is as nothing compared to the silly levity with which we tolerate poverty as if it were either a wholesome tonic for lazy people or else a virtue to be embraced as St Francis embraced it. If a man is indolent, let him be poor. If he is drunken, let him be poor. If he is not a gentleman, let him be poor. If he is addicted to the fine arts or to pure science instead of to trade and finance, let him be poor. If he chooses to spend his urban eighteen shillings a week or his agricultural thirteen shillings a week on his beer and his family instead of saving it up for his old age, let him be poor. Let nothing be done for 'the undeserving': let him be poor. Serve him right! Also—somewhat inconsistently—blessed are the poor!

Now what does this Let Him Be Poor mean? It means let him be weak. Let him be ignorant. Let him become a nucleus of disease. Let him be a standing exhibition and example of ugliness and dirt. Let him have rickety children. Let him be cheap, and drag his fellows down to his own price by selling himself to do their work. Let his habitations turn our cities into poisonous congeries of slums. Let his daughters infect our young men with the diseases of the streets, and his sons revenge him by turning the nation's manhood into scrofula, cowardice, cruelty, hypocrisy, political imbecility, and all the other fruits of oppression and malnutrition. Let the undeserving become still less deserving; and let the deserving lay up for himself, not treasures in heaven, but horrors in hell upon earth. This being so, is it really wise to let him be poor? Would he not do ten times less harm as a prosperous burglar, incendiary, ravisher or murderer, to the utmost limits of humanity's comparatively negligible impulses in these directions? Suppose we were to abolish all penalties for such activities, and decide that poverty is the one thing we will not tolerate—that every adult with less than, say, £365 a year, shall be painlessly but inexorably killed, and every hungry half naked child forcibly fattened and clothed, would not that be an enormous improvement on our existing system, which has already destroyed so many civilizations, and is visibly destroying ours in the same way?

Is there any radicle of such legislation in our parliamentary system? Well, there are two measures just sprouting in the political soil, which may conceivably grow to something valuable. One is the institution of a Legal Minimum Wage. The other, Old Age Pensions. But there is a better plan than either of these. Some time ago I mentioned the subject of Universal Old Age Pensions to my fellow Socialist Cobden-Sanderson, famous as an artist-craftsman in bookbinding and printing. 'Why not Universal Pensions for Life?' said Cobden-Sanderson. In saying this, he solved the industrial problem at a stroke. At present we say callously to each citizen 'If you want money, earn it' as if his having or not having it were a matter that concerned himself alone. We do not even secure for him the opportunity of earning it: on the contrary, we allow our industry to be organized in open dependence on the maintenance of 'a reserve army of unemployed' for the sake of 'elasticity.' The sensible course would be Cobden-Sanderson's: that is, to give every man enough to live well on, so as to guarantee the community against the possibility of a case of the malignant disease of poverty, and then (necessarily) to see that he earned it.

Undershaft, the hero of Major Barbara, is simply a man who, having grasped the fact that poverty is a crime, knows that when society offered him the alternative of poverty or a lucrative trade in death and destruction, it offered him, not a choice between opulent villainy and humble virtue, but between energetic enterprise and cowardly infamy. His conduct stands the Kantian test, which Peter Shirley's does not. Peter Shirley is what we call the honest poor man. Undershaft is what we call the wicked rich one: Shirley is Lazarus, Undershaft Dives. Well, the misery of the world is due to the fact that the great mass of men act and believe as Peter Shirley acts and believes. If they acted and believed as Undershaft acts and believes, the immediate result would be a revolution of incalculable beneficence. To be wealthy, says Undershaft, is with me a point of honor for which I am prepared to kill at the risk of my own life. This preparedness is, as he says, the final test of sincerity. Like Froissart's medieval hero, who saw that 'to rob and pill was a good life' he is not the dupe of that public sentiment against killing which is propagated and endowed by people who would otherwise be killed themselves, or of the mouth-honor paid to poverty and obedience by rich and insubordinate donothings who want to rob the poor without courage and command them without superiority. Froissart's knight, in placing the achievement of a good life before all the other duties—which indeed are not duties at all when they conflict with it, but plain wickedness—behaved bravely, admirably, and, in the final analysis, public-spiritedly. Medieval society, on the other hand, behaved very badly indeed in organizing itself so stupidly that a good life could be achieved by robbing and pilling. If the knight's contemporaries had been all as resolute as he, robbing and pilling would have been the shortest way to the gallows, just as, if we were all as resolute and clearsighted as Undershaft, an attempt to live by means of what is called 'an indecent income' would be the shortest way to the lethal chamber. But as, thanks to our political imbecility and personal cowardice (fruits of poverty, both), the best imitation of a good life now procurable is life on an independent income, all sensible people aim at securing such an income, and are, of course, careful to legalize and moralize both it and all the actions and sentiments which lead to it and support it as an institution. What else can they do? They know, of course, that they are rich because others are poor. But they cannot help that: it is for the poor to repudiate poverty when they have had enough of it. The thing can be done easily enough: the demonstrations to the contrary made by the economists, jurists, moralists and sentimentalists hired by the rich to defend them, or even doing the work gratuitously out of sheer folly and abjectness, impose only on those who want to be imposed on.

The reason why the independent income-tax payers are not solid in defence of their position is that since we are not medieval rovers through a sparsely populated country, the poverty of those we rob prevents our having the good life for which we sacrifice them. Rich men or aristocrats with a developed sense of life—men like Ruskin and William Morris and Kropotkin—have enormous social appetites and very fastidious personal ones. They are not content with handsome houses: they want handsome cities. They are not content with bediamonded wives and blooming daughters: they complain because the charwoman is badly dressed, because the laundress smells of gin, because the sempstress is anemic, because every man they meet is not a friend and every woman not a romance. They turn up their noses at their neighbor's drains, and are made ill by the architecture of their neighbor's houses. Trade patterns made to suit vulgar people do not please them (and they can get nothing else): they cannot sleep nor sit at ease upon 'slaughtered' cabinet makers' furniture.

The very air is not good enough for them: there is too much factory smoke in it. They even demand abstract conditions: justice, honor, a noble moral atmosphere, a mystic nexus to replace the cash nexus. Finally they declare that though to rob and pill with your own hand on horseback and in steel coat may have been a good life, to rob and pill by the hands of the policeman, the bailiff, and the soldier, and to underpay them meanly for doing it, is not a good life, but rather fatal to all possibility of even a tolerable one. They call on the poor to revolt, and, finding the poor shocked at their ungentlemanliness, despairingly revile the proletariat for its 'damned wantlessness' (*verdammte Bedürfnislosigkeit*).

So far, however, their attack on society has lacked simplicity. The poor do not share their tastes nor understand their art-criticisms. They do not want the simple life, nor the esthetic life; on the contrary, they want very much to wallow in all the costly vulgarities from which the elect souls among the rich turn away with loathing. It is by surfeit and not by abstinence that they will be cured of their hankering after unwholesome sweets. What they do dislike and despise and are ashamed of is poverty. To ask them to fight for the difference between the Christmas number of the Illustrated London News and the Kelmscott Chaucer is silly: they prefer the News. The difference between a stock-broker's cheap and dirty starched white shirt and collar and the comparatively costly and carefully dyed blue shirt of William Morris is a difference so disgraceful to Morris in their eyes that if they fought on the subject at all, they would fight in defence of the starch. 'Cease to be slaves, in order that you may become cranks' is not a very inspiring call to arms; nor is it really improved by substituting saints for cranks. Both terms denote men of genius; and the common man does not want to live the life of a man of genius: he would much rather live the life of a pet collie if that were the only alternative. But he does want more money. Whatever else he may be vague about, he is clear about that. He may or may not prefer Major Barbara to the Drury Lane pantomime; but he always prefers five hundred pounds to five hundred shillings.

Now to deplore this preference as sordid, and teach children that it is sinful to desire money, is to strain towards the extreme possible limit of impudence in lying and corruption in hypocrisy. The universal regard for money is the one hopeful fact in our civilization, the one sound spot in our social conscience. Money is the most important thing in the world. It represents health, strength, honor, generosity and beauty as conspicuously and undeniably as the want of it represents illness, weakness, disgrace, meanness and ugliness. Not the least of its virtues is that it destroys base people as certainly as it fortifies and dignifies noble people. It is only when it is cheapened to worthlessness for some and made impossibly dear to others, that it becomes a curse. In short, it is a curse only in such foolish social conditions that life itself is a curse. For the two things are inseparable: money is the counter that enables life to be distributed socially: it *is* life as truly as sovereigns and bank notes are money. The first duty of every citizen is to insist on having money on reasonable terms; and this demand is not complied with by giving four men three shillings each for ten or twelve hours' drudgery and one man a thousand pounds for nothing. The crying need of the nation is not for better morals, cheaper bread, temperance, liberty, culture, redemption of fallen sisters and erring brothers, nor the grace, love and fellowship of the Trinity, but simply for enough money. And the evil to be attacked is not sin, suffering, greed, priestcraft, kingcraft, demagogy, monopoly, ignorance, drink, war, pestilence, nor any other of the scapegoats which reformers sacrifice, but simply poverty.

Once take your eyes from the ends of the earth and fix them on this truth just under your nose; and Andrew Undershaft's views will not perplex you in the least. Unless indeed his constant sense that he is only the instrument of a Will or Life Force which uses him for purposes wider than his own, may puzzle you. If so, that is because you are walking either in artificial Darwinian darkness, or in mere stupidity. All genuinely religious people have that consciousness. To them Undershaft the Mystic will be quite intelligible, and his perfect comprehension of his daughter the Salvationist and her lover the Euripidean republican natural and inevitable. That, however, is not new, even on the stage. What is new, as far as I know, is that article in Undershaft's religion which recognizes in Money the first need and in poverty the vilest sin of man and society.

This dramatic conception has not, of course, been attained *per saltum*. Nor has it been borrowed from Nietzsche or from any man born beyond the Channel. The late Samuel Butler, in his own depart-

ment the greatest English writer of the latter half of the XIX century, steadily inculcated the necessity and morality of a conscientious Laodiceanism in religion and of an earnest and constant sense of the importance of money. It drives one almost to despair of English literature when one sees so extraordinary a study of English life as Butler's posthumous Way of All Flesh making so little impression that when, some years later, I produce plays in which Butler's extraordinarily fresh, free and future-piercing suggestions have an obvious share, I am met with nothing but vague cacklings about Ibsen and Nietzsche, and am only too thankful that they are not about Alfred de Musset and Georges Sand. Really, the English do not deserve to have great men. They allowed Butler to die practically unknown, whilst I, a comparatively insignificant Irish journalist, was leading them by the nose into an advertisement of me which has made my own life a burden. In Sicily there is a Via Samuele Butler. When an English tourist sees it, he either asks 'Who the devil was Samuele Butler?' or wonders why the Sicilians should perpetuate the memory of the author of Hudibras.

Well, it cannot be denied that the English are only too anxious to recognize a man of genius if somebody will kindly point him out to them. Having pointed myself out in this manner with some success, I now point out Samuel Butler, and trust that in consequence I shall hear a little less in future of the novelty and foreign origin of the ideas which are now making their way into the English theatre through plays written by Socialists. There are living men whose originality and power are as obvious as Butler's and when they die that fact will be discovered. Meanwhile I recommend them to insist on their own merits as an important part of their own business.

The Salvation Army

When Major Barbara was produced in London, the second act was reported in an important northern newspaper as a withering attack on the Salvation Army, and the despairing ejaculation of Barbara deplored by a London daily as a tasteless blasphemy. And they were set right, not by the professed critics of the theatre, but by religious and philosophical publicists like Sir Oliver Lodge and Dr Stanton Coit, and strenuous Nonconformist journalists like William Stead, who not only understood the act as well as the Salvationists themselves, but also saw it in its relation to the religious life of the nation, a life which seems to lie not only outside the sympathy of many of our theatre critics, but actually outside their knowledge of society. Indeed nothing could be more ironically curious than the confrontation Major Barbara effected of the theatre enthusiasts with the religious enthusiasts. On the one hand was the playgoer, always seeking pleasure, paying exorbitantly for it, suffering unbearable discomforts for it, and hardly ever getting it. On the other hand was the Salvationist, repudiating gaiety and courting effort and sacrifice, yet always in the wildest spirits, laughing, joking, singing, rejoicing, drumming, and tambourining: his life flying by in a flash of excitement, and his death arriving as a climax of triumph. And, if you please, the playgoer despising the Salvationist as a joyless person, shut out from the heaven of the theatre, self-condemned to a life of hideous gloom; and the Salvationist mourning over the playgoer as over a prodigal with vine leaves in his hair, careering outrageously to hell amid the popping of champagne corks and the ribald laughter of sirens! Could misunderstanding be more complete, or sympathy worse misplaced?

Fortunately, the Salvationists are more accessible to the religious character of the drama than the playgoers to the gay energy and artistic fertility of religion. They can see, when it is pointed out to them, that a theatre, as a place where two or three are gathered together, takes from that divine presence an inalienable sanctity of which the grossest and profanest farce can no more deprive it than a hypocritical sermon by a snobbish bishop can desecrate Westminster Abbey. But in our professional playgoers this indispensable preliminary conception of sanctity seems wanting. They talk of actors as mimes and mummers, and, I fear, think of dramatic authors as liars and pandars, whose main business is the voluptuous soothing of the tired city speculator when what he calls the serious business of the day is over. Passion, the life of drama, means nothing to them but primitive sexual excitement: such phrases as 'impassioned poetry' or 'passionate love of truth' have fallen quite out of their vocabulary and been replaced by 'passional crime' and the like. They assume, as far as I can gather, that people in whom passion has a larger scope are passionless and therefore uninteresting. Consequently they come to think of religious people

as people who are not interesting and not amusing. And so, when Barbara cuts the regular Salvation Army jokes, and snatches a kiss from her lover across his drum, the devotees of the theatre think they ought to appear shocked, and conclude that the whole play is an elaborate mockery of the Army. And then either hypocritically rebuke me for mocking, or foolishly take part in the supposed mockery!

Even the handful of mentally competent critics got into difficulties over my demonstration of the economic deadlock in which the Salvation Army finds itself. Some of them thought that the Army would not have taken money from a distiller and a cannon founder: others thought it should not have taken it: all assumed more or less definitely that it reduced itself to absurdity or hypocrisy by taking it. On the first point the reply of the Army itself was prompt and conclusive. As one of its officers said, they would take money from the devil himself and be only too glad to get it out of his hands and into God's. They gratefully acknowledged that publicans not only give them money but allow them to collect it in the bar—sometimes even when there is a Salvation meeting outside preaching teetotalism. In fact, they questioned the verisimilitude of the play, not because Mrs Baines took the money, but because Barbara refused it.

On the point that the Army ought not to take such money, its justification is obvious. It must take the money because it cannot exist without money, and there is no other money to be had. Practically all the spare money in the country consists of a mass of rent, interest, and profit, every penny of which is bound up with crime, drink, prostitution, disease, and all the evil fruits of poverty, as inextricably as with enterprise, wealth, commercial probity, and national prosperity. The notion that you can earmark certain coins as tainted is an unpractical individualist superstition. None the less the fact that all our money is tainted gives a very severe shock to earnest young souls when some dramatic instance of the taint first makes them conscious of it. When an enthusiastic young clergyman of the Established Church first realizes that the Ecclesiastical Commissioners receive the rents of sporting public houses, brothels, and sweating dens; or that the most generous contributor at his last charity sermon was an employer trading in female labor cheapened by prostitution as unscrupulously as a hotel keeper trades in waiters' labor cheapened by tips, or commissionaires' labor cheapened by pensions; or that the only patron who can afford to rebuild his church or his schools or give his boys' brigade a gymnasium or a library is the son-in-law of a Chicago meat King, that young clergyman has, like Barbara, a very bad quarter hour. But he cannot help himself by refusing to accept money from anybody except sweet old ladies with independent incomes and gentle and lovely ways of life. He has only to follow up the income of the sweet ladies to its industrial source, and there he will find Mrs Warren's profession and the poisonous canned meat and all the rest of it. His own stipend has the same root. He must either share the world's guilt or go to another planet. He must save the world's honor if he is to save his own. This is what all the Churches find just as the Salvation Army and Barbara find it in the play. Her discovery that she is her father's accomplice; that the Salvation Army is the accomplice of the distiller and the dynamite maker; that they can no more escape one another than they can escape the air they breathe; that there is no salvation for them through personal righteousness, but only through the redemption of the whole nation from its vicious, lazy, competitive anarchy: this discovery has been made by everyone except the Pharisees and (apparently) the professional playgoers, who still wear their Tom Hood shirts and underpay their washerwomen without the slightest misgiving as to the elevation of their private characters, the purity of their private atmospheres, and their right to repudiate as foreign to themselves the coarse depravity of the garret and the slum. Not that they mean any harm: they only desire to be, in their little private way, what they call gentlemen. They do not understand Barbara's lesson because they have not, like her, learnt it by taking their part in the larger life of the nation.

Barbara's Return to the Colors

Barbara's return to the colors may yet provide a subject for the dramatic historian of the future. To get back to the Salvation Army with the knowledge that even the Salvationists themselves are not saved yet; that poverty is not blessed, but a most damnable sin; and that when General Booth chose Blood and Fire for the emblem of Salvation instead of the Cross, he was perhaps better inspired than he knew: such knowledge, for the daughter of Andrew Undershaft, will clearly lead to something hopefuller than distributing bread and treacle at the expense of Bodger.

It is a very significant thing, this instinctive choice of the military form of organization, this substitution of the drum for the organ, by the Salvation Army. Does it not suggest that the Salvationists divine that they must actually fight the devil instead of merely praying at him? At present, it is true, they have not quite ascertained his correct address. When they do, they may give a very rude shock to that sense of security which he has gained from his experience of the fact that hard words, even when uttered by eloquent essayists and lecturers, or carried unanimously at enthusiastic public meetings on the motion of eminent reformers, break no bones. It has been said that the French Revolution was the work of Voltaire, Rousseau and the Encyclopedists. It seems to me to have been the work of men who had observed that virtuous indignation, caustic criticism, conclusive argument and instructive pamphleteering, even when done by the most earnest and witty literary geniuses, were as useless as praying, things going steadily from bad to worse whilst the Social Contract and the pamphlets of Voltaire were at the height of their vogue. Eventually, as we know, perfectly respectable citizens and earnest philanthropists connived at the September massacres because hard experience had convinced them that if they contented themselves with appeals to humanity and patriotism, the aristocracy, though it would read their appeals with the greatest enjoyment and appreciation, flattering and admiring the writers, would none the less continue to conspire with foreign monarchists to undo the revolution and restore the old system with every circumstance of savage vengeance and ruthless repression of popular liberties.

The nineteenth century saw the same lesson repeated in England. It had its Utilitarians, its Christian Socialists, its Fabians (still extant): it had Bentham, Mill, Dickens, Ruskin, Carlyle, Butler, Henry George, and Morris. And the end of all their efforts is the Chicago described by Mr Upton Sinclair and the London in which the people who pay to be amused by my dramatic representation of Peter Shirley turned out to starve at forty because there are younger slaves to be had for his wages, do not take, and have not the slightest intention of taking, any effective step to organize society in such a way as to make that everyday infamy impossible. I, who have preached and pamphleteered like any Encyclopedist, have to confess that my methods are no use, and would be no use if I were Voltaire, Rousseau, Bentham, Marx, Mill, Dickens, Carlyle, Ruskin, Butler, and Morris all rolled into one, with Euripides, More, Montaigne, Molière, Beaumarchais, Swift, Goethe, Ibsen, Tolstoy, Jesus and the prophets all thrown in (as indeed in some sort I actually am, standing as I do on all their shoulders). The problem being to make heroes out of cowards, we paper apostles and artist-magicians have succeeded only in giving cowards all the sensations of heroes whilst they tolerate every abomination, accept every plunder, and submit to every oppression. Christianity, in making a merit of such submission, has marked only that depth in the abyss at which the very sense of shame is lost. The Christian has been like Dickens' doctor in the debtor's prison, who tells the newcomer of its ineffable peace and security: no duns; no tyrannical collectors of rates, taxes, and rent; no importunate hopes nor exacting duties; nothing but the rest and safety of having no farther to fall.

Yet in the poorest corner of this soul-destroying Christendom vitality suddenly begins to germinate again. Joyousness, a sacred gift long dethroned by the hellish laughter of derision and obscenity, rises like a flood miraculously out of the fetid dust and mud of the slums; rousing marches and impetuous dithyrambs rise to the heavens from people among whom the depressing noise called 'sacred music' is a standing joke; a flag with Blood and Fire on it is unfurled, not in murderous rancor, but because fire is beautiful and blood a vital and splendid red; Fear, which we flatter by calling Self, vanishes; and transfigured men and women carry their gospel through a transfigured world, calling their leader General, themselves captains and brigadiers, and their whole body an Army: praying, but praying only for refreshment, for strength to fight, and for needful MONEY (a notable sign, that); preaching, but not preaching submission; daring ill-usage and abuse, but not putting up with more of it than is inevitable; and practising what the world will let them practise, including soap and water, color and music. There is danger in such activity; and where there is danger there is hope. Our present security is nothing, and can be nothing, but evil made irresistible.

Weaknesses of the Salvation Army

For the present, however, it is not my business to flatter the Salvation Army. Rather must I point out to it that it has almost as many weaknesses as the Church of England itself. It is building up a business organization which will compel it eventually to see that its present staff of enthusiast-commanders shall be succeeded by a bureaucracy of men of business who will be no better than bishops, and perhaps a good deal more unscrupulous. That has always happened sooner or later to great orders founded by saints; and the order founded by St William Booth is not exempt from the same danger. It is even more dependent than the Church on rich people who would cut off supplies at once if it began to preach that indispensable revolt against poverty which must also be a revolt against riches. It is hampered by a heavy contingent of pious elders who are not really Salvationists at all, but Evangelicals of the old school. It still, as Commissioner Howard affirms, 'sticks to Moses,' which is flat nonsense at this time of day if the Commissioner means, as I am afraid he does, that the Book of Genesis contains a trustworthy scientific account of the origin of species, and that the god to whom Jephthah sacrificed his daughter is any less obviously a tribal idol than Dagon or Chemosh.

Further, there is still too much other-worldliness about the Army. Like Frederick's grenadier, the Salvationist wants to live for ever (the most monstrous way of crying for the moon); and though it is evident to anyone who has ever heard General Booth and his best officers that they would work as hard for human salvation as they do at present if they believed that death would be the end of them individually, they and their followers have a bad habit of talking as if the Salvationists were heroically enduring a very bad time on earth as an investment which will bring them in dividends later on in the form, not of a better life to come for the whole world, but of an eternity spent by themselves personally in a sort of bliss which would bore any active person to a second death. Surely the truth is that the Salvationists are unusually happy people. And is it not the very diagnostic of true salvation that it shall overcome the fear of death? Now the man who has come to believe that there is no such thing as death, the change so called being merely the transition to an exquisitely happy and utterly careless life, has not overcome the fear of death at all: on the contrary, it has overcome him so completely that he refuses to die on any terms whatever. I do not call a Salvationist really saved until he is ready to lie down cheerfully on the scrap heap, having paid scot and lot and something over, and let his eternal life pass on to renew its youth in the battalions of the future.

Then there is the nasty lying habit called confession, which the Army encourages because it lends itself to dramatic oratory, with plenty of thrilling incident. For my part, when I hear a convert relating the violences and oaths and blasphemies he was guilty of before he was saved, making out that he was a very terrible fellow then and is the most contrite and chastened of Christians now, I believe him no more than I believe the millionaire who says he came up to London or Chicago as a boy with only three halfpence in his pocket. Salvationists have said to me that Barbara in my play would never have been taken in by so transparent a humbug as Snobby Price; and certainly I do not think Snobby could have taken in any experienced Salvationist on a point on which the Salvationist did not wish to be taken in. But on the point of conversion all Salvationists wish to be taken in; for the more obvious the sinner the more obvious the miracle of his conversion. When you advertize a converted burglar or reclaimed drunkard as one of the attractions at an experience meeting, your burglar can hardly have been too burglarious or your drunkard too drunken. As long as such attractions are relied on, you will have your Snobbies claiming to have beaten their mothers when they were as a matter of prosaic fact habitually beaten by them, and your Rummies of the tamest respectability pretending to a past of reckless and dazzling vice. Even when confessions are sincerely autobiographic we should beware of assuming that the impulse to make them was pious or that the interest of the hearers is wholesome. As well might we assume that the poor people who insist on shewing disgusting ulcers to district visitors are convinced hygienists, or that the curiosity which sometimes welcomes such exhibitions is a pleasant and creditable one. One is often tempted to suggest that those who pester our police superintendents with confessions of murder might very wisely be taken at their word and executed, except in the few cases in which a real murderer is seeking to be relieved of his guilt by confession and expiation. For though I am not, I hope, an unmerciful person, I do not think that the inexorability of the deed once done should be disguised by any ritual, whether in the confessional or on the scaffold.

And here my disagreement with the Salvation Army, and with all propagandists of the Cross (which I loathe as I loathe all gibbets) becomes deep indeed. Forgiveness, absolution, atonement, are figments: punishment is only a pretence of cancelling one crime by another; and you can no more have forgiveness without vindictiveness than you can have a cure without a disease. You will never get a high morality from people who conceive that their misdeeds are revocable and pardonable, or in a society where absolution and expiation are officially provided for us all. The demand may be very real; but the supply is spurious. Thus Bill Walker, in my play, having assaulted the Salvation Lass, presently finds himself overwhelmed with an intolerable conviction of sin under the skilled treatment of Barbara. Straightway he begins to try to unassault the lass and deruffianize his deed, first by getting punished for it in kind, and, when that relief is denied him, by fining himself a pound to compensate the girl. He is foiled both ways. He finds the Salvation Army as inexorable as fact itself. It will not punish him: it will not take his money. It will not tolerate a redeemed ruffian: it leaves him no means of salvation except ceasing to be a ruffian. In doing this, the Salvation Army instinctively grasps the central truth of Christianity and discards its central superstition: that central truth being the vanity of revenge and punishment, and that central superstition the salvation of the world by the gibbet.

For, be it noted, Bill has assaulted an old and starving woman also; and for this worse offence he feels no remorse whatever, because she makes it clear that her malice is as great as his own. 'Let her have the law of me, as she said she would,' says Bill: 'what I done to her is no more on what you might call my conscience than sticking a pig.' This shews a perfectly natural and wholesome state of mind on his part. The old woman, like the law she threatens him with, is perfectly ready to play the game of retaliation with him: to rob him if he steals, to flog him if he strikes, to murder him if he kills. By example and precept the law and public opinion teach him to impose his will on others by anger, violence, and cruelty, and to wipe off the moral score by punishment. That is sound Crosstianity. But this Crosstianity has got entangled with something which Barbara calls Christianity, and which unexpectedly causes her to refuse to play the hangman's game of Satan casting out Satan. She refuses to prosecute a drunken ruffian; she converses on equal terms with a blackguard to whom no lady should be seen speaking in the public street: in short, she imitates Christ. Bill's conscience reacts to this just as naturally as it does to the old woman's threats. He is placed in a position of unbearable moral inferiority, and strives by every means in his power to escape from it, whilst he is still quite ready to meet the abuse of the old woman by attempting to smash a mug on her face. And that is the triumphant justification of Barbara's Christianity as against our system of judicial punishment and the vindictive villain-thrashings and 'poetic justice' of the romantic stage.

For the credit of literature it must be pointed out that the situation is only partly novel. Victor Hugo long ago gave us the epic of the convict and the bishop's candlesticks, of the Crosstian policeman annihilated by his encounter with the Christian Valjean. But Bill Walker is not, like Valjean, romantically changed from a demon into an angel. There are millions of Bill Walkers in all classes of society today; and the point which I, as a professor of natural psychology, desire to demonstrate, is that Bill, without any change in his character or circumstances whatsoever, will react one way to one sort of treatment and another way to another.

In proof I might point to the sensational object lesson provided by our commercial millionaires today. They begin as brigands: merciless, unscrupulous, dealing out ruin and death and slavery to their competitors and employees, and facing desperately the worst that their competitors can do to them. The history of the English factories, the American Trusts, the exploitation of African gold, diamonds, ivory and rubber, outdoes in villainy the worst that has ever been imagined of the buccaneers of the Spanish Main. Captain Kidd would have marooned a modern Trust magnate for conduct unworthy of a gentleman of fortune. The law every day seizes on unsuccessful scoundrels of this type and punishes them with a cruelty worse than their own, with the result that they come out of the torture house more dangerous than they went in, and renew their evil doing (nobody will employ them at anything else) until they are again seized, again tormented, and again let loose, with the same result.

But the successful scoundrel is dealt with very differently, and very Christianly. He is not only forgiven: he is idolized, respected, made much of, all but worshipped. Society returns him good for evil in the most extravagant overmeasure. And with what result? He begins to idolize himself, to respect himself, to live up to the treatment he receives. He preaches sermons; he writes books of the most edifying advice to young men, and actually persuades himself that he got on by taking his own advice; he endows educational institutions; he supports charities; he dies finally in the odor of sanctity, leaving a will which is a monument of public spirit and bounty. And all this without any change in his character. The spots of the leopard and the stripes of the tiger are as brilliant as ever; but the conduct of the world towards him has changed; and his conduct has changed accordingly. You have only to reverse your attitude towards him—to lay hands on his property, revile him, assault him, and he will be a brigand again in a moment, as ready to crush you as you are to crush him, and quite as full of pretentious moral reasons for doing it.

In short, when Major Barbara says that there are no scoundrels, she is right: there are no absolute scoundrels, though there are impracticable people of whom I shall treat presently. Every reasonable man (and woman) is a potential scoundrel and a potential good citizen. What a man is depends on his character; but what he does, and what we think of what he does, depends on his circumstances. The characteristics that ruin a man in one class make him eminent in another. The characters that behave differently in different circumstances behave alike in similar circumstances. Take a common English character like that of Bill Walker. We meet Bill everywhere: on the judicial bench, on the episcopal bench, in the Privy Council, at the War Office and Admiralty, as well as in the Old Bailey dock or in the ranks of casual unskilled labor. And the morality of Bill's characteristics varies with these various circumstances. The faults of the burglar are the qualities of the financier: the manners and habits of a duke would cost a city clerk his situation. In short, though character is independent of circumstances, conduct is not; and our moral judgments of character are not: both are circumstantial. Take any condition of life in which the circumstances are for a mass of men practically alike: felony, the House of Lords, the factory, the stables, the gipsy encampment or where you please! In spite of diversity of character and temperament, the conduct and morals of the individuals in each group are as predicable and as alike in the main as if they were a flock of sheep, morals being mostly only social habits and circumstantial necessities. Strong people know this and count upon it. In nothing have the master-minds of the world been distinguished from the ordinary suburban season-ticket holder more than in their straightforward perception of the fact that mankind is practically a single species, and not a menagerie of gentlemen and bounders, villains and heroes, cowards and daredevils, peers and peasants, grocers and aristocrats, artisans and laborers, washerwomen and duchesses, in which all the grades of income and caste represent distinct animals who must not be introduced to one another or intermarry. Napoleon constructing a galaxy of generals and courtiers, and even of monarchs, out of his collection of social nobodies; Julius Caesar appointing as governor of Egypt the son of a freedman—one who but a short time before would have been legally disqualified for the post even of a private soldier in the Roman army; Louis XI making his barber his privy councillor: all these had in their different ways a firm hold of the scientific fact of human equality, expressed by Barbara in the Christian formula that all men are children of one father. A man who believes that men are naturally divided into upper and lower and middle classes morally is making exactly the same mistake as the man who believes that they are naturally divided in the same way socially. And just as our persistent attempts to found political institutions on a basis of social inequality have always produced long periods of destructive friction relieved from time to time by violent explosions of revolution; so the attempt— will Americans please note—to found moral institutions on a basis of moral inequality can lead to nothing but unnatural Reigns of the Saints relieved by licentious Restorations; to Americans who have made divorce a public institution turning the face of Europe into one huge sardonic smile by refusing to stay in the same hotel with a Russian man of genius who has changed wives without the sanction of South Dakota; to grotesque hypocrisy, cruel persecution, and final utter confusion of conventions and compliances with benevolence and respectability. It is quite useless to declare that all men are born free if you deny that they are born good. Guarantee a man's goodness and his liberty will take care of itself. To guarantee his freedom on condition that you approve of his moral character is formally to abolish all freedom whatsoever, as every man's liberty is at the mercy of a moral indictment which any fool can trump up against everyone who violates custom, whether as a prophet or as a rascal. This is the lesson Democracy has to learn before it can become anything but the most oppressive of all the priesthoods.

Let us now return to Bill Walker and his case of conscience against the Salvation Army. Major Barbara, not being a modern Tetzel, or the treasurer of a hospital, refuses to sell absolution to Bill for a sovereign. Unfortunately, what the Army can afford to refuse in the case of Bill Walker, it cannot refuse in the case of Bodger. Bodger is master of the situation because he holds the purse strings. 'Strive as you will,' says Bodger, in effect: 'me you cannot do without. You cannot save Bill Walker without my money.' And the Army answers, quite rightly under the circumstances, 'We will take money from the devil himself sooner than abandon the work of Salvation.' So Bodger pays his conscience-money and gets the absolution that is refused to Bill. In real life Bill would perhaps never know this. But I, the dramatist whose business it is to shew the connexion between things that seem apart and unrelated in the haphazard order of events in real life, have contrived to make it known to Bill, with the result that the Salvation Army loses its hold of him at once.

But Bill may not be lost, for all that. He is still in the grip of the facts and of his own conscience, and may find his taste for blackguardism permanently spoiled. Still, I cannot guarantee that happy ending. Walk through the poorer quarters of our cities on Sunday when the men are not working, but resting and chewing the cud of their reflections. You will find one expression common to every mature face: the expression of cynicism. The discovery made by Bill Walker about the Salvation Army has been made by everyone there. They have found that every man has his price; and they have been foolishly or corruptly taught to mistrust and despise him for that necessary and salutary condition of social existence. When they learn that General Booth, too, has his price, they do not admire him because it is a high one, and admit the need of organizing society so that he shall get it in an honorable way: they conclude that his character is unsound and that all religious men are hypocrites and allies of their sweaters and oppressors. They know that the large subscriptions which help to support the Army are endowments, not of religion, but of the wicked doctrine of docility in poverty and humility under oppression; and they are rent by the most agonizing of all the doubts of the soul, the doubt whether their true salvation must not come from their most abhorrent passions, from murder, envy, greed, stubbornness, rage, and terrorism, rather than from public spirit, reasonableness, humanity, generosity, tenderness, delicacy, pity and kindness. The confirmation of that doubt, at which our newspapers have been working so hard for years past, is the morality of militarism; and the justification of militarism is that circumstances may at any time make it the true morality of the moment. It is by producing such moments that we produce violent and sanguinary revolutions, such as the one now in progress in Russia and the one which Capitalism in England and America is daily and diligently provoking.

At such moments it becomes the duty of the Churches to evoke all the powers of destruction against the existing order. But if they do this, the existing order must forcibly suppress them. Churches are suffered to exist only on condition that they preach submission to the State as at present capitalistically organized. The Church of England itself is compelled to add to the thirtysix articles in which it formulates its religious tenets, three more in which it apologetically protests that the moment any of these articles comes in conflict with the State it is to be entirely renounced, abjured, violated, abrogated and abhorred, the policeman being a much more important person than any of the Persons of the Trinity. And this is why no tolerated Church nor Salvation Army can ever win the entire confidence of the poor. It must be on the side of the police and the military, no matter what it believes or disbelieves; and as the police and the military are the instruments by which the rich rob and oppress the poor (on legal and moral principles made for the purpose), it is not possible to be on the side of the poor and of the police at the same time. Indeed the religious bodies, as the almoners of the rich, become a sort of auxiliary police, taking off the insurrectionary edge of poverty with coals and blankets, bread and treacle, and soothing and cheering the victims with hopes of immense and inexpensive happiness in another world when the process of working them to premature death in the service of the rich is complete in this.

Christianity and Anarchism

Such is the false position from which neither the Salvation Army nor the Church of England nor any other religious organization whatever can escape except through a reconstitution of society. Nor can they merely endure the State passively, washing their hands of its sins. The State is constantly forcing the consciences of men by violence and cruelty. Not content with exacting money from us for the maintenance of its soldiers and policemen, its gaolers and executioners, it forces us to take an active personal part in its proceedings on pain of becoming ourselves the victims of its violence. As I write these lines, a sensational example is given to the world. A royal marriage has been celebrated, first by sacrament in a cathedral, and then by a bullfight having for its main amusement the spectacle of horses gored and disembowelled by the bull, after which, when the bull is so exhausted as to be no longer dangerous, he is killed by a cautious matador. But the ironic contrast between the bullfight and the sacrament of marriage does not move anyone. Another contrast—that between the splendor, the happiness, the atmosphere of kindly admiration surrounding the young couple, and the price paid for it under our abominable social arrangements in the misery, squalor and degradation of millions of other young couples—is drawn at the same moment by a novelist, Mr Upton Sinclair, who chips a corner of the veneering from the huge meat packing industries of Chicago, and shews it to us as a sample of what is going on all over the world underneath the top layer of prosperous plutocracy. One man is sufficiently moved by that contrast to pay his own life as the price of one terrible blow at the responsible parties. His poverty has left him ignorant enough to be duped by the pretence that the innocent young bride and bridegroom, put forth and crowned by plutocracy as the heads of a State in which they have less personal power than any policeman, and less influence than any Chairman of a Trust, are responsible. At them accordingly he launches his sixpennorth of fulminate, missing his mark, but scattering the bowels of as many horses as any bull in the arena, and slaying twentythree persons, besides wounding ninetynine. And of all these, the horses alone are innocent of the guilt he is avenging: had he blown all Madrid to atoms with every adult person in it, not one could have escaped the charge of being an accessory, before, at, and after the fact, to poverty and prostitution, to such wholesale massacre of infants as Herod never dreamt of, to plague, pestilence and famine, battle, murder and lingering death—perhaps not one who had not helped, through example, precept, connivance, and even clamor, to teach the dynamiter his well-learnt gospel of hatred and vengeance, by approving every day of sentences of years of imprisonment so infernal in their unnatural stupidity and panic-stricken cruelty, that their advocates can disavow neither the dagger nor the bomb without stripping the mask of justice and humanity from themselves also.

Be it noted that at this very moment there appears the biography of one of our dukes, who, being a Scot, could argue about politics, and therefore stood out as a great brain among our aristocrats. And what, if you please, was his grace's favorite historical episode, which he declared he never read without intense satisfaction? Why, the young General Bonapart's pounding of the Paris mob to pieces in 1795, called in playful approval by our respectable classes 'the whiff of grapeshot,' though Napoleon, to do him justice, took a deeper view of it, and would fain have had it forgotten. And since the Duke of Argyll was not a demon, but a man of like passions with ourselves, by no means rancorous or cruel as men go, who can doubt that all over the world proletarians of the ducal kidney are now revelling in 'the whiff of dynamite' (the flavor of the joke seems to evaporate a little, does it not?) because it was aimed at the class they hate even as our argute duke hated what he called the mob.

In such an atmosphere there can be only one sequel to the Madrid explosion. All Europe burns to emulate it. Vengeance! More blood! Tear 'the Anarchist beast' to shreds. Drag him to the scaffold. Imprison him for life. Let all civilized States band together to drive his like off the face of the earth; and if any State refuses to join, make war on it. This time the leading London newspaper, anti-Liberal and therefore anti-Russian in politics, does not say 'Serve you right' to the victims, as it did, in effect, when Bobrikoff, and De Plehve, and Grand Duke Sergius, were in the same manner unofficially fulminated into fragments. No: fulminate our rivals in Asia by all means, ye brave Russian revolutionaries; but to aim at an English princess! monstrous! hideous! hound down the wretch to his doom; and observe, please, that we are a civilized and merciful people, and, however much we may regret it, must not treat him as Ravaillac and Damiens were treated. And meanwhile, since we have not yet caught him, let us soothe our quivering nerves with the bullfight, and comment in a courtly way on the unfailing tact and good taste of the ladies of our royal houses, who, though presumably of full normal natural tenderness, have been so effectually broken in to fashionable routine that they can be taken to see the horses slaughtered as helplessly as they could no doubt be taken to a gladiator show, if that happened to be the mode just now.

Strangely enough, in the midst of this raging fire of malice, the one man who still has faith in the kindness and intelligence of human nature is the fulminator, now a hunted wretch, with nothing, apparently, to secure his triumph over all the prisons and scaffolds of infuriate Europe except the revolver in his pocket and his readiness to discharge it at a moment's notice into his own or any other head. Think of him setting out to find a gentleman and a Christian in the multitude of human wolves howling for his blood. Think also of this: that at the very first essay he finds what he seeks, a veritable grandee of Spain, a noble, high-thinking, unterrified, malice-void soul, in the guise—of all masquerades in the world!—of a modern editor. The Anarchist wolf, flying from the wolves of plutocracy, throws himself on the honor of the man. The man, not being a wolf (nor a London editor), and therefore not having enough sympathy with his exploit to be made bloodthirsty by it, does not throw him back to the pursuing wolves—gives him, instead, what help he can to escape, and sends him off acquainted at last with a force that goes deeper than dynamite, though you cannot buy so much of it for sixpence. That righteous and honorable high human deed is not wasted on Europe, let us hope, though it benefits the fugitive wolf only for a moment. The plutocratic wolves presently smell him out. The fugitive shoots the unlucky wolf whose nose is nearest; shoots himself; and then convinces the world, by his photograph, that he was no monstrous freak of reversion to the tiger, but a good looking young man with nothing abnormal about him except his appalling courage and resolution (that is why the terrified shriek Coward at him): one to whom murdering a happy young couple on their wedding morning would have been an unthinkably unnatural abomination under rational and kindly human circumstances.

Then comes the climax of irony and blind stupidity. The wolves, balked of their meal of fellow-wolf, turn on the man, and proceed to torture him, after their manner, by imprisonment, for refusing to fasten his teeth in the throat of the dynamiter and hold him down until they came to finish him.

Thus, you see, a man may not be a gentleman nowadays even if he wishes to. As to being a Christian, he is allowed some latitude in that matter, because, I repeat, Christianity has two faces. Popular Christianity has for its emblem a gibbet, for its chief sensation a sanguinary execution after torture, for its central mystery an insane vengeance bought off by a trumpery expiation. But there is a nobler and profounder Christianity which affirms the sacred mystery of Equality, and forbids the glaring futility and folly of vengeance, often politely called punishment or justice. The gibbet part of Christianity is tolerated. The other is criminal felony. Connoisseurs in irony are well aware of the fact that the only editor in England who denounces punishment as radically wrong, also repudiates Christianity; calls his paper The Freethinker; and has been imprisoned for 'bad taste' under the law against blasphemy.

Sane Conclusions

And now I must ask the excited reader not to lose his head on one side or the other, but to draw a sane moral from these grim absurdities. It is not good sense to propose that laws against crime should apply to principals only and not to accessories whose consent, counsel, or silence may secure impunity to the principal. If you institute punishment as part of the law, you must punish people for refusing to punish. If you have a police, part of its duty must be to compel everybody to assist the police. No doubt if your laws are unjust, and your policemen agents of oppression, the result will be an unbearable violation of the private consciences of citizens. But that cannot be helped: the remedy is, not to license everybody to thwart the law if they please, but to make laws that will command the public assent, and not to deal cruelly and stupidly with law-breakers. Everybody disapproves of burglars; but the modern burglar, when caught and overpowered by a householder, usually appeals, and often, let us hope, with success,

to his captor not to deliver him over to the useless horrors of penal servitude. In other cases the law-breaker escapes because those who could give him up do not consider his breach of the law a guilty action. Sometimes, even, private tribunals are formed in opposition to the official tribunals; and these private tribunals employ assassins as executioners, as was done, for example, by Mahomet before he had established his power officially, and by the Ribbon lodges of Ireland in their long struggle with the landlords. Under such circumstances, the assassin goes free although everybody in the district knows who he is and what he has done. They do not betray him, partly because they justify him exactly as the regular Government justifies its official executioner, and partly because they would themselves be assassinated if they betrayed him: another method learnt from the official government. Given a tribunal, employing a slayer who has no personal quarrel with the slain; and there is clearly no moral difference between official and unofficial killing.

In short, all men are anarchists with regard to laws which are against their consciences, either in the preamble or in the penalty. In London our worst anarchists are the magistrates, because many of them are so old and ignorant that when they are called upon to administer any law that is based on ideas or knowledge less than half a century old, they disagree with it, and being mere ordinary homebred private Englishmen without any respect for law in the abstract, naïvely set the example of violating it. In this instance the man lags behind the law; but when the law lags behind the man, he becomes equally an anarchist. When some huge change in social conditions, such as the industrial revolution of the eighteenth and nineteenth centuries, throws our legal and industrial institutions out of date, Anarchism becomes almost a religion. The whole force of the most energetic geniuses of the time in philosophy, economics, and art, concentrates itself on demonstrations and reminders that morality and law are only conventions, fallible and continually obsolescing. Tragedies in which the heroes are bandits, and comedies in which law-abiding and conventionally moral folk are compelled to satirize themselves by outraging the conscience of the spectators every time they do their duty, appear simultaneously with economic treatises entitled 'What is Property? Theft!' and with histories of 'The Conflict between Religion and Science.'

Now this is not a healthy state of things. The advantages of living in society are proportionate, not to the freedom of the individual from a code, but to the complexity and subtlety of the code he is prepared not only to accept but to uphold as a matter of such vital importance that a lawbreaker at large is hardly to be tolerated on any plea. Such an attitude becomes impossible when the only men who can make themselves heard and remembered throughout the world spend all their energy in raising our gorge against current law, current morality, current respectability, and legal property. The ordinary man, uneducated in social theory even when he is schooled in Latin verse, cannot be set against all the laws of his country and yet persuaded to regard law in the abstract as vitally necessary to society. Once he is brought to repudiate the laws and institutions he knows, he will repudiate the very conception of law and the very groundwork of institutions, ridiculing human rights, extolling brainless methods as 'historical,' and tolerating nothing except pure empiricism in conduct, with dynamite as the basis of politics and vivisection as the basis of science. That is hideous; but what is to be done? Here am I, for instance, by class a respectable man, by common sense a hater of waste and disorder, by intellectual constitution legally minded to the verge of pedantry, and by temperament apprehensive and economically disposed to the limit of old-maidishness; yet I am, and have always been, and shall now always be, a revolutionary writer, because our laws make law impossible; our liberties destroy all freedom; our property is organized robbery; our morality is an impudent hypocrisy; our wisdom is administered by inexperienced or malexperienced dupes, our power wielded by cowards and weaklings, and our honor false in all its points. I am an enemy of the existing order for good reasons; but that does not make my attacks any less encouraging or helpful to people who are its enemies for bad reasons. The existing order may shriek that if I tell the truth about it, some foolish person may drive it to become still worse by trying to assassinate it. I cannot help that, even if I could see what worse it could do than it is already doing. And the disadvantage of that worst even from its own point of view is that society, with all its prisons and bayonets and whips and ostracisms and starvations, is powerless in the face of the Anar-

chist who is prepared to sacrifice his own life in the battle with it. Our natural safety from the cheap and devastating explosives which every Russian student can make, and every Russian grenadier has learnt to handle in Manchuria, lies in the fact that brave and resolute men, when they are rascals, will not risk their skins for the good of humanity, and, when they are not, are sympathetic enough to care for humanity, abhorring murder, and never committing it until their consciences are outraged beyond endurance. The remedy is, then, simply not to outrage their consciences.

Do not be afraid that they will not make allowances. All men make very large allowances indeed before they stake their own lives in a war to the death with society. Nobody demands or expects the millennium. But there are two things that must be set right, or we shall perish, like Rome, of soul atrophy disguised as empire.

The first is, that the daily ceremony of dividing the wealth of the country among its inhabitants shall be so conducted that no crumb shall, save as a criminal's ration, go to any able-bodied adults who are not producing by their personal exertions not only a full equivalent for what they take, but a surplus sufficient to provide for their superannuation and pay back the debt due for their nurture.

The second is that the deliberate infliction of malicious injuries which now goes on under the name of punishment be abandoned; so that the thief, the ruffian, the gambler, and the beggar, may without inhumanity be handed over to the law, and made to understand that a State which is too humane to punish will also be too thrifty to waste the life of honest men in watching or restraining dishonest ones. That is why we do not imprison dogs. We even take our chance of their first bite. But if a dog delights to bark and bite, it goes to the lethal chamber. That seems to me sensible. To allow the dog to expiate his bite by a period of torment, and then let him loose in a much more savage condition (for the chain makes a dog savage) to bite again and expiate again, having meanwhile spent a great deal of human life and happiness in the task of chaining and feeding and tormenting him, seems to me idiotic and superstitious. Yet that is what we do to men who bark and bite and steal. It would be far more sensible to put up with their vices, as we put up with their illnesses, until they give more trouble than they are worth, at which point we should, with many apologies and expressions of sympathy, and some generosity in complying with their last wishes, place them in the lethal chamber and get rid of them. Under no circumstances should they be allowed to expiate their misdeeds by a manufactured penalty, to subscribe to a charity, or to compensate the victims. If there is to be no punishment there can be no forgiveness. We shall never have real moral responsibility until everyone knows that his deeds are irrevocable, and that his life depends on his usefulness. Hitherto, alas! humanity has never dared face these hard facts. We frantically scatter conscience money and invent systems of conscience banking, with expiatory penalties, atonements, redemptions, salvations, hospital subscription lists and what not, to enable us to contract-out of the moral code. Not content with the old scapegoat and sacrificial lamb, we deify human saviors, and pray to miraculous virgin intercessors. We attribute mercy to the inexorable; soothe our consciences after committing murder by throwing ourselves on the bosom of divine love; and shrink even from our own gallows because we are forced to admit that it, at least, is irrevocable—as if one hour of imprisonment were not as irrevocable as any execution!

If a man cannot look evil in the face without illusion, he will never know what it really is, or combat it effectually. The few men who have been able (relatively) to do this have been called cynics, and have sometimes had an abnormal share of evil in themselves, corresponding to the abnormal strength of their minds; but they have never done mischief unless they intended to do it. This is why great scoundrels have been beneficent rulers whilst amiable and privately harmless monarchs have ruined their countries by trusting to the hocus-pocus of innocence and guilt, reward and punishment, virtuous indignation and pardon, instead of standing up to the facts without either malice or mercy. Major Barbara stands up to Bill Walker in that way, with the result that the ruffian who cannot get hated, has to hate himself. To relieve this agony he tries to get punished; but the Salvationist whom he tries to provoke is as merciless as Barbara, and only prays for him. Then he tries to pay, but can get nobody to take his money. His doom is the doom of Cain, who, failing to find either a savior, a policeman, or an almoner to help him to pretend that his brother's blood no longer cried from the ground, had to live and die a murderer. Cain took

care not to commit another murder, unlike our railway shareholders (I am one) who kill and maim shunters by hundreds to save the cost of automatic couplings, and make atonement by annual subscriptions to deserving charities. Had Cain been allowed to pay off his score, he might possibly have killed Adam and Eve for the mere sake of a second luxurious reconciliation with God afterwards. Bodger, you may depend on it, will go on to the end of his life poisoning people with bad whisky, because he can always depend on the Salvation Army or the Church of England to negotiate a redemption for him in consideration of a trifling percentage of his profits.

There is a third condition too, which must be fulfilled before the great teachers of the world will cease to scoff at its religions. Creeds must become intellectually honest. At present there is not a single credible established religion in the world. That is perhaps the most stupendous fact in the whole world-situation. This play of mine, Major Barbara, is, I hope, both true and inspired; but whoever says that it all happened, and that faith in it and understanding of it consist in believing that it is a record of an actual occurrence, is, to speak according to Scripture, a fool and a liar, and is hereby solemnly denounced and cursed as such by me, the author, to all posterity.

London, June 1906

———————— **ACT ONE** ————————

It is after dinner in January 1906, in the library in Lady Britomart Undershaft's house in Wilton Crescent. A large and comfortable settee is in the middle of the room, upholstered in dark leather. A person sitting on it (it is vacant at present) would have, on his right, Lady Britomart's writing table, with the lady herself busy at it; a smaller writing table behind him on his left; the door behind him on Lady Britomart's side; and a window with a window seat directly on his left. Near the window is an armchair.

Lady Britomart is a woman of fifty or thereabouts, well dressed and yet careless of her dress, well bred and quite reckless of her breeding, well mannered and yet appallingly outspoken and indifferent to the opinion of her interlocutors, amiable and yet peremptory, arbitrary, and high-tempered to the last bearable degree, and withal a very typical managing matron of the upper class, treated as a naughty child until she grew into a scolding mother, and finally settling down with plenty of practical ability and worldly experience, limited in the oddest way with domestic and class limitations, conceiving the universe exactly as if it were a large house in Wilton Crescent, though handling her corner of it very effectively on that assumption, and being quite enlightened and liberal as to the books in the library, the pictures on the walls, the music in the portfolios, and the articles in the papers.

Her son, Stephen, comes in. He is a gravely correct young man under 25, taking himself very seriously, but still in some awe of his mother, from childish habit and bachelor shyness rather than from any weakness of character.

STEPHEN
What's the matter?

LADY BRITOMART
Presently, Stephen.

[Stephen submissively walks to the settee and sits down. He takes up a Liberal weekly called The Speaker.]

LADY BRITOMART
Dont begin to read, Stephen. I shall require all your attention.

STEPHEN
It was only while I was waiting—

LADY BRITOMART
Dont make excuses, Stephen. [He puts down The Speaker.] Now! [She finishes her writing: rises; and comes to the settee.] I have not kept you waiting very long, I think.

STEPHEN
Not at all, mother.

LADY BRITOMART
Bring me my cushion. [He takes the cushion from the chair at the desk and arranges it for her as she sits down on the settee.] Sit down. [He sits down and fingers his tie nervously.] Dont fiddle with your tie, Stephen: there is nothing the matter with it.

N.B. The Euripidean verses in the second act of Major Barbara are not by me, nor even directly by Euripides. They are by Professor Gilbert Murray, whose English version of The Bacchae came into our dramatic literature with all the impulsive power of an original work shortly before Major Barbara was begun. The play, indeed, stands indebted to him in more ways than one.   G.B.S.

STEPHEN
I beg your pardon. [He fiddles with his watch chain instead.]

LADY BRITOMART
Now are you attending to me, Stephen?

STEPHEN
Of course, mother.

LADY BRITOMART
No: it's not of course. I want something much more than your everyday matter-of-course attention. I am going to speak to you very seriously, Stephen. I wish you would let that chain alone.

STEPHEN
[hastily relinquishing the chain] Have I done anything to annoy you, mother? If so, it was quite unintentional.

LADY BRITOMART
[astonished] Nonsense! [With some remorse] My poor boy, did you think I was angry with you?

STEPHEN
What is it, then, mother? You are making me very uneasy.

LADY BRITOMART
[squaring herself at him rather aggressively] Stephen: may I ask how soon you intend to realize that you are a grown-up man, and that I am only a woman?

STEPHEN
[amazed] Only a—

LADY BRITOMART
Dont repeat my words, please; it is a most aggravating habit. You must learn to face life seriously, Stephen. I really cannot bear the whole burden of our family affairs any longer. You must advise me: you must assume the responsibility.

STEPHEN
I!

LADY BRITOMART
Yes, you, of course. You were 24 last June. Youve been at Harrow and Cambridge. Youve been to India and Japan. You must know a lot of things, now; unless you have wasted your time most scandalously. Well, advise me.

STEPHEN
[much perplexed] You know I have never interfered in the household—

LADY BRITOMART

No: I should think not. I dont want you to order the dinner.

STEPHEN

I mean in our family affairs.

LADY BRITOMART

Well, you must interfere now; for they are getting quite beyond me.

STEPHEN

[troubled] I have thought sometimes that perhaps I ought; but really, mother, I know so little about them; and what I do know is so painful! it is so impossible to mention some things to you—[He stops, ashamed.]

LADY BRITOMART

I suppose you mean your father.

STEPHEN

[almost inaudibly] Yes.

LADY BRITOMART

My dear: we cant go on all our lives not mentioning him. Of course you were quite right not to open the subject until I asked you to; but you are old enough now to be taken into my confidence, and to help me to deal with him about the girls.

STEPHEN

But the girls are all right. They are engaged.

LADY BRITOMART

[complacently] Yes: I have made a very good match for Sarah. Charles Lomax will be a millionaire at 35. But that is ten years ahead; and in the meantime his trustees cannot under the terms of his father's will allow him more than £800 a year.

STEPHEN

But the will says also that if he increases his income by his own exertions, they may double the increase.

LADY BRITOMART

Charles Lomax's exertions are much more likely to decrease his income than to increase it. Sarah will have to find at least another £800 a year for the next ten years; and even then they will be as poor as church mice. And what about Barbara? I thought Barbara was going to make the most brilliant career of all of you. And what does she do? Joins the Salvation Army; discharges her maid; lives on a pound a week; and walks in one evening with a professor of Greek whom she has picked up in the street, and who pre-

tends to be a Salvationist, and actually plays the big drum for her in public because he has fallen head over ears in love with her.

STEPHEN

I was certainly rather taken aback when I heard they were engaged. Cusins is a very nice fellow, certainly: nobody would ever guess that he was born in Australia; but—

LADY BRITOMART

Oh, Adolphus Cusins will make a very good husband. After all, nobody can say a word against Greek: it stamps a man at once as an educated gentleman. And my family, thank Heaven, is not a pig-headed Tory one. We are Whigs, and believe in liberty. Let snobbish people say what they please: Barbara shall marry, not the man they like, but the man I like.

STEPHEN

Of course I was thinking only of his income. However, he is not likely to be extravagant.

LADY BRITOMART

Dont be too sure of that, Stephen. I know your quiet, simple, refined, poetic people like Adolphus: quite content with the best of everything! They cost more than your extravagant people, who are always as mean as they are second rate. No: Barbara will need at least £2000 a year. You see it means two additional households. Besides, my dear, you must marry soon. I dont approve of the present fashion of philandering bachelors and late marriages; and I am trying to arrange something for you.

STEPHEN

It's very good of you, mother; but perhaps I had better arrange that for myself.

LADY BRITOMART

Nonsense! you are much too young to begin matchmaking: you would be taken in by some pretty little nobody. Of course I dont mean that you are not to be consulted: you know that as well as I do. [Stephen closes his lips and is silent.] Now dont sulk, Stephen.

STEPHEN

I am not sulking, mother. What has all this got to do with—with—with my father?

LADY BRITOMART

My dear Stephen: where is the money to come from? It is easy enough for you and the other children to live on my income as long as we are in the same house;

but I cant keep four families in four separate houses. You know how poor my father is: he has barely seven thousand a year now; and really, if he were not the Earl of Stevenage, he would have to give up society. He can do nothing for us. He says, naturally enough, that it is absurd that he should be asked to provide for the children of a man who is rolling in money. You see, Stephen, your father must be fabulously wealthy, because there is always a war going on somewhere.

STEPHEN

You need not remind me of that, mother. I have hardly ever opened a newspaper in my life without seeing our name in it. The Undershaft torpedo! the Undershaft quick firers! the Undershaft ten inch! the Undershaft disappearing rampart gun! the Undershaft submarine! and now the Undershaft aerial battleship! At Harrow they called me the Woolwich Infant. At Cambridge it was the same. A little brute at King's who was always trying to get up revivals, spoilt my Bible—your first birthday present to me—by writing under my name, 'Son and heir to Undershaft and Lazarus, Death and Destruction Dealers: address Christendom and Judea.' But that was not so bad as the way I was kowtowed to everywhere because my father was making millions by selling cannons.

LADY BRITOMART

It is not only the cannons, but the war loans that Lazarus arranges under cover of giving credit for the cannons. You know, Stephen, it's perfectly scandalous. Those two men, Andrew Undershaft and Lazarus, positively have Europe under their thumbs. That is why your father is able to behave as he does. He is above the law. Do you think Bismarck or Gladstone or Disraeli could have openly defied every social and moral obligation all their lives as your father has? They simply wouldnt have dared. I asked Gladstone to take it up. I asked The Times to take it up. I asked the Lord Chamberlain to take it up. But it was just like asking them to declare war on the Sultan. They wouldnt. They said they couldnt touch him. I believe they were afraid.

STEPHEN

What could they do? He does not actually break the law.

LADY BRITOMART

Not break the law! He is always breaking the law. He broke the law when he was born: his parents were not married.

STEPHEN

Mother! Is that true?

LADY BRITOMART

Of course it's true: that was why we separated.

STEPHEN

He married without letting you know this!

LADY BRITOMART

[rather taken aback by this inference] Oh no. To do Andrew justice, that was not the sort of thing he did. Besides, you know the Undershaft motto: Unashamed. Everybody knew.

STEPHEN

But you said that was why you separated.

LADY BRITOMART

Yes, because he was not content with being a foundling himself: he wanted to disinherit you for another foundling. That was what I couldnt stand.

STEPHEN

[ashamed] Do you mean for—for—for—

LADY BRITOMART

Dont stammer, Stephen. Speak distinctly.

STEPHEN

But this is so frightful to me, mother. To have to speak to you about such things!

LADY BRITOMART

It's not pleasant for me, either, especially if you are still so childish that you must make it worse by a display of embarrassment. It is only in the middle classes, Stephen, that people get into a state of dumb helpless horror when they find that there are wicked people in the world. In our class, we have to decide what is to be done with wicked people; and nothing should disturb our self-possession. Now ask your question properly.

STEPHEN

Mother: have you no consideration for me? For Heaven's sake either treat me as a child, as you always do, and tell me nothing at all; or tell me everything and let me take it as best I can.

LADY BRITOMART

Treat you as a child! What do you mean? It is most unkind and ungrateful of you to say such a thing. You know I have never treated any of you as children. I have always made you my companions and friends, and allowed you perfect freedom to do and say whatever you liked, so long as you liked what I could approve of.

STEPHEN

[desperately] I daresay we have been the very imperfect children of a very perfect mother; but I do beg you to let me alone for once, and tell me about this horrible business of my father wanting to set me aside for another son.

LADY BRITOMART

[amazed] Another son! I never said anything of the kind. I never dreamt of such a thing. This is what comes of interrupting me.

STEPHEN

But you said——

LADY BRITOMART

[cutting him short] Now be a good boy, Stephen, and listen to me patiently. The Undershafts are descended from a foundling in the parish of St. Andrew Undershaft in the city. That was long ago, in the reign of James the First. Well, this foundling was adopted by an armorer and gun-maker. In the course of time the foundling succeeded to the business; and from some notion of gratitude, or some vow or something, he adopted another foundling, and left the business to him. And that foundling did the same. Ever since that, the cannon business has always been left to an adopted foundling named Andrew Undershaft.

STEPHEN

But did they never marry? Were there no legitimate sons?

LADY BRITOMART

Oh yes: they married just as your father did; and they were rich enough to buy land for their own children and leave them well provided for. But they always adopted and trained some foundling to succeed them in the business; and of course they always quarrelled with their wives furiously over it. Your father was adopted in that way; and he pretends to consider himself bound to keep up the tradition and adopt somebody to leave the business to. Of course I was not going to stand that. There may have been some reason for it when the Undershafts could only marry women in their own class, whose sons were not fit to govern great estates. But there could be no excuse for passing over my son.

STEPHEN

[dubiously] I am afraid I should make a poor hand of managing a cannon foundry.

LADY BRITOMART

Nonsense! you could easily get a manager and pay him a salary.

STEPHEN

My father evidently had no great opinion of my capacity.

LADY BRITOMART

Stuff, child! you were only a baby: it had nothing to do with your capacity. Andrew did it on principle, just as he did every perverse and wicked thing on principle. When my father remonstrated, Andrew actually told him to his face that history tells us of only two successful institutions: one the Undershaft firm, and the other the Roman Empire under the Antonines. That was because the Antonine emperors all adopted their successors. Such rubbish! The Stevenages are as good as the Antonines, I hope; and you are a Stevenage. But that was Andrew all over. There you have the man! Always clever and unanswerable when he was defending nonsense and wickedness: always awkward and sullen when he had to behave sensibly and decently!

STEPHEN

Then it was on my account that your home life was broken up, mother. I am sorry.

LADY BRITOMART

Well, dear, there were other differences. I really cannot bear an immoral man. I am not a Pharisee, I hope; and I should not have minded his merely doing wrong things: we are none of us perfect. But your father didnt exactly do wrong things: he said them and thought them: that was what was so dreadful. He really had a sort of religion of wrongness. Just as one doesnt mind men practising immorality so long as they own that they are in the wrong by preaching morality; so I couldnt forgive Andrew for preaching immorality while he practised morality. You would all have grown up without principles, without any knowledge of right and wrong, if he had been in the house. You know, my dear, your father was a very attractive man in some ways. Children did not dislike him; and he took advantage of it to put the wickedest ideas into their heads, and make them quite unmanageable. I did not dislike him myself: very far from it; but nothing can bridge over moral disagreement.

STEPHEN

All this simply bewilders me, mother. People may differ about matters of opinion, or even about religion; but how can they differ about right and wrong? Right is right; and wrong is wrong; and if a man cannot distinguish them properly, he is either a fool or a rascal: thats all.

LADY BRITOMART

[touched] Thats my own boy [she pats his cheek]! Your father never could answer that: he used to laugh and get out of it under cover of some affectionate nonsense. And now that you understand the situation, what do you advise me to do?

STEPHEN

Well, what can you do?

LADY BRITOMART

I must get the money somehow.

STEPHEN

We cannot take money from him. I had rather go and live in some cheap place like Bedford Square or even Hampstead[1] than take a farthing of his money.

LADY BRITOMART

But after all, Stephen, our present income comes from Andrew.

STEPHEN

[shocked] I never knew that.

LADY BRITOMART

Well, you surely didnt suppose your grandfather had anything to give me. The Stevenages could not do everything for you. We gave you social position. Andrew had to contribute something. He had a very good bargain, I think.

STEPHEN

[bitterly] We are utterly dependent on him and his cannons, then?

LADY BRITOMART

Certainly not: the money is settled. But he provided it. So you see it is not a question of taking money from him or not: it is simply a question of how much. I dont want any more for myself.

---

[1]Actually very expensive neighborhoods.

STEPHEN

Nor do I.

LADY BRITOMART

But Sarah does; and Barbara does. That is, Charles Lomax and Adolphus Cusins will cost them more. So I must put my pride in my pocket and ask for it, I suppose. That is your advice, Stephen, is it not?

STEPHEN

No.

LADY BRITOMART

[sharply] Stephen!

STEPHEN

Of course if you are determined—

LADY BRITOMART

I am not determined: I ask your advice; and I am waiting for it. I will not have all the responsibility thrown on my shoulders.

STEPHEN

[obstinately] I would die sooner than ask him for another penny.

LADY BRITOMART

[resignedly] You mean that I must ask him. Very well, Stephen: it shall be as you wish. You will be glad to know that your grandfather concurs. But he thinks I ought to ask Andrew to come here and see the girls. After all, he must have some natural affection for them.

STEPHEN

Ask him here!!!

LADY BRITOMART

Do not repeat my words, Stephen. Where else can I ask him?

STEPHEN

I never expected you to ask him at all.

LADY BRITOMART

Now dont tease, Stephen. Come! you see that it is necessary that he should pay us a visit, dont you?

STEPHEN

[reluctantly] I suppose so, if the girls cannot do without his money.

LADY BRITOMART

Thank you, Stephen: I knew you would give me the right advice when it was properly explained to you. I have asked your father to come this evening. [Stephen bounds from his seat.] Dont jump, Stephen: it fidgets me.

STEPHEN

[in utter consternation] Do you mean to say that my father is coming here tonight—that he may be here at any moment?

LADY BRITOMART

[looking at her watch] I said nine. [He gasps. She rises.] Ring the bell, please. [Stephen goes to the smaller writing table; presses a button on it; and sits at it with his elbows on the table and his head in his hands, outwitted and overwhelmed.] It is ten minutes to nine yet; and I have to prepare the girls. I asked Charles Lomax and Adolphus to dinner on purpose that they might be here. Andrew had better see them in case he should cherish any delusions as to their being capable of supporting their wives. [The butler enters: Lady Britomart goes behind the settee to speak to him.] Morrison: go up to the drawing room and tell everybody to come down here at once. [Morrison withdraws. Lady Britomart turns to Stephen.] Now remember, Stephen: I shall need all your countenance and authority. [He rises and tries to recover some vestige of these attributes.] Give me a chair, dear. [He pushes a chair forward from the wall to where she stands, near the smaller writing table. She sits down; and he goes to the armchair, into which he throws himself.] I dont know how Barbara will take it. Ever since they made her a major in the Salvation Army she has developed a propensity to have her own way and order people about which quite cows me sometimes. It's not ladylike: I'm sure I dont know where she picked it up. Anyhow, Barbara shant bully me; but still it's just as well that your father should be here before she has time to refuse to meet him or make a fuss. Dont look nervous, Stephen: it will only encourage Barbara to make difficulties. I am nervous enough, goodness knows; but I dont shew it.

[Sarah and Barbara come in with their respective young men, Charles Lomax and Adolphus Cusins. Sarah is slender, bored, and mundane. Barbara is robuster, jollier, much more energetic. Sarah is fashionably dressed: Barbara is in Salvation Army uniform. Lomax, a young man about town, is like many other young men about town. He is afflicted with a frivolous sense of humor which plunges him at the most inopportune moments into paroxysms of imperfectly suppressed laughter. Cusins is a spectacled student, slight, thin haired, and sweet voiced, with a more complex form of

Lomax's complaint. His sense of humor is intellectual and subtle, and is complicated by an appalling temper. The lifelong struggle of a benevolent temperament and a high conscience against impulses of inhuman ridicule and fierce impatience has set up a chronic strain which has visibly wrecked his constitution. He is a most implacable, determined, tenacious, intolerant person who by mere force of character presents himself as— and indeed actually is—considerate, gentle, explanatory, even mild and apologetic, capable possibly of murder, but not of cruelty or coarseness. By the operation of some instinct which is not merciful enough to blind him with the illusions of love, he is obstinately bent on marrying Barbara. Lomax likes Sarah and thinks it will be rather a lark to marry her. Consequently he has not attempted to resist Lady Britomart's arrangements to that end. All four look as if they had been having a good deal of fun in the drawing room. The girls enter first, leaving the swains outside. Sarah comes to the settee. Barbara comes in after her and stops at the door.]

BARBARA

Are Cholly and Dolly to come in?

LADY BRITOMART

[forcibly] Barbara: I will not have Charles called Cholly: the vulgarity of it positively makes me ill.

BARBARA

It's all right, mother: Cholly is quite correct nowadays. Are they to come in?

LADY BRITOMART

Yes, if they will behave themselves.

BARBARA

[through the door] Come in, Dolly; and behave yourself.

[Barbara comes to her mother's writing table. Cusins enters smiling, and wanders towards Lady Britomart.]

SARAH

[calling] Come in, Cholly. [Lomax enters, controlling his features very imperfectly, and places himself vaguely between Sarah and Barbara.]

LADY BRITOMART

[peremptorily] Sit down, all of you. [They sit. Cusins crosses to the window and seats himself there. Lomax takes a chair. Barbara sits at the writing table and Sarah on the settee.] I dont in the least know what you are laughing at, Adolphus. I am surprised at you, though I expected nothing better from Charles Lomax.

CUSINS

[in a remarkably gentle voice] Barbara has been trying to teach me the West Ham Salvation March.

LADY BRITOMART

I see nothing to laugh at in that; nor should you if you are really converted.

CUSINS

[sweetly] You were not present. It was really funny, I believe.

LOMAX

Ripping.

LADY BRITOMART

Be quiet, Charles. Now listen to me, children. Your father is coming here this evening.

[General stupefaction. Lomax, Sarah, and Barbara rise: Sarah scared, and Barbara amused and expectant.]

LOMAX

[remonstrating] Oh I say!

LADY BRITOMART

You are not called on to say anything, Charles.

SARAH

Are you serious, mother?

LADY BRITOMART

Of course I am serious. It is on your account, Sarah, and also on Charles's. [Silence. Sarah sits, with a shrug. Charles looks painfully unworthy.] I hope you are not going to object, Barbara.

BARBARA

I! Why should I? My father has a soul to be saved like anybody else. He's quite welcome as far as I am concerned. [She sits on the table, and softly whistles 'Onward, Christian Soldiers.']

LOMAX

[still remonstrant] But really, dont you know! Oh I say!

LADY BRITOMART

[frigidly] What do you wish to convey, Charles?

LOMAX

Well, you must admit that this is a bit thick.

LADY BRITOMART

[turning with ominous suavity to Cusins] Adolphus: you are a professor of Greek. Can you translate Charles Lomax's remarks into reputable English for us?

CUSINS

[cautiously] If I may say so, Lady Brit, I think Charles has rather happily expressed what we all feel. Homer, speaking of Autolycus, uses the same phrase. πυκινὸν δόμον ἐλθεῖν[2] means a bit thick.

LOMAX

[handsomely] Not that I mind, you know, if Sarah dont. [He sits.]

LADY BRITOMART

[crushingly] Thank you. Have I your permission, Adolphus, to invite my own husband to my own house?

CUSINS

[gallantly] You have my unhesitating support in everything you do.

LADY BRITOMART

Tush! Sarah: have you nothing to say?

SARAH

Do you mean that he is coming regularly to live here?

LADY BRITOMART

Certainly not. The spare room is ready for him if he likes to stay for a day or two and see a little more of you; but there are limits.

SARAH

Well, he cant eat us, I suppose. I dont mind.

LOMAX

[chuckling] I wonder how the old man will take it.

LADY BRITOMART

Much as the old woman will, no doubt, Charles.

LOMAX

[abashed] I didnt mean—at least—

LADY BRITOMART

You didnt think, Charles. You never do; and the result is, you never mean anything. And now please attend to me, children. Your father will be quite a stranger to us.

LOMAX

I suppose he hasnt seen Sarah since she was a little kid.

---

[2] *Pukinon domon elthein*, or "to come into a thick house." The line—actually a misquotation of Homer—was supplied to Shaw by his friend (and the role model for Cusins) Professor Gilbert Murray, the Euripidean translator.

LADY BRITOMART

Not since she was a little kid, Charles, as you express it with that elegance of diction and refinement of thought that seem never to desert you. Accordingly—er—*[impatiently]* Now I have forgotten what I was going to say. That comes of your provoking me to be sarcastic, Charles. Adolphus: will you kindly tell me where I was.

CUSINS

[sweetly] You were saying that as Mr Undershaft has not seen his children since they were babies, he will form his opinion of the way you have brought them up from their behavior tonight, and that therefore you wish us all to be particularly careful to conduct ourselves well, especially Charles.

LADY BRITOMART

[with emphatic approval] Precisely.

LOMAX

Look here, Dolly: Lady Brit didnt say that.

LADY BRITOMART

[vehemently] I did, Charles. Adolphus's recollection is perfectly correct. It is most important that you should be good; and I do beg you for once not to pair off into opposite corners and giggle and whisper while I am speaking to your father.

BARBARA

All right, mother. We'll do you credit. *[She comes off the table, and sits in her chair with ladylike elegance.]*

LADY BRITOMART

Remember, Charles, that Sarah will want to feel proud of you instead of ashamed of you.

LOMAX

Oh I say! theres nothing to be exactly proud of, dont you know.

LADY BRITOMART

Well, try and look as if there was.

[Morrison, pale and dismayed, breaks into the room in unconcealed disorder.]

MORRISON

Might I speak a word to you, my lady?

LADY BRITOMART

Nonsense! Shew him up.

MORRISON

Yes, my lady. *[He goes.]*

LOMAX

Does Morrison know who it is?

LADY BRITOMART

Of course. Morrison has always been with us.

LOMAX

It must be a regular corker for him, dont you know.

LADY BRITOMART

Is this a moment to get on my nerves, Charles, with your outrageous expressions?

LOMAX

But this is something out of the ordinary, really—

MORRISON

[at the door] The—er—Mr Undershaft. *[He retreats in confusion.]*

[Andrew Undershaft comes in. All rise. Lady Britomart meets him in the middle of the room behind the settee. Andrew is, on the surface, a stoutish, easygoing elderly man, with kindly patient manners, and an engaging simplicity of character. But he has a watchful, deliberate, waiting, listening face, and formidable reserves of power, both bodily and mental, in his capacious chest and long head. His gentleness is partly that of a strong man who has learnt by experience that his natural grip hurts ordinary people unless he handles them very carefully, and partly the mellowness of age and success. He is also a little shy in his present very delicate situation.]

LADY BRITOMART

Good evening, Andrew.

UNDERSHAFT

How d'ye do, my dear.

LADY BRITOMART

You look a good deal older.

UNDERSHAFT

[apologetically] I am somewhat older. *[Taking her hand with a touch of courtship]* Time has stood still with you.

LADY BRITOMART

[throwing away his hand] Rubbish! This is your family.

UNDERSHAFT

[surprised] Is it so large? I am sorry to say my memory is failing very badly in some things. *[He offers his hand with paternal kindness to Lomax.]*

LOMAX

[jerkily shaking his hand] Ahdedoo.

UNDERSHAFT

I can see you are my eldest. I am very glad to meet you again, my boy.

LOMAX

[remonstrating] No, but look here dont you know— [Overcome] Oh I say!

LADY BRITOMART

[recovering from momentary speechlessness] Andrew: do you mean to say that you dont remember how many children you have?

UNDERSHAFT

Well, I am afraid I—. They have grown so much— er. Am I making any ridiculous mistake? I may as well confess: I recollect only one son. But so many things have happened since, of course—er—

LADY BRITOMART

[decisively] Andrew: you are talking nonsense. Of course you have only one son.

UNDERSHAFT

Perhaps you will be good enough to introduce me, my dear.

LADY BRITOMART

That is Charles Lomax, who is engaged to Sarah.

UNDERSHAFT

My dear sir, I beg your pardon.

LOMAX

Notatall. Delighted, I assure you.

LADY BRITOMART

This is Stephen.

UNDERSHAFT

[bowing] Happy to make your acquaintance, Mr Stephen. Then [going to Cusins] you must be my son. [Taking Cusins' hands in his] How are you, my young friend? [To Lady Britomart] He is very like you, my love.

CUSINS

You flatter me, Mr Undershaft. My name is Cusins: engaged to Barbara. [Very explicitly] That is Major Barbara Undershaft, of the Salvation Army. That is Sarah, your second daughter. This is Stephen Undershaft, your son.

UNDERSHAFT

My dear Stephen, I beg your pardon.

STEPHEN

Not at all.

UNDERSHAFT

Mr Cusins: I am much indebted to you for explaining so precisely. [Turning to Sarah] Barbara, my dear—

SARAH

[prompting him] Sarah.

UNDERSHAFT

Sarah, of course. [They shake hands. He goes over to Barbara.] Barbara—I am right this time, I hope?

BARBARA

Quite right. [They shake hands.]

LADY BRITOMART

[resuming command] Sit down, all of you. Sit down, Andrew. [She comes forward and sits on the settee. Cusins also brings his chair forward on her left. Barbara and Stephen resume their seats. Lomax gives his chair to Sarah and goes for another.]

UNDERSHAFT

Thank you, my love.

LOMAX

[conversationally, as he brings a chair forward between the writing table and the settee, and offers it to Undershaft] Takes you some time to figure out exactly where you are, dont it?

UNDERSHAFT

[accepting the chair, but remaining standing] That is not what embarrasses me, Mr Lomax. My difficulty is that if I play the part of a father, I shall produce the effect of an intrusive stranger; and if I play the part of a discreet stranger, I may appear a callous father.

LADY BRITOMART

There is no need for you to play any part at all, Andrew. You had much better be sincere and natural.

UNDERSHAFT

[submissively] Yes, my dear: I daresay that will be best. [He sits down comfortably.] Well, here I am. Now what can I do for you all?

LADY BRITOMART

You need not do anything, Andrew. You are one of the family. You can sit with us and enjoy yourself.

[A painfully conscious pause. Barbara makes a face at Lomax, whose too long suppressed mirth explodes in agonized neighings.]

LADY BRITOMART

[outraged] Charles Lomax: if you can behave yourself, behave yourself. If not, leave the room.

LOMAX

I'm awfully sorry, Lady Brit; but really you know, upon my soul! *[He sits on the settee between Lady Britomart and Undershaft, quite overcome.]*

BARBARA

Why dont you laugh if you want to, Cholly? It's good for your inside.

LADY BRITOMART

Barbara: you have had the education of a lady. Please let your father see that; and dont talk like a street girl.

UNDERSHAFT

Never mind me, my dear. As you know, I am not a gentleman; and I was never educated.

LOMAX

[encouragingly] Nobody'd know it, I assure you. You look all right, you know.

CUSINS

Let me advise you to study Greek, Mr. Undershaft. Greek scholars are privileged men. Few of them know Greek; and none of them know anything else; but their position is unchallengeable. Other languages are the qualifications of waiters and commercial travellers: Greek is to a man of position what the hallmark is to silver.

BARBARA

Dolly: dont be insincere. Cholly: fetch your concertina and play something for us.

LOMAX

[jumps up eagerly, but checks himself to remark doubtfully to Undershaft] Perhaps that sort of thing isnt in your line, eh?

UNDERSHAFT

I am particularly fond of music.

LOMAX

[delighted] Are you? Then I'll get it. *[He goes upstairs for the instrument.]*

UNDERSHAFT

Do you play, Barbara?

BARBARA

Only the tambourine. But Cholly's teaching me the concertina.

UNDERSHAFT

Is Cholly also a member of the Salvation Army?

BARBARA

No: he says it's bad form to be a dissenter. But I dont despair of Cholly. I made him come yesterday to a meeting at the dock gates, and take the collection in his hat.

UNDERSHAFT

[looks whimsically at his wife] !!

LADY BRITOMART

It is not my doing, Andrew. Barbara is old enough to take her own way. She has no father to advise her.

BARBARA

Oh yes she has. There are no orphans in the Salvation Army.

UNDERSHAFT

Your father there has a great many children and plenty of experience, eh?

BARBARA

[looking at him with quick interest and nodding] Just so. How did you come to understand that? *[Lomax is heard at the door trying the concertina.]*

LADY BRITOMART

Come in, Charles. Play us something at once.

LOMAX

Righto! *[He sits down in his former place, and preludes.]*

UNDERSHAFT

One moment, Mr Lomax. I am rather interested in the Salvation Army. Its motto might be my own: Blood and Fire.

LOMAX

[shocked] But not your sort of blood and fire, you know.

UNDERSHAFT

My sort of blood cleanses: my sort of fire purifies.

BARBARA

So do ours. Come down tomorrow to my shelter— the West Ham shelter—and see what we're doing. We're going to march to a great meeting in the Assembly Hall at Mile End. Come and see the shelter and then march with us: it will do you a lot of good. Can you play anything?

UNDERSHAFT

In my youth I earned pennies, and even shillings occasionally, in the streets and in public house parlors by my natural talent for stepdancing. Later on, I became a member of the Undershaft orchestral society, and performed passably on the tenor trombone.

LOMAX

[scandalized—putting down the concertina] Oh I say!

BARBARA

Many a sinner has played himself into heaven on the trombone, thanks to the Army.

LOMAX

[to Barbara, still rather shocked] Yes; but what about the cannon business, dont you know? *[To Undershaft]* Getting into heaven is not exactly in your line, is it?

LADY BRITOMART

Charles!!!

LOMAX

Well; but it stands to reason, dont it? The cannon business may be necessary and all that: we cant get on without cannons; but it isnt right, you know. On the other hand, there may be a certain amount of tosh about the Salvation Army—I belong the the Established Church myself—but still you cant deny that it's religion; and you cant go against religion, can you? At least unless youre downright immoral, dont you know.

UNDERSHAFT

You hardly appreciate my position, Mr Lomax—

LOMAX

[hastily] I'm not saying anything against you personally—

UNDERSHAFT

Quite so, quite so. But consider for a moment. Here I am, a profiteer in mutilation and murder. I find myself in a specially amiable humor just now because, this morning, down at the foundry, we blew twenty-seven dummy soldiers into fragments with a gun which formerly destroyed only thirteen.

LOMAX

[leniently] Well, the more destructive war becomes, the sooner it will be abolished, eh?

UNDERSHAFT

Not at all. The more destructive war becomes the more fascinating we find it. No, Mr Lomax: I am obliged to you for making the usual excuse for my trade; but I am not ashamed of it. I am not one of those men who keep their morals and their business in watertight compartments. All the spare money my trade rivals spend on hospitals, cathedrals, and other receptacles for conscience money, I devote to experiments and researches in improved methods of destroying life and property. I have always done so; and I always shall. Therefore your Christmas card mor-

alities of peace on earth and goodwill among men are of no use to me. Your Christianity, which enjoins you to resist not evil, and to turn the other cheek, would make me bankrupt. My morality—my religion—must have a place for cannons and torpedoes in it.

STEPHEN

[coldly—almost sullenly] You speak as if there were half a dozen moralities and religions to choose from, instead of one true morality and one true religion.

UNDERSHAFT

For me there is only one true morality; but it might not fit you, as you do not manufacture aerial battleships. There is only one true morality for every man; but every man has not the same true morality.

LOMAX

[overtaxed] Would you mind saying that again? I didnt quite follow it.

CUSINS

It's quite simple. As Euripides says, one man's meat is another man's poison morally as well as physically.

UNDERSHAFT

Precisely.

LOMAX

Oh, that! Yes, yes, yes. True. True.

STEPHEN

In other words, some men are honest and some are scoundrels.

BARBARA

Bosh! There are no scoundrels.

UNDERSHAFT

Indeed? Are there any good men?

BARBARA

No. Not one. There are neither good men nor scoundrels: there are just children of one Father; and the sooner they stop calling one another names the better. You neednt talk to me: I know them. Ive had scores of them through my hands: scoundrels, criminals, infidels, philanthropists, missionaries, county councillors, all sorts. Theyre all just the same sort of sinner; and theres the same salvation ready for them all.

UNDERSHAFT

May I ask have you ever saved a maker of cannons?

BARBARA

No. Will you let me try?

UNDERSHAFT

Well, I will make a bargain with you. If I go to see you tomorrow in your Salvation Shelter, will you come the day after to see me in my cannon works?

BARBARA

Take care. It may end in your giving up the cannons for the sake of the Salvation Army.

UNDERSHAFT

Are you sure it will not end up in your giving up the Salvation Army for the sake of the cannons?

BARBARA

I will take my chance of that.

UNDERSHAFT

And I will take my chance of the other. *[They shake hands on it.]* Where is your shelter?

BARBARA

In West Ham. At the sign of the cross. Ask anybody in Canning Town. Where are your works?

UNDERSHAFT

In Perivale St Andrews. At the sign of the sword. Ask anybody in Europe.

LOMAX

Hadnt I better play something?

BARBARA

Yes. Give us Onward, Christian Soldiers.

LOMAX

Well, thats rather a strong order to begin with, dont you know. Suppose I sing Thourt passing hence, my brother. It's much the same tune.

BARBARA

It's too melancholy. You get saved, Cholly; and youll pass hence, my brother, without making such a fuss about it.

LADY BRITOMART

Really, Barbara, you go on as if religion were a pleasant subject. Do have some sense of propriety.

UNDERSHAFT

I do not find it an unpleasant subject, my dear. It is the only one that capable people really care for.

LADY BRITOMART

[looking at her watch] Well, if you are determined to have it, I insist on having it in a proper and respectable way. Charles: ring for prayers.

[General amazement. Stephen rises in dismay.]

LOMAX

[rising] Oh I say!

UNDERSHAFT

[rising] I am afraid I must be going.

LADY BRITOMART

You cannot go now, Andrew: it would be most improper. Sit down. What will the servants think?

UNDERSHAFT

My dear: I have conscientious scruples. May I suggest a compromise? If Barbara will conduct a little service in the drawing room, with Mr Lomax as organist, I will attend it willingly. I will even take part, if a trombone can be procured.

LADY BRITOMART

Dont mock, Andrew.

UNDERSHAFT

[shocked—to Barbara] You dont think I am mocking, my love, I hope.

BARBARA

No, of course not; and it wouldnt matter if you were: half the Army came to their first meeting for a lark. *[Rising]* Come along. *[She throws her arm round her father and sweeps him out, calling to the others from the threshold.]* Come, Dolly. Come, Cholly.

[Cusins rises.]

LADY BRITOMART

I will not be disobeyed by everybody. Adolphus: sit down. *[He does not.]* Charles: you may go. You are not fit for prayers: you cannot keep your countenance.

LOMAX

Oh I say! *[He goes out.]*

LADY BRITOMART

[continuing] But you, Adolphus, can behave yourself if you choose to. I insist on your staying.

CUSINS

My dear Lady Brit: there are things in the family prayer book that I couldnt bear to hear you say.

LADY BRITOMART

What things, pray?

CUSINS

Well, you would have to say before all the servants that we have done things we ought not to have done, and left undone things we ought to have done, and that there is no health in us. I cannot bear to hear you doing yourself such an injustice, and Barbara such an injustice. As for myself, I flatly deny it: I have done my best. I shouldnt dare to marry Barbara—I couldnt look you in the face—if it were true. So I must go to the drawing room.

LADY BRITOMART

[offended] Well, go. [He starts for the door.] And remember this, Adolphus [he turns to listen]: I have a very strong suspicion that you went to the Salvation Army to worship Barbara and nothing else. And I quite appreciate the very clever way in which you systematically humbug me. I have found you out. Take care Barbara doesnt. Thats all.

CUSINS

[with unruffled sweetness] Dont tell on me. [He steals out.]

LADY BRITOMART

Sarah: if you want to go, go. Anything's better than to sit there as if you wished you were a thousand miles away.

SARAH

[languidly] Very well, mamma. [She goes.]

[Lady Britomart, with a sudden flounce, gives way to a little gust of tears.]

STEPHEN

[going to her] Mother: whats the matter?

LADY BRITOMART

[swishing away her tears with her handkerchief] Nothing. Foolishness. You can go with him, too, if you like, and leave me with the servants.

STEPHEN

Oh, you mustnt think that, mother. I—I don't like him.

LADY BRITOMART

The others do. That is the injustice of a woman's lot. A woman has to bring up her children; and that means to restrain them, to deny them things they want, to set them tasks, to punish them when they do wrong, to do all the unpleasant things. And then the father, who has nothing to do but pet them and spoil them, comes in when all her work is done and steals their affection from her.

STEPHEN

He has not stolen our affection from you. It is only curiosity.

LADY BRITOMART

[violently] I wont be consoled, Stephen. There is nothing the matter with me. [She rises and goes towards the door.]

STEPHEN

Where are you going, mother?

LADY BRITOMART

To the drawing room, of course. [She goes out. Onward, Christian Soldiers, on the concertina, with tambourine accompaniment, is heard when the door opens.] Are you coming, Stephen?

STEPHEN

No. Certainly not. [She goes. He sits down on the settee, with compressed lips and an expression of strong dislike.]

——————— **ACT TWO** ———————

The yard of the West Ham shelter of the Salvation Army is a cold place on a January morning. The building itself, an old warehouse, is newly whitewashed. Its gabled end projects into the yard in the middle, with a door on the ground floor, and another in the loft above it without any balcony or ladder, but with a pulley rigged over it for hoisting sacks. Those who come from this central gable end into the yard have the gateway leading to the street on their left, with a stone horse-trough just beyond it, and, on the right, a penthouse shielding a table from the weather. There are forms at the table; and on them are seated a man and a woman, both much down on their luck, finishing a meal of bread (one thick slice each, with margarine and golden syrup) and diluted milk.

The man, a workman out of employment, is young, agile, a talker, a poser, sharp enough to be capable of anything in reason except honesty or altruistic considerations of any kind. The woman is a commonplace old bundle of poverty and hard-worn humanity. She looks sixty and probably is forty-five. If they were rich people, gloved and muffed and well wrapped up in furs and overcoats, they would be numbed and miserable; for it is a grindingly cold raw January day; and a glance at the background of grimy warehouses and leaden sky visible over the whitewashed walls of the yard would drive any idle rich person straight to the Mediterranean. But these two, being no more troubled with visions of the Mediterranean than of the moon, and being compelled to keep more of their clothes in the pawnshop, and less on *their persons, in winter than in summer, are not depressed by the cold: rather are they stung into vivacity, to which their meal has just now given an almost jolly turn. The man takes a pull at his mug, and then gets up and moves about the yard with his hands deep in his pockets, occasionally breaking into a stepdance.*

THE WOMAN
Feel better arter your meal, sir?

THE MAN
No. Call that a meal! Good enough for you, praps; but wot is it to me, an intelligent workin man.

THE WOMAN
Workin man! Wot are you?

THE MAN
Painter.

THE WOMAN
[sceptically] Yus, I dessay.

THE MAN
Yus, you dessay! I know. Every loafer that cant do nothink calls isself a painter. Well, I'm a real painter: grainer, finisher, thirty-eight bob a week when I can get it.

THE WOMAN
Then why dont you go and get it?

THE MAN
I'll tell you why. Fust: I'm intelligent.—ff ff f! it's rotten cold here *[he dances a step or two]*—yes: intelligent beyond the station o life into which it has pleased the capitalists to call me; and they dont like a man that sees through em. Second, an intelligent bein needs a doo share of appiness; so I drink somethink cruel when I get the chawnce. Third, I stand by my class and do as little as I can so's to leave arf the job for me fellow workers. Fourth, I'm fly enough to know wots inside the law and wots outside it; and inside it I do as the capitalists do: pinch wot I can lay me ands on. In a proper state of society I am sober, industrious, and honest: in Rome, so to speak, I do as the Romans do. Wots the consequence? When trade is bad—and it's rotten bad just now—and the employers az to sack arf their men, they generally start on me.

THE WOMAN
Whats your name?

THE MAN
Price. Bronterre O'Brien Price. Usually called Snobby Price, for short.

THE WOMAN
Snobby's a carpenter, aint it? You said you was a painter.

PRICE
Not that kind of snob, but the genteel sort. I'm too uppish, owing to my intelligence, and my father being a Chartist and a reading, thinking man: a stationer, too. I'm none of your common hewers of wood and drawers of water; and dont you forget it. *[He returns to his seat at the table, and takes up his mug.]* Wots your name?

THE WOMAN
Rummy Mitchens, sir.

PRICE
[quaffing the remains of his milk to her] Your elth, Miss Mitchens.

RUMMY
[correcting him] Missis Mitchens.

PRICE
Wot! Oh Rummy, Rummy! Respectable married woman, Rummy, gittin rescued by the Salvation Army by pretendin to be a bad un. Same old game!

RUMMY
What am I to do? I cant starve. Them Salvation lasses is dear good girls; but the better you are, the worse they likes to think you were before they rescued you. Why shouldnt they av a bit o credit, poor loves? theyre worn to rags by their work. And where would they get the money to rescue us if we was to let on we're no worse than other people? You know what ladies and gentlemen are.

PRICE
Thievin swine! Wish I ad their job, Rummy, all the same. Wot does Rummy stand for? Pet name praps?

RUMMY
Short for Romola.

PRICE
For wot!?

RUMMY
Romola. It was out of a new book. Somebody me mother wanted me to grow up like.

PRICE

We're companions in misfortune, Rummy. Both on us got names that nobody cawnt pronounce. Consequently I'm Snobby and youre Rummy because Bill and Sally wasnt good enough for our parents. Such is life!

RUMMY

Who saved you, Mr Price? Was it Major Barbara?

PRICE

No: I come here on my own. I'm going to be Bronterre O'Brien Price, the converted painter. I know wot they like. I'll tell em how I blasphemed and gambled and wopped my poor old mother—

RUMMY

[shocked] Used you to beat your mother?

PRICE

Not likely. She used to beat me. No matter: you come and listen to the converted painter, and youll hear how she was a pious woman that taught me me prayers at er knee, an how I used to come home drunk and drag her out o bed be er snow white airs, an lam into er with the poker.

RUMMY

Thats whats so unfair to us women. Your confessions is just as big lies as ours: you dont tell what you really done no more than us; but you men can tell your lies right out at the meetins and be made much of for it; while the sort o confessions we az to make az to be wispered to one lady at a time. It aint right, spite of all their piety.

PRICE

Right! Do you spose the Army'd be allowed if it went and did right? Not much. It combs our air and makes us good little blokes to be robbed and put upon. But I'll play the game as good as any of em. I'll see somebody struck by lightnin, or hear a voice sayin 'Snobby Price: where will you spend eternity?' I'll av a time of it, I tell you.

RUMMY

You wont be let drink, though.

PRICE

I'll take it out in gorspellin, then. I dont want to drink if I can get fun enough any other way.

[Jenny Hill, a pale, overwrought, pretty Salvation lass of 18, comes in through the yard gate, leading Peter Shirley, a half hardened, half worn-out elderly man, weak with hunger.]

JENNY

[supporting him] Come! pluck up. I'll get you something to eat. Youll be all right then.

PRICE

[rising and hurrying officiously to take the old man off Jenny's hands] Poor old man! Cheer up, brother: youll find rest and peace and appiness ere. Hurry up with the food, miss: e's fair done *[Jenny hurries into the shelter.]* Ere, buck up, daddy! she's fetchin y'a thick slice o breadn treacle, an a mug o skyblue. *[He seats him at the corner of the table.]*

RUMMY

[gaily] Keep up your old art! Never say die!

SHIRLEY

I'm not an old man. I'm only 46. I'm as good as ever I was. The grey patch come in my hair before I was thirty. All it wants is three pennorth o hair dye: am I to be turned on the streets to starve for it? Holy God! Ive worked ten to twelve hours a day since I was thirteen, and paid my way all through; and now am I to be thrown into the gutter and my job given to a young man that can do it no better than me because Ive black hair that goes white at the first change?

PRICE

[cheerfully] No good jawrin about it. Youre ony a jumped-up, jerked-off, orspittle-turned-out incurable of an ole workin man: who cares about you? Eh? Make the thievin swine give you a meal: theyve stole many a one from you. Get a bit o your own back. *[Jenny returns with the usual meal.]* There you are, brother. Awsk a blessin an tuck that into you.

SHIRLEY

[looking at it ravenously but not touching it, and crying like a child] I never took anything before.

JENNY

[petting him] Come, come! the Lord sends it to you: he wasnt above taking bread from his friends; and why should you be? Besides, when we find you a job you can pay us for it if you like.

SHIRLEY

[eagerly] Yes, yes: thats true. I can pay you back: it's only a loan. *[Shivering]* Oh Lord! oh Lord! *[He turns to the table and attacks the meal ravenously.]*

JENNY

Well, Rummy, are you more comfortable now?

RUMMY

God bless you, lovey! youve fed my body and saved my soul, havnt you? [Jenny, touched, kisses her.] Sit down and rest a bit: you must be ready to drop.

JENNY

Ive been going hard since morning. But theres more work than we can do. I mustnt stop.

RUMMY

Try a prayer for just two minutes. Youll work all the better after.

JENNY

[her eyes lighting up] Oh isnt it wonderful how a few minutes prayer revives you! I was quite lightheaded at twelve o'clock, I was so tired; but Major Barbara just sent me to pray for five minutes; and I was able to go on as if I had only just begun. [To Price] Did you have a piece of bread?

PRICE

[with unction] Yes, miss; but Ive got the piece that I value more; and thats the peace that passeth hall hannerstennin.

RUMMY

[fervently] Glory Hallelujah!

[Bill Walker, a rough customer of about 25, appears at the yard gate and looks malevolently at Jenny.]

JENNY

That makes me so happy. When you say that, I feel wicked for loitering here. I must get to work again.

[She is hurrying to the shelter, when the new-comer moves quickly up to the door and intercepts her. His manner is so threatening that she retreats as he comes at her truculently, driving her down the yard.]

BILL

Aw knaow you. Youre the one that took awy maw girl. Youre the one that set er agen me. Well, I'm gowin to ev er aht. Not that Aw care a carse for er or you: see? Bat Aw'll let er knaow; and Aw'll let you knaow. Aw'm gowin to give her a doin thatll teach er to cat away from me. Nah in wiv you and tell er to cam aht afore Aw cam in and kick er aht. Tell er Bill Walker wants er. She'll knaow wot thet means; and if she keeps me witin itll be worse. You stop to jawr beck at me; and Aw'll stawt on you: d'ye eah? Theres your

wy. In you gow. [He takes her by the arm and slings her towards the door of the shelter. She falls on her hand and knee. Rummy helps her up again.]

PRICE

[rising, and venturing irresolutely towards Bill] Easy there, mate. She aint doin you no arm.

BILL

Oo are you callin mite? [Standing over him threateningly] Youre gowin to stend ap for er, aw yer? Put ap your ends.

RUMMY

[running indignantly to him to scold him] Oh, you great brute— [He instantly swings his left hand back against her face. She screams and reels back to the trough, where she sits down, covering her bruised face with her hands and rocking herself and moaning with pain.]

JENNY

[going to her] Oh, God forgive you! How could you strike an old woman like that?

BILL

[seizing her by the hair so violently that she also screams, and tearing her away from the old woman] You Gawd forgimme again an Aw'll Gawd forgive you one on the jawr thetll stop you pryin for a week. [Holding her and turning fiercely on Price] Ev you ennything to sy agen it?

PRICE

[intimidated] No, matey: she aint anything to do with me.

BILL

Good job for you! Aw'd pat two meals into you and fawt you with one finger arter, you stawved cur. [To Jenny] Nah are you gowin to fetch aht Mog Ebbijem; or em Aw to knock your fice off you and fetch her meself?

JENNY

[writhing in his grasp] Oh please someone go in and tell Major Barbara— [she screams again as he wrenches her head down; and Price and Rummy flee into the shelter.]

BILL

You want to gow in and tell your Mijor of me, do you?

JENNY

Oh please dont drag my hair. Let me go.

BILL

Do you or downt you? [She stifles a scream.] Yus or nao?

JENNY

God give me strength—

BILL

[striking her with his fist in the face] Gow an shaow her thet, and tell her if she wants one lawk it to cam and interfere with me. [Jenny, crying with pain, goes into the shed. He goes to the form and addresses the old man.] Eah: finish your mess; an git aht o maw wy.

SHIRLEY

[springing up and facing him fiercely, with the mug in his hand] You take a liberty with me, and I'll smash you over the face with the mug and cut your eye out. Aint you satisfied—young whelps like you—with takin the bread out o the mouths of your elders that have brought you up and slaved for you, but you must come shovin and cheekin and bullyin in here, where the bread o charity is sickenin in our stummicks?

BILL

[contemptuously, but backing a little] Wot good are you, you aold palsy mag?[3] Wot good are you?

SHIRLEY

As good as you and better. I'll do a day's work agen you or any fat young soaker of your age. Go and take my job at Horrockses, where I worked for ten year. They want young men there: they cant afford to keep men over forty-five. Theyre very sorry—give you a character and happy to help you to get anything suited to your years—sure a steady man wont be long out of a job. Well, let em try you. Theyll find the differ. What do you know? Not as much as how to beeyave yourself—laying your dirty fist across the mouth of a respectable woman!

BILL

Downt provowk me to ly it acrost yours: d'ye eah?

SHIRLEY

[with blighting contempt] Yes: you like an old man to hit, dont you, when youve finished with the women. I aint seen you hit a young one yet.

_____
[3]Drunkard.

BILL

[stung] You loy, you aold soupkitchener, you. There was a yang menn eah. Did Aw offer to itt him or did Aw not?

SHIRLEY

Was he starvin or was he not? Was he a man or only a crosseyed thief an a loafer? Would you hit my son-in-law's brother?

BILL

Oo's ee?

SHIRLEY

Todger Fairmile o Balls Pond. Him that won £20 off the Japanese wrastler at the music hall by standin out 17 minutes 4 seconds agen him.

BILL

[sullenly] Aw'm nao music awl wrastler. Ken he box?

SHIRLEY

Yes: an you cant.

BILL

Wot! Aw cawnt, cawnt Aw? Wots thet you sy [threatening him]?

SHIRLEY

[not budging an inch] Will you box Todger Fairmile if I put him on to you? Say the word.

BILL

[subsiding with a slouch] Aw'll stend ap to enny menn alawv, if he was ten Todger Fairmawls. But Aw dont set ap to be a perfeshnal.

SHIRLEY

[looking down on him with unfathomable disdain] You box! Slap an old woman with the back o your hand! You hadnt even the sense to hit her where a magistrate couldnt see the mark of it, you silly young lump of conceit and ignorance. Hit a girl in the jaw and ony make her cry! If Todger Fairmile'd done it, she wouldnt a got up inside o ten minutes, no more than you would if he got on to you. Yah! I'd set about you myself if I had a week's feedin in me instead o two months' starvation. [He turns his back on him and sits down moodily at the table.]

BILL

[following him and stooping over him to drive the taunt in] You loy! youve the bread and treacle in you that you cam eah to beg.

SHIRLEY

[bursting into tears] Oh God! it's true: I'm only an old pauper on the scrap heap. [Furiously] But youll come to it yourself; and then youll know. Youll come to it sooner than a teetotaller like me, fillin yourself with gin at this hour o the mornin!

BILL

Aw'm nao gin drinker, you oald lawr; bat wen Aw want to give my girl a bloomin good awdin Aw lawk to ev a bit o devil in me: see? An eah Aw emm, talkin to a rotten aold blawter like you sted o givin her wot for. [Working himself into a rage] Aw'm gowin in there to fetch her aht. [He makes vengefully for the shelter door.]

SHIRLEY

Youre going to the station on a stretcher, more likely; and theyll take the gin and the devil out of you there when they get you inside. You mind what youre about: the major here is the Earl o Stevenage's granddaughter.

BILL

[checked] Garn!

SHIRLEY

Youll see.

BILL

[his resolution oozing] Well, Aw aint dan nathin to er.

SHIRLEY

Spose she said you did! who'd believe you?

BILL

[very uneasy, skulking back to the corner of the penthouse] Gawd! theres no jastice in this cantry. To think wot them people can do! Aw'm as good as er.

SHIRLEY

Tell her so. It's just what a fool like you would do.

[Barbara, brisk and businesslike, comes from the shelter with a note book, and addresses herself to Shirley. Bill, cowed, sits down in the corner on a form, and turns his back on them.]

BARBARA

Good morning.

SHIRLEY

[standing up and taking off his hat] Good morning, miss.

BARBARA

Sit down: make yourself at home. [He hesitates; but she puts a friendly hand on his shoulder and makes him obey.] Now then! since youve made friends with us, we want to know all about you. Names and addresses and trades.

SHIRLEY

Peter Shirley. Fitter. Chucked out two months ago because I was too old.

BARBARA

[not at all surprised] Youd pass still. Why didnt you dye your hair?

SHIRLEY

I did. Me age come out at a coroner's inquest on me daughter.

BARBARA

Steady?

SHIRLEY

Teetotaller. Never out of a job before. Good worker. And sent to the knackers like an old horse!

BARBARA

No matter: if you did your part God will do his.

SHIRLEY

[suddenly stubborn] My religion's no concern of anybody but myself.

BARBARA

[guessing] I know. Secularist?

SHIRLEY

[hotly] Did I offer to deny it?

BARBARA

Why should you? My own father's a Secularist, I think. Our Father—yours and mine—fulfils himself in many ways; and I daresay he knew what he was about when he made a Secularist of you. So buck up, Peter! we can always find a job for a steady man like you. [Shirley, disarmed and a little bewildered, touches his hat. She turns from him to Bill.] Whats your name?

BILL

[insolently] Wots thet to you?

BARBARA

[calmly making a note] Afraid to give his name. Any trade?

BILL

Oo's afride to give is nime? [Doggedly, with a sense of heroically defying the House of Lords in the person of Lord Stevenage] If you want to bring a chawge agen me, bring it. [She waits, unruffled.] Moy nime's Bill Walker.

BARBARA

[as if the name were familiar: trying to remember how] Bill Walker? [Recollecting] Oh, I know: youre the man that Jenny Hill was praying for inside just now. [She enters his name in her note book.]

BILL

Oo's Jenny Ill? And wot call as she to pry for me?

BARBARA

I dont know. Perhaps it was you that cut her lip.

BILL

[defiantly] Yus, it was me that cat her lip. Aw aint afride o you.

BARBARA

How could you be, since youre not afraid of God? Youre a brave man, Mr Walker. It takes some pluck to do our work here; but none of us dare lift our hand against a girl like that, for fear of her father in heaven.

BILL

[sullenly] I want nan o your kentin jawr. I spowse you think Aw cam eah to beg from you, like this demmiged lot eah. Not me. Aw downt want your bread and scripe and ketlep. Aw dont blieve in your Gawd, no more than you do yourself.

BARBARA

[sunnily apologetic and ladylike, as on a new footing with him] Oh, I beg your pardon for putting your name down, Mr Walker. I didnt understand. I'll strike it out.

BILL

[taking this as a slight, and deeply wounded by it] Eah! you let maw nime alown. Aint it good enaff to be in your book?

BARBARA

[considering] Well, you see, theres no use putting down your name unless I can do something for you, is there? Whats your trade?

BILL

[still smarting] Thets nao concern o yours.

BARBARA

Just so. [Very businesslike] I'll put you down as [writing] the man who—struck—poor little Jenny Hill—in the mouth.

BILL

[rising threateningly] See eah. Awve ed enaff o this.

BARBARA

[quite sunny and fearless] What did you come to us for?

BILL

Aw cam for maw gel, see? Aw cam to tike her aht o this and to brike er jawr for er.

BARBARA

[complacently] You see I was right about your trade. [Bill, on the point of retorting furiously, finds himself, to his great shame and terror, in danger of crying instead. He sits down again suddenly.] Whats her name?

BILL

[dogged] Er nime's Mog Ebbijem: thets wot her nime is.

BARBARA

Mog Habbijam! Oh, she's gone to Canning Town, to our barracks there.

BILL

[fortified by his resentment of Mog's perfidy] Is she? [Vindictively] Then Aw'm gowin to Kennintahn arter her. [He crosses to the gate; hesitates; finally comes back at Barbara] Are you loyin to me to git shat o me?

BARBARA

I dont want to get shut of you. I want to keep you here and save your soul. Youd better stay: youre going to have a bad time today, Bill.

BILL

Oo's gowin to give it to me? You, preps?

BARBARA

Someone you dont believe in. But youll be glad afterwards.

BILL

[slinking off] Aw'll gow to Kennintahn to be aht o reach o your tangue. [Suddenly turning on her with intense malice] And if Aw downt fawnd Mog there, Aw'll cam beck and do two years for you, selp me Gawd if Aw downt!

BARBARA

[a shade kindlier, if possible] It's no use, Bill. She's got another bloke.

BILL

Wot!

BARBARA

One of her own converts. He fell in love with her when he saw her with her soul saved, and her face clean, and her hair washed.

BILL

[surprised] Wottud she wash it for, the carroty slat? It's red.

BARBARA

It's quite lovely now, because she wears a new look in her eyes with it. It's a pity youre too late. The new bloke has put your nose out of joint, Bill.

BILL

Aw'll put his nowse aht o joint for him. Not that Aw care a carse for er, mawnd thet. But Aw'll teach her to drop me as if Aw was dirt. And Aw'll teach him to meddle with maw judy. Wotz iz bleedin nime?

BARBARA

Sergeant Todger Fairmile.

SHIRLEY

[rising with grim joy] I'll go with him, miss. I want to see them two meet. I'll take him to the infirmary when it's over.

BILL

[to Shirley, with undissembled misgiving] Is thet im you was speakin on?

SHIRLEY

Thats him.

BILL

Im that wrastled in the music awl?

SHIRLEY

The competitions at the National Sportin Club was worth nigh a hundred a year to him. He's gev em up now for religion; so he's a bit fresh for want of the exercise he was accustomed to. He'll be glad to see you. Come along.

BILL

Wots is wight?

SHIRLEY

Thirteen four.[4] [Bill's last hope expires.]

BARBARA

Go and talk to him, Bill. He'll convert you.

SHIRLEY

He'll convert your head into a mashed potato.

BILL

[sullenly] Aw aint afride of im. Aw aint afride of ennybody. Bat e can lick me. She's dan me. [He sits down moodily on the edge of the horse trough.]

––––––––––––––

[4]Thirteen stone, four pounds (186 pounds).

SHIRLEY

You aint going. I thought not. [He resumes his seat.]

BARBARA

[calling] Jenny!

JENNY

[appearing at the shelter door with a plaster on the corner of her mouth] Yes, Major.

BARBARA

Send Rummy Mitchens out to clear away here.

JENNY

I think she's afraid.

BARBARA

[her resemblance to her mother flashing out for a moment] Nonsense! she must do as she's told.

JENNY

[calling into the shelter] Rummy: the Major says you must come.

[Jenny comes to Barbara, purposely keeping on the side next Bill, lest he should suppose that she shrank from him or bore malice.]

BARBARA

Poor little Jenny! Are you tired? [Looking at the wounded cheek] Does it hurt?

JENNY

No: it's all right now. It was nothing.

BARBARA

[critically] It was as hard as he could hit, I expect. Poor Bill! You dont feel angry with him, do you?

JENNY

Oh no, no, no: indeed I dont, Major, bless his poor heart! [Barbara kisses her; and she runs away merrily into the shelter. Bill writhes with an agonizing return of his new and alarming symptoms, but says nothing. Rummy Mitchens comes from the shelter.]

BARBARA

[going to meet Rummy] Now Rummy, bustle. Take in those mugs and plates to be washed; and throw the crumbs about for the birds.

[Rummy takes the three plates and mugs; but Shirley takes back his mug from her, as there is still some milk left in it.]

RUMMY

There aint any crumbs. This aint a time to waste good bread on birds.

PRICE

[appearing at the shelter door] Gentleman come to see the shelter, Major. Says he's your father.

BARBARA

All right. Coming. *[Snobby goes back into the shelter, followed by Barbara.]*

RUMMY

[stealing across to Bill and addressing him in a subdued voice, but with intense conviction] I'd av the lor of you, you flat eared pignosed potwalloper, if she'd let me. Youre no gentleman, to hit a lady in the face. *[Bill, with greater things moving in him, takes no notice.]*

SHIRLEY

[following her] Here! in with you and dont get yourself into more trouble by talking.

RUMMY

[with hauteur] I aint ad the pleasure o being hintroduced to you, as I can remember. *[She goes into the shelter with the plates.]*

SHIRLEY

Thats the—

BILL

[savagely] Downt you talk to me, d'ye eah? You lea me alown, or Aw'll do you a mischief. Aw'm not dirt under your feet, ennywy.

SHIRLEY

[calmly] Dont you be afeerd. You aint such prime company that you need expect to be sought after. *[He is about to go into the shelter when Barbara comes out, with Undershaft on her right.]*

BARBARA

Oh, there you are, Mr Shirley! *[Between them]* This is my father: I told you he was a Secularist, didnt I? Perhaps youll be able to comfort one another.

UNDERSHAFT

[startled] A Secularist! Not the least in the world: on the contrary, a confirmed mystic.

BARBARA

Sorry, I'm sure. By the way, papa, what is your religion? in case I have to introduce you again.

UNDERSHAFT

My religion? Well, my dear, I am a Millionaire. That is my religion.

BARBARA

Then I'm afraid you and Mr Shirley wont be able to comfort one another after all. Youre not a Millionaire, are you, Peter?

SHIRLEY

No; and proud of it.

UNDERSHAFT

[gravely] Poverty, my friend, is not a thing to be proud of.

SHIRLEY

[angrily] Who made your millions for you? Me and my like. Whats kep us poor? Keepin you rich. I wouldnt have your conscience, not for all your income.

UNDERSHAFT

I wouldnt have your income, not for all your conscience, Mr Shirley. *[He goes to the penthouse and sits down on a form.]*

BARBARA

[stopping Shirley adroitly as he is about to retort] You wouldnt think he was my father, would you, Peter? Will you go into the shelter and lend the lasses a hand for a while: we're worked off our feet.

SHIRLEY

[bitterly] Yes: I'm in their debt for a meal, aint I?

BARBARA

Oh, not because youre in their debt, but for love of them, Peter, for love of them. *[He cannot understand, and is rather scandalized.]* There! dont stare at me. In with you; and give that conscience of yours a holiday *[bustling him into the shelter.]*

SHIRLEY

[as he goes in] Ah! it's a pity you never was trained to use your reason, miss. Youd have been a very taking lecturer on Secularism.

[Barbara turns to her father.]

UNDERSHAFT

Never mind me, my dear. Go about your work; and let me watch it for a while.

BARBARA

All right.

UNDERSHAFT

For instance, whats the matter with that outpatient over there?

BARBARA

[looking at Bill, whose attitude has never changed, and whose expression of brooding wrath has deepened] Oh, we shall cure him in no time. Just watch. *[She goes over to Bill and waits. He glances up at her and casts his eyes down again, uneasy, but grimmer than ever.]* It would be nice to just stamp on Mog Habbijam's face, wouldnt it, Bill?

BILL

[starting up from the trough in consternation] It's a loy: Aw never said so. *[She shakes her head.]* Oo taold you wot was in moy mawnd?

BARBARA

Only your new friend.

BILL

Wot new friend?

BARBARA

The devil, Bill. When he gets round people they get miserable, just like you.

BILL

[with a heartbreaking attempt at devil-may-care cheerfulness] Aw aint miserable. *[He sits down again, and stretches his legs in an attempt to seem indifferent.]*

BARBARA

Well, if youre happy, why dont you look happy, as we do?

BILL

[his legs curling back in spite of him] Aw'm eppy enaff, Aw tell you. Woy cawnt you lea me alown? Wot ev I dan to you? Aw aint smashed your fice, ev Aw?

BARBARA

[softly: wooing his soul] It's not me thats getting at you, Bill.

BILL

Oo else is it?

BARBARA

Somebody that doesnt intend you to smash women's faces, I suppose. Somebody or something that wants to make a man of you.

BILL

[blustering] Mike a menn o me! Aint Aw a menn? eh? Oo sez Aw'm not a menn?

BARBARA

Theres a man in you somewhere, I suppose. But why did he let you hit poor little Jenny Hill? That wasn't very manly of him, was it?

BILL

[tormented] Ev dan wiv it, Aw tell you. Chack it. Aw'm sick o your Jenny Ill and er silly little fice.

BARBARA

Then why do you keep thinking about it? Why does it keep coming up against you in your mind? Youre not getting converted, are you?

BILL

[with conviction] Not ME. Not lawkly.

BARBARA

Thats right, Bill. Hold out against it. Put out your strength. Dont lets get you cheap. Todger Fairmile said he wrestled for three nights against his salvation harder than he ever wrestled with the Jap at the music hall. He gave in to the Jap when his arm was going to break. But he didnt give in to his salvation until his heart was going to break. Perhaps youll escape that. You havnt any heart, have you?

BILL

Wot d'ye mean? Woy aint Aw got a awt the sime as ennybody else?

BARBARA

A man with a heart wouldnt have bashed poor little Jenny's face, would he?

BILL

[almost crying] Ow, will you lea me alown? Ev Aw ever offered to meddle with you, that you cam neggin and provowkin me lawk this? *[He writhes convulsively from his eyes to his toes.]*

BARBARA

[with a steady soothing hand on his arm and a gentle voice that never lets him go] It's your soul thats hurting you, Bill, and not me. Weve been through it all ourselves. Come with us, Bill. *[He looks wildly round.]* To brave manhood on earth and eternal glory in heaven. *[He is on the point of breaking down.]* Come. *[A drum is heard in the shelter; and Bill, with a gasp, escapes from the spell as Barbara turns quickly. Adolphus enters from the shelter with a big drum.]* Oh! there you are, Dolly. Let me introduce a new friend of mine, Mr Bill Walker. This is my bloke, Bill: Mr. Cusins. *[Cusins salutes with his drumstick.]*

BILL

Gowin to merry im?

BARBARA

Yes.

BILL

[fervently] Gawd elp im! Gaw-aw-aw-awd elp im!

BARBARA

Why? Do you think he wont be happy with me?

BILL

Awve aony ed to stend it for a mawnin: e'll ev to stend it for a lawftawm.

CUSINS

That is a frightful reflection, Mr Walker. But I cant tear myself away from her.

BILL

Well, Aw ken. *[To Barbara]* Eah! do you knaow where Aw'm gowin to, and wot Aw'm gowin to do?

BARBARA

Yes: youre going to heaven; and youre coming back here before the week's out to tell me so.

BILL

You loy. Aw'm gowin to Kennintahn, to spit in Todger Fairmawl's eye. Aw beshed Jenny Ill's fice; an nar Aw'll git me aown fice beshed and cam beck and shaow it to er. Ee'll itt me ardern Aw itt her. Thatll mike us square *[To Adolphus]* Is thet fair or is it not? Youre a genlmn: you oughter knaow.

BARBARA

Two black eyes wont make one white one, Bill.

BILL

Aw didnt awst you. Cawnt you never keep your mahth shat? Oy awst the genlmn.

CUSINS

[reflectively] Yes: I think youre right, Mr Walker. Yes: I should do it. It's curious: it's exactly what an ancient Greek would have done.

BARBARA

But what good will it do?

CUSINS

Well, it will give Mr Fairmile some exercise; and it will satisfy Mr Walker's soul.

BILL

Rot! there aint nao sach a thing as a saoul. Ah kin you tell wevver Awve a saoul or not? You never seen it.

BARBARA

Ive seen it hurting you when you went against it.

BILL

[with compressed aggravation] If you was maw gel and took the word aht o me mahth lawk thet, Aw'd give you sathink youd feel urtin, Aw would. *[To Adolphus]* You tike maw tip, mite. Stop er jawr; or youll doy afoah your tawm *[With intense expression]* Wore aht: thets wot youll be: wore aht. *[He goes away through the gate.]*

CUSINS

[looking after him] I wonder!

BARBARA

Dolly! *[indignant, in her mother's manner]*

CUSINS

Yes, my dear, it's very wearing to be in love with you. If it lasts, I quite think I shall die young.

BARBARA

Should you mind?

CUSINS

Not at all. *[He is suddenly softened, and kisses her over the drum, evidently not for the first time, as people cannot kiss over a big drum without practice. Undershaft coughs.]*

BARBARA

It's all right, papa, weve not forgotten you. Dolly: explain the place to papa: I havnt time. *[She goes busily into the shelter.]*

> *[Undershaft and Adolphus now have the yard to themselves. Undershaft, seated on a form, and still keenly attentive, looks hard at Adolphus. Adolphus looks hard at him.]*

UNDERSHAFT

I fancy you guess something of what is in my mind, Mr Cusins. *[Cusins flourishes his drumsticks as if in the act of beating a lively rataplan, but makes no sound.]* Exactly so. But suppose Barbara finds you out!

CUSINS

You know, I do not admit that I am imposing on Barbara. I am quite genuinely interested in the views of the Salvation Army. The fact is, I am a sort of collector of religions; and the curious thing is that I find I can believe them all. By the way, have you any religion?

UNDERSHAFT

Yes.

CUSINS

Anything out of the common?

UNDERSHAFT

Only that there are two things necessary to Salvation.

CUSINS

[disappointed, but polite]Ah, the Church Catechism. Charles Lomax also belongs to the Established Church.

UNDERSHAFT

The two things are—

CUSINS

Baptism and—

UNDERSHAFT

No. Money and gunpowder.

CUSINS

[surprised, but interested] That is the general opinion of our governing classes. The novelty is in hearing any man confess it.

UNDERSHAFT

Just so.

CUSINS

Excuse me: is there any place in your religion for honor, justice, truth, love, mercy and so forth?

UNDERSHAFT

Yes: they are the graces and luxuries of a rich, strong, and safe life.

CUSINS

Suppose one is forced to choose between them and money or gunpowder?

UNDERSHAFT

Choose money and gunpowder; for without enough of both you cannot afford the others.

CUSINS

That is your religion?

UNDERSHAFT

Yes.

[The cadence of this reply makes a full close in the conversation, Cusins twists his face dubiously and contemplates Undershaft. Undershaft contemplates him.]

CUSINS

Barbara wont stand that. You will have to choose between your religion and Barbara.

UNDERSHAFT

So will you, my friend. She will find out that that drum of yours is hollow.

CUSINS

Father Undershaft: you are mistaken: I am a sincere Salvationist. You do not understand the Salvation Army. It is the army of joy, of love, of courage: it has banished the fear and remorse and despair of the old hell-ridden evangelical sects: it marches to fight the devil with trumpet and drum, with music and dancing, with banner and palm, as becomes a sally from heaven by its happy garrison. It picks the waster out of the public house and makes a man of him: it finds a worm wriggling in a back kitchen, and lo! a woman! Men and women of rank too, sons and daughters of the Highest. It takes the poor professor of Greek, the most artificial and self-suppressed of human creatures, from his meal of roots, and lets loose the rhapsodist in him; reveals the true worship of Dionysos to him; sends him down the public street drumming dithyrambs. [He plays a thundering flourish on the drum.]

UNDERSHAFT

You will alarm the shelter.

CUSINS

Oh, they are accustomed to these sudden ecstasies. However, if the drum worries you— [He pockets the drumsticks; unhooks the drum; and stands it on the ground opposite the gateway.]

UNDERSHAFT

Thank you.

CUSINS

You remember what Euripides says about your money and gunpowder.

UNDERSHAFT

No.

CUSINS

[declaiming]One and another
　　In money and guns may outpass his brother;
　　And men in their millions float and flow
　　And seethe with a million hopes as leaven;
　　And they win their will; or they miss their will;
　　And their hopes are dead or are pined for still;
　　　　But whoe'er can know
　　　　As the long days go
　　That to live is happy, has found his heaven.

My translation: what do you think of it?

UNDERSHAFT

I think, my friend, that if you wish to know, as the long days go, that to live is happy, you must first acquire money enough for a decent life, and power enough to be your own master.

CUSINS

You are damnably discouraging. *[He resumes his declamation.]*

> Is it so hard a thing to see
> That the spirit of God—whate'er it be—
> The law that abides and changes not, ages long,
> The Eternal and Nature-born: these things be
> strong?
> What else is Wisdom? What of Man's endeavor,
> Or God's high grace so lovely and so great?
> To stand from fear set free? to breathe and wait?
> To hold a hand uplifted over Fate?
> And shall not Barbara be loved for ever?

UNDERSHAFT

Euripides mentions Barbara, does he?

CUSINS

It is a fair translation. The word means Loveliness.

UNDERSHAFT

May I ask—as Barbara's father—how much a year she is to be loved for ever on?

CUSINS

As for Barbara's father, that is more your affair than mine. I can feed her by teaching Greek: that is about all.

UNDERSHAFT

Do you consider it a good match for her?

CUSINS

[with polite obstinacy] Mr Undershaft: I am in many ways a weak, timid, ineffectual person; and my health is far from satisfactory. But whenever I feel that I must have anything, I get it, sooner or later. I feel that way about Barbara. I dont like marriage: I feel intensely afraid of it; and I don't know what I shall do with Barbara or what she will do with me. But I feel that I and nobody else must marry her. Please regard that as settled.—Not that I wish to be arbitrary; but why should I waste your time in discussing what is inevitable?

UNDERSHAFT

You mean that you will stick at nothing: not even the conversion of the Salvation Army to the worship of Dionysos.

CUSINS

The business of the Salvation Army is to save, not to wrangle about the name of the pathfinder. Dionysos or another: what does it matter?

UNDERSHAFT

[rising and approaching him] Professor Cusins: you are a young man after my own heart.

CUSINS

Mr Undershaft: you are, as far as I am able to gather, a most infernal old rascal; but you appeal very strongly to my sense of ironic humor.

[Undershaft mutely offers his hand. They shake.]

UNDERSHAFT

[suddenly concentrating himself] And now to business.

CUSINS

Pardon me. We are discussing religion. Why go back to such an uninteresting and unimportant subject as business?

UNDERSHAFT

Religion is our business at present, because it is through religion alone that we can win Barbara.

CUSINS

Have you, too, fallen in love with Barbara?

UNDERSHAFT

Yes, with a father's love.

CUSINS

A father's love for a grown-up daughter is the most dangerous of all infatuations. I apologize for mentioning my own pale, coy, mistrustful fancy in the same breath with it.

UNDERSHAFT

Keep to the point. We have to win her; and we are neither of us Methodists.

CUSINS

That doesnt matter. The power Barbara wields here—the power that wields Barbara herself—is not Calvinism, not Presbyterianism, not Methodism—

UNDERSHAFT

Not Greek Paganism either, eh?

CUSINS

I admit that. Barbara is quite original in her religion.

UNDERSHAFT

[triumphantly] Aha! Barbara Undershaft would be. Her inspiration comes from within herself.

CUSINS

How do you suppose it got there?

UNDERSHAFT

[in towering excitement]It is the Undershaft inheritance. I shall hand on my torch to my daughter. She shall make my converts and preach my gospel—

CUSINS

What! Money and gunpowder!

UNDERSHAFT

Yes, money and gunpowder. Freedom and power. Command of life and command of death.

CUSINS

[urbanely: trying to bring him down to earth]This is extremely interesting, Mr Undershaft. Of course you know that you are mad.

UNDERSHAFT

[with redoubled force] And you?

CUSINS

Oh, mad as a hatter. You are welcome to my secret since I have discovered yours. But I am astonished. Can a madman make cannons?

UNDERSHAFT

Would anyone else than a madman make them? And now [with surging energy] question for question. Can a sane man translate Euripides?

CUSINS

No.

UNDERSHAFT

[seizing him by the shoulder] Can a sane woman make a man of a waster or a woman of a worm?

CUSINS

[reeling before the storm] Father Colossus—Mammoth Millionaire—

UNDERSHAFT

[pressing him] Are there two mad people or three in this Salvation shelter today?

CUSINS

You mean Barbara is as mad as we are?

UNDERSHAFT

[pushing him lightly off and resuming his equanimity suddenly and completely] Pooh, Professor! let us call things by their proper names. I am a millionaire; you are a poet; Barbara is a savior of souls. What have we three to do with the common mob of slaves and idolators? [He sits down again with a shrug of contempt for the mob.]

CUSINS

Take care! Barbara is in love with the common people. So am I. Have you never felt the romance of that love?

UNDERSHAFT

[cold and sardonic] Have you ever been in love with Poverty, like St Francis? Have you ever been in love with Dirt, like St Simeon! Have you ever been in love with disease and suffering, like our nurses and philanthropists? Such passions are not virtues, but the most unnatural of all the vices. This love of the common people may please an earl's granddaughter and a university professor; but I have been a common man and a poor man; and it has no romance for me. Leave it to the poor to pretend that poverty is a blessing: leave it to the coward to make a religion of his cowardice by preaching humility: we know better than that. We three must stand together above the common people: how else can we help their children to climb up beside us? Barbara must belong to us, not to the Salvation Army.

CUSINS

Well, I can only say that if you think you will get her away from the Salvation Army by talking to her as you have been talking to me, you dont know Barbara.

UNDERSHAFT

My friend: I never ask for what I can buy.

CUSINS

[in a white fury] Do I understand you to imply that you can buy Barbara?

UNDERSHAFT

No; but I can buy the Salvation Army.

CUSINS

Quite impossible.

UNDERSHAFT

You shall see. All religious organizations exist by selling themselves to the rich.

CUSINS

Not the Army. That is the Church of the poor.

UNDERSHAFT

All the more reason for buying it.

CUSINS

I dont think you quite know what the Army does for the poor.

UNDERSHAFT
Oh yes I do. It draws their teeth: that is enough for me as a man of business.

CUSINS
Nonsense! It makes them sober—

UNDERSHAFT
I prefer sober workmen. The profits are larger.

CUSINS
—honest—

UNDERSHAFT
Honest workmen are the most economical.

CUSINS
—attached to their homes—

UNDERSHAFT
So much the better: they will put up with anything sooner than change their shop.

CUSINS
—happy—

UNDERSHAFT
An invaluable safeguard against revolution.

CUSINS
—unselfish—

UNDERSHAFT
Indifferent to their own interests, which suits me exactly.

CUSINS
—with their thoughts on heavenly things—

UNDERSHAFT
[rising] And not on Trade Unionism nor Socialism. Excellent.

CUSINS
[revolted] You really are an infernal old rascal.

UNDERSHAFT
[indicating Peter Shirley, who has just come from the shelter and strolled dejectedly down the yard between them] And this is an honest man!

SHIRLEY
Yes; and what av I got by it? [He passes on bitterly and sits on the form, in the corner of the penthouse.]

[Snobby Price, beaming sanctimoniously, and Jenny Hill, with a tambourine full of coppers, come from the shelter and go to the drum, on which Jenny begins to count the money.]

UNDERSHAFT
[replying to Shirley] Oh, your employers must have got a good deal by it from first to last. [He sits on the table, with one foot on the side form, Cusins, overwhelmed, sits down on the same form nearer the shelter. Barbara comes from the shelter to the middle of the yard. She is excited and a little overwrought.]

BARBARA
Weve just had a splendid experience meeting at the other gate in Cripps's lane. Ive hardly ever seen them so much moved as they were by your confession, Mr Price.

PRICE
I could almost be glad of my past wickedness if I could believe that it would elp to keep hathers stright.

BARBARA
So it will, Snobby. How much, Jenny?

JENNY
Four and tenpence, Major.

BARBARA
Oh Snobby, if you had given your poor mother just one more kick, we should have got the whole five shillings!

PRICE
If she heard you say that, miss, she'd be sorry I didnt. But I'm glad. Oh what a joy it will be to her when she hears I'm saved!

UNDERSHAFT
Shall I contribute the odd twopence, Barbara? The millionaire's mite, eh? [He takes a couple of pennies from his pocket.]

BARBARA
How did you make that twopence?

UNDERSHAFT
As usual. By selling cannons, torpedoes, submarines, and my new patent Grand Duke hand grenade.

BARBARA
Put it back in your pocket. You cant buy your salvation here for twopence: you must work it out.

UNDERSHAFT

Is twopence not enough? I can afford a little more, if you press me.

BARBARA

Two million millions would not be enough. There is bad blood on your hands; and nothing but good blood can cleanse them. Money is no use. Take it away. [She turns to Cusins.] Dolly: you must write another letter for me to the papers. [He makes a wry face.] Yes: I know you dont like it; but it must be done. The starvation this winter is beating us: everybody is unemployed. The General says we must close this shelter if we cant get more money. I force the collections at the meetings until I am ashamed: dont I, Snobby?

PRICE

It's a fair treat to see you work it, miss. The way you got them up from three-and-six to four-and-ten with that hymn, penny by penny and verse by verse, was a caution. Not a Cheap Jack on Mile End Waste could touch you at it.

BARBARA

Yes; but I wish we could do without it. I am getting at last to think more of the collection than of the people's souls. And what are those hatfuls of pence and halfpence? We want thousands! tens of thousands! hundreds of thousands! I want to convert people, not to be always begging for the Army in a way I'd die sooner than beg for myself.

UNDERSHAFT

[in profound irony] Genuine unselfishness is capable of anything, my dear.

BARBARA

[unsuspectingly, as she turns away to take the money from the drum and put it in a cash bag she carries] Yes, isn't it? [Undershaft looks sardonically at Cusins.]

CUSINS

[aside to Undershaft] Mephistopheles! Machiavelli!

BARBARA

[tears coming into her eyes as she ties the bag and pockets it] How are we to feed them? I cant talk religion to a man with bodily hunger in his eyes. [Almost breaking down] It's frightful.

JENNY

[running to her] Major, dear—

BARBARA

[rebounding] No: dont comfort me. It will be all right. We shall get the money.

UNDERSHAFT

How?

JENNY

By praying for it, of course. Mrs Baines says she prayed for it last night; and she has never prayed for it in vain: never once. [She goes to the gate and looks out into the street.]

BARBARA

[who has dried her eyes and regained her composure] By the way, dad, Mrs Baines has come to march with us to our big meeting this afternoon; and she is very anxious to meet you, for some reason or other. Perhaps she'll convert you.

UNDERSHAFT

I shall be delighted, my dear.

JENNY

[at the gate: excitedly] Major! Major! heres that man back again.

BARBARA

What man?

JENNY

The man that hit me. Oh, I hope he's coming back to join us.

[Bill Walker, with frost on his jacket, comes through the gate, his hands deep in his pockets and his chin sunk between his shoulders, like a cleaned-out gambler. He halts between Barbara and the drum.]

BARBARA

Hullo, Bill! Back already!

BILL

[nagging at her] Bin talkin ever sence, ev you?

BARBARA

Pretty nearly. Well, has Todger paid you out for poor Jenny's jaw?

BILL

Nao e aint.

BARBARA

I thought your jacket looked a bit snowy.

BILL

Sao it is snaowy. You want to knaow where the snaow cam from, downt you?

BARBARA

Yes.

BILL

Well, it cam from orf the grahnd in Pawkinses Corner in Kennintahn. It got rabbed orf be maw shaoulders: see?

BARBARA

Pity you didnt rub some off with your knees, Bill! That would have done you a lot of good.

BILL

[with sour mirthless humor] Aw was sivin another menn's knees at the tawm. E was kneelin on moy ed, e was.

JENNY

Who was kneeling on your head?

BILL

Todger was. E was pryin for me: pryin camfortable wiv me as a cawpet. Sow was Mog. Sao was the aol bloomin meetin. Mog she sez 'Ow Lawd brike is stabborn sperrit; bat downt urt is dear art.' Thet was wot she said. 'Downt urt is dear art'! An er blowk—thirteen stun four!—kneelin wiv all is wight on me. Fanny, aint it?

JENNY

Oh no, We're so sorry, Mr Walker.

BARBARA

[enjoying it frankly] Nonsense! of course it's funny. Served you right, Bill! You must have done something to him first.

BILL

[doggedly] Aw did wot Aw said Aw'd do. Aw spit in is eye. E looks ap at the skoy and sez, 'Ow that Aw should be fahnd worthy to be spit upon for the gospel's sike!' e sez; an Mog sez 'Glaory Allelloolier!'; an then e called me Braddher, an dahned me as if Aw was a kid and e was me mather worshin me a Setterda nawt. Aw ednt jast nao shaow wiv im at all. Arf the street pryed; an the tather arf larfed fit to split theirselves. [To Barbara] There! are you settisfawed nah?

BARBARA

[her eyes dancing] Wish I'd been there, Bill.

BILL

Yus: youd a got in a hextra bit o talk on me, wouldnt you?

JENNY

I'm so sorry, Mr Walker.

BILL

[fiercely]Downt you gow bein sorry for me: youve no call. Listen eah. Aw browk your jawr.

JENNY

No, it didnt hurt me: indeed it didnt, except for a moment. It was only that I was frightened.

BILL

Aw downt want to be forgive be you, or be ennybody. Wot Aw did Aw'll py for. Aw trawd to gat me aown jawr browk to settisfaw you—

JENNY

[distressed] Oh no—

BILL

[impatiently] Tell y' Aw did: cawnt you listen to wots bein taold you? All Aw got be it was bein mide a sawt of in the pablic street for me pines. Well, if Aw cawnt settisfaw you one wy, Aw ken anather. Listen eah! Aw ed two quid[5] sived agen the frost; an Awve a pahnd of it left. A mite o mawn last week ed words with the judy e's gowin to merry. E give er wot-for; an e's bin fawnd fifteen bob.[6] E ed a rawt to itt er cause they was gowin to be merrid; but Aw ednt nao rawt to itt you; sao put anather fawv bob on an call it a pahnd's worth. [He produces a sovereign.][7] Eahs the manney. Tike it; and lets ev no more o your forgivin an prying and your Mijor jawrin me. Let wot Aw dan be dan an pide for; and let there be a end of it.

JENNY

Oh, I couldnt take it, Mr Walker. But if you would give a shilling or two to poor Rummy Mitchens! you really did hurt her; and she's old.

BILL

[contemptuously] Not lawkly. Aw'd give her anather as soon as look at er. Let her ev the lawr o me as she threatened! She aint forgiven me: not mach. Wot Aw dan to er is not on me mawnd—wot she [indicating Barbara] mawt call on me conscience—no more than stickin a pig. It's this Christian gime o yours that Aw wownt ev plyed agen me: this bloomin forgivin an neggin an jawrin that mikes a menn thet sore that iz lawf's a burdn to im. Aw wownt ev it, Aw tell you; sao

---

[5]A quid is a one-pound note in English currency.

[6]A bob is a shilling, 1/20th of a pound in old English currency.

[7]A sovereign is a gold coin worth one pound.

tike your manney and stop thraowin your silly
beshed fice hap agen me.

JENNY

Major: may I take a little of it for the Army?

BARBARA

No: the Army is not to be bought. We want your soul,
Bill; and we'll take nothing less.

BILL

[bitterly] Aw knaow. Me an maw few shillins is not
good enaff for you. Youre a earl's grendorter, you are.
Nathink less than a anderd pahnd for you.

UNDERSHAFT

Come, Barbara! you could do a great deal of good
with a hundred pounds. If you will set this gentleman's mind at ease by taking his pound, I will give the
other ninety-nine.

[Bill, dazed by such opulence, instinctively touches
his cap.]

BARBARA

Oh, youre too extravagant, papa. Bill offers twenty
pieces of silver. All you need offer is the other ten.[8]
That will make the standard price to buy anybody
who's for sale. I'm not; and the Army's not. [To Bill]
Youll never have another quiet moment, Bill, until
you come round to us. You cant stand out against
your salvation.

BILL

[sullenly] Aw cawnt stend aht agen music awl wras-
tlers and awful tangued women. Awve offered to py.
Aw can do no more. Tike it or leave it. There it is. [He
throws the sovereign on the drum, and sits down on the
horse-trough. The coin fascinates Snobby Price, who
takes an early opportunity of dropping his cap on it.]

[Mrs Baines comes from the shelter. She is dressed as a
Salvation Army Commissioner. She is an earnest
looking woman of about 40, with a caressing, urgent
voice, and an appealing manner.]

BARBARA

This is my father, Mrs Baines. [Undershaft comes from
the table, taking his hat off with marked civility.] Try
what you can do with him. He wont listen to me, because he remembers what a fool I was when I was a
baby. [She leaves them together and chats with Jenny.]

---

[8] The reference is to Jesus, who was betrayed by Judas for thirty
pieces of silver.

MRS BAINES

Have you been shewn over the shelter, Mr Undershaft? You know the work we're doing, of course.

UNDERSHAFT

[very civilly] The whole nation knows it, Mrs Baines.

MRS BAINES

No, sir: the whole nation does not know it, or we
should not be crippled as we are for want of money
to carry our work through the length and breadth of
the land. Let me tell you that there would have been
rioting this winter in London but for us.

UNDERSHAFT

You really think so?

MRS BAINES

I know it. I remember 1886, when you rich gentlemen hardened your hearts against the cry of the poor.
They broke the windows of your clubs in Pall Mall.

UNDERSHAFT

[gleaming with approval of their method] And the Man-
sion House Fund went up next day from thirty thousand pounds to seventy-nine thousand! I remember
quite well.

MRS BAINES

Well, wont you help me to get at the people? They
wont break windows then. Come here, Price. Let me
shew you to this gentleman. [Price comes to be in-
spected.] Do you remember the window breaking?

PRICE

My old father thought it was the revolution, maam.

MRS BAINES

Would you break windows now?

PRICE

Oh no, maam. The windows of eaven av bin opened
to me. I know now that the rich man is a sinner like
myself.

RUMMY

[appearing above at the loft door] Snobby Price!

SNOBBY

Wot is it?

RUMMY

Your mother's askin for you at the other gate in
Cripps's Lane. She's heard about your confession.
[Price turns pale.]

MRS BAINES

Go, Mr Price; and pray with her.

JENNY
You can go through the shelter, Snobby.

PRICE
[to Mrs. Baines] I couldnt face her now, maam, with all the weight of my sins fresh on me. Tell her she'll find her son at ome, waitin for her in prayer. [He skulks off through the gate, incidentally stealing the sovereign on his way out by picking up his cap from the drum.]

MRS BAINES
[with swimming eyes] You see how we take the anger and the bitterness against you out of their hearts, Mr Undershaft.

UNDERSHAFT
It is certainly most convenient and gratifying to all large employers of labor, Mrs Baines.

MRS BAINES
Barbara: Jenny: I have good news: most wonderful news. [Jenny runs to her.] My prayers have been answered. I told you they would, Jenny, didnt I?

JENNY
Yes, yes.

BARBARA
[moving nearer to the drum] Have we got money enough to keep the shelter open?

MRS BAINES
I hope we shall have enough to keep all the shelters open. Lord Saxmundham has promised us five thousand pounds—

BARBARA
Hooray!

JENNY
Glory!

MRS BAINES
—if—

BARBARA
'If!' If what?

MRS BAINES
—if five other gentlemen will give a thousand each to make it up to ten thousand.

BARBARA
Who is Lord Saxmundham? I never heard of him.

UNDERSHAFT
[who has pricked up his ears at the peer's name, and is now watching Barbara curiously] A new creation, my dear. You have heard of Sir Horace Bodger?

BARBARA
Bodger! Do you mean the distiller? Bodger's whisky!

UNDERSHAFT
That is the man. He is one of the greatest of our public benefactors. He restored the cathedral at Hakington. They made him a baronet for that. He gave half a million to the funds of his party: they made him a baron for that.

SHIRLEY
What will they give him for the five thousand?

UNDERSHAFT
There is nothing left to give him. So the five thousand, I should think, is to save his soul.

MRS BAINES
Heaven grant it may! Oh Mr Undershaft, you have some very rich friends. Cant you help us towards the other five thousand? We are going to hold a great meeting this afternoon at the Assembly Hall in the Mile End Road. If I could only announce that one gentleman had come forward to support Lord Saxmundham, others would follow. Dont you know somebody? couldnt you? wouldnt you? [Her eyes fill with tears.] oh, think of those poor people, Mr Undershaft: think of how much it means to them, and how little to a great man like you.

UNDERSHAFT
[sardonically gallant] Mrs Baines: you are irresistible. I cant disappoint you; and I cant deny myself the satisfaction of making Bodger pay up. You shall have your five thousand pounds.

MRS BAINES
Thank God!

UNDERSHAFT
You dont thank me?

MRS BAINES
Oh sir, dont try to be cynical: dont be ashamed of being a good man. The Lord will bless you abundantly; and our prayers will be like a strong fortification round you all the days of your life. [With a touch of caution] You will let me have the cheque to shew at the meeting, wont you? Jenny: go in and fetch a pen and ink. [Jenny runs to the shelter door.]

UNDERSHAFT

Do not disturb Miss Hill: I have a fountain pen. *[Jenny halts. He sits at the table and writes the cheque. Cusins rises to make room for him. They all watch him silently.]*

BILL

[cynically, aside to Barbara, his voice and accent horribly debased] Wot prawce selvytion nah?

BARBARA

Stop. *[Undershaft stops writing: they all turn to her in surprise.]* Mrs Baines: are you really going to take this money?

MRS BAINES

[astonished] Why not, dear?

BARBARA

Why not! Do you know what my father is? Have you forgotten that Lord Saxmundham is Bodger the whisky man? Do you remember how we implored the County Council to stop him from writing Bodger's Whisky in letters of fire against the sky; so that the poor drink-ruined creatures on the Embankment could not wake up from their snatches of sleep without being reminded of their deadly thirst by that wicked sky sign? Do you know that the worst thing I have had to fight here is not the devil, but Bodger, Bodger, Bodger, with his whisky, his distilleries, and his tied houses?[9] Are you going to make our shelter another tied house for him, and ask me to keep it?

BILL

Rotten dranken whisky it is too.

MRS BAINES

Dear Barbara: Lord Saxmundham has a soul to be saved like any of us. If heaven has found the way to make a good use of his money, are we to set ourselves up against the answer to our prayers?

BARBARA

I know he has a soul to be saved. Let him come down here; and I'll do my best to help him to his salvation. But he wants to send his cheque down to buy us, and go on being as wicked as ever.

UNDERSHAFT

[with a reasonableness which Cusins alone perceives to be ironical] My dear Barbara: alcohol is a very necessary article. It heals the sick—

BARBARA

It does nothing of the sort.

UNDERSHAFT

Well, it assists the doctor: that is perhaps a less questionable way of putting it. It makes life bearable to millions of people who could not endure their existence if they were quite sober. It enables Parliament to do things at eleven at night that no sane person would do at eleven in the morning. Is it Bodger's fault that this inestimable gift is deplorably abused by less than one per cent of the poor? *[He turns again to the table; signs the cheque; and crosses it.]*

MRS BAINES

Barbara: will there be less drinking or more if all those poor souls we are saving come tomorrow and find the doors of our shelters shut in their faces? Lord Saxmundham gives us the money to stop drinking— to take his own business from him.

CUSINS

[impishly] Pure self-sacrifice on Bodger's part, clearly! Bless dear Bodger! *[Barbara almost breaks down as Adolphus, too, fails her.]*

UNDERSHAFT

[tearing out the cheque and pocketing the book as he rises and goes past Cusins to Mrs Baines] I also, Mrs Baines, may claim a little disinterestedness. Think of my business! think of the widows and orphans! the men and lads torn to pieces with shrapnel and poisoned with lyddite![10] *[Mrs Baines shrinks; but he goes on remorselessly.]* the oceans of blood, not one drop of which is shed in a really just cause! the ravaged crops! the peaceful peasants forced, women and men, to till their fields under the fire of opposing armies on pain of starvation! the bad blood of the fierce little cowards at home who egg on others to fight for the gratification of their national vanity! All this makes money for me: I am never richer, never busier than when the papers are full of it. Well, it is your work to preach peace on earth and good will to men. *[Mrs Baines's face lights up again.]* Every convert you make is a vote against

---

[9]Taverns that, by ties with a distiller, sell only "house brand" whisky.

[10]An explosive.

war. [Her lips move in prayer.] Yet I give you this money to help you to hasten my own commercial ruin. [He gives her the cheque.]

CUSINS

[mounting the form in an ecstasy of mischief] The millennium will be inaugurated by the unselfishness of Undershaft and Bodger. Oh be joyful! [He takes the drum-sticks from his pocket and flourishes them.]

MRS BAINES

[taking the cheque] The longer I live the more proof I see that there is an Infinite Goodness that turns everything to the work of salvation sooner or later. Who would have thought that any good could have come out of war and drink? And yet their profits are brought today to the feet of salvation to do its blessed work. [She is affected to tears.]

JENNY

[running to Mrs Baines and throwing her arms round her] Oh dear! how blessed, how glorious it all is!

CUSINS

[in a convulsion of irony] Let us seize this unspeakable moment. Let us march to the great meeting at once. Excuse me just an instant. [He rushes into the shelter. Jenny takes her tambourine from the drum head.]

MRS BAINES

Mr Undershaft: have you ever seen a thousand people fall on their knees with one impulse and pray? Come with us to the meeting. Barbara shall tell them that the Army is saved, and saved through you.

CUSINS

[returning impetuously from the shelter with a flag and a trombone, and coming between Mrs Baines and Undershaft] You shall carry the flag down the first street, Mrs Baines. [He gives her the flag.] Mr Undershaft is a gifted trombonist: he shall intone an Olympian diapason to the West Ham Salvation March. [Aside to Undershaft, as he forces the trombone on him] Blow, Machiavelli, blow.

UNDERSHAFT

[aside to him, as he takes the trombone] The trumpet in Zion! [Cusins rushes to the drum, which he takes up and puts on. Undershaft continues, aloud.] I will do my best. I could vamp a bass if I knew the tune.

CUSINS

It is a wedding chorus from one of Donizetti's operas; but we have converted it. We convert everything to good here, including Bodger. You remember the chorus. 'For thee immense rejoicing—immenso giubilo—immenso giubilo.' [With drum obbligato] Rum tum ti tum tum, tum tum ti ta—

BARBARA

Dolly: you are breaking my heart.

CUSINS

What is a broken heart more or less here? Dionysos Undershaft has descended. I am possessed.

MRS BAINES

Come, Barbara: I must have my dear Major to carry the flag with me.

JENNY

Yes, yes, Major darling.

CUSINS

[snatches the tambourine out of Jenny's hand and mutely offers it to Barbara]

BARBARA

[coming forward a little as she puts the offer behind her with a shudder, whilst Cusins recklessly tosses the tambourine back to Jenny and goes to the gate] I cant come.

JENNY

Not come!

MRS BAINES

[with tears in her eyes] Barbara: do you think I am wrong to take the money?

BARBARA

[impulsively going to her and kissing her] No, no: God help you, dear, you must: you are saving the Army. Go; and may you have a great meeting!

JENNY

But arnt you coming?

BARBARA

No. [She begins taking off the silver S brooch from her collar.]

MRS BAINES

Barbara: what are you doing?

JENNY

Why are you taking your badge off? You cant be going to leave us, Major.

BARBARA

[quietly] Father: come here.

UNDERSHAFT

[coming to her] My dear! [Seeing that she is going to pin the badge on his collar, he retreats to the penthouse in some alarm.]

BARBARA

[following him] Dont be frightened. [She pins the badge on and steps back towards the table, shewing him to the others.] There! It's not much for £5000, is it?

MRS BAINES

Barbara: if you wont come and pray with us, promise me you will pray for us.

BARBARA

I cant pray now. Perhaps I shall never pray again.

MRS BAINES

Barbara!

JENNY

Major!

BARBARA

[almost delirious] I cant bear any more. Quick march!

CUSINS

[calling to the procession in the street outside] Off we go. Play up, there! Immenso giubilo. [He gives the time with his drum; and the band strikes up the march, which rapidly becomes more distant as the procession moves briskly away.]

MRS BAINES

I must go, dear. Youre overworked: you will be all right tomorrow. We'll never lose you. Now Jenny: step out with the old flag. Blood and Fire! [She marches out through the gate with her flag.]

JENNY

Glory Hallelujah! [flourishing her tambourine and marching]

UNDERSHAFT

[to Cusins, as he marches out past him easing the slide of his trombone] 'My ducats and my daughter'!

CUSINS

[following him out] Money and gunpowder!

BARBARA

Drunkenness and Murder! My God: why hast thou forsaken me?

[She sinks on the form with her face buried in her hands. The march passes away into silence. Bill Walker steals across to her.]

BILL

[taunting] Wot prawce selvytion nah?

SHIRLEY

Dont you hit her when she's down.

BILL

She itt me wen aw wiz dahn. Waw shouldnt Aw git a bit o me aown beck?

BARBARA

[raising her head] I didnt take your money, Bill. [She crosses the yard to the gate and turns her back on the two men to hide her face from them.]

BILL

[sneering after her] Naow, it warnt enaff for you. [Turning to the drum, he misses the money.] Ellow! If you aint took it sammun else ez. Weres it gorn? Bly me if Jenny Ill didnt tike it arter all!

RUMMY

[screaming at him from the loft] You lie, you dirty blackguard! Snobby Price pinched it off the drum when he took up his cap. I was up here all the time an see im do it.

BILL

Wot! Stowl maw manney! Waw didnt you call thief on him, you silly aold macker you?

RUMMY

To serve you aht for ittin me acrost the fice. It's cost y'pahnd, that az. [Raising a pæan of squalid triumph] I done you. I'm even with you. Uve ad it aht o y— [Bill snatches up Shirley's mug and hurls it at her. She slams the loft door and vanishes. The mug smashes against the door and falls in fragments.]

BILL

[beginning to chuckle] Tell us, aol menn, wot o'clock this mawnin was it wen im as they call Snobby Prawce was sived?

BARBARA

[turning to him more composedly, and with unspoiled sweetness] About half past twelve, Bill. And he pinched your pound at a quarter to two. I know. Well, you cant afford to lose it. I'll send it to you.

BILL

[his voice and accent suddenly improving] Not if Aw wiz to stawve for it. Aw aint to be bought.

SHIRLEY

Aint you? Youd sell yourself to the devil for a pint o beer; only there aint no devil to make the offer.

BILL

[unashamed] Sao Aw would, mite, and often ev, cheerful. But she cawnt baw me. [Approaching Barbara] You wanted maw saoul, did you? Well, you aint got it.

BARBARA

I nearly got it, Bill. But weve sold it back to you for ten thousand pounds.

SHIRLEY

And dear at the money!

BARBARA

No, Peter: it was worth more than money.

BILL

[salvationproof] It's nao good: you cawnt get rahnd me nah. Aw downt blieve in it; and Awve seen tody that Aw was rawt. [Going] Sao long, aol soupkitchener! Ta, ta, Mijor Earl's Grendorter! [Turning at the gate] Wot prawce selvytion nah? Snobby Prawce! Ha! ha!

BARBARA

[offering her hand] Goodbye, Bill.

BILL

[taken aback, half plucks his cap off; then shoves it on again defiantly] Git aht. [Barbara drops her hand, discouraged. He has a twinge of remorse.] But thets aw rawt, you knaow. Nathink pasnl. Naow mellice. Sao long, Judy. [He goes.]

BARBARA

No malice. So long, Bill.

SHIRLEY

[shaking his head] You make too much of him, miss, in your innocence.

BARBARA

[going to him] Peter: I'm like you now. Cleaned out, and lost my job.

SHIRLEY

Youve youth an hope. Thats two better than me.

BARBARA

I'll get you a job, Peter. Thats hope for you: the youth will have to be enough for me. [She counts her money.] I have just enough left for two teas at Lockharts, a Rowton doss[11] for you, and my tram and bus home.

[11] Bed.

[He frowns and rises with offended pride. She takes his arm.] Dont be proud, Peter: it's sharing between friends. And promise me youll talk to me and not let me cry. [She draws him towards the gate.]

SHIRLEY

Well, I'm not accustomed to talk to the like of you—

BARBARA

[urgently] Yes, yes: you must talk to me. Tell me about Tom Paine's books and Bradlaugh's lectures. Come along.

SHIRLEY

Ah, if you would only read Tom Paine in the proper spirit, miss! [They go out through the gate together.]

──────── **ACT THREE** ────────

Next day after lunch Lady Britomart is writing in the library in Wilton Crescent. Sarah is reading in the armchair near the window. Barbara, in ordinary fashionable dress, pale and brooding, is on the settee. Charles Lomax enters. He starts on seeing Barbara fashionably attired and in low spirits.

LOMAX

Youve left off your uniform!

[Barbara says nothing; but an expression of pain passes over her face.]

LADY BRITOMART

[warning him in low tones to be careful]Charles!

LOMAX

[much concerned, coming behind the settee and bending sympathetically over Barbara] I'm awfully sorry, Barbara. You know I helped you all I could with the concertina and so forth. [Momentously] Still, I have never shut my eyes to the fact that there is a certain amount of tosh about the Salvation Army. Now the claims of the Church of England—

LADY BRITOMART

Thats enough, Charles. Speak of something suited to your mental capacity.

LOMAX

But surely the Church of England is suited to all our capacities.

BARBARA

[pressing his hand] Thank you for your sympathy, Cholly. Now go and spoon with Sarah.

LOMAX

[dragging a chair from the writing table and seating himself affectionately by Sarah's side] How is my ownest today?

SARAH

I wish you wouldnt tell Cholly to do things, Barbara. He always comes straight and does them. Cholly: we're going to the works this afternoon.

LOMAX

What works?

SARAH

The cannon works.

LOMAX

What? your governor's shop!

SARAH

Yes.

LOMAX

Oh I say!

[Cusins enters in poor condition. He also starts visibly when he sees Barbara without her uniform.]

BARBARA

I expected you this morning, Dolly. Didnt you guess that?

CUSINS

[sitting down beside her] I'm sorry. I have only just breakfasted.

SARAH

But weve just finished lunch.

BARBARA

Have you had one of your bad nights?

CUSINS

No: I had rather a good night: in fact, one of the most remarkable nights I have ever passed.

BARBARA

The meeting?

CUSINS

No: after the meeting.

LADY BRITOMART

You should have gone to bed after the meeting. What were you doing?

CUSINS

Drinking.

LADY BRITOMART		Adolphus!
SARAH	} {	Dolly!
BARBARA		Dolly!
LOMAX		Oh I say!

LADY BRITOMART

What were you drinking, may I ask?

CUSINS

A most devilish kind of Spanish burgundy, warranted free from added alcohol: a Temperance burgundy in fact. Its richness in natural alcohol made any addition superfluous.

BARBARA

Are you joking, Dolly?

CUSINS

[patiently] No. I have been making a night of it with the nominal head of this household: that is all.

LADY BRITOMART

Andrew made you drunk!

CUSINS

No: he only provided the wine. I think it was Dionysos who made me drunk. [To Barbara] I told you I was possessed.

LADY BRITOMART

Youre not sober yet. Go home to bed at once.

CUSINS

I have never before ventured to reproach you, Lady Brit; but how could you marry the Prince of Darkness?

LADY BRITOMART

It was much more excusable to marry him than to get drunk with him. That is a new accomplishment of Andrew's, by the way. He usent to drink.

CUSINS

He doesnt now. He only sat there and completed the wreck of my moral basis, the rout of my convictions, the purchase of my soul. He cares for you, Barbara. That is what makes him so dangerous to me.

BARBARA

That has nothing to do with it, Dolly. There are larger loves and diviner dreams than the fireside ones. You know that, dont you?

CUSINS

Yes: that is our understanding. I know it. I hold to it. Unless he can win me on that holier ground he may amuse me for a while; but he can get no deeper hold, strong as he is.

BARBARA

Keep to that; and the end will be right. Now tell me what happened at the meeting?

CUSINS

It was an amazing meeting. Mrs Baines almost died of emotion. Jenny Hill simply gibbered with hysteria. The Prince of Darkness played his trombone like a madman: its brazen roarings were like the laughter of the damned. 117 conversions took place then and there. They prayed with the most touching sincerity and gratitude for Bodger, and for the anonymous donor of the £5000. Your father would not let his name be given.

LOMAX

That was rather fine of the old man, you know. Most chaps would have wanted the advertisement.

CUSINS

He said all the charitable institutions would be down on him like kites on a battle-field if he gave his name.

LADY BRITOMART

Thats Andrew all over. He never does a proper thing without giving an improper reason for it.

CUSINS

He convinced me that I have all my life been doing improper things for proper reasons.

LADY BRITOMART

Adolphus: now that Barbara has left the Salvation Army, you had better leave it too. I will not have you playing that drum in the streets.

CUSINS

Your orders are already obeyed, Lady Brit.

BARBARA

Dolly: were you ever really in earnest about it? Would you have joined if you had never seen me?

CUSINS

[disingenuously] Well—er—well, possibly, as a collector of religions—

LOMAX

[cunningly] Not as a drummer, though, you know. You are a very clearheaded brainy chap, Dolly; and it must have been apparent to you that there is a certain amount of tosh about—

LADY BRITOMART

Charles: if you must drivel, drivel like a grown-up man and not like a schoolboy.

LOMAX

[out of countenance] Well, drivel is drivel, dont you know, whatever a man's age.

LADY BRITOMART

In good society in England, Charles, men drivel at all ages by repeating silly formulas with an air of wisdom. Schoolboys make their own formulas out of slang, like you. When they reach your age, and get political private secretaryships and things of that sort, they drop slang and get their formulas out of the Spectator or The Times. You had better confine yourself to The Times. You will find that there is a certain amount of tosh about The Times; but at least its language is reputable.

LOMAX

[overwhelmed] You are so awfully strong-minded, Lady Brit—

LADY BRITOMART

Rubbish! [Morrison comes in.] What is it?

MORRISON

If you please, my lady, Mr Undershaft has just drove up to the door.

LADY BRITOMART

Well, let him in. [Morrison hesitates.] Whats the matter with you?

MORRISON

Shall I announce him, my lady; or is he at home here, so to speak, my lady?

LADY BRITOMART

Announce him.

MORRISON

Thank you, my lady. You wont mind my asking, I hope. The occasion is in a manner of speaking new to me.

LADY BRITOMART

Quite right. Go and let him in.

MORRISON

Thank you, my lady. [He withdraws.]

LADY BRITOMART

Children: go and get ready. [Sarah and Barbara go upstairs for their out-of-door wraps.] Charles: go and tell Stephen to come down here in five minutes: you will find him in the drawing room. [Charles goes.] Adolphus: tell them to send round the carriage in about fifteen minutes. [Adolphus goes.]

MORRISON
[at the door] Mr Undershaft.

[Undershaft comes in. Morrison goes out.]

UNDERSHAFT
Alone! How fortunate!

LADY BRITOMART
[rising] Dont be sentimental, Andrew. Sit down. [She sits on the settee: he sits beside her, on her left. She comes to the point before he has time to breathe.] Sarah must have £800 a year until Charles Lomax comes into his property. Barbara will need more, and need it permanently, because Adolphus hasnt any property.

UNDERSHAFT
[resignedly] Yes, my dear: I will see to it. Anything else? for yourself, for instance?

LADY BRITOMART
I want to talk to you about Stephen.

UNDERSHAFT
[rather wearily] Dont, my dear. Stephen doesnt interest me.

LADY BRITOMART
He does interest me. He is our son.

UNDERSHAFT
Do you really think so? He has induced us to bring him into the world; but he chose his parents very incongruously, I think. I see nothing of myself in him, and less of you.

LADY BRITOMART
Andrew: Stephen is an excellent son, and a most steady, capable, highminded young man. You are simply trying to find an excuse for disinheriting him.

UNDERSHAFT
My dear Biddy: the Undershaft tradition disinherits him. It would be dishonest of me to leave the cannon foundry to my son.

LADY BRITOMART
It would be most unnatural and improper of you to leave it to anyone else, Andrew. Do you suppose this wicked and immoral tradition can be kept up for ever? Do you pretend that Stephen could not carry on the foundry just as well as all the other sons of the big business houses?

UNDERSHAFT
Yes: he could learn the office routine without understanding the business, like all the other sons; and the firm would go on by its own momentum until the real Undershaft—probably an Italian or a German—would invent a new method and cut him out.

LADY BRITOMART
There is nothing that any Italian or German could do that Stephen could not do. And Stephen at least has breeding.

UNDERSHAFT
The son of a foundling! Nonsense!

LADY BRITOMART
My son, Andrew! And even you may have good blood in your veins for all you know.

UNDERSHAFT
True. Probably I have. That is another argument in favour of a foundling.

LADY BRITOMART
Andrew: dont be aggravating. And dont be wicked. At present you are both.

UNDERSHAFT
This conversation is part of the Undershaft tradition, Biddy. Every Undershaft's wife has treated him to it ever since the house was founded. It is mere waste of breath. If the tradition be ever broken it will be for an abler man than Stephen.

LADY BRITOMART
[pouting] Then go away.

UNDERSHAFT
[deprecatory] Go away!

LADY BRITOMART
Yes: go away. If you will do nothing for Stephen, you are not wanted here. Go to your foundling, whoever he is; and look after him.

UNDERSHAFT
The fact is, Biddy—

LADY BRITOMART
Dont call me Biddy. I dont call you Andy.

UNDERSHAFT
I will not call my wife Britomart: it is not good sense. Seriously, my love, the Undershaft tradition has landed me in a difficulty. I am getting on in years; and my partner Lazarus has at last made a stand and insisted that the succession must be settled one way or the other; and of course he is quite right. You see, I havent found a fit successor yet.

LADY BRITOMART

[obstinately] There is Stephen.

UNDERSHAFT

Thats just it: all the foundlings I can find are exactly like Stephen.

LADY BRITOMART

Andrew!!

UNDERSHAFT

I want a man with no relations and no schooling: that is, a man who would be out of the running altogether if he were not a strong man. And I cant find him. Every blessed foundling nowadays is snapped up in his infancy by Barnardo homes, or School Board officers, or Boards of Guardians; and if he shews the least ability he is fastened on by schoolmasters; trained to win scholarships like a racehorse; crammed with secondhand ideas; drilled and disciplined in docility and what they call good taste; and lamed for life so that he is fit for nothing but teaching. If you want to keep the foundry in the family, you had better find an eligible foundling and marry him to Barbara.

LADY BRITOMART

Ah! Barbara! Your pet! You would sacrifice Stephen to Barbara.

UNDERSHAFT

Cheerfully. And you, my dear, would boil Barbara to make soup for Stephen.

LADY BRITOMART

Andrew: this is not a question of our likings and dislikings: it is a question of duty. It is your duty to make Stephen your successor.

UNDERSHAFT

Just as much as it is your duty to submit to your husband. Come, Biddy! these tricks of the governing class are of no use with me. I am one of the governing class myself; and it is waste of time giving tracts to a missionary. I have the power in this matter; and I am not to be humbugged into using it for your purposes.

LADY BRITOMART

Andrew: you can talk my head off; but you cant change wrong into right. And your tie is all on one side. Put it straight.

UNDERSHAFT

[disconcerted] It wont stay unless it's pinned [he fumbles at it with childish grimaces]—

[Stephen comes in.]

STEPHEN

[at the door] I beg your pardon [about to retire].

LADY BRITOMART

No: come in, Stephen. [Stephen comes forward to his mother's writing table.]

UNDERSHAFT

[not very cordially] Good afternoon.

STEPHEN

[coldly] Good afternoon.

UNDERSHAFT

[to Lady Britomart] He knows all about the tradition, I suppose?

LADY BRITOMART

Yes. [To Stephen] It is what I told you last night, Stephen.

UNDERSHAFT

[sulkily] I understand you want to come into the cannon business.

STEPHEN

I go into trade! Certainly not.

UNDERSHAFT

[opening his eyes, greatly eased in mind and manner] Oh! in that case—

LADY BRITOMART

Cannons are not trade, Stephen. They are enterprise.

STEPHEN

I have no intention of becoming a man of business in any sense. I have no capacity for business and no taste for it. I intend to devote myself to politics.

UNDERSHAFT

[rising] My dear boy: this is an immense relief to me. And I trust it may prove an equally good thing for the country. I was afraid you would consider yourself disparaged and slighted. [He moves towards Stephen as if to shake hands with him.]

LADY BRITOMART

[rising and interposing] Stephen: I cannot allow you to throw away an enormous property like this.

STEPHEN

[stiffly] Mother: there must be an end of treating me as a child, if you please. [Lady Britomart recoils, deeply wounded by his tone.] Until last night I did not take your attitude seriously, because I did not think you

meant it seriously. But I find now that you left me in the dark as to matters which you should have explained to me years ago. I am extremely hurt and offended. Any further discussion of my intentions had better take place with my father, as between one man and another.

LADY BRITOMART

Stephen! [She sits down again, her eyes filling with tears.]

UNDERSHAFT

[with grave compassion] You see, my dear, it is only the big men who can be treated as children.

STEPHEN

I am sorry, mother, that you have forced me—

UNDERSHAFT

[stopping him] Yes, yes, yes, yes: thats all right, Stephen. She wont interfere with you any more: your independence is achieved: you have won your latchkey. Dont rub it in; and above all, dont apologize. [He resumes his seat.] Now what about your future, as between one man and another—I beg your pardon, Biddy: as between two men and a woman.

LADY BRITOMART

[who has pulled herself together strongly] I quite understand, Stephen. By all means go your own way if you feel strong enough. [Stephen sits down magisterially in the chair at the writing table with an air of affirming his majority.]

UNDERSHAFT

It is settled that you do not ask for the succession to the cannon business.

STEPHEN

I hope it is settled that I repudiate the cannon business.

UNDERSHAFT

Come, come! dont be so devilishly sulky: it's boyish. Freedom should be generous. Besides, I owe you a fair start in life in exchange for disinheriting you. You cant become prime minister all at once. Havnt you a turn for something? What about literature, art, and so forth?

STEPHEN

I have nothing of the artist about me, either in faculty or character, thank Heaven!

UNDERSHAFT

A philosopher, perhaps? Eh?

STEPHEN

I make no such ridiculous pretension.

UNDERSHAFT

Just so. Well, there is the army, the navy, the Church, the Bar. The Bar requires some ability. What about the Bar?

STEPHEN

I have not studied law. And I am afraid I have not the necessary push—I believe that is the name barristers give to their vulgarity—for success in pleading.

UNDERSHAFT

Rather a difficult case, Stephen. Hardly anything left but the stage, is there? [Stephen makes an impatient movement.] Well, come! is there anything you know or care for?

STEPHEN

[rising and looking at him steadily] I know the difference between right and wrong.

UNDERSHAFT

[hugely tickled] You dont say so! What! no capacity for business, no knowledge of law, no sympathy with art, no pretension to philosophy; only a simple knowledge of the secret that has puzzled all the philosophers, baffled all the lawyers, muddled all the men of business, and ruined most of the artists: the secret of right and wrong. Why, man, youre a genius, a master of masters, a god! At twentyfour, too!

STEPHEN

[keeping his temper with difficulty] You are pleased to be facetious. I pretend to nothing more than any honorable English gentleman claims as his birthright. [He sits down angrily.]

UNDERSHAFT

Oh, thats everybody's birthright. Look at poor little Jenny Hill, the Salvation lassie! she would think you were laughing at her if you asked her to stand up in the street and teach grammar or geography or mathematics or even drawing room dancing; but it never occurs to her to doubt that she can teach morals and religion. You are all alike, you respectable people. You cant tell me the bursting strain of a ten-inch gun, which is a very simple matter; but you all think you can tell me the bursting strain of a man under temptation. You darent handle high explosives; but youre all ready to handle honesty and truth and justice and the whole duty of man, and kill one another at that game. What a country! What a world!

LADY BRITOMART

[uneasily] What do you think he had better do, Andrew?

UNDERSHAFT

Oh, just what he wants to do. He knows nothing and he thinks he knows everything. That points clearly to a political career. Get him a private secretaryship to someone who can get him an Under Secretaryship; and then leave him alone. He will find his natural and proper place in the end on the Treasury Bench.

STEPHEN

[springing up again] I am sorry, sir, that you force me to forget the respect due to you as my father. I am an Englishman and I will not hear the Government of my country insulted. [He thrusts his hands in his pockets, and walks angrily across to the window.]

UNDERSHAFT

[with a touch of brutality] The government of your country! I am the government of your country: I, and Lazarus. Do you suppose that you and half a dozen amateurs like you, sitting in a row in that foolish gabble shop, can govern Undershaft and Lazarus? No, my friend: you will do what pays us. You will make war when it suits us, and keep peace when it doesnt. You will find out that trade requires certain measures when we have decided on those measures. When I want anything to keep my dividends up, you will discover that my want is a national need. When other people want something to keep my dividends down, you will call out the police and military. And in return you shall have the support and applause of my newspapers, and the delight of imagining that you are a great statesman. Government of your country! Be off with you, my boy, and play with your caucuses and leading articles and historic parties and great leaders and burning questions and the rest of your toys. I am going back to my counting-house to pay the piper and call the tune.

STEPHEN

[actually smiling, and putting his hand on his father's shoulder with indulgent patronage] Really, my dear father, it is impossible to be angry with you. You dont know how absurd all this sounds to me. You are very properly proud of having been industrious enough to make money; and it is greatly to your credit that you have made so much of it. But it has kept you in circles where you are valued for your money and deferred to for it, instead of in the doubtless very old-fashioned

and behind-the-times public school and university where I formed my habits of mind. It is natural for you to think that money governs England; but you must allow me to think I know better.

UNDERSHAFT

And what does govern England, pray?

STEPHEN

Character, father, character.

UNDERSHAFT

Whose character? Yours or mine?

STEPHEN

Neither yours nor mine, father, but the best elements in the English national character.

UNDERSHAFT

Stephen: Ive found your profession for you. Youre a born journalist. I'll start you with a high-toned weekly review. There!

[Before Stephen can reply Sarah, Barbara, Lomax, and Cusins come in ready for walking. Barbara crosses the room to the window and looks out. Cusins drifts amiably to the armchair. Lomax remains near the door, whilst Sarah comes to her mother. Stephen goes to the smaller writing table and busies himself with his letters.]

SARAH

Go and get ready, mamma: the carriage is waiting. [Lady Britomart leaves the room.]

UNDERSHAFT

[to Sarah] Good day, my dear. Good afternoon, Mr Lomax.

LOMAX

[vaguely] Ahdedoo.

UNDERSHAFT

[to Cusins] Quite well after last night, Euripides, eh?

CUSINS

As well as can be expected.

UNDERSHAFT

Thats right. [To Barbara] So you are coming to see my death and devastation factory, Barbara?

BARBARA

[at the window] You came yesterday to see my salvation factory. I promised you a return visit.

LOMAX

[coming forward between Sarah and Undershaft] Youll find it awfully interesting. Ive been through the

Woolwich Arsenal; and it gives you a ripping feeling of security, you know, to think of the lot of beggars we could kill if it came to fighting. *[To Undershaft, with sudden solemnity]* Still, it must be rather an awful reflection for you, from the religious point of view as it were. Youre getting on, you know, and all that.

SARAH

You dont mind Cholly's imbecility, papa, do you?

LOMAX

[much taken aback] Oh I say!

UNDERSHAFT

Mr Lomax looks at the matter in a very proper spirit, my dear.

LOMAX

Just so. Thats all I meant, I assure you.

SARAH

Are you coming, Stephen?

STEPHEN

Well, I am rather busy—er—*[Magnanimously]*Oh well, yes: I'll come. That is, if there is room for me.

UNDERSHAFT

I can take two with me in a little motor I am experimenting with for field use. You wont mind its being rather unfashionable. It's not painted yet; but it's bullet proof.

LOMAX

[appalled at the prospect of confronting Wilton Crescent in an unpainted motor] Oh I say!

SARAH

The carriage for me, thank you. Barbara doesnt mind what she's seen in.

LOMAX

I say, Dolly, old chap: do you really mind the car being a guy? Because of course if you do I'll go in it. Still—

CUSINS

I prefer it.

LOMAX

Thanks awfully, old man. Come, my ownest. *[He hurries out to secure his seat in the carriage. Sarah follows him.]*

CUSINS

[moodily walking across to Lady Britomart's writing table] Why are we two coming to this Works Department of Hell? that is what I ask myself.

BARBARA

I have always thought of it as a sort of pit where lost creatures with blackened faces stirred up smoky fires and were driven and tormented by my father? Is it like that, dad?

UNDERSHAFT

[scandalized] My dear! It is a spotlessly clean and beautiful hillside town.

CUSINS

With a Methodist chapel? Oh do say theres a Methodist chapel.

UNDERSHAFT

There are two: a Primitive one and a sophisticated one. There is even an Ethical Society; but it is not much patronized, as my men are all strongly religious. In the High Explosives Sheds they object to the presence of Agnostics as unsafe.

CUSINS

And yet they dont object to you!

BARBARA

Do they obey all your orders?

UNDERSHAFT

I never give them any orders. When I speak to one of them it is 'Well, Jones, is the baby doing well? and has Mrs Jones made a good recovery?' 'Nicely, thank you, sir.' And thats all.

CUSINS

But Jones has to be kept in order. How do you maintain discipline among your men?

UNDERSHAFT

I dont. They do. You see, the one thing Jones wont stand is any rebellion from the man under him, or any assertion of social equality between the wife of the man with 4 shillings less than himself, and Mrs Jones! Of course they all rebel against me, theoretically. Practically, every man of them keeps the man below him in his place. I never meddle with them. I never bully them. I dont even bully Lazarus. I say that certain things are to be done; but I dont order anybody to do them. I dont say, mind you, that there is no ordering about and snubbing and even bullying. The men snub the boys and order them about; the carmen snub the sweepers; the artisans snub the unskilled laborers; the foremen drive and bully both the laborers and artisans; the assistant engineers find fault with the foremen; the chief engineers drop on the assistants; the departmental managers worry the chiefs; and the clerks have tall hats and hymnbooks and keep up the social tone by refusing to associate on equal terms with anybody. The result is a colossal profit, which comes to me.

CUSINS

[revolted] You really are a—well, what I was saying yesterday.

BARBARA

What was he saying yesterday?

UNDERSHAFT

Never mind, my dear. He thinks I have made you unhappy. Have I?

BARBARA

Do you think I can be happy in this vulgar silly dress? I! who have worn the uniform. Do you understand what you have done to me? Yesterday I had a man's soul in my hand. I set him in the way of life with his face to salvation. But when we took your money he turned back to drunkenness and derision. [With intense conviction] I will never forgive you that. If I had a child, and you destroyed its body with your explosives—if you murdered Dolly with your horrible guns—I could forgive you if my forgiveness would open the gates of heaven to you. But to take a human soul from me, and turn it into the soul of a wolf! that is worse than any murder.

UNDERSHAFT

Does my daughter despair so easily? Can you strike a man to the heart and leave no mark on him?

BARBARA

[her face lighting up] Oh, you are right: he can never be lost now: where was my faith?

CUSINS

Oh, clever clever devil!

BARBARA

You may be a devil; but God speaks through you sometimes. [She takes her father's hands and kisses them.] You have given me back my happiness: I feel it deep down now, though my spirit is troubled.

UNDERSHAFT

You have learnt something. That always feels at first as if you had lost something.

BARBARA

Well, take me to the factory of death; and let me learn something more. There must be some truth or other

behind all this frightful irony. Come, Dolly. [She goes out.]

CUSINS

My guardian angel! [To Undershaft] Avaunt! [He follows Barbara.]

STEPHEN

[quietly, at the writing table] You must not mind Cusins, father. He is a very amiable good fellow; but he is a Greek scholar and naturally a little eccentric.

UNDERSHAFT

Ah, quite so. Thank you, Stephen. Thank you. [He goes out.]

[Stephen smiles patronizingly; buttons his coat responsibly; and crosses the room to the door. Lady Britomart, dressed for out-of-doors, opens it before he reaches it. She looks round for the others; looks at Stephen; and turns to go without a word.]

STEPHEN

[embarrassed] Mother—

LADY BRITOMART

Dont be apologetic, Stephen. And dont forget that you have outgrown your mother. [She goes out.]

[Perivale St Andrews lies between two Middlesex hills, half climbing the northern one. It is an almost smokeless town of white walls, roofs of narrow green slates or red tiles, tall trees, domes, campaniles, and slender chimney shafts, beautifully situated and beautiful in itself. The best view of it is obtained from the crest of a slope about half a mile to the east, where the high explosives are dealt with. The foundry lies hidden in the depths between, the tops of its chimneys sprouting like huge skittles into the middle distance. Across the crest runs an emplacement of concrete, with a firestep, and a parapet which suggests a fortification, because there is a huge cannon of the obsolete Woolwich Infant pattern peering across it at the town. The cannon is mounted on an experimental gun carriage: possibly the original model of the Undershaft disappearing rampart gun alluded to by Stephen. The firestep, being a convenient place to sit, is furnished here and there with straw disc cushions; and at one place there is the additional luxury of a fur rug.
Barbara is standing on the firestep, looking over the parapet towards the town. On her right is the cannon; on her left the end of a shed raised on piles, with a ladder of three or four steps up to the door, which*

opens outwards and has a little wooden landing at the threshold, with a fire bucket in the corner of the landing. Several dummy soldiers more or less mutilated, with straw protruding from their gashes, have been shoved out of the way under the landing. A few others are nearly upright against the shed; and one has fallen forward and lies, like a grotesque corpse, on the emplacement. The parapet stops short of the shed, leaving a gap which is the beginning of the path down the hill through the foundry to the town. The rug is on the firestep near this gap. Down on the emplacement behind the cannon is a trolley carrying a huge conical bombshell with a red band painted on it. Further to the right is the door of an office, which, like the sheds, is of the lightest possible construction. Cusins arrives by the path from the town.]

BARBARA
Well?

CUSINS
Not a ray of hope. Everything perfect! wonderful! real! It only needs a cathedral to be a heavenly city instead of a hellish one.

BARBARA
Have you found out whether they have done anything for old Peter Shirley?

CUSINS
They have found him a job as gatekeeper and timekeeper. He's frightfully miserable. He calls the timekeeping brainwork, and says he isnt used to it; and his gate lodge is so splendid that he's ashamed to use the rooms, and skulks in the scullery.

BARBARA
Poor Peter!

[Stephen arrives from the town. He carries a fieldglass.]

STEPHEN
[enthusiastically] Have you two seen the place? Why did you leave us?

CUSINS
I wanted to see everything I was not intended to see, and Barbara wanted to make the men talk.

STEPHEN
Have you found anything discreditable?

CUSINS
No. They call him Dandy Andy and are proud of his being a cunning old rascal; but it's all horribly, frightfully, immorally, unanswerably perfect.

[Sarah arrives.]

SARAH
Heavens! what a place! *[She crosses to the trolley.]* Did you see the nursing home!? *[She sits down on the shell.]*

STEPHEN
Did you see the libraries and schools!?

SARAH
Did you see the ball room and the banqueting chamber in the Town Hall!?

STEPHEN
Have you gone into the insurance fund, the pension fund, the building society, the various applications of cooperation!?

[Undershaft comes from the office, with a sheaf of telegrams in his hand.]

UNDERSHAFT
Well, have you seen everything? I'm sorry I was called away. *[Indicating the telegrams]* Good news from Manchuria.

STEPHEN
Another Japanese victory?

UNDERSHAFT
Oh, I dont know. Which side wins does not concern us here. No: the good news is that the aerial battleship is a tremendous success. At the first trial it has wiped out a fort with three hundered soldiers in it.

CUSINS
[from the platform] Dummy soldiers?

UNDERSHAFT
[striding across to Stephen and kicking the prostrate dummy brutally out of his way] No: the real thing.

[Cusins and Barbara exchange glances. Then Cusins sits on the step and buries his face in his hands. Barbara gravely lays her hand on his shoulder. He looks up at her in whimsical desperation.]

UNDERSHAFT
Well, Stephen, what do you think of the place?

STEPHEN
Oh, magnificent. A perfect triumph of modern industry. Frankly, my dear father, I have been a fool: I

had no idea of what it all meant: of the wonderful forethought, the power of organization, the administrative capacity, the financial genius, the colossal capital it represents. I have been repeating to myself as I came through your streets 'Peace hath her victories no less renowned than War.' I have only one misgiving about it all.

UNDERSHAFT

Out with it.

STEPHEN

Well, I cannot help thinking that all this provision for every want of your workmen may sap their independence and weaken their sense of responsibility. And greatly as we enjoyed our tea at that splendid restaurant—how they gave us all that luxury and cake and jam and cream for threepence I really cannot imagine!—still you must remember that restaurants break up home life. Look at the continent, for instance! Are you sure so much pampering is really good for the men's characters?

UNDERSHAFT

Well you see, my dear boy, when you are organizing civilization you have to make up your mind whether trouble and anxiety are good things or not. If you decide that they are, then, I take it, you simply dont organize civilization; and there you are, with trouble and anxiety enough to make us all angels! But if you decide the other way, you may as well go through with it. However, Stephen, our characters are safe here. A sufficient dose of anxiety is always provided by the fact that we may be blown to smithereens at any moment.

SARAH

By the way, papa, where do you make the explosives?

UNDERSHAFT

In separate little sheds, like that one. When one of them blows up, it costs very little; and only the people quite close to it are killed.

[Stephen, who is quite close to it, looks at it rather scaredly, and moves away quickly to the cannon. At the same moment the door of the shed is thrown abruptly open; and a foreman in overalls and list slippers comes out on the little landing and holds the door for Lomax, who appears in the doorway.]

LOMAX

[with studied coolness] My good fellow: you neednt get into a state of nerves. Nothing's going to happen to you; and I suppose it wouldnt be the end of the world if anything did. A little bit of British pluck is what you want, old chap. [He descends and strolls across to Sarah.]

UNDERSHAFT

[to the foreman] Anything wrong, Bilton?

BILTON

[with ironic calm] Gentleman walked into the high explosives shed and lit a cigaret, sir: thats all.

UNDERSHAFT

Ah, quite so. [Going over to Lomax] Do you happen to remember what you did with the match?

LOMAX

Oh come! I'm not a fool. I took jolly good care to blow it out before I chucked it away.

BILTON

The top of it was red hot inside, sir.

LOMAX

Well, suppose it was! I didn't chuck it into any of your messes.

UNDERSHAFT

Think no more of it, Mr Lomax. By the way, would you mind lending me your matches.

LOMAX

[offering his box] Certainly.

UNDERSHAFT

Thanks. [He pockets the matches.]

LOMAX

[lecturing to the company generally] You know, these high explosives dont go off like gunpowder, except when theyre in a gun. When theyre spread loose, you can put a match to them without the least risk: they just burn quietly like a bit of paper. [Warming to the scientific interest of the subject] Did you know that, Undershaft? Have you ever tried?

UNDERSHAFT

Not on a large scale, Mr Lomax. Bilton will give you a sample of gun cotton when you are leaving if you ask him. You can experiment with it at home. [Bilton looks puzzled.]

SARAH

Bilton will do nothing of the sort, papa. I suppose it's your business to blow up the Russians and Japs; but you might really stop short of blowing up poor Cholly. [Bilton gives it up and retires into the shed.]

LOMAX

My ownest, there is no danger. [He sits beside her on the shell.]

[Lady Britomart arrives from the town with a bouquet.]

LADY BRITOMART

[impetuously] Andrew: you shouldnt have let me see this place.

UNDERSHAFT

Why, my dear?

LADY BRITOMART

Never mind why: you shouldnt have: thats all. To think of all that [indicating the town] being yours! and that you have kept it to yourself all these years!

UNDERSHAFT

It does not belong to me. I belong to it. It is the Undershaft inheritance.

LADY BRITOMART

It is not. Your ridiculous cannons and that noisy banging foundry may be the Undershaft inheritance; but all that plate and linen, all that furniture and those houses and orchards and gardens belong to us. They belong to me: they are not a man's business. I wont give them up. You must be out of your senses to throw them all away; and if you persist in such folly, I will call in a doctor.

UNDERSHAFT

[stooping to smell the bouquet] Where did you get the flowers, my dear?

LADY BRITOMART

Your men presented them to me in your William Morris Labor Church.

CUSINS

Oh! It needed only that. A Labor Church! [He mounts the firestep distractedly, and leans with his elbows on the parapet, turning his back to them.]

LADY BRITOMART

Yes, with Morris's words in mosaic letters ten feet high round the dome. NO MAN IS GOOD ENOUGH TO BE ANOTHER MAN'S MASTER. The cynicism of it!

UNDERSHAFT

It shocked the men at first, I am afraid. But now they take no more notice of it than of the ten commandments in church.

LADY BRITOMART

Andrew: you are trying to put me off the subject of the inheritance by profane jokes. Well, you shant. I dont

ask it any longer for Stephen: he has inherited far too much of your perversity to be fit for it. But Barbara has rights as well as Stephen. Why should not Adolphus succeed to the inheritance? I could manage the town for him; and he can look after the cannons, if they are really necessary.

UNDERSHAFT

I should ask nothing better if Adolphus were a foundling. He is exactly the sort of new blood that is wanted in English business. But he's not a foundling; and theres an end of it. [He makes for the office door.]

CUSINS

[turning to them] Not quite. [They all turn and stare at him.] I think—Mind! I am not committing myself in any way as to my future course—but I think the foundling difficulty can be got over. [He jumps down to the emplacement.]

UNDERSHAFT

[coming back to him] What do you mean?

CUSINS

Well, I have something to say which is in the nature of a confession.

SARAH
LADY BRITOMART
BARBARA
STEPHEN
} Confession!

LOMAX

Oh I say!

CUSINS

Yes, a confession. Listen, all. Until I met Barbara I thought myself in the main an honorable, truthful man, because I wanted the approval of my conscience more than I wanted anything else. But the moment I saw Barbara, I wanted her far more than the approval of my conscience.

LADY BRITOMART

Adolphus!

CUSINS

It is true. You accused me yourself, Lady Brit, of joining the Army to worship Barbara; and so I did. She bought my soul like a flower at a street corner; but she bought it for herself.

UNDERSHAFT

What! Not for Dionysos or another?

CUSINS

Dionysos and all the others are in herself. I adored what was divine in her, and was therefore a true worshipper. But I was romantic about her too. I thought she was a woman of the people, and that a marriage with a professor of Greek would be far beyond the wildest social ambitions of her rank.

LADY BRITOMART

Adolphus!!

LOMAX

Oh I say!!!

CUSINS

When I learnt the horrible truth—

LADY BRITOMART

What do you mean by the horrible truth, pray?

CUSINS

That she was enormously rich; that her grandfather was an earl; that her father was the Prince of Darkness—

UNDERSHAFT

Chut!

CUSINS

—and that I was only an adventurer trying to catch a rich wife, then I stooped to deceive her about my birth.

BARBARA

[rising] Dolly!

LADY BRITOMART

Your birth! Now Adolphus, dont dare to make up a wicked story for the sake of these wretched cannons. Remember: I have seen photographs of your parents; and the Agent General for South Western Australia knows them personally and has assured me that they are most respectable married people.

CUSINS

So they are in Australia; but here they are outcasts. Their marriage is legal in Australia, but not in England. My mother is my father's deceased wife's sister; and in this island I am consequently a foundling. [Sensation][12]

---

[12] At the time, English law prohibited marriage between a widower and his deceased wife's sister.

BARBARA

Silly! [She climbs to the cannon, and leans, listening, in the angle it makes with the parapet.]

CUSINS

Is the subterfuge good enough, Machiavelli?

UNDERSHAFT

[thoughtfully] Biddy: this may be a way out of the difficulty.

LADY BRITOMART

Stuff! A man cant make cannons any the better for being his own cousin instead of his proper self. [She sits down on the rug with a bounce that expresses her downright contempt for their casuistry.]

UNDERSHAFT

[to Cusins] You are an educated man. That is against the tradition.

CUSINS

Once in ten thousand times it happens that the schoolboy is a born master of what they try to teach him. Greek has not destroyed my mind: it has nourished it. Besides, I did not learn it at an English public school.

UNDERSHAFT

Hm! Well, I cannot afford to be too particular: you have cornered the foundling market. Let it pass. You are eligible, Euripides: you are eligible.

BARBARA

Dolly: yesterday morning, when Stephen told us all about the tradition, you became very silent; and you have been strange and excited ever since. Were you thinking of your birth then?

CUSINS

When the finger of Destiny suddenly points at a man in the middle of his breakfast, it makes him thoughtful.

UNDERSHAFT

Aha! You have had your eye on the business, my young friend, have you?

CUSINS

Take care! There is an abyss of moral horror between me and your accursed aerial battleships.

UNDERSHAFT

Never mind the abyss for the present. Let us settle the practical details and leave your final decision open. You know that you will have to change your name. Do you object to that?

CUSINS

Would any man named Adolphus—any man called Dolly!—object to being called something else?

UNDERSHAFT

Good. Now, as to money! I propose to treat you handsomely from the beginning. You shall start at a thousand a year.

CUSINS

[with sudden heat, his spectacles twinkling with mischief] A thousand! You dare offer a miserable thousand to the son-in-law of a millionaire! No, by Heavens, Machiavelli! you shall not cheat me. You cannot do without me; and I can do without you. I must have two thousand five hundred a year for two years. At the end of that time, if I am a failure, I go. But if I am a success, and stay on, you must give me the other five thousand.

UNDERSHAFT

What other five thousand?

CUSINS

To make the two years up to five thousand a year. The two thousand five hundred a year is only half pay in case I should turn out a failure. The third year I must have ten per cent on the profits.

UNDERSHAFT

[taken aback] Ten per cent! Why, man, do you know what my profits are?

CUSINS

Enormous, I hope: otherwise I shall require twenty-five per cent.

UNDERSHAFT

But, Mr Cusins, this is a serious matter of business. You are not bringing any capital into the concern.

CUSINS

What! no capital! Is my mastery of Greek no capital? Is my access to the subtlest thought, the loftiest poetry yet attained by humanity, no capital? My character! my intellect! my life! my career! what Barbara calls my soul! are these no capital? Say another word; and I double my salary.

UNDERSHAFT

Be reasonable—

CUSINS

[peremptorily] Mr Undershaft: you have my terms. Take them or leave them.

UNDERSHAFT

[recovering himself] Very well. I note your terms; and I offer you half.

CUSINS

[disgusted] Half!

UNDERSHAFT

[firmly] Half.

CUSINS

You call yourself a gentleman; and you offer me half!!

UNDERSHAFT

I do not call myself a gentleman; but I offer you half.

CUSINS

This to your future partner! your successor! your son-in-law!

BARBARA

You are selling your own soul, Dolly, not mine. Leave me out of the bargain, please.

UNDERSHAFT

Come! I will go a step further for Barbara's sake. I will give you three fifths; but that is my last word.

CUSINS

Done!

LOMAX

Done in the eye! Why, I get only eight hundred, you know.

CUSINS

By the way, Mac, I am a classical scholar, not an arithmetical one. Is three fifths more than half or less?

UNDERSHAFT

More, of course.

CUSINS

I would have taken two hundred and fifty. How you can succeed in business when you are willing to pay all that money to a University don who is obviously not worth a junior clerk's wages!—well! What will Lazarus say?

UNDERSHAFT

Lazarus is a gentle romantic Jew who cares for nothing but string quartets and stalls at fashionable theatres. He will be blamed for your rapacity in money matters, poor fellow! as he has hitherto been blamed for mine. You are a shark of the first order, Euripides. So much the better for the firm!

BARBARA

Is the bargain closed, Dolly? Does your soul belong to him now?

CUSINS

No: the price is settled: that is all. The real tug of war is still to come. What about the moral question?

LADY BRITOMART

There is no moral question in the matter at all, Adolphus. You must simply sell cannons and weapons to people whose cause is right and just, and refuse them to foreigners and criminals.

UNDERSHAFT

[determinedly] No: none of that. You must keep the true faith of an Armorer, or you dont come in here.

CUSINS

What on earth is the true faith of an Armorer?

UNDERSHAFT

To give arms to all men who offer an honest price for them, without respect of persons or principles: to aristocrat and republican, to Nihilist and Tsar, to Capitalist and Socialist, to Protestant and Catholic, to burglar and policeman, to black man, white man and yellow man, to all sorts and conditions, all nationalities, all faiths, all follies, all causes and all crimes. The first Undershaft wrote up in his shop IF GOD GAVE THE HAND, LET NOT MAN WITHHOLD THE SWORD. The second wrote up ALL HAVE THE RIGHT TO FIGHT: NONE HAVE THE RIGHT TO JUDGE. The third wrote up TO MAN THE WEAPON: TO HEAVEN THE VICTORY. The fourth had no literary turn; so he did not write up anything; but he sold cannons to Napoleon under the nose of George the Third. The fifth wrote up PEACE SHALL NOT PREVAIL SAVE WITH A SWORD IN HER HAND. The sixth, my master, was the best of all. He wrote up NOTHING IS EVER DONE IN THIS WORLD UNTIL MEN ARE PREPARED TO KILL ONE ANOTHER IF IT IS NOT DONE. After that, there was nothing left for the seventh to say. So he wrote up, simply, UNASHAMED.

CUSINS

My good Machiavelli, I shall certainly write something up on the wall; only, as I shall write it in Greek, you wont be able to read it. But as to your Armorer's faith, if I take my neck out of the noose of my own morality I am not going to put it into the noose of yours. I shall sell cannons to whom I please and refuse them to whom I please. So there!

UNDERSHAFT

From the moment when you become Andrew Undershaft, you will never do as you please again. Dont come here lusting for power, young man.

CUSINS

If power were my aim I should not come here for it. You have no power.

UNDERSHAFT

None of my own, certainly.

CUSINS

I have more power than you, more will. You do not drive this place: it drives you. And what drives the place?

UNDERSHAFT

[enigmatically] A will of which I am a part.

BARBARA

[startled] Father! Do you know what you are saying; or are you laying a snare for my soul?

CUSINS

Dont listen to his metaphysics, Barbara. The place is driven by the most rascally part of society, the money hunters, the pleasure hunters, the military promotion hunters; and he is their slave.

UNDERSHAFT

Not necessarily. Remember the Armorer's Faith. I will take an order from a good man as cheerfully as from a bad one. If you good people prefer preaching and shirking to buying my weapons and fighting the rascals, dont blame me. I can make cannons: I cannot make courage and conviction. Bah! you tire me, Euripides, with your morality mongering. Ask Barbara: she understands. [He suddenly reaches up and takes Barbara's hands, looking powerfully into her eyes] Tell him, my love, what power really means.

BARBARA

[hypnotized] Before I joined the Salvation Army, I was in my own power; and the consequence was that I never knew what to do with myself. When I joined it, I had not enough time for all the things I had to do.

UNDERSHAFT

[approvingly] Just so. And why was that, do you suppose?

BARBARA

Yesterday I should have said, because I was in the power of God. [She resumes her self-possession, withdrawing her hands from his with a power equal to his own.] But you came and shewed me that I was in the power of Bodger and Undershaft. Today I feel—oh! how can I put it into words? Sarah: do you remember the earthquake at Cannes, when we were little children? —how little the surprise of the first shock mattered compared to the dread and horror of waiting for the second? That is how I feel in this place today. I stood on the rock I thought eternal; and without a word of warning it reeled and crumbled under me. I was safe with an infinite wisdom watching me, an army marching to Salvation with me; and in a moment, at a stroke of your pen in a cheque book, I stood alone; and the heavens were empty. That was the first shock of the earthquake: I am waiting for the second.

UNDERSHAFT
Come, come, my daughter! dont make too much of your little tinpot tragedy. What do we do here when we spend years of work and thought and thousands of pounds of solid cash on a new gun or an aerial battleship that turns out just a hairsbreadth wrong after all? Scrap it. Scrap it without wasting another hour or another pound on it. Well, you have made for yourself something that you call a morality or a religion or what not. It doesnt fit the facts. Well, scrap it. Scrap it and get one that does fit. That is what is wrong with the world at present. It scraps its obsolete steam engines and dynamos; but it wont scrap its old prejudices and its old moralities and its old religions and its old political constitutions. Whats the result? In machinery it does very well; but in morals and religion and politics it is working at a loss that brings it nearer bankruptcy every year. Dont persist in that folly. If your old religion broke down yesterday, get a newer and a better one for tomorrow.

BARBARA
Oh how gladly I would take a better one to my soul! But you offer me a worse one. [Turning on him with sudden vehemence] Justify yourself: shew me some light through the darkness of this dreadful place, with its beautifully clean workshops, and respectable workmen, and model homes.

UNDERSHAFT
Cleanliness and respectability do not need justification, Barbara: they justify themselves. I see no darkness here, no dreadfulness. In your Salvation shelter I saw poverty, misery, cold and hunger. You gave them bread and treacle and dreams of heaven. I give from thirty shillings a week to twelve thousand a year. They find their own dreams; but I look after the drainage.

BARBARA
And their souls?

UNDERSHAFT
I save their souls just as I saved yours.

BARBARA
[revolted]You saved my soul! What do you mean?

UNDERSHAFT
I fed you and clothed you and housed you. I took care that you should have money enough to live handsomely—more than enough; so that you could be wasteful, careless, generous. That saved your soul from the seven deadly sins.

BARBARA
[bewildered] The seven deadly sins!

UNDERSHAFT
Yes, the deadly seven. [Counting on his fingers] Food, clothing, firing, rent, taxes, respectability and children. Nothing can lift those seven millstones from Man's neck but money; and the spirit cannot soar until the mill stones are lifted. I lifted them from your spirit. I enabled Barbara to become Major Barbara; and I saved her from the crime of poverty.

CUSINS
Do you call poverty a crime?

UNDERSHAFT
The worst of crimes. All the other crimes are virtues beside it: all the other dishonors are chivalry itself by comparison. Poverty blights whole cities; spreads horrible pestilences; strikes dead the very souls of all who come within sight, sound, or smell of it. What you call crime is nothing: a murder here and a theft there, a blow now and a curse then: what do they matter? they are only the accidents and illnesses of life: there are not fifty genuine professional criminals in London. But there are millions of poor people, abject people, dirty people, ill fed, ill clothed people. They poison us morally and physically: they kill the happiness of society: they force us to do away with our own liberties and to organize unnatural cruelties for fear they should rise against us and drag us down into their abyss. Only fools fear crime: we all fear poverty. Pah! [turning on Barbara] you talk of your half-saved ruffian in West Ham: you accuse me of dragging his soul back to perdition. Well, bring him to me here; and I will drag his soul back again to salvation for you. Not by words and dreams; but by thirtyeight shillings a week, a sound house in a handsome street, and a permanent job. In three weeks he will have a fancy waistcoat; in three months a tall hat and a

chapel sitting; before the end of the year he will shake hands with a duchess at a Primrose League meeting, and join the Conservative Party.

BARBARA

And will he be the better for that?

UNDERSHAFT

You know he will. Dont be a hypocrite, Barbara. He will be better fed, better housed, better clothed, better behaved; and his children will be pounds heavier and bigger. That will be better than an American cloth mattress in a shelter, chopping firewood, eating bread and treacle, and being forced to kneel down from time to time to thank heaven for it: knee drill, I think you call it. It is cheap work converting starving men with a Bible in one hand and a slice of bread in the other. I will undertake to convert West Ham to Mahometanism on the same terms. Try your hand on my men: their souls are hungry because their bodies are full.

BARBARA

And leave the east end to starve?

UNDERSHAFT

[his energetic tone dropping into one of bitter and brooding remembrance] I was an east ender. I moralized and starved until one day I swore that I would be a full-fed free man at all costs; that nothing should stop me except a bullet, neither reason nor morals nor the lives of other men. I said 'Thou shalt starve ere I starve'; and with that word I became free and great. I was a dangerous man until I had my will: now I am a useful, beneficent, kindly person. That is the history of most self-made millionaires, I fancy. When it is the history of every Englishman we shall have an England worth living in.

LADY BRITOMART

Stop making speeches, Andrew. This is not the place for them.

UNDERSHAFT

[punctured] My dear: I have no other means of conveying my ideas.

LADY BRITOMART

Your ideas are nonsense. You got on because you were selfish and unscrupulous.

UNDERSHAFT

Not at all. I had the strongest scruples about poverty and starvation. Your moralists are quite unscrupulous about both: they make virtues of them. I had rather be a thief than a pauper. I had rather be a murderer than a slave. I dont want to be either; but if you force the alternative on me, then, by Heaven, I'll choose the braver and more moral one. I hate poverty and slavery worse than any other crimes whatsoever. And let me tell you this. Poverty and slavery have stood up for centuries to your sermons and leading articles: they will not stand up to my machine guns. Dont preach at them: dont reason with them. Kill them.

BARBARA

Killing. Is that your remedy for everything?

UNDERSHAFT

It is the final test of conviction, the only lever strong enough to overturn a social system, the only way of saying Must. Let six hundred and seventy fools loose in the streets; and three policemen can scatter them. But huddle them together in a certain house in Westminster; and let them go through certain ceremonies and call themselves certain names until at last they get the courage to kill; and your six hundred and seventy fools become a government. Your pious mob fills up ballot papers and imagines it is governing its masters; but the ballot paper that really governs is the paper that has a bullet wrapped up in it.

CUSINS

That is perhaps why, like most intelligent people, I never vote.

UNDERSHAFT

Vote! Bah! When you vote, you only change the names of the cabinet. When you shoot, you pull down governments, inaugurate new epochs, abolish old orders and set up new. Is that historically true, Mr Learned Man, or is it not?

CUSINS

It is historically true. I loathe having to admit it. I repudiate your sentiments. I abhor your nature. I defy you in every possible way. Still, it is true. But it ought not to be true.

UNDERSHAFT

Ought! ought! ought! ought! ought! Are you going to spend your life saying ought, like the rest of our moralists? Turn your oughts into shalls, man. Come and make explosives with me. Whatever can blow men up can blow society up. The history of the world is the history of those who had courage enough to embrace this truth. Have you the courage to embrace it, Barbara?

LADY BRITOMART

Barbara: I positively forbid you to listen to your father's abominable wickedness. And you, Adolphus, ought to know better than to go about saying that wrong things are true. What does it matter whether things are true if they are wrong?

UNDERSHAFT

What does it matter whether they are wrong if they are true?

LADY BRITOMART

[rising] Children: come home instantly. Andrew: I am exceedingly sorry I allowed you to call on us. You are wickeder than ever. Come at once.

BARBARA

[shaking her head] It's no use running away from wicked people, Mamma.

LADY BRITOMART

It is every use. It shews your disapprobation of them.

BARBARA

It does not save them.

LADY BRITOMART

I can see that you are going to disobey me. Sarah: are you coming home or are you not?

SARAH

I daresay it's very wicked of papa to make cannons; but I dont think I shall cut him on that account.

LOMAX

[pouring oil on the troubled waters] The fact is, you know, there is a certain amount of tosh about this notion of wickedness. It doesnt work. You must look at facts. Not that I would say a word in favor of anything wrong; but then, you see, all sorts of chaps are always doing all sorts of things; and we have to fit them in somehow, dont you know. What I mean is that you cant go cutting everybody; and thats about what it comes to. [Their rapt attention to his eloquence makes him nervous.] Perhaps I dont make myself clear.

LADY BRITOMART

You are lucidity itself, Charles. Because Andrew is successful and has plenty of money to give to Sarah, you will flatter him and encourage him in his wickedness.

LOMAX

[unruffled] Well, where the carcase is, there will the eagles be gathered, dont you know. [To Undershaft] Eh? What?

UNDERSHAFT

Precisely. By the way, may I call you Charles?

LOMAX

Delighted. Cholly is the usual ticket.

UNDERSHAFT

[to Lady Britomart] Biddy—

LADY BRITOMART

[violently] Dont dare call me Biddy. Charles Lomax: you are a fool. Adolphus Cusins: you are a Jesuit. Stephen: you are a prig. Barbara: you are a lunatic. Andrew: you are a vulgar tradesman. Now you all know my opinion; and my conscience is clear, at all events. [She sits down with a vehemence that the rug fortunately softens.]

UNDERSHAFT

My dear: you are the incarnation of morality. [She snorts.] Your conscience is clear and your duty done when you have called everybody names. Come, Euripides! it is getting late; and we all want to go home. Make up your mind.

CUSINS

Understand this, you old demon—

LADY BRITOMART

Adolphus!

UNDERSHAFT

Let him alone, Biddy. Proceed, Euripides.

CUSINS

You have me in a horrible dilemma. I want Barbara.

UNDERSHAFT

Like all young men, you greatly exaggerate the difference between one young woman and another.

BARBARA

Quite true, Dolly.

CUSINS

I also want to avoid being a rascal.

UNDERSHAFT

[with biting contempt] You lust for personal righteousness, for self-approval, for what you call a good conscience, for what Barbara calls salvation, for what I call patronizing people who are not so lucky as yourself.

CUSINS

I do not: all the poet in me recoils from being a good man. But there are things in me that I must reckon with. Pity—

UNDERSHAFT

Pity! The scavenger of misery.

CUSINS

Well, love.

UNDERSHAFT

I know. You love the needy and the outcast: you love the oppressed races, the negro, the Indian ryot,[13] the underdog everywhere. Do you love the Japanese? Do you love the French? Do you love the English?

CUSINS

No. Every true Englishman detests the English. We are the wickedest nation on earth; and our success is a moral horror.

UNDERSHAFT

That is what comes of your gospel of love, is it?

CUSINS

May I not love even my father-in-law?

UNDERSHAFT

Who wants your love, man? By what right do you take the liberty of offering it to me? I will have your due heed and respect, or I will kill you. But your love! Damn your impertinence!

CUSINS

[grinning] I may not be able to control my affections, Mac.

UNDERSHAFT

You are fencing, Euripides. You are weakening: your grip is slipping. Come! try your last weapon. Pity and love have broken in your hand: forgiveness is still left.

CUSINS

No: forgiveness is a beggar's refuge. I am with you there: we must pay our debts.

UNDERSHAFT

Well said. Come! you will suit me. Remember the words of Plato.

CUSINS

[starting] Plato! You dare quote Plato to me!

---

[13] Tenant farmer.

UNDERSHAFT

Plato says, my friend, that society cannot be saved until either the Professors of Greek take to making gunpowder, or else the makers of gunpowder become Professors of Greek.

CUSINS

Oh, tempter, cunning tempter!

UNDERSHAFT

Come! choose, man, choose.

CUSINS

But perhaps Barbara will not marry me if I make the wrong choice.

BARBARA

Perhaps not.

CUSINS

[desperately perplexed] You hear!

BARBARA

Father: do you love nobody?

UNDERSHAFT

I love my best friend

LADY BRITOMART

And who is that, pray?

UNDERSHAFT

My bravest enemy. That is the man who keeps me up to the mark.

CUSINS

You know, the creature is really a sort of poet in his way. Suppose he is a great man, after all!

UNDERSHAFT

Suppose you stop talking and make up your mind, my young friend.

CUSINS

But you are driving me against my nature. I hate war.

UNDERSHAFT

Hatred is the coward's revenge for being intimidated. Dare you make war on war? Here are the means: my friend Mr Lomax is sitting on them.

LOMAX

[springing up] Oh I say! You dont mean that this thing is loaded, do you? My ownest: come off it.

SARAH

[sitting placidly on the shell] If I am to be blown up, the more thoroughly it is done the better. Dont fuss, Cholly.

LOMAX

[to Undershaft, strongly remonstrant] Your own daughter, you know!

UNDERSHAFT

So I see. [To Cusins] Well, my friend, may we expect you here at six tomorrow morning?

CUSINS

[firmly] Not on any account. I will see the whole establishment blown up with its own dynamite before I will get up at five. My hours are healthy, rational hours: eleven to five.

UNDERSHAFT

Come when you please: before a week you will come at six and stay until I turn you out for the sake of your health. [Calling] Bilton! [He turns to Lady Britomart, who rises.] My dear: let us leave these two young people to themselves for a moment. [Bilton comes from the shed.] I am going to take you through the gun cotton shed.

BILTON

[barring the way] You cant take anything explosive in here, sir.

LADY BRITOMART

What do you mean? Are you alluding to me?

BILTON

[unmoved] No, maam. Mr Undershaft has the other gentleman's matches in his pocket.

LADY BRITOMART

[abruptly] Oh! I beg your pardon. [She goes into the shed.]

UNDERSHAFT

Quite right, Bilton, quite right: here you are. [He gives Bilton the box of matches.] Come, Stephen. Come, Charles. Bring Sarah. [He passes into the shed.]

[Bilton opens the box and deliberately drops the matches into the fire-bucket.]

LOMAX

Oh! I say. [Bilton stolidly hands him the empty box.] Infernal nonsense! Pure scientific ignorance! [He goes in.]

SARAH

Am I all right, Bilton?

BILTON

Youll have to put on list slippers, miss: thats all. Weve got em inside. [She goes in.]

STEPHEN

[very seriously to Cusins] Dolly, old fellow, think. Think before you decide. Do you feel that you are a sufficiently practical man? It is a huge undertaking, an enormous responsibility. All this mass of business will be Greek to you.

CUSINS

Oh, I think it will be much less difficult than Greek.

STEPHEN

Well, I just want to say this before I leave you to yourselves. Dont let anything I have said about right and wrong prejudice you against this great chance in life. I have satisfied myself that the business is one of the highest character and a credit to our country. [Emotionally] I am very proud of my father. I—[Unable to proceed, he presses Cusins' hand and goes hastily into the shed, followed by Bilton.]

[Barbara and Cusins, left alone together, look at one another silently.]

CUSINS

Barbara: I am going to accept this offer.

BARBARA

I thought you would.

CUSINS

You understand, dont you, that I had to decide without consulting you. If I had thrown the burden of the choice on you, you would sooner or later have despised me for it.

BARBARA

Yes: I did not want you to sell your soul for me any more than for this inheritance.

CUSINS

It is not the sale of my soul that troubles me: I have sold it too often to care about that. I have sold it for a professorship. I have sold it for an income. I have sold it to escape being imprisoned for refusing to pay taxes for hangmen's ropes and unjust wars and things that I abhor. What is all human conduct but the daily and hourly sale of our souls for trifles? What I am now selling it for is neither money nor position nor comfort, but for reality and for power.

BARBARA

You know that you will have no power, and that he has none.

CUSINS

I know. It is not for myself alone. I want to make power for the world.

BARBARA

I want to make power for the world too; but it must be spiritual power.

CUSINS

I think all power is spiritual: these cannons will not go off by themselves. I have tried to make spiritual power by teaching Greek. But the world can never be really touched by a dead language and a dead civilization. The people must have power; and the people cannot have Greek. Now the power that is made here can be wielded by all men.

BARBARA

Power to burn women's houses down and kill their sons and tear their husbands to pieces.

CUSINS

You cannot have the power for good without having power for evil too. Even mother's milk nourishes murderers as well as heroes. This power which only tears men's bodies to pieces has never been so horribly abused as the intellectual power, the imaginative power, the poetic, religious power that can enslave men's souls. As a teacher of Greek I gave the intellectual man weapons against the common man. I now want to give the common man weapons against the intellectual man. I love the common people. I want to arm them against the lawyers, the doctors, the priests, the literary men, the professors, the artists, and the politicians, who, once in authority, are more disastrous and tyrannical than all the fools, rascals, and impostors. I want a power simple enough for common men to use, yet strong enough to force the intellectual oligarchy to use its genius for the general good.

BARBARA

Is there no higher power than that [pointing to the shell]?

CUSINS

Yes; but that power can destroy the higher powers just as a tiger can destroy a man: therefore Man must master that power first. I admitted this when the Turks and Greeks were last at war. My best pupil went out to fight for Hellas. My parting gift to him was not a copy of Plato's Republic, but a revolver and a hundred Undershaft cartridges. The blood of every Turk he shot—if he shot any—is on my head as well as on Undershaft's. That act committed me to this place for ever. Your father's challenge has beaten me. Dare I make war on war? I dare. I must. I will. And now, is it all over between us?

BARBARA

[touched by his evident dread of her answer] Silly baby Dolly? How could it be!

CUSINS

[overjoyed] Then you—you—you—Oh for my drum! [He flourishes imaginary drum-sticks.]

BARBARA

[angered by his levity] Take care, Dolly, take care. Oh, if only I could get away from you and from father and from it all! if I could have the wings of a dove and fly away to heaven!

CUSINS

And leave me!

BARBARA

Yes, you, and all the other naughty mischievous children of men. But I cant. I was happy in the Salvation Army for a moment. I escaped from the world into a paradise of enthusiasm and prayer and soul saving; but the moment our money ran short, it all came back to Bodger: it was he who saved our people: he, and the Prince of Darkness, my papa. Undershaft and Bodger: their hands stretch everywhere: when we feed a starving fellow creature, it is with their bread, because there is no other bread; when we tend the sick, it is in the hospitals they endow; if we turn from the churches they build, we must kneel on the stones of the streets they pave. As long as that lasts, there is no getting away from them. Turning our backs on Bodger and Undershaft is turning our backs on life.

CUSINS

I thought you were determined to turn your back on the wicked side of life.

BARBARA

There is no wicked side: life is all one. And I never wanted to shirk my share in whatever evil must be endured, whether it be sin or suffering. I wish I could cure you of middle-class ideas, Dolly.

CUSINS

[gasping] Middle cl—! A snub! A social snub to me! from the daughter of a foundling!

BARBARA

That is why I have no class, Dolly: I come straight out of the heart of the whole people. If I were middle-class I should turn my back on my father's business; and we should both live in an artistic drawing room, with you reading the reviews in one corner, and I in the other at the piano, playing Schumann: both very superior persons, and neither of us a bit of use. Sooner than that, I would sweep out the gun cotton shed, or be one of Bodger's barmaids. Do you know what would have happened if you had refused papa's offer?

CUSINS

I wonder!

BARBARA

I should have given you up and married the man who accepted it. After all, my dear old mother has more sense than any of you. I felt like her when I saw this place—felt that I must have it—that never, never, never could I let it go; only she thought it was the houses and the kitchen ranges and the linen and china, when it was really all the human souls to be saved: not weak souls in starved bodies, sobbing with gratitude for a scrap of bread and treacle, but full-fed, quarrelsome, snobbish, uppish creatures, all standing on their little rights and dignities, and thinking that my father ought to be greatly obliged to them for making so much money for him—and so he ought. That is where salvation is really wanted. My father shall never throw it in my teeth again that my converts were bribed with bread. [She is transfigured.] I have got rid of the bribe of bread. I have got rid of the bribe of heaven. Let God's work be done for its own sake: the work he had to create us to do because it cannot be done except by living men and women. When I die, let him be in my debt, not I in his; and let me forgive him as becomes a woman of my rank.

CUSINS

Then the way of life lies through the factory of death?

BARBARA

Yes, through the raising of hell to heaven and of man to God, through the unveiling of an eternal light in the Valley of The Shadow. [Seizing him with both hands] Oh, did you think my courage would never come back? did you believe that I was a deserter? that I, who have stood in the streets, and taken my people

to my heart, and talked of the holiest and greatest things with them, could ever turn back and chatter foolishly to fashionable people about nothing in a drawing room? Never, never, never, never: Major Barbara will die with the colors. Oh! and I have my dear little Dolly boy still; and he has found me my place and my work. Glory Hallelujah! [She kisses him.]

CUSINS

My dearest: consider my delicate health. I cannot stand as much happiness as you can.

BARBARA

Yes: it is not easy work being in love with me, is it? But it's good for you. [She runs to the shed, and calls, childlike.] Mamma! Mamma! [Bilton comes out of the shed, followed by Undershaft.] I want Mamma.

UNDERSHAFT

She is taking off her list slippers, dear. [He passes on to Cusins.] Well? What does she say?

CUSINS

She has gone right up into the skies.

LADY BRITOMART

[Coming from the shed and stopping on the steps, obstructing Sarah, who follows with Lomax. Barbara clutches like a baby at her mother's skirt.] Barbara: when will you learn to be independent and to act and think for yourself? I know as well as possible what that cry of 'Mamma, Mamma' means. Always running to me!

SARAH

[touching Lady Britomart's ribs with her finger tips and imitating a bicycle horn] Pip! pip!

LADY BRITOMART

[highly indignant] How dare you say Pip! pip! to me, Sarah? You are both very naughty children. What do you want, Barbara?

BARBARA

I want a house in the village to live in with Dolly. [Dragging at the skirt] Come and tell me which one to take.

UNDERSHAFT

[to Cusins] Six o'clock tomorrow morning, Euripides.

[The End]

8

CAT ON A HOT TIN ROOF

Tennessee Williams • 1955

CAT ON A HOT TIN ROOF IS, QUITE SIMPLY, A PLAY about sex. Whether this was a dramatic breakthrough or a fall from grace was hotly debated at the time of the play's 1955 premiere, but the debate has not entirely gone away; although it won the Pulitzer Prize, and was made into an acclaimed film (with Elizabeth Taylor), and has enjoyed major foreign productions and Broadway revivals over the years, *Cat* has in no way lost its power to provoke both moral outrage and aesthetic controversy.

Three playwrights dominated the American theatre in the mid-twentieth century: Eugene O'Neill, Arthur Miller, and Tenessee Williams. Of the three, Williams was the most sensual, lyrical, and, in the words favored by the press of the time, "steamy." Contemporary critical opinion was seriously mixed: it was only after fifteen years of calling his work "garish," "decadently primitive," "excessively purple," "profane," "noisomely misanthropic," "inept," "pathetic-romantic," and "a vast, specious pageant of depravity," that *Time* maga-

zine suddenly announced, in 1962, that Williams was America's greatest living playwright. What gives rise to such contradictory opinions is that Williams draws much of his dramatic power from deep sexual anguish. "The theatre," he has maintained, "has made in our time its greatest artistic advance through the unlocking and lighting up and ventilation of the closets, attics, and basements of human behavior and experience."[1] Some, though, thought Williams had only ventilated the sewers.

Williams did not invent sex in the theatre, of course. Henrik Ibsen and August Strindberg were forthright in treating sexual functions and dysfunctions, if sometimes in code language, and most of the works of Euripides, Marlowe, Shakespeare, Molière, and Racine are incomprehensible

---

[1] "Tennessee Williams Presents His POV," *New York Times Magazine*, June 12, 1960, reprinted in Tennessee Williams, *Where I Live: Selected Essays* (New York: New Directions, 1978), p. 116.

without an understanding of—and a willingness to explore—human sexuality and carnal passion. What made Williams a unique dramatist was his arrival on the stage at the time of a naturalistic revolution in American acting, centered at the New York Actors Studio. The combination of Williams's libidinous preoccupations, and the sensual intensity of such Studio-trained performers as Marlon Brando, Vivien Leigh, Geraldine Page, and Ben Gazzara, proved electrifying to contemporary audiences.

To be sure, *Cat on a Hot Tin Roof* deals with more than sex. Within the continuous action of the play—which occupies a single summer evening in the Pollitt household—we are shown a brutal intrafamily inheritance struggle; the facing and denial of imminent death; racism and sexism, both conscious and unconscious; the lying ("mendacity," as the characters prefer to call it) endemic to "gentility"; and the troubled interplay of friendship, romance, and family obligation. But the centrality of sex—and the actual sexual act—is made abundantly clear from the moment the curtain rises: on a "big double bed which staging should make a functional part of the set as often as suitable," according to the author's unsubtle instructions. And *Cat on a Hot Tin Roof* never strays far from projections as to whether or not an act of copulation will take place on that bed shortly after the curtain falls. Indeed, one might say, the cat is on the tin roof because she's not in the double bed.

It is difficult to discuss this play today without probing the sexual relationship between the character of Brick and his deceased friend, Skipper. In his later autobiographical works, Williams freely acknowledged his own lifelong homosexuality; in 1955, however, such an admission would have seriously damaged, if not ruined, his career, and Williams wisely kept his private life entirely to himself at that time. But what are we to make of Brick to-

day? Is Williams, in the play, evasive about this character, or is the character drawn with deliberate ambiguity? In a newspaper essay in 1955, Williams held to the latter viewpoint: "Was Brick homosexual? He probably—no, I would even say quite certainly—went no further in physical expression than clasping Skipper's hand across the space between their twin beds in hotel rooms—and yet his sexual nature was not innately 'normal.'"[2] Williams's explanation betrays the author's obvious discomfort; it is quite possible that had Williams tackled the subject twenty or more years later, he would have treated it very differently. Yet the conflict between carnality and delicacy, which perhaps became Williams's major theme, could easily be lost in a less tortured, more "open," and more direct writer.

Thomas Lanier Williams (his given name) was born 1914 in Columbus, Mississippi, and was raised there until the age of twelve, when he and his family moved to St. Louis, Missouri. His first major play, *The Glass Menagerie* (1945), is a frankly autobiographical "memory play" of the author's early life in St. Louis; most of his subsequent plays, however, are set deeper in the U.S. South or in other tropical climes, and most revolve around sensitive and artistic persons who are estranged, in varying degrees, from what in Williams appears as the crassness and brutality of "normal" American life. Rape, castration, suicide, unbridled lust, and even cannibalism appear with frequency in his later plays, but always as a metaphor for larger issues: the victories of mendacity, and the oppression of those too tender to survive. After great fame and success—with *A Streetcar Named Desire, Cat*

---

[2] "Critic Says 'Evasion,' Writer Says 'Mystery,' " *New York Herald Tribune*, April 17, 1955, reprinted in Tennessee Williams, *Where I Live: Selected Essays* (New York: New Directions, 1978), p. 72.

on a Hot Tin Roof, *Summer and Smoke*, and *The Night of the Iguana*—through the early 1960s, Williams's career and health began to decline, partly on account of alcoholism and drug addiction. Yet he continued to write and produce new plays, though less frequently and effectively, until his accidental death in 1983.

ABOUT THE TEXT

This is Williams's preferred version of the play. It is not, however, exactly the text that was performed on Broadway in 1955. For that production, Williams prepared a revision of the play's third act, in accordance with the wishes of the play's director, Elia Kazan. Williams pronounced himself satisfied with this Kazan-dictated rewrite, which includes a re-entrance of Big Daddy (Kazan considered the character "too vivid and important" to restrict to a single act), but when it came time to publish the text, Williams had both versions printed, inviting the reader to "make up his own mind" as to which one is better. Space prevents printing both third acts here, and the current editor, sharing Williams's opinion, has opted for the authorial version.

Otherwise the text is printed exactly as it appears, including Williams's characteristically elaborate stage directions. The older term *Negro*, where we would today say *African American* or *black*, is used by Williams as a neutral and entirely nonprejudicial term; however, the word *nigger*, where it appears, is clearly meant to depict the unthinking (and therefore brutal) racism of the characters who employ it. The word *poon-tang*, used by Big Daddy in the second act, is a southern colloquialism of the period: it means "cheap sex." The word created a gigantic scandal when the play premiered, and prevented its unabridged production in many southern cities.

✦ CAT ON A HOT TIN ROOF ✦

MARGARET

BRICK

MAE, sometimes called Sister Woman

BIG MAMA

DIXIE, a little girl

BIG DADDY

REVEREND TOOKER

GOOPER, sometimes called Brother Man

DOCTOR BAUGH, pronounced "Baw"

LACEY, a Negro servant

SOOKEY, another

Another little girl and two small boys

——— NOTES FOR THE DESIGNER ———

The set is the bed-sitting-room of a plantation home in the Mississippi Delta. It is along an upstairs gallery which probably runs around the entire house; it has two pairs of very wide doors opening onto the gallery; showing white balustrades against a fair summer sky that fades into dusk and night during the course of the play, which occupies precisely the time of its performance, excepting, of course, the fifteen minutes of intermission.

Perhaps the style of the room is not what you would expect in the home of the Delta's biggest cotton-planter. It is Victorian with a touch of the Far East. It hasn't changed much since it was occupied by the original owners of the place, Jack Straw and Peter Ochello, a pair of old bachelors who shared this room all their lives together. In other words, the room must evoke some ghosts; it is gently and poetically haunted by a relationship that must have involved a tenderness which was uncommon. This may be irrelevant or unnecessary, but I once saw a reproduction of a faded photograph of the verandah of Robert Louis Stevenson's home on that Samoan Island where he spent his last years, and there was a quality of tender light on weathered wood, such as porch furniture made of bamboo and wicker, exposed to tropical suns and tropical rains, which came to mind when I thought about the set for this play, bringing also to mind the grace and comfort of light, the reassurance it gives, on a late and fair afternoon in summer, the way that no matter what, even dread of death, is gently touched and soothed by it. For the set is the background for a play that deals with human extremities of emotion, and it needs that softness behind it.

The bathroom door, showing only pale-blue tile and silver towel racks, is in one side wall; the hall door in the opposite wall. Two articles of furniture need mention: a big double bed which staging should make a functional part of the set as often as suitable, the surface of which should be slightly raked to make figures on it seen more easily; and against the wall space between the two huge double doors upstage: a monumental monstrosity peculiar to our times, a *huge* console combination of radio-phonograph (Hi-Fi with three speakers), TV set *and* liquor cabinet, bearing and containing many glasses and bottles, all in one piece, which is a composition of muted silver tones, and the opalescent tones of reflecting glass, a chromatic link, this thing, between the sepia (tawny gold) tones of the interior and the cool (white and blue) tones of the gallery and sky. This piece of furniture (?!), this monument, is a very complete and compact little shrine to virtually all the comforts and illusions behind which we hide from such things as the characters in the play are faced with. . . . The set should be far less realistic than I have so far implied in this description of it. I think the walls below the ceiling should dissolve mysteriously into air; the set should be roofed by the sky; stars and moon suggested by traces of milky pallor, as if they were observed through a telescope lens out of focus.

Anything else I can think of? Oh, yes, fanlights (transoms shaped like an open glass fan) above all the doors in the set, with panes of blue and amber, and above all, the designer should take as many pains to give the actors room to move about freely (to show their restlessness, their passion for breaking out) as if it were a set for a ballet.

An evening in summer. The action is continuous, with two intermissions.

---------------- **ACT ONE** ----------------

At the rise of the curtain someone is taking a shower in the bathroom, the door of which is half open. A pretty young woman, with anxious lines in her face, enters the bedroom and crosses to the bathroom door.

MARGARET

[shouting above the roar of water] One of those no-neck monsters hit me with a hot buttered biscuit so I have t'change!

[Margaret's voice is both rapid and drawling. In her long speeches she has the vocal tricks of a priest delivering a liturgical chant, the lines are almost sung, always continuing a little beyond her breath so she has to gasp for another. Sometimes she intersperses the lines with a little wordless singing, such as "Da-da-daaaa!"
Water turns off and Brick calls out to her, but is still unseen. A tone of politely feigned interest, masking indifference, or worse, is characteristic of his speech with Margaret.]

BRICK

Wha'd you say, Maggie? Water was on s' loud I couldn't hearya. . . .

MARGARET

Well, I!—just remarked that!—one of th' no-neck monsters messed up m' lovely lace dress so I got t'—cha-a-ange. . . .

[She opens and kicks shut drawers of the dresser.]

BRICK

Why d'ya call Gooper's kiddies no-neck monsters?

MARGARET

Because they've got no necks! Isn't that a good enough reason?

BRICK

Don't they have any necks?

MARGARET

None visible. Their fat little heads are set on their fat little bodies without a bit of connection.

BRICK

That's too bad.

MARGARET

Yes, it's too bad because you can't wring their necks if they've got no necks to wring! Isn't that right, honey?

[She steps out of her dress, stands in a slip of ivory satin and lace.]

Yep, they're no-neck monsters, all no-neck people are monsters. . . .

[Children shriek downstairs.]

Hear them? Hear them screaming? I don't know where their voice-boxes are located since they don't have necks. I tell you I got so nervous at that table tonight I thought I would throw back my head and utter a scream you could hear across the Arkansas border an' parts of Louisiana an' Tennessee. I said to your charming sister-in-law, Mae, honey, couldn't you feed those precious little things at a separate table with an oilcloth cover? They make such a mess an' the lace cloth looks *so* pretty! She made enormous eyes at me and said, "Ohhh, noooooo! On Big Daddy's birthday? Why, he would never forgive me!" Well, I want you to know, Big Daddy hadn't been at the table two minutes with those five no-neck monsters slobbering and drooling over their food before he threw down his fork an' shouted, "Fo' God's sake, Gooper, why don't you put them pigs at a trough in th' kitchen?"—Well, I swear, I simply could have di-eed!

Think of it, Brick, they've got five of them and number six is coming. They've brought the whole bunch down here like animals to display at a county fair. Why, they have those children doin' tricks all the time! "Junior, show Big Daddy how you do this, show Big Daddy how you do that, say your little piece fo' Big Daddy, Sister. Show your dimples, Sugar. Brother, show Big Daddy how you stand on your head!"—It goes on all the time, along with constant little remarks and innuendos about the fact that you and I have not produced any children, are totally childless and therefore totally useless!—Of course it's comical but it's also disgusting since it's so obvious what they're up to!

BRICK
[without interest] What are they up to, Maggie?

MARGARET
Why, you know what they're up to!

BRICK
[appearing] No, I don't know what they're up to.

[He stands there in the bathroom doorway drying his hair with a towel and hanging onto the towel rack because one ankle is broken, plastered and bound. He is still slim and firm as a boy. His liquor hasn't started tearing him down outside. He has the additional charm of that cool air of detachment that people have who have given up the struggle. But now and then, when disturbed, something flashes behind it, like lightning in a fair sky, which shows that at some deeper level he is far from peaceful. Perhaps in a stronger light he would show some signs of deliquescence, but the fading, still warm, light from the gallery treats him gently.]

MARGARET
I'll tell you what they're up to, boy of mine!—They're up to cutting you out of your father's estate, and—

[She freezes momentarily before her next remark. Her voice drops as if it were somehow a personally embarrassing admission.]

—Now we know that Big Daddy's dyin' of— cancer. . . .

[There are voices on the lawn below: long-drawn calls across distance. Margaret raises her lovely bare arms and powders her armpits with a light sigh. She adjusts the angle of a magnifying mirror to straighten an eyelash, then rises fretfully saying:]

There's so much light in the room it—

BRICK
[softly but sharply] Do we?

MARGARET
Do we what?

BRICK
Know Big Daddy's dyin' of cancer?

MARGARET
Got the report today.

BRICK
Oh . . .

MARGARET
[letting down bamboo blinds which cast long, gold-fretted shadows over the room] Yep, got th' report just now . . . it didn't surprise me, Baby. . . .

[Her voice has range, and music; sometimes it drops low as a boy's and you have a sudden image of her playing boys' games as a child.]

I recognized the symptoms soon's we got here last spring and I'm willin' to bet you that Brother Man and his wife were pretty sure of it, too. That more than likely explains why their usual summer migration to the coolness of the Great Smokies was passed up this summer in favor of—hustlin' down here ev'ry whip-stitch with their whole screamin' tribe! And why so many allusions have been made to Rainbow Hill lately. You know what Rainbow Hill is? Place that's famous for treatin' alcoholics an' dope fiends in the movies!

BRICK
I'm not in the movies.

MARGARET
No, and you don't take dope. Otherwise you're a perfect candidate for Rainbow Hill, Baby, and that's where they aim to ship you—over my dead body! Yep, over my dead body they'll ship you there, but nothing would please them better. Then Brother Man could get a-hold of the purse strings and dole out remittances to us, maybe get power-of-attorney and sign checks for us and cut off our credit wherever, whenever he wanted! Son-of-a-bitch!—How'd you like that, Baby?—Well, you've been doin' just about ev'rything in your power to bring it about, you've just been doin' ev'rything you can think of to aid and abet them in this scheme of theirs! Quittin' work, devoting yourself to the occupation of drinkin'!—Breakin' your ankle last night on the high school athletic field:

doin' what? Jumpin' hurdles? At two or three in the morning? Just fantastic! Got in the paper. *Clarksdale Register* carried a nice little item about it, human interest story about a well-known former athlete stagin' a one-man track meet on the Glorious Hill High School athletic field last night, but was slightly out of condition and didn't clear the first hurdle! Brother Man Gooper claims he exercised his influence t' keep it from goin' out over AP or UP or every goddam "P." But, Brick? You still have one big advantage!

[*During the above swift flood of words, Brick has reclined with contrapuntal leisure on the snowy surface of the bed and has rolled over carefully on his side or belly.*]

BRICK
[*wryly*] Did you *say* something, Maggie?

MARGARET
Big Daddy dotes on you, honey. And he can't stand Brother Man and Brother Man's wife, that monster of fertility, Mae; she's downright odious to him! Know how I know? By little expressions that flicker over his face when that woman is holding fo'th on one of her choice topics such as—how she refused twilight sleep!—when the twins were delivered! Because she feels motherhood's an experience that a woman ought to experience fully!—in order to fully appreciate the wonder and beauty of it! HAH!

[*This loud "HAH!" is accompanied by a violent action such as slamming a drawer shut.*]

—and how she made Brother Man come in an' stand beside her in the delivery room so he would not miss out on the "wonder and beauty" of it either—producin' those no-neck monsters. . . .

[*A speech of this kind would be antipathetic from almost anybody but Margaret; she makes it oddly funny, because her eyes constantly twinkle and her voice shakes with laughter which is basically indulgent.*]

—Big Daddy shares my attitude toward those two! As for me, well—I give him a laugh now and then and he tolerates me. In fact!—I sometimes suspect that Big Daddy harbors a little unconscious "lech" fo' me. . . .

BRICK
What makes you think that Big Daddy has a lech for you, Maggie?

MARGARET
Way he always drops his eyes down my body when I'm talkin' to him, drops his eyes to my boobs an' licks his old chops! Ha ha!

BRICK
That kind of talk is disgusting.

MARGARET
Did anyone ever tell you that you're an ass-aching Puritan, Brick?
I think it's mighty fine that that ole fellow, on the doorstep of death, still takes in my shape with what I think is deserved appreciation!
And you wanta know something else? Big Daddy didn't know how many little Maes and Goopers had been produced! "How many kids have you got?" he asked at the table, just like Brother Man and his wife were new acquaintances to him! Big Mama said he was jokin', but that ole boy wasn't jokin', Lord, no!
And when they infawmed him that they had five already and were turning out number six!—the news seemed to come as a sort of unpleasant surprise . . .

[*Children yell below.*]

Scream, monsters!

[*Turns to Brick with a sudden, gay, charming smile which fades as she notices that he is not looking at her but into fading gold space with a troubled expression. It is constant rejection that makes her humor "bitchy."*]

Yes, you should of been at that supper-table, Baby.

[*Whenever she calls him "baby" the word is a soft caress.*]

Y'know, Big Daddy, bless his ole sweet soul, he's the dearest ole thing in the world, but he does hunch over his food as if he preferred not to notice anything else. Well, Mae an' Gooper were side by side at the table, direckly across from Big Daddy, watchin' his face like hawks while they jawed an' jabbered about the cuteness and brilliance of th' no-neck monsters!

[*She giggles with a hand fluttering at her throat and her breast and her long throat arched. She comes downstage and recreates the scene with voice and gesture.*]

And the no-neck monsters were ranged around the table, some in high chairs and some on th' *Books of Knowledge*, all in fancy little paper caps in honor of Big

Daddy's birthday, and all through dinner, well, I want you to know that Brother Man an' his partner never once, for one moment, stopped exchanging pokes an' pinches an' kicks an' signs an' signals!— Why, they were like a couple of cardsharps fleecing a sucker.—Even Big Mama, bless her ole sweet soul, she isn't th' quickest an' brightest thing in the world, she finally noticed, at last, an' said to Gooper, "Gooper, what are you an' Mae makin' all these signs at each other about?"—I swear t' goodness, I nearly choked on my chicken!

[Margaret, back at the dressing-table, still doesn't see Brick. He is watching her with a look that is not quite definable.—Amused? shocked? contemptuous?—part of those and part of something else.]

Y'know—your brother Gooper still cherishes the illusion he took a giant step up on the social ladder when he married Miss Mae Flynn of the Memphis Flynns.

[Margaret moves about the room as she talks, stops before the mirror, moves on.]

But I have a piece of Spanish news for Gooper. The Flynns never had a thing in this world but money and they lost that, they were nothing at all but fairly successful climbers. Of course, Mae Flynn came out in Memphis eight years before I made my debut in Nashville, but I had friends at Ward-Belmont who came from Memphis and they used to come to see me and I used to go to see them for Christmas and spring vacations, and so I know who rates an' who doesn't rate in Memphis society. Why, y'know ole Papa Flynn, he barely escaped doing time in the Federal pen for shady manipulations on th' stock market when his chain stores crashed, and as for Mae having been a cotton carnival queen, as they remind us so often, lest we forget, well, that's one honor that I don't envy her for!—Sit on a brass throne on a tacky float an' ride down Main Street, smilin', bowin', and blowin' kisses to all the trash on the street—

[She picks out a pair of jeweled sandals and rushes to the dressing-table.]

Why, year before last, when Susan McPheeters was singled out fo' that honor, y'know what happened to her? Y'know what happened to poor little Susie McPheeters?

BRICK

[absently] No. What happened to little Susie McPheeters?

MARGARET

Somebody spit tobacco juice in her face.

BRICK

[dreamily] Somebody spit tobacco juice in her face?

MARGARET

That's right, some old drunk leaned out of a window in the Hotel Gayoso and yelled, "Hey, Queen, hey, hey, there, Queenie!" Poor Susie looked up and flashed him a radiant smile and he shot out a squirt of tobacco juice right in poor Susie's face.

BRICK

Well, what d'you know about that.

MARGARET

[gaily] What do I know about it? I was there, I saw it!

BRICK

[absently] Must have been kind of funny.

MARGARET

Susie didn't think so. Had hysterics. Screamed like a banshee. They had to stop th' parade an' remove her from her throne an' go on with—

[She catches sight of him in the mirror, gasps slightly, wheels about to face him. Count ten.]

—Why are you looking at me like that?

BRICK

[whistling softly, now] Like what, Maggie?

MARGARET

[intensely, fearfully] The way y' were lookin' at me just now, befo' I caught your eye in the mirror and you started t' whistle! I don't know how t' describe it but it froze my blood!—I've caught you lookin' at me like that so often lately. What are you thinkin' of when you look at me like that?

BRICK

I wasn't conscious of lookin' at you, Maggie.

MARGARET

Well, I was conscious of it! What were you thinkin'?

BRICK

I don't remember thinking of anything, Maggie.

MARGARET

Don't you think I know that—? Don't you—?—Think I know that—?

BRICK

[coolly] Know what, Maggie?

MARGARET

[struggling for expression] That I've gone through this—hideous!—transformation, become—hard! Frantic!

[Then she adds, almost tenderly:]

—cruel!!

That's what you've been observing in me lately. How could y' help but observe it? That's all right. I'm not—thin-skinned any more, can't afford t' be thin-skinned any more.

[She is now recovering her power.]

—But Brick? Brick?

BRICK

Did you say something?

MARGARET

I was goin' t' say something: that I get—lonely. Very!

BRICK

Ev'rybody gets that . . .

MARGARET

Living with someone you love can be lonelier—than living entirely alone!—if the one that y' love doesn't love you. . . .

[There is a pause. Brick hobbles downstage and asks, without looking at her:]

BRICK

Would you like to live alone, Maggie?

[Another pause: then—after she has caught a quick, hurt breath:]

MARGARET

No!—God!—I wouldn't!

[Another gasping breath. She forcibly controls what must have been an impulse to cry out. We see her deliberately, very forcibly, going all the way back to the world in which you can talk about ordinary matters.]

Did you have a nice shower?

BRICK

Uh-huh.

MARGARET

Was the water cool?

BRICK

No.

MARGARET

But it made y' feel fresh, huh?

BRICK

Fresher. . . .

MARGARET

I know something would make y' feel much fresher!

BRICK

What?

MARGARET

An alcohol rub. Or cologne, a rub with cologne!

BRICK

That's good after a workout but I haven't been workin' out, Maggie.

MARGARET

You've kept in good shape, though.

BRICK

[indifferently] You think so, Maggie?

MARGARET

I always thought drinkin' men lost their looks, but I was plainly mistaken.

BRICK

[wryly] Why, thanks, Maggie.

MARGARET

You're the only drinkin' man I know that it never seems t' put fat on.

BRICK

I'm gettin' softer, Maggie.

MARGARET

Well, sooner or later it's bound to soften you up. It was just beginning to soften up Skipper when—

[She stops short.]

I'm sorry. I never could keep my fingers off a sore—I wish you would lose your looks. If you did it would make the martyrdom of Saint Maggie a little more bearable. But no such goddam luck. I actually believe you've gotten better looking since you've gone on the bottle. Yeah, a person who didn't know you would think you'd never had a tense nerve in your body or a strained muscle.

[There are sounds of croquet on the lawn below: the click of mallets, light voices, near and distant.]

Of course, you always had that detached quality as if you were playing a game without much concern over whether you won or lost, and now that you've lost the game, not lost but just quit playing, you have that rare sort of charm that usually only happens in very old or hopelessly sick people, the charm of the defeated.—You look so cool, so cool, so enviably cool.

[Music is heard.]

They're playing croquet. The moon has appeared and it's white, just beginning to turn a little bit yellow. . . .
You were a wonderful lover. . . .
Such a wonderful person to go to bed with, and I think mostly because you were really indifferent to it. Isn't that right? Never had any anxiety about it, did it naturally, easily, slowly, with absolute confidence and perfect calm, more like opening a door for a lady or seating her at a table than giving expression to any longing for her. Your indifference made you wonderful at lovemaking—*strange?*—but true. . . .
You know, if I thought you would never, never, *never* make love to me again—I would go downstairs to the kitchen and pick out the longest and sharpest knife I could find and stick it straight into my heart, I swear that I would!
But one thing I don't have is the charm of the defeated, my hat is still in the ring, and I am determined to win!

[There is the sound of croquet mallets hitting croquet balls.]

—What is the victory of a cat on a hot tin roof?—I wish I knew. . . .
Just staying on it, I guess, as long as she can. . . .

[More croquet sounds.]

Later tonight I'm going to tell you I love you an' maybe by that time you'll be drunk enough to believe me. Yes, they're playing croquet. . . .
Big Daddy is dying of cancer. . . .
What were you thinking when I caught you looking at me like that? Were you thinking of Skipper?

[Brick takes up his crutch, rises.]

Oh, excuse me, forgive me, but the laws of silence don't work! No, laws of silence don't work. . . .

[Brick crosses to the bar, takes a quick drink, and rubs his head with a towel.]

Laws of silence don't work. . . .
When something is festering in your memory or your imagination, laws of silence don't work, it's just like shutting a door and locking it on a house on fire in hope of forgetting that the house is burning. But not facing a fire doesn't put it out. Silence about a thing just magnifies it. It grows and festers in silence, becomes malignant. . . .
Get dressed, Brick.

[He drops his crutch.]

BRICK
I've dropped my crutch.

[He has stopped rubbing his hair dry but still stands hanging onto the towel rack in a white towel-cloth robe.]

MARGARET
Lean on me.

BRICK
No, just give me my crutch.

MARGARET
Lean on my shoulder.

BRICK
I don't want to lean on your shoulder, I want my crutch!

[This is spoken like sudden lightning.]

Are you going to give me my crutch or do I have to get down on my knees on the floor and—

MARGARET
Here, here, take it, take it!

[She has thrust the crutch at him.]

BRICK
[hobbling out] Thanks . . .

MARGARET
We mustn't scream at each other, the walls in this house have ears. . . .

[He hobbles directly to the liquor cabinet to get a new drink.]

—but that's the first time I've heard you raise your voice in a long time, Brick. A crack in the wall?—Of composure?—I think that's a good sign. . . .
A sign of nerves in a player on the defensive!

[Brick turns and smiles at her coolly over his fresh drink.]

BRICK
It just hasn't happened yet, Maggie.

MARGARET
What?

BRICK
The click I get in my head when I've had enough of this stuff to make me peaceful. . . .
Will you do me a favor?

MARGARET
Maybe I will. What favor?

BRICK
Just, just keep your voice down!

MARGARET
[in a hoarse whisper] I'll do you that favor, I'll speak in a whisper, if not shut up completely, if *you* will do *me* a favor and make that drink your last one till after the party.

BRICK
What party?

MARGARET
Big Daddy's birthday party.

BRICK
Is this Big Daddy's birthday?

MARGARET
You know this is Big Daddy's birthday!

BRICK
No, I don't, I forgot it.

MARGARET
Well, I remembered it for you. . . .

[They are both speaking as breathlessly as a pair of kids after a fight, drawing deep exhausted breaths and looking at each other with faraway eyes, shaking and panting together as if they had broken apart from a violent struggle.]

BRICK
Good for you, Maggie.

MARGARET
You just have to scribble a few lines on this card.

BRICK
You scribble something, Maggie.

MARGARET
It's got to be your handwriting; it's your present, I've given him my present; it's got to be your handwriting!

[The tension between them is building again, the voices becoming shrill once more.]

BRICK
I didn't get him a present.

MARGARET
I got one for you.

BRICK
All right. You write the card, then.

MARGARET
And have him know you didn't remember his birthday?

BRICK
I didn't remember his birthday.

MARGARET
You don't have to prove you didn't!

BRICK
I don't want to fool him about it.

MARGARET
Just write "Love, Brick!" for God's—

BRICK
No.

MARGARET
You've *got* to!

BRICK
I don't have to do anything I don't want to do. You keep forgetting the conditions on which I agreed to stay on living with you.

MARGARET
[out before she knows it] I'm not living with you. We occupy the same cage.

BRICK
You've got to remember the conditions agreed on.

MARGARET
They're impossible conditions!

BRICK
Then why don't you—?

MARGARET
HUSH! Who is out there? Is somebody at the door?

[There are footsteps in hall.]

MAE

[outside] May I enter a moment?

MARGARET

Oh, *you!* Sure. Come in, Mae.

[Mae enters bearing aloft the bow of a young lady's
archery set.]

MAE

Brick, is this thing yours?

MARGARET

Why, Sister Woman—that's my Diana Trophy. Won
it at the intercollegiate archery contest on the Ole
Miss campus.

MAE

It's a mighty dangerous thing to leave exposed round
a house full of nawmal rid-blooded children attracted
t'weapons.

MARGARET

"Nawmal rid-blooded children attracted t'weapons"
ought t'be taught to keep their hands off things that
don't belong to them.

MAE

Maggie, honey, if you had children of your own you'd
know how funny that is. Will you please lock this up
and put the key out of reach?

MARGARET

Sister Woman, nobody is plotting the destruction of
your kiddies. —Brick and I still have our special
archers' license. We're goin' deer-huntin' on Moon
Lake as soon as the season starts. I love to run with
dogs through chilly woods, run, run, leap over ob-
structions—

[She goes into the closet carrying the bow.]

MAE

How's the injured ankle, Brick?

BRICK

Doesn't hurt. Just itches.

MAE

Oh, my! Brick—Brick, you should've been downstairs after supper! Kiddies put on a show. Polly
played the piano, Buster an' Sonny drums, an' then
they turned out the lights an' Dixie an' Trixie
puhfawmed a toe dance in fairy costume with *spahk-
luhs!* Big Daddy just beamed! He just beamed!

MARGARET

[from the closet with a sharp laugh] Oh, I bet. It breaks
my heart that we missed it!

[She reenters.]

But Mae? Why did y'give dawgs' names to all your
kiddies?

MAE

Dogs' names?

[Margaret has made this observation as she goes to
raise the bamboo blinds, since the sunset glare has
diminished. In crossing she winks at Brick.]

MARGARET

[sweetly] Dixie, Trixie, Buster, Sonny, Polly!—
Sounds like four dogs and a parrot . . . animal act in
a circus!

MAE

Maggie?

[Margaret turns with a smile.]

Why are you so catty?

MARGARET

Cause I'm a cat! But why can't *you* take a joke, Sister
Woman?

MAE

Nothin' pleases me more than a joke that's funny. You
know the real names of our kiddies. Buster's real
name is Robert. Sonny's real name is Saunders. Trixie's real name is Marlene and Dixie's—

[Someone downstairs calls for her. "Hey, Mae!"—She
rushes to door, saying:]

Intermission is over!

MARGARET

[as Mae closes door] I wonder what Dixie's real name
is?

BRICK

Maggie, being catty doesn't help things any . . .

MARGARET

I know! *WHY!*—Am I so catty?—Cause I'm consumed with envy an' eaten up with longing?—Brick,
I've laid out your beautiful Shantung silk suit from
Rome and one of your monogrammed silk shirts. I'll
put your cuff-links in it, those lovely star sapphires I
get you to wear so rarely. . . .

BRICK
I can't get trousers on over this plaster cast.

MARGARET
Yes, you can, I'll help you.

BRICK
I'm not going to get dressed, Maggie.

MARGARET
Will you just put on a pair of white silk pajamas?

BRICK
Yes, I'll do that, Maggie.

MARGARET
Thank you, thank you so *much!*

BRICK
Don't mention it.

MARGARET
Oh, Brick! How long does it have t' go on? This punishment? Haven't I done time enough, haven't I served my term, can't I apply for a—pardon?

BRICK
Maggie, you're spoiling my liquor. Lately your voice always sounds like you'd been running upstairs to warn somebody that the house was on fire!

MARGARET
Well, no wonder, no wonder. Y'know what I feel like, Brick?

[Children's and grownups' voices are blended, below, in a loud but uncertain rendition of "My Wild Irish Rose."]

I feel all the time like a cat on a hot tin roof!

BRICK
Then jump off the roof, jump off it, cats can jump off roofs and land on their four feet uninjured!

MARGARET
Oh, yes!

BRICK
Do it!—fo' God's sake, do it . . .

MARGARET
Do what?

BRICK
Take a lover!

MARGARET
I can't see a man but you! Even with my eyes closed, I just see you! Why don't you get ugly, Brick, why don't you please get fat or ugly or something so I could stand it?

[She rushes to hall door, opens it, listens.]

The concert is still going on! Bravo, no-necks, bravo!

[She slams and locks door fiercely.]

BRICK
What did you lock the door for?

MARGARET
To give us a little privacy for a while.

BRICK
You know better, Maggie.

MARGARET
No, I don't know better. . . .

[She rushes to gallery doors, draws the rose-silk drapes across them.]

BRICK
Don't make a fool of yourself.

MARGARET
I don't mind makin' a fool of myself over you!

BRICK
I mind, Maggie. I feel embarrassed for you.

MARGARET
Feel embarrassed! But don't continue my torture. I can't live on and on under these circumstances.

BRICK
You agreed to—

MARGARET
I know but—

BRICK
—Accept that condition!

MARGARET
I CAN'T! CAN'T! CAN'T!

[She seizes his shoulder.]

BRICK
Let go!

[He breaks away from her and seizes the small boudoir chair and raises it like a lion-tamer facing a big circus cat.

Count five. She stares at him with her fist pressed to her mouth, then bursts into shrill, almost hysterical laughter. He remains grave for a moment, then grins and puts the chair down.

Big Mama calls through closed door.]

BIG MAMA
Son? Son? Son?

BRICK
What is it, Big Mama?

BIG MAMA
[outside] Oh, son! We got the most wonderful news about Big Daddy. I just had t' run up an' tell you right this—

[She rattles the knob.]

—What's this door doin', locked, faw? You all think there's robbers in the house?

MARGARET
Big Mama, Brick is dressin', he's not dressed yet.

BIG MAMA
That's all right, it won't be the first time I've seen Brick not dressed. Come on, open this door!

[Margaret, with a grimace, goes to unlock and open the hall door, as Brick hobbles rapidly to the bathroom and kicks the door shut. Big Mama has disappeared from the hall.]

MARGARET
Big Mama?

[Big Mama appears through the opposite gallery doors behind Margaret, huffing and puffing like an old bulldog. She is a short, stout woman; her sixty years and 170 pounds have left her somewhat breathless most of the time; she's always tensed like a boxer, or rather, a Japanese wrestler. Her "family" was maybe a little superior to Big Daddy's, but not much. She wears a black or silver lace dress and at least half a million in flashy gems. She is very sincere.]

BIG MAMA
[loudly, startling Margaret] Here—I come through Gooper's and Mae's gall'ry door. Where's Brick? Brick—Hurry on out of there, son, I just have a second and want to give you the news about Big Daddy.—I hate locked doors in a house. . . .

MARGARET
[with affected lightness] I've noticed you do, Big Mama, but people have got to have some moments of privacy, don't they?

BIG MAMA
No, ma'am, not in my house. [Without pause] Whacha took off you' dress faw? I thought that little lace dress was so sweet on yuh, honey.

MARGARET
I thought it looked sweet on me, too, but one of m' cute little table-partners used it for a napkin so—!

BIG MAMA
[picking up stockings on floor] What?

MARGARET
You know, Big Mama, Mae and Gooper's so touchy about those children—thanks, Big Mama . . .

[Big Mama has thrust the picked-up stockings in Margaret's hand with a grunt.]

—that you just don't dare to suggest there's any room for improvement in their—

BIG MAMA
Brick, hurry out!—Shoot, Maggie, you just don't like children.

MARGARET
I do SO like children! Adore them!—well brought up!

BIG MAMA
[gentle—loving] Well, why don't you have some and bring them up well, then, instead of all the time pickin' on Gooper's an' Mae's?

GOOPER
[shouting up the stairs]Hey, hey, Big Mama, Betsy an' Hugh got to go, waitin' t' tell yuh g'by!

BIG MAMA
Tell 'em to hold their hawses, I'll be right down in a jiffy!

[She turns to the bathroom door and calls out.]

Son? Can you hear me in there?

[There is a muffled answer.]

We just got the full report from the laboratory at the Ochsner Clinic, completely negative, son, ev'rything negative, right on down the line! Nothin' a-tall's wrong with him but some little functional thing called a spastic colon. Can you hear me, son?

MARGARET
He can hear you, Big Mama.

BIG MAMA
Then why don't he say something? God Almighty, a piece of news like that should make him shout. It made *me* shout, I can tell you. I shouted and sobbed and fell right down on my knees—Look!

[*She pulls up her skirt.*]

See the bruises where I hit my kneecaps? Took both doctors to haul me back on my feet!

[*She laughs—she always laughs like hell at herself.*]

Big Daddy was furious with me! But ain't that wonderful news?

[*Facing bathroom again, she continues:*]

After all the anxiety we been through to git a report like that on Big Daddy's birthday? Big Daddy tried to hide how much of a load that news took off his mind, but didn't fool *me*. He was mighty close to crying about it *himself*!

[*Goodbyes are shouted downstairs, and she rushes to door.*]

Hold those people down there, don't let them go!—Now, git dressed, we're all comin' up to this room fo' Big Daddy's birthday party because of your ankle.—How's his ankle, Maggie?

MARGARET
Well, he broke it, Big Mama.

BIG MAMA
I know he broke it.

[*A phone is ringing in hall. A Negro voice answers: "Mistuh Polly's res'dence."*]

I mean does it hurt him much still.

MARGARET
I'm afraid I can't give you that information, Big Mama. You'll have to ask Brick if it hurts much still or not.

SOOKEY
[*in the hall*] It's Memphis, Mizz Polly, it's Miss Sally in Memphis.

BIG MAMA
Awright, Sookey.

[*Big Mama rushes into the hall and is heard shouting on the phone:*]

Hello, Miss Sally. How are you, Miss Sally?—Yes, well, I was just gonna call you about it. *Shoot!*—

[*She raises her voice to a bellow.*]

Miss Sally? Don't ever call me from the Gayoso Lobby, too much talk goes on in that hotel lobby, no wonder you can't hear me! Now listen, Miss Sally. They's nothin' serious wrong with Big Daddy. We got the report just now, they's nothin' wrong but a thing called a—spastic! SPASTIC!—colon . . .

[*She appears at the hall door and calls to Margaret.*]

—Maggie, come out here and talk to that fool on the phone. I'm shouted breathless!

MARGARET
[*goes out and is heard sweetly at phone*] Miss Sally? This is Brick's wife, Maggie. So nice to hear your voice. Can you hear *mine*? Well, *good*!—Big Mama just wanted you to know that they've got the report from the Ochsner Clinic and what Big Daddy has is a spastic colon. Yes. Spastic colon, Miss Sally. That's right, spastic colon. *G'bye, Miss Sally, hope I'll see you real soon!*

[*Hangs up a little before Miss Sally was probably ready to terminate the talk. She returns through the hall door.*]

She heard me perfectly. I've discovered with deaf people the thing to do is not shout at them but just enunciate clearly. My rich old Aunt Cornelia was deaf as the dead but I could make her hear me just by sayin' each word slowly, distinctly, close to her ear. I read her the *Commercial Appeal* ev'ry night, read her the classified ads in it, even, she never missed a word of it. But was she a mean ole thing! Know what I got when she died? Her unexpired subscriptions to five magazines and the Book-of-the-Month Club and a LIBRARY full of ev'ry dull book ever written! All else went to her hellcat of a sister . . . meaner than she was, even!

[*Big Mama has been straightening things up in the room during this speech.*]

BIG MAMA
[*closing closet door on discarded clothes*] Miss Sally sure is a case! Big Daddy says she's always got her hand out fo' something. He's not mistaken. That poor ole thing

always has her hand out fo' somethin'. I don't think Big Daddy gives her as much as he should.

[Somebody shouts for her downstairs and she shouts:]

I'm comin'!

[She starts out. At the hall door, turns and jerks a forefinger, first toward the bathroom door, then toward the liquor cabinet, meaning: "Has Brick been drinking?" Margaret pretends not to understand, cocks her head and raises her brows as if the pantomimic performance was completely mystifying to her. Big Mama rushes back to Margaret:]

Shoot! Stop playin' so dumb!—I mean has he been drinkin' that stuff much yet?

MARGARET
[with a little laugh] Oh! I think he had a highball after supper.

BIG MAMA
Don't laugh about it!—Some single men stop drinkin' when they git married and others start! Brick never touched liquor before he—!

MARGARET
[crying out] THAT'S NOT FAIR!

BIG MAMA
Fair or not fair I want to ask you a question, one question: D'you make Brick happy in bed?

MARGARET
Why don't you ask if he makes *me* happy in bed?

BIG MAMA
Because I know that—

MARGARET
It works both ways!

BIG MAMA
Something's not right! You're childless and my son drinks!

[Someone has called her downstairs and she has rushed to the door on the line above. She turns at the door and points at the bed.]

—When a marriage goes on the rocks, the rocks are there, right *there*!

MARGARET
That's—

[Big Mama has swept out of the room and slammed the door.]

—not—*fair* . . .

[Margaret is alone, completely alone, and she feels it. She draws in, hunches her shoulders, raises her arms with fists clenched, shuts her eyes tight as a child about to be stabbed with a vaccination needle. When she opens her eyes again, what she sees is the long oval mirror and she rushes straight to it, stares into it with a grimace and says: "Who are you?"—Then she crouches a little and answers herself in a different voice which is high, thin, mocking: "I am Maggie the Cat!"— Straightens quickly as bathroom door opens a little and Brick calls out to her.]

BRICK
Has Big Mama gone?

MARGARET
She's gone.

[He opens the bathroom door and hobbles out, with his liquor glass now empty, straight to the liquor cabinet. He is whistling softly. Margaret's head pivots on her long, slender throat to watch him.
She raises a hand uncertainly to the base of her throat, as if it was difficult for her to swallow, before she speaks:]

You know, our sex life didn't just peter out in the usual way, it was cut off short, long before the natural time for it to, and it's going to revive again, just as sudden as that. I'm confident of it. That's what I'm keeping myself attractive for. For the time when you'll see me again like other men see me. Yes, like other men see me. They still see me, Brick, and they like what they see. Uh-huh. Some of them would give their—Look, Brick!

[She stands before the long oval mirror, touches her breast and then her hips with her two hands.]

How high my body stays on me!—Nothing has fallen on me—not a fraction. . . .

[Her voice is soft and trembling: a pleading child's. At this moment as he turns to glance at her—a look which is like a player passing a ball to another player, third down and goal to go—she has to capture the audience in a grip so tight that she can hold it till the first intermission without any lapse of attention.]

Other men still want me. My face looks strained, sometimes, but I've kept my figure as well as you've kept yours, and men admire it: I still turn heads on the street. Why, last week in Memphis everywhere that I went men's eyes burned holes in my clothes, at the country club and in restaurants and department stores, there wasn't a man I met or walked by that didn't just eat me up with his eyes and turn around when I passed him and look back at me. Why, at Alice's party for her New York cousins, the best lookin' man in the crowd—followed me upstairs and tried to force his way in the powder room with me, followed me to the door and tried to force his way in!

BRICK
Why didn't you let him, Maggie?

MARGARET
Because I'm not that common, for one thing. Not that I wasn't almost tempted to. You like to know who it was? It was Sonny Boy Maxwell, that's who!

BRICK
Oh, yeah, Sonny Boy Maxwell, he was a good end-runner but had a little injury to his back and had to quit.

MARGARET
He has no injury now and has no wife and still has a lech for me!

BRICK
I see no reason to lock him out of a powder room in that case.

MARGARET
And have someone catch me at it? I'm not that stupid. Oh, I might sometime cheat on you with someone, since you're so insultingly eager to have me do it!—But if I do, you can be damned sure it will be in a place and a time where no one but me and the man could possibly know. Because I'm not going to give you any excuse to divorce me for being unfaithful or anything else. . . .

BRICK
Maggie, I wouldn't divorce you for being unfaithful or anything else. Don't you know that? Hell. I'd be relieved to know that you'd found yourself a lover.

MARGARET
Well, I'm taking no chances. No, I'd rather stay on this hot tin roof.

BRICK
A hot tin roof's 'n uncomfo'table place t' stay on. . . .

[He starts to whistle softly.]

MARGARET
[through his whistle] Yeah, but I can stay on it just as long as I have to.

BRICK
You could leave me, Maggie.

[He resumes whistle. She wheels about to glare at him.]

MARGARET
Don't want to and will not! Besides if I did, you don't have a cent to pay for it but what you get from Big Daddy and he's dying of cancer!

[For the first time a realization of Big Daddy's doom seems to penetrate to Brick's consciousness, visibly, and he looks at Margaret.]

BRICK
Big Mama just said he *wasn't*, that the report was okay.

MARGARET
That's what she thinks because she got the same story that they gave Big Daddy. And was just as taken in by it as he was, poor ole things. . . .
But tonight they're going to tell her the truth about it. When Big Daddy goes to bed, they're going to tell her that he is dying of cancer.

[She slams the dresser drawer.]

—It's malignant and it's terminal.

BRICK
Does Big Daddy know it?

MARGARET
Hell, do they *ever* know it? Nobody says, "You're dying." You have to fool them. They have to fool *themselves.*

BRICK
Why?

MARGARET
Why? Because human beings dream of life everlasting, that's the reason! But most of them want it on earth and not in heaven.

[He gives a short, hard laugh at her touch of humor.]

Well. . . . *[She touches up her mascara.]* That's how it is, anyhow. . . . *[She looks about.]* Where did I put down my cigarette? Don't want to burn up the homeplace, at least not with Mae and Gooper and their five monsters in it!

[She has found it and sucks at it greedily. Blows out smoke and continues:]

So this is Big Daddy's last birthday. And Mae and Gooper, they know it, oh, *they* know it, all right. They got the first information from the Ochsner Clinic. That's why they rushed down here with their no-neck monsters. Because. Do you know something? Big Daddy's made no will? Big Daddy's never made out any will in his life, and so this campaign's afoot to impress him, forcibly as possible, with the fact that you drink and I've borne no children!

[He continues to stare at her a moment, then mutters something sharp but not audible and hobbles rather rapidly out onto the long gallery in the fading, much faded, gold light.]

MARGARET

[continuing her liturgical chant] Y'know, I'm *fond* of Big Daddy, I am genuinely fond of that old man, I really *am*, you know. . . .

BRICK

[faintly, vaguely] Yes, I know you are. . . .

MARGARET

I've always sort of admired him in spite of his coarseness, his four-letter words and so forth. Because Big Daddy *is* what he *is*, and he makes no bones about it. He hasn't turned gentleman farmer, he's still a Mississippi red neck, as much of a red neck as he must have been when he was just overseer here on the old Jack Straw and Peter Ochello place. But he got hold of it an' built it into th' biggest an' finest plantation in the Delta.—I've always *liked* Big Daddy. . . .

[She crosses to the proscenium.]

Well, this is Big Daddy's last birthday. I'm sorry about it. But I'm facing the facts. It takes money to take care of a drinker and that's the office that I've been elected to lately.

BRICK

You don't have to take care of me.

MARGARET

Yes, I do. Two people in the same boat have got to take care of each other. At least you want money to buy more Echo Spring when this supply is exhausted, or will you be satisfied with a ten-cent beer? Mae an' Gooper are plannin' to freeze us out of Big Daddy's estate because you drink and I'm childless. But we can defeat that plan. We're *going* to defeat that plan!

Brick, y'know, I've been so God damn disgustingly poor all my life!—That's the *truth*, Brick!

BRICK

I'm not sayin' it isn't.

MARGARET

Always had to suck up to people I couldn't stand because they had money and I was poor as Job's turkey. You don't know what that's like. Well, I'll tell you, it's like you would feel a thousand miles away from Echo Spring!—And had to get back to it on that broken ankle . . . without a crutch!

That's how it feels to be as poor as Job's turkey and have to suck up to relatives that you hated because they had money and all you had was a bunch of hand-me-down clothes and a few old moldy three per cent government bonds. My daddy loved his liquor, he fell in love with his liquor the way you've fallen in love with Echo Spring!—And my poor mama, having to maintain some semblance of social position, to keep appearances up, on an income of one hundred and fifty dollars a month on those old government bonds! When I came out, the year that I made my debut, I had just two evening dresses! One Mother made me from a pattern in *Vogue*, the other a hand-me-down from a snotty rich cousin I hated!

—The dress that I married you in was my grandmother's weddin' gown. . . .

So that's why I'm like a cat on a hot tin roof!

[Brick is still on the gallery. Someone below calls up to him in a warm Negro voice, "Hiya, Mistuh Brick, how yuh feelin'?" Brick raises his liquor glass as if that answered the question.]

MARGARET

You can be young without money but you can't be old without it. You've got to be old *with* money because to be old without it is just too awful, you've got to be one or the other, either *young* or *with money*, you can't be old and *without* it.—That's the truth, Brick. . . .

[Brick whistles softly, vaguely.]

Well, now I'm dressed, I'm all dressed, there's nothing else for me to do.

[Forlornly, almost fearfully.]

I'm dressed, all dressed, nothing else for me to do. . . .

[She moves about restlessly, aimlessly, and speaks, as if to herself.]

I know when I made my mistake.—What am I—? Oh!—my bracelets. . . .

[She starts working a collection of bracelets over her hands onto her wrists, about six on each, as she talks.]

I've thought a whole lot about it and now I know when I made my mistake. Yes, I made my mistake when I told you the truth about that thing with Skipper. Never should have confessed it, a fatal error, tellin' you about that thing with Skipper.

BRICK

Maggie, shut up about Skipper. I mean it, Maggie; you got to shut up about Skipper.

MARGARET

You ought to understand that Skipper and I—

BRICK

You don't think I'm serious, Maggie? You're fooled by the fact that I am saying this quiet? Look, Maggie. What you're doing is a dangerous thing to do. You're—you're—you're—foolin' with something that—nobody ought to fool with.

MARGARET

This time I'm going to finish what I have to say to you. Skipper and I made love, if love you could call it, because it made both of us feel a little bit closer to you. You see, you son of a bitch, you asked too much of people, of me, of him, of all the unlucky poor damned sons of bitches that happen to love you, and there was a whole pack of them, yes, there was a pack of them besides me and Skipper, you asked too goddam much of people that loved you, you—superior creature—you godlike being!—And so we made love to each other to dream it was you, both of us! Yes, yes, yes! Truth, truth! What's so awful about it? I like it, I think the truth is—yeah! I shouldn't have told you. . . .

BRICK

[holding his head unnaturally still and uptilted a bit] It was Skipper that told me about it. Not you, Maggie.

MARGARET

I told you!

BRICK

After he told me!

MARGARET

What does it matter who—?

[Brick turns suddenly out upon the gallery and calls:]

BRICK

Little girl! Hey, little girl!

LITTLE GIRL

[at a distance] What, Uncle Brick?

BRICK

Tell the folks to come up!—Bring everybody upstairs!

MARGARET

I can't stop myself! I'd go on telling you this in front of them all, if I had to!

BRICK

Little girl! Go on, go on, will you? Do what I told you, call them!

MARGARET

Because it's got to be told, and you, you!—you never let me!

[She sobs, then controls herself, and continues almost calmly.]

It was one of those beautiful, ideal things they tell you about in the Greek legends, it couldn't be anything else, you being you, and that's what made it so sad, that's what made it so awful, because it was love that never could be carried through to anything satisfying or even talked about plainly. Brick, I tell you, you got to believe me, Brick, I *do* understand all about it! I—I think it was—*noble*! Can't you tell I'm sincere when I say I respect it? My only point, the only point that I'm making, is life has got to be allowed to continue even after the *dream* of life is—all—over. . . .

[Brick is without his crutch. Leaning on furniture, he crosses to pick it up as she continues as if possessed by a will outside herself:]

Why I remember when we double-dated at college, Gladys Fitzgerald and I and you and Skipper, it was more like a date between you and Skipper. Gladys and I were just sort of tagging along as if it was necessary to chaperone you!—to make a good public impression—

BRICK

[turns to face her, half lifting his crutch] Maggie, you want me to hit you with this crutch? Don't you know I could kill you with this crutch?

MARGARET

Good Lord, man, d' you think I'd care if you did?

BRICK

One man has one great good true thing in his life. One great good thing which is true!—I had friendship with Skipper.—You are naming it dirty!

MARGARET

I'm not naming it dirty! I am naming it clean.

BRICK

Not love with you, Maggie, but friendship with Skipper was that one great true thing, and you are naming it dirty!

MARGARET

Then you haven't been listenin', not understood what I'm saying! I'm naming it so damn clean that it killed poor Skipper!—You two had something that had to be kept on ice, yes, incorruptible, yes!—and death was the only icebox where you could keep it. . . .

BRICK

I married you, Maggie. Why would I marry you, Maggie, if I was—?

MARGARET

Brick, don't brain me yet, let me finish!—I know, believe me I know, that it was only Skipper that harbored even any *unconscious* desire for anything not perfectly pure between you two!—Now let me skip a little. You married me early that summer we graduated out of Ole Miss, and we were happy, weren't we, we were blissful, yes, hit heaven together ev'ry time that we loved! But that fall you an' Skipper turned down wonderful offers of jobs in order to keep on bein' football heroes—pro-football heroes. You organized the Dixie Stars that fall, so you could keep on bein' team-mates forever! But somethin' was not right with it!—*Me included!*—between you. Skipper began hittin' the bottle . . . you got a spinal injury—couldn't play the Thanksgivin' game in Chicago, watched it on TV from a traction bed in Toledo. I joined Skipper. The Dixie Stars lost because poor Skipper was drunk. We drank together that night all night in the bar of the Blackstone and when cold day was comin' up over the Lake an' we were comin' out drunk to take a dizzy look at it, I said, "SKIPPER! STOP LOVIN' MY HUSBAND OR TELL HIM HE'S GOT TO LET YOU ADMIT IT TO HIM!"—one way or another!

HE SLAPPED ME HARD ON THE MOUTH!—then turned and ran without stopping once, I am sure, all the way back into his room at the Blackstone. . . .

—When I came to his room that night, with a little scratch like a shy little mouse at his door, he made that pitiful, ineffectual little attempt to prove that what I had said wasn't true. . . .

[Brick strikes at her with crutch, a blow that shatters the gemlike lamp on the table.]

—In this way, I destroyed him, by telling him truth that he and his world which he was born and raised in, yours and his world, had told him could not be told?

—From then on Skipper was nothing at all but a receptacle for liquor and drugs. . . .

—*Who shot cock-robin? I with my*—

[She throws back her head with tight shut eyes.]

—*merciful arrow!*

[Brick strikes at her; misses.]

Missed me!—Sorry,—I'm not tryin' to whitewash my behavior, Christ, no! Brick, I'm not good. I don't know why people have to pretend to be good, nobody's good. The rich or the well-to-do can afford to respect moral patterns, conventional moral patterns, but I could never afford to, yeah, but—I'm honest! Give me credit for just that, will you *please?*—Born poor, raised poor, expect to die poor unless I manage to get us something out of what Big Daddy leaves when he dies of cancer! But Brick?!—*Skipper is dead! I'm alive!* Maggie the cat is—

[Brick hops awkwardly forward and strikes at her again with his crutch.]

—*alive! I am alive, alive! I am . . .*

[He hurls the crutch at her, across the bed she took refuge behind, and pitches forward on the floor as she completes her speech.]

—*alive!*

[A little girl, Dixie, bursts into the room, wearing an Indian war bonnet and firing a cap pistol at Margaret and shouting: "Bang, bang, bang!" Laughter downstairs floats through the open hall door. Margaret had crouched gasping to bed at child's entrance. She now rises and says with cool fury:]

Little girl, your mother or someone should teach you—*[Gasping]*—to knock at a door before you come into a room. Otherwise people might think that you—lack—good breeding. . . .

DIXIE

Yanh, yanh, yanh, what is Uncle Brick doin' on th' floor?

BRICK

I tried to kill your Aunt Maggie, but I failed—and I fell. Little girl, give me my crutch so I can get up off th' floor.

MARGARET

Yes, give your uncle his crutch, he's a cripple, honey, he broke his ankle last night jumping hurdles on the high school athletic field!

DIXIE

What were you jumping hurdles for, Uncle Brick?

BRICK

Because I used to jump them, and people like to do what they used to do, even after they've stopped being able to do it. . . .

MARGARET

That's right, that's your answer, now go away, little girl.

[Dixie fires cap pistol at Margaret three times.]

Stop, you stop that, monster! You little no-neck monster!

[She seizes the cap pistol and hurls it through gallery doors.]

DIXIE

[with a precocious instinct for the cruelest thing] You're jealous!—You're just jealous because you can't have babies!

[She sticks out her tongue at Margaret as she sashays past her with her stomach stuck out, to the gallery. Margaret slams the gallery doors and leans panting against them. There is a pause. Brick has replaced his spilt drink and sits, faraway, on the great four-poster bed.]

MARGARET

You see?—they gloat over us being childless, even in front of their five little no-neck monsters!

[Pause. Voices approach on the stairs.]

Brick?—I've been to a doctor in Memphis, a—a gynecologist. . . .

I've been completely examined, and there is no reason why we can't have a child whenever we want one. And this is my time by the calendar to conceive. Are you listening to me? Are you? Are you LISTENING TO ME!

BRICK

Yes. I hear you, Maggie.

[His attention returns to her inflamed face.]

—But how in hell on earth do you imagine—that you're going to have a child by a man that can't stand you?

MARGARET

That's a problem that I will have to work out.

[She wheels about to face the hall door.]

Here they come!

[The lights dim.]

[Curtain]

ACT TWO

There is no lapse of time. Margaret and Brick are in the same positions they held at the end of Act One.

MARGARET

[at door] Here they come!

[Big Daddy appears first, a tall man with a fierce, anxious look, moving carefully not to betray his weakness even, or especially, to himself.]

BIG DADDY

Well, Brick.

BRICK

Hello, Big Daddy.—Congratulations!

BIG DADDY

—Crap. . . .

[Some of the people are approaching through the hall, others along the gallery: voices from both directions. Gooper and Reverend Tooker become visible outside gallery doors, and their voices come in clearly. They pause outside as Gooper lights a cigar.]

REVEREND TOOKER

[vivaciously] Oh, but St. Paul's in Grenada has three memorial windows, and the latest one is a Tiffany stained-glass window that cost twenty-five hundred dollars, a picture of Christ the Good Shepherd with a Lamb in His arms.

GOOPER

Who give that window, Preach?

REVEREND TOOKER

Clyde Fletcher's widow. Also presented St. Paul's with a baptismal font.

GOOPER

Y'know what somebody ought t' give your church is a *coolin'* system, Preach.

REVEREND TOOKER

Yes, siree, Bob! And y'know what Gus Hamma's family gave in his memory to the church at Two Rivers? A complete new stone parish-house with a basketball court in the basement and a—

BIG DADDY

[uttering a loud barking laugh which is far from truly mirthful] Hey, Preach! What's all this talk about memorials, Preach? Y' think somebody's about t' kick off around here? 'S that it?

[Startled by this interjection, Reverend Tooker decides to laugh at the question almost as loud as he can. How he would answer the question we'll never know, as he's spared that embarrassment by the voice of Gooper's wife, Mae, rising high and clear as she appears with "Doc" Baugh, the family doctor, through the hall door.]

MAE

[almost religiously] —Let's see now, they've had their tyyy-phoid shots, and their tetanus shots, their diphtheria shots and their hepatitis shots and their polio shots, they got *those* shots every month from May through September, and—Gooper? Hey! Gooper!— What all have the kiddies been shot faw?

MARGARET

[overlapping a bit] Turn on the Hi-Fi, Brick! Let's have some music t' start off th' party with!

[The talk becomes so general that the room sounds like a great aviary of chattering birds. Only Brick remains unengaged, leaning upon the liquor cabinet with his faraway smile, an ice cube in a paper napkin with which he now and then rubs his forehead. He doesn't respond to Margaret's command. She bounds forward and stoops over the instrument panel of the console.]

GOOPER

We gave 'em that thing for a third anniversary present, got three speakers in it.

[The room is suddenly blasted by the climax of a Wagnerian opera or a Beethoven symphony.]

BIG DADDY

Turn that damn thing off!

[Almost instant silence, almost instantly broken by the shouting charge of Big Mama, entering through the hall door like a charging rhino.]

BIG MAMA

Wha's my Brick, wha's mah precious baby!

BIG DADDY

Sorry! Turn it back on!

[Everyone laughs very loud. Big Daddy is famous for his jokes at Big Mama's expense, and nobody laughs louder at these jokes than Big Mama herself, though sometimes they're pretty cruel and Big Mama has to pick up or fuss with something to cover the hurt that the loud laugh doesn't quite cover.

On this occasion, a happy occasion because the dread in her heart has also been lifted by the false report on Big Daddy's condition, she giggles, grotesquely, coyly, in Big Daddy's direction and bears down upon Brick, all very quick and alive.]

BIG MAMA

Here he is, here's my precious baby! What's that you've got in your hand? You put that liquor down, son, your hand was made fo' holdin' somethin' better than that!

GOOPER

Look at Brick put it down.

[Brick has obeyed Big Mama by draining the glass and handing it to her. Again everyone laughs, some high, some low.]

BIG MAMA

Oh, you bad boy, you, you're my bad little boy. Give Big Mama a kiss, you bad boy, you!—Look at him shy away, will you? Brick never liked bein' kissed or made a fuss over, I guess because he's always had too much of it!

Son, you turn that thing off!

[Brick has switched on the TV set.]

I can't stand TV, radio was bad enough but TV has gone it one better, I mean—*[Plops wheezing in chair]*—one worse, ha ha! Now what'm I sittin' down here faw? I want t' sit next to my sweetheart on the sofa, hold hands with him and love him up a little!

[*Big Mama has on a black and white figured chiffon. The large irregular patterns, like the markings of some massive animal, the luster of her great diamonds and many pearls, the brilliants set in the silver frames of her glasses, her riotous voice, booming laugh, have dominated the room since she entered. Big Daddy has been regarding her with a steady grimace of chronic annoyance.*]

BIG MAMA

[*still louder*] Preacher, Preacher, hey, Preach! Give me you' hand an' help me up from this chair!

REVEREND TOOKER

None of your tricks, Big Mama!

BIG MAMA

What tricks? You give me you' hand so I can get up an'—

[*Reverend Tooker extends her his hand. She grabs it and pulls him into her lap with a shrill laugh that spans an octave in two notes.*]

Ever seen a preacher in a fat lady's lap? Hey, hey, folks! Ever seen a preacher in a fat lady's lap?

[*Big Mama is notorious throughout the Delta for this sort of inelegant horseplay. Margaret looks on with indulgent humor, sipping Dubonnet "on the rocks" and watching Brick, but Mae and Gooper exchange signs of humorless anxiety over these antics, the sort of behavior which Mae thinks may account for their failure to quite get in with the smartest young married set in Memphis, despite all. One of the Negroes, Lacy or Sookey, peeks in, cackling. They are waiting for a sign to bring in the cake and champagne. But Big Daddy's not amused. He doesn't understand why, in spite of the infinite mental relief he's received from the doctor's report, he still has these same old fox teeth in his guts. "This spastic thing sure is something," he says to himself, but aloud he roars at Big Mama:*]

BIG DADDY

BIG MAMA, WILL YOU QUIT HORSIN'?—You're too old an' too fat fo' that sort of crazy kid stuff an' besides a woman with your blood-pressure—she had two hundred last spring!—is riskin' a stroke when you mess around like that. . . .

BIG MAMA

Here comes Big Daddy's birthday!

[*Negroes in white jackets enter with an enormous birthday cake ablaze with candles and carrying buckets of champagne with satin ribbons about the bottle necks.*

Mae and Gooper strike up song, and everybody, including the Negroes and Children, joins in. Only Brick remains aloof.]

EVERYONE

Happy birthday to you.
Happy birthday to you.
Happy birthday, Big Daddy—

[*Some sing: "Dear, Big Daddy!"*]

Happy birthday to you.

[*Some sing: "How old are you?"*]

[*Mae has come down center and is organizing her children like a chorus. She gives them a barely audible: "One, two, three!" and they are off in the new tune.*]

CHILDREN

Skinamarinka—dinka—dink
Skinamarinka—do
We love you.
Skinamarinka—dinka—dink
Skinamarinka—do

[*All together, they turn to Big Daddy.*]

Big Daddy, you!

[*They turn back front, like a musical comedy chorus.*]

We love you in the morning;
We love you in the night.
We love you when we're with you,
And we love you out of sight.
Skinamarinka—dinka—dink
Skinamarinka—do.

[*Mae turns to Big Mama.*]

Big Mama, too!

[*Big Mama bursts into tears. The Negroes leave.*]

BIG DADDY

Now Ida, what the hell is the matter with you?

MAE

She's just so happy.

BIG MAMA

I'm just so happy, Big Daddy, I have to cry or something.

[Sudden and loud in the hush:]

Brick, do you know the wonderful news that Doc Baugh got from the clinic about Big Daddy? Big Daddy's one hundred per cent!

MARGARET
Isn't that wonderful?

BIG MAMA
He's just one hundred per cent. Passed the examination with flying colors. Now that we know there's nothing wrong with Big Daddy but a spastic colon, I can tell you something. I was worried sick, half out of my mind, for fear that Big Daddy might have a thing like—

[Margaret cuts through this speech, jumping up and exclaiming shrilly:]

MARGARET
Brick, honey, aren't you going to give Big Daddy his birthday present?

[Passing by him, she snatches his liquor glass from him. She picks up a fancily wrapped package.]

Here it is, Big Daddy, this is from Brick!

BIG MAMA
This is the biggest birthday Big Daddy's ever had, a hundred presents and bushels of telegrams from—

MAE
[at same time] What is it, Brick?

GOOPER
I bet 500 to 50 that Brick don't *know* what it is.

BIG MAMA
The fun of presents is not knowing what they are till you open the package. Open your present, Big Daddy.

BIG DADDY
Open it you'self. I want to ask Brick somethin'! Come here, Brick.

MARGARET
Big Daddy's callin' you, Brick.

[She is opening the package.]

BRICK
Tell Big Daddy I'm crippled.

BIG DADDY
I see you're crippled. I want to know how you got crippled.

MARGARET
[making diversionary tactics] Oh, look, oh, look, why, it's a cashmere robe!

[She hold the robe up for all to see.]

MAE
You sound surprised, Maggie.

MARGARET
I never saw one before.

MAE
That's funny.—Hah!

MARGARET
[turning on her fiercely, with a brilliant smile] Why is it funny? All my family ever had was family—and luxuries such as cashmere robes still surprise me!

BIG DADDY
[ominously] Quiet!

MAE
[heedless in her fury] I don't see how you could be so surprised when you bought it yourself at Loewenstein's in Memphis last Saturday. You know how I know?

BIG DADDY
I said, Quiet!

MAE
—I know because the salesgirl that sold it to you waited on me and said, Oh, Mrs. Pollitt, your sister-in-law just bought a cashmere robe for your husband's father!

MARGARET
Sister Woman! Your talents are wasted as a housewife and mother, you really ought to be with the FBI or—

BIG DADDY
QUIET!

[Reverend Tooker's reflexes are slower than the others'. He finishes a sentence after the bellow.]

REVEREND TOOKER
[to Doc Baugh] —the Stork and the Reaper are running neck and neck!

[He starts to laugh gaily when he notices the silence and Big Daddy's glare. His laugh dies falsely.]

BIG DADDY
Preacher, I hope I'm not butting in on more talk about memorial stained-glass windows, am I, Preacher?

[Reverend Tooker laughs feebly, then coughs dryly in the embarrassed silence.]

Preacher?

BIG MAMA
Now, Big Daddy, don't you pick on Preacher!

BIG DADDY
[raising his voice] You ever hear that expression all hawk and no spit? You bring that expression to mind with that little dry cough of yours, all hawk an' no spit. . . .

[The pause is broken only by a short startled laugh from Margaret, the only one there who is conscious of and amused by the grotesque.]

MAE
[raising her arms and jangling her bracelets] I wonder if the mosquitoes are active tonight?

BIG DADDY
What's that, Little Mama? Did you make some remark?

MAE
Yes, I said I wondered if the mosquitoes would eat us alive if we went out on the gallery for a while.

BIG DADDY
Well, if they do, I'll have your bones pulverized for fertilizer!

BIG MAMA
[quickly] Last week we had an airplane spraying the place and I think it done some good, at least I haven't had a—

BIG DADDY
[cutting her speech] Brick, they tell me, if what they tell me is true, that you done some jumping last night on the high school athletic field?

BIG MAMA
Brick, Big Daddy is talking to you, son.

BRICK
[smiling vaguely over his drink] What was that, Big Daddy?

BIG DADDY
They said you done some jumping on the high school track field last night.

BRICK
That's what they told me, too.

BIG DADDY
Was it jumping or humping that you were doing out there? What were you doing out there at three A.M., layin' a woman on that cinder track?

BIG MAMA
Big Daddy, you are off the sick-list, now, and I'm not going to excuse you for talkin' so—

BIG DADDY
Quiet!

BIG MAMA
—nasty in front of Preacher and—

BIG DADDY
QUIET!—I ast you, Brick, if you was cuttin' you'self a piece o' poon-tang last night on that cinder track? I thought maybe you were chasin' poon-tang on that track an' tripped over something in the heat of the chase—'sthat it?

[Gooper laughs, loud and false, others nervously following suit. Big Mama stamps her foot, and purses her lips, crossing to Mae and whispering something to her as Brick meets his father's hard, intent, grinning stare with a slow, vague smile that he offers all situations from behind the screen of his liquor.]

BRICK
No, sir, I don't think so. . . .

MAE
[at the same time, sweetly] Reverend Tooker, let's you and I take a stroll on the widow's walk.

[She and the preacher go out on the gallery as Big Daddy says:]

BIG DADDY
Then what the hell were you doin' out there at three o'clock in the morning?

BRICK
Jumping the hurdles, Big Daddy, runnin' and jumpin' the hurdles, but those high hurdles have gotten too high for me, now.

BIG DADDY
Cause you was drunk?

BRICK
[his vague smile fading a little] Sober I wouldn't have tried to jump the *low* ones. . . .

BIG MAMA
[quickly] Big Daddy, blow out the candles on your birthday cake!

MARGARET

[at the same time] I want to propose a toast to Big Daddy Pollitt on his sixty-fifth birthday, the biggest cotton-planter in—

BIG DADDY

[bellowing with fury and disgust] I told you to stop it, now stop it, quit this—!

BIG MAMA

[coming in front of Big Daddy with the cake] Big Daddy, I will not allow you to talk that way, not even on your birthday, I—

BIG DADDY

I'll talk like I want to on my birthday, Ida, or any other goddam day of the year and anybody here that don't like it knows what they can do!

BIG MAMA

You don't mean that!

BIG DADDY

What makes you think I don't mean it?

[Meanwhile various discreet signals have been exchanged and Gooper has also gone out on the gallery.]

BIG MAMA

I just know you don't mean it.

BIG DADDY

You don't know a goddam thing and you never did!

BIG MAMA

Big Daddy, you don't mean that.

BIG DADDY

Oh, yes, I do, oh, yes, I do, I mean it! I put up with a whole lot of crap around here because I thought I was dying. And you thought I was dying and you started taking over, well, you can stop taking over now, Ida, because I'm not gonna die, you can just stop now this business of taking over because you're not taking over because I'm not dying, I went through the laboratory and the goddam exploratory operation and there's nothing wrong with me but a spastic colon. And I'm not dying of cancer which you thought I was dying of. Ain't that so? Didn't you think that I was dying of cancer, Ida?

[Almost everybody is out on the gallery but the two old people glaring at each other across the blazing cake. Big Mama's chest heaves and she presses a fat fist to her mouth. Big Daddy continues, hoarsely:]

Ain't that so, Ida? Didn't you have an idea I was dying of cancer and now you could take control of this place and everything on it? I got that impression, I seemed to get that impression. Your loud voice everywhere, your fat old body butting in here and there!

BIG MAMA

Hush! The Preacher!

BIG DADDY

Rut the goddam preacher!

[Big Mama gasps loudly and sits down on the sofa which is almost too small for her.]

Did you hear what I said? I said rut the goddam preacher!

[Somebody closes the gallery doors from outside just as there is a burst of fireworks and excited cries from the children.]

BIG MAMA

I never seen you act like this before and I can't think what's got in you!

BIG DADDY

I went through all that laboratory and operation and all just so I would know if you or me was boss here! Well, now it turns out that I am and you ain't —and that's my birthday present—and my cake and champagne!—because for three years now you been gradually taking over. Bossing. Talking. Sashaying your fat old body around the place I made! I made this place! I was overseer on it! I was the overseer on the old Straw and Ochello plantation. I quit school at ten! I quit school at ten years old and went to work like a nigger in the fields. And I rose to be overseer of the Straw and Ochello plantation. And old Straw died and I was Ochello's partner and the place got bigger and bigger and bigger and bigger and bigger! I did all that myself with no goddam help from you, and now you think you're just about to take over. Well, I am just about to tell you that you are not just about to take over, you are not just about to take over a God damn thing. Is that clear to you, Ida? Is that very plain to you, now? Is that understood completely? I been through the laboratory from A to Z.

I've had the goddam exploratory operation, and nothing is wrong with me but a spastic colon—made spastic, I guess, by *disgust*! By all the goddam lies and liars that I have had to put up with, and all the goddam hypocrisy that I lived with all these forty years that we been livin' together!

Hey! Ida!! Blow out the candles on the birthday cake! Purse up your lips and draw a deep breath and blow out the goddam candles on the cake!

BIG MAMA
Oh, Big Daddy, oh, oh, oh, Big Daddy!

BIG DADDY
What's the matter with you?

BIG MAMA
In all these years you never believed that I loved you??

BIG DADDY
Huh?

BIG MAMA
And I did, I did so much, I did love you!—I even loved your hate and your hardness, Big Daddy!

[*She sobs and rushes awkwardly out onto the gallery.*]

BIG DADDY
[*to himself*] Wouldn't it be funny if that was true. . . .

[*A pause is followed by a burst of light in the sky from the fireworks.*]

BRICK! HEY, BRICK!

[*He stands over his blazing birthday cake. After some moments, Brick hobbles in on his crutch, holding his glass. Margaret follows him with a bright, anxious smile.*]

I didn't call you, Maggie. I called Brick.

MARGARET
I'm just delivering him to you.

[*She kisses Brick on the mouth which he immediately wipes with the back of his hand. She flies girlishly back out. Brick and his father are alone.*]

BIG DADDY
Why did you do that?

BRICK
Do what, Big Daddy?

BIG DADDY
Wipe her kiss off your mouth like she'd spit on you.

BRICK
I don't know. I wasn't conscious of it.

BIG DADDY
That woman of yours has a better shape on her than Gooper's but somehow or other they got the same look about them.

BRICK
What sort of look is that, Big Daddy?

BIG DADDY
I don't know how to describe it but it's the same look.

BRICK
They don't look peaceful, do they?

BIG DADDY
No, they sure in hell don't.

BRICK
They look nervous as cats?

BRICK
That's right, they look nervous as cats.

BRICK
Nervous as a couple of cats on a hot tin roof?

BIG DADDY
That's right, boy, they look like a couple of cats on a hot tin roof. It's funny that you and Gooper being so different would pick out the same type of woman.

BRICK
Both of us married into society, Big Daddy.

BIG DADDY
Crap . . . I wonder what gives them both that look?

BRICK
Well. They're sittin' in the middle of a big piece of land, Big Daddy, twenty-eight thousand acres is a pretty big piece of land and so they're squaring off on it, each determined to knock off a bigger piece of it than the other whenever you let it go.

BIG DADDY
I got a surprise for those women. I'm not gonna let it go for a long time yet if that's what they're waiting for.

BRICK
That's right, Big Daddy. You just sit tight and let them scratch each other's eyes out. . . .

BIG DADDY
You bet your life I'm going to sit tight on it and let those sons of bitches scratch their eyes out, ha ha ha. . . .

But Gooper's wife's a good breeder, you got to admit she's fertile. Hell, at supper tonight she had them all at the table and they had to put a couple of extra leafs in the table to make room for them, she's got five head of them, now, and another one's comin'.

BRICK
Yep, number six is comin'. . . .

BIG DADDY
Brick, you know, I swear to God, I don't know the way it happens?

BRICK
The way what happens, Big Daddy?

BIG DADDY
You git you a piece of land, by hook or crook, an' things start growin' on it, things accumulate on it, and the first thing you know it's completely out of hand, completely out of hand!

BRICK
Well, they say nature hates a vacuum, Big Daddy.

BIG DADDY
That's what they say, but sometimes I think that a vacuum is a hell of a lot better than some of the stuff that nature replaces it with.
Is someone out there by that door?

BRICK
Yep.

BIG DADDY
Who?

[He has lowered his voice.]

BRICK
Someone int'rested in what we say to each other.

BIG DADDY
Gooper?——GOOPER!

[After a discreet pause, Mae appears in the gallery door.]

MAE
Did you call Gooper, Big Daddy?

BIG DADDY
Aw, it was you.

MAE
Do you want Gooper, Big Daddy?

BIG DADDY
No, and I don't want you. I want some privacy here, while I'm having a confidential talk with my son Brick. Now it's too hot in here to close them doors, but if I have to close those rutten doors in order to have a private talk with my son Brick, just let me know and I'll close 'em. Because I hate eavesdroppers, I don't like any kind of sneakin' an' spyin'.

MAE
Why, Big Daddy—

BIG DADDY
You stood on the wrong side of the moon, it threw your shadow!

MAE
I was just—

BIG DADDY
You was just nothing but *spyin'* an' you *know* it!

MAE
[begins to sniff and sob] Oh, Big Daddy, you're so unkind for some reason to those that really love you!

BIG DADDY
Shut up, shut up, shut up! I'm going to move you and Gooper out of that room next to this! It's none of your goddam business what goes on in here at night between Brick an' Maggie. You listen at night like a couple of rutten peek-hole spies and go and give a report on what you hear to Big Mama an' she comes to me and says they say such and such and so and so about what they heard goin' on between Brick an' Maggie, and Jesus, it makes me sick. I'm goin' to move you an' Gooper out of that room, I can't stand sneakin' an' spyin', it makes me sick. . . .

[Mae throws back her head and rolls her eyes heavenward and extends her arms as if invoking God's pity for this unjust martyrdom; then she presses a handkerchief to her nose and flies from the room with a loud swish of skirts.]

BRICK
[now at the liquor cabinet] They listen, do they?

BIG DADDY
Yeah. They listen and give reports to Big Mama on what goes on in here between you and Maggie. They say that—

[He stops as if embarrassed.]

—You won't sleep with her, that you sleep on the sofa. Is that true or not true? If you don't like Maggie, get rid of Maggie!—What are you doin' there now?

BRICK
Fresh'nin' up my drink.

BIG DADDY
Son, you know you got a real liquor problem?

BRICK
Yes, sir, yes, I know.

BIG DADDY
Is that why you quit sports-announcing, because of this liquor problem?

BRICK
Yes, sir, yes, sir, I guess so.

[He smiles vaguely and amiably at his father across his replenished drink.]

BIG DADDY
Son, don't guess about it, it's too important.

BRICK
[vaguely] Yes, sir.

BIG DADDY
And listen to me, don't look at the damn chandelier. . . .

[Pause. Big Daddy's voice is husky.]

—Somethin' else we picked up at th' big fire sale in Europe.

[Another pause.]

Life is important. There's nothing else to hold onto. A man that drinks is throwing his life away. Don't do it, hold onto your life. There's nothing else to hold onto. . . .
Sit down over here so we don't have to raise our voices, the walls have ears in this place.

BRICK
[hobbling over to sit on the sofa beside him] All right, Big Daddy.

BIG DADDY
Quit!—how'd that come about? Some disappointment?

BRICK
I don't know. Do you?

BIG DADDY
I'm askin' you, God damn it! How in hell would I know if you don't?

BRICK
I just got out there and found that I had a mouth full of cotton. I was always two or three beats behind what was goin' on on the field and so I—

BIG DADDY
Quit!

BRICK
[amiably] Yes, quit.

BIG DADDY
Son?

BRICK
Huh?

BIG DADDY
[inhales loudly and deeply from his cigar; then bends suddenly a little forward, exhaling loudly and raising a hand to his forehead] —Whew!—ha ha!—I took in too much smoke, it made me a little light-headed. . . .

[The mantel clock chimes.]

Why is it so damn hard for people to talk?

BRICK
Yeah. . . .

[The clock goes on sweetly chiming till it has completed the stroke of ten.]

—Nice peaceful-soundin' clock, I like to hear it all night. . . .

[He slides low and comfortable on the sofa; Big Daddy sits up straight and rigid with some unspoken anxiety. All his gestures are tense and jerky as he talks. He wheezes and pants and sniffs through his nervous speech, glancing quickly, shyly, from time to time, at his son.]

BIG DADDY
We got that clock the summer we wint to Europe, me an' Big Mama on that damn Cook's Tour, never had such an awful time in my life, I'm tellin' you, son, those gooks over there, they gouge your eyeballs out in their grand hotels. And Big Mama bought more stuff than you could haul in a couple of boxcars, that's no crap. Everywhere she wint on this whirl-wind tour, she bought, bought, bought. Why, half that stuff she bought is still crated up in the cellar, under water last spring!

[He laughs.]

That Europe is nothin' on earth but a great big auction, that's all it is, that bunch of old worn-out places, it's just a big fire-sale, the whole rutten thing, an' Big Mama wint wild in it, why, you couldn't hold that woman with a mule's harness! Bought, bought, bought!—lucky I'm a rich man, yes siree, Bob, an' half that stuff is mildewin' in th' basement. It's lucky I'm a rich man, it sure is lucky, well, I'm a rich man, Brick, yep, I'm a mighty rich man.

[His eyes light up for a moment.]

Y'know how much I'm worth? Guess, Brick! Guess how much I'm worth!

[Brick smiles vaguely over his drink.]

Close on ten million in cash an' blue chip stocks, outside, mind you, of twenty-eight thousand acres of the richest land this side of the valley Nile!

[A puff and crackle and the night sky blooms with an eerie greenish glow. Children shriek on the gallery.]

But a man can't buy his life with it, he can't buy back his life with it when his life has been spent, that's one thing not offered in the Europe fire-sale or in the American markets or any markets on earth, a man can't buy his life with it, he can't buy back his life when his life is finished. . . .

That's a sobering thought, a very sobering thought, and that's a thought that I was turning over in my head, over and over and over—until today. . . .

I'm wiser and sadder, Brick, for this experience which I just gone through. They's one thing else that I remember in Europe.

BRICK
What is that, Big Daddy?

BIG DADDY
The hills around Barcelona in the country of Spain and the children running over those bare hills in their bare skins beggin' like starvin' dogs with howls and screeches, and how fat the priests are on the streets of Barcelona, so many of them and so fat and so pleasant, ha ha!—Y'know I could feed that country? I got money enough to feed that goddam country, but the human animal is a selfish beast and I don't reckon the money I passed out there to those howling children in the hills around Barcelona would more than upholster one of the chairs in this room, I mean pay to put a new cover on this chair!

Hell, I threw them money like you'd scatter feed corn for chickens, I threw money at them just to get rid of them long enough to climb back into th' car and—drive away. . . .

And then in Morocco, them Arabs, why, prostitution begins at four or five, that's no exaggeration, why, I remember one day in Marrakech, that old walled Arab city, I set on a broken-down wall to have a cigar, it was fearful hot there and this Arab woman stood in the road and looked at me till I was embarrassed, she stood stock still in the dusty hot road and looked at me till I was embarrassed. But listen to this. She had a naked child with her, a little naked girl with her, barely able to toddle, and after a while she set this child on the ground and give her a push and whispered something to her. This child come toward me, barely able t' walk, come toddling up to me and—Jesus, it makes you sick t' remember a thing like this! It stuck out its hand and tried to unbutton my trousers!

That child was not yet five! Can you believe me? Or do you think that I am making this up? I wint back to the hotel and said to Big Mama, Git packed! We're clearing out of this country. . . .

BRICK
Big Daddy, you're on a talkin' jag tonight.

BIG DADDY
[ignoring this remark] Yes, sir, that's how it is, the human animal is a beast that dies but the fact that he's dying don't give him pity for others, no, sir, it——Did you say something?

BRICK
Yes.

BIG DADDY
What?

BRICK
Hand me over that crutch so I can get up.

BIG DADDY
Where you goin'?

BRICK
I'm takin' a little short trip to Echo Spring.

BIG DADDY
To where?

BRICK
Liquor cabinet. . . .

BIG DADDY
Yes, sir, boy—

[He hands Brick the crutch.]

—the human animal is a beast that dies and if he's got money he buys and buys and buys and I think the reason he buys everything he can buy is that in the back of his mind he has the crazy hope that one of his purchases will be life everlasting!—Which it never can be. . . . The human animal is a beast that—

BRICK

[at the liquor cabinet] Big Daddy, you sure are shootin' th' breeze here tonight.

[There is a pause and voices are heard outside.]

BIG DADDY

I been quiet here lately, spoke not a word, just sat and stared into space. I had a something heavy weighing on my mind but tonight that load was took off me. That's why I'm talking.—The sky looks diff'rent to me. . . .

BRICK

You know what I like to hear most?

BIG DADDY

What?

BRICK

Solid quiet. Perfect unbroken quiet.

BIG DADDY

Why?

BRICK

Because it's more peaceful.

BIG DADDY

Man, you'll hear a lot of that in the grave.

[He chuckles agreeably.]

BRICK

Are you through talkin' to me?

BIG DADDY

Why are you so anxious to shut me up?

BRICK

Well, sir, ever so often you say to me, Brick, I want to have a talk with you, but when we talk, it never materializes. Nothing is said. You sit in a chair and gas about this and that and I look like I listen. I try to look like I listen, but I don't listen, not much. Communication is—awful hard between people an' —somehow between you and me, it just don't—

BIG DADDY

Have you ever been scared? I mean have you ever felt downright terror of something?

[He gets up.]

Just one moment. I'm going to close these doors. . . .

[He closes doors on gallery as if he were going to tell an important secret.]

BRICK

What?

BIG DADDY

Brick?

BRICK

Huh?

BIG DADDY

Son, I thought I had it!

BRICK

Had what? Had what, Big Daddy?

BIG DADDY

Cancer!

BRICK

Oh . . .

BIG DADDY

I thought the old man made out of bones had laid his cold and heavy hand on my shoulder!

BRICK

Well, Big Daddy, you kept a tight mouth about it.

BIG DADDY

A pig squeals. A man keeps a tight mouth about it, in spite of a man not having a pig's advantage.

BRICK

What advantage is that?

BIG DADDY

Ignorance—of mortality—is a comfort. A man don't have that comfort, he's the only living thing that conceives of death, that knows what it is. The others go without knowing which is the way that anything living should go, go without knowing, without any knowledge of it, and yet a pig squeals, but a man sometimes, he can keep a tight mouth about it. Sometimes he—

[There is a deep, smoldering ferocity in the old man.]

—can keep a tight mouth about it. I wonder if—

BRICK

What, Big Daddy?

BIG DADDY

A whiskey highball would injure this spastic condition?

BRICK

No, sir, it might do it good.

BIG DADDY

[grins suddenly, wolfishly] Jesus, I can't tell you! The sky is open! Christ, it's open again! It's open, boy, it's open!

[Brick looks down at his drink.]

BRICK

You feel better, Big Daddy?

BIG DADDY

Better? Hell! I can breathe!—All of my life I been like a doubled up fist. . . .

[He pours a drink.]

—Poundin', smashin', drivin'!—now I'm going to loosen these doubled up hands and touch things easy with them. . . .

[He spreads his hands as if caressing the air.]

You know what I'm contemplating?

BRICK

[vaguely] No, sir. What are you contemplating?

BIG DADDY

Ha ha!—Pleasure!—pleasure with women!

[Brick's smile fades a little but lingers.]

Brick, this stuff burns me!—
—Yes, boy. I'll tell you something that you might not guess. I still have desire for women and this is my sixty-fifth birthday.

BRICK

I think that's mighty remarkable, Big Daddy.

BIG DADDY

Remarkable?

BRICK

Admirable, Big Daddy.

BIG DADDY

You're damn right it is, remarkable and admirable both. I realize now that I never had me enough. I let many chances slip by because of scruples about it, scruples, convention—crap. . . . All that stuff is bull, bull, bull!—It took the shadow of death to make me see it. Now that shadow's lifted, I'm going to cut loose and have, what is it they call it, have me a—ball!

BRICK

A ball, huh?

BIG DADDY

That's right, a ball, a ball! Hell—I slept with Big Mama till, let's see, five years ago, till I was sixty and she was fifty-eight, and never even liked her, never did!

[The phone has been ringing down the hall. Big Mama enters, exclaiming:]

BIG MAMA

Don't you men hear that phone ring? I heard it way out on the gall'ry.

BIG DADDY

There's five rooms off this front gall'ry that you could go through. Why do you go through this one?

[Big Mama makes a playful face as she bustles out the hall door.]

Hunh!—Why, when Big Mama goes out of a room, I can't remember what that woman looks like, but when Big Mama comes back into the room, boy, then I see what she looks like, and I wish I didn't!

[Bends over laughing at this joke till it hurts his guts and he straightens with a grimace. The laugh subsides to a chuckle as he puts the liquor glass a little distrustfully down on the table. Brick has risen and hobbled to the gallery doors.]

Hey! Where you goin'?

BRICK

Out for a breather.

BIG DADDY

Not yet you ain't. Stay here till this talk is finished, young fellow.

BRICK

I thought it was finished, Big Daddy.

BIG DADDY

It ain't even begun.

BRICK

My mistake. Excuse me. I just wanted to feel that river breeze.

BIG DADDY

Turn on the ceiling fan and set back down in that chair.

[Big Mama's voice rises, carrying down the hall.]

BIG MAMA

Miss Sally, you're a case! You're a caution, Miss Sally. Why didn't you give me a chance to explain it to you?

BIG DADDY
Jesus, she's talking to my old maid sister again.

BIG MAMA
Well, goodbye, now, Miss Sally. You come down real soon, Big Daddy's dying to see you! Yaisss, goodbye, Miss Sally. . . .

[She hangs up and bellows with mirth. Big Daddy groans and covers his ears as she approaches. Bursting in:]

Big Daddy, that was Miss Sally callin' from Memphis again! You know what she done, Big Daddy? She called her doctor in Memphis to git him to tell her what that spastic thing is! Ha-HAAAA!—And called back to tell me how relieved she was that—Hey! Let me in!

[Big Daddy has been holding the door half closed against her.]

BIG DADDY
Naw I ain't. I told you not to come and go through this room. You just back out and go through those five other rooms.

BIG MAMA
Big Daddy? Big Daddy? Oh, Big Daddy!—You didn't mean those things you said to me, did you?

[He shuts door firmly against her but she still calls.]

Sweetheart? Sweetheart? Big Daddy? You didn't mean those awful things you said to me?—I know you didn't. I know you didn't mean those things in your heart. . . .

[The childlike voice fades with a sob and her heavy footsteps retreat down the hall. Brick has risen once more on his crutches and starts for the gallery again.]

BIG DADDY
All I ask of that woman is that she leave me alone. But she can't admit to herself that she makes me sick. That comes of having slept with her too many years. Should of quit much sooner but that old woman she never got enough of it—and I was good in bed . . . I never should of wasted so much of it on her. . . . They say you got just so many and each one is numbered. Well, I got a few left in me, a few, and I'm going to pick me a good one to spend 'em on! I'm going to pick me a choice one, I don't care how much she costs, I'll smother her in—minks! Ha ha! I'll strip her naked and smother her in minks and choke her with

diamonds! Ha ha! I'll strip her naked and choke her with diamonds and smother her with minks and hump her from hell to breakfast. *Ha aha ha ha ha!*

MAE
[*gaily at door*] Who's that laughin' in there?

GOOPER
Is Big Daddy laughin' in there?

BIG DADDY
Crap!—them two—drips. . . .

[*He goes over and touches Brick's shoulder.*]

Yes, son, Brick, boy.—I'm—*happy!* I'm happy, son, I'm happy!

[*He chokes a little and bites his under lip, pressing his head quickly, shyly against his son's head and then, coughing with embarrassment, goes uncertainly back to the table where he set down the glass. He drinks and makes a grimace as it burns his guts. Brick sighs and rises with effort.*]

What makes you so restless? Have you got ants in your britches?

BRICK
Yes, sir . . .

BIG DADDY
Why?

BRICK
—Something—hasn't—happened. . . .

BIG DADDY
Yeah? What is that!

BRICK
[*sadly*] —the click. . . .

BIG DADDY
Did you say click?

BRICK
Yes, click.

BIG DADDY
What click?

BRICK
A click that I get in my head that makes me peaceful.

BIG DADDY
I sure in hell don't know what you're talking about, but it disturbs me.

BRICK
It's just a mechanical thing.

BIG DADDY
What is a mechanical thing?

BRICK
This click that I get in my head that makes me peaceful. I got to drink till I get it. It's just a mechanical thing, something like a—like a—like a—

BIG DADDY
Like a—

BRICK
Switch clicking off in my head, turning the hot light off and the cool night on and—

[He looks up, smiling sadly.]

—all of a sudden there's—peace!

BIG DADDY
[whistles long and soft with astonishment; he goes back to Brick and clasps his son's two shoulders] Jesus! I didn't know it had gotten that bad with you. Why, boy, you're—alcoholic!

BRICK
That's the truth, Big Daddy. I'm alcoholic.

BIG DADDY
This shows how I—let things go!

BRICK
I have to hear that little click in my head that makes me peaceful. Usually I hear it sooner than this, sometimes as early as—noon, but—
—Today it's—dilatory. . . .
—I just haven't got the right level of alcohol in my bloodstream yet!

[This last statement is made with energy as he freshens his drink.]

BIG DADDY
Uh—huh. Expecting death made me blind. I didn't have no idea that a son of mine was turning into a drunkard under my nose.

BRICK
[gently] Well, now you do, Big Daddy, the news has penetrated.

BIG DADDY
UH-huh, yes, now I do, the news has—penetrated. . . .

BRICK
And so if you'll excuse me—

BIG DADDY
No, I won't excuse you.

BRICK
—I'd better sit by myself till I hear that click in my head, it's just a mechanical thing but it don't happen except when I'm alone or talking to no one. . . .

BIG DADDY
You got a long, long time to sit still, boy, and talk to no one, but now you're talkin' to me. At least I'm talking to you. And you set there and listen until I tell you the conversation is over!

BRICK
But this talk is like all the others we've ever had together in our lives! It's nowhere, nowhere!—it's—it's painful, Big Daddy. . . .

BIG DADDY
All right, then let it be painful, but don't you move from that chair!—I'm going to remove that crutch. . . .

[He seizes the crutch and tosses it across room.]

BRICK
I can hop on one foot, and if I fall, I can crawl!

BIG DADDY
If you ain't careful you're gonna crawl off this plantation and then, by Jesus, you'll have to hustle your drinks along Skid Row!

BRICK
That'll come, Big Daddy.

BIG DADDY
Naw, it won't. You're my son and I'm going to straighten you out; now that I'm straightened out, I'm going to straighten out you!

BRICK
Yeah?

BIG DADDY
Today the report come in from Ochsner Clinic. Y'know what they told me?

[His face glows with triumph.]

The only thing that they could detect with all the instruments of science in that great hospital is a little spastic condition of the colon! And nerves torn to pieces by all that worry about it.

[*A little girl bursts into room with a sparkler clutched in each fist, hops and shrieks like a monkey gone mad and rushes back out again as Big Daddy strikes at her. Silence. The two men stare at each other. A woman laughs gaily outside.*]

I want you to know I breathed a sigh of relief almost as powerful as the Vicksburg tornado!

BRICK
You weren't ready to go?

BIG DADDY
GO WHERE?—crap. . . .
—When you are gone from here, boy, you are long gone and no where! The human machine is not no different from the animal machine or the fish machine or the bird machine or the reptile machine or the insect machine! It's just a whole God damn lot more complicated and consequently more trouble to keep together. Yep. I thought I had it. The earth shook under my foot, the sky come down like the black lid of a kettle and I couldn't breathe!—To-day!!—that lid was lifted, I drew my first free breath in—how many years?—*God!*—three. . . .

[*There is laughter outside, running footsteps, the soft, plushy sound and light of exploding rockets. Brick stares at him soberly for a long moment; then makes a sort of startled sound in his nostrils and springs up on one foot and hops across the room to grab his crutch, swinging on the furniture for support. He gets the crutch and flees as if in horror for the gallery. His father seizes him by the sleeve of his white silk pajamas.*]

Stay here, you son of a bitch!—till I say go!

BRICK
I can't.

BIG DADDY
You sure in hell will, God damn it.

BRICK
No, I can't. We talk, you talk, in—circles! We get nowhere, nowhere! It's always the same, you say you want to talk to me and don't have a ruttin' thing to say to me!

BIG DADDY
Nothin' to say when I'm tellin' you I'm going to live when I thought I was dying?!

BRICK
Oh—*that!*—Is that what you have to say to me?

BIG DADDY
Why, you son of a bitch! Ain't that, aint' that—important?!

BRICK
Well, you said that, that's said, and now I—

BIG DADDY
Now you set back down.

BRICK
You're all balled up, you—

BIG DADDY
I ain't balled up!

BRICK
You are, you're all balled up!

BIG DADDY
Don't tell me what I am, you drunken whelp! I'm going to tear this coat sleeve off if you don't set down!

BRICK
Big Daddy—

BIG DADDY
Do what I tell you! I'm the boss here, now! I want you to know I'm back in the driver's seat now!

[*Big Mama rushes in, clutching her great heaving bosom.*]

What in hell do you want in here, Big Mama?

BIG MAMA
Oh, Big Daddy! Why are you shouting like that? I just cain't *stainnnnnnnd*—it. . . .

BIG DADDY
[*raising the back of his hand above his head*] GIT!—outa here.

[*She rushes back out, sobbing.*]

BRICK
[*softly, sadly*] Christ. . . .

BIG DADDY
[*fiercely*] Yeah! Christ!—is right . . .

[*Brick breaks loose and hobbles toward the gallery. Big Daddy jerks his crutch from under Brick so he steps with the injured ankle. He utters a hissing cry of anguish, clutches a chair and pulls it over on top of him on the floor.*]

Son of a—tub of—hog fat. . . .

BRICK
Big Daddy! Give me my crutch.

[Big Daddy throws the crutch out of reach.]

Give me that crutch, Big Daddy.

BIG DADDY
Why do you drink?

BRICK
Don't know, give me my crutch!

BIG DADDY
You better think why you drink or give up drinking!

BRICK
Will you please give me my crutch so I can get up off this floor?

BIG DADDY
First you answer my question. Why do you drink? Why are you throwing your life away, boy, like somethin' disgusting you picked up on the street?

BRICK
[getting onto his knees] Big Daddy, I'm in pain, I stepped on that foot.

BIG DADDY
Good! I'm glad you're not too numb with the liquor in you to feel some pain!

BRICK
You—spilled my—drink . . .

BIG DADDY
I'll make a bargain with you. You tell me why you drink and I'll hand you one. I'll pour you the liquor myself and hand it to you.

BRICK
Why do I drink?

BIG DADDY
Yeah! Why?

BRICK
Give me a drink and I'll tell you.

BIG DADDY
Tell me first!

BRICK
I'll tell you in one word.

BIG DADDY
What word?

BRICK
DISGUST!

[The clock chimes softly, sweetly. Big Daddy gives it a short, outraged glance.]

Now how about that drink?

BIG DADDY
What are you disgusted with? You got to tell me that, first. Otherwise being disgusted don't make no sense!

BRICK
Give me my crutch.

BIG DADDY
You heard me, you got to tell me what I asked you first.

BRICK
I told you, I said to kill my disgust!

BIG DADDY
DISGUST WITH WHAT!

BRICK
You strike a hard bargain.

BIG DADDY
What are you disgusted with?—an' I'll pass you the liquor.

BRICK
I can hop on one foot, and if I fall, I can crawl.

BIG DADDY
You want liquor that bad?

BRICK
[dragging himself up, clinging to bedstead] Yeah, I want it that bad.

BIG DADDY
If I give you a drink, will you tell me what it is you're disgusted with, Brick?

BRICK
Yes, sir, I will try to.

[The old man pours him a drink and solemnly passes it to him.
There is silence as Brick drinks.]

Have you ever heard the word "mendacity"?

BIG DADDY
Sure. Mendacity is one of them five dollar words that cheap politicians throw back and forth at each other.

BRICK
You know what it means?

BIG DADDY
Don't it mean lying and liars?

BRICK
Yes, sir, lying and liars.

BIG DADDY
Has someone been lying to you?

CHILDREN
[chanting in chorus offstage]
We want Big Dad-dee!
We want Big Dad-dee!

[Gooper appears in the gallery door.]

GOOPER
Big Daddy, the kiddies are shouting for you out there.

BIG DADDY
[fiercely] Keep out, Gooper!

GOOPER
'Scuse *me*!

[Big Daddy slams the doors after Gooper.]

BIG DADDDY
Who's been lying to you, has Margaret been lying to you, has your wife been lying to you about something, Brick?

BRICK
Not her. That wouldn't matter.

BIG DADDY
Then who's been lying to you, and what about?

BRICK
No one single person and no one lie. . . .

BIG DADDY
Then what, what then, for Christ's sake?

BRICK
—The whole, the whole—thing. . . .

BIG DADDY
Why are you rubbing your head? You got a headache?

BRICK
No, I'm tryin' to—

BIG DADDY
—Concentrate, but you can't because your brain's all soaked with liquor, is that the trouble? Wet brain!

[He snatches the glass from Brick's hand.]

What do you know about this mendacity thing? Hell! I could write a book on it! Don't you know that? I could write a book on it and still not cover the subject? Well, I could, I could write a goddam book on it and still not cover the subject anywhere near enough!!—Think of all the lies I got to put up with!—Pretenses! Ain't that mendacity? Having to pretend stuff you don't think or feel or have any idea of? Hav-

ing for instance to act like I care for Big Mama!—I haven't been able to stand the sight, sound, or smell of that woman for forty years now!—even when I *laid* her!—regular as a piston. . . . Pretend to love that son of a bitch of a Gooper and his wife Mae and those five same screechers out there like parrots in a jungle! Jesus! Can't stand to look at 'em!
Church!—it bores the Bejesus out of me but I go!—I go an' sit there and listen to the fool preacher! Clubs!—Elks! Masons! Rotary!—*crap!*

[A spasm of pain makes him clutch his belly. He sinks into a chair and his voice is softer and hoarser.]

You I *do* like for some reason, did always have some kind of real feeling for—affection—respect—yes, always. . . .
You and being a success as a planter is all I ever had any devotion to in my whole life!—and that's the truth. . . .
I don't know why, but it is!
I've lived with mendacity!—Why can't *you* live with it? Hell, you *got* to live with it, there's nothing *else* to *live* with except mendacity, is there?

BRICK
Yes, sir. Yes, sir, there is something else that you can live with!

BIG DADDY
What?

BRICK
[lifting his glass] This!—Liquor. . . .

BIG DADDY
That's not living, that's dodging away from life.

BRICK
I want to dodge away from it.

BIG DADDY
Then why don't you kill yourself, man?

BRICK
I like to drink. . . .

BIG DADDY
Oh, God, I can't talk to you. . . .

BRICK
I'm sorry, Big Daddy.

BIG DADDY
Not as sorry as I am. I'll tell you something. A little while back when I thought my number was up—

—before I found out it was just this—spastic—colon, I thought about you. Should I or should I not, if the jig was up, give you this place when I go—since I hate Gooper an' Mae an' know that they hate me, and since all five same monkeys are little Maes an' Goopers.—And I thought, No!—Then I thought, Yes!—I couldn't make up my mind. I hate Gooper and his five same monkeys and that bitch Mae! Why should I turn over twenty-eight thousand acres of the richest land this side of the valley Nile to not my kind?—But why in hell, on the other hand, Brick—should I subsidize a goddam fool on the bottle?—Liked or not liked, well, maybe even—*loved!*—Why should I do that? Subsidize worthless behavior? Rot? Corruption?

BRICK

[smiling] I understand.

BIG DADDY

Well, if you do, you're smarter than I am, God damn it, because I don't understand. And this I will tell you frankly. I didn't make up my mind at all on that question and still to this day I ain't made out no will!—Well, now I don't *have* to. The pressure is gone. I can just wait and see if you pull yourself together or if you don't.

BRICK

That's right, Big Daddy.

BIG DADDY

You sound like you thought I was kidding.

BRICK

[rising] No, sir, I know you're not kidding.

BIG DADDY

But you don't care—?

BRICK

[hobbling toward the gallery door] No, sir, I don't care. . . .
Now how about taking a look at your birthday fireworks and getting some of that cool breeze off the river?

[He stands in the gallery doorway as the night sky turns pink and green and gold with successive flashes of light.]

BIG DADDY

WAIT!—Brick. . . .

[His voice drops. Suddenly there is something shy, almost tender, in his restraining gesture.]

Don't let's—leave it like this, like them other talks we've had, we've always—talked around things, we've—just talked around things for some rutten reason. I don't know what, it's always like something was left not spoken, something avoided because neither of us was honest enough with the—other. . . .

BRICK

I never lied to you, Big Daddy.

BIG DADDY

Did I ever to *you?*

BRICK

No, sir. . . .

BIG DADDY

Then there is at least two people that never lied to each other.

BRICK

But we've never *talked* to each other.

BIG DADDY

We can *now.*

BRICK

Big Daddy, there don't seem to be anything much to say.

BIG DADDY

You say that you drink to kill your disgust with lying.

BRICK

You said to give you a reason.

BIG DADDY

Is liquor the only thing that'll kill this disgust?

BRICK

Now. Yes.

BIG DADDY

But not once, huh?

BRICK

Not when I was still young an' believing. A drinking man's someone who wants to forget he isn't still young an' believing.

BIG DADDY

Believing what?

BRICK

Believing. . . .

BIG DADDY

Believing *what?*

BRICK
[stubbornly evasive] Believing. . . .

BIG DADDY
I don't know what the hell you mean by believing and I don't think you know what you mean by believing, but if you still got sports in your blood, go back to sports announcing and—

BRICK
Sit in a glass box watching games I can't play? Describing what I can't do while players do it? Sweating out their disgust and confusion in contests I'm not fit for? Drinkin' a coke, half bourbon, so I can stand it? That's no goddam good any more, no help—time just outran me, Big Daddy—got there first . . .

BIG DADDY
I think you're passing the buck.

BRICK
You know many drinkin' men?

BIG DADDY
[with a slight, charming smile] I have known a fair number of that species.

BRICK
Could any of them tell you why he drank?

BIG DADDY
Yep, you're passin' the buck to things like time and disgust with "mendacity" and—crap!—if you got to use that kind of language about a thing, it's ninety-proof bull, and I'm not buying any.

BRICK
I had to give you a reason to get a drink!

BIG DADDY
You started drinkin' when your friend Skipper died.

[Silence for five beats. Then Brick makes a startled movement, reaching for his crutch.]

BRICK
What are you suggesting?

BIG DADDY
I'm suggesting nothing.

[The shuffle and clop of Brick's rapid hobble away from his father's steady, grave attention.]

—But Gooper an' Mae suggested that there was something not right exactly in your—

BRICK
[stopping short downstage as if backed to a wall] "Not right"?

BIG DADDY
Not, well, exactly normal in your friendship with—

BRICK
They suggested that, too? I thought that was Maggie's suggestion.

[Brick's detachment is at last broken through. His heart is accelerated; his forehead sweat-beaded; his breath becomes more rapid and his voice hoarse. The thing they're discussing, timidly and painfully on the side of Big Daddy, fiercely, violently on Brick's side, is the inadmissible thing that Skipper died to disavow between them. The fact that if it existed it had to be disavowed to "keep face" in the world they lived in, may be at the heart of the "mendacity" that Brick drinks to kill his disgust with. It may be the root of his collapse. Or maybe it is only a single manifestation of it, not even the most important. The bird that I hope to catch in the net of this play is not the solution to one man's psychological problem. I'm trying to catch the true quality of experience in a group of people, that cloudy, flickering, evanescent—fiercely charged!—interplay of live human beings in the thunder-cloud of a common crisis. Some mystery should be left in the revelation of character in a play, just as a great deal of mystery is always left in the revelation of character in life, even in one's own character to himself. This does not absolve the playwright of his duty to observe and probe as clearly and deeply as he legitimately can: but it should steer him away from "pat" conclusions, facile definitions which make a play just a play, not a snare for the truth of human experience. The following scene should be played with great concentration, with most of the power leashed but palpable in what is left unspoken.]

Who else's suggestion is it, is it yours? How many others thought that Skipper and I were—

BIG DADDY
[gently] Now, hold on, hold on a minute, son.—I knocked around in my time.

BRICK
What's that got to do with—

BIG DADDY
I said 'Hold on!'—I bummed, I bummed this country till I was—

BRICK
Whose suggestion, who else's suggestion is it?

BIG DADDY
Slept in hobo jungles and railroad Y's and flophouses
in all cities before I—

BRICK
Oh, *you* think so, too, you call me your son and a
queer. Oh! Maybe that's why you put Maggie and me
in this room that was Jack Straw's and Peter Ochello's, in which that pair of old sisters slept in a double
bed where both of 'em died!

BIG DADDY
Now just don't go throwing rocks at—

> *[Suddenly Reverend Tooker appears in the gallery
> doors, his head slightly, playfully, fatuously cocked,
> with a practised clergyman's smile, sincere as a bird-
> call blown on a hunter's whistle, the living embodiment
> of the pious, conventional lie.
> Big Daddy gasps a little at this perfectly timed, but
> incongruous, apparition.]*

—What're you lookin' for, Preacher?

REVEREND TOOKER
The gentleman's lavatory, ha ha!—heh, heh . . .

BIG DADDY
[with strained courtesy] —Go back out and walk
down to the other end of the gallery, Reverend
Tooker, and use the bathroom connected with my
bedroom, and if you can't find it, ask them where it
is!

REVEREND TOOKER
Ah, thanks.

> *[He goes out with a deprecatory chuckle.]*

BIG DADDY
It's hard to talk in this place . . .

BRICK
Son of a—!

BIG DADDY
[leaving a lot unspoken] —I seen all things and understood a lot of them, till 1910. Christ, the year that—
I had worn my shoes through, hocked my—I hopped
off a yellow dog freight car half a mile down the road,
slept in a wagon of cotton outside the gin—Jack
Straw an' Peter Ochello took me in. Hired me to manage this place which grew into this one.— When Jack
Straw died—why, old Peter Ochello quit eatin' like a
dog does when its master's dead, and died, too!

BRICK
Christ!

BIG DADDY
I'm just saying I understand such—

BRICK
[violently] Skipper is dead. I have not quit eating!

BIG DADDY
No, but you started drinking.

> *[Brick wheels on his crutch and hurls his glass across
> the room shouting.]*

BRICK
YOU THINK SO, TOO?

BIG DADDY
Shhh!

> *[Footsteps run on the gallery. There are women's calls.
> Big Daddy goes toward the door.]*

Go way!—Just broke a glass. . . .

> *[Brick is transformed, as if a quiet mountain blew
> suddenly up in volcanic flame.]*

BRICK
You think so, too? You think so, too? You think me an'
Skipper did, did, did!—*sodomy!*—together?

BIG DADDY
Hold—!

BRICK
That what you—

BIG DADDY
—*ON*—a minute!

BRICK
You think we did dirty things between us, Skipper
an'—

BIG DADDY
Why are you shouting like that? Why are you—

BRICK
—Me, is that what you think of Skipper, is that—

BIG DADDY
—so excited? I don't think nothing. I don't know
nothing. I'm simply telling you what—

BRICK
You think that Skipper and me were a pair of dirty old
men?

BIG DADDY
Now that's—

BRICK
Straw? Ochello? A couple of—

BIG DADDY
Now just—

BRICK
—ducking sissies? Queers? Is that what you—

BIG DADDY
Shhh.

BRICK
—think?

*[He loses his balance and pitches to his knees without
noticing the pain. He grabs the bed and drags
himself up.]*

BIG DADDY
Jesus!—Whew. . . . Grab my hand!

BRICK
Naw, I don't want your hand. . . .

BIG DADDY
Well, I want yours. Git up!

*[He draws him up, keeps an arm about him with
concern and affection.]*

You broken out in a sweat! You're panting like you'd
run a race with—

BRICK
[freeing himself from his father's hold] Big Daddy, you
shock me, Big Daddy, you, you—*shock* me! Talkin'
so—

[He turns away from his father.]

—casually!—about a—thing like that . . .
—Don't you know how people *feel* about things like
that? How, how *disgusted* they are by things like that?
Why, at Ole Miss when it was discovered a pledge to
our fraternity, Skipper's and mine, did a, *attempted* to
do a, unnatural thing with—
We not only dropped him like a hot rock!—We told
him to git off the campus, and he did, he got!—All the
way to—

[He halts, breathless.]

BIG DADDY
—Where?

BRICK
—North Africa, last I heard!

BIG DADDY
Well, I have come back from further away than that.
I have just now returned from the other side of the
moon, death's country, son, and I'm not easy to
shock by anything here.

[He comes downstage and faces out.]

Always, anyhow, lived with too much space around
me to be infected by ideas of other people. One thing
you can grow on a big place more important than cotton—is *tolerance*!—I grown it.

[He returns toward Brick.]

BRICK
Why can't exceptional friendship, *real, real, deep,
deep friendship*! between two men be respected as
something clean and decent without being thought
of as—

BIG DADDY
It can, it is, for God's sake.

BRICK
—*Fairies.* . . .

*[In his utterance of this word, we gauge the wide and pro-
found reach of the conventional mores he got from the
world that crowned him with early laurel.]*

BIG DADDY
I told Mae an' Gooper—

BRICK
Frig Mae and Gooper, frig all dirty lies and liars!—
Skipper and me had a clean, true thing between us!—
had a clean friendship, practically all our lives, till
Maggie got the idea you're talking about. Normal?
No!—It was too rare to be normal, any true thing between two people is too rare to be normal. Oh, once
in a while he put his hand on my shoulder or I'd put
mine on his, oh, maybe even, when we were touring
the country in pro-football an' shared hotel-rooms
we'd reach across the space between the two beds
and shake hands to say goodnight, yeah, one or two
times we—

BIG DADDY
Brick, nobody thinks that that's not normal!

BRICK
Well, they're mistaken, it was! It was a pure an' true
thing an' that's not normal.

[They both stare straight at each other for a long moment. The tension breaks and both turn away as if tired.]

BIG DADDY
Yeah, it's—hard t'—talk. . . .

BRICK
All right, then, let's—let it go. . . .

BIG DADDY
Why did Skipper crack up? Why have you?

[Brick looks back at his father again. He has already decided, without knowing that he has made this decision, that he is going to tell his father that he is dying of cancer. Only this could even the score between them: one inadmissible thing in return for another.]

BRICK
[ominously] All right. You're asking for it, Big Daddy. We're finally going to have that real true talk you wanted. It's too late to stop it, now, we got to carry it through and cover every subject.

[He hobbles back to the liquor cabinet.]
Uh-huh.

[He opens the ice bucket and picks up the silver tongs with slow admiration of their frosty brightness.]
Maggie declares that Skipper and I went into pro-football after we left "Ole Miss" because we were scared to grow up . . .

[He moves downstage with the shuffle and clop of a cripple on a crutch. As Margaret did when her speech became "recitative," he looks out into the house, commanding its attention by his direct, concentrated gaze—a broken, "tragically elegant" figure telling simply as much as he knows of "the Truth":]

—Wanted to—keep on tossing—-those long, long!—high, high!—passes that—couldn't be intercepted except by time, the aerial attack that made us famous! And so we did, we did, we kept it up for one season, that aerial attack, we held it high!—Yeah, but—
—that summer, Maggie, she laid the law down to me, said, Now or never, and so I married Maggie. . . .

BIG DADDY
How was Maggie in bed?

BRICK
[wryly] Great! the greatest!

[Big Daddy nods as if he thought so.]

She went on the road that fall with the Dixie Stars. Oh, she made a great show of being the world's best sport. She wore a—wore a—tall bearskin cap! A shako, they call it, a dyed moleskin coat, a moleskin coat dyed red!—Cut up crazy! Rented hotel ballrooms for victory celebrations, wouldn't cancel them when it—turned out—defeat. . . . MAGGIE THE CAT! Ha ha!

[Big Daddy nods.]

—But Skipper, he had some fever which came back on him which doctors couldn't explain and I got that injury—turned out to be just a shadow on the X-ray plate—and a touch of bursitis. . . .
I lay in a hospital bed, watched our games on TV, saw Maggie on the bench next to Skipper when he was hauled out of a game for stumbles, fumbles!—Burned me up the way she hung on his arm!—Y'know, I think that Maggie had always felt sort of left out because she and me never got any closer together than two people just get in bed, which is not much closer than two cats on a—fence humping. . . .
So! She took this time to work on poor dumb Skipper. He was a less than average student at Ole Miss, you know that, don't you?!—Poured in his mind the dirty, false idea that what we were, him and me, was a frustrated case of that ole pair of sisters that lived in this room, Jack Straw and Peter Ochello!—He, poor Skipper, went to bed with Maggie to prove it wasn't true, and when it didn't work out, he thought it *was* true!—Skipper broke in two like a rotten stick—nobody ever turned so fast to a lush—or died of it so quick. . . . —Now are you satisfied?

[Big Daddy has listened to this story, dividing the grain from the chaff. Now he looks at his son.]

BIG DADDY
Are *you* satisfied?

BRICK
With what?

BIG DADDY
That half-ass story!

BRICK
What's half-ass about it?

BIG DADDY
Something's left out of that story. What did you leave out?

[The phone has started ringing in the hall. As if it reminded him of something, Brick glances suddenly toward the sound and says:]

BRICK
Yes!—I left out a long-distance call which I had from Skipper, in which he made a drunken confession to me and on which I hung up!—last time we spoke to each other in our lives. . . .

[Muted ring stops as someone answers phone in a soft, indistinct voice in hall.]

BIG DADDY
You hung up?

BRICK
Hung up. Jesus! Well—

BIG DADDY
Anyhow now!—we have tracked down the lie with which you're disgusted and which you are drinking to kill your disgust with, Brick. You been passing the buck. This disgust with mendacity is disgust with yourself.
You!—dug the grave of your friend and kicked him in it!—before you'd face truth with him!

BRICK
His truth, not *mine*!

BIG DADDY
His truth, okay! But you wouldn't face it with him!

BRICK
Who *can* face truth? Can *you*?

BIG DADDY
Now don't start passin' the rotten buck again, boy!

BRICK
How about these birthday congratulations, these many, many happy returns of the day, when ev'rybody but you knows there won't be any!

[Whoever has answered the hall phone lets out a high, shrill laugh; the voice becomes audible saying: "no, no, you got it all wrong! Upside down! Are you crazy?"
Brick suddenly catches his breath as he realizes that he has made a shocking disclosure. He hobbles a few paces, then freezes, and without looking at his father's shocked face, says:]

Let's, let's—go out, now, and—

[Big Daddy moves suddenly forward and grabs holds of the boy's crutch like it was a weapon for which they were fighting for possession.]

BIG DADDY
Oh, no, no! No one's going out. What did you start to say?

BRICK
I don't remember.

BIG DADDY
"Many happy returns when they know there won't be any"?

BRICK
Aw, hell, Big Daddy, forget it. Come on out on the gallery and look at the fireworks they're shooting off for your birthday. . . .

BIG DADDY
First you finish that remark you were makin' before you cut off. "Many happy returns when they know there won't be any"?—Ain't that what you just said?

BRICK
Look, now. I can get around without that crutch if I have to but it would be a lot easier on the furniture an' glassware if I didn' have to go swinging along like Tarzan of th'—

BIG DADDY
FINISH! WHAT YOU WAS SAYIN'!

[An eerie green glow shows in sky behind him.]

BRICK
[sucking the ice in his glass, speech becoming thick] Leave th' place to Gooper and Mae an' their five little same little monkeys. All I want is—

BIG DADDY
"LEAVE TH' PLACE," did you say?

BRICK
[vaguely] All twenty-eight thousand acres of the richest land this side of the valley Nile.

BIG DADDY
Who said I was "leaving the place" to Gooper or anybody? This is my sixty-fifth birthday! I got fifteen years or twenty years left in me! I'll outlive *you*! I'll bury you an' have to pay for your coffin!

BRICK
Sure. Many happy returns. Now let's go watch the fireworks, come on, let's—

BIG DADDY

Lying, have they been lying? About the report from th'—clinic? Did they, did they—find something?—*Cancer*. Maybe?

BRICK

Mendacity is a system that we live in. Liquor is one way out an' death's the other. . . .

[*He takes the crutch from Big Daddy's loose grip and swings out on the gallery leaving the doors open. A song, "Pick a Bale of Cotton," is heard.*]

MAE

[*appearing in door*] Oh, Big Daddy, the field-hands are singin' fo' you!

BIG DADDY

[*shouting hoarsely*] BRICK! BRICK!

MAE

He's outside drinkin', Big Daddy.

BIG DADDY

BRICK!

[*Mae retreats, awed by the passion of his voice. Children call Brick in tones mocking Big Daddy. His face crumbles like broken yellow plaster about to fall into dust.*
There is a glow in the sky. Brick swings back through the doors, slowly, gravely, quite soberly.]

BRICK

I'm sorry, Big Daddy. My head don't work any more and it's hard for me to understand how anybody could care if he lived or died or was dying or cared about anything but whether or not there was liquor left in the bottle and so I said what I said without thinking. In some ways I'm no better than the others, in some ways worse because I'm less alive. Maybe it's being alive that makes them lie, and being almost *not* alive makes me sort of accidentally truthful—I don't know but—anyway—we've been friends . . .
—And being friends is telling each other the truth. . . .

[*There is a pause.*]

You told *me*! I told *you*!

[*A child rushes into the room and grabs a fistful of firecrackers and runs out again.*]

CHILD

[*screaming*] Bang, bang, bang, bang, bang, bang, bang, bang, bang!

BIG DADDY

[*slowly and passionately*] CHRIST—DAMN—ALL—LYING SONS OF—LYING BITCHES!

[*He straightens at last and crosses to the inside door. At the door he turns and looks back as if he had some desperate question he couldn't put into words. Then he nods reflectively and says in a hoarse voice:*]

Yes, all liars, all liars, all lying dying liars!

[*This is said slowly, slowly, with a fierce revulsion. He goes on out.*]

—Lying! Dying! Liars!

[*His voice dies out. There is the sound of a child being slapped. It rushes, hideously bawling, through room and out the hall door.*
Brick remains motionless as the lights dim out and the curtain falls.]

[*Curtain*]

ACT THREE

There is no lapse of time.
Mae enters with Reverend Tooker.

MAE

Where is Big Daddy! Big Daddy?

BIG MAMA

[*entering*] Too much smell of burnt fireworks makes me feel a little bit sick at my stomach.—Where is Big Daddy?

MAE

That's what I want to know, where has Big Daddy gone?

BIG MAMA

He must have turned in, I reckon he went to baid. . . .

[*Gooper enters.*]

GOOPER

Where is Big Daddy?

MAE

We don't know where he is!

BIG MAMA

I reckon he's gone to baid.

GOOPER
Well, then, now we can talk.

BIG MAMA
What *is* this talk, *what* talk?

[*Margaret appears on gallery, talking to Dr. Baugh.*]

MARGARET
[*musically*] My family freed their slaves ten years before abolition, my great-great-grandfather gave his slaves their freedom five years before the war between the States started!

MAE
Oh, for God's sake! Maggie's climbed back up in her family tree!

MARGARET
[*sweetly*] What, Mae?—Oh, where's Big Daddy?!

[*The pace must be very quick. Great Southern animation.*]

BIG MAMA
[*addressing them all*] I think Big Daddy was just worn out. He loves his family, he loves to have them around him, but it's a strain on his nerves. He wasn't himself tonight, Big Daddy wasn't himself, I could tell he was all worked up.

REVEREND TOOKER
I think he's remarkable.

BIG MAMA
Yaisss! Just remarkable. Did you all notice the food he ate at that table? Did you all notice the supper he put away? Why, he ate like a hawss!

GOOPER
I hope he doesn't regret it.

BIG MAMA
Why, that man—ate a huge piece of cawn-bread with molasses on it! Helped himself twice to hoppin' john.

MARGARET
Big Daddy loves hoppin' john.—We had a real country dinner.

BIG MAMA
[*overlapping Margaret*] Yais, he simply adores it! An' candied yams? That man put away enough food at that table to stuff a nigger *field*-hand!

GOOPER
[*with grim relish*] I hope he don't have to pay for it later on. . . .

BIG MAMA
[*fiercely*] What's *that*, Gooper?

MAE
Gooper says he hopes Big Daddy doesn't suffer tonight.

BIG MAMA
Oh, shoot, Gooper says, Gooper says! Why should Big Daddy suffer for satisfying a normal appetite? There's nothin' wrong with that man but nerves, he's sound as a dollar! And now he knows he is an' that's why he ate such a supper. He had a big load off his mind, knowin' he wasn't doomed t'—what he thought he was doomed to. . . .

MARGARET
[*sadly and sweetly*] Bless his old sweet soul. . . .

BIG MAMA
[*vaguely*] Yais, bless his heart, where's Brick?

MAE
Outside.

GOOPER
—Drinkin' . . .

BIG MAMA
I know he's drinkin'. You all don't have to keep tellin' *me* Brick is drinkin'. Cain't I see he's drinkin' without you continually tellin' me that boy's drinkin'?

MARGARET
Good for you, Big Mama!

[*She applauds.*]

BIG MAMA
Other people *drink* and *have* drunk an' will *drink*, as long as they make that stuff an' put it in bottles.

MARGARET
That's the truth. I never trusted a man that didn't drink.

MAE
Gooper never drinks. Don't you trust Gooper?

MARGARET
Why, Gooper, don't you drink? If I'd known you didn't drink, I wouldn't of made that remark—

BIG MAMA
Brick?

MARGARET
—at least not in your presence.

[She laughs sweetly.]

BIG MAMA

Brick!

MARGARET

He's still on the gall'ry. I'll go bring him in so we can talk.

BIG MAMA

[worriedly] I don't know what this mysterious family conference is about.

[Awkward silence. Big Mama looks from face to face, then belches slightly and mutters, "Excuse me. . . ."
She opens an ornamental fan suspended about her throat, a black lace fan to go with her black lace gown, and fans her wilting corsage, sniffing nervously and looking from face to face in the uncomfortable silence as Margaret calls "Brick?" and Brick sings to the moon on the gallery.]

I don't know what's wrong here, you all have such long faces! Open that door on the hall and let some air circulate through here, will you please, Gooper?

MAE

I think we'd better leave that door closed, Big Mama, till after the talk.

BIG MAMA

Reveren' Tooker, will *you* please open that door?!

REVEREND TOOKEER

I sure will, Big Mama.

MAE

I just didn't think we ought t' take any chance of Big Daddy hearin' a word of this discussion.

BIG MAMA

I swear! Nothing's going to be said in Big Daddy's house that he cain't hear if he wants to!

GOOPER

Well, Big Mama, it's—

[Mae gives him a quick, hard poke to shut him up. He glares at her fiercely as she circles before him like a burlesque ballerina, raising her skinny bare arms over her head, jangling her bracelets, exclaiming:]

MAE

A breeze! A breeze!

REVEREND TOOKER

I think this house is the coolest house in the Delta.—Did you all know that Halsey Banks' widow put air-

conditioning units in the church and rectory at Friar's Point in memory of Halsey?

[General conversation has resumed; everybody is chatting so that the stage sounds like a big bird-cage.]

GOOPER

Too bad nobody cools your church off for you. I bet you sweat in that pulpit these hot Sundays, Reverend Tooker.

REVEREND TOOKER

Yes, my vestments are drenched.

MAE

[at the same time to Dr. Baugh] You reckon those vitamin B_{12} injections are what they're cracked up t' be, Doc Baugh?

DOCTOR BAUGH

Well, if you want to be stuck with something I guess they're as good to be stuck with as anything else.

BIG MAMA

[at gallery door] Maggie, Maggie, aren't you comin' with Brick?

MAE

[suddenly and loudly, creating a silence] I have a strange feeling, I have a peculiar feeling!

BIG MAMA

[turning from gallery] What feeling?

MAE

That Brick said somethin' he shouldn't of said t' Big Daddy.

BIG MAMA

Now what on earth could Brick of said t' Big Daddy that he shouldn't say?

GOOPER

Big Mama, there's somethin'—

MAE

NOW, WAIT!

[She rushes up to Big Mama and gives her a quick hug and kiss. Big Mama pushes her impatiently off as the Reverend Tooker's voice rises serenely in a little pocket of silence:]

REVEREND TOOKER

Yes, last Sunday the gold in my chasuble faded into th' purple. . . .

GOOPER

Reveren', you must of been preachin' hell's fire last Sunday!

[He guffaws at this witticism but the Reverend is not sincerely amused. At the same time Big Mama has crossed over to Dr. Baugh and is saying to him:]

BIG MAMA
[her breathless voice rising high-pitched above the others] In my day they had what they call the Keeley cure for heavy drinkers. But now I understand they just take some kind of tablets, they call them "Annie Bust" tablets. But *Brick* don't need to take *nothin*'.

[Brick appears in gallery doors with Margaret behind him.]

BIG MAMA
[unaware of his presence behind her]That boy is just broken up over Skipper's death. You know how poor Skipper died. They gave him a big, big dose of that sodium amytal stuff at his home and then they called the ambulance and give him another big, big dose of it at the hospital and that and all of the alcohol in his system fo' months an' months an' months just proved too much for his heart. . . . I'm scared of needles! I'm more scared of a needle than the knife. . . . I think more people have been needled out of this world than—

[She stops short and wheels about.]

OH!—here's Brick! My precious baby—

[She turns upon Brick with short, fat arms extended, at the same time uttering a loud, short sob, which is both comic and touching.
Brick smiles and bows slightly, making a burlesque gesture of gallantry for Maggie to pass before him into the room. Then he hobbles on his crutch directly to the liquor cabinet and there is absolute silence, with everybody looking at Brick as everybody has always looked at Brick when he spoke or moved or appeared.
One by one he drops ice cubes in his glass, then suddenly, but not quickly, looks back over his shoulder with a wry, charming smile, and says:]

BRICK
I'm sorry! Anyone else?

BIG MAMA
[sadly] No, son. I *wish* you wouldn't!

BRICK
I wish I didn't have to, Big Mama, but I'm still waiting for that click in my head which makes it all smooth out!

BIG MAMA
Aw, Brick, you—BREAK MY HEART!

MARGARET
[at the same time] Brick, go sit with Big Mama!

BIG MAMA
I just cain't *staiiiiiiiii-nnnnnd*—it. . . .

[She sobs.]

MAE
Now that we're all assembled—

GOOPER
We kin talk. . . .

BIG MAMA
Breaks my heart. . . .

MARGARET
Sit with Big Mama, Brick, and hold her hand.

[Big Mama sniffs very loudly three times, almost like three drum beats in the pocket of silence.]

BRICK
You do that, Maggie. I'm a restless cripple. I got to stay on my crutch.

[Brick hobbles to the gallery door; leans there as if waiting.
Mae sits beside Big Mama, while Gooper moves in front and sits on the end of the couch, facing her.
Reverend Tooker moves nervously into the space between them; on the other side, Dr. Baugh stands looking at nothing in particular and lights a cigar.
Margaret turns away.]

BIG MAMA
Why're you all *surroundin*' me—like this? Why're you all starin' at me like this an' makin' signs at each other?

[Reverend Tooker steps back startled.]

MAE
Calm yourself, Big Mama.

BIG MAMA
Calm you'self *you'self*, Sister Woman. How could I calm myself with everyone starin' at me as if big drops of blood had broken out on m'face? What's this all about, Annh! What?

[Gooper coughs and takes a center position.]

GOOPER
Now, Doc Baugh.

MAE
Doc Baugh?

BRICK
[suddenly] SHHH!—

[Then he grins and chuckles and shakes his head
regretfully.]

—Naw!—that wasn't th' click.

GOOPER
Brick, shut up or stay out there on the gallery with
your liquor! We got to talk about a serious matter. Big
Mama wants to know the complete truth about the
report we got today from the Ochsner Clinic.

MAE
[eagerly]—on Big Daddy's condition!

GOOPER
Yais, on Big Daddy's condition, we got to face it.

DOCTOR BAUGH
Well. . . .

BIG MAMA
[terrified, rising] Is there? Something? Something that
I? Don't—Know?

[In these few words, this startled, very soft, question,
Big Mama reviews the history of her forty-five years
with Big Daddy, her great, almost embarrassingly true-
hearted and simple-minded devotion to Big Daddy, who
must have had something Brick has, who made himself
loved so much by the "simple expedient" of not loving
enough to disturb his charming detachment, also once
coupled, like Brick's, with virile beauty.
Big Mama has a dignity at this moment: she almost
stops being fat.]

DOCTOR BAUGH
[after a pause, uncomfortably] Yes?—Well—

BIG MAMA
I!!!—want to—knowwwwwww. . . .

[Immediately she thrusts her fist to her mouth as if to
deny that statement.
Then, for some curious reason, she snatches the
withered corsage from her breast and hurls it on the
floor and steps on it with her short, fat feet.]

—Somebody must be lyin'!—I want to know!

MAE
Sit down, Big Mama, sit down on this sofa.

MARGARET
[quickly] Brick, go sit with Big Mama.

BIG MAMA
What is it, what is it?

DOCTOR BAUGH
I never have seen a more thorough examination than
Big Daddy Pollitt was given in all my experience with
the Ochsner Clinic.

GOOPER
It's one of the best in the country.

MAE
It's THE best in the country—bar none!

[For some reason she gives Gooper a violent poke as she
goes past him. He slaps at her hand without removing
his eyes from his mother's face.]

DOCTOR BAUGH
Of course they were ninety-nine and nine-tenths percent sure before they even started.

BIG MAMA
Sure of what, sure of what, sure of—what?—what!

[She catches her breath in a startled sob. Mae kisses her
quickly. She thrusts Mae fiercely away from her, staring
at the doctor.]

MAE
Mommy, be a brave girl!

BRICK
[in the doorway, softly]
"By the light, by the light,
Of the sil-ve-ry mo-ooo-n . . ."

GOOPER
Shut up!—Brick.

BRICK
—Sorry. . . .

[He wanders out on the gallery.]

DOCTOR BAUGH
But now, you see, Big Mama, they cut a piece off this
growth, a specimen of the tissue and—

BIG MAMA
Growth? You told Big Daddy—

DOCTOR BAUGH
Now wait.

BIG MAMA
[fiercely] You told me and Big Daddy there wasn't a
thing wrong with him but—

MAE
Big Mama, they always—

GOOPER
Let Doc Baugh talk, will yuh?

BIG MAMA
—little spastic condition of—

[Her breath gives out in a sob.]

DOCTOR BAUGH
Yes, that's what we told Big Daddy. But we had this bit of tissue run through the laboratory and I'm sorry to say the test was positive on it. It's—well— malignant. . . .

[Pause.]

BIG MAMA
—Cancer?! Cancer?!

[Dr. Baugh nods gravely.
Big Mama gives a long gasping cry.]

MAE AND GOOPER
Now, now, now, Big Mama, you had to know. . . .

BIG MAMA
WHY DIDN'T THEY CUT IT OUT OF HIM? HANH? HANH?

DOCTOR BAUGH
Involved too much, Big Mama, too many organs affected.

MAE
Big Mama, the liver's affected and so's the kidneys, both! It's gone way past what they call a—

GOOPER
A surgical risk.

MAE
—Uh-huh. . . .

[Big Mama draws a breath like a dying gasp.]

REVEREND TOOKER
Tch, tch, tch, tch, tch!

DOCTOR BAUGH
Yes, it's gone past the knife.

MAE
That's why he's turned yellow, Mommy!

BIG MAMA
Git away from me, git away from me, Mae!

[She rises abruptly.]

I want Brick! Where's Brick? Where is my only son?

MAE
Mama! Did she say "only son"?

GOOPER
What does that make me?

MAE
A sober responsible man with five precious children—Six!

BIG MAMA
I want Brick to tell me! Brick! Brick!

MARGARET
[rising from her reflections in a corner] Brick was so upset he went back out.

BIG MAMA
Brick!

MARGARET
Mama, let me tell you!

BIG MAMA
No, no, leave me alone, you're not my blood!

GOOPER
Mama, I'm your son! Listen to me!

MAE
Gooper's your son, he's your first-born!

BIG MAMA
Gooper never liked Daddy.

MAE
[as if terribly shocked] That's not TRUE!

[There is a pause. The minister coughs and rises.]

REVEREND TOOKER
[to Mae] I think I'd better slip away at this point.

MAE
[sweetly and sadly] Yes, Doctor Tooker, you go.

REVEREND TOOKER
[discreetly] Goodnight, goodnight, everybody, and God bless you all . . . on this place. . . .

[He slips out.]

DOCTOR BAUGH
That man is a good man but lacking in tact. Talking about people giving memorial windows—if he mentioned one memorial window, he must have spoke of a dozen, and saying how awful it was when somebody died intestate, the legal wrangles, and so forth.

[Mae coughs, and points at Big Mama.]

DOCTOR BAUGH
Well, Big Mama. . . .

[He sighs.]

BIG MAMA
It's all a mistake, I know it's just a bad dream.

DOCTOR BAUGH
We're gonna keep Big Daddy as comfortable as we can.

BIG MAMA
Yes, it's just a bad dream, that's all it is, it's just an awful dream.

GOOPER
In my opinion Big Daddy is having some pain but won't admit that he has it.

BIG MAMA
Just a dream, a bad dream.

DOCTOR BAUGH
That's what lots of them do, they think if they don't admit they're having the pain they can sort of escape the fact of it.

GOOPER
[with relish] Yes, they get sly about it, they get real sly about it.

MAE
Gooper and I think—

GOOPER
Shut up, Mae!—Big Daddy ought to be started on morphine.

BIG MAMA
Nobody's going to give Big Daddy morphine.

DOCTOR BAUGH
Now, Big Mama, when that pain strikes it's going to strike mighty hard and Big Daddy's going to need the needle to bear it.

BIG MAMA
I tell you, nobody's going to give him morphine.

MAE
Big Mama, you don't want to see Big Daddy suffer, you know you—

[Gooper standing beside her gives her a savage poke.]

DOCTOR BAUGH
[placing a package on the table] I'm leaving this stuff here, so if there's a sudden attack you all won't have to send out for it.

MAE
I know how to give a hypo.

GOOPER
Mae took a course in nursing during the war.

MARGARET
Somehow I don't think Big Daddy would want Mae to give him a hypo.

MAE
You think he'd want *you* to do it?

[Dr. Baugh rises.]

GOOPER
Doctor Baugh is goin'.

DOCTOR BAUGH
Yes, I got to be goin'. Well, keep your chin up, Big Mama.

GOOPER
[with jocularity] She's gonna keep *both* chins up, aren't you Big Mama?

[Big Mama sobs.]

Now stop that, Big Mama.

MAE
Sit down with me, Big Mama.

GOOPER
[at door with Dr. Baugh] Well, Doc, we sure do appreciate all you done. I'm telling you, we're surely obligated to you for—

[Dr. Baugh has gone out without a glance at him.]

GOOPER
—I guess that doctor has got a lot on his mind but it wouldn't hurt him to act a little more human. . . .

[Big Mama sobs.]

Now be a brave girl, Mommy.

BIG MAMA
It's not true, I know that it's just not true!

GOOPER
Mama, those tests are infallible!

BIG MAMA
Why are you so determined to see your father daid?

MAE
Big Mama!

MARGARET
[gently] I know what Big Mama means.

MAE

[fiercely]Oh, do you?

MARGARET

[quietly and very sadly] Yes, I think I do.

MAE

For a newcomer in the family you sure do show a lot of understanding.

MARGARET

Understanding is needed on this place.

MAE

I guess you must have needed a lot of it in your family, Maggie, with your father's liquor problem and now you've got Brick with his!

MARGARET

Brick does not have a liquor problem at all. Brick is devoted to Big Daddy. This thing is a terrible strain on him.

BIG MAMA

Brick is Big Daddy's boy, but he drinks too much and it worries me and Big Daddy, and, Margaret, you've got to cooperate with us, you've got to cooperate with Big Daddy and me in getting Brick straightened out. Because it will break Big Daddy's heart if Brick don't pull himself together and take hold of things.

MAE

Take hold of what things, Big Mama?

BIG MAMA

The place.

[There is a quick violent look between Mae and Gooper.]

GOOPER

Big Mama, you've had a shock.

MAE

Yais, we've all had a shock, but. . . .

GOOPER

Let's be realistic—

MAE

—Big Daddy would never, would never, be foolish enough to—

GOOPER

—put this place in irresponsible hands!

BIG MAMA

Big Daddy ain't going to leave the place in anybody's hands; Big Daddy is not going to die. I want you to get that in your heads, all of you!

MAE

Mommy, Mommy, Big Mama, we're just as hopeful an' optimistic as you are about Big Daddy's prospects, we have faith in prayer—but nevertheless there are certain matters that have to be discussed an' dealt with, because otherwise—

GOOPER

Eventualities have to be considered and now's the time. . . . Mae, will you please get my briefcase out of our room?

MAE

Yes, honey.

[She rises and goes out through the hall door.]

GOOPER

[standing over Big Mama] Now Big Mom. What you said just now was not at all true and you know it. I've always loved Big Daddy in my own quiet way. I never made a show of it, and I know that Big Daddy has always been fond of me in a quiet way, too, and he never made a show of it neither.

[Mae returns with Gooper's briefcase.]

MAE

Here's your briefcase, Gooper, honey.

GOOPER

[handing the briefcase back to her] Thank you. . . . Of cou'se, my relationship with Big Daddy is different from Brick's.

MAE

You're eight years older'n Brick an' always had t'carry a bigger load of th' responsibilities than Brick ever had t'carry. He never carried a thing in his life but a football or a highball.

GOOPER

Mae, will y' let me talk, please?

MAE

Yes, honey.

GOOPER

Now, a twenty-eight thousand acre plantation's a mighty big thing t'run.

MAE

Almost singlehanded.

[Margaret has gone out onto the gallery, and can be heard calling softly to Brick.]

BIG MAMA

You never had to run this place! What are you talking about? As if Big Daddy was dead and in his grave, you had to run it? Why, you just helped him out with a few business details and had your law practice at the same time in Memphis!

MAE

Oh, Mommy, Mommy, Big Mommy! Let's be fair! Why, Gooper has given himself body and soul to keeping this place up for the past five years since Big Daddy's health started failing. Gooper won't say it, Gooper never thought of it as a duty, he just did it. And what did Brick do? Brick kept living in his past glory at college! Still a football player at twenty-seven!

MARGARET

[returning alone] Who are you talking about, now? Brick? A football player? He isn't a football player and you know it. Brick is a sports announcer on TV and one of the best-known ones in the country!

MAE

I'm talking about what he was.

MARGARET

Well, I wish you would just stop talking about my husband.

GOOPER

I've got a right to discuss my brother with other members of MY OWN family which don't include *you*. Why don't you go out there and drink with Brick?

MARGARET

I've never seen such malice toward a brother.

GOOPER

How about his for me? Why, he can't stand to be in the same room with me!

MARGARET

This is a deliberate campaign of vilification for the most disgusting and sordid reason on earth, and I know what it is! It's *avarice, avarice, greed, greed!*

BIG MAMA

Oh, I'll scream! I will scream in a moment unless this stops!

[Gooper has stalked up to Margaret with clenched fists at his sides as if he would strike her. Mae distorts her face again into a hideous grimace behind Margaret's back.]

MARGARET

We only remain on the place because of Big Mom and Big Daddy. If it is true what they say about Big Daddy we are going to leave here just as soon as it's over. Not a moment later.

BIG MAMA

[sobs]Margaret. Child. Come here. Sit next to Big Mama.

MARGARET

Precious Mommy. I'm sorry, I'm sorry, I—!

[She bends her long graceful neck to press her forehead to Big Mama's bulging shoulder under its black chiffon.]

GOOPER

How beautiful, how touching, this display of devotion!

MAE

Do you know why she's childless? She's childless because that big beautiful athlete husband of hers won't go to bed with her!

GOOPER

You jest won't let me do this in a nice way, will yah? Aw right—Mae and I have five kids with another one coming! I don't give a goddam if Big Daddy likes me or don't like me or did or never did or will or will never! I'm just appealing to a sense of common decency and fair play. I'll tell you the truth. I've resented Big Daddy's partiality to Brick ever since Brick was born, and the way I've been treated like I was just barely good enough to spit on and sometimes not even good enough for that. Big Daddy is dying of cancer, and it's spread all through him and it's attacked all his vital organs including the kidneys and right now he is sinking into uremia, and you all know what uremia is, it's poisoning of the whole system due to the failure of the body to eliminate its poisons.

MARGARET

[to herself, downstage, hissingly] Poisons, poisons! Venomous thoughts and words! In hearts and minds!—That's poisons!

GOOPER

[overlapping her] I am asking for a square deal, and I expect to get one. But if I don't get one, if there's any peculiar shenanigans going on around here behind my back, or before me, well, I'm not a corporation lawyer for nothing, I know how to protect my own interests.—OH! A late arrival!

[Brick enters from the gallery with a tranquil, blurred smile, carrying an empty glass with him.]

MAE
Behold the conquering hero comes!

GOOPER
The fabulous Brick Pollitt! Remember him?—Who could forget him!

MAE
He looks like he's been injured in a game!

GOOPER
Yep, I'm afraid you'll have to warm the bench at the Sugar Bowl this year, Brick!

[Mae laughs shrilly.]

Or was it the Rose Bowl that he made that famous run in?

MAE
The punch bowl, honey. It was in the punch bowl, the cut-glass punch bowl!

GOOPER
Oh, that's right, I'm getting the bowls mixed up!

MARGARET
Why don't you stop venting your malice and envy on a sick boy?

BIG MAMA
Now you two hush, I mean it, hush, all of you, hush!

GOOPER
All right, Big Mama. A family crisis brings out the best and the worst in every member of it.

MAE
That's the truth.

MARGARET
Amen!

BIG MAMA
I said, hush! I won't tolerate any more catty talk in my house.

[Mae gives Gooper a sign indicating briefcase. Brick's smile has grown both brighter and vaguer. As he prepares a drink, he sings softly:]

BRICK
Show me the way to go home,
I'm tired and I wanta go to bed,
I had a little drink about an hour ago—

GOOPER
[at the same time] Big Mama, you know it's necessary for me t'go back to Memphis in th' mornin' t'represent the Parker estate in a lawsuit.

[Mae sits on the bed and arranges papers she has taken from the briefcase.]

BRICK
[continuing the song]
Wherever I may roam,
On land or sea or foam.

BIG MAMA
Is it, Gooper?

MAE
Yaiss.

GOOPER
That's why I'm forced to—to bring up a problem that—

MAE
Somethin' that's too important t' be put off!

GOOPER
If Brick was sober, he ought to be in on this.

MARGARET
Brick is present; we're here.

GOOPER
Well, good. I will now give you this outline my partner, Tom Bullitt, an' me have drawn up—a sort of dummy—trusteeship.

MARGARET
Oh, that's it! You'll be in charge an' dole out remittances, will you?

GOOPER
This we did as soon as we got the report on Big Daddy from th' Ochsner Laboratories. We did this thing, I mean we drew up this dummy outline with the advice and assistance of the Chairman of the Boa'd of Directors of th' Southern Plantahs Bank and Trust Company in Memphis, C. C. Bellowes, a man who handles estates for all th' prominent fam'lies in West Tennessee and th' Delta.

BIG MAMA

Gooper?

GOOPER

[crouching in front of Big Mama] Now this is not—not final, or anything like it. This is just a preliminary outline. But it does provide a basis—a design—a—possible, feasible—*plan*!

MARGARET

Yes, I'll bet.

MAE

It's a plan to protect the biggest estate in the Delta from irresponsibility an'—

BIG MAMA

Now you listen to me, all of you, you listen here! They's not goin' to be any more catty talk in my house! And Gooper, you put that away before I grab it out of your hand and tear it right up! I don't know what the hell's in it, and I don't want to know what the hell's in it. I'm talkin' in Big Daddy's language now; I'm his *wife*, not his *widow*, I'm still his *wife*! And I'm talkin' to you in his language an'—

GOOPER

Big Mama, what I have here is—

MAE

Gooper explained that it's just a plan. . . .

BIG MAMA

I don't care what you got there. Just put it back where it came from, an' don't let me see it again, not even the outside of the envelope of it! Is that understood? Basis! Plan! Preliminary! Design! I say—what is it Big Daddy always says when he's disgusted?

BRICK

[from the bar] Big Daddy says "crap" when he's disgusted.

BIG MAMA

[rising] That's right—CRAP! I say CRAP too, like Big Daddy!

MAE

Coarse language doesn't seem called for in this—

GOOPER

Somethin' in me is *deeply outraged* by hearin' you talk like this.

BIG MAMA

Nobody's goin' to take nothin'!—till Big Daddy lets go of it, and maybe, just possibly, not—not even then! No, not even then!

BRICK

You can always hear me singin' this song,
Show me the way to go home.

BIG MAMA

Tonight Brick looks like he used to look when he was a little boy, just like he did when he played wild games and used to come home all sweaty and pink-cheeked and sleepy, with his—red curls shining. . . .

[*She comes over to him and runs her fat shaky hand through his hair. He draws aside as he does from all physical contact and continues the song in a whisper, opening the ice bucket and dropping in the ice cubes one by one as if he were mixing some important chemical formula.*]

BIG MAMA

[continuing] Time goes by so fast. Nothin' can outrun it. Death commences too early—almost before you're half-acquainted with life—you meet with the other. . . .

Oh, you know we just got to love each other an' stay together, all of us, just as close as we can, especially now that such a *black* thing has come and moved into this place without invitation.

[*Awkwardly embracing Brick, she presses her head to his shoulder.*
Gooper has been returning papers to Mae who has restored them to briefcase with an air of severely tried patience.]

GOOPER

Big Mama? Big Mama?

[*He stands behind her, tense with sibling envy.*]

BIG MAMA

[oblivious of Gooper] Brick, you hear me, don't you?

MARGARET

Brick hears you, Big Mama, he understands what you're saying.

BIG MAMA

Oh, Brick, son of Big Daddy! Big Daddy does so love you! Y'know what would be his fondest dream come true? If before he passed on, if Big Daddy has to pass on, you gave him a child of yours, a grandson as much like his son as his son is like Big Daddy!

MAE

[zipping briefcase shut: an incongruous sound] Such a pity that Maggie an' Brick can't oblige!

MARGARET

[suddenly and quietly but forcefully] Everybody listen.

[She crosses to the center of the room, holding her hands
rigidly together.]

MAE

Listen to what, Maggie?

MARGARET

I have an announcement to make.

GOOPEER

A sports announcement, Maggie?

MARGARET

Brick and I are going to—*have a child!*

[Big Mama catches her breath in a loud gasp.
Pause. Big Mama rises.]

BIG MAMA

Maggie! Brick! This is too good to believe!

MAE

That's right, too good to believe.

BIG MAMA

Oh, my, my! This is Big Daddy's dream, his dream
come true! I'm going to tell him right now before
he—

MARGARET

We'll tell him in the morning. Don't disturb him now.

BIG MAMA

I want to tell him before he goes to sleep, I'm going to
tell him his dream's come true this minute! And
Brick! A child will make you pull yourself together
and quit this drinking!

[She seizes the glass from his hand.]

The responsibilities of a father will—

[Her face contorts and she makes an excited gesture;
bursting into sobs, she rushes out, crying.]

I'm going to tell Big Daddy right this minute!

[Her voice fades out down the hall.
Brick shrugs slightly and drops an ice cube into
another glass. Margaret crosses quickly to his side,
saying something under her breath, and she pours the
liquor for him, staring up almost fiercely into his face.]

BRICK

[coolly] Thank you, Maggie, that's a nice big shot.

[Mae has joined Gooper and she gives him a fierce poke,
making a low hissing sound and a grimace of fury.]

GOOPER

[pushing her aside] Brick, could you possibly spare me
one small shot of that liquor?

BRICK

Why, help yourself, Gooper boy.

GOOPER

I will.

MAE

[shrilly] Of course we know that this is—

GOOPER

Be still, Mae!

MAE

I won't be still! I know she's made this up!

GOOPER

God damn it, I said to shut up!

MARGARET

Gracious! I didn't know that my little announcement
was going to provoke such a storm!

MAE

That woman isn't *pregnant!*

GOOPER

Who said she was?

MAE

She did.

GOOPER

The doctor didn't. Doc Baugh didn't.

MARGARET

I haven't gone to Doc Baugh.

GOOPER

Then who'd you go to, Maggie?

MARGARET

One of the best gynecologists in the South.

GOOPER

Uh huh, uh huh!—I see. . . .

[He takes out pencil and notebook.]

—May we have his name, please?

MARGARET

No, you may not, Mister Prosecuting Attorney!

MAE

He doesn't have any name, he doesn't exist!

MARGARET
Oh, he exists all right, and so does my child, Brick's baby!

MAE
You can't conceive a child by a man that won't sleep with you unless you think you're—

[Brick has turned on the phonograph. A scat song cuts Mae's speech.]

GOOPER
Turn that off!

MAE
We know it's a lie because we hear you in here; he won't sleep with you, we hear you! So don't imagine you're going to put a trick over on us, to fool a dying man with a—

[A long drawn cry of agony and rage fills the house. Margaret turns the phonograph down to a whisper. The cry is repeated.]

MAE
[awed]Did you hear that, Gooper, did you hear that?

GOOPER
Sounds like the pain has struck.

MAE
Go see, Gooper!

GOOPER
Come along and leave these love birds together in their nest!

[He goes out first. Mae follows but turns at the door, contorting her face and hissing at Margaret.]

MAE
Liar!

[She slams the door. Margaret exhales with relief and moves a little unsteadily to catch hold of Brick's arm.]

MARGARET
Thank you for—keeping still. . . .

BRICK
OK, Maggie.

MARGARET
It was gallant of you to save my face!

BRICK
—It hasn't happened yet.

MARGARET
What?

BRICK
The click. . . .

MARGARET
—the click in your head that makes you peaceful, honey?

BRICK
Uh-huh. It hasn't happened. . . . I've got to make it happen before I can sleep. . . .

MARGARET
—I—know what you—mean. . . .

BRICK
Give me that pillow in the big chair, Maggie.

MARGARET
I'll put it on the bed for you.

BRICK
No, put it on the sofa, where I sleep.

MARGARET
Not tonight, Brick.

BRICK
I want it on the sofa. That's where I sleep.

[He has hobbled to the liquor cabinet. He now pours down three shots in quick succession and stands waiting, silent. All at once he turns with a smile and says:]

There!

MARGARET
What?

BRICK
The *click*. . . .

[His gratitude seems almost infinite as he hobbles out on the gallery with a drink. We hear his crutch as he swings out of sight. Then, at some distance, he begins singing to himself a peaceful song.
Margaret holds the big pillow forlornly as if it were her only companion, for a few moments, then throws it on the bed. She rushes to the liquor cabinet, gathers all the bottles in her arms, turns about undecidedly, then runs out of the room with them, leaving the door ajar on the dim yellow hall. Brick is heard hobbling back along the gallery, singing his peaceful song. He comes back in, sees the pillow on the bed, laughs lightly, sadly, picks it up. He has it under his arm as Margaret returns to the

room. Margaret softly shuts the door and leans against it, smiling softly at Brick.]

MARGARET

Brick, I used to think that you were stronger than me and I didn't want to be overpowered by you. But now, since you've taken to liquor—you know what?—I guess it's bad, but now I'm stronger than you and I can love you more truly!
Don't move that pillow. I'll move it right back if you do!—Brick?

[She turns out all the lamps but a single rose-silk-shaded one by the bed.]

I really have been to a doctor and I know what to do and—Brick?—this is my time by the calendar to conceive!

BRICK

Yes, I understand, Maggie. But how are you going to conceive a child by a man in love with his liquor?

MARGARET

By locking his liquor up and making him satisfy my desire before I unlock it!

BRICK

Is that what you've done, Maggie?

MARGARET

Look and see. That cabinet's mighty empty compared to before!

BRICK

Well, I'll be a son of a—

[He reaches for his crutch but she beats him to it and rushes out on the gallery, hurls the crutch over the rail and comes back in, panting. There are running footsteps. Big Mama bursts into the room, her face all awry, gasping, stammering.]

BIG MAMA

Oh, my God, oh, my God, oh, my God, where is it?

MARGARET

Is this what you want, Big Mama?

[Margaret hands her the package left by the doctor.]

BIG MAMA

I can't bear it, oh, God! Oh, Brick! Brick, baby!

[She rushes at him. He averts his face from her sobbing kisses. Margaret watches with a tight smile.]

My son, Big Daddy's boy! Little Father!

[The groaning cry is heard again. She runs out, sobbing.]

MARGARET

And so tonight we're going to make the lie true, and when that's done, I'll bring the liquor back here and we'll get drunk together, here, tonight, in this place that death has come into. . . .
—What do you say?

BRICK

I don't say anything. I guess there's nothing to say.

MARGARET

Oh, you weak people, you weak, beautiful people!—who give up.—What you want is someone to—

[She turns out the rose-silk lamp.]

—take hold of you.—Gently, gently, with love! And—

[The curtain begins to fall slowly.]

I *do* love you, Brick, I *do*!

BRICK

[smiling with charming sadness] Wouldn't it be funny if that was true?

[The Curtain Comes Down]

[The End]

9

GLENGARRY GLEN ROSS

David Mamet • 1983

FEW PLAYS APPEAR LESS "LITERARY" ON THE PAGE than *Glengarry Glen Ross*. First-time readers are bound to be startled, if not shocked, by the abruptly staccato and incessantly vulgar dialogue of this play, which is set in and around an all-male real estate office in modern Chicago. There is hardly a single complete sentence in the play, and hardly a speech without one or more well-recognized obscenities and/or ethnic slurs. And rather than being led gracefully into the play's organizing story line, we are simply thrown into a series of furious and ongoing arguments. "Oh, shades of Shaw and Chekhov," the poet may very well ask, "Have we come to this?"

In a word, yes. Along with many other contemporary playwrights (but clearly as a leader among them), David Mamet (b. 1947) seeks to redefine modern dramaturgy in terms of the human society that drama both mirrors and critiques. The world of his play is not merely that of a struggling Chicago office, but of a large sector of American business in general, and of "male business" in par-

ticular: the sometimes seamy business of being a "Man." In the world of Mamet's desperate salesmen, competition is ferocious, deceit is universal, brute pressure rules, and verbal violence—shouts, oaths, insults, and interruptions—is simply the medium of communication. It is even the medium of friendship. *Glengarry Glen Ross*, though often bitter and accusatory, is also, from time to time, a comedy.

The characters of *Glengarry* may be on the edge (if not over the edge) of criminality, but Mamet also makes us reflect on an unpleasant reality of free-market economics: when business gets tough, the margin of profit is often at the margin of legality—if not beyond. Criminality is a common Mamet theme (his *American Buffalo* is also about business theft; *Oleanna* is about sexual harassment; his screenplays include, among others, the crime-ridden *Homicide* and *Hoffa*). But Mamet's plays are not whodunits as much as they are examinations of the social and economic forces that combine to create antisocial behavior, including arrant lawlessness. This is the world of white-collar crime, but also white-collar economics. It is a revelation, as well as a satire, as well as an intrigue.

Mamet's plays, although immensely successful on stage, are not always easy to read. His dialogue, which has become justly celebrated, employs conversational rather than "literary" syntax, with the stammerings, trail-offs, restarts, mutterings, obscenities, sudden halts, and fragmentary grammatical constructions that are common to daily speech, particularly in the high-stress give and take of modern life. We are probably more used to *hearing* such dialogue than reading it; a page of this play will look, in fact, more like a page from the Watergate tapes transcript (with the expletives *not* deleted) than of a playscript by Ibsen or Shaw or Tennessee Williams.

Mamet's technique of throwing us headlong into the (furious) action right from the play's first words is also unsettling, but deliberately so: Mamet doesn't just show us the urban jungle, he plunges us boldly into it; we spend the first few minutes of the play just as bewildered as James Lingk, the hapless customer who walks into the *Glengarry* office in Act 2. But the play's manifold complexities and abruptness coalesce easily and naturally in performance. *Glengarry Glen Ross* won the 1983 "Best New Play" Olivier Award in London, and the 1984 American Pulitzer Prize for Drama; it has subsequently entered the English-speaking theatre repertory as one of the best (as well as most representative) plays of the 1980s, the "Me Decade."

NOTE ON THE TEXT

Glengarry Glen Ross was initially produced at the National Theatre of England in 1983; its American premiere was in 1984, at the Goodman Theatre in Chicago, where it was directed by Gregory Mosher. That production subsequently went to Broadway in New York.

The text does not require footnoting, but readers unfamiliar with American sales jargon should understand that a "lead" is the name of a prospective customer, "closing" is the act of completing a sale, and that, in the *Glengarry* office, the "board" would be a bulletin board listing each salesman's activity for the month.

✦ GLENGARRY GLEN ROSS ✦

──────── **THE CHARACTERS** ────────

WILLIAMSON, BAYLEN, ROMA, LINGK, Men in their early
    forties.
LEVENE, MOSS, AARONOW, Men in their fifties.

──────── **THE SCENE** ────────

*The three scenes of Act One take place in a Chinese
restaurant.*
Act Two takes place in a real estate office.

Always Be Closing.
                                    Practical Sales Maxim

──────── **ACT ONE** ────────

Scene One

*A booth at a Chinese restaurant, Williamson and Levene
are seated at the booth.*

LEVENE
John . . . John . . . John. Okay. John. John. Look:
[Pause] The Glengarry Highland's leads, you're sending Roma out. Fine. He's a good man. We know what
he is. He's fine. All I'm saying, you look at the *board*,
he's throwing . . . wait, wait, wait, he's throwing
them *away*, he's throwing the leads away. All that I'm
saying, that you're wasting leads. I don't want to tell
you your *job*. All that I'm saying, things get *set*, I know
they do, you get a certain *mindset.* . . . A guy gets a
reputation. We know how this . . . all I'm saying, put
a *closer* on the job. There's more than one man for the

. . . Put a . . . wait a second, put a *proven man out* . . .
and you watch, now *wait* a second—and you watch
your *dollar* volumes. . . . You start closing them for
fifty 'stead of *twenty-five* . . . you put a *closer* on
the . . .

WILLIAMSON
Shelly, you blew the last . . .

LEVENE
No. John. No. Let's wait, let's back up here, I did . . .
will you please? Wait a second. Please. I didn't "blow"
them. No. I didn't "blow" them. No. One kicked *out*,
one I closed . . .

WILLIAMSON
. . . you didn't close . . .

LEVENE
. . . I, if you'd *listen* to me. Please. I *closed* the cocksucker. His *ex*, John, his *ex*, I didn't know he was married . . . he, the *judge* invalidated the . . .

WILLIAMSON
Shelly . . .

LEVENE
. . . and what is that, John? What? Bad *luck*. That's all
it is. I pray in your *life* you will never find it runs in
streaks. That's what it does, that's all it's doing.
Streaks. I pray it misses you. That's all I want to say.

WILLIAMSON
[Pause] What about the other two?

LEVENE
What two?

WILLIAMSON
Four. You had four leads. One kicked out, one the
judge, you say . . .

LEVENE

. . . you want to see the court records? John? Eh? You want to go down . . .

WILLIAMSON

. . . no . . .

LEVENE

. . . do you want to go down*town* . . . ?

WILLIAMSON

. . . no . . .

LEVENE

. . . then . . .

WILLIAMSON

. . . I only . . .

LEVENE

. . . then what is this "you *say*" shit, what is that? *[Pause]* What is that . . . ?

WILLIAMSON

All that I'm saying . . .

LEVENE

What is this "you *say*"? A deal kicks out . . . I got to *eat. Shit*, Williamson, *shit.* You . . . Moss . . . Roma . . . look at the *sheets* . . . look at the *sheets.* Nineteen *eighty*, eighty-*one* . . . eighty-*two* . . . six months of eighty-two . . . who's there? Who's up there?

WILLIAMSON

Roma.

LEVENE

Under him?

WILLIAMSON

Moss.

LEVENE

Bullshit. John. Bull*shit.* April, September 1981. It's *me.* It isn't *fucking* Moss. Due respect, he's an *order* taker, John. He *talks*, he talks a good game, look at the *board*, and it's *me*, John, it's me . . .

WILLIAMSON

Not lately it isn't.

LEVENE

Lately kiss my ass lately. That isn't how you build an org . . . talk, talk to Murray. Talk to Mitch. When we were on Peterson, who paid for his fucking *car*? You talk to him. The *Seville* . . . ? He came in, "You bought that for me Shelly." Out of *what*? Cold *calling. Nothing.* Sixty-*five*, when we were there, with Glen

Ross Farms? You call 'em downtown. What was that? *Luck?* That was "luck"? Bullshit, John. You're burning my ass, I can't get a fucking *lead* . . . you think that was luck. My stats for those years? Bull*shit* . . . over that period of time . . . ? Bull*shit.* It wasn't luck. It was *skill.* You want to throw that away, John . . . ? You want to throw that away?

WILLIAMSON

It isn't me . . .

LEVENE

. . . it isn't you . . . ? Who *is* it? Who is this I'm talking to? I need the *leads* . . .

WILLIAMSON

. . . after the thirtieth . . .

LEVENE

Bull*shit* the thirtieth, I don't get on the board the thirtieth, they're going to can my ass. I need the leads. I need them now. Or I'm gone, and you're going to miss me, John, I swear to you.

WILLIAMSON

Murray . . .

LEVENE

. . . you *talk* to Murray . . .

WILLIAMSON

I have. And my job is to marshal those leads . . .

LEVENE

Marshal the leads . . . marshal the leads? What the fuck, what bus did *you* get off of, we're here to fucking *sell. Fuck* marshaling the leads. What the fuck talk is that? What the fuck talk is that? Where did you learn that? In school? *[Pause.]* That's "talk," my friend, that's "talk." Our job is to *sell.* I'm the *man* to sell. I'm getting garbage. *[Pause.]*You're giving it to me, and what I'm saying is it's *fucked.*

WILLIAMSON

You're saying that I'm fucked.

LEVENE

Yes. *[Pause.]* I am. I'm sorry to antagonize you.

WILLIAMSON

Let me . . .

LEVENE

. . . and I'm going to get bounced and you're . . .

WILLIAMSON

. . . let me . . . are you listening to me . . . ?

LEVENE

Yes.

WILLIAMSON

Let me tell you something, Shelly. I do what I'm hired to do. I'm . . . wait a second. I'm *hired* to watch the leads. I'm given . . . hold on, I'm given a *policy*. *My* job is to *do that*. What I'm *told*. That's it. You, wait a second, *anybody* falls below a certain mark I'm not *permitted* to give them the premium leads.

LEVENE

Then how do they come up above that mark? With *dreck* . . . ? That's *nonsense*. Explain this to me. 'Cause it's a waste, and it's a stupid waste. I want to tell you something . . .

WILLIAMSON

You know what those leads cost?

LEVENE

The premium leads. Yes. I know what they cost. John. Because I, *I* generated the dollar revenue sufficient to *buy* them. Nineteen senny-*nine*, you know what I made? Senny-*nine*? Ninety-six thousand dollars. John? For *Murray* . . . For *Mitch* . . . look at the sheets . . .

WILLIAMSON

Murray said . . .

LEVENE

Fuck him. *Fuck* Murray. John? You know? You tell him I said so. What does *he* fucking know? He's going to have a "sales" contest . . . you know what our sales contest used to be? *Money*. A *fortune*. Money lying on the ground. Murray? When was the last time *he* went out on a sit? Sales contest? It's *laughable*. It's cold out there now, John. It's tight. Money is *tight*. This ain't sixty-five. It ain't. It just ain't. See? See? Now I'm a good *man*—but I need a . . .

WILLIAMSON

Murray said . . .

LEVENE

John. John . . .

WILLIAMSON

Will you please wait a second. Shelly. Please. Murray told me: the hot leads . . .

LEVENE

. . . ah, *fuck* this . . .

WILLIAMSON

The . . . Shelly? *[Pause.]* The hot leads are assigned according to the board. During the contest. *Period*. Anyone who beats fifty per . . .

LEVENE

That's fucked. That's fucked. You don't look at the fucking *percentage*. You look at the *gross*.

WILLIAMSON

Either way. You're out.

LEVENE

I'm out.

WILLIAMSON

Yes.

LEVENE

I'll tell you why I'm out. I'm *out*, you're giving me toilet paper. John. I've *seen* those leads. I saw them when I was at Homestead, we pitched those cocksuckers Rio Rancho nineteen sixty-*nine* they wouldn't buy. They couldn't buy a fucking *toaster*. They're *broke*, John. They're cold. They're deadbeats, you can't judge on that. Even so. Even so. Alright. Fine. Fine. Even so. I go in, FOUR FUCKING LEADS they got their money in a *sock*. They're fucking *Polacks*, John. Four leads. I close two. *Two*. Fifty per . . .

WILLIAMSON

. . . they kicked out.

LEVENE

They *all* kick out. You run in *streaks*, pal. *Streaks*. I'm . . . I'm . . . don't look at the *board*, look at *me*. Shelly Levene. *Anyone*. *Ask* them on Western. Ask Getz at Homestead. Go ask Jerry Graff. You know who I am . . . I NEED A SHOT. I got to get on the fucking board. Ask them. *Ask* them. Ask them who ever picked up a check I was flush. Moss, Jerry Graff, Mitch himself . . . Those guys *lived* on the business I brought in. They *lived* on it . . . and so did Murray, John. You were here you'd of benefited from it too. And now I'm saying this. Do I want charity? Do I want *pity*? I want *sits*. I want leads don't come right out of a *phone book*. Give me a lead hotter than that, I'll go in and close it. Give me a chance. That's all I want. I'm going to *get* up on that fucking board and all I want is a chance. It's a *streak* and I'm going to turn it around. *[Pause.]* I need your help. *[Pause.]*

WILLIAMSON

I can't do it, Shelly. *[Pause.]*

LEVENE

Why?

WILLIAMSON

The leads are assigned randomly . . .

LEVENE
Bullshit, bullshit, you assign them. . . . What are you *telling* me?

WILLIAMSON
. . . apart from the top men on the contest board.

LEVENE
Then put me on the board.

WILLIAMSON
You start closing again, you'll *be* on the board.

LEVENE
I can't close these leads, John. No one can. It's a joke. John, look, just give me a hot lead. Just give me two of the premium leads. As a "test," alright? As a "test" and I promise you . . .

WILLIAMSON
I can't do it, Shel. *[Pause.]*

LEVENE
I'll give you ten percent. *[Pause.]*

WILLIAMSON
Of what?

LEVENE
Of my end what I close.

WILLIAMSON
And what if you don't close.

LEVENE
I *will* close.

WILLIAMSON
What if you *don't* close . . . ?

LEVENE
I *will* close.

WILLIAMSON
What if you *don't*? Then I'm *fucked*. You see . . . ? Then it's *my* job. That's what I'm *telling* you.

LEVENE
I *will* close. John, John, ten percent. I can get hot. You *know* that . . .

WILLIAMSON
Not lately you can't . . .

LEVENE
Fuck that. That's defeatist. Fuck that. Fuck it. . . . Get on my side. *Go* with me. Let's *do* something. You want to run this office, *run* it.

WILLIAMSON
Twenty percent. *[Pause.]*

LEVENE
Alright.

WILLIAMSON
And fifty bucks a lead.

LEVENE
John. *[Pause.]* Listen. I want to talk to you. Permit me to do this a second. I'm older than you. A man acquires a reputation. On the street. What he does when he's *up*, what he does otherwise. . . . I said "ten," you said "no." You said "twenty." I said "fine," I'm not going to fuck with you, how can I beat that, you tell me? . . . Okay. Okay. We'll . . . Okay. Fine. We'll . . . Alright, twenty percent, and fifty bucks a lead. That's fine. For now. That's fine. A month or two we'll talk. A month from now. Next month. After the thirtieth. *[Pause.]* We'll talk.

WILLIAMSON
What are we going to say?

LEVENE
No. You're right. That's for later. We'll talk in a month. What have you got? I want two sits. Tonight.

WILLIAMSON
I'm not sure I have two.

LEVENE
I saw the board. You've got *four* . . .

WILLIAMSON
[Snaps] I've got *Roma*. Then I've got Moss . . .

LEVENE
Bullshit. They ain't been in the office yet. Give 'em some stiff. We have a deal or not? Eh? Two sits. The Des Plaines. Both of 'em, six and ten, you can do it . . . six and ten . . . eight and eleven, I don't give a shit, you set 'em up? Alright? The two sits in Des Plaines.

WILLIAMSON
Alright.

LEVENE
Good. Now we're talking. *[Pause.]*

WILLIAMSON
A hundred bucks. *[Pause.]*

LEVENE
Now? *[Pause.]* Now?

WILLIAMSON
Now. *[Pause.] Yes . . . When?*

LEVENE
Ah, *shit*, John. *[Pause.]*

WILLIAMSON
I wish I could.

LEVENE
You fucking asshole. *[Pause.]* I haven't got it. *[Pause.]* I haven't got it, John. *[Pause.]* I'll pay you tomorrow. *[Pause.]* I'm coming in here with the sales, I'll pay you *tomorrow.* *[Pause.]* I haven't *got* it, when I pay, the *gas* . . . I get back the hotel, I'll bring it in tomorrow.

WILLIAMSON
Can't do it.

LEVENE
I'll give you thirty on them now, I'll bring the rest tomorrow. I've got it at the hotel. *[Pause.]* John? *[Pause.]* We do that, for chrissake?

WILLIAMSON
No.

LEVENE
I'm asking you. As a favor to me? *[Pause.]* John. *[Long pause.]* John: my *daughter* . . .

WILLIAMSON
I can't do it, Shelly.

LEVENE
Well, I want to tell you something, fella, wasn't long I could pick up the phone, call *Murray* and I'd have your job. You know that? Not too *long* ago. For what? For *nothing.* "Mur, this new kid burns my ass." "Shelly, he's out." You're gone before I'm back from lunch. I bought him a trip to Bermuda once . . .

WILLIAMSON
I have to go . . . *[Gets up.]*

LEVENE
Wait. Alright. Fine. *[Starts going in pocket for money.]* The one. Give me the lead. Give me the one lead. The best one you have.

WILLIAMSON
I can't split them. *[Pause.]*

LEVENE
Why?

WILLIAMSON
Because I say so.

LEVENE
[Pause.] Is that it? Is that *it?* You want to do business that way . . . ?

[Williamson gets up, leaves money on the table.]

LEVENE
You want to do business that way . . . ? Alright. Alright. Alright. Alright. What is there on the other list . . . ?

WILLIAMSON
You want something off the B list?

LEVENE
Yeah. Yeah.

WILLIAMSON
Is that what you're saying?

LEVENE
That's what I'm saying. Yeah. *[Pause.]* I'd like something off the other list. Which, very least, that I'm entitled to. If I'm still *working* here, which for the moment I guess that I am. *[Pause.]* What? I'm sorry I spoke harshly to you.

WILLIAMSON
That's alright.

LEVENE
The deal still stands, our other thing.

[Williamson shrugs. Starts out of the booth.]

LEVENE
Good. Mmm. I, you know, I left my wallet back at the hotel.

Scene Two

A booth at the restaurant. Moss and Aaronow seated. After the meal.

MOSS
Polacks and deadbeats.

AARONOW
. . . Polacks . . .

MOSS
Deadbeats *all.*

AARONOW
. . . they hold on to their money . . .

MOSS
All of 'em. They, *hey*: it happens to us all.

AARONOW
Where am I going to work?

MOSS
You have to cheer up, George, you aren't out yet.

AARONOW

I'm not?

MOSS

You missed a fucking sale. Big deal. A deadbeat Polack. Big deal. How you going to sell 'em in the *first*
place . . . ? Your mistake, you shoun'a took the lead.

AARONOW

I had to.

MOSS

You had to, yeah. Why?

AARONOW

To get on the . . .

MOSS

To get on the board. Yeah. How you goan'a get on the
board sell'n a Polack? And I'll tell you, I'll tell you
what *else*. You listening? I'll tell you what else: don't
ever try to sell an Indian.

AARONOW

I'd never try to sell an Indian.

MOSS

You get those names come up, you ever get 'em,
"Patel"?

AARONOW

Mmm . . .

MOSS

You ever get 'em?

AARONOW

Well, I think I had one once.

MOSS

You did?

AARONOW

I . . . I don't know.

MOSS

You had one you'd know it. *Patel.* They keep coming
up. I don't know. They like to talk to salesmen.
[Pause.] They're *lonely*, something. *[Pause.]* They like
to feel *superior*, I don't know. Never bought a fucking
thing. You're sitting down "The Rio Rancho *this*, the
blah blah blah," "The Mountain View—" "Oh yes.
My brother told me that. . . ." They got a grapevine.
Fuckin' Indians, George. Not my cup of tea. Speaking
of which I want to tell you something: *[Pause]* I never
got a cup of tea with them. You see them in the restaurants. A supercilious race. What is this *look* on
their face all the time? I don't know. *[Pause.]* I don't

know. Their broads all look like they just got fucked
with a dead *cat*, I don't know. *[Pause.]* I don't know.
I don't like it. Christ . . .

AARONOW

What?

MOSS

The whole fuckin' thing . . . The pressure's just too
great. You're ab . . . you're absolu . . . they're too important. All of them. You go in the door. I . . . "I got
to *close* this fucker, or I don't eat lunch," "or I don't
win the *Cadillac*. . . ." We fuckin' work too hard. You
work too hard. We all, I remember when we were at
Platt . . . huh? Glen Ross Farms . . . *didn't* we sell a
bunch of that . . . ?

AARONOW

They came in and they, you know . . .

MOSS

Well, they fucked it up.

AARONOW

They did.

MOSS

They killed the goose.

AARONOW

They did.

MOSS

And now . . .

AARONOW

We're stuck with *this* . . .

MOSS

We're stuck with *this* fucking shit . . .

AARONOW

. . . *this* shit . . .

MOSS

It's too . . .

AARONOW

It is.

MOSS

Eh?

AARONOW

It's too . . .

MOSS

You get a bad month, all of a . . .

AARONOW

You're on this . . .

MOSS
All of, they got you on this "board . . ."

AARONOW
I, I . . . I . . .

MOSS
Some *contest* board . . .

AARONOW
I . . .

MOSS
It's not right.

AARONOW
It's not.

MOSS
No. *[Pause.]*

AARONOW
And it's not right to the *customers*.

MOSS
I know it's not. I'll tell you, you got, you know, you got . . . what did I learn as a kid on Western? Don't sell a guy one car. Sell him *five* cars over fifteen years.

AARONOW
That's right?

MOSS
Eh . . . ?

AARANOW
That's right?

MOSS
Goddamn right, that's right. Guys come on: "Oh, the blah blah blah, *I* know what I'll do: I'll go in and rob everyone blind and go to Argentina cause nobody ever *thought* of this before."

AARONOW
. . . that's right . . .

MOSS
Eh?

AARONOW
No. That's absolutely right.

MOSS
And so they kill the goose. I, I, I'll . . . and a fuckin' *man*, worked all his *life* has got to . . .

AARONOW
. . . that's right . . .

MOSS
. . . cower in his boots . . .

AARONOW
[simultaneously with "boots"] Shoes, boots, yes . . .

MOSS
For some fuckin' "Sell ten thousand and you win the steak knives . . ."

AARONOW
For some *sales* pro . . .

MOSS
. . . sales promotion, "You *lose*, then we fire your . . ." No. It's *medieval* . . . it's wrong. "Or we're going to fire your ass." It's wrong.

AARONOW
Yes.

MOSS
Yes, it is. And you know who's responsible?

AARONOW
Who?

MOSS
You know who it is. It's Mitch. And Murray. 'Cause it doesn't have to be this way.

AARONOW
No.

MOSS
Look at Jerry Graff. He's *clean*, he's doing business for *himself*, he's got his, that *list* of his with the *nurses* . . . see? You see? That's *thinking*. Why take ten percent? A ten percent comm . . . why are we giving the rest away? What are we giving ninety per . . . for *nothing*. For some jerk sit in the office tell you "Get out there and close." "Go win the Cadillac." Graff. He goes out and *buys*. He pays top dollar for the . . . you see?

AARONOW
Yes.

MOSS
That's *thinking*. Now, he's got the leads, he goes in business for *himself*. He's . . . that's what I . . . that's *thinking*! "Who? Who's got a steady *job*, a couple bucks nobody's touched, who?"

AARONOW
Nurses.

MOSS
So Graff buys a fucking list of nurses, one grand—if he paid two I'll eat my hat—four, five thousand nurses, and he's going *wild* . . .

AARONOW
He is?

MOSS
He's doing *very* well.

AARONOW
I heard that they were running cold.

MOSS
The nurses?

AARONOW
Yes.

MOSS
You hear a *lot* of things. . . . He's doing very well.
He's doing *very* well.

AARONOW
With River Oaks?

MOSS
River Oaks, Brook Farms. *All* of that shit. Somebody
told me, you know what he's clearing *himself*? Fourteen, fifteen grand a *week*.

AARONOW
Himself?

MOSS
That's what I'm *saying*. Why? The *leads*. He's got the
good leads . . . what are we, we're sitting in the shit
here. Why? We have to go to *them* to *get* them. Huh.
Ninety percent our sale, we're *paying* to the *office* for
the *leads*.

AARONOW
The leads, the overhead, the telephones, there's *lots*
of things.

MOSS
What do you need? A *telephone*, some broad to say
"Good morning," nothing . . . nothing . . .

AARONOW
No, it's not that simple, Dave . . .

MOSS
Yes. It *is*. It *is* simple, and you know what the hard part
is?

AARONOW
What?

MOSS
Starting up.

AARONOW
What hard part?

MOSS
Of doing the thing. The dif . . . the difference. Between me and Jerry Graff. Going to business for yourself. The hard part is . . . you know what it is?

AARONOW
What?

MOSS
Just the *act*.

AARONOW
What act?

MOSS
To say "I'm going on my own." 'Cause what you do,
George, let me tell you what you do: you find yourself
in *thrall* to someone else. And we *enslave* ourselves.
To *please*. To win some fucking *toaster* . . . to . . . to
. . . and the guy who got there first made *up* those . . .

AARONOW
That's right . . .

MOSS
He made *up* those rules, and we're working for *him*.

AARONOW
That's the truth . . .

MOSS
That's the *God's* truth. And it gets me depressed. I
swear that it does. At MY AGE. To see a goddamn:
"Somebody wins the Cadillac this month. P.S. Two
guys get fucked."

AARONOW
Huh.

MOSS
You don't *ax* your sales force.

AARONOW
No.

MOSS
You . . .

AARONOW
You . . .

MOSS
You *build* it!

AARONOW
That's what I . . .

MOSS
You fucking *build* it! Men come . . .

AARONOW
Men come *work* for you . . .

MOSS
. . . you're absolutely right.

AARONOW
They . . .

MOSS
They have . . .

AARONOW
When they. . .

MOSS
Look look look look, when they *build* your business, then you can't fucking turn around, *enslave* them, treat them like *children*, fuck them up the ass, leave them to fend for themselves . . . no. *[Pause.]* No. *[Pause.]* You're absolutely right, and I want to tell you something.

AARONOW
What?

MOSS
I want to tell you what somebody should do.

AARONOW
What?

MOSS
Someone should stand up and strike *back*.

AARONOW
What do you mean?

MOSS
Somebody . . .

AARONOW
Yes . . . ?

MOSS
Should do something to *them*.

AARONOW
What?

MOSS
Something. To pay them back. *[Pause.]* Someone, someone should hurt them. Murray and Mitch.

AARONOW
Someone should hurt them.

MOSS
Yes.

AARONOW
[Pause.] How?

MOSS
How? Do something to hurt them. Where they live.

AARONOW
What? *[Pause.]*

MOSS
Someone should rob the office.

AARONOW
Huh.

MOSS
That's what I'm *saying*. We were, if we were that kind of guys, to knock it off, and *trash* the joint, it looks like robbery, and *take* the fuckin' leads out of the files . . . go to Jerry Graff. *[Long pause.]*

AARONOW
What could somebody get for them?

MOSS
What could we *get* for them? I don't know. Buck a *throw* . . . buck-a-half a throw . . . I don't know. . . . Hey, who knows what they're worth, what do they *pay* for them? All told . . . must be, I'd . . . three bucks a throw . . . *I* don't know.

AARONOW
How many leads have we got?

MOSS
The *Glengarry* . . . the premium leads . . . ? I'd say we got five thousand. Five. Five thousand leads.

AARONOW
And you're saying a fella could take and sell these leads to Jerry Graff.

MOSS
Yes.

AARONOW
How do you know he'd buy them?

MOSS
Graff? Because I worked for him.

AARONOW
You haven't talked to him.

MOSS
No. What do you mean? Have I talked to him about *this*? *[Pause.]*

AARONOW
Yes. I mean are you actually *talking* about this, or are we just . . .

MOSS
No, we're just . . .

AARONOW
We're just "*talking*" about it.

MOSS
We're just *speaking* about it. [*Pause.*] As an *idea*.

AARONOW
As an idea.

MOSS
Yes.

AARONOW
We're not actually *talking* about it.

MOSS
No.

AARONOW
Talking about it as a . . .

MOSS
No.

AARONOW
As a *robbery*.

MOSS
As a "robbery"?! No.

AARONOW
Well. Well . . .

MOSS
Hey. [*Pause.*]

AARONOW
So all this, um, you didn't, actually, you didn't actually go talk to Graff.

MOSS
Not actually, no. [*Pause.*]

AARONOW
You didn't?

MOSS
No. Not actually.

AARONOW
Did you?

MOSS
What did I say?

AARONOW
What did you say?

MOSS
Yes. [*Pause.*] I said, "Not actually." The fuck *you* care, George? We're just *talking* . . .

AARONOW
We are?

MOSS
Yes. [*Pause.*]

AARONOW
Because, because, you know, it's a *crime*.

MOSS
That's right. It's a crime. It is a crime. It's also very safe.

AARONOW
You're actually *talking* about this?

MOSS
That's right. [*Pause.*]

AARONOW
You're going to steal the leads?

MOSS
Have I said that? [*Pause.*]

AARONOW
Are you? [*Pause.*]

MOSS
Did I say that?

AARONOW
Did you talk to Graff?

MOSS
Is that what I said?

AARONOW
What did he say?

MOSS
What did he say? He'd *buy* them. [*Pause.*]

AARONOW
You're going to steal the leads and sell the leads to him? [*Pause.*]

MOSS
Yes.

AARONOW
What will he pay?

MOSS
A buck a shot.

AARONOW
For five thousand?

MOSS
However they are, that's the deal. A buck a throw. Five thousand dollars. Split it half and half.

AARONOW
You're saying "me."

MOSS
Yes. *[Pause.]* Twenty-five hundred apiece. One night's work, and the job with Graff. Working the premium leads. *[Pause.]*

AARONOW
A job with Graff.

MOSS
Is that what I said?

AARONOW
He'd give me a job.

MOSS
He would take you on. Yes. *[Pause.]*

AARONOW
Is that the truth?

MOSS
Yes. It is, George. *[Pause.]* Yes. It's a big decision. *[Pause.]* And it's a big reward. *[Pause.]* It's a big reward. For one night's work. *[Pause.]* But it's got to be tonight.

AARONOW
What?

MOSS
What? What? The *leads*.

AARONOW
You have to steal the leads tonight?

MOSS
That's *right*, the guys are moving them downtown. After the thirtieth. Murray and Mitch. After the contest.

AARONOW
You're, you're saying so you have to go in there tonight and . . .

MOSS
You . . .

AARONOW
I'm sorry?

MOSS
You. *[Pause.]*

AARONOW
Me?

MOSS
You have to go in. *[Pause.]* *You* have to get the leads. *[Pause.]*

AARONOW
I do?

MOSS
Yes.

AARONOW
I . . .

MOSS
It's not something for nothing, George, I took you in on this, you have to go. That's your thing. I've made the deal with Graff. I can't go. I can't go in, I've spoken on this too much. I've got a big mouth. *[Pause.]* "The fucking leads" et cetera, blah blah blah ". . . the fucking tight ass company . . ."

AARONOW
They'll know when you go over to Graff . . .

MOSS
What will they know? That I stole the leads? I *didn't* steal the leads, I'm going to the *movies* tonight with a friend, and then I'm going to the Como Inn. Why did I go to Graff? I got a better deal. *Period.* Let 'em prove something. They can't prove anything that's not the case. *[Pause.]*

AARONOW
Dave.

MOSS
Yes.

AARONOW
You want me to break into the office tonight and steal the leads?

MOSS
Yes. *[Pause.]*

AARONOW
No.

MOSS
Oh, yes, George.

AARONOW
What does that mean?

MOSS
Listen to this. I have an alibi, I'm going to the Como Inn, why? Why? The place gets robbed, they're going to come looking for *me*. Why? Because I probably did it. Are you going to turn me in? *[Pause.]* George? Are you going to turn me in?

AARONOW
What if you don't get caught?

MOSS
They come to you, you going to turn me in?

AARONOW
Why would they come to me?

MOSS
They're going to come to *everyone*.

AARONOW
Why would I *do* it?

MOSS
You wouldn't, George, that's why I'm talking to you.
Answer me. They come to you. You going to turn me
in?

AARONOW
No.

MOSS
Are you sure?

AARONOW
Yes. I'm sure.

MOSS
Then listen to this: I have to get those leads tonight.
That's something I have to do. If I'm not at the *movies*
. . . if I'm not eating over at the inn . . . If you don't
do this, then *I* have to come in here . . .

AARONOW
. . . you don't have to come in . . .

MOSS
. . . and *rob* the place . . .

AARONOW
. . . I thought that we were only talking . . .

MOSS
. . . they *take* me, then. They're going to ask me who
were my accomplices.

AARONOW
Me?

MOSS
Absolutely.

AARONOW
That's ridiculous.

MOSS
Well, to the law, you're an accessory. Before the fact.

AARONOW
I didn't ask to be.

MOSS
Then tough luck, George, because you are.

AARONOW
Why? *Why*, because you only *told* me about it?

MOSS
That's right.

AARONOW
Why are you doing this to me, Dave? Why are you
talking this way to me? I don't understand. Why are
you doing this at *all* . . . ?

MOSS
That's none of your fucking business . . .

AARONOW
Well, well, well, *talk* to me, we sat down to eat *dinner*,
and here I'm a *criminal* . . .

MOSS
You *went* for it.

AARONOW
In the abstract . . .

MOSS
So I'm making it concrete.

AARONOW
Why?

MOSS
Why? Why *you* going to give me five grand?

AARONOW
Do you need five grand?

MOSS
Is that what I just said?

AARONOW
You need money? Is that the . . .

MOSS
Hey, hey, let's just keep it simple, what I need is not
the . . . what do *you* need . . . ?

AARONOW
What is the five grand? *[Pause.]* What is the, you said
that we were going to *split* five . . .

MOSS
I lied. *[Pause.]* Alright? My end is *my* business. Your
end's twenty-five. In or out. You tell me, you're out
you take the consequences.

AARONOW
I do?

MOSS
Yes. *[Pause.]*

AARONOW
And why is that?

MOSS
Because you listened.

Scene Three

The restaurant. Roma is seated alone at the booth. Lingk is at the booth next to him. Roma is talking to him.

ROMA
. . . all train compartments smell vaguely of shit. It gets so you don't mind it. That's the worst thing that I can confess. You know how long it took me to get there? A long time. When you *die* you're going to regret the things you don't do. You think you're *queer* . . . ? I'm going to tell you something: we're *all* queer. You think that you're a *thief*? So *what*? You get befuddled by a middle-class morality . . . ? Get *shut* of it. Shut it out. You cheated on your wife . . . ? You *did* it, *live* with it. *[Pause.]* You fuck little girls, so *be* it. There's an absolute morality? May *be*. And *then* what? If you *think* there is, then *be* that thing. Bad people go to hell? I don't *think* so. If you think that, act that way. A hell exists on earth? Yes. I won't live in it. That's *me*. You ever take a dump made you feel like you'd just slept for twelve hours . . . ?

LINGK
Did I . . . ?

ROMA
Yes.

LINGK
I don't know.

ROMA
Or a *piss* . . . ? A great meal fades in reflection. Everything else gains. Yout know why? 'Cause it's only food. This shit we eat, it keeps us going. But it's only food. The great fucks that you may have had. What do you remember about them?

LINGK
What do I . . . ?

ROMA
Yes.

LINGK
Mmmm . . .

ROMA
I don't know. For *me*, I'm saying, what it is, it's probably not the orgasm. Some broads, forearms on your neck, something her *eyes* did. There was a *sound* she made . . . or, me, lying, in the, I'll tell you: me lying in bed; the next day she brought me café au lait. She gives me a cigarette, my balls feel like concrete. Eh? What I'm saying, what is our life? *[Pause.]* It's looking forward or it's looking back. And that's our life. That's *it*. Where is the *moment*? *[Pause.]* And what is it that we're afraid of? Loss. What else? *[Pause.]* The *bank* closes. We get *sick*, my wife died on a plane, the stock market collapsed . . . the house burnt down . . . what of these happen . . . ? None of 'em. We worry anyway. What does this mean? I'm not *secure*. How can I be secure? *[Pause.]* Through amassing wealth beyond all measure? No. And what's beyond all measure? That's a sickness. That's a trap. There is no measure. Only greed. How can we act? The right way, we would say, to deal with this: "There is a one-in-a-million chance that so and so will happen. . . . *Fuck* it, it won't happen to *me*. . . ." No. We know that's not the right way I think. *[Pause.]* We say the *correct* way to deal with this is "There is a one-in-so-and-so chance this will happen . . . God *protect* me. I am powerless, let it not happen to me. . . ." But no to *that*. I say. There's something else. What is it? "If it happens, AS IT MAY for that is not within our powers, I will *deal* with it, just as I do *today* with what draws my concern today." I say *this* is how we must act. I do those things which seem correct to me *today*. I trust myself. And if security concerns me, I do that which *today* I think will make me secure. And every day I *do* that, when that day *arrives* that I need a reserve, (a) odds are that I have it, and (b) the *true* reserve that I have is the strength that I have of *acting each day* without fear. *[Pause.]* According to the dictates of my mind. *[Pause.]* Stocks, bonds, objects of art, real estate. Now: what are they? *[Pause.]* An opportunity. To what? To make money? Perhaps. To lose money? Perhaps. To "indulge" and to "learn" about ourselves? Perhaps. *So fucking what?* What *isn't*? They're an *opportunity*. That's all. They're an *event*. A guy comes up to you, you make a call, you send in a brochure, it doesn't matter, "There're these *properties* I'd like for you to see." What does it mean? What you *want* it to mean. *[Pause.]* Money? *[Pause.]* If that's what it signifies to you. Security? *[Pause.]* Comfort? *[Pause.]* All it is is THINGS THAT HAPPEN TO YOU. *[Pause.]* That's all it is. How are they different? *[Pause.]* Some poor newly married guy gets run down by a cab. Some *busboy* wins the lottery. *[Pause.]* All it

is, it's a carnival. What's special . . . what *draws* us? *[Pause.]* We're all different. *[Pause.]* We're not the same. *[Pause.]* We are not the same. *[Pause.]* Hmmm. *[Pause. Sighs.]* It's been a long day. *[Pause.]* What are you drinking?

LINGK
Gimlet.

ROMA
Well, let's have a couple more. My name is Richard Roma, what's yours?

LINGK
Lingk. James Lingk.

ROMA
James. I'm glad to meet you. *[They shake hands.]* I'm glad to meet you, James. *[Pause.]* I want to show you something. *[Pause.]* It might mean *nothing* to you . . . and it might not. I don't know. I don't know anymore. *[Pause. He takes out a small map and spreads it on a table.]* What is that? Florida. Glengarry Highlands. Florida. "Florida. *Bullshit.*" And maybe that's true; and that's what *I* said: but look *here*: what is this? This is a piece of land. Listen to what I'm going to tell you now:

──────── **ACT TWO** ────────

The real estate office. Ransacked. A broken plate-glass window boarded up, glass all over the floor. Aaronow and Williamson standing around, smoking.
Pause.

AARONOW
People used to say that there are numbers of such magnitude that multiplying them by two made no difference. *[Pause.]*

WILLIAMSON
Who used to say that?

AARONOW
In school. *[Pause.]*

[Baylen, a detective, comes out of the inner office.]

BAYLEN
Alright . . . ?

[Roma enters from the street.]

ROMA
Williamson . . . Williamson, they stole the *contracts* . . . ?

BAYLEN
Excuse me, sir . . .

ROMA
Did they get my contracts?

WILLIAMSON
They got . . .

BAYLEN
Excuse me, fella.

ROMA
. . . did they . . .

BAYLEN
Would you excuse us, please . . . ?

ROMA
Don't *fuck* with me, fella. I'm talking about a fuckin' Cadillac car that you owe me . . .

WILLIAMSON
They didn't get your contract. I filed it before I left.

ROMA
They didn't get my contracts?

WILLIAMSON
They—excuse me . . . *[He goes back into inner room with the Detective.]*

ROMA
Oh, *fuck.* Fuck. *[He starts kicking the desk.]* FUCK FUCK FUCK! WILLIAMSON!!! WILLIAMSON!!! *[Goes to the door Williamson went into, tries the door; it's locked.]* OPEN THE FUCKING . . . WILLIAMSON . . .

BAYLEN
[coming out] Who are you?

[Williamson comes out.]

WILLIAMSON
They didn't get the contracts.

ROMA
Did they . . .

WILLIAMSON
They got, listen to me . . .

ROMA
Th . . .

WILLIAMSON
Listen to me: They got *some* of them.

ROMA
Some of them . . .

BAYLEN
Who told you . . . ?

ROMA
Who told me wh . . . ? You've got a fuckin', you've
. . . a . . . who is this . . . ? You've got a board-up on
the window. . . . *Moss* told me.

BAYLEN
[Looking back toward the inner office.] Moss . . . Who
told him?

ROMA
How the fuck do *I* know? *[To Williamson:]* What . . .
talk to me.

WILLIAMSON
They took *some* of the con . . .

ROMA
. . . some of the contracts . . . Lingk. James Lingk. I
closed . . .

WILLIAMSON
You closed him yesterday.

ROMA
Yes.

WILLIAMSON
It went down. I filed it.

ROMA
You did?

WILLIAMSON
Yes.

ROMA
Then I'm over the fucking top and you owe me a
Cadillac.

WILLIAMSON
I . . .

ROMA
And I don't want any fucking shit and I don't give a
shit, Lingk puts me over the top, you filed it, that's
fine, any other shit kicks out *you* go back. You . . . *you*
reclose it, 'cause I *closed* it and you . . . you owe me
the car.

BAYLEN
Would you excuse us, please.

AARONOW
I, um, and may . . . maybe they're in . . . they're in
. . . you should, John, if we're ins . . .

WILLIAMSON
I'm sure that we're insured, George . . . *[Going back
inside.]*

ROMA
Fuck insured. You owe me a car.

BAYLEN
[Stepping back into the inner room] Please don't leave.
I'm going to talk to you. What's your name?

ROMA
Are you talking to me? *[Pause.]*

BAYLEN
Yes. *[Pause.]*

ROMA
My name is Richard Roma.

[Baylen goes back into the inner room.]

AARONOW
I, you know, they should be insured.

ROMA
What do *you* care . . . ?

AARONOW
Then, you know, they wouldn't be so ups . . .

ROMA
Yeah. That's swell. Yes. You're right. *[Pause.]* How are
you?

AARONOW
I'm fine. You mean the *board*? You mean the *board*
. . . ?

ROMA
I don't . . . yes. Okay, the board.

AARONOW
I'm, I'm, I'm, I'm fucked on the board. *You.* You see
how . . . I . . . *[Pause.]* I can't . . . my mind must be
in other places. 'Cause I can't do any . . .

ROMA
What? You can't do any *what?* *[Pause.]*

AARONOW
I can't close 'em.

ROMA
Well, they're old. I saw the shit that they were giving
you.

AARONOW
Yes.

ROMA
Huh?

AARONOW
Yes. They are old.

ROMA
They're ancient.

AARONOW
Clear . . .

ROMA
Clear Meadows. That shit's dead. [Pause.]

AARONOW
It *is* dead.

ROMA
It's a waste of time.

AARONOW
Yes. [Long pause.] I'm no fucking good.

ROMA
That's . . .

AARONOW
Everything I . . . *you* know . . .

ROMA
That's not . . . Fuck that shit, George. You're a, *hey*, you had a bad month. You're a good man, George.

AARONOW
I am?

ROMA
You hit a bad streak. We've all . . . look at this: fifteen units Mountain View, the fucking things get stole.

AARONOW
He said he filed . . .

ROMA
He filed half of them, he filed the *big* one. All the little ones, I have, I have to go back and . . . ah, *fuck*, I got to go out like a fucking schmuck hat in my hand and reclose the . . . [Pause.] I mean, talk about a bad streak. That would sap *anyone's* self confi . . . I got to go out and reclose all my . . . Where's the phones?

AARONOW
They stole . . .

ROMA
They stole the . . .

AARONOW
What. What kind of outfit are we running where . . . where anyone . . .

ROMA
[To himself] They stole the phones.

AARONOW
Where criminals can come in here . . . they take the . . .

ROMA
They stole the phones. They stole the leads. They're . . . *Christ.* [Pause.] What am I going to do this month? Oh, *shit* . . . [Starts for the door.]

AARONOW
You think they're going to catch . . . where are you going?

ROMA
Down the street.

WILLIAMSON
[Sticking his head out of the door] Where are you going?

ROMA
To the restaura . . . what do you fucking . . . ?

WILLIAMSON
Aren't you going out today?

ROMA
With what? [Pause.] With what, John, they took the leads . . .

WILLIAMSON
I have the stuff from last year's . . .

ROMA
Oh. Oh. Oh, your "nostalgia" file, that's fine. No. Swell. 'Cause I don't have to . . .

WILLIAMSON
. . . you want to go out today . . . ?

ROMA
'Cause I don't have to *eat* this month. No. Okay. *Give* 'em to me . . . [To himself:] Fucking Mitch and Murray going to shit a br . . . what am I going to *do* all . . .

[Williamson starts back into the office. He is accosted by Aaronow.]

AARONOW
Were the leads . . .

ROMA
. . . what am I going to *do* all month . . . ?

AARONOW
Were the leads insured?

WILLIAMSON
I don't know, George, why?

AARONOW
'Cause, you know, 'cause they weren't, I know that
Mitch and Murray uh . . . [Pause.]

WILLIAMSON
What?

AARONOW
That they're going to be upset.

WILLIAMSON
That's right. [Going back into his office. Pause. To Roma:]
You want to go out today . . . ?

[Pause. Williamson returns to his office.]

AARONOW
He said we're all going to have to go talk to the guy.

ROMA
What?

AARONOW
He said we . . .

ROMA
To the cop?

AARONOW
Yeah.

ROMA
Yeah. That's swell. *Another* waste of time.

AARONOW
A waste of time? Why?

ROMA
Why? 'Cause they aren't going to find the guy.

AARONOW
The cops?

ROMA
Yes. The cops. No.

AARONOW
They aren't?

ROMA
No.

AARONOW
Why don't you think so?

ROMA
Why? Because they're *stupid.* "Where were you last
night . . ."

AARONOW
Where were you?

ROMA
Where was *I?*

AARONOW
Yes.

ROMA
I was at home, where were *you?*

AARONOW
At home.

ROMA
See . . . ? Were you the guy who broke in?

AARONOW
Was I?

ROMA
Yes.

AARONOW
No.

ROMA
Then don't sweat it, George, you know why?

AARONOW
No.

ROMA
You have nothing to hide.

AARONOW
[Pause.] When I talk to the police, I get nervous.

ROMA
Yeah. You know who doesn't?

AARONOW
No, who?

ROMA
Thieves.

AARONOW
Why?

ROMA
They're inured to it.

AARONOW
You think so?

ROMA
Yes. [Pause.]

AARONOW
But what should I *tell* them?

ROMA
The truth, George. Always tell the truth. It's the eas-
iest thing to remember.

[*Williamson comes out of the office with leads. Roma takes one, reads it.*]

ROMA

Patel? Ravidam *Patel?* How am I going to make a living on these deadbeat *wogs?* Where did you get this, from the *morgue?*

WILLIAMSON

If you don't want it, give it back.

ROMA

I don't "want" it, if you catch my drift.

WILLIAMSON

I'm giving you *three* leads. You . . .

ROMA

What's the fucking point in *any* case . . . ? What's the *point.* I got to argue with *you,* I got to knock heads with the *cops,* I'm busting my *balls,* sell you *dirt* to fucking *deadbeats* money in the *mattress,* I come back you can't even manage to keep the contracts safe, I have to go back and close them *again.* . . . What the fuck am I wasting my time, fuck this shit. I'm going out and reclose last week's . . .

WILLIAMSON

The word from Murray is: leave them alone. If we need a new signature he'll go out himself, he'll be the *president,* just come *in,* from out of *town* . . .

ROMA

Okay, okay, okay, gimme this shit. Fine. [*Takes the leads.*]

WILLIAMSON

Now, I'm giving you three . . .

ROMA

Three? I count *two.*

WILLIAMSON

Three.

ROMA

Patel? Fuck *you.* Fuckin' *Shiva* handed him a million dollars, told him "sign the deal," he wouldn't sign. And Vishnu, too. Into the bargain. Fuck *that,* John. You know your business, I know mine. Your business is being an *asshole,* and I find out whose fucking *cousin* you are, I'm going to go to him and figure out a way to have your *ass* . . . fuck you—I'll wait for the new leads.

[*Shelly Levene enters.*]

LEVENE

Get the *chalk.* Get the *chalk* . . . get the *chalk!* I closed 'em! I *closed* the cocksucker. Get the chalk and put me on the *board.* I'm going to Hawaii! Put me on the Cadillac board, Williamson! Pick up the fuckin' chalk. Eight units. Mountain View . . .

ROMA

You sold eight Mountain View?

LEVENE

You bet your ass. Who wants to go to lunch? Who wants to go to lunch? I'm buying. [*Slaps contract down on Williamson's desk.*] Eighty-two fucking grand. And twelve grand in commission. John. [*Pause.*] On fucking deadbeat magazine subscription leads.

WILLIAMSON

Who?

LEVENE

[*Pointing to contract*] *Read* it. Bruce and Harriett Nyborg. [*Looking around.*] What happened here?

AARONOW

Fuck. I had them on River Glen.

[*Levine looks around.*]

LEVENE

What happened?

WILLIAMSON

Somebody broke in.

ROMA

Eight units?

LEVENE

That's right.

ROMA

Shelly . . . !

LEVENE

Hey, big fucking deal. Broke a bad streak . . .

AARONOW

Shelly, the Machine, Levene.

LEVENE

You . . .

AARONOW

That's great.

LEVENE

Thank you, George.

[*Baylen sticks his head out of the room; calls in,*
"Aaronow." Aaronow goes into the side room.]

LEVENE
Williamson, get on the phone, call Mitch . . .

ROMA
They took the phones . . .

LEVENE
They . . .

BAYLEN
Aaronow . . .

ROMA
They took the typewriters, they took the leads, they
took the *cash*, they took the *contracts* . . .

LEVENE
Wh . . . wh . . . Wha . . . ?

AARONOW
We had a robbery. [*Goes into the inner room.*]

LEVENE
[*Pause.*] When?

ROMA
Last night, this morning. [*Pause.*]

LEVENE
They took the leads?

ROMA
Mmm.

[*Moss comes out of the interrogation.*]

MOSS
Fuckin' asshole.

ROMA
What, they beat you with a rubber bat?

MOSS
Cop couldn't find his dick two hands and a map.
Anyone talks to this guy's an *asshole* . . .

ROMA
You going to turn State's?

MOSS
Fuck you, Ricky. I ain't going out today. I'm going
home. I'm going home because nothing's *accomplished* here. . . . Anyone *talks* to this guy is . . .

ROMA
Guess what the Machine did?

MOSS
Fuck the Machine.

ROMA
Mountain View. Eight units.

MOSS
Fuckin' cop's got no right talk to me that way. I didn't
rob the place . . .

ROMA
You hear what I said?

MOSS
Yeah. He closed a deal.

ROMA
Eight units. Mountain View.

MOSS
[*To Levene*] You did that?

LEVENE
Yeah. [*Pause.*]

MOSS
Fuck you.

ROMA
Guess who?

MOSS
When . . .

LEVENE
Just now.

ROMA
Guess who?

MOSS
You just this morning . . .

ROMA
Harriett and blah blah Nyborg.

MOSS
You did that?

LEVENE
Eighty-two thousand dollars. [*Pause.*]

MOSS
Those fuckin' *deadbeats* . . .

LEVENE
My ass. I told 'em. [*To Roma:*] Listen to this: I said . . .

MOSS
Hey, I don't want to hear your fucking war stories . . .

ROMA
Fuck *you*, Dave . . .

LEVENE
"You have to believe in your*self* . . . you"—look—
"alright . . . ?"

MOSS
[To Williamson]Give me some leads. I'm going out
. . . I'm getting out of . . .

LEVENE
". . . you have to believe in yourself . . ."

MOSS
Na, fuck the leads, I'm going home.

LEVENE
"Bruce, Harriett . . . Fuck me, believe in yourself . . ."

ROMA
We haven't got a lead . . .

MOSS
Why not?

ROMA
They took 'em . . .

MOSS
Hey, they're fuckin' garbage any case. . . . This whole
goddamn . . .

LEVENE
". . . You look around, you say, 'This one has so-and-
so, and I have nothing . . .'"

MOSS
Shit.

LEVENE
"Why? Why don't I get the opportunities . . . ?"

MOSS
And did they steal the contracts . . . ?

ROMA
Fuck you care . . . ?

LEVENE
"I want to tell you something, Harriett . . ."

MOSS
. . . the fuck is that supposed to mean . . . ?

LEVENE
Will you shut up, I'm telling you this . . .

[Aaronow sticks his head out.]

AARONOW
Can we get some coffee . . . ?

MOSS
How ya doing? [Pause.]

AARONOW
Fine.

MOSS
Uh-huh.

AARONOW
If anyone's going, I could use some coffee.

LEVENE
"You do get the . . ." [To Roma:] Huh? Huh?

MOSS
Fuck is that supposed to mean?

LEVENE
"You do get the opportunity. . . . You get them. As I
do, as anyone does . . ."

MOSS
Ricky? . . . That I don't care they stole the contracts?
[Pause.]

LEVENE
I got 'em in the kitchen. I'm eating her crumb cake.

MOSS
What does that mean?

ROMA
It means, Dave, you haven't closed a good one in a
month, none of my business, you want to push me to
answer you. [Pause.] And so you haven't got a contract to get stolen or so forth.

MOSS
You have a mean streak in you, Ricky, you know
that . . . ?

LEVENE
Rick. Let me tell you. Wait, we're in the . . .

MOSS
Shut the fuck up. [Pause.] Ricky. You have a mean
streak in you. . . . [To Levene:] And what the fuck are
you babbling about . . . ? [To Roma:] Bring that shit
up. Of my volume. You were on a bad one and I
brought it up to you you'd harbor it. [Pause.] You'd
harbor it a long long while. And you'd be right.

ROMA
Who said "Fuck the Machine"?

MOSS
"Fuck the Machine"? "Fuck the Machine"? What is this.
Courtesy class . . . ? You're fucked, Rick—are you
fucking nuts? You're hot, so you think you're the ruler
of this place . . . ?! You want to . . .

LEVENE
Dave . . .

MOSS

. . . Shut up. Decide who should be dealt with how? Is that the thing? I come into the fuckin' office today, I get humiliated by some jagoff cop. I get accused of . . . I get this *shit* thrown in my face by you, you genuine shit, because you're top name on the board . . .

ROMA

Is that what I did? Dave? I humiliated you? My *God* . . . I'm *sorry* . . .

MOSS

Sittin' on top of the *world*, sittin' on top of the *world*, everything's fucking *peach*fuzz . . .

ROMA

Oh, and I don't get a moment to spare for a bust-out *humanitarian* down on his luck lately. Fuck *you*, Dave, you know you got a big *mouth*, and *you* make a close the whole *place* stinks with your *farts* for a week. "How much you just ingested," what a big *man* you are, "Hey, let me buy you a pack of gum. I'll show you how to *chew* it." Your *pal* closes, all that comes out of your mouth is *bile*, how fucked *up* you are . . .

MOSS

Who's my pal . . . ? And what are you, Ricky, huh, what are you, Bishop *Sheean*? Who the fuck are *you*, Mr. Slick . . . ? What are you, friend to the *workingman*? Big deal. Fuck *you*, you got the memory a fuckin' *fly*. I never liked you.

ROMA

What is this, your farewell speech?

MOSS

I'm going home.

ROMA

Your farewell to the troops?

MOSS

I'm not going home. I'm going to Wis*con*sin.

ROMA

Have a good trip.

MOSS

[Simultaneously with "trip"] And fuck *you*. Fuck the *lot* of you. Fuck you *all*.

[Moss exits. Pause.]

ROMA

[To Levene] You were saying? *[Pause.]* Come on. Come on, you got them in the kitchen, you got the stats spread out, you're in your shirt-sleeves, you can

smell it. Huh? Snap out of it, you're eating her *crumb* cake. *[Pause.]*

LEVENE

I'm eating her *crumb* cake . . .

ROMA

How was it . . . ?

LEVENE

From the store.

ROMA

Fuck *her* . . .

LEVENE

"What we have to do is *admit* to ourself that we see that opportunity . . . and *take* it. *[Pause.]* And that's it." And we *sit* there. *[Pause.]* I got the pen out . . .

ROMA

"Always be closing . . ."

LEVENE

That's what I'm *saying*. The *old* ways. The *old* ways . . . convert the motherfucker . . . *sell* him . . . *sell* him . . . *make him sign the check. [Pause.]* The . . . Bruce, Harriett . . . the kitchen, blah: they got their money in *government* bonds. . . . I say *fuck* it, we're going to go the whole route. I plat it out eight units. Eighty-two grand. I tell them. "This is now. This is that *thing* that you've been dreaming of, you're going to find that suitcase on the train, the guy comes in the door, the bag that's full of money. This is it, Harriett . . ."

ROMA

[Reflectively] Harriett . . .

LEVENE

Bruce . . . "I don't want to fuck *around* with you. I don't want to go *round* this, and *pussy-foot* around the thing, you have to look back on this. I do, too. I came here to do good for you and me. For *both* of us. Why take an interim position? *The only arrangement I'll accept* is full investment. Period. The whole eight units. I know that you're saying 'be safe,' I know what you're saying. I know if I left you to yourselves, you'd say 'come back tomorrow,' and when I walked out that door, you'd make a cup of *coffee* . . . you'd sit *down* . . . and you'd think 'let's be safe . . .' and not to disappoint me you'd go *one* unit or maybe two, because you'd become scared because you'd met possibility. But this won't do, and that's not the subject. . . ." Listen to this, I actually said this. "That's not the subject of our *evening* together." Now I handed them the pen. I held it in my hand. I turned the contract, eight units eighty-two grand. "Now I want you to sign." *[Pause.]* I sat there. Five minutes. Then, I sat there, Ricky, *twenty-two minutes* by the kitchen *clock. [Pause.]* Twenty-two minutes by the kitchen clock. Not a *word*, not a *motion*. What am I thinking? "My arm's getting tired?" *No.* I *did* it. I *did* it. Like in the *old* days, Ricky. Like I was taught . . . Like, like, like I *used* to do . . . I did it.

ROMA
Like you taught me . . .

LEVENE
Bullshit, you're . . . No. That's raw . . . well, if I *did*, then I'm *glad* I did. I, *well*. I locked on them. All on them, nothing on me. All my thoughts are on them. I'm holding the last thought that I spoke: "Now is the time." *[Pause.]* They signed, Ricky. It was *great*. It was fucking great. It was like they wilted all at once. No *gesture* . . . nothing. Like together. They, I swear to God, they both kind of *imperceptibly slumped*. And he reaches and takes the pen and signs, he passes it to her, she signs. It was so fucking solemn. I just let it sit. I nod like this. I nod again. I grasp his hands. I shake his hands. I grasp *her* hands. I nod at her like this. "Bruce . . . Harriett . . ." I'm beaming at them. I'm nodding like this. I point back in the living room, back to the sideboard. *[Pause.] I didn't fucking know there was a sideboard there!!* He goes back, he brings us a drink. Little shot glasses. A pattern in 'em. And we toast. In silence. *[Pause.]*

ROMA
That was a great sale, Shelly. *[Pause.]*

LEVENE
Ah, fuck. Leads! Leads! Williamson! *[Williamson sticks his head out of the office.]* Send me *out*! Send me *out*!

WILLIAMSON
The leads are coming.

LEVENE
Get 'em to me!

WILLIAMSON
I talked to Murray and Mitch an hour ago. They're coming in, you understand they're a bit *upset* over this morning's . . .

LEVENE
Did you tell 'em my sale?

WILLIAMSON
How could I tell 'em your sale? Eh? I don't have a tel . . . I'll tell 'em your sale when they bring in the leads. Alright? Shelly. Alright? We had a little . . . You closed a deal. You made a good sale. Fine.

LEVENE
It's better than a good sale. It's a . . .

WILLIAMSON
Look: I have a lot of things on my mind, they're coming in, alright, they're very upset, I'm trying to make some *sense* . . .

LEVENE
All that I'm *telling* you: that one thing you can tell them it's a remarkable sale.

WILLIAMSON
The only thing remarkable is who you made it to.

LEVENE
What does *that* fucking mean?

WILLIAMSON
That if the sale sticks, it will be a miracle.

LEVENE
Why should the sale not stick? Hey, *fuck* you. That's what I'm saying. You have no idea of your job. A man's his job and you're *fucked* at yours. You hear what I'm saying to you? Your "end of month board . . ." You can't run an office. I don't care. You don't know what it *is*, you don't have the *sense*, you don't have the *balls*. You ever been on a sit? *Ever?* Has this cocksucker ever been . . . you ever sit down with a cust . . .

WILLIAMSON
I were you, I'd calm down, Shelly.

LEVENE
Would you? *Would* you . . . ? Or you're gonna *what*, fire me?

WILLIAMSON
It's not impossible.

LEVENE
On an eighty-thousand dollar *day*? And it ain't even *noon*.

ROMA
You closed 'em today?

LEVENE
Yes. I did. This *morning*. *[To Williamson:]* What I'm *saying* to you: things can *change*. You *see*? This is

where you fuck *up*, because this is something you don't *know*. You can't look down the *road*. And see what's *coming*. Might be someone *else*, John. It might be someone *new*, eh? Someone *new*. And you can't look *back*. 'Cause you don't know *history*. You ask them. When we were at Rio Rancho, who was top man? A month . . . ? Two months . . . ? Eight months in twelve for three years in a row. You know what that means? You know what that means? Is that *luck*? Is that some, some, some purloined leads? That's *skill*. That's *talent*, that's, that's . . .

ROMA
. . . *yes* . . .

LEVENE
. . . and you don't *remember*. 'Cause you weren't *around*. That's cold *calling*. Walk up to the door. I don't even know their *name*. I'm selling something they don't even *want*. You talk about soft sell . . . before we had a name for it . . . before we called it anything, we did it.

ROMA
That's right, Shel.

LEVENE
And, and, and, I *did* it. And I put a kid through *school*. She . . . and . . . Cold *calling*, fella. Door to door. But you don't know. You don't know. You never heard of a *streak*. You never heard of "marshaling your sales force. . . ." What are you, you're a *secretary*, John. Fuck *you*. That's my message to you. Fuck you and kiss my ass. You don't like it, I'll go talk to Jerry Graff. Period. Fuck you. Put me on the board. And I want three worthwhile leads today and I don't want any bullshit about them and I want 'em close together 'cause I'm going to hit them all today. That's all I have to say to you.

ROMA
He's right, Williamson.

[Williamson goes into a side office. Pause.]

LEVENE
It's not right. I'm sorry, and I'll tell you who's to blame is Mitch and Murray.

[Roma sees something outside the window.]

ROMA
[Sotto] Oh, Christ.

LEVENE
The hell with him. We'll go to lunch, the leads won't be up for . . .

ROMA
You're a client. I just sold you five waterfront Glengarry Farms. I rub my head, throw me the cue "Kenilworth."

LEVENE
What is it?

ROMA
Kenilw . . .

[Lingk enters the office.]

ROMA
[To Levene] I own the property, my *mother* owns the property, I put her *into* it. I'm going to show you on the plats. You look when you get home A–3 through A–14 and 26 through 30. You take your time and if you still feel.

LEVENE
No, Mr. Roma. I don't need the time, I've made a lot of *investments* in the last . . .

LINGK
I've got to talk to you.

ROMA
[Looking up] Jim! What are you doing here? Jim Lingk, D. Ray Morton . . .

LEVENE
Glad to meet you.

ROMA
I just put Jim into Black Creek . . . are you acquainted with . . .

LEVENE
No . . . Black *Creek*. Yes. In *Florida*?

ROMA
Yes.

LEVENE
I wanted to *speak* with you about . . .

ROMA
Well, we'll do that this weekend.

LEVENE
My *wife* told me to look into . . .

ROMA
Beautiful. Beautiful rolling land. I was telling Jim and Jinny, Ray, I want to tell you something. *[To Levene:]*

You, Ray, you eat in a lot of restaurants. I know you do. . . . *[To Lingk:]* Mr. Morton's with American Express . . . he's . . . *[To Levene:]* I can tell Jim what you do . . . ?

LEVENE
Sure.

ROMA
Ray is director of all European sales and services for American Ex . . . *[To Levene:]* But I'm saying you haven't had a *meal* until you've tasted . . . I was at the Lingks' last . . . as a matter of fact, what was that service feature you were talking about . . . ?

LEVENE
Which . . .

ROMA
"Home Cooking" . . . what did you call it, you said it . . . it was a tag phrase that you had . . .

LEVENE
Uh . . .

ROMA
Home . . .

LEVENE
Home cooking . . .

ROMA
The monthly interview . . . ?

LEVENE
Oh! For the *magazine* . . .

ROMA
Yes. Is this something that I can talk ab . . .

LEVENE
Well, it isn't coming *out* until the February iss . . . *sure.* Sure, go ahead, Ricky.

ROMA
You're sure?

LEVENE
[nods] Go ahead.

ROMA
Well, Ray was eating at one of his company's men's home in France . . . the man's French, isn't he?

LEVENE
No, his *wife* is.

ROMA
Ah. Ah, his wife is. Ray: what *time* do you have . . . ?

LEVENE
Twelve-fifteen.

ROMA
Oh! My God . . . I've got to get you on the *plane*!

LEVENE
Didn't I say I was taking the two o' . . .

ROMA
No. You said the one. That's why you said we couldn't talk till Kenilworth.

LEVENE
Oh, my God, you're right! I'm on the one. . . . *[Getting up.]* Well, let's *scoot* . . .

LINGK
I've got to talk to you . . .

ROMA
I've got to get Ray to O'Hare . . . *[To Levene:]* Come on, let's hustle. . . . *[Over his shoulder:]* John! Call American Express in *Pittsburgh* for Mr. Morton, will you, tell them he's on the one o'clock. *[To Lingk:]* I'll see you. . . . Christ, I'm sorry you came all the way in. . . . I'm running Ray over to O'Hare. . . . You wait here, I'll . . . no. *[To Levene:]* I'm meeting your man at the bank. . . . *[To Lingk:]* I wish you'd phoned. . . . I'll tell you, wait: are you and Jinny going to be home tonight? *[Rubs forehead.]*

LINGK
I . . .

LEVENE
Rick.

ROMA
What?

LEVENE
Kenilworth . . . ?

ROMA
I'm sorry . . . ?

LEVENE
Kenilworth.

ROMA
Oh, God . . . Oh, God . . . *[Roma takes Lingk aside, sotto]* Jim, excuse me. . . . Ray, I told you, who he is is *the* senior vice-president American Express. His family owns 32 per. . . . Over the past years I've sold him . . . I can't tell you the dollar amount, but *quite* a lot of land. I promised five *weeks* ago that I'd go to the wife's birthday party in Kenilworth tonight. *[Sighs.]* I

have to go. You understand. They treat me like a member of the family, so I have to go. It's funny, you know, you get a picture of the Corporation-Type Company Man, all business . . . this man, *no*. We'll go out to his home sometime. Let's see. *[He checks his datebook.]* Tomorrow. No. Tomorrow, I'm in L.A. . . . Monday . . . I'll take you to lunch, where would you like to go?

LINGK
My wife . . . *[Roma rubs his head.]*

LEVENE
[Standing in the door] Rick . . . ?

ROMA
I'm sorry, Jim. I can't talk now. I'll call you tonight . . . I'm sorry. I'm coming, Ray. *[Starts for the door.]*

LINGK
My wife said I have to cancel the deal.

ROMA
It's a common reaction, Jim. I'll tell you what it is, and I know that that's why you married her. One of the reasons is *prudence*. It's a sizable investment. One thinks *twice* . . . it's also something *women* have. It's just a reaction to the size of the investment. *Monday*, if you'd invite me for dinner again . . . *[To Levene:]* This woman can *cook* . . .

LEVENE
[Simultaneously] I'm sure she can . . .

ROMA
[To Lingk] We're going to talk. I'm going to *tell* you something. Because *[Sotto:]* there's something about your acreage I want you to know. I can't talk about it now. I really shouldn't. And in fact, by *law*, I . . . *[Shrugs, resigned.]* The man next to you, he bought his lot at forty-*two*, he phoned to say that he'd *already* had an offer . . . *[Roma rubs his head.]*

LEVENE
Rick . . . ?

ROMA
I'm coming, Ray . . . what a day! I'll call you this evening, Jim. I'm sorry you had to come in . . . Monday, lunch.

LINGK
My wife . . .

LEVENE
Rick, we really have to go.

LINGK
My wife . . .

ROMA
Monday.

LINGK
She called the consumer . . . the attorney, I don't know. The attorney gen . . . they said we have three days . . .

ROMA
Who did she call?

LINGK
I don't know, the attorney gen . . . the . . . some consumer office, umm . . .

ROMA
Why did she do *that*, Jim?

LINGK
I don't know. *[Pause.]* They said we have three days. *[Pause.]* They said we have three days.

ROMA
Three days.

LINGK
To . . . you know. *[Pause.]*

ROMA
No, I don't know. *Tell* me.

LINGK
To change our minds.

ROMA
Of *course* you have three days. *[Pause.]*

LINGK
So we can't talk *Monday*. *[Pause.]*

ROMA
Jim, Jim, you saw my book . . . I *can't*, *you* saw my book . . .

LINGK
But we have to *before* Monday. To get our money ba . . .

ROMA
Three *business* days. They mean three *business* days.

LINGK
Wednesday, Thursday, Friday.

ROMA
I don't understand.

LINGK

That's what they are. Three business . . . if I wait till Monday, my time limit runs out.

ROMA

You don't count Saturday.

LINGK

I'm not.

ROMA

No, I'm saying you don't include Saturday . . . in your three days. It's not a *business* day.

LINGK

But I'm not *counting* it. *[Pause.]* Wednesday. Thursday. Friday. So it would have elapsed.

ROMA

What would have elapsed?

LINGK

If we wait till Mon . . .

ROMA

When did you write the check?

LINGK

Yest . . .

ROMA

What was yesterday?

LINGK

Tuesday.

ROMA

And when was that check cashed?

LINGK

I don't know.

ROMA

What was the *earliest* it could have been cashed? *[Pause.]*

LINGK

I don't know.

ROMA

Today. *[Pause.]* *Today.* Which, in any case, it was not, as there were a couple of points on the agreement I wanted to go over with you in any case.

LINGK

The check wasn't cashed?

ROMA

I just called downtown, and it's on their desk.

LEVENE

Rick . . .

ROMA

One moment, I'll be right with you. *[To Lingk:]* In fact, a . . . *one* point, which I spoke to you of which *[Looks around.]* I can't talk to you about here.

[Detective puts his head out of the doorway.]

BAYLEN

Levene!!!

LINGK

I, I . . .

ROMA

Listen to me, the *statute*, it's for your protection. I have no complaints with that, in fact, I was a member of the board when we *drafted* it, so quite the *opposite*. It *says* that you can change your mind three working days from the time the deal is closed.

BAYLEN

Levene!

ROMA

Which, wait a second, which is not until the check is cashed.

BAYLEN

Levene!!

[Aaronow comes out of the Detective's office.]

AARONOW

I'm *through*, with *this* fucking meshugaas. No one should talk to a man that way. How are you *talking* to me that . . . ?

BAYLEN

Levene!

[Williamson puts his head out of the office.]

AARONOW

. . . how can you *talk* to me that . . . that . . .

LEVENE

[To Roma] Rick, I'm going to flag a cab.

AARONOW

I didn't rob . . .

[Williamson sees Levene.]

WILLIAMSON

Shelly: get in the office.

AARONOW

I didn't . . . why should I . . . "Where were you last . . . ." Is anybody listening to me . . . ? Where's Moss . . . ? Where . . . ?

BAYLEN
Levene? *[To Williamson:]* Is this Lev . . . *[Baylen accosts Lingk.]*

LEVENE
[Taking Baylen into the office] Ah. Ah. Perhaps I can advise you on that. . . . *[To Roma and Lingk, as he exits:]* Excuse us, will you . . . ?

AARONOW
[Simultaneous with Levene's speech above] . . . Come in here . . . I *work* here, I don't come in here to be *mistreated* . . .

WILLIAMSON
Go to *lunch*, will you . . .

AARONOW
I want to *work* today, that's why I came . . .

WILLIAMSON
The leads come in, I'll let . . .

AARONOW
. . . that's why I came in. I thought I . . .

WILLIAMSON
Just go to lunch.

AARONOW
I don't *want* to go to lunch.

WILLIAMSON
Go to lunch, George.

AARONOW
Where does he get off to talk that way to a working man? It's not . . .

WILLIAMSON
[Buttonholes him] Will you take it outside, we have people trying to do *business* here . . .

AARONOW
That's what, that's what, that's what *I* was trying to do. *[Pause.]* That's why I came *in* . . . I meet *gestapo* tac . . .

WILLIAMSON
[Going back into his office] Excuse me . . .

AARONOW
I meet *gestapo* tactics . . . I meet *gestapo* tactics. . . . That's not right. . . . No man has the right to . . . "Call an attorney," that means you're guilt . . . you're under sus . . . "Co . . . ," he says, "cooperate" or we'll go downtown. *That's* not . . . as long as I've . . .

WILLIAMSON
[Bursting out of his office] Will you get out of here. Will you get *out* of here. Will you. I'm trying to run an *office* here. Will you go to lunch? Go to lunch. Will you go to lunch? *[Retreats into office.]*

ROMA
[To Aaronow] Will you excuse . . .

AARONOW
Where did Moss . . . ? I . . .

ROMA
Will you excuse us please?

AARONOW
Uh, uh, did he go to the restaurant? *[Pause.]* I . . . I . . . *[Exits.]*

ROMA
I'm *very* sorry, Jimmy. I apologize to you.

LINGK
It's not me, it's my wife.

ROMA
[Pause.] What is?

LINGK
I told you.

ROMA
Tell me again.

LINGK
What's going on here?

ROMA
Tell me again. Your wife.

LINGK
I told you.

ROMA
You tell me again.

LINGK
She wants her money back.

ROMA
We're going to speak to her.

LINGK
No. She told me "right now."

ROMA
We'll speak to her, Jim . . .

LINGK
She won't listen.

[Detective sticks his head out.]

BAYLEN
Roma.

LINGK
She told me if not, I have to call the State's attorney.

ROMA
No, no. That's just something she "said." We don't have to do that.

LINGK
She told me I *have* to.

ROMA
No, Jim.

LINGK
I *do.* If I don't get my *money* back . . .

[Williamson points out Roma to Baylen.]

BAYLEN
Roma! *[To Roma:]* I'm talking to you . . .

ROMA
I've . . . look. *[Generally:]* Will someone get this guy off my back.

BAYLEN
You have a problem?

ROMA
Yes, I have a problem. Yes, I *do,* my fr . . . It's not me that ripped the joint off, I'm doing *business.* I'll be with you in a *while.* You got it . . . ? *[Looks back. Lingk is heading for the door.]* Where are you going?

LINGK
I'm . . .

ROMA
Where are you going . . . ? This is *me* . . . This is Ricky, Jim. Jim, anything you *want,* you *want* it, you *have* it. You understand? This is *me.* Something *upset* you. Sit down, now sit down. You tell me what it is. *[Pause.]* Am I going to help you fix it? You're god-damned right I am. Sit down. Tell you something . . . ? *Sometimes* we need someone from *outside.* It's . . . no, sit down. . . . Now *talk* to me.

LINGK
I can't negotiate.

ROMA
What does that mean?

LINGK
That . . .

ROMA
. . . what, what, *say* it. Say it to me . . .

LINGK
I . . .

ROMA
What . . . ?

LINGK
I . . .

ROMA
What . . . ? Say the words.

LINGK
I don't have the *power.* *[Pause.]* I said it.

ROMA
What power?

LINGK
The power to negotiate.

ROMA
To negotiate what? *[Pause.]* To negotiate what?

LINGK
This.

ROMA
What, "this"? *[Pause.]*

LINGK
The deal.

ROMA
The "deal," *forget* the deal. *Forget* the deal, you've got something on your mind, Jim, what is it?

LINGK
[rising] I can't talk to you, *you* met my wife, I . . . *[Pause.]*

ROMA
What? *[Pause.]* What? *[Pause.]* What, Jim: I tell you what, let's get out of here . . . let's go get a drink.

LINGK
She told me not to talk to you.

ROMA
Let's . . . no one's going to know, let's go around the *corner* and we'll get a drink.

LINGK
She told me I had to get back the check or call the State's att . . .

ROMA

Forget the deal, Jimmy. *[Pause.] Forget* the deal . . . you know me. The deal's *dead*. Am I talking about the *deal*? That's *over*. Please. Let's talk about *you*. Come on. *[Pause. Roma rises and starts walking toward the front door.]* Come on. *[Pause.]* Come on, Jim. *[Pause.]* I want to tell you something. Your life is your own. You have a contract with your wife. You have certain things you do *jointly*, you have a *bond* there . . . and there are *other* things. Those things are yours. You needn't feel *ashamed*, you needn't feel that you're being *untrue* . . . or that she would abandon you if she knew. This is your life. *[Pause.] Yes*. Now I want to *talk* to you because you're obviously upset and that *concerns* me. Now let's go. Right now.

[Lingk gets up and they start for the door.]

BAYLEN

[Sticks his head out of the door] Roma . . .

LINGK

. . . and . . . and . . . *[Pause.]*

ROMA

What?

LINGK

And the check is . . .

ROMA

What did I *tell* you? *[Pause.]* What did I say about the three days . . . ?

BAYLEN

Roma, would you, I'd like to get some lunch . . .

ROMA

I'm talking with Mr. Lingk. If you please, I'll be back in. *[Checks watch.]* I'll be back in a while . . . I told you, check with Mr. Williamson.

BAYLEN

The people downtown said . . .

ROMA

You call them again. Mr. Williamson . . . !

WILLIAMSON

Yes.

ROMA

Mr. Lingk and I are going to . . .

WILLIAMSON

Yes. Please. Please. *[To Lingk:]* The police *[Shrugs]* can be . . .

LINGK

What are the police doing?

ROMA

It's nothing.

LINGK

What are the *police* doing here . . . ?

WILLIAMSON

We had a slight burglary last night.

ROMA

It was nothing . . . I was assuring Mr. Lingk . . .

WILLIAMSON

Mr. Lingk. James Lingk. Your contract went out. Nothing to . . .

ROMA

John . . .

WILLIAMSON

Your contract went out to the bank.

LINGK

You cashed the check?

WILLIAMSON

We . . .

ROMA

. . . Mr. Williamson . . .

WILLIAMSON

Your check was cashed yesterday afternoon. And we're completely insured, as you know, in *any* case. *[Pause.]*

LINGK

[To Roma] You cashed the check?

ROMA

Not to my knowledge, no . . .

WILLIAMSON

I'm sure we can . . .

LINGK

Oh, Christ . . . *[Starts out the door.]* Don't follow me. . . . Oh, Christ. *[Pause. To Roma:]* I know I've let you down. I'm sorry. For . . . Forgive . . . for . . . I don't know anymore. *[Pause.]* Forgive me. *[Lingk exits. Pause.]*

ROMA

[To Williamson] You stupid fucking cunt. *You*, Williamson . . . I'm talking to *you*, shithead. . . . You just cost me *six thousand dollars*. *[Pause.]* Six thousand dollars. And one Cadillac. That's right. What are you

going to do about it? What are you going to do about it, asshole. You fucking *shit*. Where did you learn your *trade*. You stupid fucking *cunt*. You *idiot*. Whoever told you you could work with *men*?

BAYLEN
Could I . . .

ROMA
I'm going to have your *job*, shithead. I'm going *downtown* and talk to Mitch and Murray, and I'm going to Lemkin. I don't care *whose* nephew you are, who you know, whose dick you're sucking on. You're going *out*, I swear to you, you're going . . .

BAYLEN
Hey, fella, let's get this done . . .

ROMA
Anyone in this office lives on their *wits*. . . . *[To Baylen:]* I'm going to be with you in a second. *[To Williamson:]* What you're hired for is to *help* us—does that seem clear to you? To *help* us. *Not* to fuck us up . . . to help *men* who are going *out* there to try to earn a *living*. You *fairy*. You company man . . . I'll tell you something else. I hope you knocked the joint off, I can tell our friend here something might help him catch you. *[Starts into the room.]* You want to learn the first rule you'd know if you ever spent a day in your life . . . you never open your mouth till you know what the shot is. *[Pause.]* You fucking *child* . . . *[Roma goes to the inner room.]*

LEVENE
You *are* a shithead, Williamson . . . *[Pause.]*

WILLIAMSON
Mmm.

LEVENE
You can't think on your feet you should keep your mouth closed. *[Pause.]* You hear me? I'm *talking* to you. Do you hear me . . . ?

WILLIAMSON
Yes. *[Pause.]* I hear you.

LEVENE
You can't learn that in an office. Eh? He's right. You have to learn it on the streets. You can't *buy* that. You have to *live* it.

WILLIAMSON
Mmm.

LEVENE
Yes. Mmm. *Yes. Precisely. Precisely.* 'Cause your partner *depends* on it. *[Pause.]* I'm *talking* to you, I'm trying to tell you something.

WILLIAMSON
You are?

LEVENE
Yes, I am.

WILLIAMSON
What are you trying to tell me?

LEVENE
What Roma's trying to tell you. What I told you yesterday. Why you don't belong in this business.

WILLIAMSON
Why I don't . . .

LEVENE
You listen to me, someday you might say, "Hey . . ." No, fuck that, you just listen what I'm going to say: your partner *depends* on you. Your partner . . . a man who's your "partner" *depends* on you . . . you have to go *with* him and *for* him . . . or you're shit, you're *shit*, you can't exist alone . . .

WILLIAMSON
[Brushing past him] Excuse me . . .

LEVENE
. . . excuse you, *nothing*, you be as cold as you want, but you just fucked a good man out of six thousand dollars and his goddamn bonus 'cause you didn't know the *shot*, if you can do that and you aren't man enough that it gets you, then I don't know what, if you can't take *some thing* from that . . . *[Blocking his way.]* you're scum, you're fucking white-bread. You be as cold as you want. A *child* would know it, he's right. *[Pause.]* You're going to make something up, be sure it will *help* or keep your mouth closed. *[Pause.]*

WILLIAMSON
Mmm. *[Levene lifts up his arm.]*

LEVENE
Now I'm done with you. *[Pause.]*

WILLIAMSON
How do you know I made it up?

LEVENE
[Pause.] What?

WILLIAMSON
How do you know I made it up?

LEVENE
What are you talking about?

WILLIAMSON
You said, "You don't make something up unless it's sure to help." [*Pause.*] How did you know that I made it up?

LEVENE
What are you talking about?

WILLIAMSON
I told the customer that his contracts had gone to the bank.

LEVENE
Well, hadn't it?

WILLIAMSON
No. [*Pause.*] It hadn't.

LEVENE
Don't *fuck* with me, John, don't *fuck* with me . . . what are you saying?

WILLIAMSON
Well, I'm saying this, Shel: usually I take the contracts to the bank. Last night I didn't. How did you know that? One night in a year I left a contract on my desk. Nobody knew that but *you*. Now how did you know that? [*Pause.*] You want to talk to me, you want to talk to someone *else* . . . because this is *my* job. This is my job on the line, and you are going to *talk* to me. Now how did you know that contract was on my desk?

LEVENE
You're so full of shit.

WILLIAMSON
You robbed the office.

LEVENE
[*Laughs*] Sure! I robbed the office. Sure.

WILLIAMSON
What'd you do with the leads? [*Pause. Points to the Detective's room.*] You want to go in there? I tell him what I know, he's going to dig up *something*. . . . You got an alibi last night? You better have one. What did you do with the leads? If you tell me what you did with the leads, we can talk.

LEVENE
I don't know what you are saying.

WILLIAMSON
If you tell me where the leads are, I won't turn you in. If you *don't*, I am going to tell the cop you stole them, Mitch and Murray will see that you go to jail. Believe me they will. Now, what did you do with the leads? I'm walking in that door—you have five seconds to tell me: or you are going to jail.

LEVENE
I . . .

WILLIAMSON
I don't care. You understand? *Where are the leads?* [*Pause.*] Alright. [*Williamson goes to open the office door.*]

LEVENE
I sold them to Jerry Graff.

WILLIAMSON
How much did you get for them? [*Pause.*] How much did you get for them?

LEVENE
Five thousand. I kept half.

WILLIAMSON
Who kept the other half? [*Pause.*]

LEVENE
Do I have to tell you? [*Pause. Williamson starts to open the door.*] Moss.

WILLIAMSON
That was easy, *wasn't* it? [*Pause.*]

LEVENE
It was his idea.

WILLIAMSON
Was it?

LEVENE
I . . . I'm sure he got more than the five, actually.

WILLIAMSON
Uh-huh?

LEVENE
He told me my share was twenty-five.

WILLIAMSON
Mmm.

LEVENE
Okay: I . . . look: I'm going to make it worth your while. I am. I turned this thing around. I closed the *old* stuff, I can do it again. *I'm* the one's going to close 'em. I am! I am! 'Cause I turned this thing a . . . I can do *that*, I can do *anyth* . . . last night. I'm going to tell you, I was ready to Do the Dutch. Moss gets me, "Do this, we'll get well. . . ." Why not. Big fuckin' deal.

I'm halfway hoping to get caught. To put me out of my . . . [Pause.] But it *taught* me something. What it taught me, that you've got to get *out* there. Big deal. So I wasn't cut out to be a thief. I was cut out to be a salesman. And now I'm back, and I got my *balls* back . . . and, you know, John, you have the *advantage* on me now. Whatever it takes to make it right, we'll make it right. We're going to make it right.

WILLIAMSON
I want to tell you something, Shelly. You have a big mouth. [Pause.]

LEVENE
What?

WILLIAMSON
You've got a big mouth, and now I'm going to show you an even bigger one. [Starts toward the Detective's door.]

LEVENE
Where are you going, John? . . . you can't do that, you don't want to do that . . . hold, hold on . . . hold on . . . wait . . . wait . . . wait . . . [Pulls money out of his pockets.] Wait . . . uh, look . . . [Starts splitting money.] Look, twelve, twenty, two, twen . . . twenty-five hundred, it's . . . take it. [Pause.] Take it all. . . . [Pause.] Take it!

WILLIAMSON
No, I don't think so, Shel.

LEVENE
I . . .

WILLIAMSON
No, I think I don't want your money. I think you fucked up my office. And I think you're going away.

LEVENE
I . . . what? Are you, are you, that's why . . . ? Are you nuts? I'm . . . I'm going to *close* for you, I'm going to . . . [Thrusting money at him.] Here, here, I'm going to *make* this office . . . I'm going to be back there Number One. . . . Hey, hey, hey! This is only the beginning. . . . List . . . list . . . listen. Listen. Just one moment. List . . . here's what . . . here's what we're going to do. Twenty percent. I'm going to give you twenty percent of my sales. . . . [Pause.] Twenty percent. [Pause.] For as long as I am with the firm. [Pause.] Fifty percent. [Pause.] You're going to be my partner. [Pause.] Fifty percent. Of all my sales.

WILLIAMSON
What sales?

LEVENE
What sales . . . ? I just *closed* eighty-two *grand*. . . . Are you fuckin' . . . I'm *back* . . . I'm *back*, this is only the beginning.

WILLIAMSON
Only the beginning . . .

LEVENE
Abso . . .

WILLIAMSON
Where have you been, Shelly? Bruce and Harriett Nyborg. Do you want to see the *memos* . . . ? They're nuts . . . they used to call in every week. When I was with Webb. And we were selling Arizona . . . they're nuts . . . did you see how they were *living*? How can you delude yours . . .

LEVENE
I've got the check . . .

WILLIAMSON
Forget it. Frame it. It's worthless. [Pause.]

LEVENE
The check's no good?

WILLIAMSON
You stick around I'll pull the memo for you. [Starts for the door.] I'm busy now . . .

LEVENE
Their check's no good? They're nuts . . . ?

WILLIAMSON
Call up the bank. *I* called them.

LEVENE
You did?

WILLIAMSON
I called them when we had the lead . . . four months ago. [Pause.] The people are insane. They just like talking to salesmen. [Williamson starts for door.]

LEVENE
Don't.

WILLIAMSON
I'm sorry.

LEVENE
Why?

WILLIAMSON
Because I don't like you.

LEVENE
John: John: . . . my *daughter* . . .

WILLIAMSON

Fuck you. [Roma comes out of the Detective's door. Williamson goes in.]

ROMA

[To Baylen] Asshole . . . [To Levene:] Guy couldn't find his fuckin' couch the living room . . . Ah, Christ . . . what a day, what a day . . . I haven't even had a cup of coffee. . . . Jagoff John opens his mouth he blows my Cadillac. . . . [Sighs.] I swear . . . it's not a world of men . . . it's not a world of men, Machine . . . it's a world of clock watchers, bureaucrats, officeholders . . . what it is, it's a fucked-up world . . . there's no adventure to it. [Pause.] Dying breed. Yes it is. [Pause.] We are the members of a dying breed. That's . . . that's . . . that's why we have to stick together. Shel: I want to talk to you. I've wanted to talk to you for some time. For a long time, actually. I said, "The Machine, there's a man I would work with. There's a man. . . ." You know? I never said a thing. I should have, don't know why I didn't. And that shit you were slinging on my guy today was so good . . . it . . . it was, and, excuse me, 'cause it isn't even my place to say it. It was admirable . . . it was the old stuff. Hey, I've been on a hot streak, so what? There's things that I could learn from you. You eat today?

LEVENE

Me.

ROMA

Yeah.

LEVENE

Mm.

ROMA

Well, you want to swing by the Chinks, watch me eat, we'll talk?

LEVENE

I think I'd better stay here for a while.

[Baylen sticks his head out of the room.]

BAYLEN

Mr. Levene . . . ?

ROMA

You're done, come down and let's . . .

BAYLEN

Would you come in here, please?

ROMA

And let's put this together. Okay? Shel? Say okay. [Pause.]

LEVENE

[Softly, to himself] Huh.

BAYLEN

Mr. Levene, I think we have to talk.

ROMA

I'm going to the Chinks. You're done, come down, we're going to smoke a cigarette.

LEVENE

I . . .

BAYLEN

[Comes over] . . . Get in the room.

ROMA

Hey, hey, hey, easy friend, that's the "Machine." That is Shelly "The Machine" Lev . . .

BAYLEN

Get in the goddamn room. [Baylen starts manhandling Shelly into the room.]

LEVENE

Ricky, I . . .

ROMA

Okay, okay, I'll be at the resta . . .

LEVENE

Ricky . . .

BAYLEN

"Ricky" can't help you, pal.

LEVENE

. . . I only want to . . . .

BAYLEN

Yeah. What do you want? You want to what? [He pushes Levene into the room, closes the door behind him. Pause.]

ROMA

Williamson: listen to me: when the leads come in . . . listen to me: when the leads come in I want my top two off the list. For me. My usual two. Anything you give Levene . . .

WILLIAMSON

. . . I wouldn't worry about it.

ROMA

Well I'm going to worry about it, and so are you, so shut up and listen. [Pause.] I GET HIS ACTION. My stuff is mine, whatever he gets for himself, I'm talking half. You put me in with him.

[Aaronow enters.]

AARONOW
Did they . . . ?

ROMA
You understand?

AARONOW
Did they catch . . . ?

ROMA
Do you understand? My stuff is mine, his stuff is ours. I'm taking half of his commissions—now, *you* work it out.

WILLIAMSON
Mmm.

AARONOW
Did they find the guy who broke into the office yet?

ROMA
No. *I* don't know. [*Pause.*]

AARONOW
Did the leads come in yet?

ROMA
No.

AARONOW
[*Settling into a desk chair*] Oh, God, I hate this job.

ROMA
[*Simultaneous with "job," exiting the office*] I'll be at the restaurant.

10

THE SEARCH FOR SIGNS
OF INTELLIGENT LIFE
IN THE UNIVERSE

By Jane Wagner • 1986

FROM ITS TITLE ON, JANE WAGNER'S *THE SEARCH for Signs of Intelligent Life in the Universe* is a most unusual play.

Unusual particularly because it was originally written as a performance piece for one actress, Lily Tomlin, who performed all the roles—male, female, and canine—in the stage premiere: a stunning *tour de force*. So associated with this play is Tomlin—who is also Wagner's long-time friend and professional colleague—that the play was generally known as "the Lily Tomlin show" during its Broadway run. But although Tomlin is clearly instrumental to the play—she also created the central character of Trudy on the television show *Laugh-In*—this should not obscure Jane Wagner's achievement as the play's author, because *The Search for Signs of Intelligent Life in the Universe* is no mere extended TV sketch: it is a masterwork of

modern dramaturgy, as has been demonstrated not only in Tomlin's solo performance, but in a subsequent larger-cast production.

Search for Signs is constructed through a developing interplay of often casually related characters; their various stories eventually coalesce into an increasingly meaningful plot that increasingly focuses on its key themes. The general tone, of course, is comic: Wagner's subjects are largely topical, and her tone is highly satiric, as befits comedy in all media—stage as well as television. The quaint (and here exaggerated) immoderations of the 1970s and 1980s—aura goggles, tofu consciousness, Astroturf neckties, holistic capitalists, Bio-Bottom diapers, karmic debt, detox parties, and "sharing for the sharing-impaired"—are deftly skewered by Wagner's/Tomlin's narrator Trudy, the delightfully deranged Manhattan bagwoman who "brings in" her host of jokey characters radiophonically: on an umbrella-hat satellite dish! A comedy, yes, but there can be no mistaking Wagner's deep compassion for the human needs that bring these indulgences to life. The women's consciousness-raising movement of the 1970s, which becomes the principal subject of the second half, arrives as an alternative to addiction, despair, abuse, and suicide; if there is mild satire here, there is also a testament to human courage and sociopolitical will.

Wagner's comic swath cuts through homophobia, commercialism, hypocrisy, and meanspiritedness; serving up, in their steads, a vision of comradeship and understanding through the medium of theatre itself. *Search for Signs* culminates in a thrilling theatrical (and metatheatrical) conclusion, during which the audience is boldly invited to consider its own reaction to the play's themes and to participate in "the goose-bump experience" of a live theatrical communion. The standing—and whooping—ovation that greeted every Broadway performance of this play brought forth goose bumps indeed, and testified not only to Tomlin's brilliant performance, but the play's superb dramatic structure, its deep humanity, and its immediate social relevance.

The 1980s and 1990s have proven a "coming of age" era for women playwrights: already three women in these decades have won the Pulitzer Prize for Drama (Wendy Wasserstein, Beth Henley, and Marsha Norman), and many others (Wagner, Tina Howe, Caryl Churchill, Maria Irene Fornes, Alice Childress, and Ntozake Shange) have been widely ranked among the best contemporary dramatists in both England and America. It should not be surprising that women entered the theatre late in its history—women were legally excluded for drama's first two thousand or so years, and only admitted grudgingly (except as actresses) until relatively recent times. But the revolution has clearly arrived. *Search for Signs*, which was written by one woman to be performed by another, and which deals centrally with issues of gender discrimination and women's opportunity, is at the heart of this revolution: a truly iconic (while deeply amusing) portrait of a society in transition—if not crisis.

A NOTE ON THE TEXT

The play was developed over a two-year period of regional theatre workshops and performances—in San Diego, Los Angeles, Seattle, Portland, Houston, Lexington, Atlanta, Aspen, and Boston. It opened at the Plymouth Theatre on Broadway (which is referenced in the play itself) in 1986: what follows is the text of that production.

The text is set exactly as in the initial publication: with speech headings printed vertically at the left, and setting "locations" horizontally at top. When performed by Tomlin, however, there were neither costume changes nor scene shifts to indicate character or locale changes; all was done through mime and audience inference.

Although many of the topical references (such as "Betty Ford's") may already have become unfamiliar to the newest generation of readers, I have resisted any slight temptation to gloss the text with explanatory footnotes, as they would only take the bloom off what should remain, for at least another decade or so, a very fresh rose.

❦ THE SEARCH FOR SIGNS OF INTELLIGENT LIFE IN THE UNIVERSE ❧

CAST OF CHARACTERS
(all initially played by Lily Tomlin)

TRUDY, a homeless bag lady

LILY, herself. The performer playing the role

JUDITH BEASLEY, a suburban housewife

CHRISSY, a young and multiphobic career woman

PAUL, an ex-swinger and cokehead

KATE, a bored, rich socialite

AGNUS ANGST, a punk rock performance artist

LUD, an older suburban husband

MARIE, his wife

TINA, a prostitute

BRANDY, another prostitute

LYN, a divorcing/divorced woman; active feminist in the 1970s

EDIE, a radical feminist in Lyn's consciousness-raising group

MARGE, another member of the group

BOB, Lyn's husband

A TV VOICE

DEBBIE BOONE, a recording

PART I

TRUDY

Here we are, standing on the corner of
"Walk, Don't Walk."
You look away from me, tryin' not to catch my eye,
but you didn't turn fast enough, *did* you?

You don't like my *raspy* voice, do you?
I got this *raspy* voice
'cause I have to yell all the time
'cause nobody around here ever
LISTENS to me.

You don't like that I scratch so much; yes, and excuse me,
I scratch so much
'cause my neurons are
on *fire*.

And I admit my smile is not at its Pepsodent best
'cause I think my
caps must've somehow got
osteo*porosis*.

And if my eyes seem to be twirling around like fruit flies—
the better to see you with, my dears!

Look at me,
you mammalian-brained LUNKHEADS!
I'm not just talking to myself. I'm talking to you, too.
And to you
and you
and you
and you and you and you!

I know what you're thinkin'; you're thinkin' I'm crazy.
You think I give a hoot? You people
look at my shopping bags,
call me crazy 'cause I save this junk. What should we call the ones who
buy it?

It's my belief we all, at one time or another,
secretly ask ourselves the question,
"Am *I* crazy?"
In my case, the answer came back: A resounding
YES!

You're thinkin': How does a person know if they're crazy
or not? Well, sometimes you don't know. Sometimes you
can go through life suspecting you *are*
but never really knowing for sure. Sometimes you know for sure
'cause you got so many people tellin' you you're crazy
that it's your word against everyone else's.

Another sign is when you see life so clear sometimes
you black out.
This is your typical visionary variety
who has flashes of insight
but can't get anyone to listen to 'em
'cause their insights make 'em sound so *crazy*!

In my case,
the symptoms are subtle
but unmistakable to the trained eye. For instance,
here I am,
standing at the corner of "Walk, Don't Walk,"
waiting for these aliens from outer space to show up.
I call that crazy, don't you? If I were sane,
I should be waiting for the light like everybody else.

They're late
as usual.

You'd think,
as much as they know about time travel,
they could be on time *once* in a while.

I could kick myself,
I told 'em I'd meet 'em on the corner of "Walk, Don't Walk"
'round lunchtime.
Do they even know what "lunch" means?
I doubt it.

And " 'round." Why did I say " 'round"? Why wasn't I more
specific? This is so typical of what I do.

Now they're probably stuck somewhere in time, wondering what I meant by
" 'round lunchtime." And when they get here, they'll be
dying to know what "lunchtime" means. And when they
find out it means going to Howard Johnson's for fried
clams, I wonder, will they be just a bit let down?

I dread having to explain
tartar sauce.

This problem of time just points out
how far apart we really are.
See, our ideas about time and space are different
from theirs. When we think of time, we tend to think of
clock radios, coffee breaks, afternoon naps, leisure time,
halftime activities, parole time, doing time, Minute Rice, instant
tea, mid-life crises, that time of the month, cocktail hour.
And if I should suddenly
mention *space*—aha! I bet most of you thought of your
closets. But when they think of time and space, they really think of
Time and Space.

They asked me once my thoughts on infinity and I told 'em
with all I had to think about, infinity was not on my list
of things to think about. It could be time on an ego trip,
for all I know. After all, when you're pressed for time,
infinity may as well
not be there.
They said, to them, infinity is
time-released time.

Frankly, infinity doesn't affect
me personally one way or the other.

You think too long about infinity, you could go
stark raving mad.
But I don't ever want to sound negative about going crazy.
I don't want to overromanticize it either, but frankly,
goin' crazy was the *best* thing ever happened to me.
I don't say it's for everybody;
some people couldn't cope.

But for me it came at a time when nothing else seemed to be
working. I got the kind of madness Socrates talked about,
"A divine release of the soul from the yoke of
custom and convention." I refuse to be intimidated by
reality anymore.
After all, what is reality anyway? Nothin' but a
collective hunch. My space chums think reality was once a
primitive method of
crowd control that got out of hand.
In my view, it's absurdity dressed up
in a three-piece business suit.

I made some studies, and
reality is the leading cause of stress amongst those in
touch with it. I can take it in small doses, but as a lifestyle
I found it too confining.
It was just too needful;
it expected me to be there for it *all* the time, and with all
I have to do—
I had to let something go.

Now, since I put reality on a back burner, my days are
jam-packed and fun-filled. Like some days, I go hang out
around Seventh Avenue; I love to do this old joke:
I wait for some music-loving tourist from one of the hotels
on Central Park to go up and ask someone,
"How do I get to Carnegie Hall?"
Then I run up and yell,
"Practice!"
The expression on people's faces is priceless. I never
could've done stuff like that when I was in my *right* mind.
I'd be worried people would think I was *crazy*.
When I think of the fun I missed,
I try not to be bitter.

See, the human mind is kind of like . . .

a piñata. When it breaks open,
there's a lot of surprises inside. Once you get the piñata
perspective, you see that losing your mind
can be a peak experience.

I was not always a bag lady, you know.
I used to be a designer and creative consultant. For big companies!
Who do you think thought up the color scheme
for Howard Johnson's?
At the time, nobody was using
orange and aqua
in the same room together.
With fried clams.

Laugh tracks:
I gave TV sitcoms the idea for canned laughter.
I got the idea, one day I heard voices
and no one was there.

Who do you think had the idea to package panty hose
in a plastic goose egg?

One thing I personally don't like about panty hose:
When you roll 'em down to the ankles the way I like 'em, you
can't walk too good. People seem amused, so what's a little
loss of dignity? You got to admit:
It's a look!

The only idea I'm proud of—

my umbrella hat. Protects against sunstroke, rain and
muggers. For *some* reason, muggers steer clear of people
wearing umbrella hats.

So it should come as no shock . . . I am now creative consultant to
these aliens from outer space. They're a kinda cosmic
fact-finding committee. Amongst other projects, they've been
searching all over for Signs of Intelligent Life.

It's a lot trickier than it sounds.

We're collecting all kinds of data
about life here on Earth. We're determined to figure out,
once and for all, just what the hell it all means.
I write the data on these Post-its and then we study it.
Don't worry, before I took the consulting job, I gave 'em my whole psychohistory.

I told 'em what drove *me* crazy was my *last* creative consultant
job, with the Ritz Cracker mogul, Mr. Nabisco. It was
my job to come up with snack inspirations to increase sales.
I got this idea to give Cracker Consciousness to the entire
planet.

I said, "Mr. Nabisco, sir! You could be the first to sell the
concept of munching to the Third World. We got an untapped
market here! These countries got millions and millions of
people don't even know where their next *meal* is *coming* from.
So the idea of eatin' *between* meals is somethin' just never
occurred to 'em!"

I heard myself sayin' *this*!

Must've been when I went off the deep end.
I woke up in the nuthouse. They were hookin' me up.
One thing they don't tell you about shock treatments, for
months afterwards you got
flyaway hair. And it used to *be* my best feature.

See, those shock treatments gave me new electrical circuitry
(frankly, I think one of the doctors' hands must've been wet).
I started having these time-space continuum shifts, I guess
you'd call it. Suddenly, it was like my central nervous system
had a patio addition out back.
Not only do I have a linkup to extraterrestrial
channels. I also got a hookup with humanity as a whole.
Animals and plants, too. I used to talk to plants all the time;
then, one day, they started talking back. They said,
"Trudy,
shut up!"

I got like this . . .

built-in Betamax in my head. Records anything.
It's like somebody's using my brain to dial-switch
through humanity. I pick up signals that seem to transmit
snatches of people's lives.
My umbrella hat works as a satellite dish. I hear this
sizzling sound like white noise. Then I know it's
trance time.
That's how I met my space chums. I was in one of my trances,
watching a scene from someone's life, and I suddenly sense
others were there
watching with me.

Uh-oh.
I see this skinny
punk kid.
Got hair the color of
Froot Loops and she's wearin' a T-shirt says "Leave Me Alone."
There's a terrible family squabble going on.
If they're listening to each other,
they're all gonna get their feelings hurt.

I see glitches—
Now I see this dark-haired actress
on a Broadway stage. I know her. I see her all the time outside
the Plymouth Theater, Forty-Fifth Street.

L
I
L
Y

I'm so glad that you came tonight.
I sometimes worry no one will show up, and without you,
there'd be little point
in me being here.

I think you should know I worry a lot.
Like the Nobel sperm bank. Something bothers me about the
world's greatest geniuses
sitting around
reading pornography
and jerking off.

I worry that humanity has been "advanced" to its present level
of incompetency
because evolution works on
the Peter Principle.

I worry that Andy Warhol may be right—

And everyone *will* be famous for fifteen minutes.
How will there ever be room for us all
at Betty Ford's?

I even worry about reflective flea collars. Oh, sure, drivers can
see them glow in the dark
but so can the fleas.

I worry if peanut oil comes from peanuts
and olive oil comes from olives, where *does*
baby oil come from?

One thing I have no worry about is whether
God exists.
But it has occurred to me that God has Alzheimer's and has
forgotten
we exist.

I worry that our lives are like
soap operas. We can go for months and not
tune in to them, then six months later

we look in and the
same stuff
is still going on.

I worry whoever thought up the term "quality control"
thought if we didn't control it,
it would get out of hand.

I worry no matter how cynical you become,
it's never enough to keep up.

I worry where tonight fits in the Cosmic Scheme of things.
I worry there *is* no Cosmic Scheme to things.

T
R
U
D
Y

Dial-switch me outta this!
I got enough worries of my own.
These trances are entertaining but distracting, especially since
someone *else* has the remote control, and if the pause button
should somehow get punched, I could have a neurotransmitter
mental meltdown. Causes "lapses of the synapses." I forget
things. Never underestimate the power of the human mind to
forget. The other day, I forgot where I put my house keys—
looked everywhere, then I remembered
I don't have a house. I forget more important things, too.
Like the meaning of life.
I forget that.
It'll come to me, though.
Let's just hope when it does,
I'll be in. . . .

My space chums say they're learning so much about us
since they've begun to time-share my trances.
They said to me, "Trudy, the human mind is so-o-o strange."
I told 'em, "That's nothin' compared to the human genitals."

Next to my trances they love goin' through my shopping bags.
Once they found this old box of Cream of Wheat. I told 'em, "A
box of cereal." But they saw it as a picture of infinity. You know
how on the front is a picture of that guy holding up a box of
Cream of Wheat

and on *that* box is a picture of that guy holding up a box of
Cream of Wheat
and on *that* box is a picture of that guy holding up a box of
Cream of Wheat
and on *that* box is a picture of that guy holding up a box of
Cream of Wheat . . .

We think so different.

They find it hard to grasp some things that come easy to us,
because they simply don't have our frame of reference.
I show 'em this can of Campbell's tomato soup.
I say,
"This is soup."
Then I show 'em a picture of Andy Warhol's painting
of a can of Campbell's tomato soup.
I say,
"This is art."

"This is soup."

"And this is art."

Then I shuffle the two behind my back.

Now what is this?

No,
this is soup
and *this is art*!

Oh, there's that sound!
Here we go again. Looks like we're
somewhere . . . in suburbia. A housewife. Hey,
I've seen this woman before. She used to sell
Tupperware.

JUDITH BEASLEY

About a month ago, I was shown some products designed to
improve the sex lives of suburban housewives. I got so excited,
I just had to come on public access and tell you about it. To
look at *me*, you'd *never suspect* I was a semi-nonorgasmic
woman. This means it was *possible* for me to have an orgasm—
but highly unlikely.

To me, the term "sexual freedom" meant freedom from having to
have sex. And then along came Good Vibrations. And was I
surprised! Now I am a regular
Cat on a Hot Tin Roof.

As a love object,
it surpasses my husband Harold by a country mile.
But please,
this is no threat to the family unit;
think of it as a kind of
Hamburger Helper for the boudoir.

Can you afford one, you say?
Can you afford *not* to have one, I say.
Why, the *time* it saves alone is worth the price.
I'd rank it up there with Minute Rice,
Reddi-Whip
and Pop-Tarts.

Ladies, it simply takes the guesswork out of making love.

"But doesn't it kill romance?" you say.
And I say,
"What doesn't?"

So what'll it be? This deluxe kit? Or this purse-size model
for the "woman on the go"? Fits anywhere and comes with a
silencer to avoid
curious onlookers.

Ladies, it can be a real help to the busy married woman who has
a thousand chores and simply does not need the extra burden of
trying to have an
orgasm.

But what about guilt, you say? Well, that thought did cross
my mind.

But at one time I felt guilty using a cake mix instead of
baking from scratch.

I learned to live with that.
I can learn to live with this.

❦

T
R
U
D
Y

I hear . . . music . . .
I see this young woman
at her aerobics class. She's the only one working out
in dangling earrings
and clanking bracelets.

❦

C
H
R
I
S
S
Y

Whooo!

Shake it out!

I've been on four job interviews today, Eileen; I've got one more to go.
I lost my job with the answering service because I would not
lie for people who wanted me to say they were out
when they weren't. These days,
integrity is not a required skill.

This may sound like a cop-out, but some of my job probs are not
my fault. I'm dyslexic, they tell me.

I don't type, file or spell well. It's hard to type when you
can't spell
and it's hard to file when everything you've typed looks like
alphabet soup.

I'd do better at something creative, and I feel I *am* somewhat
creative, but some*how* I *lack* talent to go with it, and *being*
creative without talent is a bit like being a perfectionist
and not being able to do anything right.

All my life I've always wanted to *be* somebody.
But I see now I should have been more
specific.

It's not that I lack ambition. I *am* ambitious in the sense that I
want to be more than I am now. But if I were truly
ambitious, I think I'd already *be* more than I am now.

A sobering thought, Eileen:
What if, right at this very moment,
I *am* living up to my full potential?

I've about reached the conclusion if I'm ever going to make
something of my life, chances are it won't be through work.
It will have to be through personal growth stuff.

Go for the burn!

I've been trying to get into positive thinking in a really big way.
Frankly, I think it's my only hope.

My seminar leader said to me, "Chrissy, you should learn
to be happy
one day at a time." But what I learned from that is that you can
also be *miserable*
one day at a time.

This seminar I'm in, Eileen, has opened me up like some kind of
bronchial *spray*. I got clear:
my expectations about life are simply way too high. So are yours,
I bet, Eileen, because we
are all being *force-fed* a lot of false hopes about romance,
success, sex, life—you name it.

My seminar leader said to me, "Chrissy, you are a classic
'false hope' case" . . . because not only do I not have a very firm
grasp on reality, see,
but I have sort of a loose grip on my fantasies, too.

We had this exercise, Eileen.
We played this mind game called
"We know everything we need to know
if only we knew it."
We were told to be silent and our minds would tell
us whatever we needed to know.

I flashed on the time I lost my contact lens. There I was
looking for my contact lens
which I couldn't find
because I had lost my contact lens.
I thought: Wow, the story of my *life*.

You can't expect insights, even the big ones,
to suddenly make you understand
everything. But I figure: Hey, it's a step if they leave you
confused
in a deeper way.

The seminar ends tonight. To get us to face our fears,
we're supposed to walk over this bed of really red-hot coals—
barefoot. Quite a test! You name
it; I've feared it.
Except walking over hot coals . . . I never had that fear
till just now.

I'm working on overcoming my fears, Eileen,
but it's not easy.
At the Phobia Institute once,
this guy in group told about a friend who was terrified
of driving on the freeway,
but finally she conquered her fear and got so she thought
nothing of driving on the freeway.
And guess what?
She died
in a freeway accident.
That story has always stuck with me.

But *my* fears are more subtle. Like I fear being out of work,
and yet when I'm working, I have this constant fear
of being fired. The worst fear I have
is that this feeling I once had may come back.

[At the lockers]

Once . . . I've been wanting to tell someone this, Eileen . . .
once I came *this* close
to committing suicide.
That's how down and low I felt.
I would have, too. There was just one thing stopped me.
Fear. I was just plain too afraid.
So, if I ever did commit suicide, I'd have to be so desperate
I wouldn't even let fear of suicide
stand in my way.

And yet if I could overcome a fear like that
I could overcome
all my fears, I bet.

And then, of course—
and here's the irony—probably
if I weren't afraid, I'd really want to live.
Only, by then, if I'd really conquered my fear of suicide,
it might be too late.
I might already, you know,
have done it.

Life can be so ironic. Sometimes, to make any move at all seems
totally pointless. I bet the worst part about dying is the part where
your whole life passes before you.

I hope I don't ever feel that low again. At the moment, I feel
pretty up about the work I'm doing on myself. I used to be so
sensitive; sometimes I would think of the Kennedy family and I
would just burst out in tears. I'm not so sensitive anymore; I
don't burst out in tears as much as I used to and I hardly ever
think of the Kennedys anymore. So these seminars have been
good for me, Eileen, which is more than I can say for any job I've
ever had.

Course, *I* don't want to be a seminar-*hopper*, like this
ex-friend I used to know. She had no time for *anything* but
self-improvement. She felt she had outgrown everyone,
especially *me*. Behind my back, she told this person that *I* was an
Upwardly
Immobile Asshole. And then, to add insult to injury,
she said it to my face. That did it—
I get enough insults on job interviews.

Well, I guess I'll see you tomorrow. How they lied about
this health club! Talk about false hopes. "The *place* to get
thin and meet good-looking men." The good-looking men here
are mostly looking at themselves.

I have never gotten so much as a date for cappuccino.

Yet I keep coming. I'm keeping really fit, I tell myself.
But the truth is,
I pig out one week and starve the next.

I have gained and lost
the same ten pounds
so many times over and over again
my cellulite must have déjà vu.

And all that business about exercise releasing endorphins.
I have not felt so much as *one* endorphin being released. Once
more, false hopes.

But hey, if it weren't for false hopes, the economy would
just collapse, I bet. Oh. I better hurry. My job interview! This
time I could get lucky. Requires no skills;
I'll just be hooking people up to
bio-feedback machines. At least I won't be lying to them.
Well, slinkydinks, I'm outta here.

P
A
U
L

This body-building bit, Ted: lately I've been thinking
what's the point a lot.
Like what's the point being a health nut by day if you're a coke
head at night. What worries me, I'm getting burned out
on both. I used to get a charge knowing my body was so great
I could turn heads. Now, when I sense some girl digging me,
I don't get so turned on; instead, I get this
trapped feeling.

The thought occurs, Ted: What if I run out
of things to get off on?

Even sports. Sure, I still watch the
games, but I don't root so much anymore,
just watch. Hell, it was the rooting that made it worthwhile.

It's the same with sex!
Yeah, my sex urge is still industrial strength,
but where's the desire?
I miss the disco scene, man.
I feel about the disco days what
hippies must feel about Woodstock.

I blame a lot of what I'm going through on Penny—
the divorce thing sure threw me for a loop.
Took the wind outta my sails. You mind if I talk, Ted?
You got time? I still can't get over it: Penny and I, we had
a romance like something Lionel Ritchie might sing
about. Then it just all started to fall
apart. One day, I'm in the den, waiting for the
game to start, I see this magazine quiz
Penny's been filling out: "On a Scale
of One to Ten, How Do You Rate Your Man?"
As a dresser, a dancer, a conversationalist, a lover? She'd
given me a three on everything. A three!
After that, making love with her
was never the same. A three!

Hell, who knows what's considered a good
lover these days anyway? Every time you turn around
there's a new erogenous zone you gotta go explore:
clitoris, vaginal, X marks the G spot, the back
of the knee. Hell, these days, a guy needs his
cock hooked up to an Apple computer.

Okay, all right, I was no angel.
One night—Penny was pregnant; she wasn't
feeling well. We'd just moved;
there was a lot of tension. So I pop into this disco to decompress.
I see this hot-looking chick, Marge. I'd seen her there before—
a real knockout. So we do some coke—seemed innocent
enough at the time—she keeps coming on to me.
In a moment of weakness, I go with her to her pad over her plant
store. We smoke some wacko weed she grew herself. This is the
kind of woman . . .
I wake up with the imprint of her Mark Cross rape whistle
on my chest.

She starts asking me all kind of questions
about my family background—my talents, my IQ. She loves it
that I have these eyes like David Bowie. See, look, Ted,
one green and one blue? You never noticed? Turns out she wants
me to be a sperm donor to these two friends of hers who want a
baby. So, I'm in a weird mood, I say, "Hell, why not?"
Then she gives me this turkey baster, wants me to
ejaculate into it. I freaked at first, but then she explained it
and it made perfect sense. So I did it. The drugs and all.
I got caught up in the moment.
Then, of course, when I came down, I think of
Penny . . . pregnant and all . . . the guilt hits me
like a karate chop. So I go home and tell Penny
everything that happened
'cause we'd made this promise that we wouldn't let lies start
building up between us.
That was my real mistake—telling her. I was so sure she'd
forgive me and we'd be back on track. Well, I was wrong;
I should've just let the lies pile up. The one time in my life I
make a conscious effort to be honest
and it blows up in my face.

Few weeks later, Penny has the baby. Can I
show you something? See this? Polaroid. Nurse
took it at the moment of my son's birth.
That's me and Penny in the delivery
room, breathing like two hippos with
a chest cold. I was right there. Penny wanted
the bonding thing that's
supposed to happen. You know what?
The bonding thing did happen, but then,
a few years later, so did the divorce. That's Paul
Junior—see, there's his little head peeping out. Isn't
life too much? Now I can see the beauty!
But at the time I almost passed out.

Penny's remarried, moved to Georgia;
I haven't seen little Paulie since . . . too long. Lately I been
thinking of that Marge chick and her friends—
the thought occurs, Ted, that maybe I've got this secret kid.
Chances are I have, 'cause I probably got a sperm count
like the national deficit.

There was one time on TV I see this genius—child prodigy or
something—playing the violin
like he was possessed. I almost switch channels, when it
suddenly hits me like a karate chop—
the kid looks like me when I was *his* age. I just about freak. I try
to get a close look at his eyes.
I could swear one was blue and one was green. I even go call
the station,
but they said they weren't allowed to take messages like that. So
anyway the girl I'm with tells me
I'm nutto and shows me how much coke I'd done. So I guess I let
my imagination run away with me,
but I still think, you know, "What if?"

Once, I obsessed to the point I go back to
the plant store thinking maybe I could talk Marge into
telling me, do I have this secret kid or not? All they
tell me at the store is Marge is dead. Blew me away.
She'd practically be
the godmother of my kid.

But I get these psychic flashes sometimes; I feel almost sure,
except for the genius part,
that could've been my kid.
I am very psychic, Ted.
Like sometimes, I can tune in to a rerun of *Twilight Zone* and I
somehow will sense before it begins
which episode it's going to be.

I can't stop thinking about it.
I ask myself, "What's he like?"
"Is he happy?" "Does he have the proper male role model?"
"Did the bonding thing happen,
I wonder?"

T R U D Y

You've all had the
experience like somebody's on your wavelength . . .
well, think of how *I* must feel. . . . An elegant woman.
Rich type. Fendi bag, looks like. Jewelry.
Beautiful hands, too. Except the little finger on the
left hand has no tip.
Sits impatient . . . some beauty salon . . . could be the one
in Tramp's Tower. . . .

K A T E

How much longer *must* I wait? I have read *all* the magazines.

I will *have* to be shampooed again.

Lonnie? Lonnie!
It's Kate.
No, I wasn't sure that that was *you*, either.

That's what comes of letting Bucci "the Arrogant" do our hair,
I suppose. I am here hoping Anouk
can do something to undo the
harm he's done. I mean, what is this?

This side ends
well above the left ear,
and this side ends,
as you can see, at the collarbone.

I am *sick* of being the victim
of trends I reflect
but don't even understand.

I tell *you*, coming here today was so humiliating. There were
people in the streets actually *staring* at my haircut.
People who normally would be *intimidated*.

Oh, I said to him, "*Please*, Bucci, nothing too radical." But
by *that* time, this side was *already* too radical. That's why
this side
looks *less* radical. Oh, well, I have gotten *scads* of
compliments. Especially when they see just *this* side
and not *this* side.

I have been waiting here so *long* today that soon this side
will *look* like this side.

Since I've been sitting here, two new age spots have appeared.
I hope they heard that.
Oh, well, I *do* like what it does for my cheekbones.
Well, *one* of my cheekbones. But you see, my left ear *juts*
out just where the cut is most radical. I'd like to say to him, "As
long as you *insist* on calling yourself an *artist*,
then go to Palm Beach and do oil portraits."
Well, no, no, I have never actually talked to him that way; can
you imagine what I would look like
if I ever actually talked to him that way?

Lonnie, you must read this article I've just finished.
Fascinating. It's all about how you can actually die
from boredom. Yes, "a slow, agonizing death."
They've done studies.

Have you ever used the expression "I am dying of boredom"?
Well, so have I; I have used it *all* my life. It says here if you
use it that often, that may be *exactly* what you are doing.

Even as I was *reading* this very *article*, in the back of my mind
I suddenly caught myself thinking:
How *boring*!

Guess who was at Rafael's last night?
With someone who was *not* her husband?
No, no, I will not *tell* you.
I will only say that she is someone you know. Rather well.
Now can you guess?

Her left ear *juts* out!
Yes, I am having an affair. But not for long,
I think. It's one thing to tolerate a boring marriage,
but a boring affair does *not* make sense.

I guess I'm talking about it because I think I *want* Freddie to
hear about it and get upset. Of course it has occurred to me
he might hear about it and *not* get upset.

Last year, I lost the tip off my little finger . . .

in a dreadful Cuisinart accident.
To this day, he has yet to notice.

And this haircut, Lonnie, hard to miss *this* haircut. Not a
word. I look at my disfigured fingertip. I think
how terrible that this should have happened
and yet it could have been worse. I have always loved music.
As a little girl I dreamed of being a concert violinist.
What a tragedy if my dream
had come true.

I'm going to L.A. next weekend to see a plastic surgeon
about a new fingertip. Maybe I should get him to operate
on this haircut while he is at it.
I can't stand the thought of going to L.A.
If you think I'm bored here,
you should see me there.

And I've got to go to the theater tonight, this actress/comedy
thing. They say it's
uplifting, but still I dread it. The last time they said
something was uplifting I must have dozed off during the
uplifting part. I don't know, Lonnie, am I so jaded
I can't be uplifted anymore,
or do I find being uplifted ultimately boring?
That is *really* jaded.
I don't know why I bother going; I can see it now—
I'll be just one big yawn
with a bad haircut.

Give me that magazine. Don't put it back.
I want to rip out that article
on boredom.

I'm going to have it Xeroxed and give copies to all my friends.
Now I know what's wrong with us all.
It says here—did you read?—"Having *everything* can
sometimes make you stop wanting *anything*."

It's called
"Rich People's Burn-Out.'"

And if *Town & Country* is writing about it,
a magazine not known for its psychological insight, well,
it must be of *epidemic* proportions, don't you think?

TRUDY

Uh-oh, irregular brain waves . . . another trance coming on.
I see that young woman again—the one with job probs.
She looks up from the classifieds.
I see tears in her eyes.
Now she takes up the newspapers . . .
throws them into the trash can. I don't like the look on her face.
She begins writing something . . .
a letter, looks like . . . now she stops, scratches something out.
Now she takes the dictionary, starts to look up a word,
now she's frantically thumbing through, having trouble trying to
find the word she wants.

New channel!
It's the skinny punk Froot Loop kid again.
Seems upset.

AGNUS ANGST

Hello, Charlotte, listen, it is *vital* I stay
over at your house tonight!
Don't ask me to explain.
You've got to make your mom let me stay over!
Can't you force her to say yes?

Look, my parents think you're a bad influence on *me*,
too.

Just for that, you can't run the equipment at my gig tonight.

You are out of my life, Charlotte;

you are *her*story. You are the "crumb de la crumb." Drop off my
tapes at the Un-Club, or I'll sue you for all you're worth.
It is vital, Charlotte!

Don't you eyeball me, you *speck*! Can't you see I am USING this
PHONE!! And don't you *touch* that cage.
That's my parakeet in there.

Hello?
Look, it's vital I talk to the radio shrink. My name's Agnus.
I'm fifteen. My *parents* locked me out of the house today.
I want to find out if that is *legal*. I'm in the
ladies' room, House of Pancakes. I can't wait long.

Hello? Is this Dr. Kassorla, the psychologist? Look, Doctor,
for years I've been going home after school, nobody
would be there—

I'd take my key
from around my neck and
let myself in.
But today I go home,
I put my key in the door . . .

THEY CHANGED THE LOCKS ON ME!

Yeah, maybe it *was* something I did. I didn't say I was innocent.

Whatever I do is wrong, anyway. Like, last night, my stepmom,
she accuses me of leaving dirty fingerprints on the *cheese*.
Even getting an innocent piece of cheese becomes a criminal act.
But the problem goes deeper: My real mother's not around
much right now. She's in Europe, Germany or someplace,
doing her art thing. She's a performance artist. Like me.
There was this big custody beef, see, 'cause
my real mother's a lesbian. So the *court* gave me to my dad.
He's a gene-splicer, a bio-businessman at this research lab of
*mis*applied science. Where he's working on some new bio-form
he thinks he'll be able to patent.
He doesn't get that *I* am a new bio-form.

I AM USING THIS PHONE!! You IHOP speck!

So today I go by my dad's lab, to get some money for some gear
for my act,
and I see this like glob of bio-plasm
quivering there in this petri dish.
I don't know why I did it.
Maybe it was sibling rivalry.
But I leaned over
and I spit into it.
And of course, my dad had a MAD SCIENTIST ALERT! He says I've
ruined years of research.
The truth is he loves that *bio-form* more than *me*.

Yeah, I thought of calling the hot line for runaways, but I'm
worried maybe they don't take
throwaways like me. I have other family, my grandparents,
but we have nothing in common, except that we are all
carbon-based life forms.

What?
A commercial?
I can't believe you're brushing me off.
To sell some product
that probably killed some poor *lab rat.*
You've been about as helpful as an acid FLASHBACK!

T
R
U
D
Y

She hangs up. Now she's walking out. She stops. She's thinking.
Now she takes the latchkey from around her neck
and throws it in the trash can.

A **A**
G **N**
N **G**
U **S**
S **T**

Hey, where's my parakeet! Conway Tweety!

THAT CREEP! STOLE MY PARAKEET! Hey, you IHOP specks, you *must*
have seen somebody leave
with a cage. You all saw me come in with one. Don't you stare
at me with those *blueberry syrup mustaches!*

T
R
U
D
Y

In suburbia. An older couple sits watching TV. They're watching
that woman who used to sell Tupperware.

L
U
D

Talkin' about vibrators that way!
The things you see on TV these days.
What kind of crazy world do we live in?

M
A
R
I
E

Lud, who was it said . . . ? that quote about, oh, you know . . .
What was that quote?
Do you remember, Lud?

L
U
D

Did you just hear what you said, Marie?

MARIE   I reckon so. I just said it. . . .
What?

LUD   You were about to say somethin' *somebody* said—you couldn't
think who said it or what it was they said.

MARIE   And that never happens to you, I suppose.
That never happens to him, does it, Fluffy?

LUD   Well, if I couldn't think who it was said somethin',
or what it was they said, I simply would not bring up the subject,
Marie. I'd simply keep my mouth shut.
Somethin' I wish *you'd* consider more often.

MARIE   I *used* to *tolerate* that kind of talk, because I told myself it was
your hernia made you act so *hateful*.
I have let you walk all over me.
Janet used to beg me, she'd say, "*Mama*, please join a
consciousness-raising group." I'd say, "Honey, what on earth
would I do at a consciousness-raising group?"

I missed out on it like I did everything else.

LUD   You know what your problem is, Marie?

MARIE   Yes. You!

LUD   You can't concentrate.
You've got a brain like a hummingbird. . . .
Makes you appear dense and at the same time flighty. Did you
ever see a hummingbird try to make up its mind which flower to
land on? Well, picture your brain
in place of that *bird*
and you have a clue as to what I have to put up with.

Some people have hare brains, some people have pea brains.
And some people . . .

MARIE

have the brains of a male chauvinist pig! Oink! Oink!
Oink! Oink! Oink!

LUD

Now who's bein' hateful?

Shh! What was that sound just then?

Sounds like the garage door flapped up! Well, give me them
damn glasses.

I see somethin' glowing out there.

Somethin's comin' up the driveway. . . . I never seen anything
like it.

AGNUS

Granddaddy Speck . . .

LET! ME! IN!

TRUDY

This is soup
and this is art.
Art.
Soup.
Soup.
Art.
No,
That's Cream of Wheat.
This is soup and this is art.

We must dash soon! We're on our way to Stonehenge. I like to
plan it so we have at least one *peak* experience each day. When
you got aliens in from out of town, you want to do something
special.

It's great traveling with 'em. You go faster than the speed
of speed.

To them, a journey of a thousand miles begins with bio-astral
projection. I said, "*So*, you folks believe in astral projection?"
They said, "If something's true,
you don't need to believe in it."

I'm talkin' *advanced*. They are so advanced they can be
in three different places at once
and still be at one with the universe.

They are so advanced they don't even *try* to prove how advanced
they are. I told 'em we're pretty advanced ourselves. We got
physicists trying to find out more about quarks. They said,
"Trudy, tell your physicists a quark is just one of nature's
little quirks."

They got such a powerful electromagnetic field . . .

just hangin' out with 'em has helped my facial neuralgia.

Only drawback,
I got a severe case of static cling.

They are just about perfect,
except for *one* weak spot:

Their personal appearance. They look like
a gelatinous mass of ribonucleic acid
been poured out of a Jell-O mold too soon.
Plus they got no
eyelids.
That alone would drive *me* up the wall.

We are delving deeply into the history of humanity.

I'm a mound of information.
Yesterday we stumbled across the first recorded history of
when humankind made an ass of itself. Then we discovered
when
humankind first laughed. Guess what!
We first laughed the day we first made an ass of ourselves. They
love that about us!

Right after we laughed, we began to reflect on ourselves.
Around this time we discovered evidence of the first
"knock-knock" joke.
"Knock-knock."
"Who's there?"

"We're not sure—we're new at this."

Not very witty, but it does give us insight into the size and
shape of Cro-Magnon man's funny bone.

I don't know what I'd do without these Post-its. I've got the
facts right at my fingertips. Let me read you some data we found.

· "Did you know, the RNA/DNA molecule can be found throughout
space in *many* galaxies . . .
only everybody spells it different?"

· "You *are* what you think."
Jeez, that's frightening.

· "What goes up must come down.
But don't expect it to come down
where you can find it."
Murphy's Law applied to Newton's.

· "Did you know, in the *entire* universe, we are the only
intelligent life forms
thought to have a Miss Universe contest?"

· "Did you know, throughout the cosmos they found intelligent
life forms that play to play.
We are the only ones that play to win." Explains why we have
more than our share
of losers.

Oh, they're pretty critical of us, but they said they had to admit
we're *way* out front
when it comes to stuff you can make with a blender.

· "Did you know what *most* distinguishes us humans from lower animals
is our desire to take drugs?"

That was for you, Tina.

Nice outfit you barely have on. How's tricks? Pun intended.

You look beautiful, Tina; you smell good. I never know what
drug you're on, but smells like you're *wearing* Opium.
Mind if I sit close?
Mind if I sit *real* close? You mind if I lay down and look up
your nose? You mind if I lay in your lap and take a nap?

T
I   All right now, Trudy, don't mess with me.
N   I am coasting on my own chemistry and I am
A   volatile, baby.

I woke up today I felt like I had had *brain surgery* done over my entire body. I'm thinkin' half the damn day, "What chemicals did I take to make me feel so wrecked?" Then I remembered, I hadn't taken *anything*.

Here I was trying to blame a drug for what it feels like to be straight.

Girl, I am seriously thinking of doing the detox trip again.
I have *never* been so
high as in detox. Those chemicals, before they leave your
.bloodstream, baby, they throw *quite* a bon voyage party.

TRUDY

My space chums are very careful what chemicals they put into their bodies.
Or to use their term, bio-container.

We were havin' a cup of coffee.
I see this strange look come over 'em.
They pointed to the label on this nondairy creamer.
They said, "*Trudy*,
this is *exactly* what we are made of."

LUD

Agnus! Turn that junk music *down*! You better learn some manners, young lady, or else . . .

AGNUS

or else WHAT, Granddaddy Speck?

MARIE

Or else people aren't gonna *like* you, honey. You do want to be *liked*, don't you, honey? Everybody wants to be liked.

AGNUS

NOT ME!
I'M DIF-FER-ENT!

LUD

Well, I can't argue with that.

MARIE	Lud, do you realize that nothing has turned out the way we planned it? Not our retirement plan. Not those Astroturf neckties. "Gonna be such a hit with sports fans, at half time." Not that cedar closet you built with *artificial* cedar. The moths just laughed. Not our patio addition out back, not our daughter, and now not our granddaughter. There's not one thing that panned out right.
LUD	You know what your problem is, Marie? Too negative. You're negative *about* ninety-two percent of the time.
MARIE	Yes, and *about* ninety-two percent of the time I am *dead* right.
LUD	Oh, hell, if you're so damn right all the time, how come we have a daughter we don't understand too good, and a pink-haired punk granddaughter got the manners of a terrorist? Leaves dirty fingerprints on the cheese? Wears somethin' makes the garage door flap up? Old man Sanders stopped me today; says he saw somethin' odd lookin' in the yard—says it was downright eerie! Worried we might have poltergeists. I had to say, "No, that wasn't no poltergeist, that was my granddaughter. She glows in the dark 'cause her necklace is a reflective flea collar." How do you think that makes me feel?
MARIE	Well, how do you think that makes *me* feel? Oh, Lud! Why didn't you just go on and let him think it was poltergeists? Well, speak of the devil! Agnus, I demand to know where you are going at this time of night looking like that!
AGNUS	YOU! WOULDN'T! WANT TO KNOW!

LUD | Young lady, you tell me where you're going
or you can march that little Day-Glo fanny back in that bedroom
and stay there till the paddy wagon comes.

AGNUS | I'm going to a gig, okay?
DON'T WAIT UP!!

MARIE | Lud, look! She has taken the candle out of my good centerpiece. I can't keep anything nice.

LUD | Well, come on to bed. You been stooped over that sewing, got eyes like two cherry tomatoes.

MARIE | You go on to bed. I'm gonna sit up here till she gets back.
Lud . . .

Remember when she was little? She'd stay over. I'd make chocolate milk,
and I'd make me a little milk mustache, and
pretend I didn't notice,
and then you'd make one and there we'd be—the two of us with little chocolate milk mustaches. Used to just tickle her to death.

You know, she's had a lot to deal with in her short lifetime.

LUD | Oh, hell. I've had *more* to deal with in my *long* lifetime. I don't take it out on the world.

MARIE | No, you take it out on *me*.
I called today—
her daddy says they've tried *everything* to get through to her.
They've washed their hands. It's in our laps now.

LUD | Well, I bet they haven't tried little milk mustaches. I'll shut that garage door. When she comes in, we'll hear it flap up.
We'll get up. Have some chocolate milk.
You and me make little milk mustaches,
see if she remembers.

✦

Onstage at the Un-Club

A
G
N
U
S

I'm getting my act together;
throwing it in your FACE.
I want to insult every member
of the human race. I'm Agnus ANGST.
I don't kiss ass
I don't say thanks.

This will be a night of sharing for the
sharing-impaired. We're all soulmates, after all,
in the vast cosmic dustbin of intergalactic space.
The universe contains at least
one hundred billion galaxies, each galaxy contains at least
one hundred billion stars, and we are
micro-SPECKS
on SPECK-ship earth.

So the fact that my
parents kicked me out of the house
and someone stole my parakeet
should mean very little in the scheme of things, but
"No, I am *quite* UPSET about IT.

T   V
V   O
     I
     C
     E

"To boldly go where no 'punk' has gone before.
Suburbia!"

A
G
N
U
S

As I was leaving to come to the Un-Club tonight,
my grandmother speck said,
"As long as you're going out, take out the trash."

I look around the room. I see her seashells shadow box and her
lima bean and split pea mosaic and decoupage
hanging over granddaddy's speck's Berkline recliner rocker, the
kind they give away on game shows.
I see her imitation Early American maple coffee table
in the shape of a
wagon wheel.
I see her salt and pepper shaker collection on the
simu–Early American knickknack shelf.
I see this wrought-iron lamppost with this
ceramic drunk
leaning against it.
I see it, but I don't believe it.
Take out the *trash*? I wanted to say,
"I wouldn't know where to begin."

TV VOICE   "And *these*
are the *days*
of our *lives*."

AGNUS   What's coming up for me is something from my own soap opera.

I look at my family,
I feel like a detached retina.

The last really deep conversation I had with my dad
was between our T-shirts. His said "Science Is Truth Found
Out." Mine said "The Truth Can Be Made Up If You Know How."

Even as a fetus, I had womb angst. Inside the amniotic sac,
the fetus has this headset
that is plugged into this DNA tape loop
that plays
over and over, auto-reverse, all the rotten things
that have happened throughout
history.

I knew the world I was coming into was liable to be a
tampered-with-Tylenol, pins-in-girl-scout-cookies, ground-
zero kind of place.

I wanted *everything* to be perfect. What's coming up for me
is my dinner.

TV VOICE   "And *these*
are the *days*
of our *lives*."

AGNUS   On the radio, I heard the weatherman say,

"The air today is unacceptable. People with breathing problems
should not go out."

I wanted to shout,
"What's unacceptable
is that the *air* is unacceptable!"
I think: Wow, breathing is a bio-hazard.

If we don't take in air every few minutes, we die,
but the air we are taking in
is killing us.

I rush to my Behavior Modification Center, hoping they can
help me
cut down on my habit
of *breathing*.

In the cubicle next to mine I hear: "Do you want to stop
drinking?"
"No."
"Do you want to stop *smoking*?"
"No."
"Do you want to stop *overeating*?"
"No. I want to stop caring
that I eat and drink and smoke too much!"

Flash: New Marketing Business Venture: Start behavior-
modification-type religion
where people can go to learn to stop caring.

(That's the music cue, you techno-nerd!
That's it, now turn up the volume, louder, louder—that's better.)

THE CANDLELIGHT SERVICE IS
ABOUT TO BEGIN
ANYONE WHO WANTS TO
IS WELCOME TO COME IN

D   B   " 'Cause you
E   O   *Light up my life.*
B   O   *You give me hope*
B   N   *To carry on.*
I   E   *You light up my days*
E   *And fill my nights*
             with song."

I want to share something vital
I just read in this self-help book
I took from the trash can
in the ladies' room at the
House of Pancakes.
Will, by G. Gordon Liddy,
Master of the Watergate caper.

My new guru.
Who, when holding his hand
over a lit candle, said,
"The trick is not to mind it."

And I don't mind it
when I first came into
this world
Elvis was already fat.

And I didn't mind it
when I heard that Ozzy Osbourne
bit the head
off a bat.

I don't mind
I was born
at the time of the crime
known as Watergate.

And must've missed out
on most things
that made America great.
But I don't mind it.

And I don't mind
no matter how much contempt
I have for society
it's nothing compared
to the contempt
society has for me.

I don't mind
that the phrase "truth in advertising"
was probably just some lie
thought up by some guy
in advertising.

I don't mind that
there's no more avant-garde
(but my mom took it pretty hard).

I used to be proud
I stuck out from the crowd
now everyone's marching
to a different drummer
what a bummer!
But *I* don't mind it.

I don't mind that I took my goldfish
and I put it in water
from the faucet
and it died;
our drinking water
caused it.

I tried my mouth-to-mouth
resuscitation skills.
My dad said, "*You* are the
daughter of a scientist;
it should've been
mouth-to-gills."
But I don't mind it.

I don't mind
each morning I get up
I feel like I want to vomit.

I don't mind that
the teenage suicide rate
is soaring
like Halley's comet.

The boy in school
that I loved the most
died last year of an overdose.
But I don't mind it.

I have set as my goal
to get so strong
I could peel onions
all day long
and never shed one tear—

I want my skin to thicken
so if I am panic-stricken
when post-nuke day gets here
I won't even feel the fear
as I watch me and the world disappear.

The trick is not to mind it—
if you're looking for peace
this is where you'll find it.

Gordon Liddy showed me the way:
I have been on
heavy metaphor maintenance
all day.

For life
is like that candle flame
and we
are like Gordon Liddy's hand
hovering
over it.

And it hurts
like hell,

but the trick

is not

A
G
N
U
S

I MIND IT!!

─────────────────────────────── **PART II** ───────────────────────────────

T
R
U
D
Y

Excuse me while I fluff up. My space chums are due any minute.

We're having drinks with Richard Leakey. Settle some questions
that we got about evolution.

They asked *me*, was man still looking for the missing link?

I told *them*, "I thought man *was* the missing link."

They think, like me:

If evolution was worth its salt,
by now it should've evolved something better than
survival of the fittest. Yeah, I told 'em I think
a better idea would be survival of the
wittiest. At least, that way,
the creatures that didn't survive could've died *laughing*.
You'd think by now evolution could've at least evolved us to the
place where we could change
ourselves.

Seems like
evolution has just kinda plateaued out,
left mankind with a middle management problem.

Or maybe evolution's got burnout. Or *maybe* evolution figures
it'll let the bio-engineers do the work for a change.

For a long time now, it appears we've been a species
on auto-snooze.

My space chums think my unique hookup with
humanity could be
evolution's awkward attempt to jump-start itself up again.

They're thinking just maybe, going crazy could be the
evolutionary process trying to hurry up mind expansion.

Maybe my mind didn't snap. Maybe it was just trying to stretch itself
into a new shape.
The cerebral cortex trying to grow a thumb of sorts.

It might seem like I got delusions of grandeur on top of
everything else, but maybe I didn't have a
breakdown—maybe I had a break*through*. Maybe
evolution's using my mind in some kind of scientific
experiment.

Sure feels like it.
But look, if I can be of service to humankind's progress, the
loss of my mind is a small price to pay.
I just think I should have been consulted.

My space chums are concerned about our evolvement
because they say we're all connected.
"Everything is part of everything."
They started talking about a little something they call
"interstellar interspecies symbiosis." To hold up my end of
the conversation, I asked them to
elaborate.

So they brought up the Quantum Inseparability Principle.
"Every particle affects every other particle everywhere."

They tried to bring quantum physics down to a level I could more clearly
misunderstand. Then one of them mentioned the Bootstrap
Theory, and at the point they got into the Superstring Theory,
frankly, I think even *they* were in over their heads.
But here's what I got from it all:

Seems like there's some kind of cosmic Krazy Glue
connecting everything to everything.

We all time-share the same atoms. "There is only one sky."
"That which is above is also in that which is below."
"What is there is also here." So said the Upanishads.

But the question remains, "Where the *hell* are the Upanishads?"
Come to think of it, I don't know where *Leakey* is, either.

Oh, here come my space chums now, late as usual.
I've been waiting for you guys. Listen, I think we'll scratch Leakey;
I'm really all you need. Besides, too many cooks spoil the soup.

Soup!

This is soup and this is art! Art! Soup! Soup! Art!

Uh-oh, thunder!
Quick, it's gonna pour! Put up your umbrella hats . . .

and follow me.

Hi, Tina. Hi, Brandy.
Keep a sharp eye out—
the fuzz is buzzin' the nabe tonight.

B
R
A
N
D
Y

Tina, Tina, hurry. Hurry, Tina, he wants you, too!

Quick, get in the backseat.

Hey. Hey, you're not a trick. What are you? A writer?
Tina, tape recorder. Another writer type.
Everybody's doing an article on
the life. You're lucky you got me; I got so many stories
you won't have to interview no one else.

Drive up Ninth.
You're the second guy this month wants to take out trade in
this bizarre fashion. Last one was more normal. He ended up
wantin' my life history
and a blowjob.

What you said before—you wasn't interested what's between my legs, huh?

Just my life history?

T
I
N
A

I got news. What's between her legs
is her life history. But me and Brandy are gettin'
out of this genital jive; we got entrepreneurial
plans . . .
telephone sex . . .
reach millions. Yeah, that's the wave of the
future. No germs and no
hand-to-hand combat. 'Cause eventually,
it could be any day now, people are not gonna want
to take the chance to go out.

When we get around the block,
let's stop for a chocolate soda;
I got the craves for something sweet.

Brandy, look at that pitiful scrawny punk kid. . . .

Hey, you skinny teenybopper punkette! Get off the streets
and go back to school!

She won't be no good at hookin', all punked out like that.
All the dudes I've talked with say the punk thing
makes 'em go limp.
And she oughta choose *one* color for her hair
and stick with it.

B
R
A
N
D
Y

What'd she call us, Tina? Some kind of "speck"?
That baby brat ain't in the life—not yet. She's just another
runaway. But in a few weeks, she'll be *all* different . . .
Ever see a stray *dog* on the streets? I can tell just like *that*
which ones will survive and which ones won't. I don't know how
I can tell but I can tell. Right, Tina?

Like there was this dog Princess, belonged to this
ol' wino dude Jim.
Delivered take-outs for this Greek place over on Eighth. Lunch
hour they put him through the ringer . . . . take this to 1650
Broadway . . . take that to the Brill . . . go here, go there . . . 'cause
everyone loves
that eggplant and grape leaves. Notorious. Him and Princess—
like Siamese twins.

Fade out, fade in. Jim gets so stressed out one lunch hour, he just
keels over in a hump like that.

T
I
N
A

You put too much stress on the human body, baby, it simply
rebels. *Tell* me about it.

B
R
A
N
D
Y

Long story short: paramedics come, they announce him dead as
a doornail, pour him into one of those plastic body bags. You
know, like a Hefty only for dead people. The paramedics quick
toss Jim in the ambulance, then run, jump in, start the motor.
Princess sees 'em moving out with Jim inside, now she freaks,
howlin' and yowlin', she all of a sudden jerks herself loose and
tears out after 'em.

Fade out, fade in. They're takin' the body bag out of the
ambulance . . . when . . .

T
I
N
A

Girl, girl, let *me* tell the rest. This dog with her bony ass,
she runs up to the body bag, she starts whinin' and scratchin'.
She gets the bag open, starts lickin' Jim's face, and
that old wino he all of a sudden pops up out the bag like an old
rusty bedspring. Well, baby, those medics just about had *heart
failure* theyselves.

B R A N D Y	But they make Jim go inside for a checkup, 'cause even though, true, he's not dead . . .
T I N A	Still he don't look all that *well*, either.
B R A N D Y	Fade in, fade out. Nobody around here ever sees Jim again. Maybe he died, maybe he didn't. None of us couldn't be sure. We didn't know his last name. Hospital's notorious for bad records, anyway, so even if *we'd* known his last name and even his mother's maiden name, the hospital might still have drawn a blank.
T I N A	Some people surmise it's *always* such a long wait, maybe he died in the waiting room. *I* am convinced what did it was being stuffed into a body bag while he was still alive. He came to, he thought: Body bag. I must be dead. And the thought that he was dead could be the very thing that killed him.
	The mind is a powerful tool. I think when something happens to somebody to that drastic extent, I think it must be astrological. Haven't you had days when things go so wrong. there's just no other explanation?
B R A N D Y	Anyway, fade out, fade in. Next day on the corner I see Princess. Shakin'. Like I never saw her before. She don't know what hit her. That's the look on her face. She just knows the wino's not there. The look they get on their face when they give up, I know. I know that look. I said to myself, "This dog is not gonna last out here." Sure enough, she didn't, and it wasn't she lacked for food, Tina, the Greeks fed her, I checked.
T I N A	Yeah, but what kind of food is that for a dog— grape leaves and baklava?

B R A N D Y	She just never kicked into that survival mode like you need to— to survive—like you and me did, Tina— you either do or you don't. Here, slow down.
T I N A	Well, don't you ever let 'em put *me* into a body bag, Brandy, unless you prepared to catch that ambulance, rip that bag open and lick my face, 'cause I don't have no pet to look out for me.
B R A N D Y	Pull over. Hey, Trudy. Trudy. Run inside Howard Johnson's, get Tina a chocolate soda, yourself fried clams. Don't get wet.
T I N A	But you know, the tune that keeps playin' over in my mind: That dog had the dumbest look on her face, but she was smart enough to know Jim was alive, which was more than you can say for us! The medics, too. And life and death is their expertise. That dog knew *some*thing about life didn't none of *us* know.
B R A N D Y	That dog. You can't say that dog knew more about life than *us*, Tina. It's just that she knew somethin' more about . . . Jim. We know about life. While you're writin' about life, we're out here on the streets living life on a gut-level basis. I could be a shrink. I should hang out a shingle. People tell me things. Forget it. Things they don't even tell to people they're close to, *especially* to people they're close to, because . . . I don't know, they'd be too embarrassed maybe, I guess, but they tell me because I swear people don't want sex so much as they want somebody who'll listen to 'em about, I don't know, their problems, you know. People don't need sex so much as they need to be listened to. People don't realize that's the secret of our business.
T I N A	Yeah, that's the first thing you learn after fellatio is how to listen.

B **R** **A** **N** **D** **Y**	Can the vulgarity! We've got a sensitive writer here. One time a bunch of us was doin' a stroll around the waterfront. This guy shows up, sensitive type, soft . . . type of guy I go for. He just wants to talk. Talks to me not like I'm a prostitute; he talks to me like I'm his . . . I don't know, sister, maybe. Fade out, fade in. Turns out he don't know what to do with his life . . . he's thinkin' maybe he'd do some hustlin', put himself through beauty school, which was an ambition he had, only where would he get the money, right? So he's askin' me would I give him some pointers on the life? You know, wise him up and all.
T **I** **N** **A**	Girl, you're too open with people. It's one thing tellin' about Jim, Jim's dead, but . . .
B **R** **A** **N** **D** **Y**	I'm not gonna tell his real name, don't worry. So we're walkin' across the pier to this bar when this car pulls up and this guy yells, "Hey, sweetie, could I get a ferry here?" I go over to the car, I come back, and the kid's standing there with this look on his face like if you was to see right before your very eyes, all at once, every sad movie that was ever made. This is the look he had. I said, "Bucci, what's wrong?" Oh, Tina . . . I said his name. Turns out he thinks the guy was makin' fun of him, see, makin' a crack, you know, "ferry"—"fairy." He was gay, and it hurt him. 'Cause inside he had a lot of unfinished business. I told him the guy really wanted directions to the Staten Island ferry—that there was no reason to feel so hurt. He starts tellin' me his whole life story. How he could never do nothin' right . . . how his macho he-man father once caught him wearin' his mom's bathing suit. And he describes the shame he felt. And I said, "Like the shame you felt just now?" And he just nodded. And I told him the only thing he should be ashamed of is being ashamed.

Yeah, I should hang out a shingle.
People's insecurities! I *tell* ya. Him on the streets? No way, I told him. He
wouldn't last three weeks. He'd go the way of Princess.

Fade out, fade in. I end up stakin' him to beauty school. The
deal, in return he pays me back when he can, which he did, and
for interest he would have to do my hair free for the rest of my
life.
My hair, don't ask. I didn't have split ends.
I had split roots. But now . . . .

here, feel, don't be shy, feel. Isn't it soft and shiny? I mean,
beauty school, it's not like he was gonna be a cardiologist,
right?

Fade in, fade out. He is now *the* top hair stylist at a
certain Fifth Avenue salon which shall be nameless, but if we
cross to
Fifth and drive by Trump's I could show it to you.

TINA Brandy, we gotta get back, meet that telephone dude.

BRANDY Oh, yeah. Listen, Bucci's real name must not be used.
Or mine.
You swear? Come on, swear.
But when you're talkin' about me, I do want to know. I know,
why don't
you call me "the girl with the exquisite hair." Then I'll
know. Pull over, we'll get out here.

Watch it gettin' out, Tina.
Don't step in that big puddle.
Ciao!

TINA Brandy, you're too open with people. If you noticed, I held back.
I'm not selling the screenplay to my life for no fifty dollars.
We could get a tape recorder.
We can be writers, too.
You don't need to know how to type no more.
We can write as good as he can write if what he's writing is
what we're talking. We should've got co-credit, or something.

When that article comes out, it's gonna say,
Written by him.

It should at least say,
Lived by Brandy and Tina.

BRANDY Tina, I forgot to ask him what magazine he's writin' for.

TINA Yeah, be just our damn luck, we could get famous and not even know it. Fade in, fade out, baby.

Howard Johnson's, Forty-Sixth and Broadway

TRUDY Chocolate soda. Side of clams. I got money. Hey, and make it snappy, Howard.

I got a big night planned for my space chums.
Should be a peak experience: violin concert, all kids.
Howard, you mind if I spread out here on the counter? I gotta get these Post-its collated. My secretary's out sick. Everywhere I look, Post-its. I got Post-its comin' out of my ear. I must collate my notes. As per usual, we came out of our last meeting more confused than ever.

They started asking me a lot of deep questions
about God, movies, you name it.

"Did Adam have a navel?" "Was it a innie or a outie?"

Let me read you some of our latest findings:

· We think Peking Man may be even more advanced than we
originally thought. Not only did we discover bones and ashes
which prove he cooked his meat, but we also found traces of
what appears to be
barbecue sauce.

· When a person dies of thirst, their eyes tear up.

· When a man gets hanged, he gets an erection, but when a
woman gets hanged, the *last* thing on her mind
is sex.

· Here's another: As soon as humankind began to discover the
truth about itself, we began to find ways
to cover up that truth. But maybe that's for the best: Our ability to
delude ourselves may be an important
survival tool.

Some of this stuff we find I'd just as soon not know. We got new
evidence as to what motivated man to walk upright: to free his
hands for masturbation.

We did some studies, Howard. We're still working on when
superficiality began showing up in human nature.
Nothin' in our studies gives us a clear picture as to the chain of
events that must've taken place.
We can only speculate. At one point, Howard,
we were hunters and gatherers and then seems like, all of a
sudden, we became
partygoers.

We speculated what it was like before we got language skills:
When we humans had our first thought, most
likely we didn't know what to think. It's hard to think
without words 'cause you haven't got a clue as to what you're
thinking. So if you think we suffer from a lack of communication
now,
think what it must've been like then, when people lived in a
verbal void—
made worse by the fact that there were no words such as
"verbal void."

They figure language happened maybe something like this.
One day man was walking along barefoot
as they did in those days, and suddenly stubbed his toe.
He said, "Ouch." Then he must've thought: Gee, I wonder what I
meant by that?
Pretty soon he felt his toe *throbbing* and he knew
the meaning of "ouch." When primitive man had his "ouch"
experience, Howard, he couldn't have known he was paving the
way years later for Helen Keller to have her "wa-wa"
experience.

I personally think we
developed language because of our deep inner need
to complain.

499

Right after we started talking to each other we began to talk
behind each other's backs. Sometimes it was vicious gossip,
other times a casual critical remark, like "Jeez, did you see
the hair on his back?" When it dawned on everybody that not
only could they talk,
but they could also be talked *about*,
primitive man began showing signs of
paranoia. With everyone so paranoid, war soon broke out.
With war came stress, and the rest is history.

My space chums are really quite concerned about the Stress
Factor we're so susceptible to. They worry about us. They even
worry more than that
actress on stage at the Plymouth Theatre.
They said to me, "Trudy, beyond any bio-force we have ever
encountered, Human Nature is the most thought-stirring, neuro-
numbing, heart-boggling of all."

They say just as the whole chemistry of the ocean
can be found in each drop of sea water,
all the profound emotional polarities of Human Nature are
crammed into each bio-container—or, to use our term, human
body.

It could be just *too* much for any one
bio-container to grapple with.

Frankly, I think *they're* showing signs of stress, too. Hard to deal
with their mood swings. Lately, I've been walking on eggs
'cause the least little thing can set 'em off on a crying jag.
I think they may be getting too emotionally involved with us.
They keep wanting me to dial-switch back to certain people so
they can see what happened to them. I think
the bonding thing might be happening.

We're *all* overworked; I just don't know how long we
can keep up this pace.
Something they said the other day gave me a pang—
makes me wonder if they're thinking of leaving here.
They said they wanted to pick up a few souvenirs and some
postcards.
So we went to some shops around Broadway, and frankly,
I was embarrassed for my species. Everything was in such
bad taste. But they understand.
They said, "Earth is a planet still in its puberty." In fact,
from their planet,
Earth looks like it has pimples.

I did have some I ♡ MANKIND T-shirts made up, but something
in their electromagnetic field caused the fabric to
demolecularize, if that's the word.

So I'm still lookin' for suitable souvenirs.
I hate to think of them going,
but frankly, all this data leaves us with more questions
than answers. It's a back-breaking task just collating all this info,
not to mention trying to make sense out of it.

Here's one that gave me pause:
"Did you know Weltschmerz exists throughout the universe?"

I turned to 'em point-blank and asked 'em,
"Okay, you've learned a lot about us
but tell me this, and be honest:
what do you think of people
as a whole?"

They said they thought it would be
a excellent idea.
Hey, Howard, when Tina comes in give her the soda and the rest
of my clams.
I must dash soon.
Almost time for the concert.
You know how I like to impress 'em with all the
miraculous stuff we humans are capable of.
Tonight we're gonna see a bunch of little kids playing
violin. If that doesn't impress 'em, I'll eat
my umbrella hat.

One peak experience coming up!
Uh-oh, irregular brain activity. Static white noise . . .

Now where am I? . . .
Reception coming in strong . . . Looks like a yard sale . . .
See boxes, price tags, toys . . . People milling around . . .
There's a woman packing up books.
She takes the last one, *Free to Be You and Me*,
and puts it into a box.
People go over, ask her questions:
Where's the top to this?
How much is this? This is cracked; what about a dollar off?
Does this work? Where's the cord to the toaster?
Is this for sale? . . .

Garage Sale, Los Angeles, 1985

L
Y
N

How could anyone accumulate so much junk?

No, I still have to go through those tapes, but everything on
this side of the yard is for sale. *Those?* Those are the twins'
Bataca encounter bats. You can have those for nothing.
And these Geraldine Ferraro buttons.
Yes, the water bed goes too. There must be a price tag
somewhere.
This? Oh, look at this.
My journal. I've been looking everywhere for it.

From Lyn's Journal, 1970, N.Y.C.

The "Women's Strike for Equality" march.
I taped all the speeches—Kate Millett, Bella Abzug—
but nothing came out clear except Betty Friedan saying:
>   "We, today . . . have learned
>   the *power* of our Sisterhood!"
And we did! I'm so glad we made the trip—even though at times
I didn't think we were going to make it in Edie's
old VW. It was worth risking our lives. I think the only thing that
kept that old junkheap moving was Edie singing
"Ain't No Mountain High Enough"
at the top of her lungs.

We've been on a high since we got here. Giddy, in fact.
But I can't wait to get back to L.A. We're going to form
a consciousness-raising group just like
thousands of women all over the country are doing.

From Lyn's Journal, 1971

I can't believe Henry Kissinger actually said
"Power is the ultimate aphrodisiac." I loved Edie's comment:
"The bombing in Vietnam shows what it takes for *him* to get it up!"
Women don't want to fight. As Marge says,
"We'd rather sit around in a circle and process."
I really feel when women get equality—
social and economic equality—
there'll be no more wars.
This is about moving the *whole* species forward,
not just half of it.

A Consciousness-Raising Group, Los Angeles, 1972

LYN Sisters! Progress report:

"Boy Scouts of America allow girls into its
Explorer Scouts division!"

EDIE *"Ain't no mountain high enough."*

LYN "Girls are appointed as Senate pages for the first time in
history!"

EDIE Make that "herstory."

LYN And oh, is this a breakthrough, or what?

Since 1920, the Big Ten has had only men in their marching
bands during football season.
This season the University of Minnesota has decided to let
women march with the men during football games.

MARGE What more could you want? *"I am Woman, hear me roar."*

LYN *"Oh, thank you, University of Minnesota. Being just a
majorette was sapping my 'woman-strength.'"*

And, Sisters, I've got a surprise.
Ms. magazine. Premier issue! Look,
I got Gloria Steinem herself to autograph them.
Here's yours, Edie, for you, Marge,
and this one is for
me.

A Neighborhood Hangout, 1973

[The jukebox: Al Green, "Let's Stay Together"]

EDIE

Let's have champagne! This is a night for celebration.
Not only did the Sisters get to watch Billy Jean
bust Bobby Riggs's chauvinistic butt
but guess what? I got a job at *The Free Press* doing my
own feature:
"Boycotts of the Month"!

MARGE

Well, it sounds like we got our own West Coast
Jill Johnston. You're lucky you got a job at that kind of place
—now you won't have to give up those
camouflage fatigues you love so much.
I mean, honey, you couldn't *be* more antiwar,
but if it weren't for army surplus
you'd have *nothing* to wear.
Lyn, I'm not exaggerating. Edie was in my plant store yesterday
in those camouflage overalls.
I almost watered her.

LYN

Okay, are you two going to rib each other all night or can we get
down to some real issues.

EDIE

I'm proud that I've never been a slave to the tyranny of
fashion trends, like you, Marge.

MARGE

Unless camouflage fatigues, political rhetoric and
boycotts of the month could be called
fashion trends.

EDIE

Marge, your problem is
your role models
were models.

LYN

Edie, you and I should only have Marge's taste in clothes.

E D I E	Oh, Marge has great taste in everything, except when it comes to men. Marge, the "Lib" in Women's Lib stands for liberation, not *libido*. I mean, what good is it, Sis, to have sexual freedom if you become a slave to it? You've got *Cosmo* damage. You should boycott those women's magazines and start reading my column.

L Y N	At least Marge has figured out from those women's magazines what shape face she has, Edie— something *I've* never been sure of.

E D I E	So she can apply makeup to overcome flaws? If your face is oval, they tell you to make it square. If it's square, they tell you to make it longer. Sometimes you make it too long and got to make it square again which was how you looked at the start only now you got a square face that's too made up where before you had a nice natural-looking square face. I don't care if I got the cheekbones of an isosceles triangle or the forehead of a Pithecanthropus. I look at myself and I don't see any flaws; that's what these consciousness-raising self-examinations are all about.

Consciousness-Raising Session

M A R G E	Okay, Edie, you say you don't see any flaws, but I'm looking at my breasts, I'm looking at Lyn's—and they do not point upwards like they're "supposed to."

L Y N	Marge, I just don't give a shit anymore.

E D I E	Hey, and mine aren't big enough to point in any direction, and I never did give a shit, and who says we need to shave under our arms? Ta-dah!

M A R G E	Oh, no! What is that—Spanish moss? How did you *manage* that much growth? I mean, the Women's Movement is still *young*.

EDIE

Your plant food, Marge . . . and a Gro-Lite.

LYN

Body hair! A sure way to tell the radicals from the
middle-of-the-roaders, like me.
*May*be I could let hair grow a few days on my legs, but under
the *arms*? Edie, you're probably on some FBI list of the
politically dangerous.

On the Phone

LYN

Edie is becoming more radical by the minute, Marge.
Today we had lunch at this restaurant. She had on a tank top, she
leaned back, and I saw one armpit as smooth-shaven as a
bathing suit model, and in the other armpit, this
shock of hair. I'm not sure *what* it meant politically,
but it *did* have visual impact.

From Lyn's Journal, 1974

I don't know what Edie wants. She thinks Marge and I are too
middle-of-the-road, and maybe we are. But I have marched and
rallied till I'm *bleary*-eyed. For Shirley Chisholm. For
Bella. I've licked so many envelopes, my tongue has paper cuts.
I'm just going to have to tell her I'm sorry about the
Jo Ann Little thing, but I promised Peter I'd go skiing and I'm
keeping that promise.
I cannot be what Edie wants and still
be all Peter needs me to be.

Edie's right when she says Peter's suppressive.
He is.
But no more so than Edie (I'd like to tell her).
Why do I always put myself in a place where I'm trying to
please people who seem impossible to please?
I saw a *Mary Tyler Moore* rerun tonight,
and I couldn't help seeing how much I'm like Mary,
and Peter is self-involved like Ted Knight,
and Edie is just like Lou Grant.
I must work on this with Dr. Stein.
Glad I finally made an appointment—only wish I'd
been in therapy *long* before now.

I guess I should tell everything, right, Doctor?
Well, Janet turned out to be a regular "Don Juanita."
She *loves* to make love, and when *she* gets tired she has an old
vibrator that heats up to such an extent I have to get up, go into
the kitchen and get an oven mitt.

She's a multimedia performance artist,
heavy into video documents. Her latest art piece,
Life Imitates the Avant-Garde,
earned her a paragraph in *Chrysalis*.

The Next Session

She's making a docu-diary of our relationship . . .
she tapes *everything*
and now she's putting me
in her performance-art pieces.

Last night she put white greasepaint on my face,
draped me in gauze veils,
put on a John Cage tape
and I had to sit in a downtown gallery
on a stack of Harvard Classics
while dazed art patrons milled around me,
cocking their heads this way and that,
whispering to each other about
what it all meant.
I said to her, "Janet, no one, including me, knows what's
going on."
But she says that was the whole point—
that *my* not knowing
and no one *else* knowing
was what it was all about.
She makes me feel so . . . so . . . *linear*.
See, her theory is if *no* one knows
what it's about, it might jolt us out of our normal
mode of perceiving,
and in having *no* information whatsoever,
we'd be forced to confront *new* information. . . .

Of course, Edie cut through it all;
she looked Janet straight in the eye and said,
"New information about what . . . ?"

I sat for forty minutes under the veils
and then Janet's little five-year-old, Agnus, came in
carrying a candle, which, for reasons known only to Janet,
was burning at both ends.
I took the candle
and that's when my veil caught on fire.
I grabbed Agnus up,
trying to protect her, but she ran away.
I swear she was worried we'd
ruined her mother's performance piece.

At the Gallery

LYN

Marge, how come no one lifted a finger to help?

MARGE

Frankly, honey, we were confused. We thought it could've been
part of the act. But I loved it. Daniel loved
it. We all *loved* it.

EDIE

Hey, Marge, let's face it, Sis, since you fell
in love with Disco Danny over there, you love
everything.

At the Therapist's

LYN

So, Doctor, we started fighting on the ski lift and Peter let
slip he didn't think a woman could make a good President and
that the feminist movement was making a monster of me.

It was the worst fight we ever had.
He said Edie was poisoning my mind.
That my CR sessions were making me conscious of everything
but his dissatisfaction with the relationship.
And he said . . . and this is what really hurt . . .
he said that I *used* to be so sexy, but now I'd even lost
my sex appeal.

I bolted off that ski lift so mad. Halfway down, I slammed
smack into a pine stump. I know he saw it, but he skied right
past me.

Okay, Doctor, but Gestalt therapy is new to me.
In this chair, I role-play Peter; in this chair, I role-play
myself right? And in that chair,
you role-play the doctor?

"Peter, I am sick of this suppressive, you-do-as-I-say macho
number you have been putting me through."

Now I'm me. No, I'm Peter. "And I'm sick of this
suppressive feminist trip you've been dumping on me."

Doctor, who said that? Is this Peter's chair?

"I'd like a *glimpse* of the nurturant female you and your
butch/rad/fem friends harp on so much. I want a woman,
not a feminist!"

"Ah ha! All it is with you is sex, sex, sex!"

"And all it is with you is sex, sex,
sexual politics! I have *had* it!"

I don't know exactly *what* happened, Doctor,
but I feel like I've just walked out on myself.

The Next Session

L
Y
N

Then, Doctor, I went to this Holly Near concert.
I saw Edie waving me over . . . she looked so *different*.

She was wearing Indian cotton drawstring pants,
Birkenstock sandals
and a "Sisters of Silkwood" T-shirt. She introduced me to her
friend Pam. She's clearly into a new phase.

And then someone very attractive came over, passing out
candles. An artist from the Woman's Building, Janet.

She was wearing Indian cotton drawstring pants,
Birkenstock sandals
and a "Lesbians Ignite" T-shirt. She'd made the candles
herself.

Not the usual phallic-shaped.

They were formed like a . . . a beautiful labia majora.

The wick, Edie pointed out,
symbolized a tampon string.

The evening took a strange turn.
Maybe it was my breakup with Peter or maybe I just felt like
widening the parameters of my sexuality.

At the Therapist's

L
Y
N

The evening ended in total chaos, Doctor.
We hear fire trucks. Suddenly firemen were everywhere.
Agnus had called them to put out the veil.
Patrons were fleeing the gallery.
Janet got the whole thing on video, including our
breakup.
And I asked her to dub me off a copy.

Two suppressive relationships in a row have put me
under a lot of stress, Doctor, and frankly, this
therapy is stressful all on its own. I'm thinking
of trying TM. It won't interfere with our sessions,
will it?

Another Session, 1975

L
Y
N

I met somebody, Doctor. . . .

I'm at the TM center in Santa Monica waiting to
get my mantra
and I meet this really great-looking guy
who's waiting to have *his* mantra checked.
He was wearing Indian cotton drawstring pants,
Birkenstock sandals
and a T-shirt that said "Whales Save Us."

I liked him right off. He has kind of a, I don't know, a post-
psychedelic air about him like somebody who
maybe in college one time had read Gurdjieff
or the Tibetan Book of the Dead
on acid.
We split to this vegetarian place nearby, the Golden Temple.
I had something that tasted like a tofu melt.
Talking with him was such a high.
He *listens* with an intensity most other people have only when
talking. Doctor, I knew he was "getting" me on so
many different levels. He could just look at me
and it was like I could feel all my
chakras opening.
I remember our exact conversation—word for word.
I felt so totally comfortable talking about myself—

I know it may not seem so to you, but it's
not something I do that easily—I mean, I find I'm
not that open with most people, not really. That's why I keep
a journal, I guess.

I told him I have a master's in Art History, but I realized too
late it didn't exactly insure my future.
So I'm getting a degree in marketing.
Out of high school,
I'd gone to art school, but somewhere along the way
I developed creative block. Then later I worked in
a gallery where they sold all this terrific art and
I realized that some people
when they develop creative block
may be doing the world a favor.

He laughed at that, then he told me he was building
a Samadhi flotation tank, that I should use it
when he finished it because it was good for creative
blocks. He invited me to his place.

I told him I'd love to another time,
but that I had my shift on the Rape Crisis Hot Line.
Then he asked about the weekend;
I told him I had my est training,
and we got up to leave.
Then the funniest thing happened—I looked down, and
realized I had picked up Bob's bag
and he'd picked up mine.
We *even* have the same taste in shoulder bags!

And I split, my heart was pounding.
The herb tea had been caffeine-free.
If it wasn't the tea, what was happening to me?

Oh, Doctor, remember, this will have to be our last session
for a while. I'm not supposed to be in therapy when I'm in est.

At the Neighborhood Hangout

LYN

Next to you, Edie, Bob is the truest feminist I've ever met.
He's the only man I've ever known who knew where he was
when Sylvia Plath died.

He has a master's in Business, but what changed his life: he
read *The Wall Street Journal* on acid.

Bob has this dream; to be a holistic
capitalist.

EDIE

Well, I'll believe this Prince Charming when I see him.

MARGE

How come I never meet a guy like that?

EDIE

Because you go to the discos instead of the TM center, Marge.

MARGE

You're right. The last guy I went to bed with, I woke up in
the morning, I practically had the imprint of his coke spoon on
my chest.

EDIE

You have "heterosexual damage," Sis. I mean, all that
Ortho-Novum is bound to seep into your bloodstream.

From Lyn's Journal, 1975

In the hallway, outside his apartment, I heard New Age music.
I smelled musk-scented candles. When he opened the door, his
face was flushed; I knew that he'd just come down from his
anti-gravity boots. . . .

We talked about est. I joked and told him
I got several things. I got whatever you get even if
you're not sure what it is you got or even that you
got it, then that's what you're *supposed* to get.

I also got that he was the kind of person I could share what I
got *with* . . . even if we weren't sharing it
in bed.

Bob showed me the Samadhi isolation tank and then I stretched
out on his water bed.

He gave me a shiatsu massage.

He knew I had seminar stiffness.

We smoked some paraquat-free Panama Red and then
we made love.

Afterwards, we talked into the night. Bob poured
out all his feelings about things that concerned him:
megavitamin therapy, solar energy, the ecosystem
and ending world hunger through tofu consciousness.

We made love again. And then stopped and had a Trail Mix
snack.

We talked till dawn, exchanging Patti Hearst theories, and then
we fell asleep.

By morning we were in love. Bob is a dream come true . . .
a New Age Ward Cleaver.

Their Wedding, 1976

MARGE

I knew that my store was the right place for the wedding, all
these plants the perfect metaphor for growth and nurturance.
Lyn, let's get some photos over here by the carrot cake. And
where's your mother?—she should
be in this. I thought she was coming from Colorado.

LYN

Mom couldn't make it. She's getting *married*
herself. Isn't that fantastic? A masseur she met at Club Med.
Can you believe it?

EDIE

Hey, but Janet's here, so we'll get a video document of the whole
thing and send it to her.

M
A
R
G
E   Edie, did you bring the contract?

Lyn, I told Edie to bring a contract like the one she has with Pam;
I want you and Bob to sign it. They've thought of everything.

Okay now,
over here by the cake.

From Lyn's Journal

Was there ever a more wonderful wedding? Marge said we made
her believe in romance again.
Edie said we looked like organic Ken and Barbie
dolls. But whatever possessed us to
go on this transformational wilderness backpacking retreat?
It was a package deal—promising
higher consciousness and body awareness through mountain
climbing and transcendental trout fishing. Money back
guaranteed; the brochure said we would find ourselves.
Not only did we *not* find *ourselves*, we lost contact with the
rest of the group and spent our wedding night in the woods
sleeping on a bed of leaves that turned out to be poison ivy.
But we couldn't ask for our money back. Between our sexual
attraction for one another
and the poison ivy,
we had never *known* such body awareness.

After the Honeymoon

L
Y
N   Whatever it is, Bob, it's the perfect wedding gift because it
comes from you. What is it?
A Geodesic Dome Home?
Kit? We have to build it ourselves?
But, Bob, you've been working on that isolation tank since before
we met
and it still leaks.

From Lyn's Journal

The look on Bob's face when I made that remark about
his Samadhi tank is still with me.
It was the first squelching thing I've ever said to him.

At the Rape Crisis Center

L
Y
N   Hey, Edie, did Marge tell you about the great new P.R. job I have
with this big new clothing chain?

Well, okay, look, I mean . . . the job itself isn't all that great
but the person I'll be working under has a great
job, so there's lots of growth potential . . .

for *him* and then for *me*, I'm sure.

[Telephone rings]

Rape Crisis Hot Line.

Oh, no.
Oh, God. I can't believe it.
We'll be there in just a few minutes.

[Redialing]

> Pam, meet us at Cedars.
> The emergency room.
> It's Marge.

A Few Weeks Later

L
Y
N

Bob, honey, Marge called and wanted to come over.
She sounded so down. Daniel's left her; I said yes. I told her we
were finishing up the house and could use her touch and to
bring a plant or two.
This area really needs something, but no matter what I do, it still
looks like the living room of a flying saucer . . .
and have you noticed when you talk with your head tilted *up*,
there's an echo . . . echo . . . echo . . .
Maybe the ceiling wasn't meant to be this high, Bob . . . Bob . . .
Bob. I bet we added the garage pieces to the ceiling by mistake.
Now all we have left for the garage are these pieces
that are supposed to be
our closet.

Oh, well, since it's new, we'll have to give the Honda Civic our
closet space. I like their politics,
but we never should have bought a home advertised in
Mother Jones.

If we can't find the Dome Owner's Manual, we'll
just have to write for another.
Oh, there's Marge. I'll let her in. Honey, you
keep working on the tank.

MARGE
For Christ's sake,
you don't need plants, you need Yosemite Park.
Hi. Bob, make me a drink, and make it a stiff one.
C'mon, you two, don't give me that look.
I've discovered a great medical cure for sobriety—
alcoholism!

But you don't have to pack me off to
Raleigh Hills treatment center quite yet. Hey, Bob, how's the
isolation tank?
You think it would help me? Hell, my whole life feels like one big
isolation tank. Okay, please, don't go to any trouble, you two;
I'll pour my own drink.

LYN
Marge, it's so ironic. I mean, that a woman as
nurturant as you could be so
self-destructive.

MARGE
I'll tell *you* what's ironic . . .
The rapist made off with my Mark Cross rape whistle.

BOB
I'm glad to see you looking so good.

LYN
The bruises are all gone.

MARGE
Yeah, the bruises *are* all gone.
Come on, let's unload the van.
Plants are gonna thrive here. They're gonna
think they died and went to heaven.

I've got japonicas, ficus, wonderful palms. Don't worry about the
tank, we'll cover it with ivy.

LYN
Thank heaven you're helping. My idea of what to do with a
room stops at throw pillows.

MARGE
All this room needs is a few decorative touches.
Like some right angles.
You two go on. I'm just gonna freshen my drink.

From Lyn's Journal

Marge is drinking more and more. Edie thinks she's doing
coke a lot and drinks to take the edge off. Whatever
it is, I'm worried.

In the Dome Home

L
Y
N

Oh, Bob, I'm so excited. I'm getting a bigger office—no
partitions, real walls and a *door*. I think Sindell is
impressed. Oh, he still thinks I'm not a good
team player, that I do things my own way, but he's less
threatened by that now,
I think. But listen, let's not talk about my promotion when Edie
and Pam get here. Edie's newspaper's been bought out by Rupert
Murdoch. Pam said she's just heartsick.
There's the bell, at least that works. Try to be nice to Edie. I don't
know what it is with you two.

Edie, you know we're both so proud of you for quitting
your job. It was the only thing to do.

E
D
I
E

Quit, shit! I didn't get to quit. They *fired* my radical ass before I
could get the satisfaction.
Now I'm back working on my book,
"What's Left of the Left."
It's gonna be a slim volume, y'all.

Hey, did you hear, Pam's pioneer work in teaching men
to cry at her sensitivity seminars earned
her a paragraph in *Psychology Today*? I brought y'all a copy.
Bob, does this tank still leak, 'cause listen, now
it squeaks, too.
Lyn, you know, you should sign up Bob for Pam's next seminar,
"Anima, Animus, Animosity."
I got to commend you, Bob: Your solar thing you're into is
admirable, but this catalogue here, "Karma-Krafts."
Some of this stuff you're selling is New Age
chotchkes. I mean, there's some worthwhile stuff
here. These Bio-Bottom diapers—that sounds
okay. But most of this stuff is just New Age kitsch,
now admit it.
Look at this—aura goggles.
Here's some pyramid salt and pepper shakers.
"Key to the Universe" key chains. Oh, and these patchouli-
scented candles—guess that covers Indian philosophy.

Bumper stickers:
"If you think you are on the path, you are lost;
this is the Hollywood Freeway." Here's one I think I'll order:
"Honk! Honk! Honk! is not a mantra."

Bob, what yellow brick path are *you* on? Trying to mix
consumerism with higher consciousness,
you're liable to have a *big* karmic debt to pay. Hell, Bob, I recall
how you used to say
how we all had to look at success in a new way
or we'd never be truly successful. I used to dig you talkin' like
that 'cause it felt like you meant it.
I thought you were one of a handful of people left who cared
about not selling out. Remember all that shit about
"only wanting to do well if you could do good"?

You'll be interested to know I'm not doing
either. Now, isn't there a Flo Kennedy lecture or something you
have to rush off to?

Bob, please stop yelling. Pam, you're the shrink. What's with
these two?

Aw, it's my fault. You know me. Pam says I get on my high horse
and stomp anything in sight. I'm sorry. Look, I've got Jiminy
Cricket damage.

She's too self-righteous for her own good, but we're
working on it.

From Lyn's Journal

I feel bad that I didn't defend Bob when Edie picked on
him. I know Edie was hurting about her job, still I
should have tried to stop her.
She says herself she only lights into people she really cares for.
It's okay that she wants us to be more than we are; I want that,
too. But sometimes it's like she wants us to be more than we
can be. I don't really try to earn her approval anymore, but her
disapproval still bothers me.

A Few Months Later, on the Phone

L
Y
N

Marge?
Guess what?
I'm pregnant!
We're thrilled!
Even though we had planned to wait.

Bob's been singing "Having My Baby" all day.
I told him, "Keep singing that and I *will* throw up.
Again."

No, I haven't told the office, it might affect my job. This
morning I threw up at a board meeting. I was sure the cat was
out of the bag, but no one seemed to think anything about it;
apparently it's quite common for people to throw up
at board meetings.

What! How great! You helped? How?

Bob, Pam and Edie are having a baby, too!
Artificial insemination. Marge says it was easy.
They used a turkey baster, and now they're just letting nature
take its course.

From Lyn's Journal

Bob and I are so happy. Pam gave us a Piaget
book we're reading to each other.
Bob is being so sweet to me. He's going to be such a good father.
And I'm going to be such a good mother.

Seven Months Later

L
Y
N

Twin boys! Honey, it must have been the water bed.

The doctor says they may both be hyperactive, but how bad could
these two little angels . . . be . . . Oh, you little tadpole!
Bob, quick—take one of them!
Honey, we have our hands full!
We can do it. We'll get superorganized; *this* time we'll
split the chores right down the middle.
We can have it all. We *already* have it all.
We just got it all at once, that's all.

One Morning at Breakfast

L
Y
N

Sweetheart, be honest—do you think I'm a good
mother? I mean, do *you* find it hard sometimes to tell the
twins apart?
Hildy says that I mix them up; of course, it's her word against
mine. We're not going to push them, but I want them to
have *all* the things we never had. Pam and Edie are already
giving Ivan violin lessons
and they're signing him up for a Tiny Tot
Transformation Seminar.

It's expensive, but let's sign up the twins.
Listen, I've got to run. Hildy will be here any minute.
Don't worry, I'm getting an assistant.
I've *asked* Sindell. Take some of the work load off.

Oh, no! Look at this—we bought the same bag again.

A Month Later, at the Office

L
Y
N

But, Bob, how could you forget that you have the twins tonight?
But you finished your sensitivity training last week. Why
would you sign up for an advanced class?
Honey, I don't think I can take you being any more *sensitive*.

Oh, I'm sorry. Listen, you're not tearing up, are you?
Look, I need this assertiveness training, Bob. I've got to
confront Sindell about that raise, and I've got to confront my
assistant, Tom.
He made a pass at me.
In front of everyone.
I think he really meant it as a put-down—
like some kind of perverse
power play. What do you think I should do? Confront him?
Let it slide? Or what?

What do you mean, "However I handle it is the way I should
handle it"?

From Lyn's Journal

I worry sometimes,
maybe Bob has gotten too much in touch with
his feminine side. Last night, I'm pretty sure,
he faked an orgasm.

Marge picked the boys up at the office today, and when she
brought them back they were wearing little Indian cotton
drawstring pants, little baby Birkenstock sandals, their
T-shirts said "Small Is Beautiful." She must've had them made.
They looked just like Bob
did when we first met. She's so crazy about the twins, but
I worry when she has them; what if she should drink
too much?
Sometimes when the twins are sleeping I look down at them and
I feel this rush of tenderness and I am amazed at the love I
feel.

And *then* they wake up!

At the Office, on Coffee Break

L
Y
N

You don't know what it's like!
Hyperactive twins!
When they turned three, my doctor prescribed Ritalin—
I wouldn't dream of giving drugs to my children,
but it does help when I take it myself.
I can't keep up with them.
At some point, they looked at one another,
realized there were two of them
and only *one* of me. Sometimes it gets so bad, I brew up some
Sleepytime herb tea, pour it over ice, serve it in Spiderman
glasses and
tell them it's a new-flavor
Kool-Aid.

I feel so guilty as I watch their little heads nod out.

Remember that rainy day last month I stayed home from the
office, sick?
They were unusually hyper. That day, I was desperate.
I said, "Do you want Mommy to teach you a new game?"

And I actually dragged them out to my car in the pouring rain,
put them in the backseat and told them,

"Stay there and play car wash."

[Everyone around the coffee machine breaks up.]

And Hildy is no help.
She lets them get away with murder.

I came home one day to find her stretched out on the floor,
motionless. I feared the worst. Suddenly, they leaped out,
jumped on Hildy, marked her earlobe with a Magic Marker.
Turns out they were playing *Wild Kingdom*,
Hildy was an elephant dying of thirst; she had to be tagged
and moved to a waterhole.

From Lyn's Journal

When I'm telling people about the twins, it suddenly
hits me how adorable they are. But when I'm actually
dealing with them, sometimes I go into such overwhelm.
I feel jittery and tired at the same time.
I wanted to be this wonderfully understanding mother—always
loving, patient.
Maybe if I cut out coffee—drink decaf and maybe some
B-complex.

I don't want Bob and the twins to look back and
remember me this way.

Funny,
I went into public relations because I have a way with people.
Just not the people I'm closest to.

My therapist told me this journal writing sometimes
relieves depression.

But it's the things that come up when I'm writing in my journal
that seem to depress me.
This morning I went to kiss the twins
goodbye, they saw Hildy coming in, left me
and ran to kiss her hello.

At the Office, on the Phone

L
Y
N

Marge, I'm so sorry to cancel lunch again.
It's been a terrible day.
I just had to fire Chrissy. Oh, it's been building up
ever since I hired her. Can you use someone
with no skills?

She gets everything confused. She got my
lunch date with an important client mixed
up with where the twins were to go for a
birthday party.

So I arrive and see my client waiting for me
outside Chuck E. Pizza-Time Theatre.

No, this weekend is out.
Sindell really wants me to do this
seminar/conference thing. I'm embarrassed to tell you:
"Woman on the Way Up." I felt insulted at first,
but it's just his way of telling me he wants me to be a corporate
clone. I know he's got bigger and better things in mind.
I can't let up now. I feel like I'm being watched every second to
see if I make
the right moves.

Oh, I know the twins would love to go,
but they've got a busier weekend than mine.

No, not tonight.
Tonight I've got Bob. Seems like we never
see each other lately unless we sign up for the same seminar.

This morning at breakfast,
I was going over my calendar.

He asked me if I was going to pencil him in
for sex
on the weekend.
How is it being back with Daniel? Is it working out?

Oh.
I'm sorry, but maybe it's for the best.

I mean, I know you say you love him,
but you haven't been happy with him.
Can't you just let him go this time without all the pain?
Oh, there's my phone. Sindell, I bet. I have to go.
Call you later. Yes, yes, I *promise*.

In the Dome Home

L
Y
N

Bob, I'm home! Honey, I'm sorry to be late.
The last lecture just went on and on. I'll try to get home early
tomorrow; I'll fix something special for dinner. Right now, I just
want to get these shoes off
and fix a drink. I don't know how I functioned before this
seminar, Bob.
I learned "desktop gardening," "office isometrics" and "power
dressing," a new fashion trend where you
wear something around the neck that looks
sort of like a scarf
and sort of like a tie
and sort of like a ruffle
and doesn't threaten anyone,
because you don't look good in it.
Look! I'm proof. Does this look like a woman on the way up?
Bob, what's wrong?

Where are you going? Your aikido class? I didn't even know you
were taking aikido.
When did you start taking aikido?

You're not mad, are you?

Later That Night, on the Phone

L
Y
N

Edie, Marge called the other day.
I can't stop worrying about her. She wanted
to take the twins someplace again. I had
to say no. Bob says he doesn't even want the twins
to be around her anymore at all. I think she knows we're cutting
her off from them.
but what can we do? She adores them, and they adore her,
bu the last time I picked them up, I found her
on the floor. I thought they were playing *Wild Kingdom* again,
but turns out she was drunk and had fallen.
We think now she's taking pills
along with everything else.

Did you know Daniel split again? He just never
got over the rape. I don't think she has, either.
And I don't know that she'll ever get over Daniel.
Could you go by tonight, see if she's okay?
Bob's just walked out in a huff, so I've got the kids, or I'd go.

Just a minute.
Come on, boys! Supper's almost ready. Settle
down. You know our agreement—if you're going to fight,
use your Bataca encounter bats.

Edie, is that little Ivan I hear playing the
violin? Amazing! I'd swear it was Isaac Stern.
I'll get him a set of Bataca bats. Bob sells them.
We better
start protecting those genius hands.
I tell you, the twins are *much* less aggressive.

Listen, if you know of someone, I need a housekeeper. I
can't afford it, but Hildy won't lift a finger to help around the
house, except for the twins. Somehow, a cluttered dome home
looks worse
than a cluttered tract house; all the clutter seems to
circle back on itself. Last week, in desperation, I
just picked up all the junk, tossed it into the
Samadhi tank, and forgot about it. That is, until
Bob started testing it, and filled the tank with water. Oh, God,
Edie, it began to overflow and out came all the stuff I'd
forgotten about.
And I'm not proud of this,
but, well, I let Bob think
the twins had done it.

If I'd known this is what it would be like to
have it all,
I might have been willing to settle
for less.

In the Dome Home

LYN

Please don't complain about the cleaning not being back;
I can't take one more complaint! I'll tell you why the cleaning's
not back.
I forgot to take it, okay? Bob, you expect too much
of me. It's one thing to be a modern housewife,
career woman, mother. I could handle being
modern. Modern is popping a frozen dinner into
the microwave, but modern isn't good enough for
you. No, I have to be organic,
holistic,
learn millet recipes,
grow wheat grass, make *beet* juice,
wait around for sourdough to rise. Well, it just so happens the
last sourdough we had wasn't sourdough—
it was Play-Doh.

Oh, the twins have a highly developed sense of humor, and *we*
didn't even notice the *difference*, Bob. So much for
conscious cooking.

And the Ecology Pageant at school. Robert wants to go as
a nuclear reactor,
McCord wants to go as the hundredth monkey.
You think I can
buy costumes like that at K Mart? No, I have
to *make* them. Edie and Pam don't sew, of course, so I told
them I'd make Ivan a Solar Energy costume—
only now he doesn't want to go as that.
He wants to go as an endangered species!

And wok cooking! You said it was fast! It *is*
fast. *What takes time*
is having to go to
Chinatown
for all those Chinese vegetables!
I'm so sick of your disappointment in me; I'm disappointed too.
I see now you're not so damn Zen, after all; you're passive-
aggressive. Somehow, we both mistook that for
spirituality.

And your acting like you've transcended your
ego is the biggest ego trip of all!

From Lyn's Journal

I don't think I've ever seen Bob so angry.
He threw things up to me:
All the times I'd been late.
All the weekends I'd been gone.
He threw things up to me I'd totally forgotten about.
He brought up that time I let the clothes pile up for so long,
by the time I got around to it, the twins had outgrown the
ironing.

It's clear what Bob and I both need:
a *wife*!

Two Phone Calls

L
Y
N

I had no idea they'd taken the bats to school with
them. Believe me, it will *not* happen again.

Look, just give me a *list* of the damage and I will
pay for it.

I'm sorry, I'm raising two Darth Vaders.

[The other call]

L
Y
N

Oh, Bob, something terrible.
Marge is dead!
She's hanged herself.
They found her hanging from a macramé planter.
What do you mean, *how?*
I guess she took the plant *out* and put her *head* in!
Oh, Bob, if only I hadn't put off seeing her; I shouldn't have cut
her off from the twins.

From Lyn's Journal, 1982

I knew she was in pain. How could I have thought I was getting
through to her when all I did was nag and criticize, and when
that didn't work, I just withdrew. Bob said I did all I could to help
her, but I have to face the fact it's not true.

We had a memorial service at her store.
We cried and then we got stoned on her sinsemilla.
Then we laughed until we cried again.

Janet was there. I asked about Agnus. She told
me that she'd lost custody, that Agnus had been
living with her father and his new wife, but had
run away. The look on her face when she talked
about Agnus. I can't stop thinking about it—
all those missing children you hear so much about. To
think now Agnus is one of them.

I felt so grateful for Bob and the kids. From now on,
I will be *Mega*-Mom,
Wonder
Working
Woman,
Willing Wife.

I will even be the Total Woman . . .
at least for a night or two.
I don't want us to lose
what we have.

A Few Months Later, at the Office

L
Y
N

Oh, Edie, I can't go to the conference this weekend.
I've got to finish this campaign.

[Office buzzer]

Hear that?
Just a second.

I told you to tell Sindell I will be there in
a moment.

[Back with Edie]

Look, I'll write a check right now. How should I make it out?
Oh, I can't find my checkbook—oh, no wonder, I've got Bob's bag
again . . .
uh, look, I'll call you later.

[Office buzzer buzzes again and again]

Tell Sindell I'll be right in.

I really have to say to you I was sure you were
thinking of me for that promotion. I mean, for you
to hire someone from outside the company
to do a job you *know* I can do because I have been
doing it . . . *and* my own job . . .

But I'm really glad it's all out in the open.
You've been holding out this new position, making me try to
prove myself to you
over and over again by outperforming everybody else,
staying late, taking work home . . .

Later That Night

L
Y
N

I wanted to take the scarf-ruffle-tie thing from
around my neck
and *strangle* him.
I had no choice but to quit.

I'ts been a *great* day, Bob . . . oh, by the way, here—
I took your bag again today, by mistake.

I tore up the letter, if that's what you're looking for.

How could I not have known you were involved with someone. I
can't believe it. How long?

Who is it? Some horny herbalist?
Is it that checkout girl at the Health-Mart?

All those nights you were gone . . . I should've known
you couldn't have that many
aikido classes each week.
Who is it?!

Your aikido instructor?

Oh, I can just imagine what she's like.
If she knows aikido,
she probably knows the *Kamasutra*.
You're probably having this great tantric sex thing.
Are you?

I'm sure she's *more evolved* than I am, isn't she? *More
centered!* Isn't that their big thing, centeredness?

She probably has time to make good money *and* to meditate.

Don't *tell* me her tofu tastes like lasagna. She knows what
shape face she has and where she's going
and how to get there
neatly.

If only I'd been taking karate classes; I would love for these
hands to be *weapons*!

Feel free to interrupt me at any time.

From Lyn's Journal

How could I not have known?
All those disagreements, irritations, misunderstandings,
expectations, disappointments, complaints—always
unresolved. Where did I think all this would lead?
I can forgive Bob;
it's harder to forgive myself. I could change my thinking
and decide to release it. I could change myself, but I can't
change the fact
that Bob really *is* involved.

At the Doctor's

L
Y
N

You're sure, Doctor?
Premenstrual syndrome?
I mean, I'm getting divorced.
My mother's getting divorced.
I'm raising twin boys.
I have a lot of job pressure—
I've got to find one.
The ERA didn't pass,
not long ago I lost a very dear friend, and . . . and
my husband is involved . . .
not just involved, but in love, I'm afraid . . . with this
woman . . .
who's quite a bit younger than I am.

And you *think* it's my *period*
and *not* my life?

The Old Hangout

[The jukebox: Tina Turner, "Let's Stay Together"]

E
D
I
E

Promise me you won't cry at what I've got to tell you.
'Cause if *you* do, *I* will,
and you know what an ugly sight *that* is.
Pam and I are moving to New York. Ivan
got that violin scholarship, and Pam's got a good offer—new
magazine they're starting, *Today's Mind.*
They want Pam on the staff. And me? I got stuff cooking there;
Bella may run again.
We got Janet's loft while she's away on some worldwide tour
with that damn art piece of hers.
Now she calls it "A Get-Well Card to the Avant-Garde."
I hear she does that part under the veil herself. Yeah, Ivan's
gonna play a solo with that Suzuki group of kids at Carnegie
Hall. Can you believe that turkey-baster kid is a prodigy? I
knew we had something special when he was born on
Thanksgiving.
He cries about leaving the twins; they've been his good
buddies. Ah, you know how those bullies at school gang up on
him, playing the violin the way he does.
Got one green eye, one blue.
Got two mommies and no daddy.
Pam and I should never have gone to that
PTA meeting together.
But anybody picked on him, those twins were like two little

Charlie Bronsons with Bataca bats.
So what about you?
You're back in the work farce, huh?

L
Y
N

Import/export. I'm a partner, Edie.
They put in all the money
and I put in all my time.

We import ethnic clothing, mostly from South
America. And no, don't say it; I don't think we're exploiting
cheap labor, so much as I think we're giving work to people
who would be out of work . . .
if *we* weren't exploiting cheap labor.
Oh, Edie, I know what you're thinking, but
it's hard to be politically conscious and upwardly mobile
at the same time.

How naive. To think there was a time when we actually thought
we were going to change the system. And all the time . . .

From Lyn's Journal, August 1984

Bob and I told the twins
that since we'd be seeing them at different times,
they'd have twice as much "quality time." But
they didn't buy it.
All I can think of is all
the mistakes I've made
and is this divorce going to be
another one.

I called Edie tonight during the nomination.
We stayed on the phone together.

When we heard "Ladies and gentlemen of the
convention, my name is
Geraldine Ferraro,"
we cried. Earlier, when the newscaster
on ABC had said,
"She's kept her maiden name,
not for any feminist reason,
but because she feels she owes
her mother so much,"
we laughed.

I thought to myself: There was a time when Edie
wouldn't have laughed at that.
It was so good to hear her voice.
I must remember to send Ivan a telegram
about his concert at Carnegie Hall.

With Bob at the Lawyer's

L
Y
N

I took the boys to see Santa Claus. When Santa Claus asked
Robert what he wanted for Christmas, Robert said,
"A nuclear freeze."
And then McCord yanked Santa's beard off and said,
"What animal got killed for this?"
I knew you'd be proud.

I mean, for a kid that age to have the spirit to confront Santa
Claus on what he thought was a *moral* issue . . . Well . . .

Maybe we did *some* things right, after all.

Back at the Garage Sale

L
Y
N

Yes, there *is* something odd-looking about a garage sale outside a
dome home. Especially when it's in your closet.

Yes, everything goes, even the house. Look, over there we still
have the boxes that it *came* in.

This? This is a Samadhi flotation tank. It leaks. But, look,
it makes a wonderful . . . storage bin. It's a little hard to open now,
because of all that ivy growing over the door.
Yes, everything inside goes.
Oh, except this—
this old autographed copy of *Ms.* magazine . . .
and this T-shirt,
"Whales Save Us."
I'm keeping these.

What a concert!
We've been having an electromagnetic
field day.
Pun intended.

Just listen . . . amazing . . . in my head, I can still hear
that violin concert.
What *is* it in our brains that lets us recall the music
after it's over? Why is it when we hear certain music
we get a lump in our throat? My space chums wonder how come
we don't get the lump in our ear. They're impressed with
our ability to get lumps in the throat. Apparently, we're
unique in that respect. They wanted to know if it felt
anything like goose bumps. I said, "You never felt goose bumps,
either?" They said, "No." They asked me to explain goose bumps—
do they come from the heart?
Do they come from the soul? Do they come from the brain?
Or do they come from
geese?
This set us waxing philosophic! All this searching. All these
trances, all this data, and all we *really* know is
how *little* we know about what it *all* means. Plus, there's the
added question of what it *means* to *know* something.
Scientists say for every deep truth discovered, the opposite is also
true. So when we get the feeling we're going around in circles—
no wonder, we *are*!
They said, "Trudy, we see now, intelligence is just the tip
of the iceberg. The more you know,
the less knowing the *meaning* of things means.
So *forget* the meaning of life."
I didn't tell them, of course,
I had.
See, it's not so much *what* we know,
but *how* we know, and what
it is about us that *needs* to know.

The intriguing part: Of all the things we've learned, we still
haven't learned
where did this desire to *want* to know *come from*?
Oh, don't look at me. This is the way they *talk*.

We know a lot about the beginnings of life. Bio-genesis.
But so what? What's more impressive is that from bio-genesis
evolved life forms intelligent enough to think up a word like
"bio-genesis."

So no matter how much we know, there's more to knowing than
we could ever know.

Sir Isaac Newton . . . secretly admitted to some friends: He
understood how gravity *behaved*, but not how it *worked*!

The operative word here is what?
Apple!
Who said "Soup"?

We're thinking maybe the secrets about life we don't understand
are the "cosmic carrots" in front of our noses that keep us going.
So maybe we should stop trying to figure out the *meaning* of
life and sit back and enjoy
the *mystery* of life.
The operative word
here is what?
Mystery!
Not meaning.

This should be comforting, especially to those who think life is
meaningless. It just might *be*, which could explain
why we have so many
meaningless things in our lives.

And yet, if life is *meaningless*—
this is the greatest *mystery* of all!

Even this feeling we get in the pit of our stomach
when we contemplate how meaningless it all seems
is part of the mystery.

And the more meaningless,
then the greater the mystery.

But if all this is meaningless, then why the hell bring up
the subject? If *life* is meaningless, this *discussion* is even
more so.

This is so *typical* of what I *do*.
I feel like a mammalian-brained lunkhead.
We thought about all this, but not for long,
because no matter how expanded your mind gets,
your span of concentration remains
as short as ever.

Next, they insisted I take them somewhere
so they could get goose bumps. They were dying to see
what it was like.

I decided maybe we should take in a play.
I got goose bumps once that way.
So we headed back toward Shubert Alley.

On the way to the play, we stopped to look at the stars.
And as usual,
I felt in awe.
And then I felt even deeper in awe at this capacity we have to be
in awe about something.

Then I became even more awestruck
at the thought that I was,
in some small way,
a part of that
which I was in awe about.

And this feeling went on
and on
and on. . . .
My space chums got a word for it:
"awe infinitum."

Because at the point you can comprehend how
incomprehensible it all is,
You're about as smart as you need to be.

Suddenly I burst into song:
"*Awe,*
sweet mystery of life,
at last I've found thee."

And I felt so good inside
and my heart felt so full,
I decided I would set time aside each day to do
awe-robics.

Because at the moment you are most in awe of all there is
about life that you don't understand,
you are closer to understanding it all
than at any other time.

K
A
T
E Oh, Lonnie, you look drenched, but doesn't the rain feel good?
I've had the most extraordinary evening.
Waiter, two brandies.
Since I've seen you, so much has happened
I feel like a new person.

No, it's not my new fingertip.

Good, though, isn't it?

No, this evening, first this little boy played the violin—
absolute genius!

Before I forget, here's that article I had Xeroxed for you—all
about boredom, remember?

Oh, no, no, no, no. Sorry, that's not it. That's my suicide note.

Well, not *my* suicide note . . .
It's one I've been keeping because,
well, I found it,
and I haven't been able to throw it away, because . . .
well, I don't know exactly, it's the strangest effect. . . .
Where shall I start?

When I was in L.A. I found this suicide note in the
street where my exercise class is. I don't know why I
picked it up. You know, it's more my nature to step *over*
things.

But something compelled me. . . .

I thought
it could be a sign.
Lately, I seem to look for signs; the closer I get to
menopause, the more metaphysical I'm becoming.

I had no idea who it belonged to. *Anyone* living in *that*
neighborhood had *reason* to want to end it all. I couldn't
bring myself to throw it away. There should be a
service one could use in cases like this, but there isn't.

I was saddened by what she said in the note—
but I felt even worse when I realized that losing the
note could only *add* to her feelings of low self-esteem.
Further evidence she could never do
anything right. I should
imagine there's only one thing more depressing than writing a
suicide note,
and that's *losing* the one you've just written.

For a while, I kept it in my wallet. And then I grew concerned.
Well, supposing I got hit by a car, or, in that neighborhood, a
beer bottle, I go unconscious, the paramedics come, they
discover the note, they think it's mine and they give it to
Freddie.

Well, it would seem very strange that I just happened to be
carrying someone else's suicide note.

So I started keeping it at home.
In one of those fireproof boxes with my important papers. Then
the thought, again, what if something happened?

The note would be discovered and be given great importance
because it was with my important papers.

So I began moving it around the house.
Lonnie, I am becoming so forgetful. I was so afraid I would
misplace it. So I wrote myself a note telling me where I'd put
it.

Now I had the suicide note *and* the note telling me *where* the
suicide note was hidden.
So I have decided it is best kept in my purse. But don't worry—
I've written a note explaining the whole business.

Go ahead and say it: I am *possessed*. What is it about this
phantom person that is so compelling?
She seemed so fragile and yet courageous, too. Ironically,
there is in this suicide note more feeling, more forgiveness,
more capacity for life . . .
Whatever this person is, or was, she was *not* jaded. She was
not bored. Her only real complaint was something she called
"false hopes."
If she ever *did* commit suicide, it would be out of feeling too
much—not too little.

There's hardly a trace of bitterness or petty *anything*. That's
really something, don't you think?
I mean, in writing a suicide note, the *real* person must come
out.

There was nothing dramatic—
no big tragedy,
no terminal illness—
it seems, just,
a lifetime of being . . .

dismissed . . . by everyone, apparently . . .
except me.

Lonnie, this experience has had such an effect on me. Made me
aware of just how closed off I've been to people's suffering,
even my own.

This evening, after the concert, I saw these two prostitutes on the corner . . . talking with this street crazy, this bag lady. And I actually stopped to watch them. Even though it had begun to rain.

And I remembered something I think it was Kafka wrote about having been filled with a sense of endless astonishment at simply seeing a group of people cheerfully assembled.

I saw this young man go up, obviously from out of town, and he asked them, "How do I get to Carnegie Hall?" And the bag lady said, "Practice!" And we caught each other's eyes—the prostitutes, the bag lady, the young man and I. We all burst out laughing.

There we were, laughing together, in the pouring rain, and then the bag lady did the dearest thing— she offered me her umbrella hat.

She said that I needed it more than she did, because one side of my hair was beginning to shrink.

And, Lonnie, I did the strangest thing.

I took it!

Hey, what's this?

"Dear Trudy, thanks for making our stay here so jam-packed and fun-filled. Sorry to abort our mission—it is not over, just temporarily scrapped.

We have orders to go to a higher bio-vibrational plane.

Just wanted you to know, the neurochemical imprints of our cardiocortical experiences here on earth will remain with us always, but what we take with us into space that we cherish the most is the 'goose bump' experience."

Did I tell you what happened at the play? We were at the back of the theater, standing there in the dark, all of a sudden I feel one of 'em tug my sleeve, whispers, "Trudy, look." I said, "Yeah, goose bumps. You definitely got goose bumps. You really like the play that much?" They said it wasn't the play gave 'em goose bumps, it was the audience.

I forgot to tell 'em to watch the play; they'd been watching
the *audience*!

Yeah, to see a group of strangers sitting together in the dark,
laughing and crying about the same things . . . that just knocked
'em out.
They said, "Trudy,
the play was soup . . .
the audience . . .
art."

So they're taking goose bumps
home with 'em.
Goose bumps!
Quite a souvenir.

I like to think of them out there
in the dark, watching us.
Sometimes we'll do something and they'll laugh.
Sometimes we'll do something and they'll cry.
And maybe one day we'll do something so magnificent,
everyone in the universe will get
goose bumps.

11

JOE TURNER'S COME AND GONE

August Wilson • 1988

THE 1980S AND 1990S HAVE SEEN A FLOOD OF IM-
portant American playwrights, but none has dominated the field as has August Wilson, who in less
than a decade has received five Tony award nomi-
nations (for five different plays) and two Pulitzer
Prizes, as well as enormous critical and public ac-
claim. He is unquestionably the finest African-
American playwright of his time, and by most accounts the best American playwright as well.

Born of an interracial couple in Pittsburgh,
Pennsylvania, in 1945, and earning a modest reputation as a poet in the 1970s, Wilson began his remarkable rise as a dramatist when his work came
to the attention of Lloyd Richards, director of the
Eugene O'Neill Theatre Center in Waterford, Con-
necticut, in 1981. Richards, who was already a major figure in the American theatre (he had directed
Lorraine Hansberry's *A Raisin in the Sun*, an ep-
ochal African-American work, in 1959), quickly
saw Wilson's writing potential and encouraged it;
in the ensuing ten years Richards directed (first at
the Yale Repertory Theatre, and subsequently on

Broadway and on national tours) the astonishing
series of five prize-winning Wilson plays: *Ma Rain-
ey's Black Bottom, Fences, Joe Turner's Come and
Gone, The Piano Lesson,* and *Two Trains Running.* In
combination, these plays—outstanding just by
themselves—comprise a series of works that detail
African-American experiences and travails, decade by decade, since the beginning of the twentieth century.

Wilson's commitment to explore African-
American culture is both political and aesthetic.
He is not interested in postulating abstract theories, synthesizing the races, or glossing over real
cultural differences (and cultural glories): "I find in
black life a very elegant kind of logical language,
based on the logical order of things," he says. A
poet still, Wilson blends language, action, and social observations into a richly textured and profound drama.

Like most of Wilson's plays, *Joe Turner's Come
and Gone* portrays characters living in a tender
equilibrium of two worlds: theirs is a pragmatic,

commercial, white-ruled "America" lying opposite and parallel to a spiritual black world, still nourished by African roots. Dustpans, sheet metal, and a $2-a-week boardinghouse on the one hand; people finders, shiny men, bones people, and binding songs on the other. Wilson's characters virtually straddle the hyphen of the term "African-American," they struggle in the latter world, but get their sustenance from the former. "*Bertha moves about the kitchen as though blessing it . . . It is a dance and demonstration of her own magic, her own remedy that is centuries old and to which she is connected by the muscles of her heart and the blood's memory,*" says Wilson in a memorable stage direction. What is remarkable (and enlightening) is that Wilson's two worlds are not locked in mortal conflict; straddling the hyphen, for most of his characters, can be joyous as well as scary. Bertha's dance, Wilson goes on to show, results in "*a near-hysterical laughter that is a celebration of life, both its pain and its blessing.*" And this act of celebration is at the core of all Wilson's plays, most notably this one.

Joe Turner is not a lighthearted work. It is a virtual disquisition on black slavery and its aftermaths, on oppression and disenfranchisement, and it describes events—and in fact they are *real* events—of unspeakable cruelty. But Wilson's theme is redemption, not retribution. Wilson's efforts are those of the classic tragedians: to purge evil through the therapeutic abrasion of cruelty. To cleanse the soul with blood, and to bind the wounds with ritual song. *Joe Turner's Come and Gone* is fashioned on grand lines, somewhat parallel to Shakespeare's late redemptive plays: *The Winter's Tale* (which in the last scene *Joe Turner* resembles) and *The Tempest*. The play you are about to read is an American tragedy of the highest order.

❖ JOE TURNER'S COME AND GONE ❖

———— CAST OF CHARACTERS ————

SETH HOLLY, owner of the boardinghouse

BERTHA HOLLY, his wife

BYNUM WALKER, a rootworker

RUTHERFORD SELIG, a peddler

JEREMY FURLOW, a resident

HERALD LOOMIS, a resident

ZONIA LOOMIS, his daughter

MATTIE CAMPBELL, a resident

REUBEN SCOTT, boy who lives next door

MOLLY CUNNINGHAM, a resident

MARTHA LOOMIS, Herald Loomis's wife

———— SETTING ————

August, 1911. A boardinghouse in Pittsburgh. At right is a kitchen. Two doors open off the kitchen. One leads to the outhouse and Seth's workshop. The other to Seth's, and Bertha's bedroom. At left is a parlor. The front door opens into the parlor, which gives access to the stairs leading to the upstairs rooms.

There is a small outside playing area.

———— THE PLAY ————

It is August in Pittsburgh, 1911. The sun falls out of heaven like a stone. The fires of the steel mill rage with a combined sense of industry and progress. Barges loaded with coal and iron ore trudge up the river to the mill towns that dot the Monongahela and return with fresh, hard, gleaming steel. The city flexes its muscles. Men throw countless bridges across the rivers, lay roads and carve tunnels through the hills sprouting with houses.

From the deep and the near South the sons and daughters of newly freed African slaves wander into the city. Isolated, cut off from memory, having forgotten the names of the gods and only guessing at their faces, they arrive dazed and stunned, their heart kicking in their chest with a song worth singing. They arrive carrying Bibles and guitars, their pockets lined with dust and fresh hope, marked men and women seeking to scrape from the narrow, crooked cobbles and the fiery blasts of the coke furnace a way of bludgeoning and shaping the malleable parts of themselves into a new identity as free men of definite and sincere worth.

Foreigners in a strange land, they carry as part and parcel of their baggage a long line of separation and dispersement which informs their sensibilities and marks their conduct as they search for ways to reconnect, to reassemble, to give clear and luminous meaning to the song which is both a wail and a yelp of joy.

———— ACT ONE ————

Scene One

The lights come up on the kitchen. Bertha busies herself with breakfast preparations. Seth stands looking out the window at Bynum in the yard. Seth is in his early fifties.

Born of Northern free parents, a skilled craftsman, and owner of the boardinghouse, he has a stability that none of the other characters have. Bertha is five years his junior. Married for over twenty-five years, she has learned how to negotiate around Seth's apparent orneriness.

SETH

[At the window, laughing.] If that ain't the damndest thing I seen. Look here, Bertha.

BERTHA

I done seen Bynum out there with them pigeons before.

SETH

Naw . . . naw . . . look at this. That pigeon flopped out of Bynum's hand and he about to have a fit.

[Bertha crosses over to the window.]

He down there on his hands and knees behind that bush looking all over for that pigeon and it on the other side of the yard. See it over there?

BERTHA

Come on and get your breakfast and leave that man alone.

SETH

Look at him . . . he still looking. He ain't seen it yet. All that old mumbo jumbo nonsense. I don't know why I put up with it.

BERTHA

You don't say nothing when he bless the house.

SETH

I just go along with that 'cause of you. You around here sprinkling salt all over the place . . . got pennies lined up across the threshold . . . all that heebie-jeebie stuff. I just put up with that 'cause of you. I don't pay that kind of stuff no mind. And you going down there to the church and wanna come home and sprinkle salt all over the place.

BERTHA

It don't hurt none. I can't say if it help . . . but it don't hurt none.

SETH

Look at him. He done found that pigeon and now he's talking to it.

BERTHA

These biscuits be ready in a minute.

SETH

He done drew a big circle with that stick and now he's dancing around. I know he'd better not . . .

[Seth bolts from the window and rushes to the back door.]

Hey, Bynum! Don't be hopping around stepping in my vegetables.

Hey, Bynum . . . Watch where you stepping!

BERTHA

Seth, leave that man alone.

SETH

[Coming back into the house.] I don't care how much he be dancing around . . . just don't be stepping in my vegetables. Man got my garden all messed up now . . . planting them weeds out there . . . burying them pigeons and whatnot.

BERTHA

Bynum don't bother nobody. He ain't even thinking about your vegetables.

SETH

I know he ain't! That's why he out there stepping on them.

BERTHA

What Mr. Johnson say down there?

SETH

I told him if I had the tools I could go out here and find me four or five fellows and open up my own shop instead of working for Mr. Olowski. Get me four or five fellows and teach them how to make pots and pans. One man making ten pots is five men making fifty. He told me he'd think about it.

BERTHA

Well, maybe he'll come to see it your way.

SETH

He wanted me to sign over the house to him. You know what I thought of that idea.

BERTHA

He'll come to see you're right.

SETH

I'm going up and talk to Sam Green. There's more than one way to skin a cat. I'm going up and talk to him. See if he got more sense than Mr. Johnson. I can't get nowhere working for Mr. Olowski and selling Selig five or six pots on the side. I'm going up and see Sam Green. See if he loan me the money.

[Seth crosses back to the window.]

Now he got that cup. He done killed that pigeon and now he's putting its blood in that little cup. I believe he drink that blood.

BERTHA

Seth Holly, what is wrong with you this morning? Come on and get your breakfast so you can go to bed. You know Bynum don't be drinking no pigeon blood.

SETH

I don't know what he do.

BERTHA

Well, watch him, then. He's gonna dig a little hole and bury that pigeon. Then he's gonna pray over that blood . . . pour it on top . . . mark out his circle and come on into the house.

SETH

That's what he doing . . . he pouring that blood on top.

BERTHA

When they gonna put you back working daytime? Told me two months ago he was gonna put you back working daytime.

SETH

That's what Mr. Olowski told me. I got to wait till he say when. He tell me what to do. I don't tell him. Drive me crazy to speculate on the man's wishes when he don't know what he want to do himself.

BERTHA

Well, I wish he go ahead and put you back working daytime. This working all hours of the night don't make no sense.

SETH

It don't make no sense for that boy to run out of here and get drunk so they lock him up either.

BERTHA

Who? Who they got locked up for being drunk?

SETH

That boy that's staying upstairs . . . Jeremy. I stopped down there on Logan Street on my way home from work and one of the fellows told me about it. Say he seen it when they arrested him.

BERTHA

I was wondering why I ain't seen him this morning.

SETH

You know I don't put up with that. I told him when he came . . .

[Bynum enters from the yard carrying some plants. He is a short, round man in his early sixties. A conjure man, or rootworker, he gives the impression of always being in control of everything. Nothing ever bothers him. He seems to be lost in a world of his own making and to swallow any adversity or interference with his grand design.]

What you doing bringing them weeds in my house? Out there stepping on my vegetables and now wanna carry them weeds in my house.

BYNUM

Morning, Seth. Morning, Sister Bertha.

SETH

Messing up my garden growing them things out there. I ought to go out there and pull up all them weeds.

BERTHA

Some gal was by here to see you this morning, Bynum. You was out there in the yard . . . I told her to come back later.

BYNUM

[To Seth.] You look sick. What's the matter, you ain't eating right?

SETH

What if I was sick? You ain't getting near me with none of that stuff.

[Bertha sets a plate of biscuits on the table.]

BYNUM

My . . . my . . . Bertha, your biscuits getting fatter and fatter.

[Bynum takes a biscuit and begins to eat.]

Where Jeremy? I don't see him around this morning. He usually be around riffing and raffing on Saturday morning.

SETH

I know where he at. I know just where he at. They got him down there in the jail. Getting drunk and acting a fool. He down there where he belong with all that foolishness.

BYNUM

Mr. Piney's boys got him, huh? They ain't gonna do nothing but hold on to him for a little while. He's gonna be back here hungrier than a mule directly.

SETH

I don't go for all that carrying on and such. This is a respectable house. I don't have no drunkards or fools around here.

BYNUM

That boy got a lot of country in him. He ain't been up here but two weeks. It's gonna take a while before he can work that country out of him.

SETH

These niggers coming up here with that old backward country style of living. It's hard enough now without all that ignorant kind of acting. Ever since slavery got over with there ain't been nothing but foolish-acting niggers. Word get out they need men to work in the mill and put in these roads . . . and niggers drop everything and head North looking for freedom. They don't know the white fellows looking too. White fellows coming from all over the world. White fellow come over and in six months got more than what I got. But these niggers keep on coming. Walking . . . riding . . . carrying their Bibles. That boy done carried a guitar all the way from North Carolina. What he gonna find out? What he gonna do with that guitar? This the city.

[There is a knock on the door.]

Niggers coming up here from the backwoods . . . coming up here from the country carrying Bibles and guitars looking for freedom. They got a rude awakening.

[Seth goes to answer the door. Rutherford Selig enters. About Seth's age, he is a thin white man with greasy hair. A peddler, he supplies Seth with the raw materials to make pots and pans which he then peddles door to door in the mill towns along the river. He keeps a list of his customers as they move about and is known in the various communities as the People Finder. He carries squares of sheet metal under his arm.]

Ho! Forgot you was coming today. Come on in.

BYNUM

If it ain't Rutherford Selig . . . the People Finder himself.

SELIG

What say there, Bynum?

BYNUM

I say about my shiny man. You got to tell me something. I done give you my dollar . . . I'm looking to get a report.

SELIG

I got eight here, Seth.

SETH

[Taking the sheet metal.] What is this? What you giving me here? What I'm gonna do with this?

SELIG

I need some dustpans. Everybody asking me about dustpans.

SETH

Gonna cost you fifteen cents apiece. And ten cents to put a handle on them.

SELIG

I'll give you twenty cents apiece with the handles.

SETH

Alright. But I ain't gonna give you but fifteen cents for the sheet metal.

SELIG

It's twenty-five cents apiece for the metal. That's what we agreed on.

SETH

This low-grade sheet metal. They ain't worth but a dime. I'm doing you a favor giving you fifteen cents. You know this metal ain't worth no twenty-five cents. Don't come talking that twenty-five cent stuff to me over no low-grade sheet metal.

SELIG

Alright, fifteen cents apiece. Just make me some dustpans out of them.

[Seth exits with the sheet metal out the back door.]

BERTHA

Sit on down there, Selig. Get you a cup of coffee and a biscuit.

BYNUM

Where you coming from this time?

SELIG

I been upriver. All along the Monongahela. Past Rankin and all up around Little Washington.

BYNUM

Did you find anybody?

SELIG

I found Sadie Jackson up in Braddock. Her mother's staying down there in Scotchbottom say she hadn't heard from her and she didn't know where she was at. I found her up in Braddock on Enoch Street. She bought a frying pan from me.

BYNUM

You around here finding everybody how come you ain't found my shiny man?

SELIG

The only shiny man I saw was the Nigras working on the road gang with the sweat glistening on them.

BYNUM

Naw, you'd be able to tell this fellow. He shine like new money.

SELIG

Well, I done told you I can't find nobody without a name.

BERTHA

Here go one of these hot biscuits, Selig.

BYNUM

This fellow don't have no name. I call him John 'cause it was up around Johnstown where I seen him. I ain't even so sure he's one special fellow. That shine could pass on to anybody. He could be anybody shining.

SELIG

Well, what's he look like besides being shiny? There's lots of shiny Nigras.

BYNUM

He's just a man I seen out on the road. He ain't had no special look. Just a man walking toward me on the road. He come up and asked me which way the road went. I told him everything I knew about the road, where it went and all, and he asked me did I have anything to eat 'cause he was hungry. Say he ain't had nothing to eat in three days. Well, I never be out there on the road without a piece of dried meat. Or an orange or an apple. So I give this fellow an orange. He take and eat that orange and told me to come and go along the road a little ways with him, that he had something he wanted to show me. He had a look about him made me wanna go with him, see what he gonna show me.

We walked on a bit and it's getting kind of far from where I met him when it come up on me all of a sudden, we wasn't going the way he had come from, we

was going back my way. Since he said he ain't knew nothing about the road, I asked him about this. He say he had a voice inside him telling him which way to go and if I come and go along with him he was gonna show me the Secret of Life. Quite naturally I followed him. A fellow that's gonna show you the Secret of Life ain't to be taken lightly. We get near this bend in the road . . .

[Seth enters with an assortment of pots.]

SETH

I got six here, Selig.

SELIG

Wait a minute, Seth. Bynum's telling me about the secret of life. Go ahead, Bynum. I wanna hear this.

[Seth sets the pots down and exits out the back.]

BYNUM

We get near this bend in the road and he told me to hold out my hands. Then he rubbed them together with his and I looked down and see they got blood on them. Told me to take and rub it all over me . . . say that was a way of cleaning myself. Then we went around the bend in that road. Got around that bend and it seem like all of a sudden we ain't in the same place. Turn around that bend and everything look like it was twice as big as it was. The trees and everything bigger than life! Sparrows big as eagles! I turned around to look at this fellow and he had this light coming out of him. I had to cover up my eyes to keep from being blinded. He shining like new money with that light. He shined until all the light seemed like it seeped out of him and then he was gone and I was by myself in this strange place where everything was bigger than life.

I wandered around there looking for that road, trying to find my way back from this big place . . . and I looked over and seen my daddy standing there. He was the same size he always was, except for his hands and his mouth. He had a great big old mouth that look like it took up his whole face and his hands were as big as hams. Look like they was too big to carry around. My daddy called me to him. Said he had been thinking about me and it grieved him to see me in the world carrying other people's songs and not having one of my own. Told me he was gonna show me how to find my song. Then he carried me further into this big place until we come to this ocean. Then he showed me something I ain't got words to tell you.

But if you stand to witness it, you done seem something there. I stayed in that place awhile and my daddy taught me the meaning of this thing that I had seen and showed me how to find my song. I asked him about the shiny man and he told me he was the One Who Goes Before and Shows the Way. Said there was lots of shiny men and if I ever saw one again before I died then I would know that my song had been accepted and worked its full power in the world and I could lay down and die a happy man. A man who done left his mark on life. On the way people cling to each other out of the truth they find in themselves. Then he showed me how to get back to the road. I came out to where everything was its own size and I had my song. I had the Binding Song. I choose that song because that's what I seen most when I was traveling . . . people walking away and leaving one another. So I takes the power of my song and binds them together.

[Seth enters from the yard carrying cabbages and tomatoes.]

Been binding people ever since. That's why they call me Bynum. Just like glue I sticks people together.

SETH
Maybe they ain't supposed to be stuck sometimes. You ever think of that?

BYNUM
Oh, I don't do it lightly. It cost me a piece of myself every time I do. I'm a Binder of What Clings. You got to find out if they cling first. You can't bind what don't cling.

SELIG
Well, how is that the Secret of Life? I thought you said he was gonna show you the secret of life. That's what I'm waiting to find out.

BYNUM
Oh, he showed me alright. But you still got to figure it out. Can't nobody figure it out for you. You got to come to it on your own. That's why I'm looking for the shiny man.

SELIG
Well, I'll keep my eye out for him. What you got there, Seth?

SETH
Here go some cabbage and tomatoes. I got some green beans coming in real nice. I'm gonna take and start me a grapevine out there next year. Butera says he gonna give me a piece of his vine and I'm gonna start that out there.

SELIG
How many of them pots you got?

SETH
I got six. That's six dollars minus eight on top of fifteen for the sheet metal come to a dollar twenty out the six dollars leave me four dollars and eighty cents.

SELIG
[Counting out the money.] There's four dollars . . . and . . . eighty cents.

SETH
How many of them dustpans you want?

SELIG
As many as you can make out them sheets.

SETH
You can use that many? I get to cutting on them sheets figuring how to make them dustpans . . . ain't no telling how many I'm liable to come up with.

SELIG
I can use them and you can make me some more next time.

SETH
Alright, I'm gonna hold you to that, now.

SELIG
Thanks for the biscuit, Bertha.

BERTHA
You know you welcome anytime, Selig.

SETH
Which way you heading?

SELIG
Going down to Wheeling. All through West Virginia there. I'll be back Saturday. They putting in new roads down that way. Makes traveling easier.

SETH
That's what I hear. All up around here too. Got a fellow staying here working on that road by the Brady Street Bridge.

SELIG
Yeah, it's gonna make traveling real nice. Thanks for the cabbage, Seth. I'll see you on Saturday. *[Selig exits.]*

SETH

[To Bynum.] Why you wanna start all that nonsense talk with that man? All that shiny man nonsense.

BYNUM

You know it ain't no nonsense. Bertha know it ain't no nonsense. I don't know if Selig know or not.

BERTHA

Seth, when you get to making them dustpans make me a coffeepot.

SETH

What's the matter with your coffee? Ain't nothing wrong with your coffee. Don't she make some good coffee, Bynum?

BYNUM

I ain't worried about the coffee. I know she makes some good biscuits.

SETH

I ain't studying no coffeepot, woman. You heard me tell the man I was gonna cut as many dustpans as them sheets will make . . . and all of a sudden you want a coffeepot.

BERTHA

Man, hush up and go on and make me that coffeepot.

[Jeremy enters the front door. About twenty-five, he gives the impression that he has the world in his hand, that he can meet life's challenges head on. He smiles a lot. He is a proficient guitar player, though his spirit has yet to be molded into song.]

BYNUM

I hear Mr. Piney's boys had you.

JEREMY

Fined me two dollars for nothing! Ain't done nothing.

SETH

I told you when you come on here everybody know my house. Know these is respectable quarters. I don't put up with no foolishness. Everybody know Seth Holly keep a good house. Was my daddy's house. This house been a decent house for a long time.

JEREMY

I ain't done nothing, Mr. Seth. I stopped by the Workmen's Club and got me a bottle. Me and Roper Lee from Alabama. Had us a half pint. We was fixing to cut that half in two when they came up on us. Asked us if we was working. We told them we was putting in the road over yonder and that it was our payday.

They snatched hold of us to get that two dollars. Me and Roper Lee ain't even had a chance to take a drink when they grabbed us.

SETH

I don't go for all that kind of carrying on.

BERTHA

Leave the boy alone, Seth. You know the police do that. Figure there's too many people out on the street they take some of them off. You know that.

SETH

I ain't gonna have folks talking.

BERTHA

Ain't nobody talking nothing. That's all in your head. You want some grits and biscuits. Jeremy?

JEREMY

Thank you, Miss Bertha. They didn't give us a thing to eat last night. I'll take one of them big bowls if you don't mind.

[There is a knock at the door. Seth goes to answer it. Enter Herald Loomis and his eleven-year-old daughter, Zonia. Herald Loomis is thirty-two years old. He is at times possessed. A man driven not by the hellhounds that seemingly bay at his heels, but by his search for a world that speaks to something about himself. He is unable to harmonize the forces that swirl around him, and seeks to recreate the world into one that contains his image. He wears a hat and a long wool coat.]

LOOMIS

Me and my daughter looking for a place to stay, mister. You got a sign say you got rooms.

[Seth stares at Loomis, sizing him up.]

Mister, if you ain't got no rooms we can go somewhere else.

SETH

How long you plan on staying?

LOOMIS

Don't know. Two weeks or more maybe.

SETH

It's two dollars a week for the room. We serve meals twice a day. It's two dollars for room and board. Pay up in advance.

[Loomis reaches into his pocket.]

It's a dollar extra for the girl.

LOOMIS
The girl sleep in the same room.

SETH
Well, do she eat off the same plate? We serve meals twice a day. That's a dollar extra for food.

LOOMIS
Ain't got no extra dollar. I was planning on asking your missus if she could help out with the cooking and cleaning and whatnot.

SETH
Her helping out don't put no food on the table. I need that dollar to buy some food.

LOOMIS
I'll give you fifty cents extra. She don't eat much.

SETH
Okay . . . but fifty cents don't buy but half a portion.

BERTHA
Seth, she can help me out. Let her help me out. I can use some help.

SETH
Well, that's two dollars for the week. Pay up in advance. Saturday to Saturday. You wanna stay on then it's two more come Saturday.

[Loomis pays Seth the money.]

BERTHA
My name's Bertha. This my husband, Seth. You got Bynum and Jeremy over there.

LOOMIS
Ain't nobody else live here?

BERTHA
They the only ones live here now. People come and go. They the only ones here now. You want a cup of coffee and a biscuit?

LOOMIS
We done ate this morning.

BYNUM
Where you coming from, Mister . . . I didn't get your name.

LOOMIS
Name's Herald Loomis. This my daughter, Zonia.

BYNUM
Where you coming from?

LOOMIS
Come from all over. Whicheverway the road take us that's the way we go.

JEREMY
If you looking for a job, I'm working putting in that road down there by the bridge. They can't get enough mens. Always looking to take somebody on.

LOOMIS
I'm looking for a woman named Martha Loomis. That's my wife. Got married legal with the papers and all.

SETH
I don't know nobody named Loomis. I know some Marthas but I don't know no Loomis.

BYNUM
You got to see Rutherford Selig if you wanna find somebody. Selig's the People Finder. Rutherford Selig's a first-class People Finder.

JEREMY
What she look like? Maybe I seen her.

LOOMIS
She a brownskin woman. Got long pretty hair. About five feet from the ground.

JEREMY
I don't know. I might have seen her.

BYNUM
You got to see Rutherford Selig. You give him one dollar to get her name on his list . . . and after she get her name on his list Rutherford Selig will go right on out there and find her. I got him looking for somebody for me.

LOOMIS
You say he find people. How you find him?

BYNUM
You just missed him. He's gone downriver now. You got to wait till Saturday. He's gone downriver with his pots and pans. He come to see Seth on Saturdays. You got to wait till then.

SETH
Come on, I'll show you to your room

[Seth, Loomis, and Zonia exit up the stairs.]

JEREMY
Miss Bertha, I'll take that biscuit you was gonna give that fellow, if you don't mind. Say, Mr. Bynum, they got somebody like that around here sure enough? Somebody that find people?

BYNUM

Rutherford Selig. He go around selling pots and pans and every house he come to he write down the name and address of whoever lives there. So if you looking for somebody, quite naturally you go and see him . . . 'cause he's the only one who know where everybody live at.

JEREMY

I ought to have him look for this old gal I used to know. It be nice to see her again.

BERTHA

[Giving Jeremy a biscuit.] Jeremy, today's the day for you to pull them sheets off the bed and set them outside your door. I'll set you out some clean ones.

BYNUM

Mr. Piney's boys done ruined your good time last night, Jeremy . . . what you planning for tonight?

JEREMY

They got me scared to go out, Mr. Bynum. They might grab me again.

BYNUM

You ought to take your guitar and go down to Seefus. Seefus got a gambling place down there on Wylie Avenue. You ought to take your guitar and go down there. They got guitar contest down there.

JEREMY

I don't play no contest, Mr. Bynum. Had one of them white fellows cure me of that. I ain't been nowhere near a contest since.

BYNUM

White fellow beat you playing guitar?

JEREMY

Naw, he ain't beat me. I was sitting at home just fixing to sit down and eat when somebody come up to my house and got me. Told me there's a white fellow say he was gonna give a prize to the best guitar player he could find. I take up my guitar and go down there and somebody had gone up and got Bobo Smith and brought him down there. Him and another fellow called Hooter. Old Hooter couldn't play no guitar, he do more hollering than playing, but Bobo could go at it awhile.

This fellow standing there say he the one that was gonna give the prize and me and Bobo started playing for him. Bobo play something and then I'd try to play something better than what he played. Old Hooter,

he just holler and bang at the guitar. Man was the worst guitar player I ever seen. So me and Bobo played and after a while I seen where he was getting the attention of this white fellow. He'd play something and while he was playing it he be slapping on the side of the guitar, and that made it sound like he was playing more than he was. So I started doing it too. White fellow ain't knew no difference. He ain't knew as much about guitar playing as Hooter did. After we play awhile, the white fellow called us to him and said he couldn't make up his mind, say all three of us was the best guitar player and we'd have to split the prize between us. Then he give us twenty-five cents. That's eight cents apiece and a penny on the side. That cured me of playing contest to this day.

BYNUM

Seefus ain't like that. Seefus give a whole dollar and a drink of whiskey.

JEREMY

What night they be down there?

BYNUM

Be down there every night. Music don't know no certain night.

BERTHA

You go down to Seefus with them people and you liable to end up in a raid and go to jail sure enough. I don't know why Bynum tell you that.

BYNUM

That's where the music at. That's where the people at. The people down there making music and enjoying themselves. Some things is worth taking the chance going to jail about.

BERTHA

Jeremy ain't got no business going down there.

JEREMY

They got some women down there, Mr. Bynum?

BYNUM

Oh, they got women down there, sure. They got women everywhere. Women be where the men is so they can find each other.

JEREMY

Some of them old gals come out there where we be putting in that road. Hanging around there trying to snatch somebody.

BYNUM

How come some of them ain't snatched hold of you?

JEREMY

I don't want them kind. Them desperate kind. Ain't nothing worse than a desperate woman. Tell them you gonna leave them and they get to crying and carrying on. That just make you want to get away quicker. They get to cutting up your clothes and things trying to keep you staying. Desperate women ain't nothing but trouble for a man.

[Seth enters from the stairs.]

SETH

Something ain't setting right with that fellow.

BERTHA

What's wrong with him? What he say?

SETH

I take him up there and try to talk to him and he ain't for no talking. Say he been traveling . . . coming over from Ohio. Say he a deacon in the church. Say he looking for Martha Pentecost. Talking about that's his wife.

BERTHA

How you know it's the same Martha? Could be talking about anybody. Lots of people named Martha.

SETH

You see that little girl? I didn't hook it up till he said it, but that little girl look just like her. Ask Bynum. *[To Bynum.]* Bynum. Don't that little girl look just like Martha Pentecost?

BERTHA

I still say he could be talking about anybody.

SETH

The way he described her wasn't no doubt about who he was talking about. Described her right down to her toes.

BERTHA

What did you tell him?

SETH

I ain't told him nothing. The way that fellow look I wasn't gonna tell him nothing. I don't know what he looking for her for.

BERTHA

What else he have to say?

SETH

I told you he wasn't for no talking. I told him where the outhouse was and to keep that gal off the front porch and out of my garden. He asked if you'd mind setting a hot tub for the gal and that was about the gist of it.

BERTHA

Well, I wouldn't let it worry me if I was you. Come on get your sleep.

BYNUM

He says he looking for Martha and he a deacon in the church.

SETH

That's what he say. Do he look like a deacon to you?

BERTHA

He might be, you don't know. Bynum ain't got no special say on whether he a deacon or not.

SETH

Well, if he the deacon I'd sure like to see the preacher.

BERTHA

Come on get your sleep. Jeremy, don't forget to set them sheets outside the door like I told you.

[Bertha exits into the bedroom.]

SETH

Something ain't setting right with that fellow, Bynum. He's one of them mean-looking niggers look like he done killed somebody gambling over a quarter.

BYNUM

He ain't no gambler. Gamblers wear nice shoes. This fellow got on clodhoppers. He been out there walking up and down them roads.

[Zonia enters from the stairs and looks around.]

BYNUM

You looking for the back door, sugar? There it is. You can go out there and play. It's alright.

SETH

[Showing her the door.] You can go out there and play. Just don't get in my garden. And don't go messing around in my workshed.

[Seth exits into the bedroom. There is a knock on the door.]

JEREMY

Somebody at the door.

[Jeremy goes to answer the door. Enter Mattie Campbell. She is a young woman of twenty-six whose attractiveness is hidden under the weight and concerns of a dissatisfied life. She is a woman in an honest search for love and companionship. She has suffered many defeats in her search, and though not always uncompromising, still believes in the possibility of love.]

MATTIE

I'm looking for a man named Bynum. Lady told me to come back later.

JEREMY

Sure, he here. Mr. Bynum, somebody here to see you.

BYNUM

Come to see me, huh?

MATTIE

Are you the man they call Bynum? The man folks say can fix things?

BYNUM

Depend on what need fixing. I can't make no promises. But I got a powerful song in some matters.

MATTIE

Can you fix it so my man come back to me?

BYNUM

Come on in . . . have a sit down.

MATTIE

You got to help me. I don't know what else to do.

BYNUM

Depend on how all the circumstances of the thing come together. How all the pieces fit.

MATTIE

I done everything I knowed how to do. You got to make him come back to me.

BYNUM

It ain't nothing to make somebody come back. I can fix it so he can't stand to be away from you. I got my roots and powders, I can fix it so wherever he's at this thing will come up on him and he won't be able to sleep for seeing your face. Won't be able to eat for thinking of you.

MATTIE

That's what I want. Make him come back.

BYNUM

The roots is a powerful thing. I can fix it so one day he'll walk out his front door . . . won't be thinking of nothing. He won't know what it is. All he knows is that a powerful dissatisfaction done set in his bones and can't nothing he do make him feel satisfied. He'll set his foot down on the road and the wind in the trees be talking to him and everywhere he step on the road, that road'll give back your name and something will pull him right up to your doorstep. Now, I can do that. I can take my roots and fix that easy. But maybe he ain't supposed to come back. And if he ain't supposed to come back . . . then he'll be in your bed one morning and it'll come up on him that he's in the wrong place. That he's lost outside of time from his place that he's supposed to be in. Then both of you be lost and trapped outside of life and ain't no way for you to get back into it. 'Cause you lost from yourselves and where the places come together, where you're supposed to be alive, your heart kicking in your chest with a song worth singing.

MATTIE

Make him come back to me. Make his feet say my name on the road. I don't care what happens. Make him come back.

BYNUM

What's your man's name?

MATTIE

He go by Jack Carper. He was born in Alabama then he come to West Texas and find me and we come here. Been here three years before he left. Say I had a curse prayer on me and he started walking down the road and ain't never come back. Somebody told me, say you can fix things like that.

BYNUM

He just got up one day, set his feet on the road, and walked away?

MATTIE

You got to make him come back, mister.

BYNUM

Did he say goodbye?

MATTIE

Ain't said nothing. Just started walking. I could see where he disappeared. Didn't look back. Just keep walking. Can't you fix it so he come back? I ain't got no curse prayer on me. I know I ain't.

BYNUM

What made him say you had a curse prayer on you?

MATTIE

'Cause the babies died. Me and Jack had two babies. Two little babies that ain't lived two months before they died. He say it's because somebody cursed me not to have babies.

BYNUM

He ain't bound to you if the babies died. Look like somebody trying to keep you from being bound up and he's gone on back to whoever it is 'cause he's already bound up to her. Ain't nothing to be done. Somebody else done got a powerful hand in it and ain't nothing to be done to break it. You got to let him go find where he's supposed to be in the world.

MATTIE

Jack done gone off and you telling me to forget about him. All my life I been looking for somebody to stop and stay with me. I done already got too many things to forget about. I take Jack Carper's hand and it feel so rough and strong. Seem like he's the strongest man in the world the way he hold me. Like he's bigger than the whole world and can't nothing bad get to me. Even when he act mean sometimes he still make everything seem okay with the world. Like there's part of it that belongs just to you. Now you telling me to forget about him?

BYNUM

Jack Carper gone off to where he belong. There's somebody searching for your doorstep right now. Ain't no need you fretting over Jack Carper. Right now he's a strong thought in your mind. But every time you catch yourself fretting over Jack Carper you push that thought away. You push it out your mind and that thought will get weaker and weaker till you wake up one morning and you won't even be able to call him up on your mind.

[Bynum gives her a small cloth pocket.]

Take this and sleep with it under your pillow and it'll bring good luck to you. Draw it to you like a magnet. It won't be long before you forget all about Jack Carper.

MATTIE

How much . . . do I owe you?

BYNUM

Whatever you got there . . . that'll be alright.

[Mattie hands Bynum two quarters. She crosses to the door.]

You sleep with that under your pillow and you'll be alright.

[Mattie opens the door to exit and Jeremy crosses over to her. Bynum overhears the first part of their conversation, then exits out the back.]

JEREMY

I overheard what you told Mr. Bynum. Had me an old gal did that to me. Woke up one morning and she was gone. Just took off to parts unknown. I woke up that morning and the only thing I could do was look around for my shoes. I woke up and got out of there. Found my shoes and took off. That's the only thing I could think of to do.

MATTIE

She ain't said nothing?

JEREMY

I just looked around for my shoes and got out of there.

MATTIE

Jack ain't said nothing either. He just walked off.

JEREMY

Some mens do that. Womens too. I ain't gone off looking for her. I just let her go. Figure she had a time to come to herself. Wasn't no use of me standing in the way. Where you from?

MATTIE

Texas. I was born in Georgia but I went to Texas with my mama. She dead now. Was picking peaches and fell dead away. I come up here with Jack Carper.

JEREMY

I'm from North Carolina. Down around Raleigh where they got all that tobacco. Been up here about two weeks. I likes it fine except I still got to find me a woman. You got a nice look to you. Look like you have mens standing in your door. Is you got mens standing in your door to get a look at you?

MATTIE

I ain't got nobody since Jack left.

JEREMY

A woman like you need a man. Maybe you let me be your man. I got a nice way with the women. That's what they tell me.

MATTIE

I don't know. Maybe Jack's coming back.

JEREMY

I'll be your man till he come. A woman can't be by her lonesome. Let me be your man till he come.

MATTIE

I just can't go through live piecing myself out to different mens. I need a man who wants to stay with me.

JEREMY

I can't say what's gonna happen. Maybe I'll be the man. I don't know. You wanna go along the road a little ways with me?

MATTIE

I don't know. Seem like life say it's gonna be one thing and end up being another. I'm tired of going from man to man.

JEREMY

Life is like you got to take a chance. Everybody got to take a chance. Can't nobody say what's gonna be. Come on . . . take a chance with me and see what the year bring. Maybe you let me come and see you. Where you staying?

MATTIE

I got me a room up on Bedford. Me and Jack had a room together.

JEREMY

What's the address? I'll come by and get you tonight and we can go down to Seefus. I'm going down there and play my guitar.

MATTIE

You play guitar?

JEREMY

I play guitar like I'm born to it.

MATTIE

I live at 1727 Bedford Avenue. I'm gonna find out if you can play guitar like you say.

JEREMY

I plays it, sugar, and that ain't all I do. I got a ten-pound hammer and I knows how to drive it down. Good god . . . you ought to hear my hammer ring!

MATTIE

Go on with that kind of talk, now. If you gonna come by and get me I got to get home and straighten up for you.

JEREMY

I'll be by at eight o'clock. How's eight o'clock? I'm gonna make you forget all about Jack Carper.

MATTIE

Go on, now. I got to get home and fix up for you.

JEREMY

Eight o'clock, sugar.

[The lights go down in the parlor and come up on the yard outside. Zonia is singing and playing a game.]

ZONIA

> I went downtown
> To get my grip
> I came back home
> Just a pullin' the skiff
>
> I went upstairs
> To make my bed
> I made a mistake
> And I bumped my head
> Just a pullin' the skiff
>
> I went downstairs
> To milk the cow
> I made a mistake
> And I milked the sow
> Just a pullin' the skiff
>
> Tomorrow, tomorrow
> Tomorrow never comes
> The marrow the marrow
> The marrow in the bone.

[Reuben enters.]

REUBEN

Hi.

ZONIA

Hi.

REUBEN

What's your name?

ZONIA

Zonia.

REUBEN

What kind of name is that?

ZONIA

It's what my daddy named me.

REUBEN

My name's Reuben. You staying in Mr. Seth's house?

ZONIA

Yeah.

REUBEN

That your daddy I seen you with this morning?

ZONIA

I don't know. Who you see me with?

REUBEN
I saw you with some man had on a great big old coat. And you was walking up to Mr. Seth's house. Had on a hat too.

ZONIA
Yeah, that's my daddy.

REUBEN
You like Mr. Seth?

ZONIA
I ain't see him much.

REUBEN
My grandpap say he a great big old windbag. How come you living in Mr. Seth's house? Don't you have no house?

ZONIA
We going to find my mother.

REUBEN
Where she at?

ZONIA
I don't know. We got to find her. We just go all over.

REUBEN
Why you got to find her? What happened to her?

ZONIA
She ran away.

REUBEN
Why she run away?

ZONIA
I don't know. My daddy say some man named Joe Turner did something bad to him once and that made her run away.

REUBEN
Maybe she coming back and you don't have to go looking for her.

ZONIA
We ain't there no more.

REUBEN
She could have come back when you wasn't there.

ZONIA
My daddy said she ran off and left us so we going looking for her.

REUBEN
What he gonna do when he find her?

ZONIA
He didn't say. He just say he got to find her.

REUBEN
Your daddy say how long you staying in Mr. Seth's house?

ZONIA
He don't say much. But we never stay too long nowhere. He say we got to keep moving till we find her.

REUBEN
Ain't no kids hardly live around here. I had me a friend but he died. He was the best friend I ever had. Me and Eugene used to keep secrets. I still got his pigeons. He told me to let them go when he died. He say, "Reuben, promise me when I die you'll let my pigeons go." But I keep them to remember him by. I ain't never gonna let them go. Even when I get to be grown up. I'm just always gonna have Eugene's pigeons.

[Pause.]

Mr. Bynum a conjure man. My grandpap scared of him. He don't like me to come over here too much. I'm scared of him too. My grandpap told me not to let him get close enough to where he can reach out his hand and touch me.

ZONIA
He don't seem scary to me.

REUBEN
He buys pigeons from me . . . and if you get up early in the morning you can see him out in the yard doing something with them pigeons. My grandpap say he kill them. I sold him one yesterday. I don't know what he do with it. I just hope he don't spook me up.

ZONIA
Why you sell him pigeons if he's gonna spook you up?

REUBEN
I just do like Eugene do. He used to sell Mr. Bynum pigeons. That's how he got to collecting them to sell to Mr. Bynum. Sometime he give me a nickel and sometime he give me a whole dime.

[Loomis enters from the house.]

LOOMIS
Zonia!

ZONIA
Sir?

LOOMIS
What you doing?

ZONIA

Nothing.

LOOMIS

You stay around this house, you hear? I don't want you wandering off nowhere.

ZONIA

I ain't wandering off nowhere.

LOOMIS

Miss Bertha set that hot tub and you getting a good scrubbing. Get scrubbed up good. You ain't been scrubbing.

ZONIA

I been scrubbing.

LOOMIS

Look at you. You growing too fast. Your bones getting bigger everyday. I don't want you getting grown on me. Don't you get grown on me too soon. We gonna find your mamma. She around here somewhere. I can smell her. You stay on around this house now. Don't you go nowhere.

ZONIA

Yes, sir.

[Loomis exits into the house.]

REUBEN

Wow, your daddy's scary!

ZONIA

He is not! I don't know what you talking about.

REUBEN

He got them mean-looking eyes!

ZONIA

My daddy ain't got no mean-looking eyes!

REUBEN

Aw, girl, I was just messing with you. You wanna go see Eugene's pigeons? Got a great big coop out the back of my house. Come on, I'll show you.

[Reuben and Zonia exit as the lights go down.]

Scene Two

It is Saturday morning, one week later. The lights come up on the kitchen. Bertha is at the stove preparing breakfast while Seth sits at the table.

SETH

Something ain't right about that fellow. I been watching him all week. Something ain't right, I'm telling you.

BERTHA

Seth Holly, why don't you hush up about that man this morning?

SETH

I don't like the way he stare at everybody. Don't look at you natural like. He just be staring at you. Like he trying to figure out something about you. Did you see him when he come back in here?

BERTHA

That man ain't thinking about you.

SETH

He don't work nowhere. Just go out and come back. Go out and come back.

BERTHA

As long as you get your boarding money it ain't your cause about what he do. He don't bother nobody.

SETH

Just go out and come back. Going around asking everybody about Martha. Like Henry Allen seen him down at the church last night.

BERTHA

The man's allowed to go to church if he want. He say he a deacon. Ain't nothing wrong about him going to church.

SETH

I ain't talking about him going to church. I'm talking about him hanging around *outside* the church.

BERTHA

Henry Allen say that?

SETH

Say he be standing around outside the church. Like he be watching it.

BERTHA

What on earth he wanna be watching the church for, I wonder?

SETH

That's what I'm trying to figure out. Looks like he fixing to rob it.

BERTHA

Seth, now do he look like the kind that would rob the church?

SETH

I ain't saying that. I ain't saying how he look. It's how he do. Anybody liable to do anything as far as I'm concerned. I ain't never thought about how no church robbers look . . . but now that you mention it, I don't see where they look no different than how he look.

BERTHA
Herald Loomis ain't the kind of man who would rob no church.

SETH
I ain't even so sure that's his name.

BERTHA
Why the man got to lie about his name?

SETH
Anybody can tell anybody anything about what their name is. That's what you call him . . . Herald Loomis. His name is liable to be anything.

BERTHA
Well, until he tell me different that's what I'm gonna call him. You just getting yourself all worked up about the man for nothing.

SETH
Talking about Loomis: Martha's name wasn't no Loomis nothing. Martha's name is Pentecost.

BERTHA
How you so sure that's her right name? Maybe she changed it.

SETH
Martha's a good Christian woman. This fellow here look like he owe the devil a day's work and he's trying to figure out how he gonna pay him. Martha ain't had a speck of distrust about her the whole time she was living here. They moved the church out there to Rankin and I was sorry to see her go.

BERTHA
That's why he be hanging around the church. He looking for her.

SETH
If he looking for her, why don't he go inside and ask? What he doing hanging around outside the church acting sneakily like?

[Bynum enters from the yard.]

BYNUM
Morning, Seth. Morning, Sister Bertha.

[Bynum continues through the kitchen and exits up the stairs.]

BERTHA
That's who you should be asking the questions. He been out there in that yard all morning. He was out there before the sun come up. He didn't even come in for breakfast. I don't know what he's doing. He had three of them pigeons line up out there. He dance around till he get tired. He sit down awhile then get up and dance some more. He came through here a little while ago looking like he was mad at the world.

SETH
I don't pay Bynum no mind. He don't spook me up with all that stuff.

BERTHA
That's how Martha come to be living here. She come to see Bynum. She come to see him when she first left from down South.

SETH
Martha was living here before Bynum. She ain't come on here when she first left from down there. She come on here after she went back to get her little girl. That's when she come on here.

BERTHA
Well, where was Bynum? He was here when she came.

SETH
Bynum ain't come till after her. That boy Hiram was staying up there in Bynum's room.

BERTHA
Well, how long Bynum been here?

SETH
Bynum ain't been here no longer than three years. That's what I'm trying to tell you. Martha was staying up there and sewing and cleaning for Doc Goldblum when Bynum came. This the longest he ever been in one place.

BERTHA
How you know how long the man been in one place?

SETH
I know Bynum. Bynum ain't no mystery to me. I done seen a hundred niggers like him. He's one of them fellows never could stay in one place. He was wandering all around the country till he got old and settled here. The only thing different about Bynum is he bring all this heebie-jeebie stuff with him.

BERTHA

I still say he was staying here when she came. That's why she came . . . to see him.

SETH

You can say what you want. I know the facts of it. She come on here four years ago all heartbroken 'cause she couldn't find her little girl. And Bynum wasn't nowhere around. She got mixed up in that old heebie-jeebie nonsense with him after he came.

BERTHA

Well, if she came on before Bynum I don't know where she stayed. 'Cause she stayed up there in Hiram's room. Hiram couldn't get along with Bynum and left out of here owing you two dollars. Now, I know you ain't forgot about that!

SETH

Sure did! You know Hiram ain't paid me that two dollars yet. So that's why he be ducking and hiding when he see me down on Logan Street. You right. Martha did come on after Bynum. I forgot that's why Hiram left.

BERTHA

Him and Bynum never could see eye to eye. They always rubbed each other the wrong way. Hiram got to thinking that Bynum was trying to put a fix on him and he moved out. Martha came to see Bynum and ended up taking Hiram's room. Now, I know what I'm talking about. She stayed on here three years till they moved the church.

SETH

She out there in Rankin now. I know where she at. I know where they moved the church to. She right out there in Rankin in that place used to be shoe store. Used to be Wolf's shoe store. They moved to a bigger place and they put that church in there. I know where she at. I know just where she at.

BERTHA

Why don't you tell the man? You see he looking for her.

SETH

I ain't gonna tell that man where that woman is! What I wanna do that for? I don't know nothing about that man. I don't know why he looking for her. He might wanna do her a harm. I ain't gonna carry that on my hands. He looking for her, he gonna have to find her for himself. I ain't gonna help him. Now, if he had come and presented himself as a gentleman—the

way Martha Pentecost's husband would have done—then I would have told him. But I ain't gonna tell this old wild-eyed mean-looking nigger nothing!

BERTHA

Well, why don't you get a ride with Selig and go up there and tell her where he is? See if she wanna see him. If that's her little girl . . . you say Martha was looking for her.

SETH

You know me, Bertha. I don't get mixed up in nobody's business.

[Bynum enters from the stairs.]

BYNUM

Morning, Seth. Morning, Bertha. Can I still get some breakfast? Mr. Loomis been down here this morning?

SETH

He done gone out and come back. He up there now. Left out of here early this morning wearing that coat. Hot as it is, the man wanna walk around wearing a big old heavy coat. He come back in here paid me for another week, sat down there waiting on Selig. Got tired of waiting and went on back upstairs.

BYNUM

Where's the little girl?

SETH

She out there in the front. Had to chase her and that Reuben off the front porch. She out there somewhere.

BYNUM

Look like if Martha was around here he would have found her by now. My guess is she ain't in the city.

SETH

She ain't! I know where she at. I know just where she at. But I ain't gonna tell him. Not the way he look.

BERTHA

Here go your coffee, Bynum.

BYNUM

He says he gonna get Selig to find her for him.

SETH

Selig can't find her. He talk all that . . . but unless he get lucky and knock on her door he can't find her. That's the only way he find anybody. He got to get lucky. But I know just where she at.

BERTHA

Here go some biscuits, Bynum.

BYNUM

What else you got over there, Sister Bertha? You got some grits and gravy over there? I could go for some of that this morning.

BERTHA

[Sets a bowl on the table.] Seth, come on and help me turn this mattress over. Come on.

SETH

Something ain't right with that fellow, Bynum. I don't like the way he stare at everybody.

BYNUM

Mr. Loomis alright, Seth. He just a man got something on his mind. He just got a straightforward mind, that's all.

SETH

What's that fellow that they had around here? Moses, that's Moses Houser. Man went crazy and jumped off the Brady Street Bridge. I told you when I seen him something wasn't right about him. And I'm telling you about this fellow now.

[There is a knock on the door. Seth goes to answer it. Enter Rutherford Selig.]

Ho! Come on in, Selig.

BYNUM

If it ain't the People Finder himself.

SELIG

Bynum, before you start . . . I ain't seen no shiny man now.

BYNUM

Who said anything about that? I ain't said nothing about that. I just called you a first-class People Finder.

SELIG

How many dustpans you get out of that sheet metal, Seth?

SETH

You walked by them on your way in. They sitting out there on the porch. Got twenty-eight. Got four out of each sheet and made Bertha a coffeepot out the other one. They a little small but they got nice handles.

SELIG

That was twenty cents apiece, right? That's what we agreed on.

SETH

That's five dollars and sixty cents. Twenty on top of twenty-eight. How many sheets you bring me?

SELIG

I got eight out there. That's a dollar twenty makes me owe you . . .

SETH

Four dollars and forty cents.

SELIG

[Paying him.] Go on and make me some dustpans. I can use all you can make.

[Loomis enters from the stairs.]

LOOMIS

I been watching for you. He say you find people.

BYNUM

Mr. Loomis here wants you to find his wife.

LOOMIS

He say you find people. Find her for me.

SELIG

Well, let see here . . . find somebody, is it?

[Selig rummages through his pockets. He has several notebooks and he is searching for the right one.]

Alright now . . . what's the name?

LOOMIS

Martha Loomis. She my wife. Got married legal with the paper and all.

SELIG

[Writing.] Martha . . . Loomis. How tall is she?

LOOMIS

She five feet from the ground.

SELIG

Five feet . . . Young or old?

LOOMIS

She a young woman. Got long pretty hair.

SELIG

Young . . . long . . . pretty . . . hair. Where did you last see her?

LOOMIS

Tennessee. Nearby Memphis.

SELIG

When was that?

LOOMIS

Nineteen hundred and one.

SELIG

Nineteen . . . hundred and one. I'll tell you, mister
. . . you better off without them. Now you take me
. . . old Rutherford Selig could tell you a thing or two
about these women. I ain't met one yet I could understand. Now, you take Sally out there. That's all a
man needs is a good horse. I say giddup and she go.
Say whoa and she stop. I feed her some oats and she
carry me wherever I want to go. Ain't had a speck of
trouble out of her since I had her. Now, I been married. A long time ago down in Kentucky. I got up one
morning and I saw this look on my wife's face. Like
way down deep inside her she was wishing I was
dead. I walked around that morning and every time
I looked at her she had that look on her face. It seem
like she knew I could see it on her. Every time I
looked at her I got smaller and smaller. Well, I wasn't
gonna stay around there and just shrink away. I
walked out on the porch and closed the door behind
me. When I closed the door she locked it. I went out
and bought me a horse. And I ain't been without one
since! Martha Loomis, huh? Well now, I'll do the best
I can do. That's one dollar.

LOOMIS

[Holding out dollar suspiciously.] How you find her?

SELIG

Well now, it ain't no easy job like you think. You can't
just go out there and find them like that. There's a lot
of little tricks to it. It's not an easy job keeping up with
you Nigras the way you move about so. Now you take
this woman you looking for . . . this Martha Loomis.
She could be anywhere. Time I find her, if you don't
keep your eye on her, she'll be gone off someplace
else. You'll be thinking she over here and she'll be
over there. But like I say there's a lot of little tricks to
it.

LOOMIS

You say you find her.

SELIG

I can't promise anything but we been finders in my
family for a long time. Bringers and finders. My great-
granddaddy used to bring Nigras across the ocean on
ships. That wasn't no easy job either. Sometimes the
winds would blow so hard you'd think the hand of
God was set against the sails. But it set him well in pay
and he settled in this new land and found him a wife
of good Christian charity with a mind for kids and the
like and well . . . here I am, Rutherford Selig. You're

in good hands, mister. Me and my daddy have found
plenty Nigras. My daddy, rest his soul, used to find
runaway slaves for the plantation bosses. He was the
best there was at it. Jonas B. Selig. Had him a reputation stretched clean across the country. After Abra-
ham Lincoln give you all Nigras your freedom papers
and with you all looking all over for each other . . .
we started finding Nigras for Nigras. Of course, it
don't pay as much. But the People Finding business
ain't so bad.

LOOMIS

[Hands him the dollar.] Find her. Martha Loomis. Find
her for me.

SELIG

Like I say, I can't promise you anything. I'm going
back upriver, and if she's around in them parts I'll
find her for you. But I can't promise you anything.

LOOMIS

When you coming back?

SELIG

I'll be back on Saturday. I come and see Seth to pick
up my order on Saturday.

BYNUM

You going upriver, huh? You going up around my
way. I used to go all up through there. Blawknox . . .
Clairton. Used to go up to Rankin and take that first
righthand road. I wore many a pair of shoes out walking around that way. You'd have thought I was a missionary spreading the gospel the way I wandered all
around them parts.

SELIG

Okay, Bynum. See you on Saturday.

SETH

Here, let me walk out with you. Help you with them
dustpans.

[Seth and Selig exit out the back. Bertha enters from the
stairs carrying a bundle of sheets.]

BYNUM

Herald Loomis got the People Finder looking for
Martha.

BERTHA

You can call him a People Finder if you want to. I
know Rutherford Selig carries people away too. He
done carried a whole bunch of them away from here.
Folks plan on leaving plan by Selig's timing. They
wait till he get ready to go, then they hitch a ride on

his wagon. Then he charge folks a dollar to tell them where he took them. Now, that's the truth of Rutherford Selig. This old People Finding business is for the birds. He ain't never found nobody he ain't took away. Herald Loomis, you just wasted your dollar.

[Bertha exits into the bedroom.]

LOOMIS

He say he find her. He say he find her by Saturday. I'm gonna wait till Saturday.

[The lights fade to black.]

Scene Three

It is Sunday morning, the next day. The lights come up on the kitchen. Seth sits talking to Bynum. The breakfast dishes have been cleared away.

SETH

They can't see that. Neither one of them can see that. Now, how much sense it take to see that? All you got to do is be able to count. One man making ten pots is five men making fifty pots. But they can't see that. Asked where I'm gonna get my five men. Hell, I can teach anybody how to make a pot. I can teach you. I can take you out there and get you started right now. Inside of two weeks you'd know how to make a pot. All you got to do is want to do it. I can get five men. I ain't worried about getting no five men.

BERTHA

[Calls from the bedroom.] Seth. Come on and get ready now. Reverend Gates ain't gonna be holding up his sermon 'cause you sitting out there talking.

SETH

Now, you take the boy, Jeremy. What he gonna do after he put in that road? He can't do nothing but go put in another one somewhere. Now, if he let me show him how to make some pots and pans . . . then he'd have something can't nobody take away from him. After a while he could get his own tools and go off somewhere and make his own pots and pans. Find him somebody to sell them to. Now, Selig can't make no pots and pans. He can sell them but he can't make them. I get me five men with some tools and we'd make him so many pots and pans he'd have to open up a store somewhere. But they can't see that. Neither Mr. Cohen nor Sam Green.

BERTHA

[Calls from the bedroom.] Seth . . . time be wasting. Best be getting on.

SETH

I'm coming, woman! *[To Bynum.]* Want me to sign over the house to borrow five hundred dollars. I ain't that big a fool. That's all I got. Sign it over to them and then I won't have nothing.

[Jeremy enters waving a dollar and carrying his guitar.]

JEREMY

Look here, Mr. Bynum . . . won me another dollar last night down at Seefus! Me and that Mattie Campbell went down there again and I played contest. Ain't no guitar players down there. Wasn't even no contest. Say, Mr. Seth, I asked Mattie Campbell if she wanna come by and have Sunday dinner with us. Get some fried chicken.

SETH

It's gonna cost you twenty-five cents.

JEREMY

That's alright. I got a whole dollar here. Say, Mr. Seth . . . me and Mattie Campbell talked it over last night and she gonna move in with me. If that's alright with you.

SETH

Your business is your business . . . but it's gonna cost her a dollar a week for her board. I can't be feeding nobody for free.

JEREMY

Oh, she know that, Mr. Seth. That's what I told her, say she'd have to pay for her meals.

SETH

You say you got a whole dollar there . . . turn loose that twenty-five cents.

JEREMY

Suppose she move in today, then that make seventy-five cents more, so I'll give you the whole dollar for her now till she gets here.

[Seth pockets the money and exits into the bedroom.]

BYNUM

So you and that Mattie Campbell gonna take up together?

JEREMY

I told her she don't need to be by her lonesome, Mr. Bynum. Don't make no sense for both of us to be by our lonesome. So she gonna move in with me.

BYNUM

Sometimes you got to be where you supposed to be. Sometimes you can get all mixed up in life and come to the wrong place.

JEREMY

That's just what I told her, Mr. Bynum. It don't make no sense for her to be all mixed up and lonesome. May as well come here and be with me. She a fine woman too. Got them long legs. Knows how to treat a fellow too. Treat you like you wanna be treated.

BYNUM

You just can't look at it like that. You got to look at the whole thing. Now, you take a fellow go out there, grab hold to a woman and think he got something 'cause she sweet and soft to the touch. Alright. Touching's part of life. It's in the world like everything else. Touching's nice. It feels good. But you can lay your hand upside a horse or a cat, and that feels good too. What's the difference? When you grab hold to a woman, you got something there. You got a whole world there. You got a way of life kicking up under your hand. That woman can take and make you feel like something. I ain't just talking about in the way of jumping off into bed together and rolling around with each other. Anybody can do that. When you grab hold to that woman and look at the whole thing and see what you got . . . why, she can take and make something out of you. Your mother was a woman. That's enough right there to show you what a woman is. Enough to show you what she can do. She made something out of you. Taught you converse, and all about how to take care of yourself, how to see where you at and where you going tomorrow, how to look out to see what's coming in the way of eating, and what to do with yourself when you get lonesome. That's a mighty thing she did. But you just can't look at a woman to jump off into bed with her. That's a foolish thing to ignore a woman like that.

JEREMY

Oh, I ain't ignoring her, Mr. Bynum. It's hard to ignore a woman got legs like she got.

BYNUM

Alright. Let's try it this way. Now, you take a ship. Be out there on the water traveling about. You out there on that ship sailing to and from. And then you see some land. Just like you see a woman walking down the street. You see that land and it don't look like nothing but a line out there on the horizon. That's all

it is when you first see it. A line that cross your path out there on the horizon. Now, a smart man know when he see that land, it ain't just a line setting out there. He know that if you get off the water to go take a good look . . . why, there's a whole world right there. A whole world with everything imaginable under the sun. Anything you can think of you can find on that land. Same with a woman. A woman is everything a man need. To a smart man she water and berries. And that's all a man need. That's all he need to live on. You give me some water and berries and if there ain't nothing else I can live a hundred years. See, you just like a man looking at the horizon from a ship. You just seeing a part of it. But it's a blessing when you learn to look at a woman and see in maybe just a few strands of her hair, the way her cheek curves . . . to see in that everything there is out of life to be gotten. It's a blessing to see that. You know you done right and proud by your mother to see that. But you got to learn it. My telling you ain't gonna mean nothing. You got to learn how to come to your own time and place with a woman.

JEREMY

What about your woman, Mr. Bynum? I know you done had some woman.

BYNUM

Oh, I got them in memory time. That lasts longer than any of them ever stayed with me.

JEREMY

I had me an old gal one time . . .

[There is a knock at the door. Jeremy goes to answer it. Enter Molly Cunningham. She is about twenty-six, the kind of woman that "could break in on a dollar anywhere she goes." She carries a small cardboard suitcase, and wears a colorful dress of the fashion of the day. Jeremy's heart jumps out of his chest when he sees her.]

MOLLY

You got any rooms here? I'm looking for a room.

JEREMY

Yeah . . . Mr. Seth got rooms. Sure . . . wait till I get Mr. Seth. [Calls.] Mr. Seth! Somebody here to see you! [To Molly.] Yeah, Mr. Seth got some rooms. Got one right next to me. This a nice place to stay, too. My name's Jeremy. What's yours?

[Seth enters dressed in his Sunday clothes.]

SETH
Ho!

JEREMY
This here woman looking for a place to stay. She say you got any rooms.

MOLLY
Mister, you got any rooms? I seen your sign say you got rooms.

SETH
How long you plan to staying?

MOLLY
I ain't gonna be here long. I ain't looking for no home or nothing. I'd be in Cincinnati if I hadn't missed my train.

SETH
Rooms cost two dollars a week.

MOLLY
Two dollars!

SETH
That includes meals. We serve two meals a day. That's breakfast and dinner.

MOLLY
I hope it ain't on the third floor.

SETH
That's the only one I got. Third floor to the left. That's pay up in advance week to week.

MOLLY
[Going into her bosom.] I'm gonna pay you for one week. My name's Molly. Molly Cunningham.

SETH
I'm Seth Holly. My wife's name is Bertha. She do the cooking and taking care of around here. She got sheets on the bed. Towels twenty-five cents a week extra if you ain't got none. You get breakfast and dinner. We got fried chicken on Sundays.

MOLLY
That sounds good. Here's two dollars and twenty-five cents. Look here, Mister . . . ?

SETH
Holly. Seth Holly.

MOLLY
Look here, Mr. Holly. I forgot to tell you. I likes me some company from time to time. I don't like being by myself.

SETH
Your business is your business. I don't meddle in no-body's business. But this is a respectable house. I don't have no riffraff around here. And I don't have no women hauling no men up to their rooms to be making their living. As long as we understand each other then we'll be alright with each other.

MOLLY
Where's the outhouse?

SETH
Straight through the door over yonder.

MOLLY
I get my own key to the front door?

SETH
Everybody get their own key. If you come in late just don't be making no whole lot of noise and carrying on. Don't allow no fussing and fighting around here.

MOLLY
You ain't got to worry about that, mister. Which way you say that outhouse was again?

SETH
Straight through that door over yonder.

[Molly exits out the back door. Jeremy crosses to watch her.]

JEREMY
Mr. Bynum, you know what? I think I know what you was talking about now.

[The lights go down on the scene.]

Scene Four

The lights come up on the kitchen. It is later the same evening. Mattie and all the residents of the house, except Loomis, sit around the table. They have finished eating and most of the dishes have been cleared.

MOLLY
That sure was some good chicken.

JEREMY
That's what I'm talking about. Miss Bertha, you sure can fry some chicken. I thought my mama could fry some chicken. But she can't do half as good as you.

SETH
I know it. That's why I married her. She don't know that, though. She think I married her for something else.

BERTHA

I ain't studying you, Seth. Did you get your things moved in alright, Mattie?

MATTIE

I ain't had that much. Jeremy helped me with what I did have.

BERTHA

You'll get to know your way around here. If you have any questions about anything just ask me. You and Molly both. I get along with everybody. You'll find I ain't no trouble to get along with.

MATTIE

You need some help with the dishes?

BERTHA

I got me a helper. Ain't I, Zonia? Got me a good helper.

ZONIA

Yes, ma'am.

SETH

Look at Bynum sitting over there with his belly all poked out. Ain't saying nothing. Sitting over there half asleep. Ho, Bynum!

BERTHA

If Bynum ain't saying nothing what you wanna start him up for?

SETH

Ho, Bynum!

BYNUM

What you hollering at me for? I ain't doing nothing.

SETH

Come on, we gonna Juba.

BYNUM

You know me, I'm always ready to Juba.

SETH

Well, come on, then.

[Seth pulls out a harmonica and blows a few notes.]

Come on there, Jeremy. Where's your guitar? Go get your guitar. Bynum say he's ready to Juba.

JEREMY

Don't need no guitar to Juba. Ain't you never Juba without a guitar?

[Jeremy begins to drum on the table.]

SETH

It ain't that. I ain't never Juba with one! Figured to try it and see how it worked.

BYNUM

[Drumming on the table.] You don't need no guitar. Look at Molly sitting over there. She don't know we Juba on Sunday. We gonna show you something tonight. You and Mattie Campbell both. Ain't that right, Seth?

SETH

You said it! Come on, Bertha, leave them dishes be for a while. We gonna Juba.

BYNUM

Alright. Let's Juba down!

[The Juba is reminiscent of the Ring Shouts of the African slaves. It is a call and response dance. Bynum sits at the table and drums. He calls the dance as others clap hands, shuffle and stomp around the table. It should be as African as possible, with the performers working themselves up into a near frenzy. The words can be improvised, but should include some mention of the Holy Ghost. In the middle of the dance Herald Loomis enters.]

LOOMIS

[In a rage.] Stop it! Stop!

[They stop and turn to look at him.]

You all sitting up here singing about the Holy Ghost. What's so holy about the Holy Ghost? You singing and singing. You think the Holy Ghost coming? You singing for the Holy Ghost to come? What he gonna do, huh? He gonna come with tongues of fire to burn up your woolly heads? You gonna tie onto the Holy Ghost and get burned up? What you got then? Why God got to be so big? Why he got to be bigger than me? How much big is there? How much big do you want?

[Loomis starts to unzip his pants.]

SETH

Nigger, you crazy!

LOOMIS

How much big you want?

SETH

You done plumb lost your mind!

[Loomis begins to speak in tongues and dance around the kitchen. Seth starts after him.]

BERTHA

Leave him alone, Seth. He ain't in his right mind.

LOOMIS

[Stops suddenly.] You all don't know nothing about me. You don't know what I done seen. Herald Loomis done seen some things he ain't got words to tell you.

[Loomis starts to walk out the front door and is thrown back and collapses, terror-stricken by his vision. Bynum crawls to him.]

BYNUM

What you done seen, Herald Loomis?

LOOMIS

I done seen bones rise up out the water. Rise up and walk across the water. Bones walking on top of the water.

BYNUM

Tell me about them bones, Herald Loomis. Tell me what you seen.

LOOMIS

I come to this place . . . to this water that was bigger than the whole world. And I looked out . . . and I seen these bones rise up out the water. Rise up and begin to walk on top of it.

BYNUM

Wasn't nothing but bones and they walking on top of the water.

LOOMIS

Walking without sinking down. Walking on top of the water.

BYNUM

Just marching in a line.

LOOMIS

A whole heap of them. They come up out the water and started marching.

BYNUM

Wasn't nothing but bones and they walking on top of the water.

LOOMIS

One after the other. They just come up out the water and start to walking.

BYNUM

They walking on the water without sinking down. They just walking and walking. And then . . . what happened, Herald Loomis?

LOOMIS

They just walking across the water.

BYNUM

What happened, Herald Loomis? What happened to the bones?

LOOMIS

They just walking across the water . . . and then . . . they sunk down.

BYNUM

The bones sunk into the water. They all sunk down.

LOOMIS

All at one time! They just all fell in the water at one time.

BYNUM

Sunk down like anybody else.

LOOMIS

When they sink down they made a big splash and this here wave come up . . .

BYNUM

A big wave, Herald Loomis. A big wave washed over the land.

LOOMIS

It washed them out of the water and up on the land. Only . . . only . . .

BYNUM

Only they ain't bones no more.

LOOMIS

They got flesh on them! Just like you and me!

BYNUM

Everywhere you look the waves is washing them up on the land right on top of one another.

LOOMIS

They black. Just like you and me. Ain't no difference.

BYNUM

Then what happened, Herald Loomis?

LOOMIS

They ain't moved or nothing. They just laying there.

BYNUM

You just laying there. What you waiting on, Herald Loomis?

LOOMIS
I'm laying there . . . waiting.

BYNUM
What you waiting on, Herald Loomis?

LOOMIS
I'm waiting on the breath to get into my body.

BYNUM
The breath coming into you, Herald Loomis. What
you gonna do now?

LOOMIS
The wind's blowing the breath into my body. I can
feel it. I'm starting to breathe again.

BYNUM
What you gonna do, Herald Loomis?

LOOMIS
I'm gonna stand up. I got to stand up. I can't lay here
no more. All the breath coming into my body and I
got to stand up.

BYNUM
Everybody's standing up at the same time.

LOOMIS
The ground's starting to shake. There's a great shaking. The world's busting half in two. The sky's splitting open. I got to stand up.

[Loomis attempts to stand up.]

My legs . . . my legs won't stand up!

BYNUM
Everybody's standing and walking toward the road.
What you gonna do, Herald Loomis?

LOOMIS
My legs won't stand up.

BYNUM
They shaking hands and saying goodbye to each
other and walking every whichaway down the road.

LOOMIS
I got to stand up!

BYNUM
They walking around here now. Mens. Just like you
and me. Come right up out the water.

LOOMIS
Got to stand up.

BYNUM
They walking, Herald Loomis. They walking around
here now.

LOOMIS
I got to stand up. Get up on the road.

BYNUM
Come on, Herald Loomis.

[Loomis tries to stand up.]

LOOMIS
My legs won't stand up! My legs won't stand up!

*[Loomis collapses on the floor as the lights go down
to black.]*

Scene One

*The lights come up on the kitchen. Bertha busies herself
with breakfast preparations. Seth sits at the table.*

SETH
I don't care what his problem is! He's leaving here!

BERTHA
You can't put the man out and he got that little girl.
Where they gonna go then?

SETH
I don't care where he go. Let him go back where he
was before he come here. I ain't asked him to come
here. I knew when I first looked at him something
wasn't right with him. Dragging that little girl around
with him. Looking like he be sleeping in the woods
somewhere. I knew all along he wasn't right.

BERTHA
A fellow get a little drunk he's liable to say or do anything. He ain't done no big harm.

SETH
I just don't have all that carrying on in my house.
When he come down here I'm gonna tell him. He got
to leave here. My daddy wouldn't stand for it and I
ain't gonna stand for it either.

BERTHA
Well, if you put him out you have to put Bynum out
too. Bynum right there with him.

SETH
If it wasn't for Bynum ain't no telling what would have
happened. Bynum talked to that fellow just as nice
and calmed him down. If he wasn't here ain't no telling what would have happened. Bynum ain't done

nothing but talk to him and kept him calm. Man acting all crazy with that foolishness. Naw, he's leaving here.

BERTHA

What you gonna tell him? How you gonna tell him to leave?

SETH

I'm gonna tell him straight out. Keep it nice and simple. Mister, you got to leave here!

[Molly enters from the stairs.]

MOLLY

Morning.

BERTHA

Did you sleep alright in that bed?

MOLLY

Tired as I was I could have slept anywhere. It's a real nice room, though. This is a nice place.

SETH

I'm sorry you had to put up with all that carrying on last night.

MOLLY

It don't bother me none. I done seen that kind of stuff before.

SETH

You won't have to see it around here no more.

[Bynum is heard singing offstage.]

I don't put up with all that stuff. When that fellow come down here I'm gonna tell him.

BYNUM

[singing]

Soon my work will all be done
Soon my work will all be done
Soon my work will all be done
I'm going to see the king.

BYNUM

[Enters.] Morning, Seth. Morning, Sister Bertha. I see we got Molly Cunningham down here at breakfast.

SETH

Bynum, I wanna thank you for talking to that fellow last night and calming him down. If you hadn't been here ain't no telling what might have happened.

BYNUM

Mr. Loomis alright, Seth. He just got a little excited.

SETH

Well, he can get excited somewhere else 'cause he leaving here.

[Mattie enters from the stairs.]

BYNUM

Well, there's Mattie Campbell.

MATTIE

Good morning.

BERTHA

Sit on down there, Mattie. I got some biscuits be ready in a minute. The coffee's hot.

MATTIE

Jeremy gone already?

BYNUM

Yeah, he leave out of here early. He got to be there when the sun come up. Most working men got to be there when the sun come up. Everybody but Seth. Seth work at night. Mr. Olowski so busy in his shop he got fellows working at night.

[Loomis enters from the stairs.]

SETH

Mr. Loomis, now . . . I don't want no trouble. I keeps me a respectable house here. I don't have no carrying on like what went on last night. This has been a respectable house for a long time. I'm gonna have to ask you to leave.

LOOMIS

You got my two dollars. That two dollars say we stay till Saturday.

[Loomis and Seth glare at each other.]

SETH

Alright. Fair enough. You stay till Saturday. But come Saturday you got to leave here.

LOOMIS

[Continues to glare at Seth. He goes to the door and calls.] Zonia. You stay around this house, you hear? Don't you go anywhere.

[Loomis exits out the front door.]

SETH

I knew it when I first seen him. I knew something wasn't right with him.

BERTHA

Seth, leave the people alone to eat their breakfast. They don't want to hear that. Go on out there and make some pots and pans. That's the only time you satisfied is when you out there. Go on out there and make some pots and pans and leave them people alone.

SETH

I ain't bothering anybody. I'm just stating the facts. I told you, Bynum.

[Bertha shoos Seth out the back door and exits into the bedroom.]

MOLLY

[To Bynum.] You one of them voo-doo people?

BYNUM

I got a power to bind folks if that what you talking about.

MOLLY

I thought so. The way you talked to that man when he started all that spooky stuff. What you say you had the power to do to people? You ain't the cause of him acting like that, is you?

BYNUM

I binds them together. Sometimes I help them find each other.

MOLLY

How do you do that?

BYNUM

With a song. My daddy taught me how to do it.

MOLLY

That's what they say. Most folks be what they daddy is. I wouldn't want to be like my daddy. Nothing ever set right with him. He tried to make the world over. Carry it around with him everywhere he go. I don't want to be like that. I just take life as it come. I don't be trying to make it over.

[Pause.]

Your daddy used to do that too, huh? Make people stay together?

BYNUM

My daddy used to heal people. He had the Healing Song. I got the Binding Song.

MOLLY

My mama used to believe in all that stuff. If she got sick she would have gone and saw your daddy. As long as he didn't make her drink nothing. She wouldn't drink nothing nobody give her. She was al-ways afraid somebody was gonna poison her. How your daddy heal people?

BYNUM

With a song. He healed people by singing over them. I seen him do it. He sung over this little white girl when she was sick. They made a big to-do about it. They carried the girl's bed out in the yard and had all her kinfolk standing around. The little girl laying up there in the bed. Doctors standing around can't do nothing to help her. And they had my daddy come up and sing his song. It didn't sound no different than any other song. It was just somebody singing. But the song was its own thing and it come out and took upon this little girl with its power and it healed her.

MOLLY

That's sure something else. I don't understand that kind of thing. I guess if the doctor couldn't make me well I'd try it. But otherwise I don't wanna be bothered with that kind of thing. It's too spooky.

BYNUM

Well, let me get on out here and get to work.

[Bynum gets up and heads out the back door.]

MOLLY

I ain't meant to offend you or nothing. What's your name . . . Bynum? I ain't meant to say nothing to make you feel bad now.

[Bynum exits out the back door.]

[To Mattie.] I hope he don't feel bad. He's a nice man. I don't wanna hurt nobody's feelings or nothing.

MATTIE

I got to go on up to Doc Goldblum's and finish this ironing.

MOLLY

Now, that's something I don't never wanna do. Iron no clothes. Especially somebody else's. That's what I believe killed my mama. Always ironing and working, doing somebody else's work. Not Molly Cunningham.

MATTIE

It's the only job I got. I got to make it someway to fend for myself.

MOLLY

I thought Jeremy was your man. Ain't he working?

MATTIE

We just be keeping company till maybe Jack come back.

MOLLY

I don't trust none of these men. Jack or nobody else. These men liable to do anything. They wait just until they get one woman tied and locked up with them . . . then they look around to see if they can get another one. Molly don't pay them no mind. One's just as good as the other if you ask me. I ain't never met one that meant nobody no good. You got any babies?

MATTIE

I had two for my man, Jack Carper. But they both died.

MOLLY

That be the best. These men make all these babies, then run off and leave you to take care of them. Talking about they wanna see what's on the other side of the hill. I make sure I don't get no babies. My mama taught me how to do that.

MATTIE

Don't make me no mind. That be nice to be a mother.

MOLLY

Yeah? Well, you go on, then. Molly Cunningham ain't gonna be tied down with no babies. Had me a man one time who I thought had some love in him. Come home one day and he was packing his trunk. Told me the time come when even the best of friends must part. Say he was gonna send me a Special Delivery some old day. I watched him out the window when he carried that trunk out and down to the train station. Said if he was gonna send me a Special Delivery I wasn't gonna be there to get it. I done found out the harder you try to hold onto them, the easier it is for some gal to pull them away. Molly done learned that. That's why I don't trust nobody but the good Lord above, and I don't love nobody but my mama.

MATTIE

I got to get on. Doc Goldblum gonna be waiting.

[Mattie exits out the front door. Seth enters from his workshop with his apron, gloves, goggles, etc. He carries a bucket and crosses to the sink for water.]

SETH

Everybody gone but you, huh?

MOLLY

That little shack out there by the outhouse . . . that's where you make them pots and pans and stuff?

SETH

Yeah, that's my workshed. I go out there . . . take these hands and make something out of nothing. Take that metal and bend and twist it whatever way I want. My daddy taught me that. He used to make pots and pans. That's how I learned it.

MOLLY

I never knew nobody made no pots and pans. My uncle used to shoe horses.

[Jeremy enters at the front door.]

SETH

I thought you was working? Ain't you working today?

JEREMY

Naw, they fired me. White fellow come by told me to give him fifty cents if I wanted to keep working. Going around to all the colored making them give him fifty cents to keep hold to their jobs. Them other fellows, they was giving it to him. I kept hold to mine and they fired me.

SETH

Boy, what kind of sense that make? What kind of sense it make to get fired from a job where you making eight dollars a week and all it cost you is fifty cents. That's seven dollars and fifty cents profit! This way you ain't got nothing.

JEREMY

It didn't make no sense to me. I don't make but eight dollars. Why I got to give him fifty cents of it? He go around to all the colored and he got ten dollars extra. That's more than I make for a whole week.

SETH

I see you gonna learn the hard way. You just looking at the facts of it. See, right now, without the job, you ain't got nothing. What you gonna do when you can't keep a roof over your head? Right now, come Saturday, unless you come up with another two dollars, you gonna be out there in the streets. Down up under one of them bridges trying to put some food in your belly and wishing you had given that fellow that fifty cents.

JEREMY

Don't make me no difference. There's a big road out there. I can get my guitar and always find me another place to stay. I ain't planning on staying in one place for too long noway.

SETH

We gonna see if you feel like that come Saturday!

[Seth exits out the back. Jeremy sees Molly.]

JEREMY

Molly Cunningham. How you doing today, sugar?

MOLLY

You can go on back down there tomorrow and go back to work if you want. They won't even know who you is. Won't even know it's you. I had me a fellow did that one time. They just went ahead and signed him up like they never seen him before.

JEREMY

I'm tired of working anyway. I'm glad they fired me. You sure look pretty today.

MOLLY

Don't come telling me all that pretty stuff. Beauty wanna come in and sit down at your table asking to be fed. I ain't hardly got enough for me.

JEREMY

You know you pretty. Ain't no sense in you saying nothing about that. Why don't you come on and go away with me?

MOLLY

You tied up with that Mattie Campbell. Now you talking about running away with me.

JEREMY

I was just keeping her company 'cause she lonely. You ain't the lonely kind. You the kind that know what she want and how to get it. I need a woman like you to travel around with. Don't you wanna travel around and look at some places with Jeremy? With a woman like you beside him, a man can make it nice in the world.

MOLLY

Moll can make it nice by herself too. Molly don't need nobody leave her cold in hand. The world rough enough as it is.

JEREMY

We can make it better together. I got my guitar and I can play. Won me another dollar last night playing guitar. We can go around and I can play at the dances and we can just enjoy life. You can make it by yourself alright, I agrees with that. A woman like you can make it anywhere she go. But you can make it better if you got a man to protect you.

MOLLY

What places you wanna go around and look at?

JEREMY

All of them! I don't want to miss nothing. I wanna go everywhere and do everything there is to be got out of life. With a woman like you it's like having water and berries. A man got everything he need.

MOLLY

You got to be doing more than playing that guitar. A dollar a day ain't hardly what Molly got in mind.

JEREMY

I gambles real good. I got a hand for it.

MOLLY

Molly don't work. And Molly ain't up for sale.

JEREMY

Sure, baby. You ain't got to work with Jeremy.

MOLLY

There's one more thing.

JEREMY

What's that, sugar?

MOLLY

Molly ain't going South.

[The lights go down on the scene.]

Scene Two

The lights come up on the parlor. Seth and Bynum sit playing a game of dominoes. Bynum sings to himself.

BYNUM

[Singing.] They tell me Joe Turner's come and gone
Ohhh Lordy
They tell me Joe Turner's come and gone
Ohhh Lordy
Got my man and gone

Come with forty links of chain
Ohhh Lordy
Come with forty links of chain
Ohhh Lordy
Got my man and gone

SETH

Come on and play if you gonna play.

BYNUM

I'm gonna play. Soon as I figure out what to do.

SETH

You can't figure out if you wanna play or you wanna sing.

BYNUM

Well sir, I'm gonna do a little bit of both.

[Playing.]

There. What you gonna do now?

[Singing.]

They tell me Joe Turner's come and gone
Ohhh Lordy
They tell me Joe Turner's come and gone
Ohhh Lordy

SETH

Why don't you hush up that noise.

BYNUM

That's a song the women sing down around Memphis. The women down there made up that song. I picked it up down there about fifteen years ago.

[Loomis enters from the front door.]

BYNUM

Evening, Mr. Loomis.

SETH

Today's Monday, Mr. Loomis. Come Saturday your time is up. We done ate already. My wife roasted up some yams. She got your plate sitting in there on the table. *[To Bynum.]* Whose play is it?

BYNUM

Ain't you keeping up with the game? I thought you was a domino player. I just played so it got to be your turn.

[Loomis goes into the kitchen, where a plate of yams is covered and set on the table. He sits down and begins to eat with his hands.]

SETH

[Plays.] Twenty! Give me twenty! You didn't know I had that ace five. You was trying to play around that. You didn't know I had that lying there for you.

BYNUM

You ain't done nothing. I let you have that to get mine.

SETH

Come on and play. You ain't doing nothing but talking. I got a hundred and forty points to your eighty.

You ain't doing nothing but talking. Come on and play.

BYNUM

[Singing.] They tell me Joe Turner's come and gone
Ohhh Lordy
They tell me Joe Turner's come and gone
Ohhh Lordy
Got my man and gone
He come with forty links of chain
Ohhh Lordy

LOOMIS

Why you singing that song? Why you singing about Joe Turner?

BYNUM

I'm just singing to entertain myself.

SETH

You trying to distract me. That's what you trying to do.

BYNUM

[Singing.] Come with forty links of chain
Ohhh Lordy
Come with forty links of chain
Ohhh Lordy

LOOMIS

I don't like you singing that song, mister!

SETH

Now, I ain't gonna have no more disturbance around here, Herald Loomis. You start any more disturbance and you leavin' here, Saturday or no Saturday.

BYNUM

The man ain't causing no disturbance, Seth. He just say he don't like the song.

SETH

Well, we all friendly folk. All neighborly like. Don't have no squabbling around here. Don't have no disturbance. You gonna have to take that someplace else.

BYNUM

He just say he don't like the song. I done sung a whole lot of songs people don't like. I respect everybody. He here in the house too. If he don't like the song, I'll sing something else. I know lots of songs. You got "I Belong to the Band," "Don't You Leave Me Here." You got "Praying on the Old Campground," "Keep Your Lamp Trimmed and Burning" . . . I know lots of songs.

[Sings.]
Boys, I'll be so glad when payday come
Captain, Captain, when payday comes
Gonna catch that Illinois Central
Going to Kankakee

SETH

Why don't you hush up that hollering and come on and play dominoes.

BYNUM

You ever been to Johnstown, Herald Loomis? You look like a fellow I seen around there.

LOOMIS

I don't know no place with that name.

BYNUM

That's around where I seen my shiny man. See, you looking for this woman. I'm looking for a shiny man. Seem like everybody looking for something.

SETH

I'm looking for you to come and play these dominoes. That's what I'm looking for.

BYNUM

You a farming man, Herald Loomis? You look like you done some farming.

LOOMIS

Same as everybody. I done farmed some, yeah.

BYNUM

I used to work at farming . . . picking cotton. I reckon everybody done picked some cotton.

SETH

I ain't! I ain't never picked no cotton. I was born up here in the North. My daddy was a freedman. I ain't never even seen no cotton!

BYNUM

Mr. Loomis done picked some cotton. Ain't you, Herald Loomis? You done picked a bunch of cotton.

LOOMIS

How you know so much about me? How you know what I done? How much cotton I picked?

BYNUM

I can tell from looking at you. My daddy taught me how to do that. Say when you look at a fellow, if you taught yourself to look for it, you can see his song written on him. Tell you what kind of man he is in the world. Now, I can look at you, Mr. Loomis, and see you a man who done forgot his song. Forgot how to

sing it. A fellow forget that and he forget who he is. Forget how he's supposed to mark down life. Now, I used to travel all up and down this road and that . . . looking here and there. Searching. Just like you, Mr. Loomis. I didn't know what I was searching for. The only thing I knew was something was keeping me dissatisfied. Something wasn't making my heart smooth and easy. Then one day my daddy gave me a song. That song had a weight to it that was hard to handle. That song was hard to carry. I fought against it. Didn't want to accept that song. I tried to find my daddy to give him back the song. But I found out it wasn't his song. It was my song. It had come from way deep inside me. I looked long back in memory and gathered up pieces and snatches of things to make that song. I was making it up out of myself. And that song helped me on the road. Made it smooth to where my footsteps didn't bite back at me. All the time that song getting bigger and bigger. That song growing with each step of the road. It got so I used all of myself up in the making of that song. Then I was the song in search of itself. That song rattling in my throat and I'm looking for it. See, Mr. Loomis, when a man forgets his song he goes off in search of it . . . till he find out he's got it with him all the time. That's why I can tell you one of Joe Turner's niggers. 'Cause you forgot how to sing your song.

LOOMIS

You lie! How you see that? I got a mark on me? Joe Turner done marked me to where you can see it? You telling me I'm a marked man. What kind of mark you got on you?

[Bynum begins singing.]

BYNUM

They tell me Joe Turner's come and gone
Ohhh Lordy
They tell me Joe Turner's come and gone
Ohhh Lordy
Got my man and gone

LOOMIS

Had a whole mess of men he catched. Just go out hunting regular like you go out hunting possum. He catch you and go home to his wife and family. Ain't thought about you going home to yours. Joe Turner catched me when my little girl was just born. Wasn't nothing but a little baby sucking on her mama's titty when he catched me. Joe Turner catched me in nineteen hundred and one. Kept me seven years until nineteen hundred and eight. Kept everybody seven years. He'd go out hunting and bring back forty men at a time. And keep them seven years.

I was walking down this road in this little town outside of Memphis. Come up on these fellows gambling. I was a deacon in the Abundant Life Church. I stopped to preach to these fellows to see if maybe I could turn some of them from their sinning when Joe Turner, brother of the Governor of the great sovereign state of Tennessee, swooped down on us and grabbed everybody there. Kept us all seven years.

My wife Martha gone from me after Joe Turner catched me. Got out from under Joe Turner on his birthday. Me and forty other men put in our seven years and he let us go on his birthday. I made it back to Henry Thompson's place where me and Martha was sharecropping and Martha's gone. She taken my little girl and left her with her mama and took off North. We been looking for her ever since. That's been going on four years now we been looking. That's the only thing I know to do. I just wanna see her face so I can get me a starting place in the world. The world got to start somewhere. That's what I been looking for. I been wandering a long time in somebody else's world. When I find my wife that be the making of my own.

BYNUM
Joe Turner tell why he caught you? You ever asked him that?

LOOMIS
I ain't never seen Joe Turner. Seen him to where I could touch him. I asked one of them fellows one time why he catch niggers. Asked him what I got he want? Why don't he keep on to himself? Why he got to catch me going down the road by my lonesome? He told me I was worthless. Worthless is something you throw away. Something you don't bother with. I ain't seen him throw me away. Wouldn't even let me stay away when I was by my lonesome. I ain't tried to catch him when he going down the road. So I must got something he want. What I got?

SETH
He just want you to do his work for him. That's all.

LOOMIS
I can look at him and see where he big and strong enough to do his own work. So it can't be that. He must want something he ain't got.

BYNUM
That ain't hard to figure out. What he wanted was your song. He wanted to have that song to be his. He thought by catching you he could learn that song. Every nigger he catch he's looking for the one he can learn that song from. Now he's got you bound up to where you can't sing your own song. Couldn't sing it them seven years 'cause you was afraid he would snatch it from under you. But you still got it. You just forgot how to sing it.

LOOMIS
[To Bynum.] I know who you are. You one of them bones people.

[The lights go down to black.]

Scene Three

The lights come up on the kitchen. It is the following morning. Mattie and Bynum sit at the table. Bertha busies herself at the stove.

BYNUM
Good luck don't know no special time to come. You sleep with that up under your pillow and good luck can't help but come to you. Sometimes it come and go and you don't even know it's been there.

BERTHA
Bynum, why don't you leave that gal alone? She don't wanna be hearing all that. Why don't you go on and get out the way and leave her alone?

BYNUM
[Getting up.] Alright, alright. But you mark what I'm saying. It'll draw it to you just like a magnet.

[Bynum exits up the stairs and Loomis enters.]

BERTHA
I got some grits here, Mr. Loomis.

[Bertha sets a bowl on the table.]

If I was you, Mattie, I wouldn't go getting all tied up with Bynum in that stuff. That kind of stuff, even if it do work for a while, it don't last. That just get people more mixed up than they is already. And I wouldn't waste my time fretting over Jeremy either. I seen it coming. I seen it when she first come here. She that kind of woman run off with the first man got a dollar to spend on her. Jeremy just young. He don't know what he getting into. That gal don't mean him no good. She's just using him to keep from being by her-self. That's the worst use of a man you can have. You ought to be glad to wash him out of your hair. I done seen all kind of men. I done seen them come and go through here. Jeremy ain't had enough to him for you. You need a man who's got some understanding and who willing to work with that understanding to come to the best he can. You got your time coming. You just tries too hard and can't understand why it don't work for you. Trying to figure it out don't do nothing but give you a troubled mind. Don't no man want a woman with a troubled mind.

You get all that trouble off your mind and just when it look like you ain't never gonna find what you want . . . you look up and it's standing right there. That's how I met my Seth. You gonna look up one day and find everything you want standing right in front of you. Been twenty-seven years now since that hap-pened to me. But life ain't no happy-go-lucky time where everything be just like you want it. You got your time coming. You watch what Bertha's saying.

[Seth enters.]

SETH
Ho!

BERTHA
What you doing come in here so late?

SETH
I was standing down there on Logan Street talking with the fellows. Henry Allen tried to sell me that old piece of horse he got.

[He sees Loomis.]

Today's Tuesday, Mr. Loomis.

BERTHA
[Pulling him toward the bedroom.] Come on in here and leave that man alone to eat his breakfast.

SETH
I ain't bothering nobody. I'm just reminding him what day it is.

[Seth and Bertha exit into the bedroom.]

LOOMIS
That dress got a color to it.

MATTIE
Did you really see them things like you said? Them people come up out the ocean?

LOOMIS
It happened just like that, yeah.

MATTIE
I hope you find your wife. It be good for your little girl for you to find her.

LOOMIS
Got to find her for myself. Find my starting place in the world. Find me a world I can fit in.

MATTIE
I ain't never found no place for me to fit. Seem like all I do is start over. It ain't nothing to find no starting place in the world. You just start from where you find yourself.

LOOMIS
Got to find my wife. That be my starting place.

MATTIE
What if you don't find her? What you gonna do then if you don't find her?

LOOMIS
She out there somewhere. Ain't no such thing as not finding her.

MATTIE
How she got lost from you? Jack just walked away from me.

LOOMIS
Joe Turner split us up. Joe Turner turned the world upside-down. He bound me on to him for seven years.

MATTIE
I hope you find her. It be good for you to find her.

LOOMIS
I been watching you. I been watching you watch me.

MATTIE
I was just trying to figure out if you seen things like you said.

LOOMIS
[Getting up.] Come here and let me touch you. I been watching you. You a full woman. A man needs a full woman. Come on and be with me.

MATTIE
I ain't got enough for you. You'd use me up too fast.

LOOMIS
Herald Loomis got a mind seem like you a part of it since I first seen you. It's been a long time since I seen

a full woman. I can smell you from here. I know you got Herald Loomis on your mind, can't keep him apart from it. Come on and be with Herald Loomis.

[Loomis has crossed to Mattie. He touches her awkwardly, gently, tenderly. Inside he howls like a lost wolf pup whose hunger is deep. He goes to touch her but finds he cannot.]

I done forgot how to touch.

[The lights fade to black.]

Scene Four

It is early the next morning. The lights come up on Zonia and Reuben in the yard.

REUBEN
Something spookly going on around here. Last night Mr. Bynum was out in the yard singing and talking to the wind . . . and the wind it just be talking back to him. Did you hear it?

ZONIA
I heard it. I was scared to get up and look. I thought it was a storm.

REUBEN
That wasn't no storm. That was Mr. Bynum. First he say something . . . and the wind it say back to him.

ZONIA
I heard it. Was you scared? I was scared.

REUBEN
And then this morning . . . I seen Miss Mabel!

ZONIA
Who Miss Mabel?

REUBEN
Mr. Seth's mother. He got her picture hanging up in the house. She been dead.

ZONIA
How you seen her if she been dead?

REUBEN
Zonia . . . if I tell you something you promise you won't tell anybody?

ZONIA
I promise.

REUBEN
It was early this morning . . . I went out to the coop to feed the pigeons. I was down on the ground like this to open up the door to the coop . . . when all of a sudden I seen some feets in front of me. I looked up . . . and there was Miss Mabel standing there.

ZONIA
Reuben, you better stop telling that! You ain't seen nobody!

REUBEN
Naw, it's the truth. I swear! I seen her just like I see you. Look . . . you can see where she hit me with her cane.

ZONIA
Hit you? What she hit you for?

REUBEN
She says, "Didn't you promise Eugene something?" Then she hit me with her cane. She say, "Let them pigeons go." Then she hit me again. That's what made them marks.

ZONIA
Jeez man . . . get away from me. You done see a haunt!

REUBEN
Shhhh. You promised, Zonia!

ZONIA
You sure it wasn't Miss Bertha come over there and hit you with her hoe?

REUBEN
It wasn't no Miss Bertha. I told you it was Miss Mabel. She was standing right there by the coop. She had this light coming out of her and then she just melted away.

ZONIA
What she had on?

REUBEN
A white dress. Ain't even had no shoes or nothing. Just had on that white dress and them big hands . . . and that cane she hit me with.

ZONIA
How you reckon she knew about the pigeons? You reckon Eugene told her?

REUBEN
I don't know. I sure ain't asked her none. She say Eugene was waiting on them pigeons. Say he couldn't go back home till I let them go. I couldn't get the door to the coop open fast enough.

ZONIA

Maybe she an angel? From the way you say she look with that white dress. Maybe she an angel.

REUBEN

Mean as she was . . . how she gonna be an angel? She used to chase us out her yard and frown up and look evil all the time.

ZONIA

That don't mean she can't be no angel 'cause of how she looked and 'cause she wouldn't let no kids play in her yard. It go by if you got any spots on your heart and if you pray and go to church.

REUBEN

What about she hit me with her cane? An angel wouldn't hit me with her cane.

ZONIA

I don't know. She might. I still say she was an angel.

REUBEN

You reckon Eugene the one who sent old Miss Mabel?

ZONIA

Why he send her? Why he don't come himeself?

REUBEN

Figured if he send her maybe that'll make me listen. 'Cause she old.

ZONIA

What you think it feel like?

REUBEN

What?

ZONIA

Being dead.

REUBEN

Like being sleep only you don't know nothing and can't move no more.

ZONIA

If Miss Mabel can come back . . . then maybe Eugene can come back too.

REUBEN

We can go down to the hideout like we used to! He could come back everyday! It be just like he ain't dead.

ZONIA

Maybe that ain't right for him to come back. Feel kinda funny to be playing games with a haunt.

REUBEN

Yeah . . . what if everybody came back? What if Miss Mabel came back just like she ain't dead? Where you and your daddy gonna sleep then?

ZONIA

Maybe they go back at night and don't need no place to sleep.

REUBEN

It still don't seem right. I'm sure gonna miss Eugene. He's the bestest friend anybody ever had.

ZONIA

My daddy say if you miss somebody too much it can kill you. Say he missed me till it liked to killed him.

REUBEN

What if your mama's already dead and all the time you looking for her?

ZONIA

Naw, she ain't dead. My daddy say he can smell her.

REUBEN

You can't smell nobody that ain't here. Maybe he smelling old Miss Bertha. Maybe Miss Bertha your mama?

ZONIA

Naw, she ain't. My mamma got long pretty hair and she five feet from the ground!

REUBEN

Your daddy say when you leaving?

[Zonia doesn't respond.]

Maybe you gonna stay in Mr. Seth's house and don't go looking for your mama no more.

ZONIA

He say we got to leave on Saturday.

REUBEN

Dag! You just only been here for a little while. Don't seem like nothing ever stay the same.

ZONIA

He say he got to find her. Find him a place in the world.

REUBEN

He could find him a place in Mr. Seth's house.

ZONIA

It don't look like we never gonna find her.

REUBEN

Maybe he find her by Saturday then you don't have to go.

ZONIA
I don't know.

REUBEN
You look like a spider!

ZONIA
I ain't no spider!

REUBEN
Got them long skinny arms and legs. You look like one of them Black Widows.

ZONIA
I ain't no Black Window nothing! My name is Zonia!

REUBEN
That's what I'm gonna call you . . . Spider.

ZONIA
You can call me that, but I don't have to answer.

REUBEN
You know what? I think maybe I be your husband when I grow up.

ZONIA
How you know?

REUBEN
I ask my grandpap how you know and he say when the moon falls into a girl's eyes that how you know.

ZONIA
Did it fall into my eyes?

REUBEN
Not that I can tell. Maybe I ain't old enough. Maybe you ain't old enough.

ZONIA
So there! I don't know why you telling me that lie!

REUBEN
That don't mean nothing 'cause I can't see it. I know it's there. Just the way you look at me sometimes look like the moon might have been in your eyes.

ZONIA
That don't mean nothing if you can't see it. You supposed to see it.

REUBEN
Shucks, I see it good enough for me. You ever let anybody kiss you?

ZONIA
Just my daddy. He kiss me on the cheek.

REUBEN
It's better on the lips. Can I kiss you on the lips?

ZONIA
I don't know. You ever kiss anybody before?

REUBEN
I had a cousin let me kiss her on the lips one time. Can I kiss you?

ZONIA
Okay.

[Reuben kisses her and lays his head against her chest.]

What you doing?

REUBEN
Listening. Your heart singing!

ZONIA
It is not.

REUBEN
Just beating like a drum. Let's kiss again.

[They kiss again.]

Now you mine, Spider. You my girl, okay?

ZONIA
Okay.

REUBEN
When I get grown, I come looking for you.

ZONIA
Okay.

[The lights fade to black.]

Scene Five

The lights come up on the kitchen. It is Saturday. Bynum, Loomis, and Zonia sit at the table. Bertha prepares breakfast. Zonia has on a white dress.

BYNUM
With all this rain we been having he might have ran into some washed-out roads. If that wagon got stuck in the mud he's liable to be still upriver somewhere. If he's upriver then he ain't coming until tomorrow.

LOOMIS
Today's Saturday. He say he be here on Saturday.

BERTHA
Zonia, you gonna eat your breakfast this morning.

ZONIA
Yes, ma'am.

BERTHA

I don't know how you expect to get any bigger if you don't eat. I ain't never seen a child that didn't eat. You about as skinny as a bean pole.

[Pause.]

Mr. Loomis, there's a place down on Wylie. Zeke Mayweather got a house down there. You ought to see if he got any rooms.

[Loomis doesn't respond.]

Well, you're welcome to some breakfast before you move on.

[Mattie enters from the stairs.]

MATTIE

Good morning.

BERTHA

Morning, Mattie. Sit on down there and get you some breakfast.

BYNUM

Well, Mattie Campbell, you been sleeping with that up under your pillow like I told you?

BERTHA

Bynum, I done told you to leave that gal alone with all that stuff. You around here meddling in other people's lives. She don't want to hear all that. You ain't doing nothing but confusing her with that stuff.

MATTIE

[To Loomis.] You all fixing to move on?

LOOMIS

Today's Saturday. I'm paid up till Saturday.

MATTIE

Where you going to?

LOOMIS

Gonna find my wife.

MATTIE

You going off to another city?

LOOMIS

We gonna see where the road take us. Ain't no telling where we wind up.

MATTIE

Eleven years is a long time. Your wife . . . she might have taken up with someone else. People do that when they get lost from each other.

LOOMIS

Zonia. Come on, we gonna find your mama.

[Loomis and Zonia cross to the door.]

MATTIE

[To Zonia.] Zonia, Mattie got a ribbon here match your dress. Want Mattie to fix your hair with her ribbon?

[Zonia nods. Mattie ties the ribbon in her hair.]

There . . . it got a color just like your dress. *[To Loomis.]* I hope you find her. I hope you be happy.

LOOMIS

A man looking for a woman be lucky to find you. You a good woman, Mattie. Keep a good heart.

[Loomis and Zonia exit.]

BERTHA

I been watching that man for two weeks . . . and that's the closest I come to seeing him act civilized. I don't know what's between you all, Mattie . . . but the only thing that man needs is somebody to make him laugh. That's all you need in the world is love and laughter. That's all anybody needs. To have love in one hand and laughter in the other.

[Bertha moves about the kitchen as though blessing it and chasing away the huge sadness that seems to envelop it. It is a dance and demonstration of her own magic, her own remedy that is centuries old and to which she is connected by the muscles of her heart and the blood's memory.]

You hear me, Mattie? I'm talking about laughing. The kind of laugh that comes from way deep inside. To just stand and laugh and let life flow right through you. Just laugh to let yourself know you're alive.

[She begins to laugh. It is a near-hysterical laughter that is a celebration of life, both its pain and its blessing. Mattie and Bynum join in the laughter. Seth enters from the front door.]

SETH

Well, I see you all having fun.

[Seth begins to laugh with them.]

That Loomis fellow standing up there on the corner watching the house. He standing right up there on Manila Street.

BERTHA

Don't you get started on him. The man done left out of here and that's the last I wanna hear of it. You about to drive me crazy with that man.

SETH

I just say he standing up there on the corner. Acting sneaky like he always do. He stand up there all he want. As long as he don't come back in here.

[There is a knock on the door. Seth goes to answer it. Enter Martha Loomis (Pentecost). She is a young woman about twenty-eight. She is dressed as befitting a member of an Evangelist church. Rutherford Selig follows.]

SETH

Look here, Bertha. It's Martha Pentecost. Come on in, Martha. Who that with you? Oh . . . that's Selig. Come on in, Selig.

BERTHA

Come on in, Martha. It's sure good to see you.

BYNUM

Rutherford Selig, you a sure enough first-class People Finder!

SELIG

She was right out there in Rankin. You take that first righthand road . . . right there at that church on Wooster Street. I started to go right past and something told me to stop at the church and see if they needed any dustpans.

SETH

Don't she look good, Bertha.

BERTHA

Look all nice and healthy.

MARTHA

Mr. Bynum . . . Selig told me my little girl was here.

SETH

There's some fellow around here say he your husband. Say his name is Loomis. Say you his wife.

MARTHA

Is my little girl with him?

SETH

Yeah, he got a little girl with him. I wasn't gonna tell him where you was. Not the way this fellow look. So he got Selig to find you.

MARTHA

Where they at? They upstairs?

SETH

He was standing right up there on Manila Street. I had to ask him to leave 'cause of how he was carrying on. He come in here one night—

[The door opens and Loomis and Zonia enter. Martha and Loomis stare at each other.]

LOOMIS

Hello, Martha.

MARTHA

Herald . . . Zonia?

LOOMIS

You ain't waited for me, Martha. I got out the place looking to see your face. Seven years I waited to see your face.

MARTHA

Herald, I been looking for you. I wasn't but two months behind you when you went to my mama's and got Zonia. I been looking for you ever since.

LOOMIS

Joe Turner let me loose and I felt all turned around inside. I just wanted to see your face to know that the world was still there. Make sure everything still in its place so I could reconnect myself together. I got there and you was gone, Martha.

MARTHA

Herald . . .

LOOMIS

Left my little girl motherless in the world.

MARTHA

I didn't leave her motherless, Herald. Reverend Tolliver wanted to move the church up North 'cause of all the trouble the colored folks was having down there. Nobody knew what was gonna happen traveling them roads. We didn't even know if we was gonna make it up here or not. I left her with my mama so she be safe. That was better than dragging her out on the road having to duck and hide from people. Wasn't no telling what was gonna happen to us. I didn't leave her motherless in the world. I been looking for you.

LOOMIS

I come up on Henry Thompson's place after seven years of living in hell, and all I'm looking to do is see your face.

MARTHA

Herald, I didn't know if you was ever coming back. They told me Joe Turner had you and my whole world split half in two. My whole life shattered. It was like I had poured it in a cracked jar and it all leaked out the bottom. When it go like that there ain't nothing you can do put it back together. You talking about Henry Thompson's place like I'm still gonna be working the land by myself. How I'm gonna do that? You wasn't gone but two months and Henry Thompson kicked me off his land and I ain't had no place to go but to my mama's. I stayed and waited there for five years before I woke up one morning and decided that you was dead. Even if you weren't, you was dead to me. I wasn't gonna carry you with me no more. So I killed you in my heart. I buried you. I mourned you. And then I picked up what was left and went on to make life without you. I was a young woman with life at my beckon. I couldn't drag you behind me like a sack of cotton.

LOOMIS

I just been waiting to look on your face to say my goodbye. That goodbye got so big at times, seem like it was gonna swallow me up. Like Jonah in the whale's belly I sat up in that goodbye for three years. That goodbye kept me out on the road searching. Not looking on women in their houses. It kept me bound up to the road. All the time that goodbye swelling up in my chest till I'm about to bust. Now that I see your face I can say my goodbye and make my own world.

[Loomis takes Zonia's hand and presents her to Martha.]

Martha . . . here go your daughter. I tried to take care of her. See that she had something to eat. See that she was out of the elements. Whatever I know I tried to teach her. Now she need to learn from her mother whatever you got to teach her. That way she won't be no one-sided person.

[Loomis stoops to Zonia.]

Zonia, you go live with your mama. She a good woman. You go on with her and listen to her good. You my daughter and I love you like a daughter. I hope to see you again in the world somewhere. I'll never forget you.

ZONIA

[Throws her arms around Loomis in a panic.] I won't get no bigger! My bones won't get no bigger! They won't!

I promise! Take me with you till we keep searching and never finding. I won't get no bigger! I promise!

LOOMIS

Go on and do what I told you now.

MARTHA

[Goes to Zonia and comforts her.] It's alright, baby. Mama's here. Mama's here. Don't worry. Don't cry.

[Martha turns to Bynum.]

Mr. Bynum, I don't know how to thank you. God bless you.

LOOMIS

It was you! All the time it was you that bind me up! You bound me to the road!

BYNUM

I ain't bind you, Herald Loomis. You can't bind what don't cling.

LOOMIS

Everywhere I go people wanna bind me up. Joe Turner wanna bind me up! Reverend Tolliver wanna bind me up. You wanna bind me up. Everybody wanna bind me up. Well, Joe Turner's come and gone and Herald Loomis ain't for no binding. I ain't gonna let nobody bind me up!

[Loomis pulls out a knife.]

BYNUM

It wasn't you, Herald Loomis. I ain't bound you. I bound the little girl to her mother. That's who I bound. You binding yourself. You bound onto your song. All you got to do is stand up and sing it, Herald Loomis. It's right there kicking at your throat. All you got to do is sing it. Then you be free.

MARTHA

Herald . . . look at yourself! Standing there with a knife in your hand. You done gone over to the devil. Come on . . . put down the knife. You got to look to Jesus. Even if you done fell away from the church you can be saved again. The Bible say, "The Lord is my shepherd I shall not want. He maketh me to lie down in green pastures. He leads me beside the still water. He restoreth my soul. He leads me in the path of righteousness for His name's sake. Even though I walk through the shadow of death—"

LOOMIS

That's just where I be walking!

MARTHA

"I shall fear no evil. For Thou art with me. Thy rod and thy staff, they comfort me."

LOOMIS

You can't tell me nothing about no valleys. I done been all across the valleys and the hills and the mountains and the oceans.

MARTHA

"Thou preparest a table for me in the presence of my enemies."

LOOMIS

And all I seen was a bunch of niggers dazed out of their woolly heads. And Mr. Jesus Christ standing there in the middle of them, grinning.

MARTHA

"Thou anointest my head with oil, my cup runneth over."

LOOMIS

He grin that big old grin . . . and niggers wallowing at his feet.

MARTHA

"Surely goodness and mercy shall follow me all the days of my life, and I shall dwell in the house of the Lord forever."

LOOMIS

Great big old white man . . . your Mr. Jesus Christ. Standing there with a whip in one hand and tote board in another, and them niggers swimming in a sea of cotton. And he counting. He tallying up the cotton. "Well, Jeremiah . . . what's the matter, you ain't picked but two hundred pounds of cotton today? Got to put you on half rations." And Jeremiah go back and lay up there on his half rations and talk about what a nice man Mr. Jesus Christ is 'cause he give him salvation after he die. Something wrong here. Something don't fit right!

MARTHA

You got to open up your heart and have faith, Herald. This world is just a trial for the next. Jesus offers you salvation.

LOOMIS

I been wading in the water. I been walking all over the River Jordan. But what it get me, huh? I done been baptized with blood of the lamb and the fire of the Holy Ghost. But what I got, huh? I got salvation? My enemies all around me picking the flesh from my bones. I'm choking on my own blood and all you got to give me is salvation?

MARTHA

You got to be clean, Herald. You got to be washed with the blood of the lamb.

LOOMIS

Blood make you clean? You clean with blood?

MARTHA

Jesus bled for you. He's the Lamb of God who takest away the sins of the world.

LOOMIS

I don't need nobody to bleed for me! I can bleed for myself.

MARTHA

You got to be something, Herald. You just can't be alive. Life don't mean nothing unless it got a meaning.

LOOMIS

What kind of meaning you got? What kind of clean you got, woman? You want blood? Blood make you clean? You clean with blood?

[Loomis slashes himself across the chest. He rubs the blood over his face and comes to a realization.]

I'm standing! I'm standing. My legs stood up! I'm standing now!

[Having found his song, the song of self-sufficiency, fully resurrected, cleansed and given breath, free from any encumbrance other than the workings of his own heart and the bonds of the flesh, having accepted the responsibility for his own presence in the world, he is free to soar above the environs that weighed and pushed his spirit into terrifying contractions.]

Goodbye, Martha.

[Loomis turns and exits, the knife still in his hands. Mattie looks about the room and rushes out after him.]

BYNUM

Herald Loomis, you shining! You shining like new money!

[The lights go down to BLACK.]

12

M. BUTTERFLY

David Henry Hwang • 1988

DAVID HWANG WAS A STANFORD UNDERGRADUATE when he wrote—"on a lark" he says—his first play, entitled *FOB* (*Fresh Off the Boat*). This biting, honest, and angry reaction to hidden (and not-so-hidden) American racism was quickly produced by the Stanford Asian-American Theatre Project, and subsequently produced professionally at the New York Public Theatre, where it won the 1980 "Obie" (Off-Broadway) award for best new play of the year.

Neither *FOB* nor a subsequent series of short, experimental plays (*The House of Sleeping Beauties*, *The Sound of a Voice*, *Family Devotions*), however, prepared the American theatre-going public for the enormous success of his first Broadway play, *M. Butterfly*, which won the 1988 Tony Award, as well as the Outer Circle Drama Critics and Drama Desk new play awards. With this play, elaborately constructed as a series of interwoven flashbacks, Hwang has taken a reportedly true historical incident, and fashioned it into a brilliantly theatrical disquisition on the major social and sexual dialec-tics of modern life: East versus West, male versus female, straight versus gay, political versus personal, and the "mainstream" versus "the Other." The actual incident was certainly bizarre: it seems that a French diplomat based in Beijing (Peking), Bernard Bouriscot by name, had apparently been duped for more than twenty years by his lover, a Chinese actress, who turned out not only to be a spy, but—completely unknown to Bouriscot—a man! Both were convicted of espionage in Paris. Rationalizing his failure to see through the sexual deception, Bouriscot told the court that he had never seen his lover naked, explaining, "I thought she was very modest. I thought it was a Chinese custom." The anatomical problems this deception may have caused were, presumably, unusual, but obviously not wholly beyond the realm of possibility. (A similar theme animates at least part of the very successful 1992 film *The Crying Game*.)

When Hwang heard the story during a dinner conversation, he, being of Chinese ancestry himself, knew that such "modesty" was *not* a Chinese custom and that Asian women are no more shy than their Western counterparts. But Hwang also realized that Bouriscot's assumption "was consistent with a certain stereotyped view of Asians as bowing, blushing flowers." Hwang's play, though in all other respects wholly original, takes off from this incident and the false stereotype.

What gives *M. Butterfly* its brilliant theatrical texture is Hwang's invention that the diplomat's lover is a star of the Peking Opera (where men traditionally played women); a star, moreover, trained also in Western music. We first see Song, the diplomat's lover-to-be, singing an aria from Puccini's *Madame Butterfly*, and it is this fantasy of the beautiful but submissive Asian woman, in love with a Western man, that centers the action. What follows is, in Hwang's own words, "a deconstructivist *Madame Butterfly*," where the stereotype is exploded, and commingled with other stereotypes: political, cultural, and sexual; all to be revealingly foregrounded against diplomatic conspiracies during the Vietnam War, the Red Guard Cultural Revolution, and the Me Decade. "We are all prisoners of our time and place," says Gallimard, as the French diplomat is here renamed, and it is Hwang's achievement to make us aware of our own ethnocentrisms and egocentrisms (our social and personal prejudices, one might say) even as he entertains our minds with their most enchanting creations. Blending the strains of Puccini with Chinese opera, and classical Asian art with Maoist militarism, Hwang has fashioned an elegant work of sexual nuance, political intrigue, and deep cultural observation. A play of ideas, and filled with (successful) theatrical experimentation and innovation in virtually every scene, *M. Butterfly* earned leaping (not just standing) ovations almost every night of its year-long Broadway run.

Does *M. Butterfly* signal the start of a brilliant lifelong career for the young Mr. Hwang? No one can tell for certain at this point, of course. Hwang's subsequent plays have been received with respectful but distinctively mixed response. His *1000 Airplanes on the Roof*, a "science-fiction music-drama" written in collaboration with composer Philip Glass and designer Jerome Sirlin, is a boldly imaginative fantasy monologue, with music and projections, that toured the world following its 1988 premiere in a Vienna airplane hangar. His backstage drama *Face Value*, however, which concerns racial considerations in theatrical casting—a subject on which Hwang has recently taken strong, well-publicized positions—closed before its scheduled 1993 Broadway opening, a victim of relatively poor reviews in its Boston premiere. Clearly, Hwang has superabundant talent and provocative, original ideas, together with the ability (and courage) to express them vividly in the theatre. Whether he can again capitalize upon them as brilliantly as in *M. Butterfly* is a subject of intense speculation in the contemporary theatre world.

⚹ M. BUTTERFLY ⚹

Playwright's Notes

*"A former French diplomat and a Chinese opera
singer have been sentenced to six years in jail for
spying for China after a two-day trial that traced a
story of clandestine love and mistaken sexual
identity. . . . Mr. Bouriscot was accused of passing
information to China after he fell in love with Mr.
Shi, whom he believed for twenty years to be a
woman."*

—The New York Times, May 11, 1986

This play was suggested by international newspaper
accounts of a recent espionage trial. For purposes of
dramatization, names have been changed, characters
created, and incidents devised or altered, and this
play does not purport to be a factual record of real
events or real people.

> *"I could escape this feeling
> With my China girl . . .*
> —David Bowie & Iggy Pop

SETTING

The action of the play takes place in a Paris prison in
the present, and in recall, during the decade 1960 to
1970 in Beijing, and from 1966 to the present in
Paris.

ACT ONE

Scene 1

M. Gallimard's prison cell. Paris. Present.

*Lights fade up to reveal René Gallimard, 65, in a
prison cell. He wears a comfortable bathrobe, and looks
old and tired. The sparsely furnished cell contains a
wooden crate upon which sits a hot plate with a kettle, and
a portable tape recorder. Gallimard sits on the crate
staring at the recorder, a sad smile on his face.*

*Upstage Song, who appears as a beautiful woman in
traditional Chinese garb, dances a traditional piece from
the Peking Opera, surrounded by the percussive clatter of
Chinese music.*

*Then, slowly, lights and sound cross-fade; the
Chinese opera music dissolves into a Western opera, the
"Love Duet" from Puccini's* Madame Butterfly. *Song
continues dancing, now to the Western accompaniment.
Though her movements are the same, the difference in
music now gives them a balletic quality.*

*Gallimard rises, and turns upstage towards the
figure of Song, who dances without acknowledging him.*

GALLIMARD
Butterfly, Butterfly . . .

[He forces himself to turn away, as the image of Song fades out, and talks to us.]

GALLIMARD
The limits of my cell are as such: four-and-a-half meters by five. There's one window against the far wall; a door, very strong, to protect me from autograph hounds. I'm responsible for the tape recorder, the hot plate, and this charming coffee table.

When I want to eat, I'm marched off to the dining room—hot, steaming slop appears on my plate. When I want to sleep, the light bulb turns itself off—the work of fairies. It's an enchanted space I occupy. The French—we know how to run a prison.

But, to be honest, I'm not treated like an ordinary prisoner. Why? Because I'm a celebrity. You see, I make people laugh.

I never dreamed this day would arrive. I've never been considered witty or clever. In fact, as a young boy, in an informal poll among my grammar school classmates, I was voted "least likely to be invited to a party." It's a title I managed to hold onto for many years. Despite some stiff competition.

But now, how the tables turn! Look at me: the life of every social function in Paris. Paris? Why be modest? My fame has spread to Amsterdam, London, New York. Listen to them! In the world's smartest parlors. I'm the one who lifts their spirits!

[With a flourish, Gallimard directs our attention to another part of the stage.]

Scene 2

A party. Present.

Lights go up on a chic-looking parlor, where a well-dressed trio, two men and one woman, make conversation. Gallimard also remains lit; he observes them from his cell.

WOMAN
And what of Gallimard?

MAN 1
Gallimard?

MAN 2
Gallimard!

GALLIMARD
[To us] You see? They're all determined to say my name, as if it were some new dance.

WOMAN
He still claims not to believe the truth.

MAN 1
What? Still? Even since the trial?

WOMAN
Yes. Isn't it mad?

MAN 2
[Laughing] He says . . . it was dark . . . and she was very modest!

[The trio break into laughter.]

MAN 1
So—what? He never touched her with his hands?

MAN 2
Perhaps he did, and simply misidentified the equipment. A compelling case for sex education in the schools.

WOMAN
To protect the National Security—the Church can't argue with that.

MAN 1
That's impossible! How could he not know?

MAN 2
Simple ignorance.

MAN 1
For twenty years?

MAN 1
Time flies when you're being stupid.

WOMAN
Well, I thought the French were ladies' men.

MAN 2
It seems Monsieur Gallimard was overly anxious to live up to his national reputation.

WOMAN
Well, he's not very good-looking.

MAN 1
No, he's not.

MAN 2
Certainly not.

WOMAN
Actually, I feel sorry for him.

MAN 2
A toast! To Monsieur Gallimard!

WOMAN
Yes! To Gallimard!

MAN 1
To Gallimard!

MAN 2
Vive la différence!

[They toast, laughing. Lights down on them.]

Scene 3

M. Gallimard's cell.

GALLIMARD
[Smiling] You see? They toast me. I've become patron saint of the socially inept. Can they really be so foolish? Men like that—they should be scratching at my door, begging to learn my secrets! For I, René Gallimard, you see, I have known, and been loved by . . . the Perfect Woman.

Alone in this cell, I sit night after night, watching our story play through my head, always searching for a new ending, one which redeems my honor, where she returns at last to my arms. And I imagine you—my ideal audience—who come to understand and even, perhaps just a little, to envy me.

[He turns on his tape recorder. Over the house speakers, we hear the opening phrases of Madame Butterfly.]

GALLIMARD
In order for you to understand what I did and why, I must introduce you to my favorite opera: *Madame Butterfly*. By Giacomo Puccini. First produced at La Scala, Milan, in 1904, it is now beloved throughout the Western world.

[As Gallimard describes the opera, the tape segues in and out to sections he may be describing.]

GALLIMARD
And why not? Its heroine, Cio-Cio-San, also known as Butterfly, is a feminine ideal, beautiful and brave. And its hero, the man for whom she gives up everything, is—[He pulls out a naval officer's cap from under his crate, pops it on his head, and struts about]—not very good-looking, not too bright, and pretty much a wimp: Benjamin Franklin Pinkerton of the U.S. Navy. As the curtain rises, he's just closed on two great bargains: one on a house, the other on a woman—call it a package deal.

Pinkerton purchased the rights to Butterfly for one hundred yen—in modern currency, equivalent to about . . . sixty-six cents. So, he's feeling pretty pleased with himself as Sharpless, the American consul, arrives to witness the marriage.

[Marc, wearing an official cap to designate Sharpless, enters and plays the character.]

SHARPLESS/MARC
Pinkerton!

PINKERTON/GALLIMARD
Sharpless! How's it hangin'? It's a great day, just great. Between my house, my wife, and the rickshaw ride in from town, I've saved nineteen cents just this morning.

SHARPLESS
Wonderful. I can see the inscription on your tombstone already: "I saved a dollar, here I lie." [He looks around] Nice house.

PINKERTON
It's artistic. Artistic, don't you think? Like the way the shoji screens slide open to reveal the wet bar and disco mirror ball? Classy, huh? Great for impressing the chicks.

SHARPLESS
"Chicks"? Pinkerton, you're going to be a married man!

PINKERTON
Well, sort of.

SHARPLESS
What do you mean?

PINKERTON
This country—Sharpless, it is okay. You got all these geisha girls running around—

SHARPLESS
I know! I live here!

PINKERTON
Then, you know the marriage laws, right? I split for one month, it's annulled!

SHARPLESS
Leave it to you to read the fine print. Who's the lucky girl?

PINKERTON
Cio-Cio-San. Her friends call her Butterfly. Sharpless, she eats out of my hand!

SHARPLESS
She's probably very hungry.

PINKERTON
Not like American girls. It's true what they say about Oriental girls. They want to be treated bad!

SHARPLESS
Oh, please!

PINKERTON
It's true!

SHARPLESS
Are you serious about this girl?

PINKERTON
I'm marrying her, aren't I?

SHARPLESS
Yes—with generous trade-in terms.

PINKERTON
When I leave, she'll known what it's like to have loved a real man. And I'll even buy her a few nylons.

SHARPLESS
You aren't planning to take her with you?

PINKERTON
Huh? Where?

SHARPLESS
Home!

PINKERTON
You mean, America? Are you crazy? Can you see her trying to buy rice in St. Louis?

SHARPLESS
So, you're not serious.

[Pause.]

PINKERTON/GALLIMARD
[As Pinkerton] Consul, I am a sailor in port. [As Gallimard] They then proceed to sing the famous duet, "The Whole World Over."

[The duet plays on the speakers. Gallimard, as Pinkerton, lip-syncs his lines from the opera.]

GALLIMARD
To give a rough translation: "The whole world over, the Yankee travels, casting his anchor wherever he wants. Life's not worth living unless he can win the hearts of the fairest maidens, then hotfoot it off the premises ASAP." [He turns towards Marc] In the preceding scene, I played Pinkerton, the womanizing

cad, and my friend Marc from school . . . [Marc bows grandly for our benefit] played Sharpless, the sensitive soul of reason. In life, however, our positions were usually—no, always—reversed.

Scene 4

Ecole Nationale. Aix-en-Provence. 1947.

GALLIMARD
No, Marc, I think I'd rather stay home.

MARC
Are you crazy?! We are going to Dad's condo in Marseille! You know what happened last time?

GALLIMARD
Of course I do.

MARC
Of course you don't! You never know. . . . They stripped, René!

GALLIMARD
Who stripped?

MARC
The girls!

GALLIMARD
Girls? Who said anything about girls?

MARC
René, we're a buncha university guys goin' up to the woods. What are we gonna do—talk philosophy?

GALLIMARD
What girls? Where do you get them?

MARC
Who cares? The point is, they come. On trucks. Packed in like sardines. The back flips open, babes hop out, we're ready to roll.

GALLIMARD
You mean, they just—?

MARC
Before you know it, every last one of them—they're stripped and splashing around my pool. There's no moon out, they can't see what's going on, their boobs are flapping, right? You close your eyes, reach out—it's grab bag, get it? Doesn't matter whose ass is between whose legs, whose teeth are sinking into who. You're just in there, going at it, eyes closed, on and on for as long as you stand. [Pause] Some fun, huh?

GALLIMARD
What happens in the morning?

MARC
In the morning, you're ready to talk some philosophy. [Beat] So how 'bout it?

GALLIMARD
Marc, I can't . . . I'm afraid they'll say no—the girls. So I never ask.

MARC
You don't have to ask! That's the beauty—don't you see? They don't have to say yes. It's perfect for a guy like you, really.

GALLIMARD
You go ahead . . . I may come later.

MARC
Hey, René—it doesn't matter that you're clumsy and got zits—they're not looking!

GALLIMARD
Thank you very much.

MARC
Wimp.

[Marc walks over to the other side of the stage, and starts waving and smiling at women in the audience.]

GALLIMARD
[To us] We now return to my version of Madame Butterfly and the events leading to my recent conviction for treason.

[Gallimard notices Marc making lewd gestures.]

GALLIMARD
Marc, what are you doing?

MARC
Huh? [Sotto voce] René, there're a lotta great babes out there. They're probably lookin' at me and thinking, "What a dangerous guy."

GALLIMARD
Yes—how could they help but be impressed by your cool sophistication?

[Gallimard pops the Sharpless cap on Marc's head, and points him offstage. Marc exits, leering.]

Scene 5

M. Gallimard's cell.

GALLIMARD
Next, Butterfly makes her entrance. We learn her age—fifteen . . . but very mature for her years.

[Lights come up on the area where we saw Song dancing at the top of the play. She appears there again, now dressed as Madame Butterfly, moving to the "Love Duet." Gallimard turns upstage slightly to watch, transfixed.]

GALLIMARD
But as she glides past him, beautiful, laughing softly behind her fan, don't we who are men sigh with hope? We, who are not handsome, nor brave, nor powerful, yet somehow belive, like Pinkerton, that we deserve a Butterfly. She arrives with all her possessions in the folds of her sleeves, lays them all out, for her man to do with as he pleases. Even her life itself—she bows her head as she whispers that she's not even worth the hundred yen he paid for her. He's already given too much, when we know he's really had to give nothing at all.

[Music and lights on Song out. Gallimard sits at his crate.]

GALLIMARD
In real life, women who put their total worth at less than sixty-six cents are quite hard to find. The closest we come is in the pages of these magazines. [He reaches into his crate, pulls out a stack of girlie magazines, and begins flipping through them.] Quite a necessity in prison. For three or four dollars, you get seven or eight women.

I first discovered these magazines at my uncle's house. One day, as a boy of twelve. The first time I saw them in his closet . . . all lined up—my body shook. Not with lust—no, with power. Here were women—a shelf-full—who would do exactly as I wanted.

[The "Love Duet" creeps in over the speakers. Special comes up, revealing, not Song this time, but a pinup girl in a sexy negligée, her back to us. Gallimard turns upstage and looks at her.]

GIRL
I know you're watching me.

GALLIMARD
My throat . . . it's dry.

GIRL
I leave my blinds open every night before I go to bed.

GALLIMARD
I can't move.

GIRL
I leave my blinds open and the lights on.

GALLIMARD
I'm shaking. My skin is hot, but my penis is soft. Why?

GIRL
I stand in front of the window.

GALLIMARD
What is she going to do?

GIRL
I toss my hair, and I let my lips part . . . barely.

GALLIMARD
I shouldn't be seeing this. It's so dirty. I'm so bad.

GIRL
Then, slowly, I lift off my nightdress.

GALLIMARD
Oh, god. I can't believe it. I can't—

GIRL
I toss it to the ground.

GALLIMARD
Now, she's going to walk away. She's going to—

GIRL
I stand there, in the light, displaying myself.

GALLIMARD
No. She's—why is she naked?

GIRL
To you.

GALLIMARD
In front of a window? This is wrong. No—

GIRL
Without shame.

GALLIMARD
No, she must . . . like it.

GIRL
I like it.

GALLIMARD
She . . . she wants me to see.

GIRL
I want you to see.

GALLIMARD
I can't believe it! She's getting excited!

GIRL
I can't see you. You can do whatever you want.

GALLIMARD
I can't do a thing. Why?

GIRL
What would you like me to do . . . next?

[Lights go down on her. Music off. Silence, as Gallimard puts away his magazines. Then he resumes talking to us.]

GALLIMARD
Act Two begins with Butterfly staring at the ocean. Pinkerton's been called back to the U.S., and he's given his wife a detailed schedule of his plans. In the column marked "return date," he's written "when the robins nest." This failed to ignite her suspicions. Now, three years have passed without a peep from him. Which brings a response from her faithful servant, Suzuki.

[Comrade Chin enters, playing Suzuki.]

SUZUKI
Girl, he's a loser. What'd he ever give you? Nineteen cents and those ugly Day-Glo stockings? Look, it's finished! Kaput! Done! And you should be glad! I mean, the guy was a woofer! He tried before, you know—before he met you, he went down to geisha central and plunked down his spare change in front of the usual candidates—everyone else gagged! These are hungry prostitutes, and they were not interested, get the picture? Now, stop slathering when an American ship sails in, and let's make some bucks—I mean, yen! We are broke!

Now, what about Yamadori? Hey, hey—don't look away—the man is a prince—figuratively, and, what's even better, literally. He's rich, he's handsome, he says he'll die if you don't marry him—and he's even willing to overlook the little fact that you've been deflowered all over the place by a foreign devil. What do you mean, "But he's Japanese?" You're Japanese! You think you've been touched by the whitey god? He was a sailor with dirty hands!

[Suzuki stalks offstage.]

GALLIMARD
She's also visited by Consul Sharpless, sent by Pinkerton on a minor errand.

[Marc enters, as Sharpless.]

SHARPLESS
I hate this job.

GALLIMARD
This Pinkerton—he doesn't show up personally to tell his wife he's abandoning her. No, he sends a government diplomat . . . at taxpayer's expense.

SHARPLESS
Butterfly? Butterfly? I have some bad—I'm going to be ill. Butterfly, I came to tell you—

GALLIMARD
Butterfly says she knows he'll return and if he doesn't she'll kill herself rather than go back to her own people. [Beat][1] This causes a lull in the conversation.

SHARPLESS
Let's put it this way . . .

GALLIMARD
Butterfly runs into the next room, and returns holding—

[Sound cue: a baby crying. Sharpless, "seeing" this, backs away.]

SHARPLESS
Well, good. Happy to see things going so well. I suppose I'll be going now. Ta ta. Ciao. [He turns away. Sound cue out] I hate this job. [He exits]

GALLIMARD
At that moment, Butterfly spots in the harbor an American ship—the Abramo Lincoln!

[Music cue: "The Flower Duet." Song, still dressed as Butterfly, changes into a wedding kimono, moving to the music.]

GALLIMARD
This is the moment that redeems her years of waiting. With Suzuki's help, they cover the room with flowers—

[Chin, as Suzuki, trudges onstage and drops a lone flower without much enthusiasm.]

GALLIMARD
—and she changes into her wedding dress to prepare for Pinkerton's arrival.

---

[1] A momentary pause.

[Suzuki helps Butterfly change. Helga enters, and helps Gallimard change into a tuxedo.]

GALLIMARD
I married a woman older than myself—Helga.

HELGA
My father was ambassador to Australia. I grew up among criminals and kangaroos.

GALLIMARD
Hearing that brought me to the altar—

[Helga exits.]

GALLIMARD
—where I took a vow renouncing love. No fantasy woman would ever want me, so, yes, I would settle for a quick leap up the career ladder. Passion, I banish, and in its place—practicality!

But my vows had long since lost their charm by the time we arrived in China. The sad truth is that all men want a beautiful woman, and the uglier the man, the greater the want.

[Suzuki makes final adjustments of Butterfly's costume, as does Gallimard of his tuxedo.]

GALLIMARD
I married late, at age thirty-one. I was faithful to my marriage for eight years. Until the day when, as a junior-level diplomat in puritanical Peking, in a parlor at the German ambassador's house, during the "Reign of a Hundred Flowers," I first saw her . . . singing the death scene from Madame Butterfly.

[Suzuki runs offstage.]

Scene 6

German ambassador's house. Beijing. 1960.

The upstage special area now becomes a stage. Several chairs face upstage, representing seating for some twenty guests in the parlor. A few "diplomats"—René, Marc, Toulon—in formal dress enter and take seats.

Gallimard also sits down, but turns towards us and continues to talk. Orchestral accompaniment on the tape is now replaced by a simple piano. Song picks up the death scene from the point where Butterfly uncovers the hara-kiri knife.

GALLIMARD
The ending is pitiful. Pinkerton, in an act of great courage, stays home and sends his American wife to

pick up Butterfly's child. The truth, long deferred, has come up to her door.

[Song, playing Butterfly, sings the lines from the opera in her own voice—which, though not classical, should be decent.]

SONG
"Con onor muore/ chi non puo serbar/ vita con onore."

GALLIMARD
[Simultaneously] "Death with honor/ Is better than life/ Life with dishonor."

[The stage is illuminated; we are now completely within an elegant diplomat's residence. Song proceeds to play out an abbreviated death scene. Everyone in the room applauds. Song, shyly, takes her bows. Others in the room rush to congratulate her. Gallimard remains with us.]

GALLIMARD
They say in opera the voice is everything. That's probably why I'd never before enjoyed opera. Here . . . here was a Butterfly with little or no voice—but she had the grace, the delicacy . . . I believed this girl. I believed her suffering. I wanted to take her in my arms—so delicate, even I could protect her, take her home, pamper her until she smiled.

[Over the course of the preceding speech, Song has broken from the upstage crowd and moved directly upstage of Gallimard.]

SONG
Excuse me. Monsieur . . . ?

[Gallimard turns upstage, shocked.]

GALLIMARD
Oh! Gallimard. Mademoiselle . . . ? A beautiful . . .

SONG
Song Liling.

GALLIMARD
A beautiful performance.

SONG
Oh, please.

GALLIMARD
I usually—

SONG
You make me blush. I'm no opera singer at all.

GALLIMARD
I usually don't like Butterfly.

SONG
I can't blame you in the least.

GALLIMARD
I mean, the story—

SONG
Ridiculous.

GALLIMARD
I like the story, but . . . what?

SONG
Oh, you like it?

GALLIMARD
I . . . what I mean is, I've always seen it played by huge women in so much bad makeup.

SONG
Bad makeup is not unique to the West.

GALLIMARD
But, who can believe them?

SONG
And you believe me?

GALLIMARD
Absolutely. You were utterly convincing. It's the first time—

SONG
Convincing? As a Japanese woman? The Japanese used hundreds of our people for medical experiments during the war, you know. But I gather such an irony is lost on you.

GALLIMARD
No! I was about to say, it's the first time I've seen the beauty of the story.

SONG
Really?

GALLIMARD
Of her death. It's a . . . a pure sacrifice. He's unworthy, but what can she do? She loves him . . . so much. It's a very beautiful story.

SONG
Well, yes, to a Westerner.

GALLIMARD
Excuse me?

SONG
It's one of your favorite fantasies, isn't it? The submissive Oriental woman and the cruel white man.

GALLIMARD
Well, I didn't quite mean . . .

SONG
Consider it this way: what would you say if a blonde homecoming queen fell in love with a short Japanese businessman? He treats her cruelly, then goes homes for three years, during which time she prays to his picture and turns down marriage from a young Kennedy. Then, when she learns he has remarried, she kills herself. Now, I believe you would consider this girl to be a deranged idiot, correct? But because it's an Oriental who kills herself for a Westerner—ah!—you find it beautiful.

[Silence.]

GALLIMARD
Yes . . . well . . . I see your point . . .

SONG
I will never do Butterfly again, Monsieur Gallimard. If you wish to see some real theatre, come to the Peking Opera sometime. Expand your mind.

[Song walks offstage.]

GALLIMARD
[To us] So much for protecting her in my big Western arms.

Scene 7

M. Gallimard's apartment. Beijing. 1960.
    Gallimard changes from his tux into a casual suit. Helga enters.

GALLIMARD
The Chinese are an incredibly arrogant people.

HELGA
They warned us about that in Paris, remember?

GALLIMARD
Even Parisians consider them arrogant. That's a switch.

HELGA
What is it that Madame Su says? "We are a very old civilization." I never know if she's talking about her country or herself.

GALLIMARD
I walk around here, all I hear every day, everywhere is how *old* this culture is. The fact that "old" may be synonymous with "senile" doesn't occur to them.

HELGA
You're not going to change them. "East is east, west is west, and . . ." whatever that guy said.

GALLIMARD
It's just that—silly. I met . . . at Ambassador Koening's tonight—you should've been there.

HELGA
Koening? Oh god, no. Did he enchant you all again with the history of Bavaria?

GALLIMARD
No. I met, I suppose, the Chinese equivalent of a diva. She's a singer in the Chinese opera.

HELGA
They have an opera, too? Do they sing in Chinese? Or maybe—in Italian?

GALLIMARD
Tonight, she did sing in Italian.

HELGA
How'd she manage that?

GALLIMARD
She must've been educated in the West before the Revolution. Her French is very good also. Anyway, she sang the death scene from *Madame Butterfly*.

HELGA
Madame Butterfly! Then I should have come. [She begins humming, floating around the room as if dragging long kimono sleeves.] Did she have a nice costume? I think it's a classic piece of music.

GALLIMARD
That's what *I* thought, too. Don't let her hear you say that.

HELGA
What's wrong?

GALLIMARD
Evidently the Chinese hate it.

HELGA
She hated it, but she performed it anyway? Is she perverse?

GALLIMARD
They hate it because the white man gets the girl. Sour grapes if you ask me.

HELGA
Politics again? Why can't they just hear it as a piece of beautiful music? So, what's in their opera?

GALLIMARD

I don't know. But, whatever it is, I'm sure it must be *old.*

[*Helga exits.*]

Scene 8

Chinese opera house and the streets of Beijing. 1960.
The sound of gongs clanging fills the stage.

GALLIMARD

My wife's innocent question kept ringing in my ears. I asked around, but no one knew anything about the Chinese opera. It took four weeks, but my curiosity overcame my cowardice. This Chinese diva—this unwilling Butterfly—what did she do to make her so proud?

The room was hot, and full of smoke. Wrinkled faces, old women, teeth missing—a man with a growth on his neck, like a human toad. All smiling, pipes falling from their mouths, cracking nuts between their teeth, a live chicken pecking at my foot—all looking, screaming, gawking . . . at her.

[*The upstage area is suddenly hit with a harsh white light. It has become the stage for the Chinese opera performance. Two dancers enter, along with Song. Gallimard stands apart, watching. Song glides gracefully amidst the two dancers. Drums suddenly slam to a halt. Song strikes a pose, looking straight at Gallimard. Dancers exit. Light change. Pause, then Song walks right off the stage and straight up to Gallimard.*]

SONG

Yes. You. White man. I'm looking straight at you.

GALLIMARD

Me?

SONG

You see any other white men? It was too easy to spot you. How often does a man in my audience come in a tie?

[*Song starts to remove her costume. Underneath, she wears simple baggy clothes. They are now backstage. The show is over.*]

SONG

So, you are an adventurous imperialist?

GALLIMARD

I . . . thought it would further my education.

SONG

It took you four weeks. Why?

GALLIMARD

I've been busy.

SONG

Well, education has always been undervalued in the West, hasn't it?

GALLIMARD

[*Laughing*] I don't think it's true.

SONG

No, you wouldn't. You're a Westerner. How can you objectively judge your own values?

GALLIMARD

I think it's possible to achieve some distance.

SONG

Do you? [*Pause*] It stinks in here. Let's go.

GALLIMARD

These are the smells of your loyal fans.

SONG

I love them for being my fans, I hate the smell they leave behind. I too can distance myself from my people. [*She looks around, then whispers in his ear*] "Art for the masses" is a shitty excuse to keep artists poor. [*She pops a cigarette in her mouth*] Be a gentlemen, will you? And light my cigarette.

[*Gallimard fumbles for a match.*]

GALLIMARD

I don't . . . smoke.

SONG

[*Lighting her own*] Your loss. Had you lit my cigarette, I might have blown a puff of smoke right between your eyes. Come.

[*They start to walk about the stage. It is a summer night on the Beijing streets. Sounds of the city play on the house speakers.*]

SONG

How I wish there were even a tiny cafe to sit in. With cappuccinos, and men in tuxedos and bad expatriate jazz.

GALLIMARD

If my history serves me correctly, you weren't even allowed into the clubs in Shanghai before the Revolution.

SONG

Your history serves you poorly, Monsieur Gallimard. True, there were signs reading "No dogs and Chinamen." But a woman, especially a delicate Oriental woman—we always go where we please. Could you imagine it otherwise? Clubs in China filled with pasty, big-thighed white women, while thousands of slender lotus blossoms wait just outside the door? Never. The clubs would be empty. *[Beat]* We have always held a certain fascination for you Caucasian men, have we not?

GALLIMARD

But . . . that fascination is imperialist, or so you tell me.

SONG

Do you believe everything I tell you? Yes. It is always imperialist. But sometimes . . . sometimes, it is also mutual. Oh—this is my flat.

GALLIMARD

I didn't even—

SONG

Thank you. Come another time and we will further expand your mind.

[Song exits. Gallimard continues roaming the streets as he speaks to us.]

GALLIMARD

What was that? What did she mean, "Sometimes . . . it is mutual?" Women do not flirt with me. And I normally can't talk to them. But tonight, I held up my end of the conversation.

Scene 9

Gallimard's bedroom. Beijing. 1960.
Helga enters.

HELGA

You didn't tell me you'd be home late.

GALLIMARD

I didn't intend to. Something came up.

HELGA

Oh? Like what?

GALLIMARD

I went to the . . . to the Dutch ambassador's home.

HELGA

Again?

GALLIMARD

There was a reception for a visiting scholar. He's writing a six-volume treatise on the Chinese revolution. We all gathered that meant he'd have to live here long enough to actually write six volumes, and we all expressed our deepest sympathies.

HELGA

Well, I had a good night too. I went with the ladies to a martial arts demonstration. Some of those men—when they break those thick boards—*[She mimes fanning herself]* whoo-whoo!

[Helga exits. Lights dim.]

GALLIMARD

I lied to my wife. Why? I've never had any reason to lie before. But what reason did I have tonight? I didn't do anything wrong. That night, I had a dream. Other people, I've been told, have dreams where angels appear. Or dragons, or Sophia Loren in a towel. In my dream, Marc from school appeared.

[Marc enters, in a nightshirt and cap.]

MARC

René! You met a girl!

[Gallimard and Marc stumble down the Beijing streets. Night sounds over the speakers.]

GALLIMARD

It's not that amazing, thank you.

MARC

No! It's so monumental, I heard about it halfway around the world in my sleep!

GALLIMARD

I've met girls before, you know.

MARC

Name one. I've come across time and space to congratulate you. *[He hands Gallimard a bottle of wine.]*

GALLIMARD

Marc, this is expensive.

MARC

On those rare occasions when you become a formless spirit, why not steal the best?

[Marc pops open the bottle, begins to share it with Gallimard.]

GALLIMARD

You embarrass me. She . . . there's no reason to think she likes me.

MARC
"Sometimes, it is mutual"?

GALLIMARD
Oh.

MARC
"Mutual"? "Mutual"? What does that mean?

GALLIMARD
You heard!

MARC
It means the money is in the bank, you only have to write the check!

GALLIMARD
I am a married man!

MARC
And an excellent one too. I cheated after . . . six months. Then again and again, until now—three hundred girls in twelve years.

GALLIMARD
I don't think we should hold that up as a model.

MARC
Of course not! My life—it is disgusting! Phooey! Phooey! But, you—you are the model husband.

GALLIMARD
Anyway, it's impossible. I'm a foreigner.

MARC
Ah, yes. She cannot love you, it is taboo, but something deep inside her heart . . . she cannot help herself . . . she must surrender to you. It is her destiny.

GALLIMARD
How do you imagine all this?

MARC
The same way you do. It's an old story. It's in our blood. They fear us, René. Their women fear us. And their men—their men hate us. And, you know something? They are all correct.

[They spot a light in a window.]

MARC
There! There, René!

GALLIMARD
It's her window.

MARC
Late at night—it burns. The light—it burns for you.

GALLIMARD
I won't look. It's not respectful.

MARC
We don't have to be respectful. We're foreign devils.

[Enter Song, in a sheer robe. The "One Fine Day" aria creeps in over the speakers. With her back to us, Song mimes attending to her toilette. Her robe comes loose, revealing her white shoulders.]

MARC
All your life you've waited for a beautiful girl who would lay down for you. All your life you've smiled like a saint when it's happened to every other man you know. And you see them in magazines and you see them in movies. And you wonder, what's wrong with me? Will anyone beautiful ever want me? As the years pass, your hair thins and you struggle to hold onto even your hopes. Stop struggling, René. The wait is over. *[He exits.]*

GALLIMARD
Marc? Marc?

[At that moment, Song, her back still towards us, drops her robe. A second of her naked back, than a sound cue: a phone ringing, very loud. Blackout, followed in the next beat by a special up on the bedroom area, where a phone now sits. Gallimard stumbles across the stage and picks up the phone. Sound cue out. Over the course of his conversation, area lights fill the vicinity of his bed. It is the following morning.]

GALLIMARD
Yes? Hello?

SONG
[Offstage] Is it very early?

GALLIMARD
Why, yes.

SONG
[Offstage] How early?

GALLIMARD
It's . . . it's 5:30. Why are you—?

SONG
[Offstage] But it's light outside. Already.

GALLIMARD
It is. The sun must be in confusion today.

[Over the course of Song's next speech, her upstage special comes up again. She sits in a chair, legs crossed, in a robe, telephone to her ear.]

SONG
I waited until I saw the sun. That was as much discipline as I could manage for one night. Do you forgive me?

GALLIMARD
Of course . . . for what?

SONG
Then I'll ask you quickly. Are you really interested in the opera?

GALLIMARD
Why, yes. Yes I am.

SONG
Then come again next Thursday. I am playing *The Drunken Beauty*. May I count on you?

GALLIMARD
Yes. You may.

SONG
Perfect. Well, I must be getting to bed. I'm exhausted. It's been a very long night for me.

[Song hangs up; special on her goes off. Gallimard begins to dress for work.]

Scene 10

Song Liling's apartment. Beijing. 1960.

GALLIMARD
I returned to the opera that next week, and the week after that . . . she keeps our meetings so short—perhaps fifteen, twenty minutes at most. So I am left each week with a thirst which is intensified. In this way, fifteen weeks have gone by. I am starting to doubt the words of my friend Marc. But no, not really. In my heart, I know she has . . . an interest in me. I suspect this is her way. She is outwardly bold and outspoken, yet her heart is shy and afraid. It is the Oriental in her at war with her Western education.

SONG
[Offstage] I will be out in an instant. Ask the servant for anything you want.

GALLIMARD
Tonight, I have finally been invited to enter her apartment. Though the idea is almost beyond belief, I believe she is afraid of me.

[Gallimard looks around the room. He picks up a picture in a frame, studies it. Without his noticing, Song enters, dressed elegantly in a black gown from the twenties. She stands in the doorway looking like Anna May Wong.]

SONG
That is my father.

GALLIMARD
[Surprised] Mademoiselle Song . . .

[She glides up to him, snatches away the picture.]

SONG
It is very good that he did not live to see the Revolution. They would, no doubt, have made him kneel on broken glass. Not that he didn't deserve such a punishment. But he is my father. I would've hated to see it happen.

GALLIMARD
I'm very honored that you've allowed me to visit your home.

[Song curtseys.]

SONG
Thank you. Oh! Haven't you been poured any tea?

GALLIMARD
I'm really not—

SONG
[To her offstage servant] Shu-Fang! Cha! Kwai-lah! [To Gallimard] I'm sorry. You want everything to be perfect—

GALLIMARD
Please.

SONG
—and before the evening even begins—

GALLIMARD
I'm really not thirsty.

SONG
—it's ruined.

GALLIMARD
[Sharply] Mademoiselle Song!

[Song sits down.]

SONG
I'm sorry.

GALLIMARD
What are you apologizing for now?

[Pause; Song starts to giggle.]

SONG
I don't know!

[Gallimard laughs.]

GALLIMARD
Exactly my point.

SONG
Oh, I am silly. Lightheaded. I promise not to apologize for anything else tonight, do you hear me?

GALLIMARD
That's a good girl.

[Shu-Fang, a servant girl, comes out with a tea tray and starts to pour.]

SONG
[To Shu-Fang] No! I'll pour myself for the gentleman!

[Shu-Fang, staring at Gallimard, exits.]

SONG
No, I . . . I don't even know why I invited you up.

GALLIMARD
Well, I'm glad you did.

[Song looks around the room.]

SONG
There is an element of danger to your presence.

GALLIMARD
Oh?

SONG
You must know.

GALLIMARD
It doesn't concern me. We both know why I'm here.

SONG
It doesn't concern me either. No . . . well perhaps . . .

GALLIMARD
What?

SONG
Perhaps I am slightly afraid of scandal.

GALLIMARD
What are we doing?

SONG
I'm entertaining you. In my parlor.

GALLIMARD
In France, that would hardly—

SONG
France. France is a country living in the modern era. Perhaps even ahead of it. China is a nation whose soul is firmly rooted two thousand years in the past. What I do, even pouring the tea for you now . . . it has . . . implications. The walls and windows say so. Even my own heart, strapped inside this Western dress . . . even it says things—things I don't care to hear.

[Song hands Gallimard a cup of tea. Gallimard puts his hand over both the teacup and Song's hand.]

GALLIMARD
This is a beautiful dress.

SONG
Don't.

GALLIMARD
What?

SONG
I don't even know if it looks right on me.

GALLIMARD
Believe me—

SONG
You are from France. You see so many beautiful women.

GALLIMARD
France? Since when are the European women—?

SONG
Oh! What am I trying to do, anyway?!

[Song runs to the door, composes herself, then turns towards Gallimard.]

SONG
Monsieur Gallimard, perhaps you should go.

GALLIMARD
But . . . why?

SONG
There's something wrong about this.

GALLIMARD
I don't see what.

SONG
I feel . . . I am not myself.

GALLIMARD
No. You're nervous.

SONG
Please. Hard as I try to be modern, to speak like a man, to hold a Western woman's strong face up to my

own . . . in the end, I fail. A small, frightened heart beats too quickly and gives me away. Monsieur Gallimard, I'm a Chinese girl. I've never . . . never invited a man up to my flat before. The forwardness of my actions makes my skin burn.

GALLIMARD
What are you afraid of? Certainly not me, I hope.

SONG
I'm a modest girl.

GALLIMARD
I know. And very beautiful. [He touches her hair.]

SONG
Please—go now. The next time you see me, I shall again be myself.

GALLIMARD
I like you the way you are right now.

SONG
You are a cad.

GALLIMARD
What do you expect? I'm a foreign devil.

[Gallimard walks downstage. Song exits.]

GALLIMARD
[To us] Did you hear the way she talked about Western women? Much differently than the first night. She does—she feels inferior to them—and to me.

Scene 11

The French embassy. Beijing. 1960.
    Gallimard moves towards a desk.

GALLIMARD
I determined to try an experiment. In Madame Butterfly, Cio-Cio-San fears that the Western man who catches a butterfly will pierce its heart with a needle, then leave it to perish. I began to wonder: had I, too, caught a butterfly who would writhe on a needle?

[Marc enters, dressed as a bureaucrat, holding a stack of papers. As Gallimard speaks, Marc hands papers to him. He peruses, then signs, stamps or rejects them.]

GALLIMARD
Over the next five weeks, I worked like a dynamo. I stopped going to the opera, I didn't phone or write her. I knew this little flower was waiting for me to call, and, as I wickedly refused to do so, I felt for the first time that rush of power—the absolute power of a man.

[Marc continues acting as the bureaucrat, but he now speaks as himself.]

MARC
René! It's me!

GALLIMARD
Marc—I hear your voice everywhere now. Even in the midst of work.

MARC
That's because I'm watching you—all the time.

GALLIMARD
You were always the most popular guy in school.

MARC
Well, there's no guarantee of failure in life like happiness in high school. Somehow I knew I'd end up in the suburbs working for Renault and you'd be in the Orient picking exotic women off the trees. And they say there's no justice.

GALLIMARD
That's why you were my friend?

MARC
I gave you a little of my life, so that now you can give me some of yours. [Pause] Remember Isabelle?

GALLIMARD
Of course I remember! She was my first experience.

MARC
We all wanted to ball her. But she only wanted me.

GALLIMARD
I had her.

MARC
Right. You balled her.

GALLIMARD
You were the only one who ever believed me.

MARC
Well, there's a good reason for that. [Beat] C'mon. You must've guessed.

GALLIMARD
You told me to wait in the bushes by the cafeteria that night. The next thing I knew, she was on me. Dress up in the air.

MARC
She never wore underwear.

GALLIMARD
My arms were pinned to the dirt.

MARC
She loved the superior position. A girl ahead of her time.

GALLIMARD
I looked up, and there was this woman . . . bouncing up and down on my loins.

MARC
Screaming, right?

GALLIMARD
Screaming, and breaking off the branches all around me, and pounding my butt up and down into the dirt.

MARC
Huffing and puffing like a locomotive.

GALLIMARD
And in the middle of all this, the leaves were getting into my mouth, my legs were losing circulation, I thought, "God. So this is *it*?"

MARC
You thought that?

GALLIMARD
Well, I was worried about my legs falling off.

MARC
You didn't have a good time?

GALLIMARD
No, that's not what I—I had a great time!

MARC
You're sure?

GALLIMARD
Yeah. Really.

MARC
'Cuz I wanted you to have a good time.

GALLIMARD
I did.

[Pause.]

MARC
Shit. [Pause.] When all is said and done, she was kind of a lousy lay, wasn't she? I mean, there was a lot of energy there, but you never knew what she was doing with it. Like when she yelled "I'm coming!"—hell, it was so loud, you wanted to go "Look, it's not that big a deal."

GALLIMARD
I got scared. I thought she meant someone was actually coming. [Pause.] But, Marc?

MARC
What?

GALLIMARD
Thanks.

MARC
Oh, don't mention it.

GALLIMARD
It was my first experience.

MARC
Yeah. You got her.

GALLIMARD
I got her.

MARC
Wait! Look at that letter again!

[Gallimard picks up one of the papers he's been stamping, and rereads it.]

GALLIMARD
[To us] After six weeks, they began to arrive. The letters.

[Upstage special on Song, as Madame Butterfly. The scene is underscored by the "Love Duet."]

SONG
Did we fight? I do not know. Is the opera no longer of interest to you? Please come—my audiences miss the white devil in their midst.

[Gallimard looks up from the letter, towards us.]

GALLIMARD
[To us] A concession, but much too dignified. [Beat; he discards the letter] I skipped the opera again that week to complete a position paper on trade.

[The bureaucrat hands him another letter.]

SONG
Six weeks have passed since last we met. Is this your practice—to leave friends in the lurch? Sometimes I hate you, sometimes I hate myself, but always I miss you.

GALLIMARD
[To us] Better, but I don't like the way she calls me "friend." When a woman calls a man her "friend," she's calling him a eunuch or a homosexual. [Beat; he

discards the letter] I was absent from the opera for the seventh week, feeling a sudden urge to clean out my files.

[Bureaucrat hands him another letter.]

SONG

Your rudeness is beyond belief. I don't deserve this cruelty. Don't bother to call. I'll have you turned away at the door.

GALLIMARD

[To us] I didn't. *[He discards the letter; bureaucrat hands him another]* And then finally, the letter that concluded my experiment.

SONG

I am out of words. I can hide behind dignity no longer. What do you want? I have already given you my shame.

[Gallimard gives the letter back to Marc, slowly. Special on Song fades out.]

GALLIMARD

[To us] Reading it, I became suddenly ashamed. Yes, my experiment had been a success. She was turning on my needle. But the victory seemed hollow.

MARC

Hollow?! Are you crazy?

GALLIMARD

Nothing, Marc. Please go away.

MARC

[Exiting, with papers] Haven't I taught you anything?

GALLIMARD

"I have already given you my shame." I had to attend a reception that evening. On the way, I felt sick. If there is a God, surely he would punish me now. I had finally gained power over a beautiful woman, only to abuse it cruelly. There must be justice in the world. I had the strange feeling that the ax would fall this very evening.

Scene 12

Ambassador Toulon's residence. Beijing. 1960.

Sound cue: party noises. Light change. We are now in a spacious residence. Toulon, the French ambassador, enters and taps Gallimard on the shoulder.

TOULON

Gallimard? Can I have a word? Over here.

GALLIMARD

[To us] Manuel Toulon. French ambassador to China. He likes to think of us all as his children. Rather like God.

TOULON

Look, Gallimard, there's not much to say. I've liked you. From the day you walked in. You were no leader, but you were tidy and efficient.

GALLIMARD

Thank you, sir.

TOULON

Don't jump the gun. Okay, our needs in China are changing. It's embarrassing that we lost Indochina. Someone just wasn't on the ball there. I don't mean you personally, of course.

GALLIMARD

Thank you, sir.

TOULON

We're going to be doing a lot more information-gathering in the future. The nature of our work here is changing. Some people are just going to have to go. It's nothing personal.

GALLIMARD

Oh.

TOULON

Want to know a secret? Vice-Consul LeBon is being transferred.

GALLIMARD

[To us] My immediate superior!

TOULON

And most of his department.

GALLIMARD

[To us] Just as I feared! God has seen my evil heart—

TOULON

But not you.

GALLIMARD

[To us]—and he's taking her away just as . . . *[To Toulon]* Excuse me, sir?

TOULON

Scare you? I think I did. Cheer up, Gallimard. I want you to replace LeBon as vice-consul.

GALLIMARD

You—? Yes, well, thank you, sir.

TOULON
Anytime.

GALLIMARD
I . . . accept with great humility.

TOULON
Humility won't be part of the job. You're going to co-ordinate the revamped intelligence division. Want to know a secret? A year ago, you would've been out. But the past few months, I don't know how it happened, you've become this new aggressive confident . . . thing. And they also tell me you get along with the Chinese. So I think you're a lucky man, Gallimard. Congratulations.

[They shake hands. Toulon exits. Party noises out. Gallimard stumbles across a darkened stage.]

GALLIMARD
Vice-consul? Impossible! As I stumbled out of the party, I saw it written across the sky: There is no God. Or, no—say that there is a God. But that God . . . understands. Of course! God who creates Eve to serve Adam, who blesses Solomon with his harem but ties Jezebel to a burning bed—that God is a man. And he understands! At age thirty-nine, I was suddenly initiated into the way of the world.

Scene 13

Song Liling's apartment. Beijing. 1960.
Song enters, in a sheer dressing gown.

SONG
Are you crazy?

GALLIMARD
Mademoiselle Song—

SONG
To come here—at this hour? After . . . after eight weeks?

GALLIMARD
It's the most amazing—

SONG
You bang on my door? Scare my servants, scandalize the neighbors?

GALLIMARD
I've been promoted. To vice-consul.

[Pause.]

SONG
And what is that supposed to mean to me?

GALLIMARD
Are you my Butterfly?

SONG
What are you saying?

GALLIMARD
I've come tonight for an answer: are you my Butterfly?

SONG
Don't you know already?

GALLIMARD
I want you to say it.

SONG
I don't want to say it.

GALLIMARD
So, that is your answer?

SONG
You know how I feel about—

GALLIMARD
I do remember one thing.

SONG
What?

GALLIMARD
In the letter I received today.

SONG
Don't.

GALLIMARD
"I have already given you my shame."

SONG
It's enough that I even wrote it.

GALLIMARD
Well, then—

SONG
I shouldn't have it splashed across my face.

GALLIMARD
—if that's all true—

SONG
Stop!

GALLIMARD
Then what is one more short answer?

SONG
I don't want to!

GALLIMARD
Are you my Butterfly? [Silence; he crosses the room and begins to touch her hair] I want from you honesty.

There should be nothing false between us. No false pride.

[Pause.]

SONG
Yes, I am. I am your Butterfly.

GALLIMARD
Then let me be honest with you. It is because of you that I was promoted tonight. You have changed my life forever. My little Butterfly, there should be no more secrets: I love you.

[He starts to kiss her roughly. She resists slightly.]

SONG
No . . . no . . . gently . . . please, I've never . . .

GALLIMARD
No?

SONG
I've tried to appear experienced, but . . . the truth is . . . no.

GALLIMARD
Are you cold?

SONG
Yes. Cold.

GALLIMARD
Then we will go very, very slowly.

[He starts to caress her; her gown begins to open.]

SONG
No . . . let me . . . keep my clothes . . .

GALLIMARD
But . . .

SONG
Please . . . it all frightens me. I'm a modest Chinese girl.

GALLIMARD
My poor little treasure.

SONG
I am your treasure. Though inexperienced, I am not . . . ignorant. They teach us things, our mothers, about pleasing a man.

GALLIMARD
Yes?

SONG
I'll do my best to make you happy. Turn off the lights.

[Gallimard gets up and heads for a lamp. Song, propped up on one elbow, tosses her hair back and smiles.]

SONG
Monsieur Gallimard?

GALLIMARD
Yes, Butterfly?

SONG
"Vieni, vieni!"

GALLIMARD
"Come, darling."

SONG
"Ah! Dolce notte!"

GALLIMARD
"Beautiful night."

SONG
"Tutto estatico d'amor ride il ciel!"

GALLIMARD
"All ecstatic with love, the heavens are filled with laughter."

[He turns off the lamp. Blackout.]

──────── ACT TWO ────────

Scene 1

M. Gallimard's cell. Paris. Present.
    Lights up on Gallimard. He sits in his cell, reading from a leaflet.

GALLIMARD
This, from a contemporary critic's commentary on *Madame Butterfly*: "Pinkerton suffers from . . . being an obnoxious bounder whom every man in the audience itches to kick." Bully for us men in the audience! Then, in the same note: "Butterfly is the most irresistibly appealing of Puccini's 'Little Women.' Watching the succession of her humiliations is like watching a child under torture. [He tosses the pamphlet over his shoulder] I suggest that, while we men may all want to kick Pinkerton, very few of us would pass up the opportunity to *be* Pinkerton.

[Gallimard moves out of his cell.]

Scene 2

Gallimard and Butterfly's flat. Beijing. 1960.

    We are in a simple but well-decorated parlor. Gallimard moves to sit on a sofa, while Song, dressed in a chong sam, enters and curls up at his feet.

GALLIMARD

[*To us*] We secured a flat on the outskirts of Peking. Butterfly, as I was calling her now, decorated our "home" with Western furniture and Chinese antiques. And there, on a few stolen afternoons or evenings each week, Butterfly commenced her education.

SONG

The Chinese men—they keep us down.

GALLIMARD

Even in the "New Society"?

SONG

In the "New Society," we are all kept ignorant equally. That's one of the exciting things about loving a Western man. I know you are not threatened by a woman's education.

GALLIMARD

I'm no saint, Butterfly.

SONG

But you come from a progressive society.

GALLIMARD

We're not always reminding each other how "old" we are, if that's what you mean.

SONG

Exactly. We Chinese—once, I suppose, it is true, we ruled the world. But so what? How much more exciting to be part of the society ruling the world today. Tell me—what's happening in Vietnam?

GALLIMARD

Oh, Butterfly—you want me to bring my work home?

SONG

I want to know what you know. To be impressed by my man. It's not the particulars so much as the fact that you're making decisions which change the shape of the world.

GALLIMARD

Not the world. At best, a small corner.

[Toulon enters, and sits at a desk upstage.]

Scene 3

French embassy. Beijing. 1961.

    Gallimard moves downstage, to Toulon's desk. Song remains upstage, watching.

TOULON

And a more troublesome corner is hard to imagine.

GALLIMARD

So, the Americans plan to begin bombing?

TOULON

This is very secret, Gallimard: yes. The Americans don't have an embassy here. They're asking us to be their eyes and ears. Say Jack Kennedy signed an order to bomb North Vietnam, Laos. How would the Chinese react?

GALLIMARD

I think the Chinese will squawk—

TOULON

Uh-huh.

GALLIMARD

—but, in their hearts, they don't even like Ho Chi Minh.

[Pause.]

TOULON

What a bunch of jerks. Vietnam was *our* colony. Not only didn't the Americans help us fight to keep them, but now, seven years later, they've come back to grab the territory for themselves. It's very irritating.

GALLIMARD

With all due respect, sir, why should the Americans have won our war for us back in '54 if we didn't have the will to win it ourselves?

TOULON

You're kidding, aren't you?

[Pause.]

GALLIMARD

The Orientals simply want to be associated with whoever shows the most strength and power. You live with the Chinese, sir. Do you think they like Communism?

TOULON

I live in China. Not with the Chinese.

GALLIMARD
Well, I—

TOULON
You live with the Chinese.

GALLIMARD
Excuse me?

TOULON
I can't keep a secret.

GALLIMARD
What are you saying?

TOULON
Only that I'm not immune to gossip. So, you're keeping a native mistress. Don't answer. It's none of my business. *[Pause]* I'm sure she must be gorgeous.

GALLIMARD
Well . . .

TOULON
I'm impressed. You have the stamina to go out into the streets and hunt one down. Some of us have to be content with the wives of the expatriate community.

GALLIMARD
I do feel . . . fortunate.

TOULON
So, Gallimard, you've got the inside knowledge—what *do* the Chinese think?

GALLIMARD
Deep down, they miss the old days. You know, cappuccinos, men in tuxedos—

TOULON
So what do we tell the Americans about Vietnam?

GALLIMARD
Tell them there's a natural affinity between the West and the Orient.

TOULON
And that you speak from experience?

GALLIMARD
The Orientals are people too. They want the good things we can give them. If the Americans demonstrate the will to win, the Vietnamese will welcome them into a mutually beneficial union.

TOULON
I don't see how the Vietnamese can stand up to American firepower.

GALLIMARD
Orientals will always submit to a greater force.

TOULON
I'll note your opinions in my report. The Americans always love to hear how "welcome" they'll be. *[He starts to exit]*

GALLIMARD
Sir?

TOULON
Mmmm?

GALLIMARD
This . . . rumor you've heard.

TOULON
Uh-huh?

GALLIMARD
How . . . widespread do you think it is?

TOULON
It's only widespread within this embassy. Where nobody talks because everybody is guilty. We were worried about you, Gallimard. We thought you were the only one here without a secret. Now you go and find a lotus blossom . . . and top us all. *[He exits]*

GALLIMARD
[To us] Toulon knows! And he approves! I was learning the benefits of being a man. We form our own clubs, sit behind thick doors, smoke—and celebrate the fact that we're still boys. *[He starts to move downstage, towards Song]* So, over the—

[Suddenly Comrade Chin enters. Gallimard backs away.]

GALLIMARD
[To Song] No! Why does she have to come in?

SONG
René, be sensible. How can they understand the story without her? Now, don't embarrass yourself.

[Gallimard moves down center.]

GALLIMARD
[To us] Now, you will see why my story is so amusing to so many people. Why they snicker at parties in disbelief. Please—try to understand it from my point of view. We are all prisoners of our time and place. *[He exits]*

Scene 4

Gallimard and Butterfly's flat. Beijing. 1961.

SONG
[To us] 1961. The flat Monsieur Gallimard rented for us. An evening after he has gone.

CHIN
Okay, see if you can find out when the Americans plan to start bombing Vietnam. If you can find out what cities, even better.

SONG
I'll do my best, but I don't want to arouse his suspicions.

CHIN
Yeah, sure, of course. So, what else?

SONG
The Americans will increase troops in Vietnam to 170,000 soldiers with 120,000 militia and 11,000 American advisors.

CHIN
[Writing] Wait, wait. 120,000 militia and—

SONG
—11,000 American—

CHIN
—American advisors. *[Beat]* How do you remember so much?

SONG
I'm an actor.

CHIN
Yeah. *[Beat]* Is that how come you dress like that?

SONG
Like what, Miss Chin?

CHIN
Like that dress! You're wearing a dress. And every time I come here, you're wearing a dress. Is that because you're an actor? Or what?

SONG
It's a . . . disguise, Miss Chin.

CHIN
Actors, I think they're all weirdos. My mother tells me actors are like gamblers or prostitutes or—

SONG
It helps me in my assignment.

[Pause.]

CHIN
You're not gathering information in any way that violates Communist Party principles, are you?

SONG
Why would I do that?

CHIN
Just checking. Remember: when working for the Great Proletarian State, you represent our Chairman Mao in every position you take.

SONG
I'll try to imagine the Chairman taking my positions.

CHIN
We all think of him this way. Good-bye, comrade. *[She starts to exit]* Comrade?

SONG
Yes?

CHIN
Don't forget: there is no homosexuality in China!

SONG
Yes, I've heard.

CHIN
Just checking. *[She exits]*

SONG
[To us] What passes for a woman in modern China.

[Gallimard sticks his head out from the wings.]

GALLIMARD
Is she gone?

SONG
Yes, René. Please continue in your own fashion.

Scene 5

Beijing. 1961–1963.

Gallimard moves to the couch where Song still sits. He lies down in her lap, and she strokes his forehead.

GALLIMARD
[To us] And so, over the years 1961, '62, '63, we settled into our routine, Butterfly and I. She would always have prepared a light snack and then, ever so delicately, and only if I agreed, she would start to pleasure me. With her hands, her mouth . . . too many ways to explain, and too sad, given my present situation. But mostly we would talk. About my life.

Perhaps there is nothing more rare than to find a woman who passionately listens.

[Song remains upstage, listening, as Helga enters and plays a scene downstage with Gallimard.]

HELGA
René, I visited Dr. Bolleart this morning.

GALLIMARD
Why? Are you ill?

HELGA
No, no. You see, I wanted to ask him . . . that question we've been discussing.

GALLIMARD
And I told you, it's only a matter of time. Why did you bring a doctor into this? We just have to keep trying—like a crapshoot, actually.

HELGA
I went, I'm sorry. But listen: he says there's nothing wrong with me.

GALLIMARD
You see? Now, will you stop—?

HELGA
René, he says he'd like you to go in and take some tests.

GALLIMARD
Why? So he can find there's nothing wrong with both of us?

HELGA
René, I don't ask for much. One trip! One visit! And then, whatever you want to do about it—you decide.

GALLIMARD
You're assuming he'll find something defective!

HELGA
No! Of course not! Whatever he finds—if he finds nothing, we decide what to do about nothing! But go!

GALLIMARD
If he finds nothing, we keep trying. Just like we do now.

HELGA
But at least we'll know! *[Pause]* I'm sorry. *[She starts to exit]*

GALLIMARD
Do you really want me to see Dr. Bolleart?

HELGA
Only if you want a child, René. We have to face the fact that time is running out. Only if you want a child. *[She exits]*

GALLIMARD
[To Song] I'm a modern man, Butterfly. And yet, I don't want to go. It's the same old voodoo. I feel like God himself is laughing at me if I can't produce a child.

SONG
You men of the West—you're obsessed by your odd desire for equality. Your wife can't give you a child, and *you're* going to the doctor?

GALLIMARD
Well, you see, she's already gone.

SONG
And because this incompetent can't find the defect, you now have to subject yourself to him? It's unnatural.

GALLIMARD
Well, what is the "natural" solution?

SONG
In Imperial China, when a man found that one wife was inadequate, he turned to another—to give him his son.

GALLIMARD
What do you—? I can't . . . marry you, yet.

SONG
Please. I'm not asking you to be my husband. But I am already your wife.

GALLIMARD
Do you want to . . . have my child?

SONG
I thought you'd never ask.

GALLIMARD
But, your career . . . your—

SONG
Phooey on my career! That's your Western mind, twisting itself into strange shapes again. Of course I love my career. But what would I love most of all? To feel something inside me—day and night—something I know is yours. *[Pause]* Promise me . . . you won't go to this doctor. Who is this Western quack to set himself as judge over the man I love? I know who is a man, and who is not. *[She exits]*

GALLIMARD

[To us] Dr. Bolleart? Of course I didn't go. What man would?

Scene 6

Beijing. 1963.

    Party noises over the house speakers. Renee enters, wearing a revealing gown.

GALLIMARD

1963. A party at the Austrian embassy. None of us could remember the Austrian ambassador's name, which seemed somehow appropriate. *[To Renee]* So, I tell the Americans, Diem must go. The U.S. wants to be respected by the Vietnamese, and yet they're propping up this nobody seminarian as her president. A man whose claim to fame is his sister-in-law imposing fanatic "moral order" campaigns? Oriental women—when they're good, they're very good, but when they're bad, they're Christians.

RENEE

Yeah.

GALLIMARD

And what do you do?

RENEE

I'm a student. My father exports a lot of useless stuff to the Third World.

GALLIMARD

How useless?

RENEE

You know. Squirt guns, confectioner's sugar, hula hoops . . .

GALLIMARD

I'm sure they appreciate the sugar.

RENEE

I'm here for two years to study Chinese.

GALLIMARD

Two years?

RENEE

That's what everybody says.

GALLIMARD

When did you arrive?

RENEE

Three weeks ago.

GALLIMARD

And?

RENEE

I like it. It's primitive, but . . . well, this is the place to learn Chinese, so here I am.

GALLIMARD

Why Chinese?

RENEE

I think it'll be important someday.

GALLIMARD

You do?

RENEE

Don't ask me when, but . . . that's what I think.

GALLIMARD

Well, I agree with you. One hundred percent. That's very farsighted.

RENEE

Yeah. Well of course, my father thinks I'm a complete weirdo.

GALLIMARD

He'll thank you someday.

RENEE

Like when the Chinese start buying hula hoops?

GALLIMARD

There're a billion bellies out there.

RENEE

And if they end up taking over the world—well, then I'll be lucky to know Chinese too, right?

[Pause]

GALLIMARD

At this point, I don't see how the Chinese can possibly take—

RENEE

You know what I *don't* like about China?

GALLIMARD

Excuse me? No—what?

RENEE

Nothing to do at night.

GALLIMARD

You come to parties at embassies like everyone else.

RENEE

Yeah, but they get out at ten. And then what?

608   *DAVID HENRY HWANG*

GALLIMARD
I'm afraid the Chinese idea of a dance hall is a dirt floor and a man with a flute.

RENEE
Are you married?

GALLIMARD
Yes. Why?

RENEE
You wanna . . . fool around?

[Pause.]

GALLIMARD
Sure.

RENEE
I'll wait for you outside. What's your name?

GALLIMARD
Gallimard. René.

RENEE
Weird. I'm Renee too. [She exits]

GALLIMARD
[To us] And so, I embarked on my first extra-extramarital affair. Renee was picture perfect. With a body like those girls in the magazines. If I put a tissue paper over my eyes, I wouldn't have been able to tell the difference. And it was exciting to be with someone who wasn't afraid to be seen completely naked. But is it possible for a woman to be *too* uninhibited, *too* willing, so as to seem almost too . . . masculine?

[Chuck Berry blares from the house speakers, then comes down in volume as Renee enters, toweling her hair.]

RENEE
You have a nice weenie.

GALLIMARD
What?

RENEE
Penis. You have a nice penis.

GALLIMARD
Oh. Well, thank you. That's very . . .

RENEE
What—can't take a compliment?

GALLIMARD
No, it's very . . . reassuring.

RENEE
But most girls don't come out and say it, huh?

GALLIMARD
And also . . . what did you call it?

RENEE
Oh. Most girls don't call it a "weenie," huh?

GALLIMARD
It sounds very—

RENEE
Small, I know.

GALLIMARD
I was going to say, "young."

RENEE
Yeah. Young, small, same thing. Most guys are pretty, uh, sensitive about that. Like, you know, I had a boyfriend back home in Denmark. I got mad at him once and called him a little weeniehead. He got so mad! He said at least I should call him a great big weeniehead.

GALLIMARD
I suppose I just say "penis."

RENEE
Yeah. That's pretty clinical. There's "cock," but that sounds like a chicken. And "prick" is painful, and "dick" is like you're talking about someone who's not in the room.

GALLIMARD
Yes. It's a . . . bigger problem than I imagined.

RENEE
I—I think maybe it's because I really don't know what to do with them—that's why I call them "weenies."

GALLIMARD
Well, you did quite well with . . . mine.

RENEE
Thanks, but I mean, really *do* with them. Like, okay, have you ever looked at one? I mean, really?

GALLIMARD
No, I suppose when it's part of you, you sort of take it for granted.

RENEE
I guess. But, like, it just hangs there. This little . . . flap of flesh. And there's so much fuss that we make about it. Like, I think the reason we fight wars is because we wear clothes. Because no one knows—be-

tween the men, I mean—who has the bigger . . . weenie. So, if I'm a guy with a small one, I'm going to build a really big building or take over a really big piece of land or write a really long book so the other men don't know, right? But, see, it never really works, that's the problem. I mean, you conquer the country, or whatever, but you're still wearing clothes, so there's no way to prove absolutely whose is bigger or smaller. And that's what we call a civilized society. The whole world run by a bunch of men with pricks the size of pins. [She exits]

GALLIMARD
[To us] This was simply not acceptable.

[A high-pitched chime rings through the air. Song, dressed as Butterfly, appears in the upstage special. She is obviously distressed. Her body swoons as she attempts to clip the stems of flowers she's arranging in a vase.]

GALLIMARD
But I kept up our affair, wildly, for several months. Why? I believe because of Butterfly. She knew the secret I was trying to hide. But, unlike a Western woman, she didn't confront me, threaten, even pout. I remembered the words of Puccini's Butterfly:

SONG
"Noi siamo gente avvezza/ alle piccole cose/ umili e silenziose."

GALLIMARD
"I come from a people/ Who are accustomed to little/ Humble and silent." I saw Pinkerton and Butterfly, and what she would say if he were unfaithful . . . nothing. She would cry, alone, into those wildly soft sleeves, once full of possessions, now empty to collect her tears. It was her tears and her silence that excited me, every time I visited Renee.

TOULON
[Offstage] Gallimard!

[Toulon enters. Gallimard turns towards him. During the next section, Song, up center, begins to dance with the flowers. It is a drunken dance, where she breaks small pieces off the stems.]

TOULON
They're killing him.

GALLIMARD
Who? I'm sorry? What?

TOULON
Bother you to come over at this late hour?

GALLIMARD
No . . . of course not.

TOULON
Not after you hear my secret. Champagne?

GALLIMARD
Um . . . thank you.

TOULON
You're surprised. There's something that you've wanted, Gallimard. No, not a promotion. Next time. Something in the world. You're not aware of this, but there's an informal gossip circle among intelligence agents. And some of ours heard from some of the Americans—

GALLIMARD
Yes?

TOULON
That the U.S. will allow the Vietnamese generals to stage a coup . . . and assassinate President Diem.

[The chime rings again. Toulon freezes. Gallimard turns upstage and looks at Butterfly, who slowly and deliberately clips a flower off its stem. Gallimard turns back towards Toulon.]

GALLIMARD
I think . . . that's a very wise move!

[Toulon unfreezes.]

TOULON
It's what you've been advocating. A toast?

GALLIMARD
Sure. I consider this a vindication.

TOULON
Not exactly. "To the test. Let's hope you pass."

[They drink. The chime rings again. Toulon freezes. Gallimard turns upstage, and Song clips another flower.]

GALLIMARD
[To Toulon] The test?

TOULON
[Unfreezing] It's a test of everything you've been saying. I personally think the generals probably will stop the Communists. And you'll be a hero. But if anything goes wrong, then your opinions won't be worth

a pig's ear. I'm sure that won't happen. But sometimes it's easier when they don't listen to you.

GALLIMARD
They're your opinions too, aren't they?

TOULON
Personally, yes.

GALLIMARD
So we agree.

TOULON
But my opinions aren't on that report. Yours are. Cheers.

[Toulon turns away from Gallimard and raises his glass. At that instant Song picks up the vase and hurls it to the ground. It shatters. Song sinks down amidst the shards of the vase, in a calm, childlike trance. She sings softly, as if reciting a child's nursery rhyme.]

SONG
[Repeat as necessary] "The whole world over, the white man travels, setting anchor, wherever he likes. Life's not worth living, unless he finds, the finest maidens, of every land . . ."

[Gallimard turns downstage towards us. Song continues singing.]

GALLIMARD
I shook as I left his house. That coward! That worm! To put the burden for his decisions on my shoulders!
    I started for Renee's. But no, that was all I needed. A schoolgirl who would question the role of the penis in modern society. What I wanted was revenge. A vessel to contain my humiliation. Though I hadn't seen her in several weeks, I headed for Butterfly's.

[Gallimard enters Song's apartment.]

SONG
Oh! René . . . I was dreaming!

GALLIMARD
You've been drinking?

SONG
If I can't sleep, then yes, I drink. But then, it gives me these dreams which—René, it's been almost three weeks since you visited me last.

GALLIMARD
I know. There's been a lot going on in the world.

SONG
Fortunately I am drunk. So I can speak freely. It's not the world, it's you and me. And an old problem. Even the softest skin becomes like leather to a man who's touched it too often. I confess I don't know how to stop it. I don't know how to become another woman.

GALLIMARD
I have a request.

SONG
Is this a solution? Or are you ready to give up the flat?

GALLIMARD
It may be a solution. But I'm sure you won't like it.

SONG
Oh well, that's very important. "Like it?" Do you think I "like" lying here alone, waiting, always waiting for your return? Please—don't worry about what I may not "like."

GALLIMARD
I want to see you . . . naked.

[Silence.]

SONG
I thought you understood my modesty. So you want me to—what—strip? Like a big cowboy girl? Shiny pasties on my breasts? Shall I fling my kimono over my head and yell "ya-hoo" in the process? I thought you respected my shame!

GALLIMARD
I believe you gave me your shame many years ago.

SONG
Yes—and it is just like a white devil to use it against me. I can't believe it. I thought myself so repulsed by the passive Oriental and the cruel white man. Now I see—we are always most revolted by the things hidden within us.

GALLIMARD
I just mean—

SONG
Yes?

GALLIMARD
—that it will remove the only barrier left between us.

SONG
No, René. Don't couch your request in sweet words. Be yourself—a cad—and know that my love is enough, that I submit—submit to the worst you can

give me. *[Pause]* Well, come. Strip me. Whatever happens, know that you have willed it. Our love, in your hands. I'm helpless before my man.

[Gallimard starts to cross the room.]

GALLIMARD
Did I not undress her because I knew, somewhere deep down, what I would find? Perhaps. Happiness is so rare that our mind can turn somersaults to protect it.

At the time, I only knew that I was seeing Pinkerton stalking towards his Butterfly, ready to reward her love with his lecherous hands. The image sickened me, pulled me to my knees, so I was crawling towards her like a worm. By the time I reached her, Pinkerton . . . had vanished from my heart. To be replaced by something new, something unnatural, that flew in the face of all I'd learned in the world—something very close to love.

[He grabs her around the waist; she strokes his hair.]

GALLIMARD
Butterfly, forgive me.

SONG
René . . .

GALLIMARD
For everything. From the start.

SONG
I'm . . .

GALLIMARD
I want to—

SONG
I'm pregnant. *[Beat]* I'm pregnant. *[Beat]* I'm pregnant. *[Beat.]*

GALLIMARD
I want to marry you!

Scene 7

Gallimard and Butterfly's flat. Beijing. 1963.

Downstage, Song paces as Comrade Chin reads from her notepad. Upstage, Gallimard is still kneeling. He remains on his knees throughout the scene, watching it.

SONG
I need a baby.

CHIN
[From pad] He's been spotted going to a dorm.

SONG
I need a baby.

CHIN
At the Foreign Language Institute.

SONG
I need a baby.

CHIN
The room of a Danish girl . . . What do you mean, you need a baby?!

SONG
Tell Comrade Kang—last night, the entire mission, it could've ended.

CHIN
What do you mean?

SONG
Tell Kang—he told me to strip.

CHIN
Strip?!

SONG
Write!

CHIN
I tell you, I don't understand nothing about this case anymore. Nothing.

SONG
He told me to strip, and I took a chance. Oh, we Chinese, we know how to gamble.

CHIN
[Writing] ". . . told him to strip."

SONG
My palms were wet, I had to make a split-second decision.

CHIN
Hey! Can you slow down?!

[Pause]

SONG
You write faster, I'm the artist here. Suddenly, it hit me—"All he wants is for her to submit. Once a woman submits, a man is always ready to become 'generous.'"

CHIN
You're just gonna end up with rough notes.

SONG

And it worked! He gave in! Now, if I can just present him with a baby. A Chinese baby with blond hair—he'll be mine for life!

CHIN

Kang will never agree! The trading of babies has to be a counterrevolutionary act!

SONG

Sometimes, a counterrevolutionary act is necessary to counter a counterrevolutionary act.

[Pause.]

CHIN

Wait.

SONG

I need one . . . in seven months. Make sure it's a boy.

CHIN

This doesn't sound like something the Chairman would do. Maybe you'd better talk to Comrade Kang yourself.

SONG

Good. I will.

[Chin gets up to leave.]

SONG

Miss Chin? Why, in the Peking Opera, are women's roles played by men?

CHIN

I don't know. Maybe, a reactionary remnant of male—

SONG

No. [Beat] Because only a man knows how a woman is supposed to act.

[Chin exits. Song turns upstage, towards Gallimard.]

GALLIMARD

[Calling after Chin] Good riddance! [To Song] I could forget all that betrayal in an instant, you know. If you'd just come back and become Butterfly again.

SONG

Fat chance. You're here in prison, rotting in a cell. And I'm on a plane, winging my way back to China. Your President pardoned me of our treason, you know.

GALLIMARD

Yes, I read about that.

SONG

Must make you feel . . . lower than shit.

GALLIMARD

But don't you, even a little bit, wish you were here with me?

SONG

I'm an artist, René. You were my greatest . . . acting challenge. [She laughs] It doesn't matter how rotten I answer, does it? You still adore me. That's why I love you, René. [She points to us] So—you were telling your audience about the night I announced I was pregnant.

[Gallimard puts his arms around Song's waist. He and Song are in the positions they were in at the end of Scene 6.]

Scene 8

Same.

GALLIMARD

I'll divorce my wife. We'll live together here, and then later in France.

SONG

I feel so . . . ashamed.

GALLIMARD

Why?

SONG

I had begun to lose faith. And now, you shame me with your generosity.

GALLIMARD

Generosity? No, I'm proposing for very selfish reasons.

SONG

Your apologies only make me feel more ashamed. My outburst a moment ago!

GALLIMARD

Your outburst? What about my request?!

SONG

You've been very patient dealing with my . . . eccentricities. A Western man, used to women freer with their bodies—

GALLIMARD

It was sick! Don't make excuses for me.

SONG

I have to. You don't seem willing to make them for yourself.

M. BUTTERFLY   613

GALLIMARD
You're crazy.

SONG
I'm happy. Which often looks like crazy.

GALLIMARD
Then make me crazy. Marry me.

[Pause.]

SONG
No.

GALLIMARD
What?

SONG
Do I sound silly, a slave, if I say I'm not worthy?

GALLIMARD
Yes. In fact you do. No one has loved me like you.

SONG
Thank you. And no one ever will. I'll see to that.

GALLIMARD
So what is the problem?

SONG
René, we Chinese are realists. We understand rice, gold, and guns. You are a diplomat. Your career is skyrocketing. Now, what would happen if you divorced your wife to marry a Communist Chinese actress?

GALLIMARD
That's not being realistic. That's defeating yourself before you begin.

SONG
We must conserve our strength for the battles we can win.

GALLIMARD
That sounds like a fortune cookie!

SONG
Where do you think fortune cookies come from?

GALLIMARD
I don't care.

SONG
You do. So do I. And we should. That is why I say I'm not worthy. I'm worthy to love and even to be loved by you. But I am not worthy to end the career of one of the West's most promising diplomats.

GALLIMARD
It's not that great a career! I made it sound like more than it is!

SONG
Modesty will get you nowhere. Flatter yourself, and you flatter me. I'm flattered to decline your offer. [She exits]

GALLIMARD
[To us] Butterfly and I argued all night. And, in the end, I left, knowing I would never be her husband. She went away for several months—to the countryside, like a small animal. Until the night I received her call.

[A baby's cry from offstage. Song enters, carrying a child.]

SONG
He looks like you.

GALLIMARD
Oh! [Beat; he approaches the baby] Well, babies are never very attractive at birth.

SONG
Stop!

GALLIMARD
I'm sure he'll grow more beautiful with age. More like his mother.

SONG
"Chi vide mai/ a bimbo del Giappon . . ."

GALLIMARD
"What baby, I wonder, was ever born in Japan"—or China, for that matter—

SONG
". . . occhi azzurrini?"

GALLIMARD
"With azure eyes"—they're actually sort of brown, wouldn't you say?

SONG
"E il labbro."

GALLIMARD
"And such lips!" [He kisses Song] And such lips.

SONG
"E i ricciolini d'oro schietto?"

GALLIMARD
"And such a head of golden"—if slightly patchy—"curls?"

SONG

I'm going to call him "Peepee."

GALLIMARD

Darling, could you repeat that because I'm sure a rickshaw just flew by overhead.

SONG

You heard me.

GALLIMARD

"Song Peepee"? May I suggest Michael, or Stephan, or Adolph?

SONG

You may, but I won't listen.

GALLIMARD

You can't be serious. Can you imagine the time this child will have in school?

SONG

In the West, yes.

GALLIMARD

It's worse than naming him Ping Pong or Long Dong or——

SONG

But he's never going to live in the West, is he?

[Pause.]

GALLIMARD

That wasn't my choice.

SONG

It is mine. And this is my promise to you: I will raise him, he will be our child, but he will never burden you outside of China.

GALLIMARD

Why do you make these promises? I want to be burdened! I want a scandal to cover the papers!

SONG

[To us] Prophetic.

GALLIMARD

I'm serious.

SONG

So am I. His name is as I registered it. And he will never live in the West.

[Song exits with the child.]

GALLIMARD

[To us] It is possible that her stubbornness only made me want her more. That drawing back at the moment of my capitulation was the most brilliant strategy she could have chosen. It is possible. But it is also possible that by this point she could have said, could have done . . . anything, and I would have adored her still.

Scene 9

Beijing. 1966.

A driving rhythm of Chinese percussion fills the stage.

GALLIMARD

And then, China began to change. Mao became very old, and his cult became very strong. And, like many old men, he entered his second childhood. So he handed over the reins of state to those with minds like his own. And children ruled the Middle Kingdom with complete caprice. The doctrine of the Cultural Revolution implied continuous anarchy. Contact between Chinese and foreigners became impossible. Our flat was confiscated. Her fame and my money now counted against us.

[Two dancers in Mao suits and red-starred caps enter, and begin crudely mimicking revolutionary violence, in an agitprop fashion.]

GALLIMARD

And somehow the American war went wrong too. Four hundred thousand dollars were being spent for every Viet Cong killed; so General Westmoreland's remark that the Oriental does not value life the way Americans do was oddly accurate. Why weren't the Vietnamese people giving in? Why were they content instead to die and die and die again?

[Toulon enters.]

TOULON

Congratulations, Gallimard.

GALLIMARD

Excuse me, sir?

TOULON

Not a promotion. That was last time. You're going home.

GALLIMARD

What?

TOULON

Don't say I didn't warn you.

GALLIMARD
I'm being transferred . . . because I was wrong about the American war?

TOULON
Of course not. We don't care about the Americans. We care about your mind. The quality of your analysis. In general, everything you've predicted here in the Orient . . . just hasn't happened.

GALLIMARD
I think that's premature.

TOULON
Don't force me to be blunt. Okay, you said China was ready to open to Western trade. The only thing they're trading out there are Western heads. And, yes, you said the Americans would succeed in Indochina. You were kidding, right?

GALLIMARD
I think the end is in sight.

TOULON
Don't be pathetic. And don't take this personally. You were wrong. It's not your fault.

GALLIMARD
But I'm going home.

TOULON
Right. Could I have the number of your mistress? [Beat] Joke! Joke! Eat a croissant for me.

[Toulon exits. Song, wearing a Mao suit, is dragged in from the wings as part of the upstage dance. They "beat" her, then lampoon the acrobatics of the Chinese opera, as she is made to kneel onstage.]

GALLIMARD
[Simultaneously] I don't care to recall how Butterfly and I said our hurried farewell. Perhaps it was better to end our affair before it killed her.

[Gallimard exits. Comrade Chin walks across the stage with a banner reading: "The Actor Renounces His Decadent Profession!" She reaches the kneeling Song. Percussion stops with a thud. Dancers strike poses.]

CHIN
Actor-oppressor, for years you have lived above the common people and looked down on their labor. While the farmer ate millet—

SONG
I ate pastries from France and sweetmeats from silver trays.

CHIN
And how did you come to live in such an exalted position?

SONG
I was a plaything for the imperialists!

CHIN
What did you do?

SONG
I shamed China by allowing myself to be corrupted by a foreigner . . .

CHIN
What does this mean? The People demand a full confession!

SONG
I engaged in the lowest perversions with China's enemies!

CHIN
What perversions? Be more clear!

SONG
I let him put it up my ass!

[Dancers look over, disgusted.]

CHIN
Aaaa-ya! How can you use such sickening language?!

SONG
My language . . . is only as foul as the crimes I committed . . .

CHIN
Yeah. That's better. So—what do you want to do now?

SONG
I want to serve the people.

[Percussion starts up, with Chinese strings.]

CHIN
What?

SONG
I want to serve the people!

[Dancers regain their revolutionary smiles, and begin a dance of victory.]

CHIN
What?!

SONG
I want to serve the people!!

[Dancers unveil a banner: "The Actor Is Rehabilitated!"
Song remains kneeling before Chin, as the dancers
bounce around them, then exit. Music out.]

Scene 10

A commune. Hunan Province. 1970.

CHIN
How you planning to do that?

SONG
I've already worked four years in the fields of Hunan,
Comrade Chin.

CHIN
So? Farmers work all their lives. Let me see your
hands.

[*Song holds them out for her inspection.*]

CHIN
Goddamn! Still so smooth! How long does it take to
turn you actors into good anythings? Hunh. You've
just spent too many years in luxury to be any good to
the Revolution.

SONG
I served the Revolution.

CHIN
Serve the Revolution? Bullshit! You wore dresses!
Don't tell me—I was there. I saw you! You and your
white vice-consul! Stuck up there in your flat, living
off the People's Treasury! Yeah, I knew what was
going on! You two . . . homos! Homos! Homos!
[*Pause; she composes herself*] Ah! Well . . . you will
serve the people, all right. But not with the Revolution's money. This time, you use your own money.

SONG
I have no money.

CHIN
Shut up! And you won't stink up China anymore with
your pervert stuff. You'll pollute the place where pol-
lution begins—the West.

SONG
What do you mean?

CHIN
Shut up! You're going to France. Without a cent in
your pocket. You find your consul's house, you make
him pay your expenses—

SONG
No.

CHIN
And you give us weekly reports! Useful information!

SONG
That's crazy. It's been four years.

CHIN
Either that, or back to rehabilitation center!

SONG
Comrade Chin, he's not going to support me! Not in
France! He's a white man! I was just his plaything—

CHIN
Oh yuck! Again with the sickening language?
Where's my stick?

SONG
You don't understand the mind of a man.

[*Pause.*]

CHIN
Oh no? No I don't? Then how come I'm married,
huh? How come I got a man? Five, six years ago, you
always tell me those kind of things, I felt very bad. But
not now! Because what does the Chairman say? He
tells us *I'm* now the smart one, you're now the nin-
compoop! *You're* the blackhead, the harebrain, the
nitwit! You think you're so smart? You understand
"The Mind of a Man"? Good! Then *you* go to France
and be a pervert for Chairman Mao!

[*Chin and Song exit in opposite directions.*]

Scene 11

Paris. 1968–70.
Gallimard enters.

GALLIMARD
And what was waiting for me back in Paris? Well, better Chinese food than I'd eaten in China. Friends and
relatives. A little accounting, regular schedule, keeping track of traffic violations in the suburbs. . . . And
the indignity of students shouting the slogans of
Chairman Mao at me—in French.

HELGA
René? René? [*She enters, soaking wet*] I've had a . . . a
problem. [*She sneezes*]

GALLIMARD
You're wet.

HELGA

Yes, I . . . coming back from the grocer's. A group of students, waving red flags, they—

[Gallimard fetches a towel.]

HELGA

—they ran by, I was caught up along with them. Before I knew what was happening—

[Gallimard gives her the towel.]

HELGA

Thank you. The police started firing water cannons at us. I tried to shout, to tell them I was the wife of a diplomat, but—you know how it is . . . *[Pause]* Needless to say, I lost the groceries. René, what's happening to France?

GALLIMARD

What's—? Well, nothing, really.

HELGA

Nothing?! The storefronts are in flames, there's glass in the streets, buildings are toppling—and I'm wet!

GALLIMARD

Nothing! . . . that I care to think about.

HELGA

And is that why you stay in this room?

GALLIMARD

Yes, in fact.

HELGA

With the incense burning? You know something? I hate incense. It smells so sickly sweet.

GALLIMARD

Well, I hate the French. Who just smell—period!

HELGA

And the Chinese were better?

GALLIMARD

Please—don't start.

HELGA

When we left, this exact same thing, the riots—

GALLIMARD

No, no . . .

HELGA

Students screaming slogans, smashing down doors—

GALLIMARD

Helga—

HELGA

It was all going on in China, too. Don't you remember?!

GALLIMARD

Helga! Please! *[Pause]* You have never understood China, have you? You walk in here with these ridiculous ideas, that the West is falling apart, that China was spitting in our faces. You come in dripping off the streets, and you leave water all over my floor. *[He grabs Helga's towel, begins mopping up the floor]*

HELGA

But it's the truth!

GALLIMARD

Helga, I want a divorce.

[Pause; Gallimard continues, mopping the floor.]

HELGA

I take it back. China is . . . beautiful. Incense, I like incense.

GALLIMARD

I've had a mistress.

HELGA

So?

GALLIMARD

For eight years.

HELGA

I knew you would. I knew you would the day I married you. And now what? You want to marry her?

GALLIMARD

I can't. She's in China.

HELGA

I see. You want to leave. For someone who's not here, is that right?

GALLIMARD

That's right.

HELGA

You can't live with her, but still you don't want to live with me.

GALLIMARD

That's right.

[Pause.]

HELGA

Shit. How terrible that I can figure that out. *[Pause.]* I never thought I'd say it. But, in China, I was happy.

I knew, in my own way, I knew you were not everything you pretended to be. But the pretense—going on your arm to the embassy ball, visiting your office and the guards saying, "Good morning, good morning, Madame Gallimard"—the pretense . . . was very good indeed. *[Pause.]* I hope everyone is mean to you for the rest of your life. *[She exits]*

GALLIMARD
[To us] Prophetic.

[Marc enters with two drinks.]

GALLIMARD
[To Marc] In China, I was different from all other men.

MARC
Sure. You were white. Here's your drink.

GALLIMARD
I felt . . . touched.

MARC
In the head? René, I don't want to hear about the Oriental love goddess. Okay? One night—can we just drink and throw up without a lot of conversation?

GALLIMARD
You still don't believe me, do you?

MARC
Sure I do. She was the most beautiful, et cetera, et cetera, blasé blasé.

[Pause.]

GALLIMARD
My life in the West has been such a disappointment.

MARC
Life in the West is like that. You'll get used to it. Look, you're driving me away. I'm leaving. Happy, now? *[He exits, then returns]* Look, I have a date tomorrow night. You wanna come? I can fix you up with—

GALLIMARD
Of course. I would love to come.

[Pause.]

MARC
Uh—on second thought, no. You'd better get ahold of yourself first.

[He exits; Gallimard nurses his drink.]

GALLIMARD
[To us] This is the ultimate cruelty, isn't it? That I can talk and talk and to anyone listening, it's only air—

too rich a diet to be swallowed by a mundane world. Why can't anyone understand? That in China, I once loved, and was loved by, very simply, the Perfect Woman.

[Song enters, dressed as Butterfly in wedding dress.]

GALLIMARD
[To Song] Not again. My imagination is hell. Am I asleep this time? Or did I drink too much?

SONG
René?

GALLIMARD
God, it's too painful! That you speak?

SONG
What are you talking about? René—touch me.

GALLIMARD
Why?

SONG
I'm real. Take my hand.

GALLIMARD
Why? So you can disappear again and leave me clutching at the air? For the entertainment of my neighbors who—?

[Song touches Gallimard.]

SONG
René?

[Gallimard takes Song's hand. Silence.]

GALLIMARD
Butterfly? I never doubted you'd return.

SONG
You hadn't . . . forgotten—?

GALLIMARD
Yes, actually, I've forgotten everything. My mind, you see—there wasn't enough room in this hard head—not for the world *and* for you. No, there was only room for one. *[Beat]* Come, look. See? Your bed has been waiting, with the Klimt poster you like, and—see? The xiang lu [incense burner] you gave me?

SONG
I . . . I don't know what to say.

GALLIMARD
There's nothing to say. Not at the end of a long trip. Can I make you some tea?

SONG

But where's your wife?

GALLIMARD

She's by my side. She's by my side at last.

[Gallimard reaches to embrace Song. Song sidesteps, dodging him.]

GALLIMARD

Why?!

SONG

[To us] So I did return to René in Paris. Where I found—

GALLIMARD

Why do you run away? Can't we show them how we embraced that evening?

SONG

Please. I'm talking.

GALLIMARD

You have to do what I say! I'm conjuring you up in *my* mind!

SONG

René, I've never done what you've said. Why should it be any different in your mind? Now split—the story moves on, and I must change.

GALLIMARD

I welcomed you into my home! I didn't have to, you know! I could've left you penniless on the streets of Paris! But I took you in!

SONG

Thank you.

GALLIMARD

So . . . please . . . don't change.

SONG

You know I have to. You know I will. And anyway, what difference does it make? No matter what your eyes tell you, you can't ignore the truth. You already know too much.

[Gallimard exits. Song turns to us.]

SONG

The change I'm going to make requires about five minutes. So I thought you might want to take this opportunity to stretch your legs, enjoy a drink, or listen to the musicians. I'll be here, when you return, right where you left me.

[Song goes to a mirror in front of which is a wash basin of water. She starts to remove her makeup as stagelights go to half and houselights come up.]

——————— ACT THREE ———————

Scene 1

A courthouse in Paris. 1986.

As he promised, Song has completed the bulk of his transformation, onstage, by the time the houselights go down and the stagelights come up full. He removes his wig and kimono, leaving them on the floor. Underneath, he wears a well-cut suit.

SONG

So I'd done my job better than I had a right to expect. Well, give him some credit, too. He's right—I was in a fix when I arrived in Paris. I walked from the airport into town, then I located, by blind groping, the Chinatown district. Let me make one thing clear: whatever else may be said about the Chinese, they are stingy! I slept in doorways three days until I could find a tailor who would make me this kimono on credit. As it turns out, maybe I didn't even need it. Maybe he would've been happy to see me in a simple shift and mascara. But . . . better safe than sorry.

That was 1970, when I arrived in Paris. For the next fifteen years, yes, I lived a very comfy life. Some relief, believe me, after four years on a fucking commune in Nowheresville, China. René supported the boy and me, and I did some demonstrations around the country as part of my "cultural exchange" cover. And then there was the spying.

[Song moves upstage, to a chair. Toulon enters as a judge, wearing the appropriate wig and robes. He sits near Song. It's 1986, and Song is testifying in a courtroom.]

SONG

Not much at first. René had lost all his high-level contacts. Comrade Chin wasn't very interested in parking-ticket statistics. But finally, at my urging, René got a job as a courier, handling sensitive documents. He'd photograph them for me, and I'd pass them on to the Chinese embassy.

JUDGE

Did he understand the extent of his activity?

SONG

He didn't ask. He knew that I needed those documents, and that was enough.

JUDGE

But he must've known he was passing classified information.

SONG

I can't say.

JUDGE

He never asked what you were going to do with them?

SONG

Nope.

[Pause.]

JUDGE

There is one thing that the court—indeed, that all of France—would like to know.

SONG

Fire away.

JUDGE

Did Monsieur Gallimard know you were a man?

SONG

Well, he never saw me completely naked. Ever.

JUDGE

But surely, he must've . . . how can I put this?

SONG

Put it however you like. I'm not shy. He must've felt around?

JUDGE

Mmmmm.

SONG

Not really. I did all the work. He just laid back. Of course we did enjoy more . . . complete union, and I suppose he *might* have wondered why I was always on my stomach, but. . . . But what you're thinking is: "Of course a wrist must've brushed . . . a hand hit . . . over twenty years!" Yeah. Well, Your Honor, it was my job to make him think I was a woman. And chew on this: it wasn't all that hard. See, my mother was a prostitute along the Bundt before the Revolution. And, uh, I think it's fair to say she learned a few things about Western men. So I borrowed her knowledge. In service to my country.

JUDGE

Would you care to enlighten the court with this secret knowledge? I'm sure we're all very curious.

SONG

I'm sure you are. [Pause] Okay, Rule One is: Men always believe what they want to hear. So a girl can tell the most obnoxious lies and the guys will believe them every time—"This is my first time"—"That's the biggest I've ever seen"—or *both*, which, if you really think about it, is not possible in a single lifetime. You've maybe heard those phrases a few times in your own life, yes, Your Honour?

JUDGE

It's not my life, Monsieur Song, which is on trial today.

SONG

Okay, okay, just trying to lighten up the proceedings. Tough room.

JUDGE

Go on.

SONG

Rule Two: As soon as a Western man comes into contact with the East—he's already confused. The West has sort of an international rape mentality towards the East. Do you know rape mentality?

JUDGE

Give us your definition, please.

SONG

Basically, "Her mouth says no, but her eyes say yes."

The West thinks of itself as masculine—big guns, big industry, big money—so the East is feminine—weak, delicate, poor . . . but good at art, and full of inscrutable wisdom—the feminine mystique.

Her mouth says no, but her eyes say yes. The West believes that the East, deep down, *wants* to be dominated—because a woman can't think for herself.

JUDGE

What does this have to do with my question?

SONG

You expect Oriental countries to submit to your guns, and you expect Oriental women to be submissive to your men. That's why you say they make the best wives.

JUDGE

But why would that make it possible for you to fool Monsieur Gallimard? Please—get to the point.

SONG

One, because when he finally met his fantasy woman, he wanted more than anything else to believe that she was, in fact, a woman. And second, I am an Oriental. And being an Oriental, I could never be completely a man.

[Pause.]

JUDGE

Your armchair political theory is tenuous, Monsieur Song.

SONG

You think so? That's why you'll lose in all your dealings with the East.

JUDGE

Just answer my question: did he know you were a man?

[Pause.]

SONG

You know, Your Honor, I never asked.

Scene 2

Same.

Music from the "Death Scene" from Butterfly blares over the house speakers. It is the loudest thing we've heard in this play.

Gallimard enters, crawling towards Song's wig and kimono.

GALLIMARD

Butterfly? Butterfly?

[Song remains a man, in the witness box, delivering a testimony we do not hear.]

GALLIMARD

[To us] In my moment of greatest shame, here, in this courtroom—with that . . . person up there, telling the world. . . . What strikes me especially is how shallow he is, how glib and obsequious . . . completely . . . without substance! The type that prowls around discos with a gold medallion stinking of garlic. So little like my Butterfly.

Yet even in this moment my mind remains agile, flip-flopping like a man on a trampoline. Even now, my picture dissolves, and I see that . . . witness . . . talking to me.

[Song suddenly stands straight up in his witness box, and looks at Gallimard.]

SONG

Yes. You. White man.

[Song steps out of the witness box, and moves downstage towards Gallimard. Light change.]

GALLIMARD

[To Song] Who? Me?

SONG

Do you see any other white men?

GALLIMARD

Yes. There're white men all around. This is a French courtroom.

SONG

So you are an adventurous imperialist. Tell me, why did it take you so long? To come back to this place?

GALLIMARD

What place?

SONG

This theatre in China. Where we met many years ago.

GALLIMARD

[To us] And once again, against my will, I am transported.

[Chinese opera music comes up on the speakers. Song begins to do opera moves, as he did the night they met.]

SONG

Do you remember? The night you gave your heart?

GALLIMARD

It was a long time ago.

SONG

Not long enough. A night that turned your world upside down.

GALLIMARD

Perhaps.

SONG

Oh, be honest with me. What's another bit of flattery when you've already given me twenty years' worth? It's a wonder my head hasn't swollen to the size of China.

GALLIMARD

Who's to say it hasn't?

SONG

Who's to say? And what's the shame? In pride? You think I could've pulled this off if I wasn't already full of pride when we met? No, not just pride. Arrogance. It takes arrogance, really—to believe you can will, with your eyes and your lips, the destiny of another. *[He dances]* C'mon. Admit it. You still want me. Even in slacks and a button-down collar.

GALLIMARD

I don't see what the point of—

SONG

You don't? Well maybe, René, just maybe—I want you.

GALLIMARD

You do?

SONG

Then again, maybe I'm just playing with you. How can you tell? *[Reprising his feminine character, he sidles up to Gallimard]* "How I wish there were even a small cafe to sit in. With men in tuxedos, and cappuccinos, and bad expatriate jazz." Now you want to kiss me, don't you?

GALLIMARD

[Pulling away] What makes you—?

SONG

—so sure? See? I take the words from your mouth. Then I wait for you to come and retrieve them. *[He reclines on the floor]*

GALLIMARD

Why?! Why do you treat me so cruelly?

SONG

Perhaps I *was* treating you cruelly. But now—I'm being nice. Come here, my little one.

GALLIMARD

I'm not your little one!

SONG

My mistake. It's I who am *your* little one, right?

GALLIMARD

Yes, I—

SONG

So come get your little one. If you like. I may even let you strip me.

GALLIMARD

I mean, you were! Before . . . but not like this!

SONG

I was? Then perhaps I still am. If you look hard enough. *[He starts to remove his clothes]*

GALLIMARD

What—what are you doing?

SONG

Helping you to see through my act.

GALLIMARD

Stop that! I don't want to! I don't—

SONG

Oh, but you asked me to strip, remember?

GALLIMARD

What? That was years ago! And I took it back!

SONG

No. You postponed it. Postponed the inevitable. Today, the inevitable has come calling.

[From the speakers, cacophony: Butterfly mixed in with Chinese gongs.]

GALLIMARD

No! Stop! I don't want to see!

SONG

Then look away.

GALLIMARD

You're only in my mind! All this is in my mind! I order you! To stop!

SONG

To what? To strip? That's just what I'm—

GALLIMARD

No! Stop! I want you—

SONG

You want me?

GALLIMARD

To stop!

SONG

You know something, René? Your mouth says no, but your eyes say yes. Turn them away. I dare you.

GALLIMARD

I don't have to! Every night, you say you're going to strip, but then I beg you and you stop!

SONG

I guess tonight is different.

GALLIMARD

Why? Why should that be?

SONG
Maybe I've become frustrated. Maybe I'm saying "Look at me, you fool!" Or maybe I'm just feeling . . . sexy. [He is down to his briefs]

GALLIMARD
Please. This is unecessary. I know what you are.

SONG
Do you? What am I?

GALLIMARD
A—a man.

SONG
You don't really believe that.

GALLIMARD
Yes I do! I knew all the time somewhere that my happiness was temporary, my love a deception. But my mind kept the knowledge at bay. To make the wait bearable.

SONG
Monsieur Gallimard—the wait is over.

[Song drops his briefs. He is naked. Sound cue out. Slowly, we and Song come to the realization that what we had thought to be Gallimard's sobbing is actually his laughter.]

GALLIMARD
Oh god! What an idiot! Of course!

SONG
René—what?

GALLIMARD
Look at you! You're a man! [He bursts into laughter again]

SONG
I fail to see what's so funny!

GALLIMARD
"You fail to see—!" I mean, you never did have much of a sense of humor, did you? I just think it's ridiculously funny that I've wasted so much time on just a man!

SONG
Wait. I'm not "just a man."

GALLIMARD
No? Isn't that what you've been trying to convince me of?

SONG
Yes, but what I mean—

GALLIMARD
And now, I finally believe you, and you tell me it's not true? I think you must have some kind of identity problem.

SONG
Will you listen to me?

GALLIMARD
Why?! I've been listening to you for twenty years. Don't I deserve a vacation?

SONG
I'm not just any man!

GALLIMARD
Then, what exactly are you?

SONG
René, how can you ask—? Okay, what about this?

[He picks up Butterfly's robes, starts to dance around. No music.]

GALLIMARD
Yes, that's very nice. I have to admit.

[Song holds out his arm to Gallimard.]

SONG
It's the same skin you've worshiped for years. Touch it.

GALLIMARD
Yes, it does feel the same.

SONG
Now—close your eyes.

[Song covers Gallimard's eyes with one hand. With the other, Song draws Gallimard's hand up to his face. Gallimard, like a blind man, lets his hands run over Song's face.]

GALLIMARD
This skin, I remember. The curve of her face, the softness of her cheek, her hair against the back of my hand . . .

SONG
I'm your Butterfly. Under the robes, beneath everything, it was always me. Now, open your eyes and admit it—you adore me. [He removes his hand from Gallimard's eyes]

GALLIMARD
You, who knew every inch of my desires—how could you, of all people, have made such a mistake?

624   DAVID HENRY HWANG

SONG
What?

GALLIMARD
You showed me your true self. When all I loved was the lie. A perfect lie, which you let fall to the ground—and now, it's old and soiled.

SONG
So—you never really loved me? Only when I was playing a part?

GALLIMARD
I'm a man who loved a woman created by a man. Everything else—simply falls short.

[Pause.]

SONG
What am I supposed to do now?

GALLIMARD
You were a fine spy, Monsieur Song, with an even finer accomplice. But now I believe you should go. Get out of my life!

SONG
Go where? René, you can't live without me. Not after twenty years.

GALLIMARD
I certainly can't live with you—not after twenty years of betrayal.

SONG
Don't be so stubborn! Where will you go?

GALLIMARD
I have a date . . . with my Butterfly.

SONG
So, throw away your pride. And come . . .

GALLIMARD
Get away from me! Tonight, I've finally learned to tell fantasy from reality. And, knowing the difference, I choose fantasy.

SONG
I'm your fantasy!

GALLIMARD
You? You're as real as hamburger. Now get out! I have a date with my Butterfly and I don't want your body polluting the room! [He tosses Song's suit at him] Look at these—you dress like a pimp.

SONG
Hey! These are Armani slacks and—! [He puts on his briefs and slacks] Let's just say . . . I'm disappointed

in you, René. In the crush of your adoration, I thought you'd become something more. More like . . . a woman.
     But no. Men. You're like the rest of them. It's all in the way we dress, and make up our faces, and bat our eyelashes. You really have so little imagination!

GALLIMARD
You, Monsieur Song? Accuse me of too little imagination? You, if anyone, should know—I am pure imagination. And in imagination I will remain. Now get out!

[Gallimard bodily removes Song from the stage, taking his kimono.]

SONG
René! I'll never put on those robes again! You'll be sorry!

GALLIMARD
[To Song] I'm already sorry! [Looking at the kimono in his hands] Exactly as sorry . . . as a Butterfly.

Scene 3

M. Gallimard's prison cell. Paris. Present.

GALLIMARD
I've played out the events of my life night after night, always searching for a new ending to my story, one where I leave this cell and return forever to my Butterfly's arms.
     Tonight I realize my search is over. That I've looked all along in the wrong place. And now, to you, I will prove that my love was not in vain—by returning to the world of fantasy where I first met her.

[He picks up the kimono; dancers enter.]

GALLIMARD
There is a vision of the Orient that I have. Of slender women in chong sams and kimonos who die for the love of unworthy foreign devils. Who are born and raised to be the perfect women. Who take whatever punishment we give them, and bounce back, strengthened by love, unconditionally. It is a vision that has become my life.

[Dancers bring the wash basin to him and help him make up his face.]

GALLIMARD
In public, I have continued to deny that Song Liling is a man. This brings me headlines, and is a source of

great embarrassment to my French colleagues, who can now be sent into a coughing fit by the mere mention of Chinese food. But alone, in my cell, I have long since faced the truth.

And the truth demands a sacrifice. For mistakes made over the course of a lifetime. My mistakes were simple and absolute—the man I loved was a cad, a bounder. He deserved nothing but a kick in the behind, and instead I gave him . . . all my love.

Yes—love. Why not admit it all? That was my undoing, wasn't it? Love warped my judgment, blinded my eyes, rearranged the very lines on my face . . . until I could look in the mirror and see nothing but . . . a woman.

[Dancers help him put on the Butterfly wig.]

GALLIMARD

I have a vision. Of the Orient. That, deep within its almond eyes, there are still women. Women willing to sacrifice themselves for the love of a man. Even a man whose love is completely without worth.

[Dancers assist Gallimard in donning the kimono. They hand him a knife.]

GALLIMARD

Death with honor is better than life . . . life with dishonor. *[He sets himself center stage, in a seppuku posi-* tion.] The love of a Butterfly can withstand many things—unfaithfulness, loss, even abandonment. But how can it face the one sin that implies all others? The devastating knowledge that, underneath it all, the object of her love was nothing more, nothing less than . . . a man. *[He sets the tip of the knife against his body]* It is 19___ ___. And I have found her at last. In a prison on the outskirts of Paris. My name is René Gallimard—also known as Madame Butterfly.

[Gallimard turns upstage and plunges the knife into his body, as music from the "Love Duet" blares over the speakers. He collapses into the arms of the dancers, who lay him reverently on the floor. The image holds for several beats. Then a tight special up on Song, who stands as a man, staring at the dead Gallimard. He smokes a cigarette; the smoke filters up through the lights. Two words leave his lips.]

SONG

Butterfly? Butterfly?

[Smoke rises as lights fade slowly to black.]

[End of Play]